MW00768474

Benchmark ADVANCE™

Creating readers who effectively

- make meaning

- build knowledge

- express understanding

- and gain a solid foundation of literacy.

Development Team

Authors

Silvia Dorta-Duque de Reyes, M.A.,
    Benchmark Education Company
Queta Fernandez, Spanish Literacy Consultant
Adria Klein, Ph.D., California State University, San Bernardino
Carrie Smith, M.S., Benchmark Education Company

Contributing Authors

Jorge Cuevas-Antillón, M.A., San Diego County
    Office of Education
Erin Bostick Mason, M.A. Ed., California State University,
    San Bernardino
Marjorie McCabe, Ph.D., California State University,
    San Bernardino
Jill Kerper Mora Ph.D., San Diego State University
Jeff Zwiers, Ed.D., Stanford University

Linguistic Consultants

Sandra Ceja, InterLingual SoLutions, Carlsbad, California
Youniss El Cheddadi, Arabic Department, San Diego
    State University
Lilly Cheng, Ph.D., University of California, San Diego
Kennon Mitchell, Ph.D., African American English consultant,
    Chino Hills, California

Program Reviewers

Patty Albañez, San Diego Unified School District
Sonia Quinn, Moreno Valley Unified School District
Maria Alzugaray, Educational Consultant, San José
Veronica Delgado, Chula Vista School District
Amanda Flores, Long Beach Unified School District
Alejandra Gomez, San Diego Unified School District
Izela Jacobo, Cajon Valley School District
Margarita Palacios, North Monterey County School District
Jennifer Alvarez, Whittier College
Elena Riviere, San Jose Unified School District
Zenaida Rosario, San Ysidro School District
Lisa Vallejos, San Luis Obispo County Office of Education
Elizabeth Wilson, Educational Consultant, Hacienda Heights

Benchmark ADVANCE™

BENCHMARK EDUCATION COMPANY
145 Huguenot Street • New Rochelle, NY 10801

For ordering information, call Toll-Free 1-877-236-2465 or visit our website at www.benchmarkeducation.com.

Table of Contents
Units 1 & 2

Program Overview

5 Themes of Literacy Instruction
Grade K Components

Unit 1:
Rules at Home and School

Why do we have rules?

Unit 2:
Every Story Has Characters

How are people different?

Additional Resources

5 Themes of Literacy Instruction

Teach reading, writing, speaking and listening and successfully reach each one of your students. *Benchmark Advance* provides materials and effective instruction that give you scaffolding techniques, routines, and dedicated EL support in a program that seamlessly weaves together all five themes of literacy instruction.

Content Knowledge

A focused, careful mapping of knowledge strands, fueling a deeper understanding of content

Driven by Essential Questions

Every unit is driven by an Essential Question, fueling a deeper understanding of content knowledge through reading, writing, and text analysis.

Mapped Across Grade Levels

- Content is carefully mapped and aligned across the grade levels.
- Each grade level contains 10 units.
- Each unit is driven by a specific knowledge strand, which is consistent across all grade levels, K-6.

To see a full alignment of content knowledge strands, please see the inside flap of this Teacher's Resource System volume.

Supports Content and Literacy Standards

The skills and content taught in *Benchmark Advance* is built to support literacy and content area standards.

- California Common Core ELA Standards (CA CCSS)
- Next Generation Science Standards (NGSS)
- California History and Social Studies Standards (HSS)

Content is carefully mapped to ensure students build deep knowledge over time.

Meaning Making

The instructional heartbeat of the program

Every unit has a predictable, consistent pulse.

Benchmark Advance provides a predictable, consistent instructional framework to develop students who successfully derive meaning from text.

- Routines to build the habits of close readers
- Texts that are worthy of close, deep analysis
- Backwards mapping in each unit to ensure students are reaching expected outcomes in vocabulary, comprehension, and critical thinking

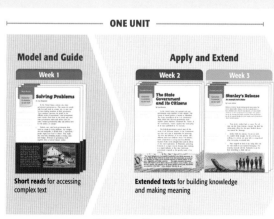

— ONE UNIT —

Model and Guide — Week 1

Apply and Extend — Week 2 — Week 3

Short reads for accessing complex text

Extended texts for building knowledge and making meaning

Every text in a unit focuses on a single topic.

Foundational Skills

Explicit and systematic instruction that lays the groundwork for literacy achievement

Kindergarten–Grade 2

Explicit phonics and high frequency word instruction.
Includes:
- Daily lessons
- Decodable texts
- Hands-on manipulatives

A	a
Am	am
An	an
and	are
at	be

Fluency and Print Concepts are taught through engaging shared readings. Includes:
- Rhymes
- Poems
- Other short texts

Reader's Theater for Kindergarten–Grade 6

Build fluency through engaging scripts for all of your students.

Grades 3–6

Multi-syllabic phonics and word analysis lessons support vocabulary development.

Language Development

Integrated, designated, and embedded throughout the program

Integrated ELD

Embedded in every mini-lesson at three levels of scaffolding intensity to provide you flexibility based on each student's need.

iELD support targets the most cognitively or linguistically demanding task, with substantial, moderate, and light support.

(iELD) Integrated ELD

Substantial Support
Explain to students that government helps protect people in the state and the country. Governments make laws and enforce laws. Governments also provide for many things that people need.
Discuss examples of responsibilities of government.

Local	State	National
• police dept.	• education	• makes and carries out laws
• fire dept.	• transportation	
• sanitation	• state parks	• meets with leaders of other countries
• local roads	• state highways	
• education		• Supreme Court

Display a list of question words and a list of terms that students can use to discuss how government influences the way we live.
- *How, who, what, where, when, why*
- *Make, protect, help, build, responsible for, tax*

Moderate Support
Display a list of question words and a list of terms that students can use to discuss how government ...

Designated ELD Components

Provide your EL's with the skills necessary for learning, thinking, and expressing in the English Language.

Designated ELD components are designed for use during a protected instructional time. They are aligned to all CA ELD standards.

Embedded Instruction

Language development is addressed within the context of reading and writing.

- Conventions of English
- Knowledge of Language
- Vocabulary acquisition strategies

Effective Expression

Tools and instructional resources to create strong communicators

Collaborative Conversation

The *Think-Speak-Listen Flip Books* and *Bookmarks* place the tools for effective, meaningful conversation directly in students' hands.

Conversation starters to support
- Sharing and building upon ideas of others
- Expressing and supporting an opinion
- Integrating knowledge and ideas

Explicit Writing Instruction

Embedded throughout the program

Writing Process Instruction
Guides students through each step of the writing process

Genre Writing Instruction
Creates effective writers in many genres, including opinions and arguments

Writing About Reading
Practice and instruction in writing text analyses and writing across multiple texts

Whole Group

Student Reads
Print & eBooks

Shared Reading Texts

Units 1–5

Units 6–10

Units 1–10

Mentor Read-Aloud Texts

Units 1–5

Units 6–10

Big Book Extended Texts

Unit 1

Unit 2

Unit 3

Unit 4

Unit 5

Unit 6

Unit 7

Unit 8

Unit 9

Unit 10

Teacher Resources
Print, eGuides & Digital tools

Units 1 & 2

Units 3 & 4

Units 5 & 6

Units 7 & 8

Units 9 & 10

Read-Aloud Handbook

Complete Library, ePlanner, Unit Videos, Assignments Pre-Built Whole Group Presentations

Phonics Resources

Picture Word Cards

Frieze Cards

Decodable Readers

Alphabet Chart

Letter Cards

High-Frequency Word Cards

Designated ELD

Student
Print & eBooks

Texts for English Language Development, Units 1–10

Think-Speak-Listen Conversation Bookmarks

Teacher
Print & eGuides

English Language Development Teacher's Resource System

English Language Development Assessment

Small Group

Leveled Texts (8 titles per unit)

Student
Print & eBooks

Unit 1   Unit 2   Unit 3   Unit 4   Unit 5   Unit 6   Unit 7   Unit 8   Unit 9   Unit 10

Teacher Guides and Text Evidence Question Cards (8 of each per unit)

Teacher
Print, eGuides & Digital tools

Unit 1   Unit 2   Unit 3   Unit 4   Unit 5   Unit 6   Unit 7   Unit 8   Unit 9   Unit 10

Reader's Theater (2 scripts per unit)

Student
Print & eBooks

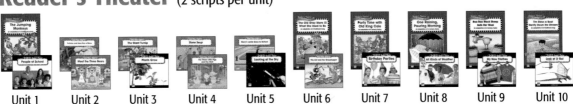

Unit 1   Unit 2   Unit 3   Unit 4   Unit 5   Unit 6   Unit 7   Unit 8   Unit 9   Unit 10

Teacher
Print, eGuides & Digital tools

Reader's Theater
Handbook, Units 1–10

Leveled Library, Small Group Manager,
ePlanner, Differentiated Assignments

Benchmarkuniverse.com

Assessment

Print & Online
Assessments

Weekly and Unit
Assessments

Interim
Assessments

Foundational
Skills Assessments

Informal
Assessments

Intervention

Teacher
Print & eGuides

Fluency and
Comprehension
Teacher's Guide

Phonics and Word
Recognition
Teacher's Guide

Phonological
Awareness
Teacher's Guide

Print Concepts
Teacher's Guide

Language
Mini-Lessons
Handbook

Grade K
20-Day Suggested Pacing

Day	Establishing Routines	Read-Aloud and Shared Reading	Shared Writing (Concepts about Print, Letter Awareness, Phonological Awareness)	Independent Reading
1	Building Good Listening Habits	Read the Big Book: *Katy's First Day of School*	Writing Prompt: How did you get ready for school today?	Model Taking Care of Books
2	Introducing Reader's Workshop	Read the Big Book: *Katy's First Day of School*	Writing Prompt: Why did you want to come to school today?	Model Reading to Self and Using the Classroom Library
3	Establishing Rules for Reader's Workshop	Read the Big Book: *Katy's First Day of School*	Writing Prompt: What is your favorite activity at school?	Model Reading to Self and Using the Classroom Library
4	Establishing Student Roles	Read the Big Book: *Katy's First Day of School*	Writing Prompt: What do you like to do at recess?	Model Reading to Self and Using the Classroom Library
5	Establishing the Teacher's Role During Reader's Workshop	Read the Big Book: *Katy's First Day of School*	Writing Prompt: What do you like to do with your friends?	Model Reading to Self and Using the Classroom Library
6	Reviewing Student and Teacher Roles During Reader's Workshop	Read the Poem: "Mary Had a Little Lamb"	Writing Prompt: What was your favorite part of the poem?	Practice Library Workstation and Introduce Writing Workstation
7	Reviewing Student and Teacher Roles during Reader's Workshop	Read the Poem: "Mary Had a Little Lamb"	Writing Prompt: What happened first in the poem?	Introduce and Practice Using Response Journals
8	Reviewing Student and Teacher Roles during Reader's Workshop	Read the Poem: "Mary Had a Little Lamb"	Writing Prompt: What part of the poem did you like best?	Introduce and Practice Using Response Journals
9	Fiction and Nonfiction text	Read the Poem: "Mary Had a Little Lamb"	Writing Prompt: What do you know about words?	Introduce and Practice Using Response Journals
10	Fiction and Nonfiction Text	Read the Poem: "Mary Had a Little Lamb"	Writing Prompt: What do you know about finding the first sound in each word?	Model Reading to Self and Using the Classroom Library
11	Respond to a Story	Read the Big Book: *Welcome to Our School*	Writing Prompt: How many words are in a sentence?	Introduce and Practice Playing Games and Puzzles Workstation
12	Readers Use Pictures	Read the Big Book: *Welcome to Our School*	Writing Prompt: What do you know about finding how many words are in a sentence?	Model Reading to Self and Using the Classroom Library
13	Readers Make Predictions	Read the Big Book: *Welcome to Our School*	Writing Prompt: How many words are in your sentence?	Computer Workstation
14	Readers Use Sounds They Know to Figure Out Words	Read the Big Book: *Welcome to Our School*	Writing Prompt: How many letters are in your word?	Computer Workstation
15	Readers Reread	Read the Big Book: *Welcome to Our School*	Writing Prompt: What do you know about words and letters?	Buddy Reading
16	Readers Visualize	Read the Poem: "A Diller, A Dollar"	Writing Prompt: What do you know about words and letters?	Workstation Rotation
17	Readers Use Chunks In Words	Read the Poem: "A Diller, A Dollar"	Writing Prompt: What do you know about words and letters?	Workstation Rotation
18	Readers Make Connections	Read the Poem: "A Diller, A Dollar"	Writing Prompt: What are a few sentences about your school?	Workstation Rotation
19	Readers Know the Difference between Fiction and Nonfiction	Read the Poem: "A Diller, A Dollar"	Writing Prompt: What are a few sentences about your school?	Workstation Rotation
20	Readers Identify Characters in a Story	Read the Poem: "A Diller, A Dollar"	Writing Prompt: What are a few sentences about your school?	Workstation Rotation

Objectives

Students will:
- Transition efficiently between mini-lessons.
- Discuss what it means to be a good listener.

Additional Materials

- Chart paper
- Markers
- Anchor Chart

Establishing Routines (20 MIN.)

Smooth Transitions

If students sit at tables or in groups, you may want to call one table at a time to transition to the rug by using a signal, such as a hand bell, clapping, a song, or flashing the lights. Begin by modeling how to push the chair in quietly and walk silently to the meeting area. Ask one table to demonstrate while the remainder of the class observes and comments.

Say: *Boys and girls, give me a thumbs-up if everyone from that table remembered to push in his or her chair.*

Once everyone is seated in the meeting area, explain your expectations for remaining seated and quiet with your eyes on the speaker.

Getting Ready for Whole-Group Instruction: Building Good Listening Habits

Say: *When we come to school, it is important to be good listeners. We need to listen so that we can learn. Today we will begin to create a chart to help us remember how to be a good listener. What is important to do when we listen?*

Begin making an anchor chart, adding one idea to the chart, such as, "A listener pays attention." Post this anchor chart as a daily reference while building routines. Reread the chart and add to it often with students to reinforce the habit of good listening.

Optional: Have students practice returning to their designated seats, or stand up to take a "brain break." You may want to ask student to stretch or to move to music at this time.

What is a Good Listener?
- A listener pays attention.
- A listener sits still.
- A listener does not bother his or her neighbor.
- A listener looks at the person who is talking.

Sample Listener Anchor Chart

Read-Aloud and Shared Reading (25 MIN.)

Read-Aloud: Build Good Listening Habits

Call students to the meeting area using the established signal.

Read any book from the Recommended Trade Books in Additional Resources or any other available book, such as *Miss Bindergarten Gets Ready for Kindergarten* by Joseph Slate.

Read and conduct a brief discussion about what people do to get ready for school. Remind students that during whole group discussions, one must raise his or her hand and wait to be called on to speak. Write these additions to the anchor chart, and reread the chart. Ask student to stretch or to move to music at this time.

Shared Reading: Build Good Listening Habits

Call students to the meeting area using the established signal.

Say: *Today we are going to read a book about a little girl named Katy. It is her first day of school, but she would rather stay in bed.*

Display the cover of the book and read the title. Explain to students that the title often helps us understand what the book is about. Help students find the names of the authors and the illustrator on the cover.

Say: *The authors wrote the words of this story, and the illustrator drew the pictures. We find important information on the book cover.*

Read the book, moving your pointer under the words and stopping in a few places where it is appropriate to support students' comprehension. When finished reading, invite students to discuss their favorite part of the story.

Return to pages 2–3, and reread these pages to students, emphasizing the words **rise** and **eyes**.

Ask: *What do you notice when I say the words* **rise** *and* **eyes***? These words rhyme. This means that the last part of the words sound alike. Say the words with me:* **rise, eyes.** *Do you hear the rhyme?*

Turn to pages 4–5.

Say: *Let's listen for one more rhyme. Read pages 4–5 as you emphasize* **said** *and* **bed***. Repeat the rhyming words with me:* **said, bed***. Do you hear the rhyme? Does* **head** *rhyme with* **said** *and* **bed***?*

Optional: Have students practice returning to their designated seats, or stand up to take a "brain break." You may want to ask student to stretch or to move to music at this time.

Katy's First Day of School

Objectives

Students will:
- Listen and respond to a story.
- Build an awareness of the information on the cover of a book: title, author, illustrator, illustration.
- Begin to recognize rhymes.

Additional Materials

- Chart paper
- Markers
- Selected book to read aloud
- Pointer

Shared Writing (15 MIN.)

Concepts about Print, Letter Awareness, Phonological Awareness

Call students to the meeting area using the established signal.

Ask students what they did to get ready for school that morning. Choose 1–2 students' responses to write.

Sample Shared Writing
Lee got dressed.
Tara got up early.

As you write, point out where on the paper you start to write. Draw attention to any letter that is a "stick letter," such as **L, I, T**. Invite students to make a stick in the air with their fingers.

As you write, emphasize the first phoneme in students' name.

Say: *Lee's sound is /l/. Tara's sound is /t/. What is your sound?*

Optional: Have students practice returning to their designated seats, or stand up to take a "brain break." You may want to ask student to stretch or to move to music at this time.

Objectives

Students will:
• Begin to differentiate stick letters within print.

Additional Materials

• Chart paper
• Markers

Independent Reading (15 MIN.)

Model Taking Care of Books

Call students to the meeting area using the established signal. Bring a basket of books to the meeting area.

Say: *In our classroom books are special so we need to take care of them.*

Model how you carefully take books out of the basket and demonstrate turning pages carefully, keeping the book flat on your lap, the floor, or on a table, and returning it carefully to the basket. Then, model how you choose and return books in the classroom library. You might use a "think aloud" to share your thinking while choosing a book and returning it to the proper basket.

Think aloud: *I love to read books about animals. I think I'll go to the basket with animal books. Look! Here's a book about cats! I have a cat. I'd like to read this book. I'm going to carefully take this book from the basket and take it to my spot to read it.*

It's time to return my book! I'll make sure I put it back in the basket where I got it. I'll also make sure to smooth all of the pages and the front and back covers so there are no wrinkles when I put it away.

Ask students to share what they noticed about how you handled books.

Optional: Create an anchor chart about taking care of books.

How do we care for books?
- We open the covers the right way.
- We put books back on the shelf when we are done reading.
- We do not turn the corners.
- We do not rip the pages.

Sample Anchor Chart

Ask a few students to practice handling books appropriately. Praise out students who are using the behaviors that were modeled.

Say: *Today you will read books that are at your tables. During independent reading, I want you to think about how you are handling the books. Think about ways we will take care of books in our classroom.*

Send students to seats using established procedures. Place a basket of books on each table and ask them to read. Observe and support the proper handling of books. Have students practice returning to their designated seats.

Objectives

Students will:
- Learn to handle books with care.

Additional Materials

- Chart paper
- Markers
- Baskets of books for independent reading

Establishing Routines (20 MIN.)

Smooth Transitions

If students sit at tables or in groups, you may want to review this transition routine by calling one table at a time to transition to the rug by using a signal. Review the procedure by showing students how to push their chair in quietly and walk silently to the meeting area. Ask one table to demonstrate while the remainder of the class observes and comments.

Model how students will sit when they come to the carpet by inviting a student to sit quietly with their legs crossed and their hands folded in their lap. Tell the rest of students that today they are going to practice sitting this way every time they come to the carpet.

Say: *Boys and girls, when we come to the carpet we want to sit quietly with our legs crossed and our hands in our laps. When I see you sitting quietly like this with your eyes on the speaker, I'll know you're ready to listen.*

Getting Ready for Whole-Group Instruction: Introducing Reader's Workshop

Say: *Every day when we are in school, we will have a very special time to learn about reading. We will call that time "Reader's Workshop." Today we will create a chart to help us remember what Reader's Workshop looks like and sounds like. What are we doing now? Yes, Reader's Workshop looks like boys and girls sitting in a group getting ready to read a book. Let's put that on our chart under 'looks like.' What does our room sound like now? Yes, it sounds like the teacher is talking. Let's put that on our chart under 'sounds like.'*

Begin making an anchor chart that looks like a T-chart. Title the T-chart *Reader's Workshop*. Title one column *Looks Like* (or draw an eye) and the other *Sounds Like* (or draw an ear.) Help students think what Reader's Workshop 'looks like' by recording phrases such as, boys and girls sitting in a group looking at a book. Help students think what Reader's Workshop 'sounds like' by recording phrases such as: hearing stories read by the teacher. Reread the chart and add to it often as students begin to better understand what Reader's Workshop looks like and sounds like.

Reader's Workshop	
Looks Like	**Sounds Like**

Sample Anchor Chart

Objectives

Students will:
• Continue practicing an efficient transition between mini-lessons.

Additional Materials

• Chart paper
• Markers

Read-Aloud and Shared Reading (25 MIN.)

Read-Aloud: Respectful Conversation Habits

Call students to the meeting area using the established signal. Read any book from the Recommended Trade Books in Additional Resources or any other available books such as, *Look Out Kindergarten, Here I Come* by Nancy Carlson. Read and introduce the concept of having a respectful conversation about a book.

Say: *When good readers talk about what they've read, they take turns telling their thoughts. We can't hear everyone at once, so only one person talks at a time. After everyone listens to one person, then another person can talk.*

Model this by sharing something you enjoyed about the book with students. Then ask one of students to share something they enjoyed. Continue having a respectful conversation about the book practicing listening and sharing.

Shared Reading: Respectful Conversation Habits

Call students to the meeting area using the established signal.

Say: *Yesterday we read a book about a little girl name Katy. It was her first day of school and she didn't think she wanted to go.*

Display the cover of the book and point to the title.

Say: *Do you remember what this is? Yes, this is the title. What else can we find on the cover of the book? Yes, we can find who wrote the book. We call this person the author. What else can we find? Yes. We can find the person who drew the pictures. We call this person the illustrator. Remember, we find important information on the cover of a book.*

Reread the book, moving the pointer under the words and stopping where it is appropriate to support students' comprehension. When finished reading, invite students to use respectful conversation habits to talk about why they thought Katy wanted to stay in bed.

Identify Rhyme

Return to pages 6–7, and reread these pages to students, emphasizing the words **eat** and **meet**.

Ask: *What do you notice when I say the words **eat** and **meet**? These words rhyme. That means that the last part of the words sound alike. Say the word with me: **eat, meat**. Do you hear the rhyme?*

Return to pages 8–9.

Say: *Let's listen for one more rhyme. Read pages 8–9 as you emphasize said and bed. Do you hear the rhyme? Repeat the words with me: **said, bed**. Do you hear the rhyme? Does **red** rhyme with **said** and **bed**?*

Katy's First Day of School

Objectives

Students will:
- Listen and respond to a story using respectful conversations.
- Recognize rhyming words.

Additional Materials

- Pointer
- Chosen read-aloud book

Shared Writing (15 MIN.)

Concepts about Print, Letter Awareness, Phonological Awareness

Call students to the meeting area using the established signal.

Ask students to tell why they wanted to come to school today. Choose 1–2 student's responses to write.

Sample Shared Writing
Kyle likes to read.
Patty likes recess.

As you write, point out where on the paper you start to write. Draw attention to any letter that is a 'stick letter'; such as **L, I,** or **T** and 'slanted letters'; such as **A, K,** and **M.** Invite students to make a straight and slanted stick in the air with their fingers.

As you write, emphasize the first phoneme in the student's name.

Say: *Kyle's sound is /k/. Patty's sound is /p/. What is your sound?*

Optional: Have students practice returning to their designated seats, or stand up to take a 'brain break.' You may want to ask students to stretch or move to music at this time.

Objectives

Students will:
• Differentiate and locate stick and slanted letters within print.

Independent Reading (10 MIN.)

Model Reading to Self and Using the Classroom Library

Call students to the meeting area using the established signal.

Say: *Today we are going to visit our classroom library and learn how to choose a book and how to put it away.*

Invite students to go with you to the library where they will be seated and show you they are ready to listen.

Say: *This is our classroom library where you will be able to look for books that you would like to read during our 'read to self' time. Let me show you how we choose a book.*

Carefully choose a book from the library. Remind students about the way they learned to handle a book yesterday. Again, model how to carefully lay the book flat on your lap, floor, or table and how to turn the pages slowly and deliberately. Ask one of the students to model how to choose a book and show the class how to take care of the book. When you are ready, model for students how to return the book to its place without bending, tearing, or misplacing it. Invite the student(s) who modeled how to choose a book to also model how to return the book correctly.

Say: *Starting tomorrow, some of you will be invited to choose a book from the library. Today, you will read books that are in the baskets at your tables. During independent reading, I want you to think about how you are handling the books. Think about ways we will take care of books and our classroom library.*

Send students to their seats using established procedures. Place a basket of books on each table and ask them to read. Observe and support the proper handling of books.

Objectives

Students will:
- Practice handling books with care.

Additional Materials

- Chart paper
- Markers
- Baskets of books for independent reading

Establishing Routines (20 MIN.)

Smooth Transitions

If students sit at tables on in groups, you may want to review this transition routine by calling one table at a time to transition to the rug by using a signal. Review the procedure by showing students how to push their chair in quietly and walk silently to the meeting area. Ask one table to demonstrate while the remainder of the class observes and comments.

Remind students how they sit when they come to the carpet. Invite one of the tables to join you at the carpet. Ask them to show the rest of the class how we move quietly in our room, push our chairs in when we leave our space, and sit with our legs crossed and our hands in our laps.

Say: *Boys and girls, I'm so glad to see that you remembered that when we come to the carpet we want to sit quietly with our legs crossed and our hands in our laps. When I see you sitting quietly like this with your eyes on the speaker, I'll know you're ready to listen. The rest of the class may quietly join the first group of students.*

Getting Ready for Whole-Group Instruction: Establishing Rules for Reader's Workshop

Say: *Let's look at our anchor chart from yesterday to help us remember what Reader's Workshop looks like and sounds like. Can you think of anything we should add to our chart? Today, I would like for us to think about how we should act during Reader's Workshop. Do you remember yesterday when we practiced having a respectful conversation? That's very important when we're learning. Only one person talks at a time. I think we should make an anchor chart with a list of ideas about how we learn best in our room. Let's call it, 'Rules for Learning.' The first thing I'll put on our chart is one person talks at a time. Can you think of another idea that would make our room a good place to learn?*

Continue taking ideas from students until they have helped create a list of 4–5 rules for learning.

Rules for Learning
One person talks at a time.
Respect each other.
Take turns when talking.
Ask questions when you do not understand something.

Sample Anchor Chart

Objectives

Students will:
• Continue practicing an efficient transition between mini-lessons
• Learn and discuss rules for Reader's Workshop.

Additional Materials

• Chart paper
• Markers

Support Tip

For students with auditory challenges, visually demonstrate what you are explaining or use models to show your expectations.

Read-Aloud and Shared Reading (10 MIN.)

Read-Aloud

Call students to the meeting area using the established signal. Read any book from the Recommended Trade Books in Additional Resources or any other available books such as, *Countdown to Kindergarten* by Alison McGhee.

Say: *Do you remember yesterday when we talked about having a respectful conversation about a book? What do you remember about that?*

Allow for 2–3 responses from students.

Say: *Today, I'd like for us to practice a special time to talk with each other and share our thoughts about many things. This special time is Turn and Talk. Turn and Talk is when you have a partner who shares respectful conversations with you. Let me show you what Turn and Talk looks like and sounds like.*

Choose one of students to model Turn and Talk with you.

Say: *When we turn and talk, the first thing we do is sit knee to knee and eye to eye, like this. Then we have a respectful conversation about something. Today, I'd like for us to turn and talk about our favorite part of the book we just read. It sounds like this; "My favorite part is_____." Model how this sounds with your partner and then ask your partner to answer with their favorite part.*

Observe to see that all students are sharing using respectful conversations. Allow a few minutes for conversations to take place.

Shared Reading

Call students to the meeting area using the established signal. Display the cover of the book and point to the title.

Say: *Do you remember what this is? Yes, this is the title. What else can we find on the cover of the book? Yes, we can find who wrote the book. We call this person the author. What else can we find? Yes. We can find the person who drew the pictures. We call this person the illustrator. Let's look at our book, **Katy's First Day of School**. Can you tell me where the front of the book is? Yes! The cover is the front of the book. Can you tell me where the back of the book is? Yes! The back of the book is on the other side.*

Reread the book, moving the pointer under the words and stopping in a few places where it is appropriate to support students' comprehension.

Say: *Today, we are going to practice retelling the story of **Katy's First Day of School**. Let me show you how that would sound.*

Do a 'think aloud' about what happened first, next, then, and last in the story.

Say: *Now let's practice having a respectful conversation by turning and talking with your partner. Each of you will retell the story. Remember, we set knee to knee and eye to eye when we turn and talk. You may Turn and Talk and retell the story to each other.*

Katy's First Day of School

Objectives

Students will:
- Listen and respond to a story using respectful conversations.
- Identify a book's title.
- Recognize front cover and back cover.

Additional Materials

- Pointer
- Chosen read-aloud book

Objectives

Students will:
• Differentiate and locate stick and slanted letters within print.

Additional Materials

• Pointer

Shared Writing (15 MIN.)

Concepts About Print, Letter Awareness, Phonological Awareness

Call students to the meeting area using the established signal.

Ask students about their favorite activity at school. Choose 1–2 student's responses to write.

Sample Shared Writing

Mary likes lunch.

Keith likes to hear stories.

As you write, point out the top of the paper, the bottom of the paper and where on the paper you start to write. Talk about starting on the left and going to the right. Draw attention to any letter that is a 'stick letter'; such as **L, I,** or **T** and 'slanted letters'; such as **A, K,** and **M**. Add the 'circle letters; such as **C** and **O**. Invite students to make a straight and slanted stick in the air with their fingers. Invite students to make a circle in the air.

As you write, emphasize the first phoneme in the student's name.

Say: *Mary's sound is /**m**/. Keith's sound is /**k**/. Turn and Talk and share your sound in a respectful conversation.*

Optional: Have students practice returning to their designated seats, or stand up to take a 'brain break.' You may want to ask students to stretch or move to music at this time.

Independent Reading (10 MIN.)

Model Reading to Self and Using the Classroom Library

Call students to the meeting area using the established signal.

Invite students to go with you to the library where they will be seated and show you they are ready to listen.

Say: *Yesterday we visited our classroom library where you looked for books you would like to read during our 'read to self' (or independent read) time. We learned about how we choose a book and how we handle our books carefully.*

Model this again by carefully choosing a book from the library. Again, model how to carefully lay the book flat on your lap, floor, or table and how to turn the pages slowly and deliberately. When you are ready, model for students how to return the book to its place without bending, tearing, or misplacing it.

Say: *Today, some of us are going to choose a book from the library and take it to our seat to read. The rest of us will use books from the baskets at our table. Tomorrow, another group will be able to choose a book, the next day, another group until all of us have had a chance to use our library. During independent reading, I want you to think about how you are handling the books, think about ways we will take care of books and our classroom library. I also want the group that borrowed books from our library to think about how we return our books so that our library stays neat, and our books stay nice.*

Ask a table group (or any group of students) to stay in the library to borrow books. The rest of the class will return to their seats and use the baskets at their table to find and read books.

After assisting students in the library, circulate, observe, and support students to ensure they handle books correctly. At the end of independent reading, assist students who borrowed books from the library return them properly. You may want to use this as a model time for the rest of the class so there is an example to follow when it is their turn.

Objectives

Students will:
• Practice handling books with care.

Additional Materials

• Chart paper
• Markers
• Baskets of books for independent reading

Objectives

Students will:
- Continue practicing an efficient transition between mini-lessons.
- Learn and discuss roles for whole groups.

Additional Materials

- Chart paper
- Markers

Establishing Routines (20 MIN.)

Smooth Transitions

Remind students how they sit when they come to the carpet. Invite one of the tables to join you at the carpet. Ask them to show the rest of the class how we move quietly in our room, push our chairs in when we leave our space, and sit with our legs crossed and our hands in our laps.

Say: *Boys and girls, I'm so glad to see that you remembered that when we come to the carpet we want to sit quietly with our legs crossed and our hands in our laps. When I see you sitting quietly like this with your eyes on the speaker, I'll know you're ready to listen. The rest of the class may quietly join the first group of students.*

Getting Ready for Whole-Group Instruction: Establishing Student Roles

Say: *Let's look at our anchor chart from yesterday that helps us think about how we act during Reader's Workshop so that we can all be learners. Can you think of anything we should add to our chart? Today, I would like for us to think about the different jobs we have during Reader's Workshop. We know that many times, we turn and talk with a partner. So one of our jobs is to be a partner.*

Say: *Let's start an anchor chart to help us remember what our jobs are during Reader's Workshop. Let's title it "Our Jobs During Reader's Workshop." First let's write 'Be a partner.' We also have respectful conversations where we have to be listeners, so another of our jobs is to be a listener. Let's write 'Be a listener.' We share with each other, so another of our jobs to take turns talking and speaking clearly. Let's add 'Be a speaker.' to our chart. A very important part of Readers' Workshop is to read books, so let's also add, 'Be a reader.'*

Our Jobs During Reader's Workshop

Be a partner.

Be a listener.

Be a speaker.

Be a reader.

Sample Anchor Chart

Say: *Let's read our chart again to make sure we have added all of our jobs. Make sure that you ask yourself which of these jobs you should be doing during Reader's Workshop, and that you are doing your very best.*

Read-Aloud and Shared Reading (30 MIN.)

Read-Aloud

Call students to the meeting area using the established signal. Read any book from the Recommended Trade Books in Additional Resources or any other available books such as, *Froggy Goes to School* by Jonathan London.

Say: *Now let's practice Turn and Talk with your partner. Today there is a very special respectful conversation I want you to have. When you talk with your partner today, please start your conversation like this: "I was nervous the first day of school because _____." Let me show you how that sounds.*

Choose a student and model using a sentence frame. Let the student use the sentence frame in return.

Say: *Now sit knee to knee and eye to eye with your Turn and Talk partner and use the sentence frame to share why you were nervous the first day of school. Remember to say, "I was nervous the first day of school because _____." Remember, also, to have a respectful conversation.*

Observe to see that all students are sharing using respectful conversations and using the sentence frame. After a couple of minutes,

Say: *Thumbs up if you had a respectful conversation with your partner!*

Shared Reading

Call students to the meeting area using the established signal.

Say: *Yesterday we read a book about a little girl name Katy. It was her first day of school and she didn't think she wanted to go.*

Display the cover of the book and review the things we can find on the cover of a book. Also review author and illustrator as well as front and back.

Say: *Let's look at our book, **Katy's First Day of School**. Do you remember what this is? (Point to the title of the book.) Yes, this is the title. What else can we find on the cover of the book? Yes, we can find who wrote the book. We call this person the author. What else can we find? Yes. We can find the person who drew the pictures. We call this person the illustrator. Remember, we find important information on the cover of a book. Who can show me the front of our book? The back of the book?*

Reread the book, inviting students to join in if they remember any of the repeated phases, moving the pointer under the words and stopping in a few places where it is appropriate to support students' comprehension.

Say: *As we read our book today, did you have a favorite part? I did! I really liked it when Katy's brother comes to the rescue! He's the one who helps Katie realize that school will be fun! Who would like to share a favorite part?*

Katy's First Day of School

Objectives

Students will:
- Listen and respond to a story using sentence frames.
- Build an awareness of the information on the cover of a book: title, author, illustrator, illustrations.
- Build an awareness of the front and back of a book.

Additional Materials
- Chart paper
- Markers
- Selected book to read aloud
- Pointer

Shared Writing (15 MIN.)

Concepts about Print, Letter Awareness, Phonological Awareness

Call students to the meeting area using the established signal. Ask students what they like to do at recess. Choose 1–2 student's responses to write.

Sample Shared Writing
Gary likes to run.
Susan likes to swing.

As you write, point out the top of the paper, the bottom of the paper and where on the paper you start to write. Talk about starting on the left and going to the right, spaces, a capital letter, return sweep if necessary, and periods. Emphasize the spaces, the number of words in each sentence, and where each word begins. Draw attention to any letter that is a 'stick letter'; such as **L, I,** or **T** and 'slanted letters'; such as **A, K,** and **M** and 'circle letters; such as **C** and **O**. Add curved letters such as **S, G, B** and **D**.

Say: *Gary's sound is /**g**/. Susan's sound is /**s**/. Turn and Talk and share your sound in a respectful conversation.*

Optional: Have students practice returning to their designated seats, or stand up to take a 'brain break.' You may want to ask students to sing, stretch, or move to music at this time.

Objectives

Students will:
• Differentiate and locate stick and slanted letters within print.

Support Tip

For our students who are learning English, avoid the use of slang and colloquialisms when explaining rules and expectations.

Independent Reading (15 MIN.)

Practice Reading to Self and Introduce Library Workstation

Call students to the meeting area using the established signal. Have the anchor chart available to use and read.

Say: *Today we are going to learn about an important way to practice what we learn about reading in our classroom. First, let's look at our anchor chart about our jobs in our classroom.*

Read the anchor chart with your students. Remind them that they will always be doing at least one of these jobs during Reader's Workshop.

Say: *Do you remember what we call this time of our day? Yes, this is Reader's Workshop. During our independent reading time, we are going to think about using workstations. A workstation is a place you will go to practice on something that will help you be a better reader. Let's say that 'Library' is our first workstation. When we think about being in a workstation, we need to remember all we know about our jobs in the classroom, how we act in our room, and our job in the workstation. Today, I'd like for us to make an anchor chart about our Library Workstation.*

Library Workstation

Handle books carefully.

Put books away where they belong.

Read quietly.

Sample Anchor Chart

Invite students to go with you to the library where they will be seated and show you they are ready to listen.

Say: *Yesterday we visited our classroom library and another group chose books to read. Today, the group that comes to the library to choose books will be able to stay in the library to read, go to their seats, or find another place in our room where they can read comfortably. We have learned about how we choose a book and how to handle our books carefully.*

Model this again by carefully choosing a book from the library. Again, model how to carefully lay the book flat on your lap, floor, or table and how to turn the pages slowly and deliberately. When you are ready, model for students how to return the book to its place without bending, tearing, or misplacing it.

Say: *The rest of us will use books from the baskets at our table. Tomorrow, another group will be able to choose a book and practice using our Library Workstation The next day, another group, until all of us have had a chance to use our Library Workstation.*

Ask a table group (or any group of students) to use the Library Workstation. The rest of the class will return to their seats and use the baskets at their table to find and read books.

Objectives

Students will:
- Practice handling books with care.
- Practice returning books to the library.

Additional Materials

- Chart paper
- Markers
- Baskets of books for independent reading

Establishing Routines (30 MIN.)

Smooth Transitions

Remind students how they sit when they come to the carpet. You may want to begin inviting the whole class to the carpet if you feel they are able to perform this routine. If not, invite one of the tables to join you at the carpet. Ask them to show the rest of the class how we move quietly in our room, push our chairs in when we leave our space, and sit with our legs crossed and our hands in our laps.

Say: *Boys and girls, I'm so glad to see that you remembered that when we come to the carpet we want to sit quietly with our legs crossed and our hands in our laps. When I see you sitting quietly like this with your eyes on the speaker, I'll know you're ready to listen.*

Getting Ready for Whole-Group Instruction: Establishing the Teacher's Role During Reader's Workshop

Say: *Let's look at our anchor chart from yesterday to help us remember our jobs while we are in Reader's Workshop.*

Read the chart with students, inviting them to join you when they know a words or remember one of the jobs.

Say: *Did you know that I (the teacher) also have jobs during Reader's Workshop? One of my jobs is to be a good listener, too. I always want to listen to you when you are speaking, just like you listen to me when I'm speaking. This time our anchor chart will say, 'My Teacher's Jobs during Reader's Workshop'. The first thing I'm going to write is to be a listener. Another job I have is to be a speaker. We have respectful conversations and that means we listen and speak, so I will write; Be a speaker. Another job is to read with you, so I will write; Be a reader. Many of my jobs looks like your jobs! If we both remember our jobs, Reader's Workshop will be a time when we can learn together. We will always need to make sure that we ask ourselves which of these jobs we should be doing during Reader's Workshop, and that we are doing your very best.*

Optional: Have students practice returning to their designated seats, or stand up to take a 'brain break.' You may want to ask students to sing, stretch, or move to music at this time.

My Teacher's Jobs During Reader's Workshop
Be a listener.
Be a speaker.
Be a reader.
Be a learner.

Sample Anchor Chart

Objectives

Students will:
- Continue practicing an efficient transition between mini-lessons.
- Understand roles for Reader's Workshop.

Additional Materials

- Chart paper
- Markers
- Selected book to read aloud
- Pointer
- Baskets of books for independent reading

Read-Aloud and Shared Reading (20 MIN.)

Read-Aloud

Call students to the meeting area using the established signal.

Read any book from the Recommended Trade Books in Additional Resources or any other available books such as, *Will I Have A Friend?* by Miriam Cohen.

Say: *Now let's practice Turn and Talk with your partner. Today there is a very special respectful conversation I want you to have. When you talk with your partner today, please start your conversation like this: "I like that Jim found a friend because ___." Let me show you how that sounds.*

Choose a student and model using a sentence frame. Let the student use the sentence frame in return.

Say: *Now sit knee to knee and eye to eye with your Turn and Talk partner and use the sentence frame to share why you liked that Jim found a friend. Remember to say, "I like that Jim found a friend because ___." Remember, also, to have a respectful conversation.*

Observe to see that all students are sharing using respectful conversations and using the sentence frame.

Shared Reading

Call students to the meeting area using the established signal.

Say: *Yesterday we read a book about a little girl name Katy. It was her first day of school and she didn't think she wanted to go.*

Display the cover of the book and review the things we can find on the cover of a book. Also review author and illustrator as well as front and back. The point to the title.

Say: *Do you remember what this is? Yes, this is the title. What else can we find on the cover of the book? Yes, we can find who wrote the book. We call this person the author. What else can we find? Yes. We can find the person who drew the pictures. We call this person the illustrator. Remember, we find important information on the cover of a book. Who can show me the front of our book? The back of the book?*

Open the book and **ask:** *Where do you think I will start reading our book?*

Reread the book, inviting students to join in if they remember any of the repeated phases, moving the pointer under the words and stopping in a few places where it is appropriate to support students' comprehension.

Say: *As we read our book today, did you have a favorite person in the story? We call the people in the story a character. For instance, Katy is a character in the story. Her mom, dad, and brother are also characters. Did you have a favorite character? I did! I really liked it Katy's brother. He was able to help Katy see that school could be fun!*

Allow three or four students to share their favorite character.

Katy's First Day of School

Student Objectives

Students will:
- Continue using the classroom library as a workstation.
- Listen and respond to a story using sentence frames.
- Build an awareness of the information on the cover of a book: title, author, illustrator, illustrations.
- Build an awareness of the front and back of a book.

Additional Materials

- Chart paper
- Markers
- Selected book to read aloud
- Pointer

Shared Writing (15 MIN.)

Concepts about Print, Letter Awareness, Phonological Awareness

Call students to the meeting area using the established signal. Ask students what they like to do with a friend. Choose 1–2 student's responses to write.

> **Sample Shared Writing**
>
> Bella likes to play.
>
> Jordan likes to use blocks.

As you write, point out the top of the paper, the bottom of the paper and where on the paper you start to write. Talk about starting on the left and going to the right. Draw attention to any letter that is a 'stick letter'; such as **L**, **I**, or **T** and 'slanted letters'; such as **A**, **K**, and **M** and 'circle letters'; such as **C** and **O**. Add curved letters such as **S**, **G**, **B**, and **D**. Invite students to make a straight, slanted, circle and curve patterns in the air with their fingers. As you write, emphasize the first phoneme in the student's name.

Say: *Bella's sound is /b/. Jordan's sound is /j/. Turn and Talk and share your sound in a respectful conversation.*

Optional: Have students practice returning to their designated seats, or stand up to take a 'brain break.' You may want to ask students to sing, stretch, or move to music at this time.

Objectives

Students will:
• Continue to differentiate and locate stick, slanted, circle and curved letters within print.

Additional Materials

• Chart paper
• Markers

Independent Reading (20 MIN.)

Model Reading to Self and Using the Classroom Library

Call students to the meeting area using the established signal. Have the anchor chart on 'student jobs' available to use and read.

Say: *Yesterday we learned about an important way to learn in our classroom. During our independent reading time, we learned about using workstations. Remember, a workstation is a place you go and work on something that will help you be a better reader. We decided that our library could be our first workstation because we go there to practice reading. When we think about being in a workstation, we need to remember all we know about our jobs in the classroom, how we act in our room, and our job in the workstation. Today, I'd like for us to look at the anchor chart we make yesterday for our library workstation.*

Read the chart with the class.

Say: *Today, a group of us are going to practice going to our Library Workstation again. Please remember what we do and how we act in our library workstation.*

Invite students who will practice being in the Library Workstation to go with you to the library where they will begin choosing books.

Say: *Today, the group that comes to the Library Workstation to choose books will be able to stay in the library to read, go to their seats, or find another place in our room where they can read comfortably. We have learned about how we choose a book and how to handle our books carefully.*

If needed, model this again by carefully choosing a book from the library. Again, model how to carefully lay the book flat on your lap, floor, or table and how to turn the pages slowly and deliberately. When you are ready, model for students how to return the book to its place without bending, tearing, or misplacing it.

Say: *The rest of us will use books from the baskets at our table. Tomorrow, another group will be able to choose a book and practice using our Library Workstation. The next day, another group, until all of us have had a chance to use our Library Workstation. During independent reading, I want you to think about how you are handling the books, think about ways we will take care of books and our classroom library. I also want the group in the Library Workstation to think about how we return our books so that our library stays neat, and our books stay nice.*

The rest of the class will return to their seats and use the baskets at their table to find and read books. After assisting students in the workstation, circulate, observe and support students to ensure they handle books correctly. At the end of independent reading (perhaps signaling with a bell, clap or any other desired means so students begin to understand the signal when workstation rotations begin), assist students who were in the library workstation return their books properly. Use this as a model time for the rest of the class so there is an example to follow when it is their turn.

Objectives

Students will:
- Practice handling books with care.
- Practice returning books to the library.

Additional Materials

- Pointer
- Baskets of books for independent reading

Support Tip

For children who are young or insecure, pair them with a partner who can help them navigate the expectations of your class.

Establishing Routines (30 MIN.)

Smooth Transitions

Remind students how they sit when they come to the carpet. You may want to begin inviting the whole class to the carpet if you feel they are able to perform this routine. If not, invite one of the tables to join you at the carpet. Ask them to show the rest of the class how we move quietly in our room, push our chairs in when we leave our space, and sit with our legs crossed and our hands in our laps.

Say: *Boys and girls, I'm so glad to see that you remembered that when we come to the carpet we want to sit quietly with our legs crossed and our hands in our laps. When I see you sitting quietly like this with your eyes on the speaker, I'll know you're ready to listen.*

Getting Ready for Whole-Group Instruction: Reviewing Student and Teacher Roles During Reader's Workshop

Say: *Let's look at our anchor charts to help us thing about our roles during Reader's Workshop. We decided that both of us, students and the teacher have very special jobs to do during Reader's Workshop. Let's read these charts.*

Read the chart with students, inviting them to join you when they know a words or remember one of the jobs.

Say: *Do you notice that being a listener is on both of our charts? I'd like for us to think about what you do to be a listener, and what I do to be a listener. We both have to make sure we look at the speaker, think about what the speaker is saying, and figure out how that helps us learn about something new. Let's practice being listeners. First, I'd like for you to show me what a listener looks like. (Model sitting quietly with hands in lap and eyes on the speaker.) Now, turn and talk to your shoulder partner about being a listener. Use this sentence frame: Listeners_____.*

Optional: Have students practice returning to their designated seats, or stand up to take a 'brain break.' You may want to ask students to sing, stretch, or move to music at this time.

My Teacher's Jobs During Reader's Workshop
Be a listener.
Be a speaker.
Be a reader.
Be a learner.

Sample Anchor Chart

Objectives

Students will:
- Continue practicing an efficient transition between mini-lessons.
- Understand roles for Reader's Workshop.

Additional Materials

- Chart paper
- Markers
- Selected book to read aloud
- Pointer
- Baskets of books for independent reading

Read-Aloud and Shared Reading (20 MIN.)

"Mary Had a Little Lamb"

Read-Aloud

Call students to the meeting area using the established signal.

Read any book from the Recommended Trade Books in Additional Resources or any other available books such as, *Chrysanthemum* by Kevin Henkes.

Say: *Now let's practice Turn and Talk with your partner. We have been practicing respectful conversations using a sentence frame. When you talk with your partner today, please start your conversation like this: Chrysanthemum was _____ because_____. Let me show you how that sounds. Chrysanthemum was brave because she went to school when the other kids made fun of her name.*

Choose a student and model using a sentence frame. Let the student use the sentence frame in return.

Say: *Now sit knee to knee and eye to eye with your Turn and Talk partner and use the sentence frame to share what you thought about Chrysanthemum. Remember, also, to have a respectful conversation.*

Observe to see that all students are sharing using respectful conversations and using the sentence frame.

Shared Reading

Call students to the meeting area using the established signal.

Say: *Today I'd like for us to read a poem.*

Display "Mary Had a Little Lamb" from the back of *Katy's First Day of School* and guide students to notice the difference between the poem and a book. Also, ask them to notice the author and tell them that we call the author of a poem a poet. Talk about the illustrator and what an illustrator does.

Say: *What do you notice about a poem? Yes, it's shorter than a book. Yes, it has fewer words. Let me read this poem to you. Let's read it again, and this time, I'd like for you to listen for your favorite part. Be ready to tell about it!*

Read the title, author and illustrator helping students to find where the poem begins, where stanzas are, and where the poem ends.

Read and then reread the poem, inviting students to join in if they remember any of the repeated phases, moving the pointer under the words and stopping in a few places where it is appropriate to support students' comprehension.

Say: *As we read our poem today, did you have a favorite part? I did! I really liked it when _____. What was your favorite part?*

Allow three or four students to share their favorite character.

Say: *Now turn and talk with your partner about your favorite part. Begin your respectful conversation with: "My favorite part is _____."*

Student Objectives

Students will:
- Continue using the classroom library as a workstation.
- Listen and respond to a story using sentence frames.
- Build an awareness of the information on the cover of a book: title, author, illustrator, illustrations.
- Build an awareness of the front and back of a book.

Additional Materials

- Chart paper
- Markers
- Selected book to read aloud
- Pointer

Shared Writing (15 MIN.)

Concepts about Print, Letter Awareness, Phonological Awareness

Call students to the meeting area using the established signal.

Say: *Today I'd like for us to remember all of the things we've been learning that good writers do when they put their thoughts on paper. (Start here (points), goes to the next line when one is full, begin with a capital, end with a period, and puts spaces between words.) Do you remember when we talked about the marks we put at the end of a thought or sentence? We called those marks punctuation. One kind of punctuation is a period. We put a period at the end of a sentence that tells us something. Watch while we practice how to make a sentence.*

Put each of the words **I**, **like**, **school** on a piece of large piece of paper. Then hand each piece of paper to a student. Have them join you and build the sentence, *I like school.* Focus on the period and where it is (at the end). Show students how the sentence would sound if you moved the student with the period to the middle of the sentence, beginning of the sentence, etc.

(Accept responses such as: start here (points), goes to the next line when one is full, begin with a capital, end with a period, puts spaces between words.)

Ask students what their favorite part of the poem was. After practicing sentences orally and checking for complete sentences, choose 1–2 student's responses to write.

Sample Shared Writing
Noel likes that it rhymes.
Dave thinks it is funny.

As you write, review student responses by pointing out the top of the paper, the bottom of the paper and where on the paper you start to write. Talk about starting on the left and going to the right, spaces, a capital letter, but focus especially on the period. Draw attention to any letter that is a 'stick letter'; such as **L, I,** or **T** and 'slanted letters'; such as **A, K,** and **M** and 'circle letters'; such as **C** and **O.** Add 'curved letters' such as **S, G, B,** and **D.** Invite students to make a straight, slanted, circle and curve patterns in the air with their fingers. As you write, emphasize the first phoneme in the student's name.

Say: *Noel's sound is /n/. Dave's sound is /d/. What is the first sound in your name?*

Optional: Have students practice returning to their designated seats, or stand up to take a 'brain break.' You may want to ask students to sing, stretch, or move to music at this time.

Objectives

Students will:
• Continue to differentiate and locate stick, slanted, circle and curved letters within print.
• Recognize ending of a sentence.

Additional Materials

• Chart paper
• Markers

Independent Reading (20 MIN.)

Practice Library Workstation and Introduce Writing Workstation

Call students to the meeting area using the established signal. Have the anchor chart on Library Workstation available to use and read.

Say: *A workstation is a place you go and work on something that will help you be a better reader. We decided that our library could be our first workstation, because we go there to practice reading. Today, I'd like for us to think about another workstation that we will have in our room. It is a Writing Workstation. Come with me to the place where we'll have a writing workstation.*

This will look different depending on your classroom. Some ideas may be a special place, or bag/basket of resources that can be moved to different places. After students are comfortable seated close to the Writing Workstation, **say:** *When we go to our Library Workstation, we read. When we come to our Writing Workstation, we write. Today, we are going to make an anchor chart about our Writing Workstation. One thing we may want to put on our chart is 'Work Quietly.'* Ask for other suggestions.

Writing Workstation
1. Work quietly.
2. Write or draw the whole time.
3. Tell others about your writing.

Sample Anchor Chart

Say: *Today, a group of us are going to practice going to our Library Workstation again. Please remember what we do and how we act in our Library Workstation.*

Invite students who will practice being in the Library Workstation to go with you to the library where they will begin choosing books.

Say: *Remember, the group that comes to the Library Workstation to choose books will be able to stay in the library to read, go to their seats, or find another place in our room where they can read comfortably. We have learned about how we choose a book and how to handle our books carefully.*

If needed, model this again by carefully choosing a book from the library.

Say: *The rest of us will use books from the baskets at our table. Tomorrow, we will begin using the Writing Workstation, too. During independent reading, I want you to think about how you are handling the books, think about ways we will take care of books and our classroom library.*

The rest of the class will return to their seats and use the baskets at their table to find and read books. After assisting students in the workstation, circulate, observe and support students to ensure they handle books correctly.

Objectives

Students will:
- Practice handling books with care.
- Practice returning books to the library.
- Practice going to Library Workstation.
- Be introduced to Writing Workstation.
- Create anchor chart for Writing Workstation.

Additional Materials

- Pointer
- Baskets of books for independent reading
- Spot and materials for Writing Workstation
- Chart
- Markers

Support Tip

For children who are cognitively challenged, break down new routines into smaller instructional steps.

Establishing Routines (30 MIN.)

Smooth Transitions

Remind students how they sit when they come to the carpet. You may want to begin inviting the whole class to the carpet if you feel they are able to perform this routine. If not, invite one of the tables to join you at the carpet. Ask them to show the rest of the class how we move quietly in our room, push our chairs in when we leave our space, and sit with our legs crossed and our hands in our laps.

Say: *Boys and girls, I'm so glad to see that you remembered that when we come to the carpet we want to sit quietly with our legs crossed and our hands in our laps. When I see you sitting quietly like this with your eyes on the speaker, I'll know you're ready to listen.*

Getting Ready for Whole-Group Instruction: Reviewing Student and Teacher Roles during Reader's Workshop

Say: *Let's look at our anchor charts to help us thing about our roles during Reader's Workshop. We decided that both of us, students and the teacher have very special jobs to do during Reader's Workshop. Let's read these charts.*

Read the student and teacher roles anchor charts created on Days 4 and 5, inviting students to join you when they know a words or remember one of the roles.

Say: *Do you notice that being a speaker is on both of our charts? I'd like for us to think about what you do to be a speaker, and what I do to be a speaker. We both have to make sure we talk about a special topic, think about what the topic is, and say the words that tell out thinking about the topic. Let's practice being speakers. First, I'd like for you to show me what a listener looks like. (Model sitting quietly with hands in lap and eyes on the speaker.) Now, turn and talk to your partner about being a speaker. Use this sentence frame: Speakers_____.*

Optional: Have students practice returning to their designated seats, or stand up to take a 'brain break.' You may want to ask students to sing, stretch, or move to music at this time.

Objectives

Students will:
- Continue practicing an efficient transition between mini-lessons.
- Understand roles for Reader's Workshop.

Additional Materials

- Chart paper
- Markers
- Selected book to read aloud
- Pointer
- Baskets of books for independent reading

Read-Aloud and Shared Reading (20 MIN.)

Read-Aloud

Call students to the meeting area using the established signal.

Read any book from the Recommended Trade Books in Additional Resources or any other available books such as, **Chicka, Chicka Boom, Boom** by Bill Martin.

Say: *Now let's practice Turn and Talk with your partner. We have been practicing respectful conversations using a sentence frame. When you talk with your partner today, please start your conversation like this:* **Chicka, Chicka, Boom, Boom** *is a good book because _____. Let me show you how that sounds.* **Chicka, Chicka Boom, Boom** *is a good book because I like to say the words,* **Chicka, Chicka, Boom, Boom**!

Choose a student and model using a sentence frame. Let the student use the sentence frame in return.

Say: *Now sit knee to knee and eye to eye with your Turn and Talk partner and use the sentence frame to share what you thought about* **Chicka, Chicka, Boom, Boom**. *Remember, also, to have a respectful conversation.*

Observe to see that all students are sharing using respectful conversations and using the sentence frame.

Shared Reading

Call students to the meeting area using the established signal. Display the poem and review the things students noticed about the poem.

Say: *What do you notice about the lines of a poem? Yes, some of them rhyme. Let's read the poem again and see if we hear some rhyming words. Did you hear any words that rhyme?*

Read and then reread the poem, inviting students to join in if they remember any of the repeated phases, moving the pointer under the words and stopping in a few places where it is appropriate to support students' comprehension. Guide a conversation about retelling the poem.

Say: *Many times, we retell what we heard by using the words* **First, Next, Then, Last**. *Listen how I show you how that sounds when I retell this poem.*

Model retelling the poem. Ask 1 or 2 children to practice retelling the poem.

Say: *Turn and talk to your partner about what happened in our poem. Use this sentence frame: First, ___ ; Next, ___ ; Then, ___ ; and Last, ___ .*

"Mary Had a Little Lamb"

Student Objectives

Students will:
- Continue using the classroom library as a workstation.
- Listen and respond to a story using sentence frames.
- Build an awareness of the information on the cover of a book: title, author, illustrator, illustrations.
- Build an awareness of the front and back of a book.

Additional Materials

- Chart paper
- Markers
- Selected book to read aloud
- Pointer

Objectives

Students will:
- Continue to differentiate and locate stick, slanted, circle and curved letters within print.

Additional Materials

- Chart paper
- Markers

Shared Writing (15 MIN.)

Concepts about Print, Letter Awareness, Phonological Awareness

Call students to the meeting area using the established signal.

Say: *Today I'd like for us to remember all of the things we've been learning that good writers do when they put their thoughts on paper. (Start here (points), goes to the next line when one is full, begin with a capital, end with a period, and puts spaces between words.) Do you remember the punctuation mark we talked about yesterday? Yes, it was a period. Today we're going to practice using a period at the end of a sentence.*

Ask students to think what happened first in the poem and write that sentence. Continue until you have retold the poem using first, next, then, last, focusing on the period at the end of the sentence.

Sample Shared Writing

First,_____.

Next, _____.

Then, _____.

Last, _____.

As you write, review student responses by pointing out the top of the paper, the bottom of the paper and where on the paper you start to write. Talk about starting on the left and going to the right, spaces, a capital letter, but focus especially on the period. Draw attention to any letter that is a 'stick letter'; such as **L, I,** or **T** and 'slanted letters'; such as **A, K,** and **M** and 'circle letters'; such as **C** and **O**. Add 'curved letters' such as **S, G, B** and **D**. Invite students to make a straight, slanted, circle and curve patterns in the air with their fingers. As you write, emphasize the first phoneme in each of the sequence words.

Say: *First begins with /f/. Next begins with /n/. Do any of our names start with these sounds?*

Optional: Have students practice returning to their designated seats, or stand up to take a 'brain break.' You may want to ask students to sing, stretch, or move to music at this time.

Independent Reading (20 MIN.)

Introduce and Practice Using Response Journals

Call students to the meeting area using the established signal. Have the anchor chart on Library Workstation available to use and read.

Say: *We are learning about an important way to learn in our classroom. During our independent reading time, we're practicing using workstations. Remember, a workstation is a place you go and work on something that will help you be a better reader. We decided that our library could be our first workstation because we go there to practice reading. When we think about being in a workstation, we need to remember all we know about our jobs in the classroom, how we act in our room, and our job in the workstation. Yesterday, we talked about another workstation that we will have in our room. It is a Writing Workstation. Come with me to the place where we'll have a writing workstation.*

Note: This will look different depending on your classroom. Some ideas may be a special place with a writing table, or bag/basket of resources that can be moved to different places. After students are comfortably seated close to the Writing Workstation, **say:** *Let's look at our anchor chart we made for the writing station. Did anyone think of something more to add? We said that when we go to the writing workstation, we write. Today, we are going to think about some of the things we write about. This is my response journal. I write down my thoughts about something I read in my response journal. (Model how you start on the first page, then use the next page – not jumping anywhere in your journal.) Let me show you what I mean. (Use a chart tablet to model independent writing.) This morning, we read a book call* **Chicka, Chicka, Boom, Boom**. *I really liked this book, so I'm going to draw a picture and write about what I liked.*

Draw a picture of the letters falling out of the tree. If appropriate for your class, use the instructional strategy of shared writing to write a sentence about your picture. For example, The letters fell out of the tree.

Say: *Today, I would like for all of you to practice drawing a picture and writing about your favorite part of* **Chicka, Chicka, Boom, Boom** *in your response journal.*

Ask the class to return to their seats. Circulate, observe and support students to ensure they understand how to handle their response journals correctly. At the end of independent reading (perhaps signaling with a bell, clap or any other desired means so students begin to understand the signal when workstation rotations begin), assist students in returning their response journals to a predetermined place. Remind them that this is where they will return their journals each time they are finished in the writing workstation.

Objectives

Students will:
- Practice handling books with care.
- Practice returning books to the library.
- Practice going to Library Workstation.
- Review anchor chart for Writing Workstation.
- Introduce response journals.

Additional Materials

- Pointer
- Baskets of books for independent reading
- Anchor chart for Library Workstation
- Spot and materials for Writing Workstation
- Chart
- Markers
- Response Journals for students

Support Tip

For children who are visually challenged, be sure to provide dark markers or crayons for drawing and writing.

Establishing Routines (30 min.)

Smooth Transitions

Remind students how they sit when they come to the carpet. You may want to begin inviting the whole class to the carpet if you feel they are able to perform this routine. If not, invite one of the tables to join you at the carpet. Ask them to show the rest of the class how we move quietly in our room, push our chairs in when we leave our space, and sit with our legs crossed and our hands in our laps.

Say: *Boys and girls, I'm so glad to see that you remembered that when we come to the carpet we want to sit quietly with our legs crossed and our hands in our laps. When I see you sitting quietly like this with your eyes on the speaker, I'll know you're ready to listen.*

Getting Ready for Whole-Group Instruction: Reviewing Student and Teacher Roles during Reader's Workshop

Say: *Let's look at our anchor charts to help us think about our roles during Reader's Workshop. We decided that both of us, students and the teacher have very special jobs to do during Reader's Workshop. Let's read these charts.*

Read the student and teacher roles anchor charts created on Days 4 and 5, inviting students to join you when they know a words or remember one of the roles.

Say: *Do you notice that being a partner is on both of our charts? I'd like for us to think about what you do to be a partner, and what I do to be a partner. We have to make sure we are ready to help each other if someone doesn't understand something or has a question. Maybe one of you would help someone in a workstation or on the playground, or if one of you asks me how to use your response journal or do something else in our room, I'd be sure to help you understand. Let's practice being good partners. First, I'd like for you to show me what a good listener looks like because we need to be a listener to know how we can help someone. (Model sitting quietly with hands in lap and eyes on the speaker.) Now, turn and talk to your partner about being a partner. Use this sentence frame: Partners_____.*

Optional: Have students practice returning to their designated seats, or stand up to take a 'brain break.' You may want to ask students to sing, stretch, or move to music at this time.

Objectives

Students will:
- Continue practicing an efficient transition between mini-lessons.
- Understand roles for Reader's Workshop.

Additional Materials

- Anchor charts with student and teacher roles from Days 4 and 5
- Selected book to read aloud
- Pointer

Read-Aloud and Shared Reading (20 Min.)

Read-Aloud

Call students to the meeting area using the established signal.

Read any book from the Recommended Trade Books in Additional Resources or any other available books, such as *The Kissing Hand* by Ruth E. Harper.

Say: *Now let's practice Turn and Talk with your partner. When you talk with your partner today, please start your conversation like this: I was afraid when _____ and _____helped me.*

Choose a student and model using a sentence frame. Let the student use the sentence frame in return.

Say: *Now sit knee to knee and eye to eye with your Turn and Talk partner and use the sentence frame to share what you thought about **Chicka, Chicka, Boom, Boom.** Remember, also, to have a respectful conversation.*

Observe to see that all students are sharing using respectful conversations and using the sentence frame.

Shared Reading

Call students to the meeting area using the established signal.

Say: *This week we have been reading a poem takes place partly in school.*

Display the poem and review the things we noticed about the poem. Then point to the title.

Say: *Listen while I read it again. If you remember any of the words, please read them with me. (Reread the poem.) Let's talk again about what we know about a poem. (Allow students time to respond to what they know about the poem. This should be a review of the first days of this week.) Yesterday we noticed that some of the lines of the poem rhyme. Did you hear any different rhymes?*

Read and then reread the poem, inviting students to join in if they remember any of the repeated phases, moving the pointer under the words and stopping in a few places where it is appropriate to support students' comprehension.

Model telling an important part of the poem. Ask 1 or 2 students to share an important part, listening for complete sentences. Model using complete sentences if necessary.

Say: *Turn and talk to your partner about an important part in the poem. Use this sentences frame: An important part of this poem is _____.*

"Mary Had a Little Lamb"

Student Objectives

Students will:
- Listen and respond to a story using sentence frames.
- Build an awareness of the information in a poem: title, author, illustrator, illustrations.
- Build an awareness a poem.

Additional Materials

- Chart paper
- Markers
- Selected book to read aloud
- Pointer

Shared Writing (15 Min.)

Concepts about Print, Letter Awareness, Phonological Awareness

Call students to the meeting area using the established signal.

Say: *Today I'd like for us to remember all of the things we've been learning that good writers do when they put their thoughts on paper. (Start here (points), goes to the next line when one is full, begin with a capital, end with a period, and puts spaces between words.) Do you remember the punctuation mark we talked about yesterday? Yes, it was a period. Today we're going to practice using a period at the end of a sentence.*

Ask students to think about a part of the poem they liked the best. Allow students to share what they liked the best, checking for complete sentences. Choose 1 or 2 sentences to use for shared writing. Focus on all concepts of print used (see below), but especially focus on complete sentences and using a period at the end of a sentence.

Sample Shared Writing
Terri thinks the school is important.
Roger thinks the boy is important.

As you write, review student responses by pointing out the top of the paper, the bottom of the paper and where on the paper you start to write. Talk about starting on the left and going to the right, spaces, a capital letter, and return sweep if necessary. Draw attention to any letter that is a 'stick letter'; such as **L, I,** or **T** and 'slanted letters'; such as **A, K,** and **M** and 'circle letters'; such as **C** and **O**. Add 'curved letters' such as **S, G, B,** and **D**. Invite students to make a straight, slanted, circle and curve patterns in the air with their fingers. As you write, emphasize the first phoneme in each of the sequence words.

Say: *Terri's name begins with /t/. Can you find other things in our room that begin with /t/? Roger starts with /r/. Can you find other things in our room that start with /r/? Do any of our names start with these letters?*

Optional: Have students practice returning to their designated seats, or stand up to take a 'brain break.' You may want to ask students to sing, stretch, or move to music at this time.

Objectives

Students will:
• Continue to differentiate and locate stick, slanted, circle and curved letters within print.

Additional Materials

• Chart paper
• Markers

Independent Reading (20 Min.)

Introduce and Practice Using Response Journals

Call students to the meeting area using the established signal. Have the anchor chart on Library Workstation available to use and read.

Say: *We are learning about an important way to learn in our classroom. During our independent reading time, we're practicing using workstations. Remember, a workstation is a place you go and work on something that will help you be a better reader. We decided that our Library could be our first workstation because we go there to practice reading. When we think about being in a workstation, we need to remember all we know about our jobs in the classroom, how we act in our room, and our job in the workstation. Yesterday, we talked about another workstation that we will have in our room. It is a Writing workstation. Come with me to the place where we'll have a writing workstation.*

Note: This will look different depending on your classroom. You may choose a special place or bag/basket of resources that can be moved to different places. After students are comfortably seated close to the Writing Workstation, **say:** *Let's look at our anchor chart we made for the writing station. Did anyone think of something more to add? We said that when we go to the writing workstation, we write. Yesterday, we practiced writing about a part we liked in Chicka, Chicka, Boom, Boom. Today we are going to think about some different things we could write about. Do you remember when we read The Kissing Hand this morning? In my response journal, I'm ready to write on this page. I'm going to write how someone helped me not be afraid to get ready for Kindergarten this year. (Model how you started on the first page and now you're ready to use the next page – not jumping anywhere in your journal.) Let me show you what I mean. (Use a chart tablet to model independent writing.) I remember how my sister helped me not be afraid to start a new year. She helped me clean our room, cut out letters, and arrange our tables.*

Draw a picture two people working in the classroom. (Or any other appropriate story.) Use the instructional strategy of shared writing to write a sentence about your picture. For example, My sister helped me in our room.

Say: *Today, I would like for all of you to practice drawing a picture and writing about how someone helped you not be afraid to start Kindergarten in your response journal.*

Ask the class to return to their seats. Circulate, observe and support students to ensure they understand how to handle their response journals correctly. At the end of independent reading (perhaps signaling with a bell, clap or any other desired means so students begin to understand the signal when workstation rotations begin), assist students in returning their response journals to a predetermined place. Remind them that this is where they will return their journals each time they are finished in the writing workstation.

Objectives

Students will:
- Practice handling books with care.
- Practice returning books to the library.
- Practice going to Library Workstation.
- Review anchor chart for Writing Workstation.
- Introduce response journals.

Additional Materials

- Pointer
- Baskets of books for independent reading
- Anchor chart for Library Workstation
- Spot and materials for Writing Workstation
- Chart
- Markers
- Response Journals for students

Support Tip

For children with social and emotional challenges, it may be necessary to revisit classroom routines and rituals frequently.

Establishing Routines (30 Min.)

Smooth Transitions

Remind students how they sit when they come to the carpet. You may want to begin inviting the whole class to the carpet if you feel they are able to perform this routine. If not, invite one of the tables to join you at the carpet. Ask them to show the rest of the class how we move quietly in our room, push our chairs in when we leave our space, and sit with our legs crossed and our hands in our laps.

Say: *Boys and girls, I'm so glad to see that you remembered that when we come to the carpet we want to sit quietly with our legs crossed and our hands in our laps. When I see you sitting quietly like this with your eyes on the speaker, I'll know you're ready to listen.*

Getting Ready for Whole-Group Instruction: Fiction and Nonfiction text

Say: *Today we're going to visit about some very special books. There are two different kinds of books that we can read. One kind of book is fiction. Do you remember this book? (perhaps* The Kissing Hand *by Ruth E. Harper) This book is a fiction book. That means it's not true or it didn't really happen. Let's look closely. Can animals talk? Does real-life school look like this? This is a book where the author used her imagination to write the story. Now let's look at this book. (perhaps a nonfiction text about animals) Do you think this is a true book? Why? Yes. I see real pictures of animals. Anything else? Yes, the table of contents tells us that we will read about what animals eat, where they live, and how they move. All of these things are real! Let's make an anchor chart about fiction and nonfiction books. We want to make sure to list things that make them different from each other.*

Fiction Books	Nonfiction Books
Not real	True
Illustrations	Real pictures

Say: *As we read books in our room, we're going to be detectives and notice whether or not they are fiction or nonfiction. As we notice how they are different, we'll add that to our chart. Turn and talk with your partner about the difference between fiction and nonfiction books. Use this sentence frame: I know a book is fiction when _____. And I know a book in nonfiction when _____. Be sure to use what we know about having a respectful conversation.*

Optional: Have students practice returning to their designated seats, or stand up to take a 'brain break.' You may want to ask students to sing, stretch, or move to music at this time.

Objectives

Students will:
• Continue practicing an efficient transition between mini-lessons.
• Understand roles for Reader's Workshop.

Additional Materials

• Anchor charts with student and teacher roles from Days 4 and 5
• Selected book to read aloud
• Pointer

Read-Aloud and Shared Reading (20 Min.)

Read-Aloud

Call students to the meeting area using the established signal.

Read any book from the Recommended Trade Books in Additional Resources or any other available books such as, *If You Take a Mouse to School* by Laura Joffe Numeroff.

Say: *We have been practicing respectful conversations using a sentence frame. When you talk with your partner today, please start your conversation like this: I was afraid when _____ and _____ helped me.*

Choose a student and model using a sentence frame. Let the student use the sentence frame in return.

Say: *With your Turn and Talk partner use the sentence frame to share what you thought about Chicka, Chicka, Boom, Boom. Remember, also, to have a respectful conversation.*

Observe to see that all students are sharing using respectful conversations and using the sentence frame.

Shared Reading

Call students to the meeting area using the established signal.

Say: *This week we have been reading a poem about school.*

Display the poem and review the things we noticed about the poem. Also review the author. Remind students that we call the author of a poem a poet. Talk about the illustrator and what an illustrator does. Then point to the title.

Say: *Listen while I read it again. If you remember any of the words, please read them with me. (Reread the poem.) Let's talk again about what we know about a poem. (Allow students time to respond to what they know about the poem. This should be a review of the first days of this week.) Yesterday we noticed that some of the lines of the poem rhyme. Did you hear any different rhymes?*

Read and then reread the poem, inviting students to join in if they remember any of the repeated phases, moving the pointer under the words and stopping in a few places where it is appropriate to support students' comprehension.

Say: *Let's put some things we know about a poem in an anchor chart. What's one idea we know? Anyone else? (Keep accepting ideas and add them to the chart.)*

What We Know about Poems

A poem has a title.

A poet writes a poem.

A poem can have rhyming words.

A poem is shorter than a book.

"Mary Had a Little Lamb"

Student Objectives

Students will:
- Listen and respond to a story using sentence frames.
- Build an awareness of the information in a poem: title, author, illustrator, illustrations.
- Create an anchor chart about poems.

Additional Materials

- Chart paper
- Markers
- Selected book to read aloud
- Pointer
- Anchor chart of rhyming words

Shared Writing (15 Min.)

Concepts about Print, Letter Awareness, Phonological Awareness

Call students to the meeting area using the established signal.

Say: *Today I'd like for us to remember all of the things we've been learning that writers do when they put their thoughts on paper. (Start here (points), goes to the next line when one is full, begin with a capital, end with a period, and puts spaces between words.) Today I want to make sure that we know where a word starts and ends. Let's look at our poem we've been reading. I know that I start reading here. What I want to think about is how many words are in the first sentence. I'm going to think aloud for you to help you know how to think about a word.*

Think aloud: *I know a word is made of letters. I can look for words by seeing where the spaces are between words, like this. (Model a word, then a space, then another word.) That helps me know where a word starts and stops. When I know that, then I can count the words in this sentence. (Model counting the words. Ask students to count with you.)*

Ask students to think about what they know about words. Allow students to share what they know, checking for complete sentences. Choose 1 or 2 sentences to use for shared writing.

Sample Shared Writing
Jennifer knows a word has letters.
Steve knows there are spaces between words.

As you write, review student responses by pointing out the top of the paper, the bottom of the paper and where on the paper you start to write. Talk about starting on the left and going to the right, spaces, a capital letter, return sweep if necessary, and periods. Emphasize the spaces and the number of words in each sentence. Draw attention to any letter that is a 'stick letter'; such as **L**, **I**, or **T** and 'slanted letters'; such as **A**, **K**, and **M** and 'circle letters'; such as **C** and **O**. Add 'curved letters' such as **S**, **G**, **B** and **D**. Invite students to make a straight, slanted, circle and curve patterns in the air with their fingers. As you write, emphasize the first phoneme in each of the sequence words.

Say: *Jennifer's name begins with /j/. Can you find other things in our room that begin with /j/? Steve's starts with /s/. Can you find other words in our sentence that start with /s/? Do any of our names start with these letters?*

Optional: Have students practice returning to their designated seats, or stand up to take a 'brain break.' You may want to ask students to sing, stretch, or move to music at this time.

Objectives

Students will:
- Continue to differentiate and locate stick, slanted, circle and curved letters within print.
- Concepts of print – identify a word

Additional Materials

- Chart paper
- Markers

Independent Reading (20 Min.)

Introduce and Practice Using Response Journals

Call students to the meeting area using the established signal. Have the anchor chart on Library Workstation available to use and read.

Say: *We are learning about an important way to learn in our classroom. During our independent reading time, we're practicing using workstations. Remember, a workstation is a place you go and work on something that will help you be a better reader. We decided that our Library could be our first workstation because we go there to practice reading. We've also been practicing another workstation called our Writing Workstation. Now, I'd like for us to think about our Word Work Workstation. Remember, when we think about being in a workstation, we need to remember all we know about our jobs in the classroom, how we act in our room, and our job in the workstation. Come with me to the place where we'll have a Word Work Workstation.*

Note: This will look different depending on your classroom. You may choose a special place or bag/basket of resources that can be moved to different places. After students are comfortably seated close to the Word Work Workstation, **say:** *Let's begin by making an anchor chart for our Word Work Station. When we are here we will practice making words with letters. Maybe the first thing we should say is that we will work with letters. Did anyone think of something more to add? Yes, we also need to practice working quietly. Anything else? Good! We want to be good partners. (Accept all reasonable responses.) We are going to practice using our letters to make our names today. We can also practice making any words we know!*

Word Work Workstation
We work with letters.
We work quietly.
We are a good partner.
We think how words go together.

Have baggies with an appropriate number of magnetic or paper letters for each child.

Ask the class to return to their seats. Circulate, observe, and support students to ensure they understand how to handle their bags of letters appropriately. At the end of independent reading (perhaps signaling with a bell, clap or any other desired means so students begin to understand the signal when workstation rotations begin), assist students in returning their letters to a predetermined place in the Word Study Workstation.. Remind them that this is where they will return their letters each time they are finished in the word study workstation.

Objectives

Students will:
- Review anchor chart for Writing Workstation.
- Introduce Word Work Workstation.
- Create anchor chart for Word Work Workstation.

Additional Materials

- Pointer
- Anchor chart for Library Workstation
- Chart
- Markers
- Bags of letters for each student

Support Tip

For children with physical challenges, make sure the room layout accommodates then with wide, open areas and access to all materials.

Objectives

Students will:
- Continue practicing an efficient transition between mini-lessons.
- Be introduced to fiction and nonfiction text.
- Create an anchor chart listing differences of fiction and nonfiction text.

Additional Materials

- Selected book to read aloud
- Several examples of fiction and nonfiction text for turn and talk partners
- Pointer

Establishing Routines (30 Min.)

Smooth Transitions

Remind students how they sit when they come to the carpet. You may want to begin inviting the whole class to the carpet if you feel they are able to perform this routine. If not, invite one of the tables to join you at the carpet. Ask them to show the rest of the class how we move quietly in our room, push our chairs in when we leave our space, and sit with our legs crossed and our hands in our laps.

Say: *I'm so glad to see that you remembered that when we come to the carpet we want to sit quietly with our legs crossed and our hands in our laps. When I see you sitting quietly like this with your eyes on the speaker, I'll know you're ready to listen.*

Getting Ready for Whole-Group Instruction: Fiction and Nonfiction Text

Have an example of fiction text (perhaps a book they've already read as a read-aloud) and nonfiction text (perhaps a subject they can connect with such as animals.)

Say: *Yesterday we started talking about some very special books. There are two different kinds of books that we can read. Do you remember what they are? Yes. One kind of book is fiction. Yes. The other book is nonfiction. Do you remember this book? (Any fiction book the class is familiar with.) This book is a fiction book. Do you remember what that means? Yes. That means it's not true or it didn't really happen. Let's look closely. (Point out features of the book that don't seem real.) This is a book where the author used her imagination to write the story. Now let's look at this book. (Perhaps a nonfiction science text) Do you think this is a true book? Why? Yes. I see real pictures. Anything else? Yes, the table of contents tells us that we will read about things that are real. All of these things are real! Let's look at the anchor chart we made yesterday about fiction and nonfiction. As we look at fiction and nonfiction books, is there anything else we could add? We want to make sure to list things that make them different from each other.*

Fiction Books	Nonfiction Books
Not real	True
Illustrations	Real pictures
Pretend people	Real people
Pretend places	Real places

Say: *As we read books in our room, we're going to be detectives and notice whether or not they are fiction or nonfiction. I'm going to hand each partner a book. I'd like for you to look at the book and use this sentence frame: We think this book is (fiction or nonfiction) because _____. Let me show you what I mean. I look at this book and notice pictures of reptiles. I think this book is nonfiction because I see pictures of real snakes. Be sure to use what we know about having a respectful conversation.*

Optional: Have students practice returning to their designated seats, or stand up to take a 'brain break.' You may want to ask students to sing, stretch, or move to music at this time.

Read-Aloud and Shared Reading (20 Min.)

Read-Aloud

Call students to the meeting area using the established signal.

Read any book from the Recommended Trade Books in Additional Resources or any other available books such as, *Kindergarten Rocks* by Katie Davies.

Say: *Now let's practice Turn and Talk with your partner. We have been practicing respectful conversations using a sentence frame. When you talk with your partner today, please start your conversation like this: I was afraid when _____ and _____ helped me.*

Choose a student and model using a sentence frame. Let the student use the sentence frame in return.

Say: *Now let's practice Turn and Talk with your partner. When you talk with your partner today, please start your conversation like this: The first day of Kindergarten, I liked _____.*

Observe to see that all students are sharing using respectful conversations and using the sentence frame.

Shared Reading

Call students to the meeting area using the established signal.

Say: *This week we have been reading a poem about school. Listen while I read it. If you remember any of the words, please read them with me. (Reread the poem.) Does this poem remind you of any other poem you know? (Allow students time to respond.) Are the poems alike? Yes. Many poems have rhyming words.*

Read and then reread the poem, inviting students to join in if they remember any of the repeated phases, moving the pointer under the words, and stopping in a few places where it is appropriate to support students' comprehension.

Say: *Let's look at our anchor chart about poems. Is there anything you'd like to add? (Keep accepting ideas and add them to the chart.)*

What We Know about Poems

A poem has a title.

A poem is written by a poet.

A poem can have rhyming words.

A poem is shorter than a book.

"Mary Had a Little Lamb"

Student Objectives

Students will:
- Build an awareness of the information in a poem: title, author, illustrator, illustrations.

Additional Materials

- Chart paper
- Markers
- Selected book to read aloud
- Pointer
- Anchor Chart about poems

Shared Writing (15 Min.)

Concepts about Print, Letter Awareness, Phonological Awareness

Objectives

Students will:
• Continue to differentiate and locate stick, slanted, circle and curved letters within print.

Additional Materials

• Chart paper
• Markers
• The first sentence of the poem written on a sentence strip for the class to see.
• Sticky dots, markers or some other way to mark beginning sounds

Call students to the meeting area using the established signal.

Say: *Today I'd like for us to remember all of the things we've been learning that good writers do when they put their thoughts on paper. Today I want to make sure that we know where a word starts and ends. Let's look at our poem we've been reading.*

Put the sentence strip with first sentence of the poem written on it in front of the class.

I know that I start reading here. What I want to think about is the first letters and sounds I hear in the words. I'm going to take this red sticky dot and put it under the first letter I see in each word. How many dots do I need? How do you know? This helps me know where a word starts. When I know that, then I can think about the sound that goes with that letter and get my mouth ready to say a word that would fit. Let me show you.

Model looking at the first word, thinking about the first letter, and saying the sound. Then begin reading using the word you see. Ask students to read with you. Continue until you have marked all of the first sounds you see in the sentence.

Ask students to think about what they know about finding the first sound in each word. Allow students to share what they know, checking for complete sentences. Choose 1 or 2 sentences to use for shared writing.

Sample Shared Writing

Liz looks for the letter after a space.

Joe thinks about the sound.

As you write, review student responses by pointing out the top of the paper, the bottom of the paper and where on the paper you start to write. Talk about starting on the left and going to the right, spaces, a capital letter, return sweep if necessary, and periods. Emphasize the spaces, the number of words in each sentence, and where each word begins. Draw attention to any letter that is a 'stick letter'; such as **L, I,** or **T** and 'slanted letters'; such as **A, K,** and **M** and 'circle letters'; such as **C** and **O**. Add 'curved letters' such as **S, G, B** and **D**. Invite students to make a straight, slanted, circle and curve patterns in the air with their fingers. As you write, emphasize the first phoneme in each of the sequence words.

Say: *Liz's name begins with /l/. Can you think where we would put a red dot to find the first sound in Liz's name? Joe starts with /j/. Can you think where we would put a red dot to find the first sound in Joe's name?*

Optional: Have students practice returning to their designated seats, or stand up to take a 'brain break.' You may want to ask students to sing, stretch, or move to music at this time.

Independent Reading (20 Min.)

Introduce and Practice Using Response Journals

Call students to the meeting area using the established signal. Have the anchor chart on Library Workstation available to use and read.

Say: *We are learning about an important way to learn in our classroom. During our independent reading time, we're practicing using workstations. Remember, a workstation is a place you go and work on something that will help you be a better reader. We decided that our Library could be our first workstation because we go there to practice reading. We've also been practicing another workstation called our Writing Workstation. Yesterday we learned about working with letters in our word work workstation. Today, I'd like for us to visit this workstation again. Today, we're going to look at our bags of letters again and write our names and words after we build them with the letters. Let me show you. I'm going to build my name. Next, I'm going to write it like this.*

Model building your name and then writing it on paper or another resource.

Note: This will look different depending on your classroom. You may choose a special place or bag/basket of resources that can be moved to different places. After students are comfortably seated close to the Word Work Workstation, **say:** *Let's begin by revisiting our anchor chart for our Word Work Workstation. Should we add anything else? We are going to practice using our letters to make our names today and then writing them on a piece of paper. We can also practice making and writing any other words we know!*

Word Work Workstation
We work with letters.
We work quietly.
We are a good partner.
We think how words go together.

Have baggies with an appropriate number of letter cards for each child.

Ask the class to return to their seats. Circulate, observe and support students to ensure they understand how to handle their bags of letters appropriately. At the end of independent reading (perhaps signaling with a bell, clap or any other desired means so students begin to understand the signal when workstation rotations begin), assist students in returning their letters to a predetermined place in the Word Study Workstation. Remind them that this is where they will return their letters each time they are finished in the word study workstation.

Objectives

Students will:
- Review anchor chart for Word Work Workstation.
- Work with letters and use resources to write letters/names.

Additional Materials

- Pointer
- Anchor chart for Library Workstation
- Anchor chart for Writing Workstation
- Letter cards
- Whiteboard, paper, markers, pencils for students
- Chart
- Markers

Support Tip

For children who are learning English, use gestures, facial expressions, visuals, and props when you are explaining new routines and concepts.

Objectives

Students will:
- Continue practicing an efficient transition between mini-lessons.
- Be introduced to fiction and nonfiction text.
- Create an anchor chart listing differences of fiction and nonfiction text.

Additional Materials

- Selected book to read aloud
- Several examples of fiction and nonfiction text for turn-and-talk partners
- Pointer

Establishing Routines (30 Min.)

Smooth Transitions

Remind students how they sit when they come to the carpet. You may want to begin inviting the whole class to the carpet if you feel they are able to perform this routine. If not, invite one of the tables to join you at the carpet. Ask them to show the rest of the class how we move quietly in our room, push our chairs in when we leave our space, and sit with our legs crossed and our hands in our laps.

Say: *Boys and girls, I'm so glad to see that you remembered that when we come to the carpet we want to sit quietly with our legs crossed and our hands in our laps. When I see you sitting quietly like this with your eyes on the speaker, I'll know you're ready to listen.*

Getting Ready for Whole-Group Instruction: Respond to a Story

Say: *Today we are going think about responding to a story. Readers are always thinking about what they read. When we think about what we read and respond to the words, it makes the book easier to understand. Let's think about a book that we've already read. Do you remember this story?*

Choose a book you've already read and read a few pages of the story that the children especially enjoyed.

Say: *I know we all liked this part because _____. One of the ways we can respond to a book to tell why we liked it. Let me show you what I mean. I could say that I really liked this part of the book because it made me laugh when the words were fun to say. That's one way to respond to a book. I could respond by saying that I didn't like it, or it made me sad. I'd like for you to respond to this book by turning and talking to your partner. Use this sentence frame: I _____(tell how you felt about this book) this book because _____. (tell why you felt that way) Remember to have a respectful conversation with your partner.*

Optional: Have students practice returning to their designated seats, or stand up to take a 'brain break.' You may want to ask students to sing, stretch, or move to music at this time.

Read-Aloud and Shared Reading (20 Min.)

Welcome to Our School

Read-Aloud

Call students to the meeting area using the established signal.

Read any book from the Recommended Trade Books in Additional Resources or any other available books such as, *The Night Before Kindergarten* by Natasha Weng.

Say: *Now let's practice Turn and Talk with your partner. We have been practicing having a respectful conversations using a sentence frame. When you talk with your partner today, please start your conversation like this: The first day of Kindergarten, I think my parents were _____ because_____.*

Choose a student and model using a sentence frame. Let the student use the sentence frame in return.

Say: *Now sit knee to knee and eye to eye with your Turn and Talk partner and use the sentence frame to talk about how you think your parents felt when you started Kindergarten.*

Observe to see that all students are sharing using respectful conversations and using the sentence frame.

Shared Reading

Call students to the meeting area using the established signal.

Say: *We are going to read a Big Book called **Welcome to Our School**.*

Display the book and review the concepts of print we have learned. Remember to start with the top of the book, reviewing the front and back of the book, reading and identifying the title, author, and illustrator. Also add a review on how many words in the title and what they think the book is about.

Read the book, moving your pointer under the words and stopping in a few places where it is appropriate to support students' comprehension. When finished reading, invite students to discuss the pictures in the book.

Say: *Listen while I read it again. If you remember any of the words, please read them with me. Please think carefully about the pictures to see if they help you understand the book.*

Say: *Did you look at the pictures carefully to see if they helped you understand the book? Let me share with you how the pictures helped me. I wasn't sure what a cafeteria was. When I looked at the picture and saw boys and girls eating, I realized the cafeteria is the same thing as our lunchroom. Who can share something the pictures helped you understand? (Accept all reasonable answers.) Turn and talk with your partner and use this sentence frame? The pictures helped me understand when _____.*

Student Objectives

Students will:
- Build an awareness of the information in a book: title, author, illustrator, illustrations.

Additional Materials

- Chart paper
- Markers
- Selected book to read aloud
- Pointer

Shared Writing (15 Min.)

Concepts about Print, Letter Awareness, Phonological Awareness

Call students to the meeting area using the established signal.

Say: *Today I'd like for us to remember all of the things we've been learning that good writers do when they put their thoughts on paper. Who will share with us one of the things we know?*

Ask several students to volunteer the following concepts of print: Start here (points), goes to the next line when one is full, begin with a capital, end with a period, and puts spaces between words.

Say: *Let's look again at the poem we read and where a word starts and ends.*

Put a sentence strip with different a sentence from the poem in front of the class.

Say: *I know that I start reading here. Let's work together to put these red dots under the first letter we see in each word. Who would like to show us where the first dot should go? This helps me know where a word starts.*

Have students continue until all of the words have a red dot under the beginning letter.

Say: *How many words are in this sentence? How did you know? Does anyone know what else we can do now? Yes. We can practice thinking about the sound we hear when we see the letter. Let me show you.*

Model looking at the first word, thinking about the first letter, and saying the sound. Ask students to read with you. Ask how many words are in a sentence. Allow students to share what they know, checking for complete sentences. Choose 1 or 2 sentences to use for shared writing.

Sample Shared Writing
Sheri counts the red dots.
Tommy looks at the spaces between words.

As you write, review student responses by pointing out the top of the paper, the bottom of the paper and where on the paper you start to write. Talk about starting on the left and going to the right, spaces, a capital letter, return sweep if necessary, and periods. Emphasize the spaces, the number of words in each sentence, and where each word begins. Draw attention to any letter that is a 'stick letter'; such as **L, I,** or **T** and 'slanted letters'; such as **A, K,** and **M** and 'circle letters'; such as **C** and **O.** Add 'curved letters' such as **S, G, B** and **D.** Invite students to make a straight, slanted, circle and curve patterns in the air with their fingers.

Say: *Sheri's name begins with /**sh**/. Where would we put a red dot for the first sound in Sheri's name? We would put it under the /**s**/ and the /**h**/! Where would we put a red dot to find the first sound in Tommy's name? Where would be put a dot in your name?*

Optional: Have students practice returning to their designated seats, or stand up to take a 'brain break.' You may want to ask students to sing, stretch, or move, to music at this time.

Objectives

Students will:
- Continue to differentiate and locate stick, slanted, circle and curved letters within print.
- Concepts of print – First letter of a word

Additional Materials

- Chart paper
- Markers
- The first sentence of the poem written on a sentence strip for the class to see.
- Sticky dots, markers or some other way to mark beginning sounds

Independent Reading (20 Min.)

Introduce and Practice Playing Games and Puzzles Workstation

Call students to the meeting area using the established signal. Have the anchor chart on Library Workstation available to use and read.

Say: *We are learning about an important way to learn in our classroom. During our independent reading time, we're practicing using workstations. Remember, a workstation is a place you go and work on something that will help you be a better reader. We decided that our Library could be our first workstation because we go there to practice reading. We've also been practiced another workstation called our Writing Workstation. Yesterday we learned about working with and writing letters in our word work workstation. Today, I'd like for you to come with me to our puzzles and games workstation. When you come to this workstation, you will practice learning the rules of a game or putting together a puzzle.*

Model building your name and then writing it on paper or another resource.

Note: This will look different depending on your classroom. You may choose a special place or bag/basket of resources that can be moved to different places. After students are comfortably seated close to the Puzzles and Games Workstation, **say:** *Let's begin by revisiting our anchor chart for our other workstations. Think about what we know about our roles in our classroom, and how we can be a partner. Let's start our Puzzles and Games Anchor Chart. I think one thing a partner does is to follow the rules of a game. Let's put that on our anchor chart. Who can think of something else?*

Accept all reasonable responses.

Puzzle and Game Workstation

We follow the rules of a game.

We take turns with our partner.

We work together to solve a puzzle.

Have enough games and puzzles for partners to use.

After the puzzles and game are distributed, ask the class to return to their seats or go to the floor with their partner. Circulate, observe, and support students to ensure they understand how to play their game. Have students take turns with a partner. At the end of independent reading (perhaps signaling with a bell, clap or any other desired means so students begin to understand the signal when workstation rotations begin), assist students in returning their puzzles and games to a predetermined place in the Puzzles and Games Workstation. Remind them that this is where they will return their puzzles and games each time they are finished in the Puzzles and Games workstation. Ask them to check and make sure all puzzle pieces and game pieces are picked up and stored correctly in the box so the games and puzzles will be ready to use the next time.

Objectives

Students will:
- Be introduced to the puzzles and games workstation.
- Create an anchor chart for the puzzles and games workstation.

Additional Materials

- Pointer
- Anchor chart for Library Workstation
- Anchor chart for Writing Workstation
- Anchor chart for Word Work Workstation
- Chart
- Markers
- Developmentally appropriate puzzles or games for partners

Support Tip

For children who are visually challenged, provide them with larger, darker print when using sentence strips

Objectives

Students will:
- Continue practicing an efficient transition between mini-lessons.
- Know what good readers do—Use pictures.

Additional Materials
- Selected book to read aloud
- Previous read-aloud book to revisit and respond to.
- Pointer

Establishing Routines (30 Min.)

Smooth Transitions

Remind students how they sit when they come to the carpet. You may want to begin inviting the whole class to the carpet if you feel they are able to perform this routine. If not, invite one of the tables to join you at the carpet. Ask them to show the rest of the class how we move quietly in our room, push our chairs in when we leave our space, and sit with our legs crossed and our hands in our laps.

Say: *Boys and girls, I'm so glad to see that you remembered that when we come to the carpet we want to sit quietly with our legs crossed and our hands in our laps. When I see you sitting quietly like this with your eyes on the speaker, I'll know you're ready to listen.*

Getting Ready for Whole-Group Instruction: Good Readers Use Pictures

Say: *Today we are going think about something that all readers do. When readers are listening to or reading a story, they use the pictures that an illustrator makes to help them understand. Let's think about a book that we've already read. Do you remember this story?*

Choose a book you've already read and read a few pages of the story that offer strong support through the use of pictures.

Say: *Did you notice all of the pictures? I think these pictures help us understand the story. Let me show you how one of the pictures helped me.*

Choose a place in the story where you could use a picture to deepen understanding. Explain to students how the picture helped you.

Say: *Now I'd like for you to choose a place in the story where the picture helped you understand the story better. Would anyone like to share? Good! Now, turn and talk with your partner and use this sentence frame: The picture of _____ helped me understand that _____.*

Optional: Have students practice returning to their designated seats, or stand up to take a 'brain break.' You may want to ask students to sing, stretch, or move to music at this time.

Read-Aloud and Shared Reading (20 MIN.)

Read-Aloud

Call students to the meeting area using the established signal.

Read any book from the Recommended Trade Books in Additional Resources or any other available books such as *Franklin Goes to School* adapted by Bob Ardiel.

Say: *Now let's practice Turn and Talk with your partner. We have been practicing having a respectful conversation using a sentence frame. When you talk with your partner today, please start your conversation like this: The first day of Kindergarten, my friends helped me _____.*

Choose a student and model using a sentence frame. Let the student use the sentence frame in return.

Say: *Now sit knee to knee and eye to eye with your Turn and Talk partner and use the sentence frame to talk about how you think your parents felt when you started Kindergarten.*

Observe to see that all students are sharing using respectful conversations and using the sentence frame.

Shared Reading

Call students to the meeting area using the established signal.

Say: *We are going to reread our Big Book called **Welcome to Our School**.*

Display the book and review the concepts of print we have learned. Remember to start with the top of the book, reviewing the front and back of the book, reading and identifying the title, author, and illustrator. Also add a review on how many words in the title.

Read the book, moving your pointer under the words and stopping in a few places where it is appropriate to support students' comprehension. When finished reading, invite students to discuss the pictures in the book.

Say: *Listen while I read it again. If you remember any of the words, please read them with me. This morning we learned that good readers use pictures to help them understand a book. Please think carefully about the pictures and see if they help you understand the book in a different place than yesterday.*

Say: *While I was reading, did you look at the pictures carefully to see if they helped you understand the book? Who can share something the pictures helped you understand?*

Accept all reasonable answers.

Say: *Turn and talk with your partner and use this sentence frame? The pictures helped me understand when _____.*

Welcome to Our School

Student Objectives

Students will:
• Build an awareness of the information in a book: title, author, illustrator, illustrations.

Additional Materials

• Chart paper
• Markers
• Selected book to read aloud
• Pointer

Objectives

Students will:
- Continue to differentiate and locate stick, slanted, circle and curved letters within print.
- Concepts of print—First letter of a word and the sound of that letter.

Additional Materials

- Chart paper
- Markers
- The first sentence of the poem written on a sentence strip for the class to see.
- Sticky dots, markers or some other way to mark beginning sounds
- Poem from week 2

Shared Writing (15 MIN.)

Concepts about Print, Letter Awareness, Phonological Awareness

Call students to the meeting area using the established signal.

Say: *Today I'd like for us to remember all of the things we've been learning that good writers do when they put their thoughts on paper. Who will share with us one of the things we know?*

Ask volunteer the following concepts of print: Start here (points), go to the next line when one is full, begin with a capital, end with a period, and put spaces between words.

Say: *Today I want to make sure that we remember where a word starts and ends. Let's look again at the poem we read.*

Put a sentence strip with different a sentence from the poem in front of the class.

Say: *I know that I start reading here. What I want to think about is the first letters and sounds I see and hear in the words in this sentence. Let's work together to put these red dots under the first letter we see in each word. Who would like to show us where the first dot should go? This helps me know where a word starts.*

Have students continue until all of the words have a red dot under the beginning letter.

Say: *How many words are in this sentence? How did you know? Now we can practice thinking about the sound we hear when we see the letter. Let me show you.*

Model looking at the first word, thinking about the first letter, and saying the sound. Ask students to read with you. Ask students to think about what they know about finding how many words are in a sentence. Choose 1 or 2 sentences to use for shared writing.

Sample Shared Writing

Addy thinks about the sound the letter makes.

Zeke looks at the letter.

As you write, review student responses about print by pointing out the top of the paper, the bottom of the paper and where on the paper you start to write. Talk about starting on the left and going to the right, spaces, a capital letter, return sweep if necessary, and periods. Emphasize the spaces, the number of words in each sentence, and where each word begins. Draw attention to any letter that is a 'stick letter'; such as **L, I,** or **T** and 'slanted letters'; such as **A, K,** and **M** and 'circle letters'; such as **C** and **O**. Add 'curved letters' such as **S, G, B,** and **D**. Invite students to make a straight, slanted, circle and curve patterns in the air with their fingers.

Say: *Addy's name begins with short /a/. Can you think where we would put a red dot to find the first letter in Addy's name? Good! Can you find another word in our sentence that begins with the same sound? Do you know that word? Let's put red dots under the rest of the first letters of words in our sentence. Now let's do the same for Zeke with /z/.*

Optional: Have students practice returning to their designated seats, or stand up to take a 'brain break.' You may want to ask students to sing, stretch, or move to music at this time.

Independent Reading (20 Min.)

Model Reading to Self and Using the Classroom Library

Call students to the meeting area using the established signal. Have the anchor chart on Library Workstation available to use and read.

Say: *We are learning about an important way to learn in our classroom. During our independent reading time, we're practicing using workstations. Remember, a workstation is a place you go and work on something that will help you be a better reader. We decided that our Library could be our first workstation because we go there to practice reading. We've also practiced another workstation called our Writing Workstation. We have also learned about working with and writing letters in our word work workstation. Today, I'd like for you to come with me again to our puzzles and games workstation. When you come to this workstation, you will practice learning the rules of a game or putting together a puzzle.*

Note: This will look different depending on your classroom. You may choose a special place or bag/basket of resources that can be moved to different places. After students are comfortably seated close to the Puzzles and Game Workstation, **say:** *Let's look again at our Puzzles and Games Anchor Chart. Can anyone think of something else to add to our anchor chart? Yes! Let's add put things away carefully. That's very important. Let's put that on our anchor chart. Who can think of something else?*

Accept all reasonable responses.

Puzzle and Game Workstation
We follow the rules of a game.
We take turns with our partner.
We work together to solve a puzzle.
Put the puzzle or game away carefully.

Have enough games and puzzles for partners to use to practice this workstation again. After the puzzles and games are distributed, ask the class to return to their seats or go to the floor with their partner. Circulate, observe and support students to ensure they understand how to play the game and work with a partner at taking turns.

If necessary, model this skill using a partner team. At the end of independent reading (perhaps signaling with a bell, clap or any other desired means so students begin to understand the signal when workstation rotations begin), assist students in returning their puzzles and games to a predetermined place in the Puzzles and Games Workstation. Remind them that this is where they will return their puzzles and games each time they are finished in the Puzzles and Games Workstation. Ask them to check and make sure all puzzle pieces and game pieces are picked up and stored correctly in the box so the game and puzzle will be ready to use the next time.

Objectives

Students will:
- Practice the puzzles and games workstation.
- Add to an anchor chart for the puzzles and games workstation.

Additional Materials

- Pointer
- Anchor chart for Library Workstation
- Anchor chart for Writing Workstation
- Anchor chart for Word Work Workstation
- Chart
- Markers
- Developmentally appropriate puzzles or games for partners

Support Tip

For children who are learning English, pair them with native English speakers to help learn routines and rituals.

Objectives

Students will:
- Continue practicing an efficient transition between mini-lessons.
- Know what good readers do—Use pictures.

Additional Materials

- Selected book to read aloud
- Previous read-aloud book to revisit and respond to.
- Pointer

Establishing Routines (30 Min.)

Smooth Transitions

Remind students how they sit when they come to the carpet. You may want to begin inviting the whole class to the carpet if you feel they are able to perform this routine. If not, invite one of the tables to join you at the carpet. Ask them to show the rest of the class how we move quietly in our room, push our chairs in when we leave our space, and sit with our legs crossed and our hands in our laps.

Say: *Boys and girls, I'm so glad to see that you remembered that when we come to the carpet we want to sit quietly with our legs crossed and our hands in our laps. When I see you sitting quietly like this with your eyes on the speaker, I'll know you're ready to listen.*

Getting Ready for Whole-Group Instruction: Good Readers Make Predictions

Say: *Today we are going think about something that all readers do. When readers get ready to read a story, they look at the book and think about what the book could be about. This is called making a prediction. There are several ways readers can make predictions. They can look at the pictures on the cover and they can read the title. They can also think about something this books reminds them of.*

Use the book that you have chosen for your read-aloud.

Say: *We are going to read this book in a while. Before we read, I'd like for us to practice making predictions about what we think this book may be about. Remember, we don't want to take a wild guess. We want to look at clues and see if we can use them to make our prediction.*

Display the book you've chosen for the read-aloud. Talk with the children about the picture you see on the front cover, read the title to the children and display the back cover to find any clues there. Use the following think-aloud.

Say: *I'm thinking that I see a (name picture) on the front cover. I also want to think about the title (read title) and now I'm going to look on the back cover. Oh! I see (another picture clue?) If I put all of these clues together, I think this book could be about_____. Now I'd like for you to think about some clues you notice. Turn and talk with your partner telling them your prediction for this book and why you made this prediction. Use this sentence frame: My prediction is _____ because _____. Remember to have a respectful conversation.*

Optional: Have students practice returning to their designated seats, or stand up to take a 'brain break.' You may want to ask students to sing, stretch, or move to music at this time.

Read-Aloud and Shared Reading (20 Min.)

Read-Aloud

Call students to the meeting area using the established signal.

Read a book from the Read aloud List, or any other available books such as *Wimberly Worried* by Kevin Henkes. Invite students to share their predictions from the lesson above.

Say: *Now let's practice Turn and Talk with your partner. We have been practicing having a respectful conversation using a sentence frame. Please start your conversation like this: When Kindergarten started, I was worried about _____.*

Model using a sentence frame. Then choose a student to use the sentence frame n.

Say: *Now sit knee to knee and eye to eye with your Turn and Talk partner and use the sentence frame to talk about how you think your parents felt when you started Kindergarten.*

Observe to see that all students are sharing using respectful conversations and using the sentence frame.

Shared Reading

Call students to the meeting area using the established signal.

Say: *Let's look at our Big Book, **Welcome to Our School**, and let's practice what we know about making predictions. Look at the picture on the front and back cover. What do you see? Yes, we see boys and girls. Does anyone remember the title? Good! Welcome to School. Can anyone make a prediction about what we might learn in our book?*

Allow two or three children to make a prediction. Display the book and review the concepts of print. Remember to start with the top and bottom of the book, reviewing the front and back of the book, reading and identifying the title, author, and illustrator. Also, review how many words in the title and how they know.

Reread the book, moving your pointer under the words and stopping in a few places where it is appropriate to support students' comprehension. Tell students to listen carefully to see if they can tell if their prediction was right.

Say: *Listen while I read it again. Be sure to look at the pictures, too, to see if your prediction about the book was right. If you remember any of the words, please read them with me.*

Say: *While I was reading, did you check to make sure your prediction was right? Who can share with us their prediction, if their prediction was right, and how you know it's right.*

Accept all reasonable answers.

Say: *Turn and talk with your partner and use this sentence frame. My prediction was right because _____.*

Welcome to Our School

Additional Materials

- Chart paper
- Markers
- Selected book to read aloud
- Pointer

Additional Materials

- Chart paper
- Markers
- Week three big book.
- Sentences from the big book written on sentence strips (two or three)

Shared Writing (15 Min.)

Concepts about Print, Letter Awareness, Phonological Awareness

Call students to the meeting area using the established signal.

Say: *Today I'd like for us to remember all of the things we've been learning that good writers do when they put their thoughts on paper.*

Ask several students to volunteer the following concepts of print: Start here (points), go to the next line when one is full, begin with a capital, end with a period, and put spaces between words.

Say: *Let's look at our big book, **Welcome to Our School**. When we read our book, we see this sentence on page 2. "This is our school." Let's look at the words in this sentence.*

Use a sentence strip for each of the sentences making large, clear letters and clear spaces between words. Reread the sentence with students, pointing to each word as you read. Review the concepts of print. Add the concepts of how many letters in each word.

Display the sentence strip with the sentence, "This is our school."

Say: *I know that I start reading here. Let's think about the word 'this.' How many letters are in "this"? Let's practice counting the letters together.*

Allow students to continue until the letters in all of the words in the sentence have been counted. Also allow students to share what they know, checking for complete sentences. Choose 1 or 2 sentences to use for shared writing.

Sample Shared Writing

Rachel looks at the word between the spaces and counts the letters.

Mike finds a word and counts the letters.

As you write, review student responses about print by pointing out the top of the paper, the bottom of the paper and where on the paper you start to write. Talk about starting on the left and going to the right, spaces, a capital letter, return sweep if necessary, and periods. Emphasize the spaces, the number of words in each sentence, and where each word begins. Draw attention to any letter that is a 'stick letter'; such as **L, I,** or **T** and 'slanted letters'; such as **A, K,** and **M** and 'circle letters'; such as **C** and **O**. Add 'curved letters' such as **S, G, B,** and **D**. Invite students to make a straight, slanted, circle and curve patterns in the air with their fingers.

Say: *Rachel's name begins with /**r**/. Can you think where we would put a red dot to find the first sound in Rachel's name? Good! Can you find how many letters are in her name? Who will come count for us? Mike starts with /**m**/. Now let's put a red dot to find the first sound in Mike's name? Can you find how many letters are in his name? Who will come count for us? As we write the rest of the sentence, think about how many words you see, and how many letters in each word.*

Optional: Have students practice returning to their designated seats, or stand up to take a 'brain break.' You may want to ask students to sing, stretch, or move to music at this time.

Independent Reading (20 Min.)

Computer Workstation

Call students to the meeting area using the established signal. Have the previously made anchor charts available to use and read.

Say: *We are learning about an important way to learn in our classroom. During our independent reading time, we're practicing using workstations. Remember, a workstation is a place you go and work on something that will help you be a better reader. We decided that our Library could be our first workstation because we go there to practice reading. We've also practiced another workstation called our Writing Workstation. We have also learned about working with and writing letters in our word work workstation. We have also learned about our Puzzles and Games Workstation. Today, I'd like for you to come with me our computers. This will be another workstation. We'll call it our Computer Workstation. When you use this workstation, you will practice reading with games and books on our computer.*

Note: This will look different depending on your classroom. The kind of technology and the amount of the technology will determine the number of students you can send to this workstation and where the workstation will be in your room. When students are seated in place where they can see the technology, **say:** *We need to make an anchor chart so we can remember how our Computer Workstation should look and sound. We need to remember is to use headphones so we don't bother other learners. Let's start with that. Does anyone have another idea?*

Accept all reasonable responses.

Computer Workstation

Use headphones when you're working on a computer.

Stay at your computer.

Work quietly.

Be a good listener.

Put students with partners for the first time at the technology workstation. Use a whole group setting for explaining the basics when using the computer.

After students are at the computers with a partner and logged in to a program, Circulate, observe and support students to ensure they understand how to use the program and work with a partner at taking turns if this is your expectation for using the computer workstation. If necessary, model this skill using a partner team. At the end of independent reading (perhaps signaling with a bell, clap or any other desired means so students begin to understand the signal when workstation rotations begin), assist students in the routine of what you'd like them to do at the end of their time in this workstation. Remind them that this is how they will store the headphones, log off, and so on when they are finished in the Computer Workstation so it is ready to use the next time.

Note: When you feel it's appropriate, you may want to begin posting the anchor charts in the correct workstation so you and students can use them for reference. Be sure to keep them fluid, adding and taking off ideas as needed.

Objectives

Students will:
- Be introduced to Computer Workstation.

Additional Materials

- Pointer
- Anchor chart for Library Workstation
- Anchor chart for Writing Workstation
- Anchor chart for Word Work Workstation
- Anchor chart for Puzzles and Games Workstation
- Chart
- Markers
- Computers and/or tablets

Support Tip

For children who are learning not familiar with technology, pair them with a student who can support them when learning the basic use of computers.

Objectives

Students will:
• Continue practicing an efficient transition between mini-lessons.
• Know what good readers do—Use sounds they know to figure out words.

Additional Materials

• Selected book to read aloud
• Pointer

Establishing Routines (30 Min.)

Smooth Transitions

Remind students how they sit when they come to the carpet. You may want to begin inviting the whole class to the carpet if you feel they are able to perform this routine. If not, invite one of the tables to join you at the carpet. Ask them to show the rest of the class how we move quietly in our room, push our chairs in when we leave our space, and sit with our legs crossed and our hands in our laps.

Say: *Boys and girls, I'm so glad to see that you remembered that when we come to the carpet we want to sit quietly with our legs crossed and our hands in our laps. When I see you sitting quietly like this with your eyes on the speaker, I'll know you're ready to listen.*

Getting Ready for Whole-Group Instruction: Good Readers Use Sounds They Know to Figure Out Words

Say: *Today we are going think about something else that all readers do. When readers are reading a story, they may come to a word that they don't know. Let's think together about what we can do if that happens. We've been learning that we can think about the first letter in the word. Do you think we could look at other letters in word to help us too? Yes! Let me show you how I can do that.*

Use the big book from week 1, Katy's First Day of School. Turn to page 5, or any other appropriate page. Read the sentence of that page.

Say: *This is a story we've ready many times. I'd like for us to look at this sentence. I'd like for us to read it together. It says, "I am going to stay in ___." I'm thinking about the word **b-e-d**. I know a few things about this word. I see it starts with /**b**/. I also see another letter I know—**d**. I think I'll add that to what I know. Let's see if that helps me with this word. I'll read the sentence again and get my mouth ready to say the word I don't know. "I am going to stay in b-d." I know! "I am going to stay in bed!" That makes sense, goes with the picture, and I used all of sounds I know to figure it out.*

Display page 7 of the book and read the sentence. Use the word 'friends'.

Say: *Use what you know about this word. Turn and Talk about the beginning sound and any other sounds you know to figure out the word. Be sure you find a word that has those sounds, makes sense in the sentence and goes with the picture. Use this sentence frame: I think the word is _____ because _____.*

Optional: Have students practice returning to their designated seats, or stand up to take a 'brain break.' You may want to ask students to sing, stretch, or move to music at this time.

Read-Aloud and Shared Reading (20 Min.)

Read-Aloud

Call students to the meeting area using the established signal.

Read any book from the Recommended Trade Books in Additional Resources or any other available books such as *The Berenstain Bears Go to School* by Stan and Jan Berenstain.

Say: *Now let's practice Turn and Talk with your partner. We have been practicing having a respectful conversation using a sentence frame. My favorite part of this book is _____.*

Choose a student and model using a sentence frame. Let the student use the sentence frame in return.

Say: *Now sit knee to knee and eye to eye with your Turn and Talk partner and use the sentence frame to talk about how you think your parents felt when you started Kindergarten.*

Observe to see that all students are sharing using respectful conversations and using the sentence frame.

Shared Reading

Call students to the meeting area using the established signal.

Say: *Let's look at our Big Book,* **Welcome to School***. Before we reread our book, I'd like to practice what we know about figuring out a word we don't know. Let's look at the title. Can you tell me what the first word is in the title? What are some clues you used to let you know that welcome is the first word? Yes. It begins with a /**w**/ sound, and you can also see an /**l**/ and a /**c**/ and an /**m**/. Good job!*

Allow two or three children to make suggestions about the words in the title and how they can figure them out. Display the book and review the concepts of print. Remember to start with the top and bottom of the book, reviewing the front and back of the book, reading and identifying the title, author, and illustrator. Also, review how many words in the title, how they know and what they've been practicing when they come to a word they don't know.

Reread the book, moving your pointer under the words and stopping in a few places where it is appropriate to support students' comprehension. Tell students look carefully for words they can figure out by looking for sounds they know in the word.

Say: *Listen while I read it again. Be sure to look for words you noticed in the book. If you remember any of the words, please read them with me.*

Say: *While I was reading, did anyone find any words you noticed that you knew? Who would like to share a word you knew. How did you know that word?*

Accept all reasonable answers.

Say: *Turn and talk with your partner and use this sentence frame. A word I knew in our story was _____.*

Welcome to Our School

Student Objectives

Students will:
- Build an awareness of the information in a book: title, author, illustrator, illustrations.

Additional Materials

- Chart paper
- Markers
- Selected book to read aloud
- Pointer

Objectives

Students will:
- Continue to differentiate and locate stick, slanted, circle and curved letters within print.
- Concepts of print – First letter of a word and the sound of that letter

Additional Materials

- Chart paper
- Markers
- Second sentence on page 2 of Welcome to School Big Book put on sentence strips for each partner

Shared Writing (15 Min.)

Concepts about Print, Letter Awareness, Phonological Awareness

Call students to the meeting area using the established signal.

Say: *Today I'd like for us to remember all of the things we've been learning that good writers do when they put their thoughts on paper. Who will share with us one of the things we know?*

Ask several students to volunteer the following concepts of print: Start here (points), goes to the next line when one is full, begin with a capital, end with a period, and puts spaces between words.

Say: *Today I'd like for us to think about words and letters. Let's look at our big book,* **Welcome to School***. When we read our book, we see this sentence on page 2. "This is our school." Let's look at the words in this sentence.*

Use a sentence strip for each of the sentences. Reread the sentences with students, pointing to each word as you read. Review the concepts of beginning letters, using the sounds of the letters to know how a word begins, spaces between words, how many words in a sentence. Add the concepts of how many letters in each word.

Display the second sentence strip with the sentence "We come here every day."

Say: *I know that I start reading here. I know that this is the first letter in the word. Let's think about the word 'we.' Model counting the letters in the word 'we.'*

Give each pair a strip with the sentence, "We come here every day." Have partners put a red dot under the first letter of each word and write how many letters are in the word.

Circulate to check that all students understand the concept of words and letters. Allow students to share what they know, checking for complete sentences. Choose 1 or 2 sentences to use for shared writing.

Sample Shared Writing

Cory counts letters.

Emma thinks about sounds.

Say: *Cory's name begins with /c̦/. Can you think where we would put a red dot to find the first sound in Cory's name? Good! How many letters in Cory's name? How do you know? Emma's name starts with a short /e/. Can you think where we would put a red dot to find the first sound in Emma's name? How many letters are in Emma's name? How do you know? How many letters are in your name?*

Optional: Have students practice returning to their designated seats, or stand up to take a 'brain break.' You may want to ask students to sing, stretch, or move to music at this time.

Independent Reading (20 Min.)

Computer Workstation

Call students to the meeting area using the established signal. Have the previously made anchor charts available to use and read.

Say: *We are learning about an important way to learn in our classroom. During our independent reading time, we're practicing using workstations. Remember, a workstation is a place you go and work on something that will help you be a better reader. We decided that our Library could be our first workstation because we go there to practice reading. We've also practiced another workstation called our Writing Workstation. We have also learned about working with and writing letters in our word work workstation. We have also learned about our Puzzles and Games Workstation. Today, we're going to visit our Computer Workstation again. Do you remember what we said we did here? Yes. When you use this workstation, you will practice reading with games and books on our computer.*

Note: This will look different depending on your classroom. The kind of technology and the amount of the technology will determine the number of students you can send to this workstation and where the workstation will be in your room. When students are seated in place where they can see the technology, **say:** *Yesterday we made an anchor chart to help remember how our Computer Workstation should look and sound. Can you think of anything else we should add? Good. Let's write, Put things away neatly. Does anyone have another idea?*

Accept all reasonable responses.

Computer Workstation
Use headphones when you're working on a computer.
Stay at your computer.
Work quietly.
Be a good listener.
Put things away neatly.

Put students with partners for the first time at the technology workstation. Use a whole group setting for explaining the basics when using the computer. (How to turn it on. Where to plug in headphones. Signing in. How to start a game…etc…)

Say: *Now let's practice working together in our Computer Workstation. Remember to use our anchor chart to be a good partner.*

After students are at the computers with a partner and logged in to a program, Circulate, observe, and support students to ensure they understand how to use the program and work with a partner at taking turns if this is your expectation for using the computer workstation. If necessary, model this skill using a partner team. At the end of independent reading (perhaps signaling with a bell, clap or any other desired means so students begin to understand the signal when workstation rotations begin), assist students in the routine of what you'd like them to do at the end of their time in this workstation. Remind them that this is how they will store the headphones, log off, etc. when they are finished in the Computer Workstation so it is ready to use the next time.

Objectives

Students will:
- Practice the puzzles and games workstation.
- Add to an anchor chart for the puzzles and games workstation.

Additional Materials

- Pointer
- Anchor chart for Library Workstation
- Anchor chart for Writing Workstation
- Anchor chart for Word Work Workstation
- Anchor chart for Puzzles and Games Workstation
- Anchor chart for Computer Workstation
- Chart
- Markers
- Computers and/or tablets – any technology that you would expect students to us

Support Tip

For children who are learning English, use visuals to help them connect the vocabulary of what they need to know about computers. (i.e. headphones, a mouse, computer, keyboard, etc)

Establishing Routines (30 Min.)

Smooth Transitions

Remind students how they sit when they come to the carpet. You may want to begin inviting the whole class to the carpet if you feel they are able to perform this routine. If not, invite one of the tables to join you at the carpet. Ask them to show the rest of the class how we move quietly in our room, push our chairs in when we leave our space, and sit with our legs crossed and our hands in our laps.

Say: *Boys and girls, I'm so glad to see that you remembered that when we come to the carpet we want to sit quietly with our legs crossed and our hands in our laps. When I see you sitting quietly like this with your eyes on the speaker, I'll know you're ready to listen.*

Getting Ready for Whole-Group Instruction: Good Readers Reread

Say: *Today we are going think about something else that all readers do. When readers are reading a story, they may come to a word they don't know. When that happens, it helps to reread the sentence to see if they can figure out the word. Let me show you what I mean..*

Use the Big Book from Week 1, *Katy's First Day of School.* Turn to pages 10-11, or any other appropriate pages. Read the sentences of those pages, but stopping at the word paint.

Say: *I'm looking this word. I know a few things about it. It starts with /**p**/ and I also see a /**n**/ and /**t**/, I'm looking at the picture, too. I think this word says paint, but I'm not sure. I'm going to reread this sentence to see if paint makes sense. It does! Rereading helps me figure out a word I don't know.*

Display page 11 of the book and read the sentence. Stop at the word said.

Say: *Use what you know about this word. Turn and Talk about everything you know about the word. Be sure to reread the sentence to help you figure out what the word says. Use this sentence frame: I think the word is _____ because _____.*

Optional: Have students practice returning to their designated seats, or stand up to take a 'brain break.' You may want to ask students to sing, stretch, or move to music at this time.

Objectives

Students will:
- Continue practicing an efficient transition between mini-lessons.
- Know what good readers do – Reread.

Additional Materials

- Selected book to read aloud
- Pointer

Read-Aloud and Shared Reading (20 Min.)

Read-Aloud

Call students to the meeting area using the established signal.

Read any book from the Recommended Trade Books in Additional Resources or any other available books such as *The Very Hungry Caterpillar* by Eric Carle.

Say: *Now let's practice Turn and Talk with your partner. We have been practicing having a respectful conversation using a sentence frame. I was surprised when _____.*

If your students are ready to proceed with modeling, allow them to continue. If not, choose a student and model using a sentence frame. Let the student use the sentence frame in return.

Say: *Now sit knee to knee and eye to eye with your Turn and Talk partner and use the sentence frame to talk about something that surprised you in our story.*

Observe to see that all students are sharing using respectful conversations and using the sentence frame.

Shared Reading

Call students to the meeting area using the established signal.

Say: *Let's look at our Big Book, **Welcome to Our School**. While we reread our book, I'd like to practice what we know about rereading to help us understand the book. Listen while I read and I'll show you what I mean.*

Reread the book and stop on page 4. Tell the class that you are a little confused by the word office. Use the following Think Aloud to model rereading.

Say: *I'm going to go on to the next page and read the sentence. Oh! It says the principal is here. I think the office is where the secretary and principal is. I'm going to reread the two pages to see if that helps. Yes. Now I understand what the author means when they said the office is here. Rereading helped me understand.*

Reread the book, moving your pointer under the words and stopping in a few places where it is appropriate to support students' comprehension. Tell students listen carefully for places they would like you to reread to help them understand.

Say: *Listen while I read the book again. Let me know if there are any place you would like for me to reread to help you understand the book.*

Accept all reasonable answers.

Say: *Turn and talk with your partner and use this sentence frame? Rereading helps me understand because_____.*

Welcome to Our School

Student Objectives

Students will:
- Build an awareness of the information in a book: title, author, illustrator, illustrations.
- Reread to help understanding.

Additional Materials

- Chart paper
- Markers
- Selected book to read aloud
- Big Book Welcome to our School
- Pointer

Shared Writing (15 Min.)

Concepts about Print, Letter Awareness, Phonological Awareness

Call students to the meeting area using the established signal.

Say: *Today I'd like for us to remember all of the things we've been learning that good writers do when they put their thoughts on paper. Who will share with us one of the things we know?*

Ask several students to volunteer the following concepts of print: Start here (points), goes to the next line when one is full, begin with a capital, end with a period, and puts spaces between words.

Say: *Today I'd like for us to think about words and letters again. Let's look at the book we read aloud. Look at the title and tell me what we know about the words in the title. How many words are there? What is the first letter in the word we will begin with? How many letters are in the word? Let's look on page ___. Do you see a word here you know about? Tell me what you know.*

Continue looking for words they know and ask how they know.

Ask students to think about what they know about words and letters. Allow students to share what they know, checking for complete sentences. Choose 1 or 2 sentences to use for shared writing.

Sample Shared Writing
Cassie knows the word 'and.'
Bart knows the word 'said.'

As you write, review student responses about print by pointing out the top of the paper, the bottom of the paper and where on the paper you start to write. Talk about starting on the left and going to the right, spaces, a capital letter, return sweep if necessary, and periods. Emphasize the spaces, the number of words in each sentence, and where each word begins. Draw attention to any letter that is a 'stick letter'; such as **L**, **I**, or **T** and 'slanted letters'; such as **A**, **K**, and **M** and 'circle letters'; such as **C** and **O**. Add 'curved letters' such as **S**, **G**, **B** and **D**. Invite students to make a straight, slanted, circle and curve patterns in the air with their fingers.

Say: *Cassandra's name begins with /c̨/. Can you think where we would put a red dot to find the first sound in Cassandra's name? Good! How many letters in Cassandra's name? How do you know? Bart's name starts with a /b/. Can you think where we would put a red dot to find the first sound in Bart's name? How many letters are in Bart's name? How do you know? How many letters are in the word 'and'? 'Said?'*

Optional: Have students practice returning to their designated seats, or stand up to take a 'brain break.' You may want to ask students to sing, stretch, or move to music at this time.

Objectives

Students will:
- Continue to differentiate and locate stick, slanted, circle and curved letters within print.
- Concepts of print – First letter of a word and the sound of that letter, difference between and word and letters

Additional Materials

- Chart paper
- Markers

Independent Reading (20 Min.)

Buddy Reading

Call students to the meeting area using the established signal. Have the previously made anchor charts available to use and read.

Say: *We are learning about an important way to learn in our classroom. During our independent reading time, we're practicing using workstations. Who can tell me the workstations we've learned about so far? Yes. We have a Library Workstation, a Writing Workstation, a Word Work Workstation, a Puzzles and Games Workstation, and a Computer Workstation. Today we are going to learn about something else we can do during this time. It is Buddy Reading. Buddy Reading is when you read or talk about your reading with a buddy.*

Note: This will look different depending on your classroom. The kind of technology and the amount of the technology will determine the number of students you can send to this workstation and where the workstation will be in your room. When students are seated in place where they can see the technology, **say:** *I would like for us to think about what buddy reading would look like and sound like in our room. Let's start with this thought. I think Buddies should be reading. Let's start an anchor chart with that. Does anyone have another thought to add?*

Accept all reasonable responses.

Buddy Reading
Buddies should read.
Buddies should sit together.
Buddies should not bother other readers.
Buddies should choose a book they want to read together.

Put students with buddies. Let them practice choosing a book from a basket, finding a place to read, and read or look at pictures quietly.

After students are reading with their buddy, Circulate, observe and support students to ensure they understand how buddy reading looks and sounds, where they can sit, and what to do if they finish the book before you ask them to put their books away. If necessary, model this skill using a partner team. At the end of independent reading (perhaps signaling with a bell, clap or any other desired means so students begin to understand the signal when workstation rotations begin), assist students in the routine of what you'd like them to do at the end of their time in this workstation. Remind them that this is how they will put the books away like they learned before in their library workstation.

Say: *Now let's practice working in our response journal about the book you read. Choose a part of your book that you really liked. Draw a picture of it. Write a sentence about your picture by putting down sounds that you hear in the words.*

Circulate, observe, and support students to ensure they understand how to use their response journals. After a few minutes, ask them to return their journals to the proper place.

Objectives

Students will:
- Introduce "Buddy Reading."
- Create an anchor chart for Buddy Reading.

Additional Materials

- Pointer
- Basket of books for Buddies to use to practice workstation
- Response Journals
- Chart
- Markers

Support Tip

For children with visual challenges, provide audio books by making your own recordings.

Objectives

Students will:
• Continue practicing an efficient transition between mini-lessons.
• Know what good readers do—Visualize.

Additional Materials

• Selected book to read aloud
• Book previously read aloud
• Pointer

Establishing Routines (30 Min.)

Smooth Transitions

Remind students how they sit when they come to the carpet. You may want to begin inviting the whole class to the carpet if you feel they are able to perform this routine. If not, invite one of the tables to join you at the carpet. Ask them to show the rest of the class how we move quietly in our room, push our chairs in when we leave our space, and sit with our legs crossed and our hands in our laps.

Say: *Boys and girls, I'm so glad to see that you remembered that when we come to the carpet we want to sit quietly with our legs crossed and our hands in our laps. When I see you sitting quietly like this with your eyes on the speaker, I'll know you're ready to listen.*

Getting Ready for Whole-Group Instruction: Good Readers Visualize

Say: *Today we are going think about something else that all readers do. When readers are reading a story, they visualize, or draw a picture in their mind about what is happening in the story. Let me show you what I mean. Let's look at this book that we've already read. Listen while I read a couple of pages to you.*

Use any book you've already read. Choose a couple of pages with particularly colorful and descriptive language. Read them with much expression and then **say:** *When I hear the words on these pages I can visualize, or draw a picture in my mind of what the author is saying. I can see that there is (fill in with a visualization that you have.)*

Read another page with colorful and descriptive language and **say:** *I'd like for you to practice visualizing or draw a picture in your mind about these pages. Turn and talk with your partner and tell them what you visualized. Use this sentence frame: I visualized _____.*

Optional: Have students practice returning to their designated seats, or stand up to take a 'brain break.' You may want to ask students to sing, stretch, or move to music at this time.

Read-Aloud and Shared Reading (20 Min.)

Read-Aloud

Call students to the meeting area using the established signal.

Read any book from the Recommended Trade Books in Additional Resources or any other available books such as *It's Time for School, Sticky Face* by Lisa McCourt.

Say: *Now let's practice Turn and Talk with your partner. We have been practicing having a respectful conversation using a sentence frame. Use this frame: I thought Kindergarten would be like _____.*

If your students are ready to proceed without modeling, allow them to continue. If not, choose a student and model using a sentence frame. Let the student use the sentence frame in return.

Say: *Now sit knee to knee and eye to eye with your Turn and Talk partner and use the sentence frame to talk about what you thought might happen in Kindergarten.*

Observe to see that all students are sharing using respectful conversations and using the sentence frame.

Shared Reading

Call students to the meeting area using the established signal.

Say: *Today we have a poem that takes place in school.*

Display the poem "A Diller, A Dollar" from the back of *Welcome to Our School* and ask students to notice the difference between the poem and a book. Read the poem for the first read through without stopping.

Say: *I'm going to reread our poem in a minute, but first I'd like for you to remember something we talked about earlier. We said that readers visualized or drew pictures in their mind to help them understand something. While I read our poem, I'd like for you to practice visualizing what's happening in the poem. Ready? Listen carefully.*

Reread the poem, moving your pointer under the words and stopping in a few places where it is appropriate to support students' comprehension. Stop in a place that you visualized and share that with your students.

Say: *While I was reading the poem, did you find a place to visualize what was happening? Who would like to share what that looked like?*

Invite a few of students to share.

Say: *Turn and talk with your partner and use this sentence frame. I visualized _____.*

"A Diller, A Dollar"

Student Objectives

Students will:
- Build an awareness of the information in a book: title, author, illustrator, illustrations.
- Visualize.

Additional Materials

- Chart paper
- Markers
- Selected book to read aloud
- Pointer

Shared Writing (15 Min.)

Concepts about Print, Letter Awareness, Phonological Awareness

Call students to the meeting area using the established signal.

Say: *Today I'd like for us to remember all of the things we've been learning that good writers do when they put their thoughts on paper. Who will share with us one of the things we know?*

Ask several students to volunteer the following concepts of print: Start here (points), goes to the next line when one is full, begin with a capital, end with a period, and put spaces between words.

Say: *Today I'd like for us to think about words and letters again. Let's look at the book we read aloud. Look at the title and tell me what we know about the words in the title. How many words are there? What is the first letter in the word we will begin with? How many letters are in the word? Let's look on page ___. Do you see a word here you know about? Tell me what you know.*

Ask students to think about what they know about words and letters. Allow students to share what they know, checking for complete sentences. Choose 1 or 2 sentences to use for shared writing.

Sample Shared Writing
Dora likes to find short words.
Frank knows words have letters.

As you write, review student responses about print by pointing out the top of the paper, the bottom of the paper and where on the paper you start to write. Talk about starting on the left and going to the right, spaces, a capital letter, return sweep if necessary, and periods. Emphasize the spaces, the number of words in each sentence, and where each word begins. Draw attention to any letter that is a 'stick letter'; such as **L**, **I**, or **T** and 'slanted letters'; such as **A**, **K**, and **M** and 'circle letters; such as **C** and **O**. Add curved letters such as **S**, **G**, **B** and **D**. Invite students to make a straight, slanted, circle and curve patterns in the air with their fingers.

Say: *Dora's name starts with /**d**/. Can you think where we would put a red dot to find the first letter in Dora's name? Good! How many letters in Dora's name? How do you know? Frank's name starts with a /**f**/. Can you think where we would put a red dot to find the first letter in Frank's name? How many letters are in Frank's name? How do you know? How many letters are in the word 'likes'? 'have?'*

Optional: Have students practice returning to their designated seats, or stand up to take a 'brain break.' You may want to ask students to sing, stretch, or move to music at this time.

Objectives

Students will:
- Continue to differentiate and locate stick, slanted, circle and curved letters within print.
- Concepts of print –First letter of a word and the sound of that letter, difference between and word and letters and beginning sounds.

Additional Materials

- Chart paper
- Markers

Independent Reading (20 Min.)

Workstation Rotation

Teachers Note: There are many types of charts you can use to help students know which workstation they are in, based on your decision for your classroom. You will want to have your rotation schedule prepared and students put in small groups. An easy way for students at this age to find their group is to have a color identification system.

Call students to the meeting area using the established signal. Have the rotation schedule available and ready to explain.

Say: *We are learning about an important way to learn in our classroom. During our independent reading time, we're practicing using workstations. Remember, a workstation is a place you go and work on something that will help you be a better reader. Who can tell me the workstations we've learned about so far? Yes. We have a Library Workstation, a Writing Workstation, a Word Work Workstation, a Puzzles and Games Workstation, and a Computer Workstation and buddy Reading. Today we are going to think about using our workstations so we all have a turn to go to each one. Do you know what rotate means? Yes. We go through each station. Today we're going to know what group we're in and the workstation we'll go to. Look at the chart and I'll explain.*

Talk to students about how to find their name and how to tell which workstation to go to. As you talk about the workstations, have the anchor charts available to remind them what to do and how to act at the workstation. Dismiss your class to their workstations one group at a time. Remind them of the signal you use when time is up, and how to clean up their spot. Since this is for 15 minutes the first week, let each group proceed through one station a day. Start small group work with you next week so you are available this week to observe and assist your students while they are working in their stations. At the end of 15 minutes, sound your signal for students to clean up and ask them to join you at your meeting place.

Say: *I would like for us to think about how our time in our workstations went. I saw boys and girls being very careful with our books in the Library Workstation. Who can share something else they thought went really well in their station? I also saw boys and girls not taking turns in our puzzles and games workstation. I think we need to talk about that. Who can share something else we need to talk about?*

Accept all reasonable responses. Talk about how to solve any problems and add to Anchor Charts for that workstation if appropriate.

Say: *You did very well for the first day in workstations! We're going to practice all week to make sure we know what to do and how to act in each of our workstations.*

Say: *Now let's practice writing in our response journal about the book we read aloud. Choose something in the book that you thought was funny. Draw a picture of it. Write a sentence about your picture by putting down sounds that you hear in the words.*

Circulate, observe, and support students to ensure they understand how to use their response journals. After a few minutes, ask them to return their journals to the proper place.

Objectives

Students will:
- Be introduced to rotation of workstations.

Additional Materials

- Pointer
- Rotation graphic
- Response Journals
- Chart
- Markers

Support Tip

For children with physical challenges, make sure the physical layout accommodates children as much as possible. Try to have wide, open areas and access to materials in the workstations.

Objectives

Students will:
- Continue practicing an efficient transition between mini-lessons.
- Know what good readers do—Use chunks in words.

Additional Materials

- Selected book to read aloud
- Pointer

Establishing Routines (30 Min.)

Smooth Transitions

Remind students how they sit when they come to the carpet. You may want to begin inviting the whole class to the carpet if you feel they are able to perform this routine. If not, invite one of the tables to join you at the carpet. Ask them to show the rest of the class how we move quietly in our room, push our chairs in when we leave our space, and sit with our legs crossed and our hands in our laps.

Say: *Boys and girls, I'm so glad to see that you remembered that when we come to the carpet we want to sit quietly with our legs crossed and our hands in our laps. When I see you sitting quietly like this with your eyes on the speaker, I'll know you're ready to listen.*

Getting Ready for Whole-Group Instruction: Good Readers Use Chunks In Words

Say: *Today we are going think about something else that all readers do. When readers are reading a story, they sometimes come to a words they don't know. One of the things they can do is to find a chunk of the word that they know and use that to help them with the rest of the word. Let me show you what I mean. Look at this word—**an**.*

Show students a word card with the word 'an' on it, or write the word 'an' on a chart tablet or white board. Ask students to look at 'an' and say the letters in the words with you. Then write the word 'can' below it. Show students that **can** has the word chunk **an** in it. Model how to use /**c**/ and put /**an**/ with it to form /**can**/. Do the same with other words with /**an**/ in them.

Say: *When I hear the words on these pages I can visualize, or draw a picture in my mind of what the author is saying. I can see that there is (fill in with a visualization that you have.)*

Read another page with colorful and descriptive language and **say:** *When I see a word I don't know I look for a chunk of the word I do know. Look at the word 'fan' and turn and talk with your partner about how you could figure out this word by finding a chunk in the word you know. Use this sentence frame: I know this word is _____ because _____.*

Optional: Have students practice returning to their designated seats, or stand up to take a 'brain break.' You may want to ask students to sing, stretch, or move to music at this time.

Read-Aloud and Shared Reading (20 Min.)

Read-Aloud

Call students to the meeting area using the established signal.

Read any book from the Recommended Trade Books in Additional Resources or any other available books such as *Bark, George* by Jules Feiffer.

Say: *Now let's practice Turn and Talk with your partner. We have been practicing having a respectful conversation using a sentence frame. Use this frame: This story really surprised me when _____.*

If your students are ready to proceed without modeling, allow them to continue. If not, choose a student and model using a sentence frame. Let the student use the sentence frame in return.

Say: *Now sit knee to knee and eye to eye with your Turn and Talk partner and use the sentence frame to talk about what surprised you in this story.*

Observe to see that all students are sharing using respectful conversations and using the sentence frame.

Shared Reading

Call students to the meeting area using the established signal.

Say: *Today we have a poem about school.*

Display the poem and ask students to notice the difference between the poem and a book. Read the poem for the first read through without stopping.

Say: *I'm going to reread our poem in a minute, but first I'd like for you to remember something we talked about earlier. We said that good readers chunked words to help them understand what they read. Listen while I reread our poem and read the words in chucks in a way I think it is easier to understand.*

Reread the poem, phrasing the words in a way that seems natural and helps with understanding.

Say: *While I was reading the poem, did you hear where I read words together in a chunk? Did that help you understand the poem any better? Listen again.*

Read a couple of phrases in a way that makes sense, and then in a way that doesn't make sense. Invite a few of students to share.

Say: *Turn and talk with your partner and use this sentence frame. I liked the way the words sounded when my teacher said _____.*

"A Diller, A Dollar"

Student Objectives

Students will:
- Build an awareness of the information in a book: title, author, illustrator, illustrations.
- Visualize.

Additional Materials

- Chart paper
- Markers
- Selected book to read aloud
- Pointer

Objectives

Students will:
- Continue to differentiate and locate stick, slanted, circle and curved letters within print.
- Concepts of print–First letter of a word and the sound of that letter, difference between and word and letters and beginning sounds.

Additional Materials
- Chart paper
- Markers

Shared Writing (15 Min.)

Concepts about Print, Letter Awareness, Phonological Awareness

Call students to the meeting area using the established signal.

Say: *Today I'd like for us to remember all of the things we've been learning that good writers do when they put their thoughts on paper. Who will share with us one of the things we know?*

Ask several students to volunteer the following concepts of print: Start here (points), goes to the next line when one is full, begin with a capital, end with a period, and put spaces between words.

Say: *Today I'd like for us to think about words and letters again. Let's look at the poem we were reading earlier. Let's look at the first line of the poem. Can you read it with me? What do you know about the words in this line?*

Let students share what they know like the number of words, the number of letters in the words, the first letter and it's sound in each word, etc.

Ask students to think about what they know about words and letters. Allow students to share what they know, checking for complete sentences. Choose 1 or 2 sentences to use for shared writing.

Sample Shared Writing

Francis knows the first letter in a word.

Gage knows that the first letter makes a sound.

Hank knows that all letters have a sound.

As you write, review student responses about print by pointing out the top of the paper, the bottom of the paper and where on the paper you start to write. Talk about starting on the left and going to the right, spaces, a capital letter, return sweep if necessary, and periods. Emphasize the spaces, the number of words in each sentence, and where each word begins. Draw attention to any letter that is a 'stick letter'; such as **L, I,** or **T** and 'slanted letters'; such as **A, K,** and M and 'circle letters'; such as **C** and **O**. Add 'curved letters' such as **S, G, B,** and **D**. Invite students to make a straight, slanted, circle and curve patterns in the air with their fingers.

Say: *who can tell me what we know about Francis, Gage, and Hank's name. Are any of their names like your name? How are they alike? How are they different?*

Optional: Have students practice returning to their designated seats, or stand up to take a 'brain break.' You may want to ask students to sing, stretch, or move to music at this time.

Independent Reading (20 Min.)

Workstation Rotation

Teachers Note: There are many types of charts you can use to help students know which workstation they are in, based on your decision for your classroom. You will want to have your rotation schedule prepared and students put in small groups. An easy way for students at this age to find their group is to have a color identification system.

Call students to the meeting area using the established signal. Have the rotation schedule available and ready to explain.

Say: *We are learning about an important way to learn in our classroom. During our independent reading time, we're practicing using workstations. Remember, a workstation is a place you go and work on something that will help you be a better reader. Who can tell me the workstations we've learned about so far? Yes. We have a Library Workstation, a Writing Workstation, a Word Work Workstation, a Puzzles and Games Workstation, and a Computer Workstation and buddy Reading. Today we are going to think about using our workstations so we all have a turn to go to each one. Do you know what rotate means? Yes. We go through each station. Today we're going to know what group we're in and the workstation we'll go to. Look at the chart and I'll explain.*

Talk to students about how to find their name and how to tell which workstation to go to. As you talk about the workstations, have the anchor charts available to remind them what to do and how to act at the workstation. Dismiss your class to their workstations one group at a time. Remind them of the signal you use when time is up, and how to clean up their spot. Since this is for 15 minutes the first week, let each group proceed through one station a day. Start small group work with you next week so you are available this week to observe and assist your students while they are working in their stations. At the end of 15 minutes, sound your signal for students to clean up and ask them to join you at your meeting place.

Say: *I would like for us to think about how our time in our workstations went. I saw boys and girls being very careful with our books in the Library Workstation. Who can share something else they thought went really well in their station? I also saw boys and girls not taking turns in our puzzles and games workstation. I think we need to talk about that. Who can share something else we need to talk about?*

Accept all reasonable responses. Talk about how to solve any problems and add to Anchor Charts for that workstation if appropriate.

Say: *You did very well in workstations! We're going to practice all week to make sure we know what to do and how to act in each of our workstations.*

Say: *Now let's practice writing in our response journal about the book we read aloud. Choose something in the book that you thought was funny. Draw a picture of it. Write a sentence about your picture by putting down sounds that you hear in the words.*

Circulate, observe, and support students to ensure they understand how to use their response journals. After a few minutes, ask them to return their journals to the proper place.

Objectives

Students will:
• Continue practicing rotation of workstations.

Additional Materials

• Pointer
• Rotation graphic
• Response Journals
• Chart
• Markers

Support Tip:

For children with social and emotional challenges, keep activities short so children and experience closure.

Objectives

Students will:
- Continue practicing an efficient transition between mini-lessons.
- Know what good readers do—Make connections.

Additional Materials

- Selected book to read aloud
- A book previously read aloud
- Pointer

Establishing Routines (30 Min.)

Smooth Transitions

Remind students how they sit when they come to the carpet. You may want to begin inviting the whole class to the carpet if you feel they are able to perform this routine. If not, invite one of the tables to join you at the carpet. Ask them to show the rest of the class how we move quietly in our room, push our chairs in when we leave our space, and sit with our legs crossed and our hands in our laps.

Say: *Boys and girls, I'm so glad to see that you remembered that when we come to the carpet we want to sit quietly with our legs crossed and our hands in our laps. When I see you sitting quietly like this with your eyes on the speaker, I'll know you're ready to listen.*

Getting Ready for Whole-Group Instruction: Good Readers Make Connections

Say: *Today we are going think about something else that all readers do. When readers are reading a story, they sometimes have trouble understanding what is happening in the story. Something that readers do to help them understand is to make a connection to something they know, or something that happened to them. Let me show you what I mean.*

Show students a book they have heard before that holds a connection to you (a pet, friend, place etc.

Say: *When I hear the words on these pages I can visualize, or draw a picture in my mind of what the author is saying. I can see that there is (fill in with a visualization that you have.)*

Read another page with colorful and descriptive language and **say:** *When we read this book, I remembered that I had a pet that was very special to me when I was growing up. I made a connection because my pet could do tricks, too. I'm wondering if you made a connection to this book. Who would like to share their connection?*

Allow one or two students to share their connection. Then **say:** *Turn and Talk with your partner and start with this sentence frame. A connection I made was _____.*

Optional: Have students practice returning to their designated seats, or stand up to take a 'brain break.' You may want to ask students to sing, stretch, or move to music at this time.

Read-Aloud and Shared Reading (20 Min.)

Read-Aloud

Call students to the meeting area using the established signal.

Read any book from the Recommended Trade Books in Additional Resources or any other available books such as *Lily's Purple Purse* by Kevin Henkes.

Say: *Now let's practice Turn and Talk with your partner. We have been practicing having a respectful conversation using a sentence frame. Use this frame: Something I want to bring to school is _____.*

If your students are ready to proceed without modeling, allow them to continue. If not, choose a student and model using a sentence frame. Let the student use the sentence frame in return.

Say: *Now sit knee to knee and eye to eye with your Turn and Talk partner and use the sentence frame to talk about what you want to bring to school.*

Observe to see that all students are sharing using respectful conversations and using the sentence frame.

Shared Reading

Call students to the meeting area using the established signal.

Say: *Today we are going to look again at our poem.*

Display the poem and ask students to notice the difference between the poem and a book. Also, ask them to notice the author and remind them that we call the author of a poem a poet. Talk about the illustrator and what an illustrator does. Read the poem for the first read through without stopping.

Say: *I'm going to reread our poem in a minute, but first I'd like for you to remember something we talked about earlier. We said that good readers make connections with things they read to help them understand. Listen while I reread our poem and think about anything in the poem that reminds you of something. Can you make a connection to this poem?*

Reread the poem.

Say: *While I was reading the poem, I made a connection when _____. Did any of you make a connection? Who would like to share a connection they made?.*

Say: *Turn and talk with your partner and use this sentence frame. I made a connection when _____.*

"A Diller, A Dollar"

Student Objectives

Students will:
- Build an awareness of the information in a book: title, author, illustrator, illustrations.
- Visualize.

Additional Materials

- Chart paper
- Markers
- Selected book to read aloud
- Poem in front of Big Book Welcome to our School
- Pointer

Objectives

Students will:
- Students will:
- Continue to differentiate and locate stick, slanted, circle and curved letters within print.

Additional Materials

- Chart paper
- Markers

Shared Writing (15 Min.)

Concepts about Print, Letter Awareness, Phonological Awareness

Call students to the meeting area using the established signal.

Say: *Today I'd like for us to remember all of the things we've been learning that good writers do when they put their thoughts on paper. Who will share with us one of the things we know?*

Ask several students to volunteer the following concepts of print: Start here (points), goes to the next line when one is full, begin with a capital, end with a period, and put spaces between words.

Say: *Today I'd like for us to think about words, letters and sentences. We've been reading a poem about school. Let's think of our own sentences about school. Think about our poems or our big books that are about schools. Do they give you some ideas about our classroom that we could write about? Let me show you what I mean. I think, 'Mr. Miller keeps our class clean.' Is a good sentence. Can you think of a sentence?*

Let students share a couple of sentences about your school. Choose 1 or 2 sentences to use for shared writing.

Sample Shared Writing

Mr. Miller keeps our class very clean.

Our class library has books.

We have six computers.

As you write, review student responses about print by pointing out the top of the paper, the bottom of the paper and where on the paper you start to write. Talk about starting on the left and going to the right, spaces, a capital letter, return sweep if necessary, and periods. Emphasize the spaces, the number of words in each sentence, and where each word begins. Talk about the sounds you hear in the words and how you know what letters to put down for each word. Draw attention to any letter that is a 'stick letter'; such as **L, I,** or **T** and 'slanted letters'; such as **A, K,** and **M** and 'circle letters'; such as **C** and **O**. Add 'curved letters' such as **S, G, B,** and **D**. Invite students to make a straight, slanted, circle and curve patterns in the air with their fingers.

Say: *Who can read the first sentence for me? Who can read the second sentence? The last sentence? Turn and talk and take turns reading the sentences to each other.*

Optional: Have students practice returning to their designated seats, or stand up to take a 'brain break.' You may want to ask students to sing, stretch, or move to music at this time.

Independent Reading (20 Min.)

Workstation Rotation

Teachers Note: There are many types of charts you can use to help students know which workstation they are in, based on your decision for your classroom. You will want to have your rotation schedule prepared and students put in small groups. An easy way for students at this age to find their group is to have a color identification system.

Call students to the meeting area using the established signal. Have the rotation schedule available and ready to explain.

Say: *We are learning about an important way to learn in our classroom. During our independent reading time, we're practicing using workstations. Remember, a workstation is a place you go and work on something that will help you be a better reader. Who can tell me the workstations we've learned about so far? Yes. We have a Library Workstation, a Writing Workstation, a Word Work Workstation, a Puzzles and Games Workstation, and a Computer Workstation and buddy Reading. Today we are going to think about using our workstations so we all have a turn to go to each one. Do you know what rotate means? Yes. We go through each station. Today we're going to know what group we're in and the workstation we'll go to. Look at the chart and I'll explain.*

Talk to students about how to find their name and how to tell which workstation to go to. As you talk about the workstations, have the anchor charts available to remind them what to do and how to act at the workstation. Dismiss your class to their workstations one group at a time. Remind them of the signal you use when time is up, and how to clean up their spot. Since this is for 15 minutes the first week, let each group proceed through one station a day. Start small group work with you next week so you are available this week to observe and assist your students while they are working in their stations. At the end of 15 minutes, sound your signal for students to clean up and ask them to join you at your meeting place.

Say: *I would like for us to think about how our time in our workstations went. I saw boys and girls being very careful with our books in the Library Workstation. Who can share something else they thought went really well in their station? I also saw boys and girls not taking turns in our puzzles and games workstation. I think we need to talk about that. Who can share something else we need to talk about?*

Accept all reasonable responses. Talk about how to solve any problems and add to Anchor Charts for that workstation if appropriate.

Say: *You did very well in workstations! We're going to practice all week to make sure we know what to do and how to act in each of our workstations.*

Say: *Now let's practice writing in our response journal about the book we read aloud. Choose something in the book that you thought was sad. Draw a picture of it. Write a sentence about your picture by putting down sounds that you hear in the words.*

Circulate, observe, and support students to ensure they understand how to use their response journals. After a few minutes, ask them to return their journals to the proper place.

Objectives

Students will:
- Continue practicing rotation of workstations.

Additional Materials

- Pointer
- Rotation graphic
- Response Journals
- Chart
- Markers

Support Tip

For children with cognitive challenges modify expectation when children are working as part of a group.

Objectives

Students will:
- Continue practicing an efficient transition between mini-lessons.
- Know what good readers do—Know the different between fiction and nonfiction.

Additional Materials

- Selected book to read aloud
- A book previously read aloud
- Pointer

Establishing Routines (30 Min.)

Smooth Transitions

Remind students how they sit when they come to the carpet. You may want to begin inviting the whole class to the carpet if you feel they are able to perform this routine. If not, invite one of the tables to join you at the carpet. Ask them to show the rest of the class how we move quietly in our room, push our chairs in when we leave our space, and sit with our legs crossed and our hands in our laps.

Say: *Boys and girls, I'm so glad to see that you remembered that when we come to the carpet we want to sit quietly with our legs crossed and our hands in our laps. When I see you sitting quietly like this with your eyes on the speaker, I'll know you're ready to listen.*

Getting Ready for Whole-Group Instruction: Good Readers Know the Difference between Fiction and Nonfiction

Say: *Today we are going think about something else that all readers do. When good readers are thinking about a story they are going to read, there is something very important that they should think about—especially when they are making a prediction! Good readers should always think about the book and ask themselves if it is fiction or nonfiction. Do you remember the difference? Yes. Fiction is pretend and nonfiction is real. Let me show you what I mean.*

Show students an example of a fiction and nonfiction book

Say: *When I look at these books and try to think what they can be about, I can look at the picture on the cover, the title, and I can also decide if I think the book is fiction or nonfiction. That will help me know what kind of book I'm going to be reading so I understand it better. I'd like for you to look at these books and help me decide.*

Show the books to students and allow some of them to share their thinking about fiction and nonfiction. Confirm if they are correct. Then **say:** *Turn and Talk with your partner and start with this sentence frame. Knowing about a book helps me understand the book better because _____.*

Optional: Have students practice returning to their designated seats, or stand up to take a 'brain break.' You may want to ask students to sing, stretch, or move to music at this time.

Read-Aloud and Shared Reading (20 Min.)

Read-Aloud

Call students to the meeting area using the established signal.

Read any book from the Recommended Trade Books in Additional Resources or any other available books such as *Sheila Rae, the Brave* by Kevin Henkes.

Say: *Now let's practice Turn and Talk with your partner. We have been practicing having a respectful conversation using a sentence frame. Use this frame: I was brave when _____.*

If your students are ready to proceed without modeling, allow them to continue. If not, choose a student and model using a sentence frame. Let the student use the sentence frame in return.

Say: *Now sit knee to knee and eye to eye with your Turn and Talk partner and use the sentence frame to talk about a time when you were brave,*

Observe to see that all students are sharing using respectful conversations and using the sentence frame.

Shared Reading

Call students to the meeting area using the established signal.

Say: *Today we are going to look again at our poem.*

Read the poem for the first read through without stopping.

Say: *When I reread our poem, I'd like for you to listen for rhyming words.*

Reread the poem.

Say: *Did anyone hear any rhyming words? Let's make an anchor chart of the words that rhyme in our poem.*

"A Diller, A Dollar"

Student Objectives

Students will:
- Visualize.
- Identify rhyming words in a poem.

Additional Materials

- Chart paper
- Markers
- Selected book to read aloud
- Pointer

Objectives

Students will:
- Continue to differentiate and locate stick, slanted, circle and curved letters within print.

Additional Materials
- Chart paper
- Markers

Shared Writing (15 MIN.)

Concepts about Print, Letter Awareness, Phonological Awareness

Call students to the meeting area using the established signal.

Say: *Today I'd like for us to remember all of the things we've been learning that good writers do when they put their thoughts on paper. Who will share with us one of the things we know?*

Ask several students to volunteer the following concepts of print: Start here (points), goes to the next line when one is full, begin with a capital, end with a period, and put spaces between words.

Say: *Today I'd like for us to think about words, letters and sentences. We've been reading a poem about school. Let's think of our own sentences about school. Think about our poems or our big books that are about schools. Do they give you some ideas about our classroom that we could write about? Let me show you what I mean. I think, 'Mr. Miller keeps our class clean.' Is a good sentence. Can you think of a sentence?*

Let students share a couple of sentences about your school. Choose 1 or 2 sentences to use for shared writing.

Sample Shared Writing

Mr. Miller keeps our room very clean.

Our class library has books.

We have six computers.

Our classroom has tables.

We have a class pet.

Our teacher is pretty.

As you write, review student responses about print by pointing out the top of the paper, the bottom of the paper and where on the paper you start to write. Talk about starting on the left and going to the right, spaces, a capital letter, return sweep if necessary, and periods. Emphasize the spaces, the number of words in each sentence, and where each word begins. Talk about the sounds you hear in the words and how you know what letters to put down for each word. Draw attention to any letter that is a 'stick letter'; such as **L**, **I**, or **T** and 'slanted letters'; such as **A**, **K**, and **M** and 'circle letters'; such as **C** and **O**. Add 'curved letters' such as **S**, **G**, **B** and **D**. Invite students to make a straight, slanted, circle and curve patterns in the air with their fingers.

Say: *Who can choose a sentence they would like to read? Anyone else? Turn and talk and take turns reading the sentences to each other.*

Optional: Have students Have students practice returning to their designated seats, or stand up to take a 'brain break.' You may want to ask students to sing, stretch, or move to music at this time.

Independent Reading (20 Min.)

Workstation Rotation

Teachers Note: There are many types of charts you can use to help students know which workstation they are, based on your decision for your classroom. You will want to have your rotation schedule prepared and students put in small groups. An easy way for students at this age to find their group is to have a color identification system.

Call students to the meeting area using the established signal. Have the rotation schedule available and ready to explain.

Say: *We are learning about an important way to learn in our classroom. During our independent reading time, we're practicing using workstations. Remember, a workstation is a place you go and work on something that will help you be a better reader. Who can tell me the workstations we've learned about so far? Yes. We have a Library Workstation, a Writing Workstation, a Word Work Workstation, a Puzzles and Games Workstation, and a Computer Workstation and buddy Reading. Today we are going to think about using our workstations so we all have a turn to go to each one. Do you know what rotate means? Yes. We go through each station. Today we're going to know what group we're in and the workstation we'll go to. Look at the chart and I'll explain.*

Talk to students about how to find their name and how to tell which workstation to go to. As you talk about the workstations, have the anchor charts available to remind them what to do and how to act at the workstation. Dismiss your class to their workstations one group at a time. Remind them of the signal you use when time is up, and how to clean up their spot. Since this is for 15 minutes the first week, let each group proceed through one station a day. Start small group work with you next week so you are available this week to observe and assist your students while they are working in their stations. At the end of 15 minutes, sound your signal for students to clean up and ask them to join you at your meeting place.

Say: *I would like for us to think about how our time in our workstations went. I saw boys and girls being very careful with our books in the Library Workstation. Who can share something else they thought went really well in their station? I also saw boys and girls not taking turns in our puzzles and games workstation. I think we need to talk about that. Who can share something else we need to talk about?*

Accept all reasonable responses. Talk about how to solve any problems and add to Anchor Charts for that workstation if appropriate.

Say: *You did very well in workstations! We're going to practice all week to make sure we know what to do and how to act in each of our workstations.*

Say: *Now let's practice writing in our response journal about the book we read aloud. Choose something in the book that you thought was sad. Draw a picture of it. Write a sentence about your picture by putting down sounds that you hear in the words.*

Circulate, observe, and support students to ensure they understand how to use their response journals. After a few minutes, ask them to return their journals to the proper place.

Objectives

Students will:
- Continue practicing rotation of workstations.

Additional Materials

- Pointer
- Rotation graphic
- Response Journals
- Chart
- Markers

Support Tip

For children who are learning English use group songs, rhymes, and chants to welcome participation.

Establishing Routines (30 Min.)

Objectives

Students will:
- Continue practicing an efficient transition between mini-lessons.
- Know what good readers do – Identify characters in a story.

Additional Materials

- Selected book to read aloud
- A book previously read aloud
- Pointer

Smooth Transitions

Remind students how they sit when they come to the carpet. You may want to begin inviting the whole class to the carpet if you feel they are able to perform this routine. If not, invite one of the tables to join you at the carpet. Ask them to show the rest of the class how we move quietly in our room, push our chairs in when we leave our space, and sit with our legs crossed and our hands in our laps.

Say: *Boys and girls, I'm so glad to see that you remembered that when we come to the carpet we want to sit quietly with our legs crossed and our hands in our laps. When I see you sitting quietly like this with your eyes on the speaker, I'll know you're ready to listen.*

Getting Ready for Whole-Group Instruction: Good Readers Identify Characters in a Story

Say: *Today we are going think about something else that all readers do. When readers are reading a story, they think about who the story is about. When we talk about who the story is about, we say they are the characters of the story. Characters can be people, animals or things.*

Show students an example of a fiction book that you have read to them such as Chrysanthemum by Kevin Henkes.

Say: *Do you remember this story? Who can remind us what this story is about? Do you think there are characters in the story? Let me show you how we can tell who characters are in the story. We can think about a name we hear in the story. We can look at the cover and see if there is a picture of the character. We can even read the title and see if there is a name in the title. Let's look closer at this book? Do we see a picture of who this book is about on the cover of the book? Listen to the title. Do we hear the name of a character? When we read the story, did you hear a name mentioned several times? Who do you think is the main character in this book? Yes, it's Chrysanthemum!*

Show another fiction read-aloud that students have heard to the children. Tell them that you will remind them about the title and story. Then **say:** *Turn and Talk with your partner and start with this sentence frame. I think the character is _____ because _____.*

Optional: Have students practice returning to their designated seats, or stand up to take a 'brain break.' You may want to ask students to sing, stretch, or move to music at this time.

Read-Aloud and Shared Reading (20 Min.)

Read-Aloud

Call students to the meeting area using the established signal.

Read any book from the Recommended Trade Books in Additional Resources or any other available books such as *A Splendid Friend, Indeed* by Suzanne Bloom.

Say: *Now let's practice Turn and Talk with your partner. We have been practicing having a respectful conversation using a sentence frame. Use this frame: My friend and I like to _____ together.*

If your students are ready to proceed without modeling, allow them to continue. If not, choose a student and model using a sentence frame. Let the student use the sentence frame in return.

Say: *Now sit knee to knee and eye to eye with your Turn and Talk partner and use the sentence frame to talk about things you and your friend like to do together.*

Observe to see that all students are sharing using respectful conversations and using the sentence frame.

Shared Reading

Call students to the meeting area using the established signal.

Say: *Today we are going to look again at our poem.*

Display the poem and ask students to notice the difference between the poem and a book. Read the poem for the first read through without stopping.

Say: *When I reread our poem, I'd like for you to listen for who the character is. Remember, knowing who the characters are can help readers better understand the poem. We can use several clues to find the character. We can look at the poem to see if there's a picture, and we can listen carefully to the poem.*

Reread the poem.

Say: *Does anyone think they know what the character in the poem does?*

Allow several students the opportunity of sharing what they think the character in the poem does.

Say: *Turn and talk with your partner about what happens that is funny in the poem.*

"A Diller, A Dollar"

Student Objectives

Students will:
- Build an awareness of the information in a book: title, author, illustrator, illustrations.
- Visualize.

Additional Materials

- Chart paper
- Markers
- Selected book to read aloud
- Pointer

Shared Writing (15 Min.)

Concepts about Print, Letter Awareness, Phonological Awareness

Call students to the meeting area using the established signal.

Say: *Today I'd like for us to remember all of the things we've been learning that good writers do when they put their thoughts on paper. Who will share with us one of the things we know?*

Ask several students to volunteer the following concepts of print: Start here (points), goes to the next line when one is full, begin with a capital, end with a period, and put spaces between words.

Say: *We have several sentences about our class. Let's read them together. I'd like for you to see that each sentence is on a sheet of this paper. You are each going to work in a small group to illustrate the sentence on the paper. Each group will need to decide what picture you want to draw that will go with the sentence and how you will each have a turn drawing. When we finish we will put our book together and put it in our class library to read.*

Let students add two or three more sentences about your class if necessary so there are enough 'pages' for small groups of 2–3 students.

Sample Shared Writing

Mr. Miller keeps our room very clean.

Our class library has books.

We have six computers.

Our classroom has tables.

We have a class pet.

Our teacher is pretty.

If you choose to write the sentences with the class instead of having them written before hand, follow this regular procedure. As you write, review student responses about print by pointing out the top of the paper, the bottom of the paper and where on the paper you start to write. Talk about starting on the left and going to the right, spaces, a capital letter, return sweep if necessary, and periods. Emphasize the spaces, the number of words in each sentence, and where each word begins. Talk about the sounds you hear in the words and how you know what letters to put down for each word. Draw attention to any letter that is a 'stick letter'; such as **L, I,** or **T** and 'slanted letters'; such as **A, K,** and **M** and 'circle letters; such as **C** and **O**. Add curved letters such as **S, G, B** and **D**. Invite students to make a straight, slanted, circle and curve patterns in the air with their fingers.

Optional: Have students practice returning to their designated seats, or stand up to take a 'brain break.' You may want to ask students to sing, stretch, or move to music at this time.

Objectives

Students will:
- Continue to differentiate and locate stick, slanted, circle and curved letters within print.
- Concepts of print – First letter of a word and the sound of that letter, difference between and word and letters and beginning sounds

Additional Materials

- Chart paper
- Markers
- Sentences about the class
- Each sentence copied on a large sheet of manila paper

Independent Reading (20 Min.)

Workstation Rotation

Teachers Note: There are many types of charts you can use to help students know which workstation they are in, based on your decision for your classroom. You will want to have your rotation schedule prepared and students put in small groups. An easy way for students at this age to find their group is to have a color identification system.

Call students to the meeting area using the established signal. Have the rotation schedule available and ready to explain.

Say: *We are learning about an important way to learn in our classroom. During our independent reading time, we're practicing using workstations. Remember, a workstation is a place you go and work on something that will help you be a better reader. Who can tell me the workstations we've learned about so far? Yes. We have a Library Workstation, a Writing Workstation, a Word Work Workstation, a Puzzles and Games Workstation, and a Computer Workstation and buddy Reading. Today we are going to think about using our workstations so we all have a turn to go to each one. Do you know what rotate means? Yes. We go through each station. Today we're going to know what group we're in and the workstation we'll go to. Look at the chart and I'll explain.*

Talk to students about how to find their name and how to tell which workstation to go to. As you talk about the workstations, have the anchor charts available to remind them what to do and how to act at the workstation. Dismiss your class to their workstations one group at a time. Remind them of the signal you use when time is up, and how to clean up their spot. Since this is for 15 minutes the first week, let each group proceed through one station a day. Start small group work with you next week so you are available this week to observe and assist your students while they are working in their stations. At the end of 15 minutes, sound your signal for students to clean up and ask them to join you at your meeting place.

Say: *I would like for us to think about how our time in our workstations went. I saw boys and girls being very careful with our books in the Library Workstation. Who can share something else they thought went really well in their station? I also saw boys and girls not taking turns in our puzzles and games workstation. I think we need to talk about that. Who can share something else we need to talk about?*

Accept all reasonable responses. Talk about how to solve any problems and add to Anchor Charts for that workstation if appropriate.

Say: *You did very well in workstations! We're going to practice all week to make sure we know what to do and how to act in each of our workstations.*

Say: *Now let's practice writing in our response journal about the book we read aloud. Choose something in the book that you thought was sad. Draw a picture of it. Write a sentence about your picture by putting down sounds that you hear in the words.*

Circulate, observe, and support students to ensure they understand how to use their response journals. After a few minutes, ask them to return their journals to the proper place.

Objectives

Students will:
- Continue practicing Rotation of workstations.

Additional Materials

- Pointer
- Rotation graphic
- Response Journals
- Chart
- Markers

Support Tip

For children who have social and emotional challenges, invite children to participate in group activities by gently describing what the other children are doing.

UNIT 1 Formative Assessment Opportunities

	Minute-By-Minute Observation	*Daily* Performance Monitoring	*Weekly* Progress Monitoring
Reading/Writing Mini-lessons	• Collaborative Conversation • Guided Practice	• Show Your Knowledge • Write Independently • Student Conferences	• Weekly Assessments *See back of Unit 1 Tab for skills assessed*
Phonics Mini-lessons	• Practice	• Independent practice activities • Read Decodable Text	• Spelling Assessment and Dictation
Small-Group Reading	• Observe and monitor student reading	• Retelling • Graphic organizers Text-Evidence Questions	• *Conduct oral reading records as appropriate*

Recommended observation forms:
• Speaking and listening observation form
• Small-Group Reading Observation Records
• Individual Reading Conference Form

UNIT 1 Vocabulary and Spelling

	Domain-Specific	General Academic	Instructional	High-Frequency Words	Spelling
Week 1	equipment	courteous enormous kick playmate winning	label predict roles		
Week 2	citizens community respect	attention clean rules safe school	chapter focus	I	I
Week 3		bumped everyone joined turns unhappy	author identify strategy	I like	I like

Week 1 Skills at a Glance

	Day 1	Day 2
Reading Mini-Lessons	**Mentor Read-Alouds:** Unit Introduction, pp. 2-3 Unit 1 Video **Introduce Unit 1: Rules at Home and School (10 Min.), p. 4** RI.K.7, RI.K.10b, SL.K.1a, SL.K.1b, SL.K.2 **Read-Aloud Handbook** **Shared Readings:** "Follow the Rules to Play Soccer," p. 2 **Read Aloud and Shared Reading (20 Min.), p. 5** RI.K.10, RI.K.10a, RI.K.10b. RF.K.1b, RF.K.3a, SL.K.2 • Fluency: Rate/Pausing • Build Unit Concepts: Following Rules • Model Print Concepts: Print Conveys Meaning • Review Phonics: Alphabet Review **Mentor Read-Alouds:** "Let's Play by the Rules!", pp. 4-7 **"Let's Play by the Rules!": Listen and Retell Key Details (10 Min.), p. 6** RI.K1, RI.K.2, RI.K.10, RI.K.10a, RI.K.10b, SL.K.1a, SL.K.1b	**Read-Aloud Handbook** **Shared Readings:** "Follow the Rules to Play Soccer," p. 2 **Read Aloud and Shared Reading (20 Min.), p. 12** RI.K.1, RI.K.10, RF.K.1d, SL.K.1a, SL.K.1b • Fluency: Rate/Pausing • Build Concepts: Following Rules • Review Phonics: Alphabet Review **Mentor Read-Alouds:** "Let's Play by the Rules!", pp. 4-7 **Describe the Relationship Between Photographs and the Text (10 Min.), p. 13** RI.K.1, RI.K.7, RI.K.10, SL.K.3 **Identify the Main Topic (10 Min.), p. 14** RI.K.1, RI.K.2, RI.K.10a, RI.K.10b
Writing Mini-Lessons	**Write Key Details (10 Min.), p. 8** W.K.2, W.K.8, SL.K.1a, SL.K.1b, L.K.1a, L.K.1b • Build Language: Nouns	**Write About School Rules (10 Min.), p. 16** W.K.3, W.K.8, SL.K.1a, SL.K.1b, L.K.1a, L.K.1b • Build Language: Nouns
Phonics Mini-Lessons	**Focus Skill: Letter Recognition: Aa, Bb, Cc, Dd, Ee (20 Min.), p. 10** RF.K.1d, RF.K.2a, RF.K.2b • Phonological Awareness: Recognize Rhyme, Syllable Blending	**Focus Skill: Letter Recognition Ff, Gg, Hh, Ii, Jj, (20 Min.), p. 18** RF.K.1d, RF.K.2a, RF.K.2b • Phonological Awareness: Recognize Rhyme, Syllable Blending

Mentor Read-Aloud 1: "Let's Play by the Rules!"

Informational Text

Quantitative	Lexile® 500L
Qualitative Analysis of Text Complexity	

Purpose and Levels of Meaning ❶
• Text has a simple purpose: to tell about the importance of following rules.

Structure ❶
• The text structure is centered around elements of sports rules and their enforcement.

Language Conventionality and Clarity ❶
• Vocabulary is either familiar or easily decodable through context.

Knowledge Demands ❷
• Prior knowledge of sports would aid students' comprehension of the text.

Day 3	Day 4	Day 5
Read-Aloud Handbook **Shared Readings:** "Making Bridges," p. 3 **Read Aloud and Shared Reading (20 Min.), p. 20** RL.K.10, RL.K.10a, RL.K.10b, RF.K.1b, RF.K.3a, SL.K.1b • Fluency: Rate/Pausing • Build Unit Concepts: Following Rules • Model Print Concepts: Print Conveys Meaning • Review Phonics: Alphabet Review **Mentor Read-Alouds:** "A New Pet," p. 8-11 **Listen and Retell Story Events(10 Min.), p. 21** RL.K.1, RL.K.2, RL.K.5, RL.K.10, RL.K.10a, RL.K.10b, RF.K.1a, SL.K.1a, SL.K.1b **Describe the Relationships Between Illustrations and the Story (10 Min.), p. 22** RL.K.1, RL.K.7	**Read-Aloud Handbook** **Shared Readings:** "Making Bridges," p. 3 **Read Aloud and Shared Reading (20 Min.), p. 27** RL.K.10, RF.K.1d, SL.K.3 • Fluency: Rate/Pacing • Build Language: Nouns • Review Phonics: Alphabet Review **Mentor Read-Alouds:** "A New Pet," pp. 8-11 **Identify Characters in a Story (10 Min.), p. 28** RL.K.1, RL.K.3, SL.K.2, SL.K.3	**Read-Aloud Handbook** **Shared Readings:** "Making Bridges," p. 3 **Read Aloud and Shared Reading (20 Min.), p. 33** RI.K.1, RF.K.3a, SL.K.1a, SL.K.1b • Fluency: Rate/Pacing • Build Concepts: Following Rules • Review Concepts of Print: Print Convey Meaning • Review Phonics: Alphabet Review **Mentor Read-Alouds:** "Let's Play by the Rules!", pp. 4-7 "A New Pet," pp. 8-11 **Compare and Contrast an Informational Text and Realistic Fiction (20 Min.), p. 34** RL.K.5, RI.K.9, RF.K.1a, SL.K.2, SL.K.3
Write About Owning a Pet (10 Min.), p. 24 W.K.2, W.K.8, SL.K.1a, SL.K.1b, L.K.1a, L.K.1b • Build Language: Nouns	**Write an Opinion (10 Min.), p. 30** W.K.1, W.K.8, SL.K.1a, SL.K.1b, L.K.1a, L.K.1b • Build Language: Nouns	**Write a Comparison and Contrast Text (10 Min.), p. 36** W.K.2, W.K.8, SL.K.1a, SL.K.1b, SL.K.6, L.K.1a, L.K.1b • Build Language: Nouns
Focus Skill: Letter Recognition Kk, Ll, Mm, Nn, Oo (20 Min.), p. 26 RF.K.1d, RF.K.2a • Phonological Awareness: Recognize and Produce Rhyme	**Pre-Decodable Reader:** *ABC* **Focus Skill: Letter Recognition Pp, Qq, Rr, Ss, Tt (20 Min.), p. 32** RF.K.1d, RF.K.2a • Phonological Awareness: Recognize and Produce Rhyme	**Pre-Decodable Reader:** *ABC* **Focus Skill: Letter Recognition: Uu, Vv, Ww, Xx, Yy, Zz (20 Min.), p. 38** RF.K.1d, RF.K.2a, RF.K.2d • Phonological Awareness: Phoneme Isolation

Mentor Read-Aloud 2: "A New Pet"

Realistic Fiction

Quantitative	Lexile 450L
Qualitative Analysis of Text Complexity	

Purpose and Levels of Meaning ❶
• The story has a simple purpose: to tell about a boy wanting, and then getting, a pet.

Structure ❶
• The narrative is structured in chronological order.

Language Conventionality and Clarity ❶
• The sentences are simple, and the language is everyday usage with no unfamiliar vocabulary.

Knowledge Demands ❶
• The text deals with a familiar situation and requires no prior knowledge.

**Mentor Read-Aloud Topic
Introduction Vol. 1, p. 2-3**

Student Objectives

I will be able to:
- Ask **what, when, where, why, how** questions about rules at home and school.
- Share what I know about rules.
- Listen carefully as others speak.

(iELD) Integrated ELD

Light Support
Have partners use the information and ideas from pages 2 and 3, *Rules at School and Home*, to ask and answer questions about why we have rules at home and school.

Moderate Support
Model exchanging information and ideas by asking and answering questions. Post question words:
What / When / Where / Why / How
Ask students to use the question words to ask and answer questions about why we follow rules at home and school. Have partners take turns asking and answering questions.
- *How do we keep safe at school? [We keep safe at school by not running in the hall.]*
- *Why do we raise our hands before speaking in class? [We raise our hands before speaking in class to be courteous.]*

Substantial Support
Model exchanging information and ideas by asking and answering questions. Post question words:
What / When / Where / Why / How
Ask students to orally complete questions about why we follow rules at home and school.
- *Why do we [buckle seatbelts]? [We buckle seatbelts to be safe in a car.]*
- *How do we keep safe [at home]? [We keep safe at home by not touching a hot stove.]*
- *When is it important [not to run]? [It is important not to run in school halls.]*

ELD.PI.K.1, ELD.PI.K.5, ELD.PI.K.6

Introduce Unit 1: Rules at Home and School (10 MIN.) RI.K.7, RI.K.10b, SL.K.1a, SL.K.1b, SL.K.2

Pose the Essential Question

Display the Topic 1 Introduction and read aloud the essential question. Explain to students that they will be thinking about this question over the next weeks.

Why do we have rules?

State Unit Objectives

Say: *In this unit, we will talk about the different rules we have at home and at school and why we have those rules. Look at the photos and listen as I read the captions. Some of these rules help us stay safe: Buckle Up! Do Not Run! Listen Up! Help a Friend. These rules can help us at school.*

Link to Prior Knowledge

Ask partners to tell about one rule they have at home and why it is important to follow that rule. Then ask them to do the same for one rule at school.

View Multimedia

Display or have students access the Unit 1 video on their devices.

Collaborative Conversation: Partner (iELD)

Tell students that you would like them to share questions they have about the unit theme. Model how to ask questions about rules at home and school.

Say: *I ask myself questions to help me get to know about this topic. When I think about rules, I have many questions: Why are some rules at school different from the rules at home? What questions do you have about rules? You can start your questions with a word, such as how, what, when, where, why, or what.*

Share

Ask volunteers to share a question about rules with the class. Make a list of the questions. Post the list in your classroom to refer to and add to during the unit. Reinforce the idea that asking and answering questions will help students learn new information.

RI.K.7 With prompting and support, describe the relationship between illustrations and the text in which they appear (e.g., what person, place, thing, or idea in the text an illustration depicts)., **RI.K.10b** Use illustrations and context to make predictions about text, **SL.K.1a** Follow agreed-upon rules for discussions (e.g., listening to others and taking turns speaking about the topics and texts under discussion)., **SL.K.1b** Continue a conversation through multiple exchanges., **SL.K.2** Confirm understanding of a text read aloud or information presented orally or through other media by asking and answering questions about key details and requesting clarification if something is not understood. **CA**

©2017 Benchmark Education Company, LLC

Read Aloud and Shared Reading (20 MIN.)

RI.K.10, RI.K.10a, RI.K.10b. RF.K.1b, RF.K.3a, SL.K.2

Read-Aloud Handbook **Shared Reading Vol. 1, p. 2 "Follow the Rules to Play Soccer"**

Read Aloud

To support the unit concept, use one of the Read-Aloud Handbook selections for Unit 1. As you read, model the metacognitive strategy for the unit, Ask Questions, guided by the samples provided. You may also wish to select a favorite read-aloud from your classroom or school library. To support the unit concept, use one of the suggested titles for Unit 1.

Shared Reading (iELD)

Introduce the Informational Text

Display "Follow the Rules to Play Soccer." Read aloud the title of the text as you point under each word. Invite students to turn to a partner and tell what they predict the text will be about. Invite a few students to share their predictions with the whole class.

Read the Informational Text

First rereading. Read aloud the text fluently and expressively, pointing under each word.

Reread for fluency: Rate/Pacing. Model reading with appropriate pacing. Point out that you do not read the text too quickly or too slowly. Lead them to pause at the end of a sentence. Invite students to choral read the text at a good pace. Provide corrective feedback and/or validate students' efforts.

Build Concepts: Following Rules

Pose questions to connect the informational text to the unit concept. For example:

- *How do you think these players learn the soccer rules?*
- *What might happen if the players did not follow the soccer rules?*
- *Why is it important to be a good sport?*

Model Concepts of Print: Print Conveys Meaning

Call on a volunteer to point to the photo. Explain that the photo shows children playing a game of soccer. Call on a volunteer to point to the words. Explain that the words have meaning. Tell students that it is the print on the page, not the photo, that gives the information the author wants us to know.

Review Phonics: Alphabet Review

Display the letters of the alphabet. Sing the "Alphabet Song," pointing to each letter as you say its name. Point out the difference between capital and lowercase letters. Randomly point to letters and lead students to say the letter name together. Then invite volunteers to name the initial letter in words, such as **Follow, ball, fast, can, and Soccer** in "Follow the Rules to Play Soccer."

Student Objectives

I will be able to:
- Read along with the correct pacing.
- Answer questions about rules in team sports.
- Understand that print has meaning.
- Identify initial letters in words.

(iELD) Integrated ELD

Light Support
Ask students to look at the print and photograph on page 2 under "Follow the Rules to Play Soccer." Then have them work with partners to take turns asking each other questions about the rules. Monitor to check their comprehension.
Discuss with students why soccer players need to know the rules of the game.

Moderate Support
Review the rules for soccer on page 2 under "Follow the Rules to Play Soccer." Have students show their comprehension of the rules by orally answering simple questions:
How should players run after the ball? [fast]
What don't players touch with their hands? [the ball]
Why do players kick the ball high? [to make a goal]
How can players be good sports? [follow the rules]
Then discuss why soccer players need to know the rules of the game.

Substantial Support
Have students look at the rules for soccer on page 2 under "Follow the Rules to Play Soccer." Read the rules aloud as students follow along. Have students point to words as you say them: **follow, rules, run, ball, kick.** Focus on the rules and have students show their comprehension by orally answering simple questions with yes-no responses:
Should players run slow? [no]
Can players touch the ball with their hands? [no]
Does a good sport know the rules? [yes]
Does a player kick the ball to make a goal? [yes]
Then discuss why soccer players need to know the rules of the game. Point out that knowing the rules helps players take part in the game, play fairly, and keep safe.

ELD.PI.K.1, ELD.PI.K.5, ELD.PI.K.6

RI.K.10 Actively engage in group reading activities with purpose and understanding., **RI.K.10a** Activate prior knowledge related to the information and events in texts. CA, **RI.K.10b** Use illustrations and context to make predictions about text. CA, **RF.K.1b** Recognize that spoken words are represented in written language by specific sequences of letters., **RF.K.3a** Know and apply grade-level phonics and word analysis skills in decoding words both in isolation and in text. CA, **SL.K.2** Confirm understanding of a text read aloud or information presented orally or through other media by asking and answering questions about key details and requesting clarification if something is not understood.,
©2017 Benchmark Education Company, LLC

"Let's Play by the Rules!": Listen and Retell Key Details (10 MIN.) RI.K.1, RI.K.2, RI.K.10, RI.K.10a, RI.K.10b, SL.K.1a, SL.K.1b

Mentor Read-Aloud Vol. 1, pp. 4–7
"Let's Play by the Rules!"

Student Objectives

I will be able to:
- Recognize features of informational text.
- Make predictions about rules.
- Listen for a purpose.
- Link my ideas to the ideas of others.
- Retell key ideas about playing by the rules.

Additional Materials

Weekly Presentation
- Two Column Chart
- Key Details Web

 Observation Checklist for Collaborative Conversation

As partners discuss the key details, use the questions below to evaluate how effectively students communicate with each other. Based on your answers, you may wish to plan future core lessons to support the collaborative conversation process.

Do partners . . .

- ❏ stay on topic throughout the discussion?
- ❏ listen respectfully?
- ❏ build on the comments of others appropriately?
- ❏ pose or respond to questions to clarify information?
- ❏ support their partners to participate?

Preview the Genre

Display "Let's Play By the Rules!" and read aloud the title. Point out that this is informational text. Review that informational text gives information about a topic. Preview the text and graphic features with students. Ask them what they might learn from the text.

Tell students to turn and talk to a partner and name features they observe and predictions they have. Make sure they explain what text or graphic feature they used to formulate their predictions. Use this opportunity to discuss specific features students may not be able to name (such as labels or captions).

Sample Informational Text Features	Sample Predictions
• title • photographs • captions • labels	I will learn about… • rules for baseball. • rules for football. • playing a team sport.

Read Aloud the Text

Ask student to listen carefully to learn key details about following the rules in team sports. Tell them that is their purpose for listening. Read aloud the text with minimal interruption. Model using a different tone of voice for dialogue and reading exclamations with excitement.

Share (iELD)

Invite one or more students in each group to share a key detail. Record students' details on the class Key Details Web and reread the part of the text where the detail was mentioned. Point out that some information may be interesting but is not necessarily important to the topic.

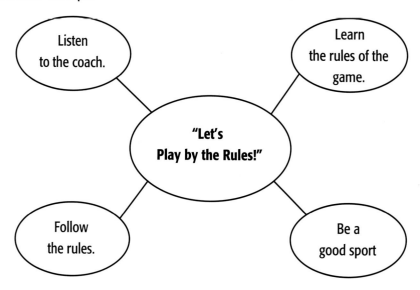

Sample Key Details Web

Reinforce or Reaffirm the Strategy

Provide modeling and/or engage students in self-reflection to build metacognitive awareness.

IF…	THEN…
students need support to retell key details from the text…	**Model to reinforce the strategy.** • *My purpose for reading was to learn about team rules. I am looking for details about following the rules in team sports.* • *The first two sentences on page 5 tell me about a rule. The rule is to listen to the coach because the coach gives important information. That is an important detail so I will write it down.* • *On page 6, I learn that following the rules makes the game fair for everybody. That is important information, too. I will write down this key detail.* Continue to model how to find key details.
students independently retell key details…	**Invite partners to reflect on their strategy by discussing one of the following questions:** • *How did you decide which facts were key details?* • *How did finding the key details help you understand about following the rules in team sports?* Ask partners to present their key details and explain how they found them.

Show Your Knowledge

Ask students to draw a picture of a key detail they learned about following the rules in team sports. Encourage them to write a word or label for their picture.

(iELD) Integrated ELD

Light Support
Provide support for partners as they locate informational text features in *Let's Play by the Rules!* Post a list to remind them of text features.
Informational Text Features
title
photographs
captions
labels

Moderate Support
Explain that informational text has features that include a title, photographs, captions, and labels. Using *Let's Play by the Rules!*, ask students to point to the title and the four photographs that help them understand the text. Identify and read aloud the captions under the photographs on pages 5 and 7. Then have students point to the labels on page 5.
Ask students to complete sentence frames orally:
The title is [Let's Play by the Rules!].
The photographs show [teams, players, sports].
A caption tells about [the photograph].
"Face mask" and "chin strap" are [labels].

Substantial Support
Explain that informational text has features that include a title, photographs, captions, and labels. Work with students to help them identify these features. Using *Let's Play by the Rules!*, page 4, read the title. Then have students read the title aloud.
Ask individuals to identify what the four photographs show by telling the sport and who is pictured. Prompt them to describe the uniforms and the difference in the baseball and football helmets. Point out that the photographs help them understand the words.
Read aloud the captions on pages 5 and 7. Point out that each one is about the photograph.
Then have students point to the labels on page 5 as you read them. Discuss what parts of the face are protected by the face mask and the chin strap.

ELD.PI.K.1, ELD.PI.K.5, ELD.PII.K.1

RL.K.1 With prompting and support, ask and answer questions about key details in a text., RL.K.2 With prompting and support, retell familiar stories, including key details, RL.K.10 Actively engage in group reading activities with purpose and understanding., RL.K.10a Activate prior knowledge related to the information and events in texts. CA, RL.K.10b Use illustrations and context to make predictions about text. CA, SL.K.1a Follow agreed-upon rules for discussions (e.g., listening to others and taking turns speaking about the topics and texts under discussion)., SL.K.1b Continue a conversation through multiple exchanges.

 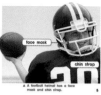

Mentor Read-Aloud Vol. 1, pp. 4–7
"Let's Play by the Rules!"

Student Objectives

I will be able to:
- Identify and share key details about playing by the rules.
- Write key details about rules.
- Identify nouns.

iELD Integrated ELD

Light Support

Explain that a noun is a word that names a person, place, or thing. Then have students use "Let's Play by the Rules!" to find words that name people, places, and things. Ask them to write at least one sentence with a noun they find. Have students underline the noun.

Moderate Support

Explain that a noun is a word that names a person, place, or thing. Post the noun chart from page 9.

Person	Place	Thing
coach	field	ball
player	school	bat
umpire	home	helmet

Work with students to compose oral sentences:
The **coach** is on the **field**.
The **player** wears a **helmet**.
The **umpire** has the **ball**.
Write the sentences as students say them.

Substantial Support

Explain that a noun is a word that names a person, place, or thing. Post the noun chart from above (see Moderate Support).

Read the nouns aloud and ask students to read them after you. Ask students to tell in their own words what the words mean. Then, with students, compose oral sentences using the words.
The **coach** helps the team.
The **player** is a good sport.
The **umpire** calls a **player** out.
Families have rules at **home**.

ELD.PI.K.2, ELD.PI.K.10, ELD.PII.K.4

Write Key Details (10 MIN.) W.K.2, W.K.8, SL.K.1a, SL.K.1b, L.K.1a, L.K.1b

Engage Thinking

Display and reread the Key Details Web with students. Remind students that they have learned important details about following rules in team sports.

Ask: *What important details have you learned about following rules in team sports?*

 Collaborative Conversation: Peer Groups

Divide students into peer groups. Tell students that before writing, you would like them to turn and talk to their peers briefly. Ask them to share a detail from the text that they found particularly interesting, a detail they would like to write about. Model how you do this.

Sample modeling: *When I tell my partner about what details I found interesting, I say, "The most interesting detail was that when your team wins, you shouldn't brag." When you talk with your partner, you can start your sentence the same way:* The most interesting detail was _____.

Write the sentence frame for students. Give students one minute to share their ideas. Then bring them together and ask volunteers to share the key details they found interesting.

Write as a Group

Based on the details your students found particularly interesting in the text, collaborate with them to agree on key details to write about as a class. Work with students to generate sentences orally that they could write. Rehearse the message orally so that students internalize it, and then model how you write the sentences. As you guide the writing, include at least one noun. Actively engage students in the writing process by thinking aloud and/or prompting them with questions. For example:

- *Who can show me where to start writing on the paper?*
- *What is the first word in our sentence?*
- *Are there any words we could add to make our sentence better?*
- *Let's reread our sentence. Is there anything we want to change?*

Sample Shared Writing

Players take turns.

Players learn how to use the equipment.

The coach teaches you how to stay safe.

Playing a team sport is fun!

Build Language: Nouns (IELD)

Explain that a noun is a word that names a person, place or thing. Display and explain the following categories of nouns.

Person	Place	Thing
coach	field	ball
player	school	bat
umpire	home	helmet

Display the following sentences. Read each sentence and underline the nouns:

- Our school has a soccer field.
- Playing baseball you take turns hitting the ball.
- Our coach makes football fun!

☑ Write Independently

Ask students to choose a sports rule and draw a picture to show it. Encourage them write a label or dictate a sentence for their drawing.

Small-Group Differentiated Instruction (15 MIN. per Group)

Meet with Small Groups

Select small-group reading titles or activities based on students' needs. See the Small-Group Instructional Planner for titles that support a range of instructional levels within the unit topic. Remind students to apply skills and strategies they learned to their small-group reading experiences.

Say: *Today we practiced finding the key details about rules and playing on a team sport. If you are reading an informational text today, pay attention to what the important details are. If you are reading a literary text, pay attention to the key events. Use strategies we have learned to help you understand the key details. You can make predictions before reading a text.*

Whole-Group Reflect and Share

Bring the class back together. Invite them to share some of the key details and events they learned about. Reinforce that strong readers use many strategies as they read.

W.K.2 Use a combination of drawing, dictating, and writing to compose informative/explanatory texts in which they name what they are writing about and supply some information about the topic., **W.K.8** With guidance and support from adults, recall information from experiences or gather information from provided sources to answer a question., **SL.K.1a** Follow agreed-upon rules for discussions (e.g., listening to others and taking turns speaking about the topics and texts under discussion)., **SL.K.1b** Continue a conversation through multiple exchanges., **L.1a** Print many upper- and lowercase letters., **L.K.1b** Use frequently occurring nouns and verbs.

Pre-Decodable Reader: *ABC*

Student Objectives

I will be able to:
• Recognize rhyme.
• Blend syllables.
• Recognize letters **Aa, Bb, Cc, Dd, Ee.**

Additional Materials

• Letter cards: **Aa, Bb, Cc, Dd, Ee**
• Pre-Decodable Reader: *ABC*
• For additional practice, see Pre-Decodable Readers: *Animal ABC, We Like Milk*

Letter Recognition: Aa, Bb, Cc, Dd, Ee

(20 MIN.) RF.K.1d, RF.K.2a, RF.K.2b

Phonological Awareness: Recognize Rhyme

Model

Say the rhyme "Hey Diddle Diddle."

Say: *Hey diddle diddle./The cat and the fiddle./The cow jumped over the moon./The little dog laughed/To see such sport./And the dish ran away with the spoon.*

Repeat the first two lines, emphasizing the last word in each line.

Say: *Listen to the words **diddle** and **fiddle**. **Diddle** and **fiddle** rhyme. They have the same sounds at the end. They both end with **-iddle.***

Practice

Say the third and last lines, emphasizing the last word in each line. Have students listen for the words that rhyme.

Say: *I will say two more lines from the rhyme. What two words rhyme? Yes, **moon** and **spoon** rhyme. They both end with **-oon**. Now I will say other words. Raise your hand if they rhyme: **cat, hat; cow, dog; pig, dig.***

Phonological Awareness: Syllable Blending

Model

Say the rhyme "Hey Diddle Diddle" again and have students join in.

Say: *Listen as I say the two parts in a word: **did-dle**. Now I will blend the parts together to say the word: **diddle**. Say it with me: **did-dle, diddle**.*

Practice

Say the syllables **fid-dle** and help students blend them together to say **fiddle**.

Repeat with the words **fun-ny, child-ren, ap-ple, pen-cil**.

Letter Recognition: Aa, Bb, Cc, Dd, Ee

Introduce Pre-Decodable Reader: *ABC*

Have students sing the Alphabet Song. Tell students that they will now read a book about the letters in the alphabet. Then display Pre-Decodable Reader: *ABC*. Run your hand under the book's title, *ABC*, and read it aloud. Discuss what students see on the cover.

Say: *What do you see on the cover? Yes, it is a train pulling letters. This book is about the letters in the alphabet just like the song we sang.*

Model: Aa, Bb, Cc, Dd, Ee

Hold up letter card **A**.

Say: *This is uppercase **A**.*

Hold up letter card **a**.

Say: *This is lowercase **a**.*

Then point to uppercase **A**.

Say: *What is the name of this letter? Yes, it is uppercase **A**.*

Point to lowercase **a**.

Say: *What is the name of this letter? Yes, it is lowercase **a**.*

Practice: Aa, Bb, Cc, Dd, Ee

Turn to page 2. Model how to match **A** and **a** on the letter cards with **A** and **a** in the book. Then have students match the letters. Repeat **Model** and **Practice** using letter cards **Bb**, **Cc**. Then turn to page 3 for letter cards **Dd**, **Ee**.

Letter Recognition in Words: Aa, Bb, Cc, Dd, Ee (iELD)

Practice: a, b, c, d, e

Display page 2 of the Pre-Decodable Reader. Name the objects on the cars of the train.

Say: *What do you see on top of **Aa**? Yes, it is an apple.*

Write the word **apple**. Have a student draw a circle around the **a** in apple and name the letter. Repeat for objects and letters **b**, **c**, **d**, **e**.

Practice: A, B, C, D, E

Then hold up the uppercase **A** letter card. Ask students whose first name begins with that letter to stand up. Write each name and have the student point to and name the uppercase **A**.

Next have students locate other places in the classroom where the names appear and identify the uppercase **A**.

Say: *Look around the classroom and see if you can find a name that begins with uppercase **A**. When you find one, raise your hand. I will have you go over and point to the uppercase **A** and say its name.*

If there are no names that begin with **A**, go on to the next letter.

Repeat for **Bb**, **Cc**, **Dd**, and **Ee**.

iELD Integrated ELD

Light Support
Display the Letter Cards **Aa**, **Bb**, **Cc**, **Dd**, **Ee**. Have students use signs and posters in the classroom to label objects that have names that include, or begin with, the letters. Also use "Let's Play by the Rules!," pages 4–7, to name words that begin with, or include, the letters.

Moderate Support
Display the Letter Cards **Aa**, **Bb**, **Cc**, **Dd**, **Ee**. Ask a student to name one of the letters and its case, such as lowercase **d**. Ask the student to go up to the display and point to the letter. Then have other students point to objects in the room that have names beginning with lowercase **d**. Continue by having students name the other letters and find examples in the room of object names that begin with the letter.

Substantial Support
Use Letter Cards **Aa**, **Bb**, **Cc**, **Dd**, **Ee**. Hold up a card and say the letter. Repeat with the other letters.
Then write the following words students listened to in the read-aloud "Let's Play by the Rules!"
coach / baseball / exciting / everybody / do / act / doesn't / buckle / about / courteous
Read the words aloud. Ask students to name the word that begins with a lowercase **D**. Continue by randomly showing letter cards for **e**, **C**, **d**, **a**, **E**, **b**, **A**, **c**, and **B**. Ask students to identify each letter and case, and to find the word that begins with the letter.

ELD.PI.K.1, ELD.PIII.1d, ELD.PIII.2b

Read-Aloud Handbook

Shared Reading Vol. 1, p. 2 "Follow the Rules to Play Soccer"

Student Objectives

I will be able to:
- Read along with the appropriate pacing.
- Answer questions about playing by the rules.
- Identify uppercase and lowercase letters.

iELD Integrated ELD

Light Support

Post question words:

How / When / Where / Why / What

Have students take turns with partners to make up and answer questions about "Follow the Rules to Play Soccer." If necessary, provide an example to get them started: *How do you run after the ball?* Then have them report their answers and compare them with the answers of other teams.

Moderate Support

Post question words:

How / When / Where / Why / What

Read the words and ask students to read them after you. Explain that these words are often used at the beginning of questions. Then have students complete sentence frames with the correct question word.

[What] rules do you follow to play soccer?

[Why] should you be a good sport?

[How] do you make a goal in soccer?

Substantial Support

Reread the text under "Follow the Rules to Play Soccer" on page 2. Post question words:

How / When / Where / Why / What

Read the words and ask students to read them after you. Explain that these words are often used at the beginning of questions.

- *Where is my jacket?*
- *What is for lunch?*

Then have students discuss which question word or words could complete each sentence frame:

[How, Where, Why] do you run?

[What] is a rule?

[When, How, Why] do you make a goal?

ELD.PI.K.1, ELD.PI.K.5, ELD.PI.K.6

Read Aloud and Shared Reading

(20 MIN.) RI.K.1, RI.K.10, RF.K.1d SL.K.1a, SL.K.1b

Read Aloud

To support the unit concept, use one of the Read-Aloud Handbook selections for Unit 1. As you read, model the metacognitive strategy for the unit: Ask Questions guided by the samples provided. You may also wish to select a favorite read-aloud from your classroom or school library. To support the unit concept, use one of the suggested titles for Unit 1.

Shared Reading iELD

Reread the Informational Text

First rereading. Read aloud the text fluently and expressively, pointing under each word.

Reread for fluency: Rate/Pacing. Explain to students that reading at a comfortable pace without hesitation helps the reader and the listener understand the text. Point out that reading too fast or too slow can make it harder to understand the information. Echo-read the selection, leading students to mimic your pacing. Provide corrective feedback and/or validate students' efforts.

Build Concepts: Following Rules

Pose questions to connect the informational text to the unit concept. For example:

- *If you can't touch the ball with your hands how do you play the game of soccer?*
- *How do you behave if your team loses, and why?*
- *Explain what it means to be a good sport.*

Review Phonics: Alphabet Review

Display the alphabet. Point out the difference between uppercase and lowercase letters. Then point to and read the word **Run** in the first sentence. Circle the first letter in **Run** and call on a volunteer to name the letter. Repeat with the words **Follow, Rules,** and **Soccer.**

RI.K.1 With prompting and support, ask and answer questions about unknown words in a text. (See grade K Language standards 4-6 additional expectations.) **RI.K.10** Actively engage in group reading activities with purpose and understanding. CA, **RF.K.1d** Recognize and name all upper- and lowercase letters of the alphabet., **SL.K.1a** Follow agreed-upon rules for discussions (e.g., listening to others and taking turns speaking about the topics and texts under discussion).,
SL.K.1b Continue a conversation through multiple exchanges.,

Describe the Relationship Between the Photographs and the Text (10 MIN.)

RI.K.1, RI.K.7, RI.K.10, SL.K.3

Engage Thinking

Display page 4 of "Let's Play by the Rules!" and explain that you are going to describe the relationships between photographs and the text. Point out that the photograph shows a team and the text says, "When you're part of a team, you learn how to get along with others."

Say: *What are some things you notice about the team in the photograph? How are the kids on the team getting along with each other?*

Model

Explain to students that photographs can give them more information that is not in the text. Explain that photographs can help them understand what they are reading. Tell students that the photographs will often show a person, place, thing, or idea that the text is also telling them about. They can look closely at the photograph to deepen their understanding of what they are reading.

Sample modeling: *Page 5 tells me that there are rules having to do with certain equipment and special gear. It says that coaches "show you how to use special gear that will keep you safe." [Point to the words.] Then, I can look at the photograph on page 5. The photograph has labels. [Point to the labels.] The labels say "face mask" and "chin strap." I think there is a relationship between these words and the photograph. I think the face mask is special gear that keeps the football player safe.*

Guided Practice (iELD)

Ask students to look at the photograph on page 5 and to use information in the photograph to develop their understanding of the text. Ask students to think about relationships between the photograph and the text having to do with the football player, the equipment, and rules. For example:

- *How could the helmet, chin strap, or face mask keep a player safe?*
- *Do you think football players must follow rules having to do with helmets, face masks, or chin straps?*
- *What do you think might be a rule having to do with helmets, face masks, or chin straps?*

☑ Show Your Knowledge

Ask students to pair off and act out a scene between a coach and a player. The coach should tell the player a rule or a way to use equipment to stay safe. Then the students should switch roles and act the scene out with a different sport.

RI.K.1 With prompting and support, ask and answer questions about unknown words in a text. (See grade K Language standards 4-6 additional expectations.) CA, **RI.K.7** With prompting and support, describe the relationship between illustrations and the text in which they appear (e.g., what person, place, thing, or idea in the text an illustration depicts)., **RI.K.10** Actively engage in group reading activities with purpose and understanding., **SL.K.3** Ask and answer questions in order to seek help, get information, or clarify something that is not understood.

MENTOR READ 1 MINI-LESSON

Mentor Reading, Vol. 1, pp. 4-7
"Let's Play by the Rules!"

Student Objectives

I will be able to:
- Describe the details in a photograph about following the rules.
- State a relationship between the details in the text and a photograph.
- Understand that rules keep us safe.

(iELD) Integrated ELD

Light Support

Explain that we use illustrations to help us understand the words we read in a text. Have students look at the photograph on page 5 as you read aloud the second paragraph of text.

Ask partners to work together to relate details they heard in the read-aloud text to the photograph. Afterward, have teams report to the class.

Moderate Support

Explain that we use illustrations to help us understand the words we read in a text. Ask students to describe what they see in the photograph on page 5.

Read aloud the second paragraph of text. If necessary, explain that **equipment** and **gear** refer to the things needed to play a sport.

Ask students to describe the "special gear" the boy is wearing. Ask:
- *How does the helmet keep the boy safe?*
- *What do the labels show?*

Substantial Support

Explain that we use illustrations to help us understand the words we read in a text. Have students look at the photograph on page 5. Ask them to describe what they see in the photograph. *[a boy wearing a football uniform and helmet while holding a football]*

Then read aloud the second paragraph of text. Explain that **equipment** includes the things needed for a job or sport. Soccer balls and baseballs are examples of equipment. Ask students to identify the "equipment" the boy is holding in the photograph. *[a football]*

Also, explain that **gear** is another word for equipment needed for a sport. Have students identify the "special gear" the boy is wearing to keep safe.

ELD.PI.K.1, ELD.PI.K.5, ELD.PI.K.6, ELD.PII.K.6

**Mentor Reading, Vol. 1, pp. 4-7
"Let's Play by the Rules!"**

Student Objectives

I will be able to:
- Identify the main topic of a text.
- Retell key details about playing by the rules.

Additional Materials

Weekly Presentation
- Word Web

Identify the Main Topic (10 MIN.) RI.K.1, RI.K.2, RI.K.10a, RI.K.10b

Engage Thinking

Explain that an informational text is about one main topic, or one big idea.

Ask: *When we read "Let's Play by the Rules!", what was the text mainly about?*

Model (iELD)

Read aloud the title, "Let's Play by the Rules!" Explain that the title of a text can help you identify what the text is mainly about. Model how to look for details in order to identify the main topic.

Sample modeling: *The title is "Let's Play by the Rules!", and the first photo shows children working together with their teammates. Maybe this text will be about working together. Let's find out.*

Take a picture walk through the text and discuss how the photos show what the text will be about. Then model how to identify the main topic.

Sample modeling: *I think this text is mainly about playing by the rules, since the title is "Let's Play by the Rules!" The photos show children following the rules, so the text will probably be about rules.*

Read aloud pages 4–5 and discuss that the text tells about rules. Write the main topic and details from the text in a web.

Guided Practice

Read aloud page 6. Ask students to think about the words and look at the photo. Use directive prompts to guide students to identify the main topic. For example:

- *Did the words tell about rules? What did you learn?*
- *Does the photo show children following rules? What rules are they following?*

Repeat the procedure for page 7. Add the details to the web.

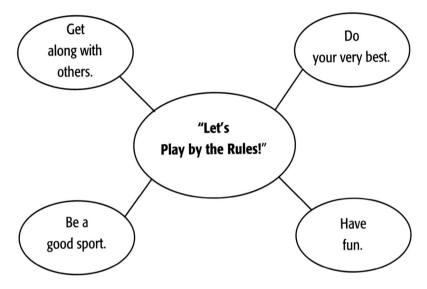

Sample Word Web

Ask students to tell in their own words what "Let's Play by the Rules!" is mainly about.

iELD **Integrated ELD**

Light Support
Using "Let's Play by the Rules," ask students to think about how the title, photographs, and words on the pages help them identify the main topic. Have them work in small groups to review the key details in the outer circles of the main topic and details web created earlier. Then have them explain in their own words what "Let's Play by the Rules!" is mainly about.

Moderate Support
Ask students to think about the web they created for main topic and key details. Prompt them to tell in their own words what "Let's Play by the Rules!" is mainly about. Ask questions such as these:

- *What clue to the main topic do you get from the title?*
- *Think about all of the details in the photographs and words on the pages. Remember that the details were in the outer circle of the web. What are the key details all about?*
- *What is the most important idea, or main topic, in "Let's Play by the Rules!"?*

Substantial Support
Review that students can look at a text's words and photos to find its main topic. Point out that the title is usually a good clue as to what a selection is about. Point out that the title is "Let's Play by the Rules!" Explain that this tells us the words probably will be about following rules and the photographs will show examples of players following rules.

Post the web created for main topic and key details and review it with students. Help them understand that the details listed in the outer circles come from words in the text and the photographs of players following rules and having fun.

Then discuss how to complete a sentence frame:
"Let's Play by the Rules!" is mainly about [following rules / why it is important to follow rules in sports / following the rules to have fun in a game].

ELD.PI.K.1, ELD.PI.K.6, ELD.PI.K.7

RI.K.1 With prompting and support, ask and answer questions about unknown words in a text. RI.K.2 With prompting and support, identify the main topic and retell key details of a text., RI.K.10 Actively engage in group reading activities with purpose and understanding.

Mentor Reading, Vol. 1, pp. 4-7
"Let's Play by the Rules!"

Student Objectives

I will be able to:
- Write about school rules.
- Use nouns in my writing.

iELD Integrated ELD

Light Support

Remind students of their discussion of playground rules. Have students choose one of the rules they talked about and draw a picture, with labels, to show the rule. Before drawing, ask them to name people, places, and things. Review that these naming words are nouns. Write examples of nouns they can use for labels for their playground rule drawing.

Moderate Support

Ask students to tell some of the playground rules they discussed. Write *We take turns on the <u>slide</u>*. Read the sentence aloud and underline the word **slide**. Explain it is a noun because it names a thing, a piece of playground equipment.

Point out that when students draw a picture of one of the rules, they may want to add a noun to label something. Ask students to name other things, places, or people they want to show in their pictures of playground rules. List appropriate word responses to help them add labels to their pictures.

Substantial Support

Remind students about the playground rules they discussed. Write *We take turns on the <u>slide</u>*. Read the sentence aloud and underline the word **slide**. Explain it is a noun because it names a thing, a piece of playground equipment.

Have students choose one of the rules they talked about and draw a picture to show the rule. To help them add a label to the picture, have them suggest words that name people, places, or things they want to show in their pictures. Write the words and read them aloud.

ELD.PI.K.1, ELD.PI.K.10, ELD.PII.K.4

Write About School Rules (10 MIN.) W.K.3, W.K.8,
SL.K.1a, SL.K.1b, L.K.1a, L.K.1b

Engage Thinking

Remind students that they have learned about rules for playing team sports.

Ask: *What are some rules we have for playing on the school playground?*

 Collaborative Conversation: Partner

Tell students that before writing, you would like them to turn and talk to a partner briefly. Ask them to talk about the rules they follow when playing on the school playground. Model how you do this.

Sample modeling: *When I talk to my partner about playground rules at school, I say, "One school playground rule is to take turns on the slide." When you speak to your partner, you can use that same sentence frame:* One school playground rule is _____.

Write the sentence frame for students. Give students two minutes to share their ideas. Then bring them together and ask volunteers to share the rules they discussed.

Write as a Group

Collaborate with students to agree on sentences to write about playground rules. Rehearse the message orally and model how you write it. As you guide the writing, include at least one noun. Actively engage students in the writing process by thinking aloud and/or prompting them with questions. For example:

- *When I start the sentence, what letter should I write first?*
- *How do we spell _____? We know that word.*
- *Is there a better word we could use here?*
- *What noun did we use in our sentence?*
- *Here is the end of the sentence. What punctuation mark do we need at the end of this sentence?*
- *Now let's read our writing. Did we include all the words we needed in our sentence? Is there anything we should fix?*

Sample Shared Writing

Hands are for helping.

Students listen to each other.

Helmets keep you safe.

Build Language: Nouns (IELD)

Remind students that a noun is a word that names a person, place, or thing. Circle a noun in your sample writing. Tell students that this word is a noun. Ask volunteers to use each of the following nouns in an oral sentence: **player**, **coach**, **helmet**, **field**.

Write Independently

Ask students to draw a picture showing a rule for the school playground. Encourage them to add a label to their picture.

Small-Group Differentiated Instruction (15 MIN. per Group)

Meet with Small Groups

Select small-group reading titles or activities based on students' needs. See the Small-Group Instructional Planner for titles that support a range of instructional levels within the unit topic. Remind students to apply skills and strategies they learned to their small-group reading experiences.

Say: *Today we learned about how photographs can help you understand the text and give the reader more information. We also learned about the main topic of a text. When you listen to informational text, think about what the text is mainly about. Remember to pay attention to the title for a clue.*

Whole-Group Reflect and Share

Bring the class back together. Ask volunteers to name the main topic from small-group reading texts they listened to.

W.K.3 Use a combination of drawing, dictating, and writing to narrate a single event or several loosely linked events, tell about the events in the order in which they occurred, and provide a reaction to what happened., **W.K.8** With guidance and support from adults, recall information from experiences or gather information from provided sources to answer a question., **SL.K.1a** Follow agreed-upon rules for discussions (e.g., listening to others and taking turns speaking about the topics and texts under discussion)., **SL.K.1b** Continue a conversation through multiple exchanges., **L.K.1a** Print many upper- and lowercase letters., **L.K.1b** Use frequently occurring nouns and verbs.

Letter Recognition Ff, Gg, Hh, Ii, Jj

(20 MIN.) RF.K.1d, RF.K.2a, RF.K.2b

Phonological Awareness: Recognize Rhyme

Model

Say the rhyme "Humpty Dumpty."

Say: *Humpty Dumpty sat on a wall./Humpty Dumpty had a great fall./ All the King's horses and all the King's men/Couldn't put Humpty together again.*

Repeat the first two lines, emphasizing the last word in each line.

Say: *Listen to the words **wall** and **fall**. **Wall** and   rhyme. They have the same sounds at the end. They both end with -all.*

Practice

Say the third and fourth lines, emphasizing the last word in each line. Have students listen for the words that rhyme.

Say: *I will say two more lines from the rhyme. What two words rhyme? Yes, **men** and **again** rhyme. They both have the same ending sounds. Now I will say other words. Raise your hand if they rhyme: **sat, mat; had, bad; pet, poke.***

Phonological Awareness: Syllable Blending

Model

Say the rhyme "Humpty Dumpty" again and have students join in.

Say: *Listen as I say two parts in a word: **hump-ty**. Now I will blend the parts together to say the word: **humpty**. Say it with me: **hump-ty, humpty.***

Practice

Say the syllables **dump-ty** and help students to blend them together to say **dumpty**.

Repeat with the words: **ti-ger**, **li-on**, **ze-bra**, **mon-key**.

Pre-Decodable Reader: *ABC*

Student Objectives

I will be able to:
- Recognize rhyme.
- Blend syllables.
- Recognize letters **Ff, Gg, Hh, Ii, Jj.**

Additional Materials

- Letter cards: **Ff, Gg, Hh, Ii, Jj**
- Pre-Decodable Reader: *ABC*

Letter Recognition: Ff, Gg, Hh, Ii, Jj

Model:
Hold up letter card **F**.

Say: *This is uppercase F.*

Hold up letter card **f**.

Say: *This is the lowercase f.*

Then point uppercase **F**.

Say: *What is the name of this letter? Yes, it is uppercase F.*

Point to lowercase **f**.

Say: *What is the name of this letter? Yes, it is lowercase f.*

Practice
Turn to page 3 in the Pre-Decodable Reader: *ABC*. Model how to match **F** and **f** on the letter cards with **F** and **f** in the book. Then have students match the letters. Repeat Model and Practice routine with letter cards **Gg**. Then turn to page 4 for letter cards **Hh**, **Ii**, and **Jj**.

Letter Recognition in Words: Ff, Gg, Hh, Ii, Jj

Practice: f, g, h, i, j
Display page 3 of the Pre-Decodable Reader. Name the objects on the cars of the train.

Say: *What do you see on top of Ff? Yes, it is a fish.*

Write the word **fish**. Have a student draw a circle around the **f** in **fish** and name the letter. Repeat for objects and letters **g, h, i, j.**

Practice: F, G, H, I, J
Hold up the uppercase **F** letter card. Ask students whose names begin with that letter to stand up. Write each name and have the student point to and name the uppercase **F**.

Next have students locate other places in the classroom where the names appear and identify the uppercase **F**.

Say: *Look around the classroom and see if you can find a name that begins with uppercase F. When you find one, raise your hand. I will have you go over and point to uppercase and say its name.*

If there are no names that begin with **F**, go on to the next letter.
Repeat for **G, H, I**, and **J**.

iELD Integrated ELD

Light Support
Use the letter cards. Ask students to identify the upper- and lowercase letters **Ff, Gg, Hh, Ii**, and **Jj**.
Ask them to find examples in the classroom of names or names of objects that begin with or include these letters.

Moderate Support
Use the letter cards. Ask students to identify the upper- and lowercase letters **Ff, Gg, Hh, Ii**, and **Jj**.
Write the following words that begin with upper- and lowercase letters. Ask students to identify the word that begins with an uppercase **F** and read the word. Give help as needed. Continue with the initial letters of the other words. Provide additional examples if necessary.
game / How / Follow / important / Is / jet

Substantial Support
Use the upper- and lowercase letter cards. Hold or display **F** and **f**. Ask students to identify the uppercase **F** and then the lowercase **f**. Follow the same procedure for **Gg, Hh, Ii**, and **Jj**.
Post the following list of words. Read aloud the first word and ask students to identify the uppercase letter that begins the word or name.

Go
He
I
Get
James
Fun
Judith
Follow
How
It

ELD.PI.K.1, ELD.PIII.K.10

RF.K.1d Recognize and name all upper- and lowercase letters of the alphabet., **RF.K.2a** Recognize and produce rhyming words., **RF.K.2b** Count, pronounce, blend, and segment syllables in spoken words.

Read-Aloud Handbook

Shared Reading Vol. 1, p. 3 "Making Bridges"

Student Objectives

I will be able to:
- Read along with the appropriate pacing and expression.
- Answer questions about how friends can help one another.
- Understand that print has meaning.
- Identify consonants.

iELD Integrated ELD

Light Support
Reread "Making Bridges" and ask students to tell what it is about in their own words. *[New neighbors will teach each other games.]* Talk with students about the title and how it relates to what the text is about.

Moderate Support
Reread "Making Bridges" on page 3 of *Shared Reading*, and encourage students to talk about the words they heard in the poem. Discuss:
- *Who are the playmates in the poem? [the new neighbors]*
- *What does the line "I'm glad you are here" mean? [One child is saying it's good to have a new neighbor.]*
- *What will the neighbors teach each other? [games]*

Substantial Support
To help students understand that print has meaning, reread the first four lines of "Making Bridges" on page 3 of *Shared Reading*. Prompt students to talk about the meaning of the words.
Ask: *Why haven't the neighbors known each other long? [They are "new" neighbors, and one comes from "over the sea."]*
What is a playmate? [a friend you play with]
Now read the last four lines aloud.
Ask: *The words say, "I'm glad you are here." What does the word **glad** mean? [happy or pleased]*
The text says, "Oh, won't it be fine / To learn all your games." What do you think the playmates will teach each other? [new games]

ELD.PI.K.1, ELD.PI.K.3, ELD.PII.K.6

Read Aloud and Shared Reading

(20 MIN.) RL.K.10, RL.K.10a, RL.K.10b, RF.K.1b, RF.K.3a, SL.K.1b

Read Aloud

To support the unit concept, use one of the Read-Aloud Handbook selections for Unit 1. As you read, model the metacognitive strategy for the unit: Ask Questions, guided by the samples provided. You may also wish to select a favorite read-aloud from your classroom or school library. To support the unit concept, use one of the suggested titles for Unit 1.

Shared Reading (iELD)

Introduce the Poem
Display "Making Bridges." Read aloud the title of the poem as you point under each word. Invite students to turn to a partner and tell what they predict the poem will be about. Invite a few students to share their predictions with the whole class.

Read the Poem
First rereading. Read aloud the text fluently and expressively, pointing under each word.

Reread for fluency: Rate/Pacing. Explain to students that reading a poem at a comfortable pace helps the reader and the listener understand the poem's beat. Lead students to be aware of how you slow your pace at punctuation marks, pausing at the end of sentences. Echo-read the selection with students following along at an appropriate pace. Provide corrective feedback and/or validate students' efforts.

Build Concepts: Following Rules
Pose questions to connect the poem to the unit concept. For example:
- *What might the girl teach the boy?*
- *What might the boy teach the girl?*
- *Is it important to follow the rules for flying a kite and playing baseball? Why?*

Model Print Concepts: Print Conveys Meaning
Ask a volunteer to point to the illustration. Point out that the illustration shows two children—a girl with a kite and a boy with a baseball and baseball glove. Ask a volunteer to point to the words. Point out that the words tell the meaning of the poem. Remind students that the print carries the author's message.

Review Phonics: Alphabet Review

Point to the word **have**. Read word with students. Circle the first letter in **have** and call on a volunteer to name the letter. Repeat with the words **playmate**, **sea**, **learn**, **games**.

RL.K.10 Actively engage in group reading activities with purpose and understanding., **RL.K.10a** Activate prior knowledge related to the information and events in texts. CA, **RL.K.10b** Use illustrations and context to make predictions about text. CA, **RF.K.1b** Recognize that spoken words are represented in written language by specific sequences of letters., **RF.K.3a** Demonstrate basic knowledge of letter-sound correspondences by producing the primary or most frequent sound for each consonant., **SL.K.1b** Continue a conversation through multiple exchanges.

©2017 Benchmark Education Company, LLC

"A New Pet": Listen and Retell Story Events (10 MIN.) RL.K.1, RL.K.2, RL.K.5, RL.K.10, RL.K.10a, RL.K.10b, RF.K.1a, SL.K.1a, SL.K.1b

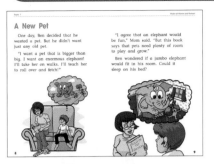

Mentor Read-Aloud, Vol. 1, pp. 8-11
"A New Pet"

Preview the Genre

Display "A New Pet "and read aloud the title. Point out that this selection is a story. It is realistic fiction, which means the characters are like real people and the events could happen in real life. Ask partners to look at the illustrations and make predictions about the story. Invite partners to share their ideas with the group.

Read Aloud the Story

Ask students to listen carefully to identify the events in the story. Remind them that this is their purpose for listening. Read aloud the text with minimal interruption. Model how you read with anticipation when you come to exciting parts of the story.

Collaborative Conversation: Partner

Give partners about two minutes to tell each other three events from the story. Call on students to share events with the whole class. Encourage them to try to retell the events in the order in which they happened in the story. Make a list of the events students retell.

 Reinforce or Reaffirm the Strategy (iELD)

Provide modeling and/or engage students in self-reflection to build metacognitive awareness.

IF...	THEN...
students need support to retell story events from the text...	**Model to reinforce the strategy.** • *I think about what happened at the beginning of the story. From the text and the illustration on page 8, I know that Ben wanted a big pet, bigger than an elephant. That is an important story event.* • *I use the text and the illustration on the next page to find the next important event. Mom tells Ben pets need room to grow. The text lets me know that and the illustration does, too.* Continue to model how you recognize the sequence of events.
students independently retell story events...	**Invite partners to reflect on their strategy by discussing one of the following questions:** • *How did you use both the text and the illustrations to understand the important events?* • *What helped you retell the events in your own words?* Invite partners to retell the events and ask them to share how they identified the events.

Student Objectives

I will be able to:
• Identify the features of a story.
• Make predictions about owning a pet.
• Listen for a purpose.
• Link my ideas to the ideas of others.
• Retell story events about rules of pet owners.

(iELD) Integrated ELD

Light Support
Explain that a story has a beginning, a middle, and an end. Using "A New Pet," have students look for an event in the beginning, an event in the middle, and an event in the end. Have them choose only the most important events that happened and retell these events in order. Using the events they chose, have partners work on a retelling of the story.

Moderate Support
Explain that a story has a beginning, a middle, and an end. Keeping this in mind, have students reread "A New Pet." Point out that when a story is retold, only important events are given.
Ask: *What important event happened in the beginning of the story?*
Tell students that events are told in order so listeners can follow what happens. Invite partners to work on a retelling of an important event from the beginning, middle, and end of the story.

Substantial Support
Help students understand that a story has a beginning, a middle, and an end. Reread page 8 in "A New Pet." Then ask students to tell what happened first in the story. Explain that if students were retelling this story to a friend, they would tell this event first. Then reread page 9 and the first paragraph on page 10.
Ask: *What happened next in the story?*
Point out that "Ben decided to get a medium elephant" would be the second important event students would want to retell. Finally, reread the rest of the story.
Ask: *What happens in the end?*
Tell students this would be the last event to retell.
Invite a volunteer to retell the three events in order.

ELD.PI.K.1, ELD.PI.K.6, ELD.PI.K.1

RL.K.1 With prompting and support, ask and answer questions about key details in a text., RL.K.2 With prompting and support, retell familiar stories, including key details, RL.K.5 Recognize common types of texts (e.g., storybooks, poems, fantasy, realistic text). CA)., RL.K.10 Actively engage in group reading activities with purpose and understanding., RL.K.10a Activate prior knowledge related to the information and events in texts. CA, RL.K.10b Use illustrations and context to make predictions about text. CA, RF.K.1a Follow words from left to right, top to bottom, and page by page., SL.K.1a Follow agreed-upon rules for discussions (e.g., listening to others and taking turns speaking about the topics and texts under discussion)., SL.K.1b Continue a conversation through multiple exchanges.

Mentor Read-Aloud, Vol. 1, pp. 8-11
"A New Pet"

Student Objectives

I will be able to:
- Describe how illustrations and text are connected.
- Use the illustrations to learn more information about taking care of pets.

Additional Materials

Weekly Presentation
- Two-Column Chart

Describe the Relationships Between Illustrations and the Story (10 MIN.) RL.K.1, RL.K.7

Engage Thinking

Explain that the illustrations in a story go along with the words. When we read the poem "Making Bridges" we looked at the illustrations of the girl and the boy.

Say: *How did looking at the illustration of the girl and the boy help you understand what games they would teach each other?*

Model

Explain to students that illustrations can give them more information that is not in the text. Explain that illustrations can help them understand what they are reading. Tell students that the illustrations will often show characters or ideas that the text is also telling them about. They can look closely at the illustrations to deepen their understanding of what they are reading. Display page 8. Model how to make a connection between the illustration and the words.

Sample modeling: *After I read that Ben wants an enormous elephant for a pet, I look at the illustration. [Point to the thought bubble.] This is a thought bubble. It shows what Ben is thinking. The thought bubble shows an elephant much bigger than Ben and Mom. And that goes along with the words: "I want an enormous elephant!"*

Guided Practice

Display page 9. Read aloud the text and ask students to examine the illustration. Read aloud the name of Mom's book. Use directive prompts to guide students to make the connection between the illustration (including the thought bubble) and the words. For example:

- *The text says Mom learned about pets from a book. What is the name of the book? How do you know?*
- *Which words on the page go along with what Ben is thinking in the thought bubble?*

Repeat the procedure for page 10 and page 11.

Illustration	Text
page 9, Mom holding a book called *Rules of Pet Owners*	*"But this book says that pets need plenty of room to play and grow."*
page 9, Ben's thought bubble	*"Ben wondered if a jumbo elephant would fit in his room."*
page 10, Ben's thought bubble	*"My elephant will be so popular on Pet Day"*

Sample Two Column Chart

☑ Show Your Knowledge

Display and read aloud page 11. Ask students to tell how the illustration goes along with the text. Remind them to look at Ben's thought bubble as they respond.

---

iELD Integrated ELD

Light Support

Explain that readers connect illustrations and the words in the text to understand what they read. Point out the pet store scene and thought bubble on page 11. Ask students to explain how the illustration, including the thought bubble, connects with the words on the page. Reread the page aloud if students cannot readily make the connection.

Moderate Support

Explain that readers connect illustrations and the words in the text to understand what they read. Call students' attention to page 11.

Ask students to describe the scene in the pet store and talk about the information they learn from Ben's thoughts in the bubble. Help students connect the illustration to the words on the page.

Ask: *How does Ben's wish to have a pet elephant connect with the name he wants to give the puppy?*

Substantial Support

Explain that readers connect illustrations and the words in the text to understand what they read. Point out the pet store scene and thought bubble on page 11.

Ask: *Where are Ben and his mother in the scene on this page? [a pet store]. What kind of pet is in the store and in Ben's thought bubble? [a puppy] What is Ben's new pet wearing in his thoughts? [an elephant costume]*

Connect the illustration to the words on the page. Reread the first paragraph aloud and ask students how the puppy in the store got Ben's attention. *[yipping, yapping, rolling over, and wagging her tail]* Reread the second paragraph aloud.

Ask: *What rule from the book is Ben following? [Be a responsible pet owner.] How does Ben's wish to have a pet elephant connect with the name he wants to give the puppy? [Ellie Phant]*

ELD.PI.K.1, ELD.PI.K.6, ELD.PII.K.1

RL.K.1 With prompting and support, ask and answer questions about key details in a text., **RL.K.7** With prompting and support, describe the relationship between illustrations and the text in which they appear (e.g., what moment in a story an illustration depicts.)

Mentor Read-Aloud, Vol. 1, pp. 8–11
"A New Pet"

Student Objectives

I will be able to:
- Write about how pet owners take care of pets.
- Use nouns in my writing.

iELD Integrated ELD

Light Support

Explain that students can write about taking care of a pet, or they can draw a picture to show what they would do. Give partners a few minutes to discuss different ways to care for a pet before students begin writing or drawing. Remind them to include labels.

Moderate Support

Explain that students can write about taking care of a pet, or they can draw a picture to show what they would do. Have students think back to "A New Pet" and name the ways the reading mentions how to care for a pet. Have students think of other ways as well. Remind them to try to add a label if they choose to draw a picture.

Substantial Support

Remind students of the shared writing activity they did as a group. Tell them to keep in mind the techniques they used while writing. Briefly review the prompts if necessary.

Explain that students can write about taking care of a pet or they can draw a picture to show what they would do to take care of a pet. Discuss with them some possible choices such as feeding the pet, brushing the pet, and giving the pet water. Remind them to try to add a label if they choose to draw a picture. Post some useful nouns on the board:
food / water / brush / toys / dish / name

ELD.PI.K.3, ELD.PI.K.10, ELD.PII.K.4

Write about Owning a Pet (10 MIN.) W.K.2, W.K.8,

SL.K.1a, SL.K.1b, L.K.1a, L.K.1b

Engage Thinking

Remind students that they have learned about what it means to be a responsible pet owner.

Ask: *What are some things pet owners do to take care of their pets?*

Page through "A New Pet" for ideas. Tell students they will write about how pet owners take care of their pets.

Collaborative Conversation: Partner

Tell students that before writing, you would like them to turn and talk to a partner briefly. Ask them to talk about some of the things pet owners need to do for their pets. Model how to share ideas.

Sample modeling: *Here is how I would tell my partner an idea about taking care of a pet. I would say, "A pet owner gives a pet food_____." When it is your turn to talk to your partner, you can use the same sentence frame:* A pet owner gives _____.

Write the sentence frame for students. Give students one minute to share ideas. Then bring them together and ask volunteers to share ideas they discussed.

Write as a Group

Collaborate with students to agree on ideas to write about. Rehearse each sentence orally and model how to write it. As you guide the writing, include at least one noun. Actively engage students in the writing process by thinking aloud and/or prompting them with questions. For example:

- *What letter should I write in the first word?*
- *This word was in the text. Let's go back and check how to spell it.*
- *Is there a better word we can use here? What is it?*
- *What punctuation mark will we write at the end of the sentence?*
- *Is there anything we want to change in our sentences?*

Sample Shared Writing

A pet owner gives a pet space to grow.
Water is important for all pets.
A puppy needs a name.

Build Language: Nouns

Circle a noun in your sample writing. Point out that this word is a noun. Remind students that a noun is a word that names a person, place, or thing. Ask volunteers to use each of the following nouns in an oral sentence: **pet**, **food**, **water**, **puppy**.

Write Independently (iELD)

Ask students to draw one way a pet owner takes care of a pet. Students can write a simple label or caption.

Small-Group Differentiated Instruction (15 MIN. per Group)

Meet with Small Groups

Select small-group reading titles or activities based on students' needs. See the Small-Group Instructional Planner for titles that support a range of instructional levels within the unit topic. Remind students to apply skills and strategies they learned to their small-group reading experiences.

Say: *Remember that today we practiced finding important events in a story about pet owners. We also learned how illustrations go along with the words in a story. If you listen to a story today, pay attention to the important events. Look at the illustrations and think about how they connect to the text.*

Whole-Group Reflect and Share

Bring the class back together. Ask volunteers to retell important story events from a small-group reading text they listened to. Discuss the connection between illustrations and text.

W.K.2 Use a combination of drawing, dictating, and writing to compose informative/explanatory texts in which they name what they are writing about and supply some information about the topic., W.K.8 With guidance and support from adults, recall information from experiences or gather information from provided sources to answer a question., SL.K.1a Follow agreed-upon rules for discussions (e.g., listening to others and taking turns speaking about the topics and texts under discussion)., SL.K.1b Continue a conversation through multiple exchanges., L.K.1a Print many upper- and lowercase letters., L.K.1b Use frequently occurring nouns and verbs.

Pre-Decodable Reader: *ABC*

Student Objectives

I will be able to:
• Recognize and produce rhyme.
• Recognize letters **Kk, Ll, Mm, Nn, Oo.**

Additional Materials

• Letter cards: **Kk, Ll, Mm, Nn, Oo**
• Pre-Decodable Reader: *ABC*

iELD Integrated ELD

Light Support

Post the letter cards for **Kk, Ll, Mm, Nn**, and **Oo.** Ask teams to work together to find an example of each upper- and lowercase letter in a sign, name tag, or poster in the room, or, alternatively, to find an example in a text in the room. You might want to suggest they use books in the classroom library. Ask each team to report on one of the examples, naming the letter and reading the word.

Moderate Support

Use the upper- and lowercase letter cards. Ask students to identify each upper- and lowercase letter. Then write the following sentences and read them aloud. Repeat the underlined word and ask students to identify the initial letter.

Ben didn't want any <u>old</u> pet. <u>Mom</u> read a book of rules. A pet will <u>need</u> food. Be <u>kind</u> to pets!

Substantial Support

Use the upper- and lowercase letter cards. Hold or display **K** and **k**. Ask students to identify the uppercase **K** and then the lowercase **k**. Follow the same procedure for **Ll, Mm, Nn**, and **Oo.**
Then post a list of words beginning with these upper- and lowercase letters:
• Old, old; Mom, mom
• Lunch, lunch; Need, need; Kind, kind
Read each word aloud. Have students read the word after you and identify the initial letter.

ELD.PI.K.1, ELD.PIII.K.1d

Letter Recognition Kk, Ll, Mm, Nn, Oo (20 MIN.) RF.K.1d, RF.K.2a

Phonological Awareness: Recognize and Produce Rhyme

Model

Say the rhyme "Little Miss Muffet."

Say: *Little Miss Muffet/Sat on a tuffet,/Eating her curds and whey;/Along came a spider,/Who sat down beside her,/And frightened Miss Muffet away.*

Repeat the first two lines emphasizing the last word in each line.

Say: *Listen to the words* **Muffet** *and* **tuffet.** **Muffet** *and* **tuffet** *rhyme. They have the same sounds at the end. They both end with* **-uffet.**

Practice

Say the third and last lines, emphasizing the last word in each line. Have students listen for the words that rhyme.

Say: *I will say two more lines from the rhyme. What two words rhyme? Yes,* **whey** *and* **away** *rhyme. They both have the same ending sounds. Now I will say other words. Raise your hand if they rhyme:* **cat, pat; pet, let; hit, hill.**

Have students say other words that rhyme with **cat** and **pat**.

Letter Recognition: Kk, Ll, Mm, Nn, Oo iELD

Model

Hold up letter card **K.**

Say: *This is uppercase* **K.**

Repeat with lowercase **k.**

Then point to uppercase **K.**

Say: *What is the name of this letter? Yes, it is uppercase* **K.**

Repeat with lowercase **k.** Repeat with **Ll, Mm, Nn, Oo.**

Practice: K, L, M, N, O

Turn to page 4 in the Pre-Decodable Reader: *ABC.* Model how to match **K** and **k** on the letter cards with **K** and **k** in the book. Then have students match the letters. Then turn to page 5 for letter cards **Ll, Mm, Nn**, and **Oo.**

Practice: k, l, m, n, o

Display page 4 of the Pre-Decodable Reader. Name the objects on the cars of the train.

Say: *What do you see on top of* **Kk**? *Yes, it is a kite.*

Write the word **kite.** Have a student draw a circle around the **k** in kite and name the letter. Repeat for objects and letters **l, m, n, o** on page 5.

RF.K.1d Recognize and name all upper- and lowercase letters of the alphabet., **RF.K.2a** Recognize and produce rhyming words.

Read Aloud and Shared Reading

(20 MIN.) RL.K.10, RF.K.1d, SL.K.3

Read-Aloud Handbook

Shared Reading, Vol 1, p. 3 "Making Bridges"

Read Aloud

To support the unit concept, use one of the Read-Aloud Handbook selections for Unit 1. As you read, model the metacognitive strategy for the unit, Ask Questions, guided by the samples provided. You may also wish to select a favorite read-aloud from your classroom or school library. To support the unit concept, use one of the suggested titles for Unit 1.

Shared Reading (iELD)

Reread the Poem

First rereading. Read aloud the text fluently and expressively, pointing under each word.

Reread for fluency: Rate/Pacing. Model reading the poem at a comfortable pace. Point out that you do not hesitate at the end of a line, continuing the steady pace unless there's a punctuation mark. Echo-read the selection several times allowing students time to read at a pace that reflects the rhythm of the poem. Provide corrective feedback and/or validate students' efforts.

Build Concepts: Following Rules

Pose questions to connect the poem to the unit concepts. For example:

- *Who do you think the little new neighbor is? Why?*
- *What other games do you think the boy will teach the girl?*
- *How do you introduce yourself to a new friend?*

Review Language: Nouns

Read aloud the title of the poem and highlight the word **Bridges**. Remind students that they have been learning about nouns, or naming words. Point out that the word **Bridges** is a noun because it names a thing. Call on volunteers to use the word **bridges** in oral sentences.

Review Phonics: Alphabet Review

Review the uppercase and lowercase letters of the alphabet. Then point to the word **new** in the poem. Read **new** with students. Circle the first letter in **new** and call on a volunteer to name the letter. Repeat with the words **come**, **be**, **mine**, **fine**.

Student Objectives

I will be able to:
- Read along with the appropriate pacing.
- Answer questions about friends.
- Use nouns.
- Identify consonants.

(iELD) Integrated ELD

Light Support
Review with students the poem "Making Bridges," and point out that the word bridges in the title is called a noun because it names a thing.
Explain that the words *neighbor, playmate, sea,* and *games* are also nouns. Ask students to provide an oral sentence for each word.

Moderate Support
Review with students the poem "Making Bridges." Point out that the word *bridges* in the title is called a noun because it names a thing.
Reread the poem aloud and ask students to orally complete the following sentence frames with nouns from the poem.
- *A person who lives nearby is a [neighbor].*
- *A large body of water is called a [sea].*
- *Baseball and soccer are two [games].*
- *Someone you play with is a [playmate].*

Substantial Support
Ask students to recall the poem "Making Bridges." Remind them that nouns are words that name people, places, and things. They learned that *bridges* is a noun because it names a thing.
Post these other nouns from "Making Bridges":
- *neighbor*
- *playmate*
- *sea*
- *games*

Point to *neighbor*. Ask students if this noun names a person, place, or thing. Follow the same procedure with the nouns *playmate* for a person and *sea* and *games* for things.

ELD.PI.K.5, ELD.PI.K.6, ELD.PII.K.4

RL.K.10 Actively engage in group reading activities with purpose and understanding., RF.K.1d Recognize and name all upper- and lowercase letters of the alphabet., SL.K.3 Ask and answer questions in order to seek help, get information, or clarify something that is not understood.

Identify Characters in a Story (10 MIN.)

RL.K.1, RL.K.3, SL.K.2, SL.K.3

Engage Thinking

Explain to students that characters in a story can be people or animals.

Ask: *What characters can you name from stories you have read or heard?*

Model

Read aloud page 8 of "A New Pet." Explain that a story can have several characters, and the characters are usually people or animals. Tell students that the characters act, think, feel, and say things in the story. Explain to students that every story has a main character, and the main character is the character who the story is mostly about. Remind students that they can find out about the characters by reading the text and looking at the illustrations.

Sample modeling: *First, I am going to think about who the characters are in this story. To do this, I can look at the illustrations and read the text. I see that the illustrations show a boy on a couch. I think this is Ben. I also see that he is sitting next to a woman, and I think this is his mom. The illustrations show that Ben is thinking about an elephant. I know that animals can be characters, too. So using the illustrations, I can figure out that Ben, his mom, and an elephant are all characters in the story.*

Now, I can read the text to figure out more about the characters. I'm going to try to figure out who is the main character. The beginning of the story says "One day, Ben decided that he wanted a pet." So this tells me about the character Ben. Then the story tells us about the type of pet Ben wants, so we learn more about Ben. The story says "I'll take her on walks." So now I know what Ben wants to do with a pet. I've learned about the character Ben, and I haven't learned much about the other characters. So I think Ben is the main character of this story.

Guided Practice (IELD)

Read aloud page 9 of "A New Pet." Remind students that they can find out about the characters in a story by looking at the illustrations and reading the text. Review how students can look for what characters say, think, feel, and do in the story. Also, encourage students to continue to think about the main character in the story. Ask them to consider who the story is mainly about. Use directive and corrective feedback as needed. For example:

- *What characters do you see in the illustration on page 9?*
- *What characters speak on page 9?*
- *Do you learn more about what Ben wants?*
- *Do you learn more about what Ben feels?*
- *What character do you find out the most about in this story?*
- *Who is the main character of the story?*

Mentor Read Aloud Vol 1, pp. 8-11
"A New Pet"

Student Objectives

I will be able to:
- Identify the characters in a story.

Additional Materials

Weekly Presentation
- Three Column Chart

Ben	His Mother	The Elephant
says …	says …	says …
thinks …	thinks …	thinks …
feels …	feels …	feels …
does …	does …	does …

Sample Three Column Chart

 Show Your Knowledge

Tell students that you are going to make some statements about characters and the story "A New Pet." Ask students to give a thumbs up if they agree with your statement and a thumbs down if they do not agree.

- *A character can be a person or an animal.*
- *The main character in a story is always a person.*
- *The main character is who the story is mostly about.*
- *There can be lots of characters in a story.*
- *Every character must say something at some point in the story.*

(iELD) Integrated ELD

Light Support
Ask students to identify the characters in "A New Pet." Remind them to consider what the characters say, think, feel, and do by using the details in the illustrations and the words in the text. Have them identify the main character (Ben). If necessary, explain that Mom and the puppy are important characters but are not the main character.

Moderate Support
Remind students that they can understand the characters in a story by identifying what the characters say, think, feel, and do. Have students look at page 11 in "A New Pet."
Ask them to describe the scene and recall what Ben says, thinks, feels, and does. If they have difficulty answering, reread aloud the last paragraph. Point out that the thought balloon shows what he is thinking and the smile on his face shows his feelings as he holds up *Rules of Pet Owners*.
Emphasize that students can get information from both the words and the pictures.

Substantial Support
Remind students that they can understand the characters in a story by identifying what the characters say, think, feel, and do. Have students look at page 11 in "A New Pet."
Ask: *What is Ben doing? [showing Mom Rules of Pet Owners].*
Ask: *What is Ben thinking? [He'd like to get the puppy and give her an elephant outfit.].*
Ask: *What does Ben say to his mom? [He'll be a "responsible pet owner." He'll give his pet "the coolest name" and call her "Ellie Phant."]*
Ask: *What words in the text tell how the puppy feels about Ben? ["yipped and yapped to get Ben's attention," "rolled over," "wagged her tail"]*
Emphasize the importance of both the words on the page and the details in the illustration. Point out that readers use the words and the pictures to understand the characters and what the characters say, think, feel, and do.

ELD.PI.K.5, ELD.PI.K.6

RL.K.1 With prompting and support, ask and answer questions about key details in a text., **RL.K.3** With prompting and support, identify characters, settings, and major events in a story., **SL.K.2** Confirm understanding of a text read aloud or information presented orally or through other media by asking and answering questions about key details and requesting clarification if something is not understood., **SL.K.3** Ask and answer questions in order to seek help, get information, or clarify something that is not understood.

Write an Opinion (10 MIN.) W.K.1, W.K.8, SL.K.1a, SL.K.1b, L.K.1a, L.K.1b

Mentor Read Aloud Vol 1, pp. 8–11
"A New Pet"

Student Objectives

I will be able to:
• Write an opinion about a pet for Ben.
• Use nouns in my writing.

iELD Integrated ELD

Light Support

Have students write or draw about being a responsible pet owner. If they draw, students should include labels. Remind students of the shared writing activity they did as a group. Ask them to think about some of the things they did to complete the writing activity.

Moderate Support

Remind students of the shared writing activity they did as a group. Ask them to think about some of the things they did to complete the writing activity. Ask students to explain what *responsible* means. Explain that they can write about Ben being a responsible pet owner, or they can draw a picture to show what he should do. Give partners a few minutes to discuss different ways to care for a pet before students begin writing or drawing. Remind them to add a label if they choose to draw a picture.

Substantial Support

Remind students of the shared writing they did as a group. Have them recall the activity by orally completing sentence frames.

Make sure students know that responsible means being dependable or being trusted to do a job, such as caring for a pet. Explain that students can draw a picture to show what Ben should do. Discuss with them some possible choices, such as Ben taking Ellie Phant for a walk or playing fetch with her.

Remind them to try to add a label if they choose to draw a picture. Post the following useful nouns and others that students suggest: *Ben / Ellie Phant / ball / water / bowl / grass /park*

ELD.PI.K.3, ELD.PI.K.10, ELD.PII.K.4

Engage Thinking

Explain that an opinion is what a person thinks about something. When a person tells an opinion, he or she should give a reason for why they think that way.

Ask: *What animal do you think is a good pet? Why?*

Tell students that today they will write an opinion about a good pet for Ben.

Collaborative Conversation: Share Opinions

Tell students that before writing, you would like them to turn and talk to a partner briefly. Ask them to talk about the kind of pet they think Ben should get and to tell why. Model how you do this.

Sample modeling: *When I tell my partner my opinion, I say, "I think Ben should get a pet hamster because a hamster is fun to watch." Notice that I told why I think a hamster is a good pet. When you talk to your partner, you can use the same sentence frame:* I think Ben should get a pet _____ because _____.

Write the sentence frame for students. After partners have shared ideas for one minute, gather them together to voice their opinions to the group.

Write as a Group

Collaborate with students to agree on a class opinion and reason. Rehearse the message orally, and then model how you write the sentence. As you guide the writing, include at least one noun. Actively engage students in the writing process by thinking aloud and/or prompting them with questions. For example:

• *Who can show me where to start writing on the paper?*
• *What is the first (last) letter in the word _____?*
• *What word could we add to make this sentence better?*
• *Did we include a reason for our opinion?*
• *Let's reread our sentence. Is there anything we want to change?*

Sample Shared Writing

I think Ben should get a dog because he will give it a cool name.
Ben will be a responsible dog owner because he will feed his dog.
Ben will walk his dog and teach it tricks.

Build Language: Nouns

Circle a noun in your sample writing. Explain that this word is a noun. Remind students that a noun is a word that names a person, place, or thing. Ask volunteers for oral sentences using these nouns: **boy**, **book**, **store**, **elephant**.

 Write Independently (iELD)

Invite students to draw a picture showing Ben being a responsible pet owner. Ask students to label their pictures and explain their drawing to a friend.

Small-Group Differentiated Instruction (15 MIN. per Group)

Meet with Small Groups

Select small-group reading titles or activities based on students' needs. See the Small-Group Instructional Planner for titles that support a range of instructional reading levels within the unit topic. Remind students to apply skills and strategies they learned to their small-group reading experiences.

Say: *One strategy we learned today was identifying the characters in a story. We used the text and the illustrations to figure out who a story was about. Pay attention to stories you hear today and figure out who the characters are. Remember that characters can be people or animals.*

Whole-Group Reflect and Share

Bring the class back together. Ask volunteers to tell about characters that were in small-group reading text they listened to.

W.K.1 Use a combination of drawing, dictating, and writing to compose opinion pieces in which they tell a reader the topic or the name of the book they are writing about and state an opinion or preference about the topic or book (e.g., My favorite book is...)., **W.K.8** With guidance and support from adults, recall information from experiences or gather information from provided sources to answer a question., **SL.K.1a** Follow agreed-upon rules for discussions (e.g., listening to others and taking turns speaking about the topics and texts under discussion)., **SL.K.1b** Continue a conversation through multiple exchanges., **L.K.1a** Print many upper- and lowercase letters., **L.K.1b** Use frequently occurring nouns and verbs.

Pre-Decodable Reader: *ABC*

Student Objectives

I will be able to:
- Recognize and produce rhyme.
- Recognize letters **Pp, Qq, Rr, Ss, Tt.**

Additional Materials
- Letter cards: **Pp, Qq, Rr, Ss, Tt**
- Pre-Decodable Reader: *ABC*

iELD Integrated ELD

Light Support
Post the upper- and lowercase letter cards for **Pp, Qq, Rr, Ss,** and **Tt.** Ask teams to work together to find an example of each letter in a word in a book. You might want to suggest that students use books in the school or classroom library. Ask each team to report on one of their examples, naming the letter and reading the word.

Moderate Support
Post the upper- and lowercase letter cards for **Pp, Qq, Rr, Ss,** and **Tt.**
Then ask teams to work together to find examples of each letter in a sign, name tag, or poster in the room. Have each team report to the class by pointing out one of the letters they found in print. They may not find examples with **Qq.**

Substantial Support
Use the upper- and lowercase letter cards for **Pp, Qq, Rr, Ss,** and **Tt..** Hold or display **P** and **p.** Ask students to identify the uppercase **P** and then the lowercase **p.** Follow the same procedure for **Qq, Rr, Ss,** and **Tt.**
Then post a list of words and names beginning with these upper- and lowercase letters:
- *Pug's pet*
- *Queen question*
- *Roberto room*
- *Sara store*
- *Tom tail*

ELD.PI.K.1, ELD.PIII.K.3a

Letter Recognition Pp, Qq, Rr, Ss, Tt (20 MIN.) RF.K.1d, RF.K.2a

Phonological Awareness: Recognize and Produce Rhyme

Model
Say the rhyme "Pease Porridge Hot."

Say: *Pease porridge hot,/Pease porridge cold./Pease porridge in the pot,/Nine days old.*

Repeat the first and third lines emphasizing the last word in each line.

Say: *Listen to the words **hot** and **pot**. **Hot** and **pot** rhyme. They have the same sounds at the end. They both end with **-ot.***

Practice
Say the second and last lines, emphasizing the last word in each line. Have students listen for the words that rhyme.

Say: *I will say two more lines from the rhyme. What two words rhyme? Yes, **cold** and **old** rhyme. They both have the same ending sounds. Now I will say other words. Raise your hand if they rhyme: **man, can; fish, frog; bake, cake.***

Have students say other words that rhyme with **bake** and **cake**.

Letter Recognition: Pp, Qq, Rr, Ss, Tt (iELD)

Model
Hold up letter card **P.**

Say: *This is uppercase **P.***

Hold up letter card **p.**

Say: *this is lowercase **p.***

Then point to uppercase **P.**

Say: *What is the name of this letter? Yes, it is uppercase **P.***

Repeat with lowercase **p.** Repeat with **Qq, Rr, Ss, Tt.**

Practice: P, Q, R, S, T
Turn to page 5 in the Pre-Decodable Reader: *ABC.* Model how to match **P** and **p** on the letter cards with **P** and **p** in the book. Then have students match the letters. Turn to page 6 for letter cards. Repeat with **Qq, Rr, Ss,** and **Tt.**

Practice: p, q, r, s, t
Display page 5 of the Pre-Decodable Reader. Name the objects on the cars of the train.

Say: *What do you see on top of **Pp**? Yes, it is a pumpkin.*

Write the word **pumpkin.** Have a student draw a circle around the two letters **p** in **pumpkin** and name the letter. Repeat for objects and letters **q, r, s,** and **t** on page 6.

RF.K.1d Recognize and name all upper- and lowercase letters of the alphabet., **RF.K.2a** Recognize and produce rhyming words.

Read Aloud and Shared Reading (20 MIN.)

RL.K.1, RF.K.3a, SL.K.1a, SL.K.1b

Read-Aloud Handbook   **Shared Reading, Vol 1, p. 3 "Making Bridges"**

Read Aloud

To support the unit concept, use one of the Read-Aloud Handbook selections for Unit 1. As you read, model the metacognitive strategy for the unit, Ask Questions, guided by the samples provided. You may also wish to select a favorite read-aloud from your classroom or school library. To support the unit concept, use one of the suggested titles for Unit 1.

Shared Reading (iELD)

Shared Reading

Reread the Informational Text

First rereading. Read aloud the text fluently and expressively, pointing under each word.

Reread for fluency: Rate/Pacing. Read with appropriate pacing. Point out that you do not read the text too quickly or too slowly. Lead them to pause at the end of a sentence. Invite students to choral read the text at a good pace. Provide corrective feedback and/or validate students' efforts.

Build Concepts: Following Rules

Read the text and pose questions to connect the text to the unit concept. For example:

- *What are some other words the author could have used for "playmate"?*
- *Why do you think the author included the words "I'm glad you are here."*

Review Concepts of Print: Print Conveys Meaning

Ask a volunteer to point to the illustration. Point out that the illustration shows a girl and a boy. Ask a volunteer to point to the words. Point out that the words tell the meaning of the selection.

Ask: *Which gives the author's message—the illustration or the words?*

Review Phonics: Alphabet Review

Point to the word **you**. Read word with students. Circle the first letter in **you** and call on a volunteer to name the letter. Repeat with the words **fine**, **mine**, **new**, **sea**.

Student Objectives

I will be able to:
- Read along with the appropriate pacing.
- Answer questions about friends.
- Understand that print has meaning.
- Identify consonants.

(iELD) Integrated ELD

Light Support
Remind students that players on a team and in other games follow rules. Have partners work together to discuss "Making Bridges" on page 3 of *My Shared Reading*. Have them talk about why this poem is in a unit about following rules. If necessary, give them the hint to connect games and rules.

Moderate Support
Remind students that players on a team and in other games follow rules. Have students recall the poem "Making Bridges" by looking at page 3 in *My Shared Reading*. Discuss with them what the new neighbors will learn from each other and how games and rules are connected. Then have students tell in their own words how the poem is connected to the idea of following rules.

Substantial Support
Remind students that players on a team and in other games follow rules. Have students look at *My Shared Reading*, page 3. Read the poem aloud and ask *wh-* and *yes-no* questions to connect the words and illustration to the concept of following rules. For example:
- Think about the poem "Making Bridges." *What* will the new neighbors learn from each other? [games]
- Does the poem connect to the idea of following rules? *Why*? [Yes. To teach someone a game, you have to explain the rules of the game.]
- Should you fly a kite on a windy day? [yes]
- *Why* should you stand in an open place to fly a kite? [You want the kite to fly high.]

ELD.PI.K.11, ELD.PI.K.5, ELD.PI.K.6

RL.K.1 With prompting and support, ask and answer questions about key details in a text., **RF.K.3a** Demonstrate basic knowledge of letter-sound correspondences by producing the primary or most frequent sound for each consonant., **SL.K.1a** Follow agreed-upon rules for discussions (e.g., listening to others and taking turns speaking about the topics and texts under discussion)., **SL.K.1b** Continue a conversation through multiple exchanges.

Compare and Contrast Informational Text and Realistic Fiction (20 MIN.) RL.K.5, RI.K.9,

RF.K.1a, SL.K.2, SL.K.3

Mentor Read Aloud "Let's Play by the Rules!" and "A New Pet"

Student Objectives

I will be able to:
• Answer questions about details in texts.
• Recognize similarities and differences between two texts.

Additional Materials

Weekly Presentation
• Compare and Contrast Chart

Engage Thinking

Display "Let's Play by the Rules!" and "A New Pet." Remind students that they know both of these texts very well and now they are going to think about both texts—ways in which they are alike and ways in which they are different. Remind students that when they think about how two or more texts are similar to each other, they are comparing them. When they think about how two or more texts are different from each other, they are contrasting them. Tell students that today, they will compare and contrast these two texts.

Model

Display a three-column chart and read the column headings. Point to the first and third columns and tell students that here you will list ways the two texts are different. Point to the middle column and tell students that here you will list ways the two texts are the same. You may wish to use the following samples to model how you compare and contrast texts.

Sample modeling: *To compare, I will think about how these two texts are alike.* "Let's Play by the Rules!" *tells about rules. In* "A New Pet," *Mom has a book called* Rules of Pet Owners. *Both texts tell about rules so that is one way they are the same. I will write this similarity in the chart.*

Sample modeling: *To contrast, I will think about how these two texts are different.* "Let's Play by the Rules!" *tells about rules for team sports.* A New Pet *tells about rules for having a pet. Even though the two texts tell about rules, they tell about rules for different things. That is one way these two texts are different. I will write this difference in the chart.*

Guided Practice

Use directive and corrective prompts as needed to guide students to:

Compare and contrast types of text.

• *"Let's Play by the Rules!" is an informational text. Is "A New Pet" an informational text, too? Or is it a story?*
• *Are "Let's Play by the Rules!" and "A New Pet" the same kind of text or different kinds of text? How do you know?*

Compare and contrast the graphic features in each text.

- *Are there photos or illustrations in "Let's Play by the Rules!"? Are there photos or illustrations in "A New Pet"? Does that make the texts the same or different?*
- *"A New Pet" has thought bubbles. Does "Let's Play by the Rules!" have thought bubbles?*
- *"Let's Play by the Rules!" has labels and captions. Does "A New Pet" have those things?*

If necessary, continue to model how you think about these comparisons and contrasts. Collaborate with students to complete the chart. Reread the comparisons and contrasts together.

"Let's Play by the Rules!"	Both Texts	"A New Pet"
Tells about rules for team sports	Tell about rules	Tells about rules for having a pet
Informational text		Story
Photos		Illustrations with thought bubbles
Labels and captions		No labels or captions

Sample Compare and Contrast Chart

 **Show Your Knowledge** (iELD)

State an entry from the chart. Call on volunteers to tell if one or both texts have the element. For example:

- *It tells about rules.*
- *It has illustrations.*
- *It tells rules about team sports.*
- *It has thought bubbles.*

(iELD) Integrated ELD

Light Support
Post the compare and contrast chart from the guided practice activity. State an entry from the Show Your Knowledge activity. Have students identify which text is an example of the statement. If students have difficulty, have them look back at the two texts.

Moderate Support
Post the compare and contrast chart from the guided practice activity. State an entry from the Show Your Knowledge activity and demonstrate how to decide which text or texts it is about.
Say: *It tells about rules.*
Ask: *What is "A New Pet" about? [rules for pet owners]*
Ask: *What is "Let's Play by the Rules!" about? [rules for team sports]*
Ask: *Which text is about rules? [Both texts are about rules.]*
If necessary, continue scaffolding the items to provide support.

Substantial Support
Post the compare and contrast chart from the guided practice activity. State an element from the chart for the Show Your Knowledge activity and demonstrate how to decide which text or texts it is about.
Ask: *How do you know "A New Pet" is about rules? [Mom is reading a book called Rules of Pet Owners. One rule in the book is that pets need room to play and grow. Another rule is that pets need water and food.]*
Ask: *Does "Let's Play by the Rules!" tell rules for team sports? [yes]*
Ask: *How do you know the text is about rules? [One rule is about doing your best for the team. Another is to wear a helmet to be safe. The words say that players need to know the rules of the game.]*
Say: *Both "A New Pet" and "Let's Play by the Rules!" tell about rules. This is how the two texts are alike.*
Continue drawing out specific examples for other items in the chart.

ELD.PI.K.5, ELD.PI.K.6, ELD.PII.K.1

RL.K.5 Recognize common types of texts (e.g., storybooks, poems, fantasy, realistic text). **CA., RI.K.9** With prompting and support, identify basic similarities in and differences between two texts on the same topic (e.g., in illustrations, descriptions, or procedures)., **RF.K.1a** Follow words from left to right, top to bottom, and page by page., **SL.K.2** Confirm understanding of a text read aloud or information presented orally or through other media by asking and answering questions about key details and requesting clarification if something is not understood., **SL.K.3** Ask and answer questions in order to seek help, get information, or clarify something that is not understood.

Mentor Read Aloud "Let's Play by the Rules!" and "A New Pet"

Student Objectives

I will be able to:
- Discuss how two texts are alike and different.
- Write comparison and contrast sentences as a class activity.
- Use nouns in my writing.

iELD Integrated ELD

Light Support
Ask partners to talk about other ways "Let's Play by the Rules!" and "A New Pet" are alike and different. Help them by writing sentences they dictate to you.

Moderate Support
Remind students how the texts "Let's Play by the Rules!" and "A New Pet" are alike and different. Have them review the texts to find similarities and differences. Guide them to say sentences that tell another way the texts are alike and another way they are different. Write the sentences they say and read them with the students.

Substantial Support
Remind students how the texts "Let's Play by the Rules!" and "A New Pet" are alike and different. Have students brainstorm to find other ways the texts are alike, such as they both have titles or they both have words. Then list ways they are different, such as "Let's Play by the Rules!" is about real people while "A New Pet" is about made-up people, or "Let's Play by the Rules!" is about sports, but "A New Pet" is about pets. Prompt them to say a sentence that tells how the texts are alike. Write the sentence. Then prompt them to say a sentence that tells how the texts are different.

Sample Shared Writing
The texts are alike because they both have titles. The texts are different because "Let's Play by the Rules!" is about real people, but "A New Pet" is about made-up characters.

ELD.PI.K.2, ELD.PI.K.10, ELD.PII.K.4

Write a Comparison and Contrast Text (10 MIN.) W.K.2, W.K.8, SL.K.1a, SL.K.1b, SL.K.6, L.K.1a, L.K.1b

Engage Thinking

Remind students that they learned ways in which "Let's Play by the Rules!" and A "New Pet" are alike and different.

Ask: *What is one way "Let's Play by the Rules!" and "A New Pet" are alike and one way they are different?*

Tell students they will think about and write an answer to this question.

💬 Collaborative Conversation: Compare and Contrast

Tell students they will talk to a partner about how the two texts are the same and how they are different. Model how to compare and contrast.

Sample modeling: *To tell my partner how the two texts are alike, I say, "Both texts tell about rules." To tell my partner how the two texts are different, I say, "Let's Play by the Rules!" tells rules about team sports, but "A New Pet" tells rules about having a pet." When you speak to your partner, you can use the same sentence frames:* Both texts _____. "Let's Play by the Rules!" _____, but "A New Pet" _____.

Write the sentence frames for students. Give partners one minute to discuss their ideas. Then bring students together and ask volunteers to share what they discussed.

Write as a Group (iELD)

Collaborate with students to agree on one similarity and one difference between the texts. Rehearse the message orally and model how you write the sentences. As you guide the writing, include at least one noun. Actively engage students in the writing process by thinking aloud and/or prompting them with questions. For example:

- *What do I need to do when I start the first word in the sentence?*
- *We have learned the word _____. How do we spell that word?*
- *What is a better word for _____?*
- *What nouns did we include in our writing?*
- *What punctuation mark should I write at the end of this sentence?*
- *Now let's read our writing. Did we include all the words we needed in our sentences?*

Sample Shared Writing
The texts are alike because they both tell about rules. The texts are different because "Let's Play by the Rules!" has photos, but "A New Pet" has illustrations.

©2017 Benchmark Education Company, LLC

Build Language: Nouns

Circle a noun in your sample writing and identify it as a noun. Remind students that a noun is a word that names a person, place, or thing. Ask volunteers for oral sentences using these nouns: **baseball, football, team, fun**.

 **Write Independently**

Ask students to draw and label a picture to show another way the texts are different.

Small-Group Differentiated Instruction (15 MIN. per Group)

Meet with Small Groups

Select small-group reading titles or activities based on students' needs. See the Small-Group Instructional Planner for titles that support a range of instructional reading levels within the unit topic. Remind students to apply skills and strategies they learned to their small-group reading experiences.

Say: *This week, we learned how to find key details and the main topic about rules and team sports. We learned to name the characters in a story. Use these and other strategies we have learned. Also, remember to compare and contrast texts—think about ways they are the same and different.*

Whole-Group Reflect and Share

Bring the class back together. Invite volunteers to share what they learned from texts they heard read aloud. Have students name strategies they used to understand texts.

W.K.2 Use a combination of drawing, dictating, and writing to compose informative/explanatory texts in which they name what they are writing about and supply some information about the topic., **W.K.8** With guidance and support from adults, recall information from experiences or gather information from provided sources to answer a question., **SL.K.1a** Follow agreed-upon rules for discussions (e.g., listening to others and taking turns speaking about the topics and texts under discussion)., **SL.K.1b** Continue a conversation through multiple exchanges., **SL.K.6** Speak audibly and express thoughts, feelings, and ideas clearly., **L.K.1a** Print many upper- and lowercase letters., **L.K.1b** Use frequently occurring nouns and verbs.

Pre-Decodable Reader: *ABC*

Student Objectives

I will be able to:
- Recognize and produce rhyme.
- Isolate phonemes.
- Recognize letters **Uu, Vv, Ww, Xx, Yy, Zz.**

Additional Materials

- Letter cards: **Uu, Vv, Ww, Xx, Yy, Zz**
- Pre-Decodable Reader: *ABC*

Letter Recognition: Uu, Vv, Ww, Xx, Yy, Zz (20 MIN.) RF.K.1d, RF.K.2a, RF.K.2d

Phonological Awareness: Recognize and Produce Rhyme

Model
Say the rhyme "Wee Willie Winkie."

Say: *Wee Willie Winkie runs through the town,/Upstairs and downstairs in his nightgown,/Rapping at the window, crying through the lock,/Are the children all in bed, for now it's eight o'clock?*

Repeat the first two lines, emphasizing the last word in each line.

Say: *Listen to the words* **town** *and* **nightgown. Town** *and* **nightgown** *rhyme. They have the same sounds at the end. They both end with* **-own.**

Practice
Say the third and fourth lines, emphasizing the last word in each line. Have students listen for the words that rhyme.

Say: *I will say two more lines from the rhyme. What two words rhyme? Yes,* **lock** *and* **clock** *rhyme. They both end with* **-ock***. Now I will say other words. Raise your hand if they rhyme:* **ring, sing; tub, cub; bike, bird.**

Have students say other words that rhyme with **bike.**

Phonological Awareness: Phoneme Isolation

Model
Say the rhyme "Wee Willie Winkie" again and have students join in. Repeat the first line. Then say the word **Wee.**

Say: *The first sound in the word* **Wee** *is* **/w/.** *Say the sound with me:* **/w/.** *Now say the word with me:* **Wee.**

Practice
Repeat the routine with the word **Willie** and **Winkie.** Guide students to say the first sound, **/w/.**

Letter Recognition: Uu, Vv, Ww, Xx, Yy, Zz

Model

Hold up letter card **U.**

Say: *This is uppercase* **U.**

Repeat with lowercase **u.**

Then point to uppercase **U.**

Say: *What is the name of this letter? Yes, it is uppercase* **U.**

Repeat with lowercase **u.**

Practice

Turn to page 6. Model how to match **U** and **u** on the letter cards with **U** and **u** in the book. Then have students match the letters. Repeat **Model** and **Practice** using letter cards **Vv, Ww, Xx, Yy,** and **Zz** on page 7.

Letter Recognition in Words: Uu, Vv, Ww, Xx, Yy, Zz (iELD)

Practice: u, v, w, x, y, z

Display page 6 of the Pre-Decodable Reader. Name the objects on the cars of the train.

Say: *What do you see on top of* **Uu***? Yes, it is an umbrella.*

Write the word **umbrella**. Have a student draw a circle around the **u** in **umbrella** and name the letter. Repeat for objects and letters **v, w, x, y, z.**

Practice: U, V, W, X, Y, Z

Then hold up the uppercase **U** letter card. Ask students whose first name begins with that letter to stand up. Write each name and have the student point to and name the uppercase **U.**

Next have students locate other places in the classroom where the names appear and identify the uppercase **U.**

Say: *Look around the classroom and see if you can find a name that begins with uppercase* **U***. When you find one, raise your hand. I will have you go over and point to the uppercase* **U** *and say its name.*

If there are no names that begin with **U,** go on to the next letter.

Repeat for **V, W, X, Y, Z.**

RF.K.1d Recognize and name all upper- and lowercase letters of the alphabet., **RF.K.2a** Recognize and produce rhyming words., **RF.K.2d** Isolate and pronounce the initial, medial vowel, and final sounds (phonemes) in three-phoneme (consonant-vowel-consonant, or CVC) words. (This does not include CVCs ending with /l/, /r/, or /x/.)

Week 2 Skills at a Glance

	Day 1	Day 2
Reading Mini-Lessons	**Mentor Read-Alouds:** Topic Introduction, pp. 2-3 **Unit 1 Video** **Build Knowledge and Review Week 1 Strategies (10 Min.), p. 42** RL.K.3, RL.K.7, SL.K.1a, SL.K.1b, SL.K.2 **Read-Aloud Handbook** **Shared Readings:** "School Rules," p. 4 **Read Aloud and Shared Reading (20 Min.), p. 43** RL.K.1, RI.K.10, RI.K.10a, RI.K.10b, RF.K.1a, SL.K.1a, SL.K.3 • Fluency: Accuracy/Self-Correct • Build Concepts: Following Rules • Review Print Concepts: Directionality: Print Conveys Meaning • Review Phonics: Alphabet Review What Are Some Rules at School? **What Are Some Rules at School?: Listen and Retell Key Details (10 Min.), p. 44** RI.K.1, RI.K.2, RI.K.10, RI.K.10a, RI.K.10b, SL.K.1a, SL.K.1b, SL.K.3, SL.K.6	**Read-Aloud Handbook** **Shared Readings:** "School Rules," p. 4 **Read Aloud and Shared Reading (20 Min.), p. 50** RI.K.1, RI.K.10, RF.K.3a, RF.K.3c, SL.K.1a, SL.K.1b • Fluency: Accuracy/Self-Correct • Build Concepts: Following Rules • Review Phonics: Initial m What Are Some Rules at School? **Identify Parts of a Book (10 Min.), p. 51** RI.K.1, RI.K.5, RI.K.6, RI.K.10, RI.K.10a, RI.K.10b, SL.K.1a, SL.K.3, **Identify the Author's Reasons (10 Min.), p. 52** RI.K.1, RI.K.8
Writing Mini-Lessons	**Write Key Details (10 Min.), p. 46** W.K.2, W.K.8, SL.K.1a, SL.K.1b, L.K.1b • Build Language: Verbs	**Write School Rules (10 Min.), p. 54** W.K.3, W.K.8, SL.K.1a, SL.K.1b, L.K.1b • Build Language: Verbs
Phonics Mini-Lessons	**Focus Skill: m/m/ (20 Min.), p. 48** RF.K.2d, RF.K.3a, RF.K.3c, L.K.1a • Phonological Awareness: Phoneme Isolation • High-Frequency Words: *I*	**Focus Skill: m/m/ (20 Min.), p. 56** RF.K.2d, RF.K.3a, RF.K.3c, L.K.1a • Phonological Awareness: Phoneme Isolation • High-Frequency Words: *I*

Extended Read 1: "What Are Some Rules at School?"

Informational Text

Quantitative	Lexile® 500L
Qualitative Analysis of Text Complexity	

Purpose and Levels of Meaning ❶
• Text has a simple purpose: to tell about rules at school and why we have them.

Structure ❷
• The text is structured in sequential chapters, each dealing with a different aspect of rules at school.
• Readers encounter some sidebars and questions to provoke thought and discussion.

Language Conventionality and Clarity ❷
• Few complex or compound sentences, language is common usage.
• Non-technical vocabulary words such as citizen, community, and rules are defined in context through direct definitions.

Knowledge Demands ❶
• The familiar nature of the topic and setting means no prior knowledge is needed for understanding.

Day 3	Day 4	Day 5
Read-Aloud Handbook **Shared Readings:** "Rules for Talking and Listening," p. 5 **Read Aloud and Shared Reading (20 Min.), p. 58** RI.K.10. RI.K.10a, RI.K.10b, RF.K.1b, RF.K.3a, SL.K.1a, SL.K.1b • Fluency: Accuracy/Self-Correct • Build Unit Concepts: Following Rules • Model Print Concepts: Print Conveys Meaning • Review Phonics: Final m What Are Some Rules at School? **Use Text Features: Glossary (10 Min.), p. 59** RI.K.1, RI.K.5 **Find Text Evidence: Make Connections Between Illustrations and Text (10 Min.), p. 60** RI.K.7, RF.K.1a, SL.K.1a, SL.K.1b	**Read Aloud Handbook** **Shared Readings:** "Rules for Talking and Listening," p. 5 **Read Aloud and Shared Reading (20 Min.), p. 65** RI.K.1, RI.K.10, RF.K.3a, SL.K.1a, SL.K.1b, L.K.1b • Fluency: Accuracy/Self-Correct • Build Concepts: Following Rules • Review Language: Verbs What Are Some Rules at School? **Identify and Use Text Features (10 Min.), p. 66** RI.K.1, RI.K.5, SL.K.1a, SL.K.1b, SL.K.2, SL.K.6	**Read Aloud Handbook** **Shared Readings:** "School Rules," p. 5 **Read Aloud and Shared Reading (20 Min.), p. 71** RI.K.10, RF.K.3a, RF.K.3c, SL.K.1a, SL.K.1b, L.K.1b • Fluency: Accuracy/Self-Correct • Build Concepts: Following Rules • Review Phonics: Initial and Final m • Review High-Frequency Words: I **Mentor Read-Alouds:** "Let's Play by the Rules!", pp. 4-7 What Are Some Rules at School? **Compare and Contrast Two Texts on the Same Topic (20 Min.), p. 72** RI.K.1, RI.K.9, SL.K.3, SL.K.4, SL.K.6
Write an Opinion about School Rules (10 Min.), p. 62 W.K.1, W.K.8, SL.K.1a, SL.K.1b, L.K.1a, L.K.1b • Build Language: Verbs	**Write a List About Respect (10 Min.), p. 68** W.K.2, W.K.8, L.K.1a, L.K.1b, SL.K.1a, SL.K.1b • Build Language: Verbs	**Plan and Draft a Response to the Essential Question (10 Min.), p. 74** W.K.2, W.K.5, W.K.8, SL.K.1a, SL.K.1b, SL.K.3, SL.K.6, L.K.1a, L.K.1b
Focus Skill: m/m/ (20 Min.), p. 64 RF.K.2d, RF.K.3a, RF.K.3c • Phonological Awareness: Phoneme Isolation • High-Frequency Words: I	**Pre-Decodable Reader: I** **Focus Skill: m/m/ (20 Min.), p. 70** RI.K.1, RI.K.10, RF.K.2c, RF.K.3c, RF.K.4 • Phonological Awareness: Onset and Rime Blending • High-Frequency Words: I	**Pre-Decodable Reader: I** **Focus Skill: m/m/ (20 Min.), p. 76** RI.K.1, RI.K.10, RF.K.2d, RF.K.3a, RF.K.3c, RF.K.4, L.K.1a • Phonological Awareness: Phoneme Categorization • High-Frequency Words: I

**Mentor Read-Aloud Topic
Introduction Vol. 1, pp. 2-3**

Student Objectives

I will be able to:
- Reflect on strategies I have learned to help me learn about rules.
- Identify characters in a story.
- Discuss connections between illustrations and text.

iELD Integrated ELD

Light Support
Preparation: An enlarged copy of "Follow the Rules to Play Soccer." Read and choral-read the title.
Ask: What is this story about? Which text tells you what the story is about? What does the photo tell you about this story? Who is playing soccer in the photo?
Read/choral-read each relevant line after the group answers the questions above.

Moderate Support
Preparation: An enlarged copy of "Follow the Rules to Play Soccer." Read and choral-read the title. Prompt and point as you ask for answers to *wh-* questions that elicit text details.
Ask: What are the children doing in the photo? What is the main topic? Where do you look to find what the story is about? Where do you look to find the rules?
Read/choral-read each relevant line after the group answers the questions above.

Substantial Support
Preparation: An enlarged copy of "Follow the Rules to Play Soccer." Read and choral-read the title. Point to the photo and title. Provide the meaning of the words *photo* and *text*.
Ask: What do we know by looking at this photograph? What main idea does this text give us? Where can we find more information about soccer? Point to and read one rule.

Say: The words give me details about soccer rules.

ELD.PI.K.1, ELD.PI.K.5, ELD.PI.K.6, ELD.PI.K.7

Build Knowledge and Review Week 1
Strategies (10 MIN.) RL.K.3, RL.K.7, SL.K.1a, SL.K.1b, SL.K.2

Discuss the Essential Question iELD

Display the Topic 1 Introduction and read aloud the essential question. Then flip through the selections from Week 1. Ask students to turn and talk to a partner about three things they learned about why we have rules. Provide a sentence frame for students to use:

I learned that _____.

Ask volunteers to share what their partners said. Then explain that Week 2 will focus on rules at school.

Review Week 1 Strategies

Identify Characters in a Story
Remind students that they learned about characters in a story.

Say: *We learned that characters are the people or animals that a story is about. And most stories have a main character whom the story is mainly about.*

Display "A New Pet" and have a volunteer name the main character in the story and ask what in the text tells us that Ben is the main character. Then ask volunteers to name the other characters in the story.

Make Connections between Illustrations and Text
Remind students that they also learned how illustrations and text are connected. Display page 8 of "A New Pet."

Say: *Remember we read that Ben wanted an enormous elephant. When we looked at the thought bubble in the illustration, it showed how huge the elephant was compared to Ben and Mom.*

Choose another page from the text. Call on volunteers to describe the connection between the illustration and the words.

Tell students that being able to identify story characters and make connections between illustrations and text will help them understand the extended text you will read aloud this week.

RL.K.3 With prompting and support, identify characters, settings, and major events in a story., **RL.K.7** With prompting and support, describe the relationship between illustrations and the text in which they appear (e.g., what moment in a story an illustration depicts)., **SL.K.1a** Follow agreed-upon rules for discussions (e.g., listening to others and taking turns speaking about the topics and texts under discussion)., **SL.K.1b** Continue a conversation through multiple exchanges., **SL.K.2** Confirm understanding of a text read aloud or information presented orally or through other media by asking and answering questions about key details and requesting clarification if something is not understood.

Read Aloud and Shared Reading

(20 MIN.) RI.K.1, RI.K.10, RI.K.10a, RI.K.10b, RF.K.1a, SL.K.1a, SL.K.3

Read-Aloud Handbook

Shared Reading Vol. 1, p. 4 "School Rules"

Read Aloud

To support the unit concept, use one of the Read-Aloud Handbook selections for Unit 1. As you read, model the metacognitive strategy for the unit, Ask Questions, guided by the samples provided. You may also wish to select a favorite read-aloud from your classroom or school library. To support the unit concept, use one of the suggested titles for Unit 1.

Shared Reading (iELD)

Introduce the Poem

Display "School Rules." Read aloud the title of the poem text as you point under each word. Invite students to look at the photo and then turn to a partner and tell what they predict the poem will be about. Invite a few students to share their predictions with the whole class.

Read the Poem

First reading. Read aloud the informational text fluently and expressively, pointing under each word

Reread for Fluency: Accuracy/Self-Correct Point out and say words that students may have difficulty pronouncing. Then model reading aloud the text for accuracy. At first, slow down at difficult words and purposefully make a mistake or two to model self-correcting. With students, reread the text several times with accuracy and at a steady rate. Provide corrective feedback and/or validate students' efforts.

Build Concepts: Following Rules

Pose questions to connect the poem to the unit concept. For example:

- *Look at the photo. What rules are the children following? Why are those rules important?*
- *How do the rules at school help everyone?*

Review Print Concepts: Print Conveys Meaning

Ask a volunteer to point to the photo. Point out that the photo shows children at school walking in line. Ask a volunteer to point to the words. Point out that the words tell the meaning of the poem. Remind students that the print, not the photo, carries the author's message.

Review Phonics: Alphabet Review

Point to the word **run**. Read the word with students. Circle the first letter in **run** and call on a volunteer to name the letter. Repeat with the words **my**, **walk**, **hand**, **put**, **school**.

Student Objectives

I will be able to:
- Read along with accuracy.
- Answer questions about school rules.
- Understand that print has meaning.
- Identify consonants.

(iELD) Integrated ELD

Light Support

Preparation: An enlarged copy of the poem "School Rules," sentence frame worksheets, and an oversize copy of the worksheet.

Act out the poem and point to each word. Have students read along and act out the poem with you. Branch after reading/acting out the poem. Pass out a worksheet to each group. Have each group work together to complete the worksheet. When students are done, display your large copy of the worksheet. Read the questions together. Ask students for their answers. Fill out your large worksheet, modifying student answers.

Moderate Support

Preparation: An enlarged copy of the poem "School Rules," sentence frame worksheets, and an oversize copy of the worksheet. Follow the light support activity until, "When students are done...."

Display your large copy of the worksheet. Read the questions together. Ask students for answers. Use these sentence frames to act out the verbs.

- *Do students run in the classroom? (No, they _____.)*
- *Do students leave their things out? (No, they _____ their things away.)*

Substantial Support

Preparation: An enlarged copy of the poem "School Rules," poster with *yes/no* questions about the poem. Follow the light support activity until, "Branch after reading/acting out the poem...." Display the poster with yes/no questions about the poem. Ask the group each question. Write the answer next to the question in big letters.

- *Do the children walk?*
- *Do the children talk without raising their hands?*

ELD.PI.K.6, ELD.PI.K.1

RL.K.1 With prompting and support, ask and answer questions about key details in a text., RI.K.10 Actively engage in group reading activities with purpose and understanding., RI.K.10a Activate prior knowledge related to the information and events in texts. CA, RI.K.10b Use illustrations and context to make predictions about text. CA, RF.K.1a Demonstrate understanding of the organization and basic features of print:.a, SL.K.1a Follow agreed-upon rules for discussions (e.g., listening to others and taking turns speaking about the topics and texts under discussion)., SL.K.3 Ask and answer questions in order to seek help, get information, or clarify something that is not understood.

What Are Some Rules at School?: Listen and Retell Key Details (10 MIN.) RI.K.1,

RI.K.2, RI.K.10, RI.K.10a, RI.K.10b, SL.K.1a, SL.K.1b, SL.K.3, SL.K.6

What Are Some Rules at School?

Student Objectives

I will be able to:
- Recognize features of an informational text about school rules.
- Make predictions about rules at school.
- Listen for a purpose.
- Link my ideas to the ideas of others.
- Retell key ideas and details about school rules.

Additional Materials

Weekly Presentation
- Two Column Chart
- Key Idea Web

 Observation Checklist for Collaborative Conversation

As partners discuss the key details, use the questions below to evaluate how effectively students communicate with each other. Based on your answers, you may wish to plan future core lessons to support the collaborative conversation process.

Do partners . . .
- ❏ stay on topic throughout the discussion?
- ❏ listen respectfully?
- ❏ build on the comments of others appropriately?
- ❏ pose or respond to questions to clarify information?
- ❏ support their partners to participate?

Preview the Genre

Display the cover of *What Are Some Rules at School?* and read aloud the title and name of the author. Point out that this is informational text. Preview the pages and graphic features with students.

Have students turn and talk to a partner and name features they observe and predictions they have. Make sure they explain what text or graphic feature they used to formulate their predictions. Use this opportunity to discuss specific features students may not be able to name (such as the glossary).

Sample Informational Features	Sample Predictions
• title • table of contents • photos • labels and captions • glossary • index	I predict that I will learn... • about different rules for the classroom. • how teachers help us learn rules. • how rules helps us at school.

Read Aloud the Text

Ask student to listen carefully to learn about rules at school. Explain that this is their purpose for listening. Read aloud the text with minimal interruption. Model how you pause after each chapter heading, emphasize the words in bold print, and pause to examine the photos closely after reading the captions. Review the predictions students made before reading.

Collaborative Conversation: Partners ⓘELD

Ask students to recall key details from the text. Model how students can build on partners' talk by listening carefully and linking their ideas to what they have said. For example, *[Name] mentioned _____. Another key detail is _____. I agree with [Name] that _____ is a key detail. Another key detail is _____.*

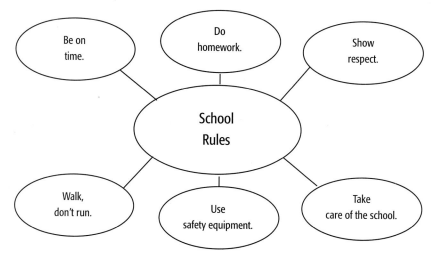

Sample Key Idea Web

Share

Invite students to share the key details. Record them on a class web and reread the part of the text where the detail was mentioned.

Reinforce or Reaffirm the Strategy

Provide modeling and/or engage students in self-reflection to build metacognitive awareness.

IF…	THEN…
students need support to retell key details from the text…	**Model to reinforce the strategy.** • *My purpose for reading was to learn about rules at school. I am looking for details that tell school rules.* • *When I read the chapter title on page 6, I know I will find out about some rules for learning. The first sentence tells these rules: get to school on time and pay attention. These are important facts about school rules. I will write down these key details.* • *In the next sentence, the text says that students need to do their homework. This is also an important detail. I will this down, too.* Continue to model how to find key details.
students independently retell key details…	**Invite partners to reflect on their strategy by discussing the following questions:** • *How did the chapter titles help you think about key details?* • *How did retelling the key details help you learn about school rules?* Have partners present their key details and explain how they found them.

☑ Show Your Knowledge

Ask students to draw a picture to show one key detail about school rules. Encourage them to write a simple word or label that tells about their picture.

(iELD) Integrated ELD

Light Support
Ask and answer detailed questions using *What Are Some Rules at School?* Read a heading from the book, and then ask students to provide details that support the heading.
Say: *Rules keep you safe. How do they keep us safe?*
Ask students to provide details from the book that explain how rules keep students safe. To prompt, ask sentence completion questions (e.g., If you run in the hall, you can _____).
Ask students to read a heading. Ask other students to provide details that explain the idea in the heading.

Moderate Support
Ask and answer questions using *What Are Some Rules at School?* Have students take turns reading several school rules. When they are done reading, model asking a question about rules by completing a sentence. For example, "At school, we _____."
Say: *Take turns.*
Ask another sentence completion question and ask the students to complete the sentence. Using the book and sentence completion cards as support, have students take turns asking classmates sentence completion questions. If necessary, support the student by acting out the missing word/verb.

Substantial Support
Ask and answer questions using *What Are Some Rules at School?* Hold up the cover of *What Are Some Rules at School?* Read the title and cup your ear with your hand to indicate careful listening. Open the book to a page with a rule (e.g., Walk, don't run). Read the rule.
Ask: *Should you walk inside? [Reply: Yes.]*
Say: *I am going to read more rules now. Listen carefully and help me finish the rule. Then tell me "yes" or "no" if it is a school rule.*
Be on _____ [time]. Is this a school rule?
Walk, don't _____ [run]. Is this a school rule?
Take care of the _____ [school]. Is this a school rule?
Do your _____ [homework]. Is this a school rule?
Say: *I like school rules! They help us learn and stay _____ [safe]. Can you help me with the last word? That's right! Rules help us learn and stay safe!*

ELD.PI.K.1, ELD.PI.K.5

RI.K.1 With prompting and support, ask and answer questions about unknown words in a text., RI.K.2 With prompting and support, identify the main topic and retell key details of a text., RI.K.10 Actively engage in group reading activities with purpose and understanding., RI.K.10a Activate prior knowledge related to the information and events in texts.CA, RI.K.10b Use illustrations and context to make predictions about text. CA, SL.K.1a Follow agreed-upon rules for discussions (e.g., listening to others and taking turns speaking about the topics and texts under discussion)., SL.K.1b Continue a conversation through multiple exchanges., SL.K.3 Ask and answer questions in order to seek help, get information, or clarify something that is not understood., SL.K.6 Speak audibly and express thoughts, feelings, and ideas clearly.

What Are Some Rules at School?

Student Objectives

I will be able to:
- Identify and share key details about school rules.
- Write key details about school rules.
- Identify verbs.

iELD Integrated ELD

Light Support

Preparation: Large copy of page 8 in *What Are Some Rules at School?*; worksheet copies of page 8 with all verbs replaced with a word-indicator line.
Say: *What am I doing?*
Model walking. Tell students that *walk* is a verb. Point to the students walking in the top photo on page 8. Tell students there are many verbs on the page. Point to/read the first sentence.
Say: *I see three verbs in this sentence.*
Circle *run*. Complete the first sentence in the paragraph. Hand out worksheets. Have them fill in the verbs, using the large copy as a reference.

Moderate Support

Preparation: Five verb cards, each with a verb from a school rule in *What Are Some Rules at School?*; copies of pictures showing students following each of the five rules (print the rule below the photo; replace the verb with a word-indicator line).
Ask: *What am I doing?*
Model walking. Reinforce/provide the answer. Hold up a card with the verb written in large print. Read the word, pointing to key letters/sounds. Tell students the word is a verb and remind them of the function of verbs. Model and show cards for/ask about the rest of the verbs embedded in rules.

Substantial Support

Preparation: Three verb cards, each with a verb from a school rule in *What Are Some Rules at School?*; copies of pictures showing students following each of the three rules (print the rule below the photo; replace the verb with a word-indicator line). Follow the moderate support activity.

ELD.PI.K.1, ELD.PI.K.3, ELD.PI.K.10, ELD.PII.K.2

Write Key Details (10 MIN.) W.K.2, W.K.8, SL.K.1a, SL.K.1b, L.K.1b

Engage Thinking

Display and reread the key details web with students. Remind students that they have learned and retold important details about school rules.

Ask: *How do rules keep you safe?*

Say: *Now we will identify and write the key details from* What Are Some Rules at School?

Collaborative Conversation: Peer Groups

Divide students into peer groups. Tell them that before writing, you would like them to turn and talk to a partner briefly. Ask them to share a detail from the text they thought was interesting, a detail they would like to write down. Tell students that when they speak to their partner, they should use complete sentences. Model how you do this.

Sample modeling: *Here is how I tell my partner about an interesting detail. I say, "The most interesting detail was the rule about using safety equipment to keep from getting hurt." When you talk with your partner, you can start your sentence the same way:* The most interesting detail was _____.

Write the sentence frame for students. Give students one minute to share their ideas. Then bring them together and ask volunteers to share they key details they found interesting.

Write as a Group

Collaborate with students to agree on one detail to write about as a class. Rehearse the message orally and model how you write the sentence. As you guide the writing, include at least one verb. Actively engage students in the writing process by thinking aloud and/or prompting them with questions. For example:

- *What is the first word in our sentence?*
- *I will leave a space before I write the next word. Why do I do that?*
- *Are there any words we could add to make our sentence better?*
- *What punctuation mark do we use at the end of the sentence?*
- *Let's reread our sentence. Is there anything we want to change?*

Sample Shared Writing

Walk in the hall.
Show respect to others.
Raise your hand.

Build Language: Verbs

Circle a verb in your sample writing. Tell students that this word is a verb. Explain that a verb is a word that names an action. Name a few verbs and ask students to act them out, such as **march**, **clap**, **spin**, **sit**.

Read aloud the first sentence on page 4 of *What Are Some Rules at School?* Point out the verb in the sentence, **follow**. Call on volunteers to use the word **follow** in oral sentences. Repeat the process with the verb **tell i**n the second sentence on the page.

☑ Write Independently

Ask students to choose another key detail from the text about school rules. Direct them to draw and label the detail.

Small-Group Differentiated Instruction (15 MIN. per Group)

Meet with Small Groups

Select small-group reading titles or activities based on students' needs. See the Small-Group Instructional Planner for titles that support a range of instructional levels within the unit topic. Remind students to apply skills and strategies they learned to their small-group reading experiences.

Say: *Today we practiced finding the key details about rules at school. If you are listening to an informational text today, pay attention to what the important details are. If you are listening to a literary text, pay attention to the key events. Use strategies we have learned to help you understand the rules at school. You can ask yourself questions to help you remember ideas in texts.*

Whole-Group Reflect and Share

Bring the class back together. Ask volunteers to share some of the key details and events they learned about in their small-group reading texts. Reinforce that strong readers use many strategies as they read.

W.K.2 Use a combination of drawing, dictating, and writing to compose informative/explanatory texts in which they name what they are writing about and supply some information about the topic., **W.K.8** With guidance and support from adults, recall information from experiences or gather information from provided sources to answer a question., **SL.K.1a** Follow agreed-upon rules for discussions (e.g., listening to others and taking turns speaking about the topics and texts under discussion)., **SL.K.1b** Continue a conversation through multiple exchanges., **L.K.1b** Use frequently occurring nouns and verbs.

Focus Skill: m/m/ (20 MIN.) RF.K.2d, RF.K.3a, RF.K.3c, L.K.1a

Phonological Awareness: Phoneme Isolation

Model

Say: *Listen to the beginning sound in* **monkey:** */m/. I'll say /mmm/ because I hear /m/ at the beginning of* **monkey.** *Say the sound: /m/. What is the sound?*

Display frieze card **Mm.**

Say: *Listen for the sound at the beginning of this word,* **magnet.** *Say the sound with me, /mmm/.* **Magnet** *has /m/ at the beginning.*

Read the poem "Melons and Muffins." Have students listen to the **/m/** sound while you read the sentence: *"Melons and muffins are yummy!" said Monkey merrily.*

Reread the poem.

Say: *Say /mmm/ each time you hear /m/ at the beginning of a word.*

Letter-Sound Correspondences (IELD)

Introduce: Mm

Display frieze card **Mm.**

Say: *The name of this letter is* **m.** *The letter* **m** *stands for the /m/ sound. Say the sound with me, /mmm/. This is the sound at the beginning of the word* **magnet.** *What is the name of this letter? (**m**) What sound does this letter stand for? (/**mmm**/)*

Model: Mm

Reread the poem "Melons and Muffins" and invite students to read along with you. Point to words in the poem that begin with the letter **m.** Say each word aloud.

Practice: Mm

Place two letter cards **m** in the pocket chart.

Place picture cards **magnet** and **drum** under the letter **m** while you say the name of the letter and pictures.

Hold up the picture card **mitten.** Have students say **mitten** with you. Ask if **mitten** begins like **magnet** or ends like **drum.**

Place picture card **mitten** under picture card **magnet.**

Say: **Mitten** *begins like* **magnet,** *so I am putting picture card* **mitten** *under the picture card* **magnet.**

Repeat with picture cards **mop, map, moon, jam, yam.**

Student Objectives

I will be able to:
- Isolate initial sound **/m/.**
- Identify letter-sound correspondence for **m /m/.**
- Sort picture names with initial m/m/ and final **m/m/.**
- Learn high-frequency word: **I.**
- Print uppercase and lowercase **Mm.**

Additional Materials

- Poetry poster: "Melons and Muffins"
- Letter card: **m**
- Sound-spelling card **Mm**
- For additional practice, see Pre-Decodable Reader: *I Can*

Weekly Presentation
- Picture cards: **drum, jam, magnet, map, mitten, mop, yam**
- Frieze card: **Mm**
- High-frequency word card: *I*

Poetry Poster

Model: Mm

Write uppercase **M** on two sticky notes and lowercase **m** on two other sticky notes. Read the poem, stopping after each line. Have students place the appropriate sticky note below each word that begins with the letter **M** or **m**. Remove the sticky notes before you go on to the next line.

Say: *I am going to read the poem "Melons and Muffins" again. I'm going to stop after the first line. I will ask you to choose one of these sticky notes, uppercase M or lowercase m, and place it under a word that begins with that letter.*

High-Frequency Words

Introduce/Practice: *I*

Display the high-frequency word card. Point to it and read the word.

Use the following routine: Point to the letter in the word and have students say the letter name with you. Say the word together.

Say: *When I say the word I, I will hold up the word card. Read the word with me. I see the girl. Can I go to the movies? I am six.*

Handwriting

Write and identify the uppercase and lowercase **Mm**. Hold up your writing hand. Write the uppercase and lowercase **Mm**. Trace the letters as you say **/m/**.

Then have students write **M** and **m** in the air as they say **/m/** several times. Finally have students write both forms of the letter several times, saying **/m/** every time they write the letter.

(iELD) Integrated ELD

Light Support
Preparation: Enlarged copy of the poem "Melons and Muffins."
Make cards that have all **m** words from the poem and other key words that do not have an **m**.
Read the poem title. Emphasize the **m** sound. Point to the letter **m**. Tell students the letter **m** makes the "mmm" sound.
Read/dramatize the poem. Emphasize **m** sounds and act out actions (e.g., yummy: rub your stomach and smile).
Have students choral-read and act out the poem with you.
Say: *I am going to circle a word that starts with **m** with this marker. Hmmm. Here's a word!* **Melon.** *Yummy. I like melons.*
Ask student volunteers to come up one by one to circle a word that starts with **m**. Choral-read the word each time. Emphasize "mmm" as you read.

Moderate Support
Preparation: Enlarged copy of the poem "Melons and Muffins."
Make cards that have all **m** words from the poem.
Follow Light Support activity.
Say: I'm impressed! You know a lot about the letter **m** now! Show me what you know!
Hold up a word card. Ask students to read it. [Prompt as necessary.]
Choral-read each word before moving on to the next word card. Emphasize "mmm" as you read.

Substantial Support
Preparation: Enlarged copy of the poem "Melons and Muffins."
Follow the Light Support activity.

ELD.PII.K.3, ELD.PII.K.4, ELD.PII.K.5, ELD.PII.K.6, ELD. PIII.K.1d

---

RF.K.2d Isolate and pronounce the initial, medial vowel, and final sounds (phonemes) in three-phoneme (consonant-vowel-consonant, or CVC) words. (This does not include CVCs ending with /l/, /r/, or /x/.), **RF.K.3a** Demonstrate basic knowledge of letter-sound correspondences by producing the primary or most frequent sound for each consonant., **RF.K.3c** Read common high-frequency words by sight (e.g., the, of, to, you, she, my, is, are, do, does)., **L.K.1a** Print many upper- and lowercase letters.

Read-Aloud Handbook

Shared Reading Vol. 1, p. 4 "School Rules"

Student Objectives

I will be able to:
- Read along with accuracy.
- Answer questions about rules.
- Identify initial **m.**
- Recognize the high-frequency word **I.**

(iELD) Integrated ELD

Light Support

Preparation: Enlarged version of "School Rules." Add worksheet for this activity.

Read the poem title; comment on the photo.

Say: *Hmmmm. I wonder what this poem is going to be about. Who has some ideas? [Prompt/reinforce.]*

Read/act out "School Rules," pointing to each word as you read. Point out the poem is about school rules. Choral-read with students. Point to yourself each time you read **I.**

Say: *Who is this girl/boy? [Prompt/reinforce] Yes! S/he is one of the students telling us the rules. She says: "I don't run in my classroom—I walk."*

Choral-read the rule. Reread and circle each **I.** Branch after reading.

Create student dyads. On their small worksheets, have each student choose a photo to tape next to each line in the poem, then circle the **I**s in the line.

Moderate Support

Preparation: Use Light Support prep. Follow light support activity until, "Branch after reading."

Read and choral-read the next line.

Ask: *Who is telling us this rule?*

Point to the students in the photo.

Read and choral-read the line. Have the student circle the two **I**s in the second line. Ask students to circle the two **I**s on their small copy.

Substantial Support

Preparation: Use Light Support prep.

Follow light support activity until, "Branch after reading."

ELD.PI.K.1, ELD.PI.K.3, ELD.PIII.K.3c

Read Aloud and Shared Reading

(20 MIN.) RI.K.1, RI.K.10, RF.K.3a, RF.K.3c, SL.K.1a, SL.K.1b

Read Aloud

To support the unit concept, use one of the Read-Aloud Handbook selections for Unit 1. As you read, model the metacognitive strategy for the unit: Ask Questions, guided by the samples provided. You may also wish to select a favorite read-aloud from your classroom or school library. To support the unit concept, use one of the suggested titles for Unit 1.

Shared Reading (iELD)

Reread the Poem

First reading. Read aloud the informational text fluently and expressively, pointing under each word.

Reread for Fluency: Accuracy/Self-Correct.

Discuss what would happen if a reader added, skipped, or changed words while reading. As you read the text aloud, demonstrate adding, omitting, or changing some words and then self-correcting. Lead students to understand that accurate reading makes the meaning of the text more clear. Together, choral read the text accurately at a steady pace. Provide corrective feedback and/or validate students' efforts.

Build Concepts: Following Rules

Pose questions to connect the poem to the unit concept. For example:

- *Why is walking safer than running?*
- *Why do you think that putting your things away and cleaning up are rules at school?*

Review Phonics: Initial m

Highlight the word **my** in the first line. Have students read the word aloud with you. Ask volunteers to name the letter at the beginning of **my** and the sound the letter **m** stands for. Do the same for **me** in the last line.

Review High-Frequency Words: I

Tell students that this text contains some words they have learned. Point to the previously-taught high-frequency word **I** in the third sentence. Ask students to turn to a partner and tell their partner the high-frequency word. Remind students to look for high-frequency words they know as they read a new text.

RI.K.1 With prompting and support, ask and answer questions about key details in a text., **RI.K.10** Actively engage in group reading activities with purpose and understanding., **RF.K.3a** Demonstrate basic knowledge of letter-sound correspondences by producing the primary or most frequent sound for each consonant., **RF.K.3c** Read common high-frequency words by sight (e.g., the, of, to, you, she, my, is, are, do, does)., **SL.K.1a** Follow agreed-upon rules for discussions (e.g., listening to others and taking turns speaking about the topics and texts under discussion)., **SL.K.1b** Continue a conversation through multiple exchanges.,

©2017 Benchmark Education Company, LLC

Identify Parts of a Book (10 MIN.) RI.K.1, RI.K.5,

RI.K.6, RI.K.10, RI.K.10a, RI.K.10b, SL.K.1a, SL.K.3

Engage Thinking

Remind students that a book has different parts.

Ask: *How does knowing the different parts of a book help us read?*

Model

Display *What Are Some Rules at School?* Model how to identify the parts of a book.

Sample modeling: *[Display the front cover.] This is the front cover of the book. This is where we begin reading. [Point to and read the title.] This is the title. By thinking about the title and looking at the illustration, we can make predictions about what the book is about. [Point to and read the author's name.] This is the name of the author. The author is the person who wrote the words in this book. [Display the title page.] This is the title page. It shows the title of the book, the author's name, and the table of contents. [Display the back cover.] This is the back cover of the book. It is where the book ends.*

Guided Practice (iELD)

Continue working with *What Are Some Rules at School?* Use directive and corrective feedback to help students identify the parts of a book and their purposes. For example:

- [Display the front cover.] *What part of the book is this?*
- [Point to and read the title.] *What is this called? Think about the title and look at the cover photo. What do you think this book will be about?*
- [Point to the author's name.] *Whose name is this? What does an author do?*
- [Display the title page.] *What things do you see on the title page?*
- [Display the back cover.] *What part of the book is this?*

☑ Show Your Word Knowledge

Call on volunteers to do the following:

- Find the front (back) cover.
- Point to the title on the front cover.
- Point to the author's name on the front cover.
- Find the title page.

RI.K.1 With prompting and support, ask and answer questions about unknown words in a text., **RI.K.5** Identify the front cover, back cover, and title page of a book., **RI.K.6** Name the author and illustrator of a text and define the role of each in presenting the ideas or information in a text., **RI.K.10** Actively engage in group reading activities with purpose and understanding., **RI.K.10a** Activate prior knowledge related to the information and events in texts.CA, **RI.K.10b** Use illustrations and context to make predictions about text. CA, **SL.K.1a** Follow agreed-upon rules for discussions (e.g., listening to others and taking turns speaking about the topics and texts under discussion)., **SL.K.3** Ask and answer questions in order to seek help, get information, or clarify something that is not understood.

EXTENDED READ 1 MINI-LESSON

What Are Some Rules at School?

Student Objectives

I will be able to:
- Identify the parts of a book.
- Tell the purpose of each part of a book.
- Find the author's name and tell what an author does.

(iELD) Integrated ELD

Light Support

Preparation: Copy parts of *What Are Some Rules at School?* that illustrate book parts students have learned (cover, title, author's name, etc.); write words for the selected book parts on separate sticky notes. If appropriate for class level, add additional sheets and cards; duplicate one set of material for student groups.

Talk aloud: *Look at this. Copies of the rules book! Oh, dear. It's not in the right order! Can you help me put it in the right order?*

Ask each student group to work together to put their sheets in order and label the book part with the sticky notes. Lead a discussion of the purpose of each book part.

Moderate Support

Preparation: Use light support materials. Place the sheets of paper upside down on the table. Have students take turns turning over a sheet and telling the group what book part it is.

When the correct book part is identified, ask a student to find the corresponding sticky note.

Substantial Support

Preparation: Write five book-vocabulary words on the sticky side of large sticky note and stick the notes to the corresponding part of the book. Hold up the book.

Say: *We've learned a lot about school rules from this book. We can also learn about all books from our rules book. Watch and listen carefully!*

Think aloud: *I'm touching the front of the book. What is the word for this part of the book?*

Say: *You all have very good ideas! Let's find out if we were correct!*

Hold up the note and read the word. Ask students to read the word together. Comment on the purpose of the cover. Continue until all notes have been turned over and read.

ELD.PI.K.1, ELD.PI.K.3, ELD.PI.K.6, ELD.PI.K.11, ELD.PI.K.12, ELD.PII.K.2

Identify the Author's Reasons (10 MIN.)

RI.K.1, RI.K.8

What Are Some Rules at School?

Engage Thinking

Tell students you would like them to listen quietly as you tell about the next lesson. The reason they should be quiet is so that everyone can hear what you have to say. Point out that is easier for students to understand what you want them to do when you give them a reason.

Ask: *Has a friend asked for you do something? What reason did they give?*

Explain that an author does the same thing in a book. When an author tells her ideas, she gives reasons to back up her ideas.

Model

Read aloud page 4. Model for students how to identify the author's reason.

Sample modeling: *The author writes that good citizens follow the rules. I want to find out what reason the author gives for this idea. I find a reason in the next sentence: "Rules tell people what they should and shouldn't do." The reason good citizens follow the rules is so they know how to act. Now I understand why the author thinks good citizens should follow the rules.*

Guided Practice (iELD)

Work with students to find reasons that support more of the author's points in the text. Use directive and corrective feedback to help students identify the reasons. For example:

• *Why do teachers make rules?*
• *Why do schools make safety rules?*
• *Why do schools want you to be a good citizen?*
• *How do rules help you take care of your school?*

Add the text evidence to the chart.

Student Objectives

I will be able to:
• Identify reasons for an author's ideas in a text.

Additional Materials

Weekly Presentation
• Author's Reasons Chart

Author's Idea	Author's Reason
Good citizens follow the rules.	Rules tell what people should and shouldn't do.
Teachers make rules.	Teachers want you to do your best.
Schools make safety rules.	Safety rules tell you how to be safe.
Schools want you to be a good citizen.	School rules teach you respect.
Rules help you take care of your school.	Rules tell you how to keep the school clean and make it better.

Sample Author's Reasons Chart

 Show Your Knowledge

Name one of the author's points about rules, such as, "Teachers make rules." Ask students to explain in their own words the reason the author gives for this idea.

iELD Integrated ELD

Light Support

Preparation: Large magnifying glass; enlarged copies of pages 6, 8, 10, and 12 from *What Are Some Rules at School?*

Say: *Who remembers how to find the author? Listen carefully now. Where do you find the main topics?* Use the magnifying glass to "discover" the table of contents. Show and read together.

Say: *I wonder if the author has reasons or rules that help you [summarize TOC benefits]. Let's find out!* Divide students into four groups. Give each group an enlarged page and colored markers.

In their groups, have students identify each reason that supports the heading. Have students underline each reason in a different color.

Moderate Support

Preparation: Large magnifying glass; enlarged copy of page 6 from *What Are Some Rules at School?* One poster sheet with the heading from page 8. One poster sheet with the heading from page 10. Strips of paper. Write one author reason on a strip until all reasons on pages 8 and 10 are written down. Hold the magnifying glass up to your eye.

Say: *I can't find the author of this book! Where should I look?*

Search for the author. Students may tell you to look on the front cover.

Say: *It's Margaret McNamara! I wonder why the author wrote this book?*

Put the magnifying glass to your eye. Look at page 6.

Say: *Here the author says rules help you learn. But why? Oh, here she tells me!*

Point to and read the reasons.

Think aloud: Those reasons would help me learn: get to school on time, pay attention, and do homework. Create student dyads. Give each dyad a strip. Have students tape the strip on the poster sheet under the appropriate heading.

Read the results together.

Say: *I think the author has good reasons to have rules. Who agrees with me?*

Substantial Support

Preparation: large magnifying glass; enlarged copies of pages 6 and 8 from *What Are Some Rules at School?*

Follow the moderate support activity until, "Create student dyads...."

Say: *Now it's your turn to be detectives!*

Put up the enlarged copy of page 8. Work as a class to find the reasons the author gives to support her idea.

Highlight each reason in a different color.

ELD.PI.K.6, ELD.PI.K.7

RI.K.1 With prompting and support, ask and answer questions about unknown words in a text., **RI.K.8** With prompting and support, identify the reasons an author gives to support points in a text.

What Are Some Rules at School?

Student Objectives

I will be able to:
- Write signs for school rules.
- Use verbs in my writing.

(iELD) Integrated ELD

Light Support

Preparation: Make copies from the rules book of photos of students following rules. Prepare sentence-completion cards for each rule. Omit the verb and one other word. Include cues for the number of words and letters. Indicate verb placement in red (e.g., _ _ _ _ _ your _ _ _ _ for Raise your hand, etc.).
Divide students into small groups. Give each group one photograph. Have students work as a group to decide the rule.
Wrap up: Each group presents to the class.

Moderate Support

Preparation: Make copies from the rules book of photos of students following rules. Prepare sentence-completion cards for each rule. Omit the verb. Include cues for the number of letters in the verb (e.g., _ _ safe for Be safe, etc.). Divide students into groups. Give each group one photograph. Have students work in their groups to identify the rule. Then have each student complete a sentence-completion card.

Substantial Support

Preparation: Make large flashcards for verbs in school rules. Pick verbs that can be acted out (e.g., walk, raise, listen). Copy photos from the rules book for each verb/rule. Write the rule on the copy of the photo in large print. Prepare sentence-completion sheets for each rule. Omit only the verb. Include cues for completion (e.g., R _ _ _ _). Remind students that verbs name actions. Demonstrate: walk.
Say: *I walk.*
Hold up one card at a time. Ask the children to say and act out each verb. Prompt as necessary by acting/speaking.
Say: *These verbs are in our school rules! Let's find out where.*

ELD.PI.K.10, ELD.PII.K.5, ELD.PII.K.6,

Write School Rules (10 MIN.) W.K.3, W.K.8, SL.K.1a, SL.K.1b, L.K.1b

Engage Thinking

Direct students to think about some of the rules in your own school.

Ask: *What signs do we have in our classroom that tell about rules?*

Remind students that they read about rules in *What Are Some Rules at School?* Tell them that today they will write signs for school rules from the text.

Collaborative Conversation: Peer Groups

Divide the class into four groups and assign each group one chapter from the text. Tell students that before writing, you would like them to briefly talk to the other members of their group. Ask each group to think of a sign they could write for one rule in their chapter. Model how you do this.

Sample modeling: *This is one way I could tell about a rule, "The sign will say, Pay attention." When you talk with your group, you can use that same sentence frame:* The sign will say, _____.

Write the sentence frame for students. Give students one minute to share their ideas. Then reconvene the groups and call on volunteers from each group to share their ideas for signs.

Write as a Group

Work with each group to generate an idea for a sign. Rehearse the text for each sign orally and model how you write the sentences. As you guide the writing, include at least one verb. Actively engage students in the writing process by thinking aloud and/or prompting them with questions. For example:

- *How do I begin the first word in our sentence?*
- *Should I write a small letter or a capital letter at the beginning of the word?*
- *Let's go back to the text to find the word _____. How do we spell it? We can use what we know about letters and sounds.*
- *What word could we use here to make our ideas more clear?*
- *Let's reread our sentences. Did we include all the words we needed?*

Sample Shared Writing
Do your homework.
Walk in the halls.
Show respect.
Keep our school clean.

Build Language: Verbs

Circle a verb in your sample writing. Tell students that this word is a verb. Remind them that a verb is a word that names an action. Ask volunteers to use each of the following verbs in an oral sentence: **learn**, **teach**, **work**, **play**.

☑ Write Independently

Ask students to make their own sign. They can write one of the school rules and draw a picture to go with it.

Small-Group Differentiated Instruction (15 MIN. per Group)

Meet with Small Groups

Select appropriate small-group reading titles or reinforcement activities based on students' needs. See the Small-Group Instructional Planner for titles that support a range of instructional reading levels within the unit topic. Remind students to apply what they learned to their small-group reading experiences.

Say: *Remember, today we learned how to find an author's reasons for the ideas she writes about rules at school. If you listen to an informational text today, pay attention to the author's ideas and how she backs them up. What are some other strategies that will help you understand a text you are listening to?*

Whole-Group Reflect and Share

Bring the class back together. Call on volunteers to tell about ideas authors wrote about in their small-group reading texts. Ask students to name the reasons the authors gave for their ideas.

W.K.3 Use a combination of drawing, dictating, and writing to narrate a single event or several loosely linked events, tell about the events in the order in which they occurred, and provide a reaction to what happened., **W.K.8** With guidance and support from adults, recall information from experiences or gather information from provided sources to answer a question., **SL.K.1a** Follow agreed-upon rules for discussions (e.g., listening to others and taking turns speaking about the topics and texts under discussion)., **SL.K.1b** Continue a conversation through multiple exchanges., **L.K.1b** Use frequently occurring nouns and verbs.

Focus Skill: m/m/ (20 MIN.) RF.K.2d, RF.K.3a, RF.K.3c, L.K.1a

Phonological Awareness: Phoneme Isolation

Model/Practice

Show students the picture on the back of the poetry poster and have them name all the objects in the picture. Point to the magnet in the picture and say the word **magnet**.

Ask: *What sound do you hear at the beginning of the word?*

Have students point to things in the picture whose name starts with /**m**/.

Say: *Now listen as I say the word* **broom.** *I can hear the* /**m**/ *sound at the end of the word* **broom.** *I am going to say some words. If you hear* /**m**/ *at the beginning of the word raise your hand. If you hear* /**m**/ *at the end of the word, clap your hands.*

Use the following words: **mitt, mop, him, make, him, team.**

Letter-Sound Correspondences

Review: m/m/

Hold up frieze card **Mm** and have students tell you the sound the letters stand for. Encourage students to think of words that start with /**m**/. Record the words, underlining the letter **m**. Then have students think of words that end with /**m**/. Record these words, underlining the letter **m**.

Reread the poem "Melons and Muffins," emphasizing the initial /**m**/ sounds. Have volunteers find words that begin with the letter **m**.

Identify Words with m/m/

Model: m

Have each student write lowercase **m** on a sticky note.

Say: *I am going to say some words. If you hear* /**m**/ *at the beginning of the word, hold up your letter* **m.**

Say: *these words:* **match, money, zebra, meat, rock, move, me.**

Repeat for words with final **m: drum, room, team, milk, plum, ham, nest.**

Practice: m

Show students the picture on the back of the poetry poster. Have students, one at a time, place his or her sticky note **m** on a picture whose name begins with /**m**/. Then ask students to name objects beginning with /**m**/ that could be added to the picture.

Student Objectives

I will be able to:
- Isolate initial and final sound /**m**/.
- Practice letter-sound correspondences for **m/m/.**
- Read high-frequency word: **I.**
- Print uppercase and lowercase **Mm.**

Additional Materials

- Poetry poster: "Melons and Muffins"

Weekly Presentation
- Frieze card: **m**
- High-frequency word card: **I**

High-Frequency Words (iELD)

Practice: *I*

Display high-frequency word card **I** and read the word. Point to the letter **I** in the word and have students say the letter name with you. Say the word together.

Say: *I am going to read some sentences. When I say the word I, I will hold up the word card. Read the word with me. I am going to the playground. Can I go on the swings? I like fruit.*

Handwriting

Have students write the uppercase and lowercase **Mm**. Observe students' pencil grip and paper position. Have students say **/m/** every time they write the letters **Mm**.

(iELD) Integrated ELD

Light Support

Preparation: Enlarged copy of the poem "School Rules"; an **I** word card for each student; worksheet with four short sentences that each include **I** and a verb (replace **I** with a line).

Point to the poem. Remind students that earlier in the week, you identified **I** in the poem. Read/choral-read the poem. Each time you say **I**, hold up your **I** card.

Give each student an **I** card. Ask students to hold up their **I** cards with you each time you read the word **I**.

Tell students they did a great job and that now you are going to make their jobs harder. Tell them to listen very carefully (emphasize by cupping your ear).

Tell them to hold up their **I** card each time you say the word **I**.

Create student dyads. Hand out worksheets. Review the worksheet by reading each short sentence, including the word **I** (e.g., _ walk; _ listen; _ clean up; etc.).

Have each dyad work together to add the **I** to their own sheets. Review as a class.

Moderate Support

Preparation: Enlarged copy of the poem "School Rules"; an **I** word card for each student; two cards with short sentences that include the word **I** and an active verb (e.g., I walk; I listen). Cards should be large enough to hold up for the class.

Follow Light Support activity until, "Create student dyads...."

Hold up and read one of the sentence cards. Point to and emphasize **I**.

Ask students to hold up their **I** cards when they hear the word **I**. Read the short sentence on the card.

Use the same procedure for the last card.

Repeat or wrap up based on time and student level.

Substantial Support

Preparation: Enlarged copy of the poem "School Rules"; an **I** word card for each student.

Follow Light Support activity until "Create student dyads...."

Say: *I think you did a great job! Give yourselves a pat on the back. [Prompt by acting out patting yourself on the back.]*

Tell children to say, "I did a great job!" while they pat themselves on their backs. Model and prompt.

ELD.PI.K.1, ELD.PI.K.5, ELD.PI.K.6, ELD.PI.K.8

RF.K.2d Isolate and pronounce the initial, medial vowel, and final sounds (phonemes) in three-phoneme (consonant-vowel-consonant, or CVC) words. (This does not include CVCs ending with /l/, /r/, or /x/.), **RF.K.3a** Demonstrate basic knowledge of letter-sound correspondences by producing the primary or most frequent sound for each consonant., **RF.K.3c** Read common high-frequency words by sight (e.g., the, of, to, you, she, my, is, are, do, does)., **L.K.1a** Print many upper- and lowercase letters.

Read Aloud and Shared Reading (20 MIN.)

RI.K.10. RI.K.10a, RI.K.10b, RF.K.1b, RF.K.3a, SL.K.1a, SL.K.1b

Read Aloud

To support the unit concept, use one of the Read-Aloud Handbook selections for Unit 1. As you read, model the metacognitive strategy for the unit, Ask Questions, guided by the samples provided. You may also wish to select a favorite read-aloud from your classroom or school library. To support the unit concept, use one of the suggested titles for Unit 1.

Shared Reading (iELD)

Introduce the Informational Text

Display "Rules for Talking and Listening." Read aloud the title as you point under each word. Invite students to look at the photo and then turn to a partner and tell what they predict the text will be about. Invite a few students to share their predictions with the whole class.

Read the Informational Text
Day 3

First reading. Read aloud the informational text fluently and expressively, pointing under each word.

Reread for Fluency: Accuracy/Self-Correct. Demonstrate how to preview this text for difficult words, such as **attraction** or **magnetic**. Lead students to echo the pronunciation of these words and unlock their meaning. Choral-read the text together, slowing down the rate as you allow students the opportunity to say and self-correct their pronunciations of difficult words. Provide corrective feedback and/or validate students' efforts.

Build Concepts: Following Rules

Pose questions to connect the informational text to the unit concept. For example:

- *Why are rules important for listening and talking?*
- *Can two people talk at the same time? Why or Why not?*

Review Print Concepts: Print Conveys Meaning

Point out that the photo shows two family members talking and listening. Ask a volunteer to point to the words. Point out that the words tell the meaning of the informational text.

Ask: *Which gives the author's message—the photo or the words?*

Review Phonics: Final m

Highlight the word **from** in the last sentence. Have students read the word aloud with you. Ask volunteers to name the letter at the end of **from** and the sound the letter **m** stands for.

Read-Aloud Handbook   **Shared Reading, Vol. 1, p. 5 "Rules for Talking and Listening"**

Student Objectives

I will be able to:
- Read along with accuracy.
- Answer questions about talking and listening.
- Understand that print has meaning.
- Identify final **m.**

(iELD) Integrated ELD

Light Support
Display "Rules for Talking and Listening." Point to the photograph.
Think aloud: *What do I see? A father and son. What are they doing?* Encourage students to provide ideas.
Say: *Great ideas! The photograph is giving you ideas! Where can we look to see if our predictions are right?* Prompt by pointing to the text. Read the title slowly. Reinforce that the words give the meaning.

Moderate Support
Display "Rules for Talking and Listening." Hold a sheet of paper over the text. Point to the photograph.
Think aloud: *What do I see? A father and son. They look happy! I wonder why!*
Ask: *Who has an idea?* Encourage students to provide ideas.
Say: *Great ideas! The photograph is giving you ideas! Are our predictions right? Let's read to find out.*
Uncover the text. Read the title slowly. Choral-read with students.

Substantial Support
Display "Rules for Talking and Listening." Hold a sheet of paper over the text. Point to the photograph.
Think aloud: *What do I see? A father and son. I wonder what they're doing.*
Ask: *Who has an idea?* Encourage students to provide lots of ideas.
Say: *You are using the photograph! The photograph is giving you ideas! Who knows how we can learn more?* Prompt by peeking under the sheet that covers the text.

ELD.PI.K.1, ELD.PI.K.3, ELD.PI.K.5, ELD.PI.K.9, ELD.PI.K.11, ELD.PI.K.12

RI.K.10 Actively engage in group reading activities with purpose and understanding.. **RI.K.10a** Activate prior knowledge related to the information and events in texts.CA, **RI.K.10b** Use illustrations and context to make predictions about text. CA, **RF.K.1b** Recognize that spoken words are represented in written language by specific sequences of letters., **RF.K.3a** Demonstrate basic knowledge of letter-sound correspondences by producing the primary or most frequent sound for each consonant., **SL.K.1a** Follow agreed-upon rules for discussions (e.g., listening to others and taking turns speaking about the topics and texts under discussion)., **SL.K.1b** Continue a conversation through multiple exchanges.

Use Text Features: Glossary (10 MIN.) RI.K.1, RI.K.5

Engage Thinking

Remind students that they have learned about different parts of a book. Tell them that today they will learn about another part of a book called a glossary. Explain that a glossary is like a little dictionary at the end of a book.

Ask: *How does a dictionary help us understand words?*

Model

Turn to the Glossary on page 16. Point to and read the heading **Glossary.** Explain that the words in the Glossary are same words found in this book. Model for students how to use the Glossary.

Sample modeling: *[Point to the word* **citizens.** *] I see that the first word in the Glossary is* **citizens.** *The Glossary shows and tells me the meaning of* **citizens,** *"the people who are part of a community." Below, the Glossary tells me that the word* **citizens** *first appears in the book, on page 4. [Turn to page 4.] Here is the word* **citizens** *in bold print on the page. All the words in bold print in the text are Glossary words.*

Guided Practice

Point to the word **community** on page 4 and read it. Then display page 16 and guide students to use the Glossary:

- *Find the Glossary.*
- *Find the word* **community (rules, school)** *in the Glossary.*
Listen to the definition. [Read the definition.] Tell me what a **community (rules, school)** *is.*

- *Tell me on what page* **rules (school)** *first appears.*

Show Your Knowledge (iELD)

Point to the word **respect** in the Glossary. Read the word and its definition. Call on volunteers to tell what the word means and on which page it first appears in the text. Ask another volunteer to find the word **respect** in bold print on page 10.

What Are Some Rules at School?

Student Objectives

I will be able to:
- Understand what a glossary is.
- Find and use a glossary in a text.

(iELD) Integrated ELD

Light Support
Preparation: Large glossary-words cards; enlarged copy of *What Are Some Rules at School?*
Hold up page 2 of the book. Point to the girl saying, "Shhh." Ask what she is doing. Encourage responses.
Say: *What does this word mean? (Point to "citizens" and read photo caption.) Where can I find out what "citizens" means?*
Hold up your book open to page 16.
Say: *Here is where it tells me. (Point to/ read* **Glossary.** *)* Have children turn to their glossaries. Read the definition. Choral-read. Branch after choral-reading the definition of **citizens.** Hold up and read the words on the large cards. Create student dyads. Give each dyad a card. Have each dyad find its word in the glossary and one example in the text. Have each dyad show the class where the word is in the glossary and in the text. Read the definition to the class. Choral-read the definition and related text.

Moderate Support
Preparation: Large glossary-words cards; enlarged copy of *What Are Some Rules at School?*
Follow Light Support activity until "Branch after choral-reading...."
Branch after choral-reading the definition of **citizens.** Hold up and read the words on the large cards. Create student dyads. Give each dyad a card. Have each dyad find its word in the glossary. Have each dyad show the class where the word is in the glossary. Read the definition to the class. Choral-read the definition.

Substantial Support
Preparation: Enlarged copy of *What Are Some Rules at School?*
Follow Light Support activity until "Branch after choral-reading...."

ELD.PI.K.6, ELD.PII.K.2

RI.K.1 With prompting and support, ask and answer questions about unknown words in a text., **RI.K.5** Identify the front cover, back cover, and title page of a book.

What Are Some Rules at School?

Student Objectives

I will be able to:
- Describe how text and illustrations are related.
- Use evidence from the text to support my answers about school rules.

☑ Observation Checklist for Productive Engagement

Is the Productive Engagement Productive?

As partners discuss their understanding of making connections between illustrations and text, look for evidence that they are truly engaged in the task.

Partners are engaged productively if…

- ❏ they ask questions and use feedback to address the task.
- ❏ they demonstrate engagement and motivation.
- ❏ they apply strategies with some success.
- ❏ *If the discussion is productive, continue the task.*

Partners are not engaged productively if…

- ❏ they apply no strategies to the task.
- ❏ they show frustration or anger.
- ❏ they give up.

If the discussion is unproductive, end the task, and provide support.

Find Text Evidence: Make Connections between Illustrations and Text (10 MIN.) RI.K.7, RF.K.1a, SL.K.1a, SL.K.1b

Engage Thinking

Remind students that they have learned about how illustrations and text are connected. Explain that sometimes illustrations can give more information.

Ask: *How can the illustrations in books help you learn about the text?*

Model

Display and read aloud a text evidence question. Tell students that to answer this question they will need to pay attention to the text. Underline the key words in the question: **small photo,** and **page 6.** Explain that the words **page 6** help students know where to look in the text. The words **small photo** let students know they should look at the photo and listen to the text on the page.

> **Text Evidence Question:** How does the small photo of the students on page 6 help you understand how they are using rules?

Direct students to look at the small photo on page 6 and listen carefully as you reread the text and the caption.

Sample modeling: *The text tells about one rule that helps students learn: they need to do their homework. The small photo shows a girl doing her homework at home with her brother's help. This photo helps me understand what the text says: that when a student follows the rules and does her homework, she will learn.*

Guided Practice (iELD)

Display and read aloud a second text evidence question. Tell students that this is another question for which they will need to pay attention to the text. Underline the key words **two small photos** and **page 8,** in the question. Tell students that they should focus on the photos and the text on page 8.

Text Evidence Question: How do the two small photos of the students on page 8 help you understand how rules keep you safe?

Ask students to look closely at the two small photos and listen carefully as you reread page 8. Provide directive feedback as needed. For example:

- *What does the text say about moving in the halls at school?*
- *What does the top photo show? What does the bottom photo show?*
- *Which photo shows students following a rule for safety? Which photo shows students not following the rule?*

Highlight the evidence in the text. Guide students to see that the text tells what can happen when students don't follow safety rules and the bottom photo shows this idea.

Productive Engagement: Partner Activity

Display and read aloud a third text evidence question. Underline and read the words **photo** and **page 12** to help students focus their attention.

Text Evidence Question: How does the photo on page 12 help you understand how students take care of their school?

Tell students to look at the photo on page 12 and listen carefully as you reread the page. After reading, reread the text evidence question. Ask students to turn and talk to a partner to answer the question. Invite partners to share their answers with the group.

☑ Show Your Knowledge

Display and read aloud page 5. Invite volunteers to explain how the photos of the students following the rules and the text are connected.

(iELD) Integrated ELD

Light Support

Preparation: Large key-word cards (safe, run, walk, fall, bump); enlarged copy of page 8.

Circle **8** in a bright color on the enlarged copy. Ask students to find page **8** in their books by looking for the 8 in a star at the bottom of the page.

Circle the top small photo. Ask students to look closely at the photo. Ask questions about the photo (e.g., *Where are the students? What are they doing?*). Summarize: Students are walking in the hall.

Circle the lower small photo. Ask students to look closely at the photo. Ask students questions about the photo (*Where are the students? Are the students walking?*).

Say: *Remember, one reason for rules is to be safe. When are students safe? Let's read the text to find out. [Point to and read the text.]*

Create small work groups. Give each group a key word card. Have each group decide and report which photo shows what the card says. A volunteer from each group tapes their cards next to the appropriate photo.

Ask: *Which photo shows students following the rules and being safe?*

Reinforce students' ideas and comment on how photos help you understand the text.

Moderate Support

Preparation: Large key-word cards (safe, run, walk, fall, bump); enlarged copy of page 8.

Follow Light Support activity through photo-circling activities, then branch to:

Say: *Remember, one reason for rules is to be safe. Which students are safe? Let's read the text to find out. [Point to and read the text.]*

Hold up key word cards one at a time. For each card, ask students which photo shows what the card says. Tape the cards in place.

Ask: *Which photo shows students following the rules and being safe?*

Reinforce students' ideas and comment on how photos help you understand the text.

Substantial Support

Preparation: Enlarged copy of page 8 from *What Are Some Rules at School?*

Follow Light Support activity through photo-circling activities, then branch to:

Summarize: *The students are running.*

Ask: *Which photo shows students following the rules? Let's find out by reading the words. Remember, words give us the meaning. [Point to and read the text.]*

ELD.PI.K.1, ELD.PI.K.5, ELD.PI.K.6

RI.K.7 With prompting and support, describe the relationship between illustrations and the text in which they appear (e.g., what person, place, thing, or idea in the text an illustration depicts)., **RF.K.1a** Follow words from left to right, top to bottom, and page by page., **SL.K.1a** Follow agreed-upon rules for discussions (e.g., listening to others and taking turns speaking about the topics and texts under discussion)., **SL.K.1b** Continue a conversation through multiple exchanges.

What Are Some Rules at School?

Student Objectives

I will be able to:
- Write an opinion about school rules.
- Use verbs in my writing.

 **Integrated ELD**

Light Support

Preparation: Create large three-column (C) chart with a row for each rule on page 11 of "What Are Some Rules at School?" In C1: photo of rule; C2: corresponding school rule; C3: the verb in the school rule. Cover each cell with separate pieces of paper. Draw large smiley faces on yellow paper and cut out. Uncover the first photo. Ask students to tell you the rule. Act out the verb while you ask.

Hold up the verb card that says, "Listen." Say "Listen" and tape the smiley face next to the matching photo. Say the rule. Continue with other rules.

Moderate Support

Preparation: Use Light Support material. Uncover the first photo. Ask students to tell you the rule. Act out the verb while you ask. Uncover the rule in C2. Read/choral-read the rule. Uncover the verb and read/choral-read. Continue for all/some rules on chart.
Say: *I have a favorite rule.*
Tape a smiley face next to "Listen to…."
Say: *When I listen, I learn a lot!*
Give each student a smiley face. Have students take turns taping a smiley face next to a favorite rule.

Substantial Support

Preparation: Use Light Support materials.
Say: *We've been learning about school rules.*
Uncover and point to the photo of "Raise your hand" on the chart.
Say: *This photo tells us about a school rule. Can you tell me what the rule is?*
Uncover C2. Point to/read the rule. Ask students to identify the verb in the rule. Remind students that a verb names an action. Raise your hand to demonstrate. Uncover "Raise" in C3. Point to/say "raise." Choral-read. Uncover/discuss more rules.

ELD.PI.K.1, ELD.PI.K.3, ELD.PI.K.9, ELD.PI.K.11

Write an Opinion about School Rules

(10 MIN.) W.K.1, W.K.8, SL.K.1a, SL.K.1b, L.K.1a, L.K.1b

Engage Thinking

Remind students that they have learned about how different rules help them at school.

Ask: *How do rules help you at school?*

Explain that today you would like students to talk about which school rule they think is the most important. Remind students that when they tell what they think, they are giving their opinion. When they give their opinion, they should give a reason telling why they think that way.

Collaborative Conversation: Partners

Tell students that before writing, you would like them to turn and talk to a partner briefly. Ask them to talk about which school rule they think is the most important. Remind them that when they tell their opinion, they should give a reason to back it up. Model how to do this.

Sample modeling: *When I tell my partner my opinion about the most important school rule, I say, "I think the most important school rule is to show respect because you want to treat your classmates well." Notice that I included a reason for my opinion. When you speak to your partner, you can use that same sentence frame:* I think the most important school rule is _____ because _____.

Write the sentence frame for students. Allow one minute for partner discussion. Then bring students together and ask volunteers to share the opinions they discussed.

Write as a Group

Collaborate with students to agree on an opinion and supporting reason to write. Rehearse the sentence orally and model how to write it. As you guide the writing, include at least one verb. Actively engage students in the writing process by thinking aloud and/or prompting them with questions. For example:

- *What do I need to do when I start the first word in the sentence?*
- *What is the first (last) letter in the word _____?*
- *Is there a better word we can use here? What is it?*
- *What punctuation mark will we write at the end of the sentence?*
- *Is there anything we want to change in our sentences?*

> **Sample Shared Writing**
> We think the most important school rule is to pay attention because this is one of the best ways to learn. Listen to your teacher and walk in the halls are also important things to do in school.

Build Language: Verbs

Circle a verb in your sample writing. Tell students that this word is a verb. Remind students that a verb is a word that names an action. Ask volunteers to use each of the following verbs in an oral sentence: **run, walk, sit, stand.**

☑ Write Independently

Direct students to draw the school rule they think is most important. Encourage them to write a label for their picture. Then ask them to give a reason for their opinion.

Small-Group Differentiated Instruction (15 MIN. per Group)

Meet with Small Groups

Select appropriate small-group reading titles or reinforcement activities based on students' needs. See the Small-Group Instructional Planner for titles that support a range of instructional reading levels within the unit topic. Remind students to apply what they learned in the core lessons to their small-group reading experiences.

Say: *As you listen to texts in your small groups today, think about how the illustrations help you understand the text. Remember that sometimes illustrations can give you more information about what is described in the text.*

Whole-Group Reflect and Share

Bring the class back together. Ask volunteers to tell how the illustrations and the text were connected in some of their small-group texts. Encourage students to share any additional information the illustrations provided.

W.K.1 Use a combination of drawing, dictating, and writing to compose opinion pieces in which they tell a reader the topic or the name of the book they are writing about and state an opinion or preference about the topic or book (e.g., My favorite book is...)., **W.K.8** With guidance and support from adults, recall information from experiences or gather information from provided sources to answer a question., **SL.K.1a** Follow agreed-upon rules for discussions (e.g., listening to others and taking turns speaking about the topics and texts under discussion)., **SL.K.1b** Continue a conversation through multiple exchanges., **L.K.1a** Print many upper- and lowercase letters., **L.K.1b** Use frequently occurring nouns and verbs.

Focus Skill: m/m/ (20 MIN.) RF.K.2d, RF.K.3a, RF.K.3c

Phonological Awareness: Phoneme Isolation

Model/Practice

Say the words **man, mitt,** and **sit.** Have students repeat the words. Ask students if they hear the same sound at the beginning of each word. Have them identify the word that starts with a different sound. Then have them identify the /**m**/ sound at the beginning of the other two words.

Say the words **Sam, book,** and **beam.** Have students repeat the words. Ask students if they hear the same sound at the end of each word. Have them identify the word that ends with a different sound. Then have them identify the /**m**/ sound at the end of the other two words.

Repeat the process with the words **made, map, sat; mind, find, map; farm.**

Letter-Sound Correspondences

Review m/m/

Display letter card **m.**

Say: *This is the letter **m.** The letter m stands for the /**m**/ sound you hear at the beginning of **magnet** and the end of **drum.***

Read the poem "School Rules." Have students identify the letter **m** at the beginning or the end of words by coming up and tracing the letter **m** with their finger as the rest of the class writes the letter **m** in the air.

Picture Sort m/m/ (iELD)

Model

Place picture cards **monkey** and **yam** next to each other in the pocket chart. Point to the monkey.

Say: *The letter **m** stands for the /**m**/ sound you hear at the beginning of **monkey.***

Point to the yam.

Say: *The letter **m** stands for the /**m**/ sound you hear at the end of **yam.***

Hold up the picture card for drum.

Say: *This is a picture of a drum. **drum** ends with the /**m**/ sound like **yam.** I'll place the picture of the drum under the yam.*

Practice: Show students picture cards **map, jam, man, milk.** Have students sort the pictures by placing them in the correct column for initial or final **m.**

High-Frequency Words

Review: I Display the high-frequency word card **I.** Have students read the word. Have students identify the five times the word **I** appears in the poem.

RF.K.2d Isolate and pronounce the initial, medial vowel, and final sounds (phonemes) in three-phoneme (consonant-vowel-consonant, or CVC) words. (This does not include CVCs ending with /l/, /r/, or /x/.), **RF.K.3a** Demonstrate basic knowledge of letter-sound correspondences by producing the primary or most frequent sound for each consonant., **RF.K.3c** Read common high-frequency words by sight (e.g., the, of, to, you, she, my, is, are, do, does).

Student Objectives

I will be able to:
- Isolate initial and final /**m**/.
- Practice letter-sound correspondence **m/m/.**
- Sort picture names with initial and final /**m**/.
- Read high-frequency word: **I.**

Additional Materials

- Letter card: **m**

Weekly Presentation
- Picture cards: **drum, jam, man, map, milk, monkey, yam**
- High-frequency word card: **I**

Integrated ELD

Light Support

Preparation: Gather **m** picture cards; large **m** card; enlarged copy of "School Rules" poem.

Hold up the **m** card. Hold up an initial-letter **m** word card (e.g., man). Read the word. Trace an **m** shape in the air. Choral-read and trace with the students. Do the same for one more card. Hold up a card with a word with a final letter **m.** Use the same speak/trace steps as above. Point out that this word ends with **m.** Hold up a bright green marker. Ask for a volunteer to come up and circle an **m** in the poem. Point to the **m** and ask the class if the **m** sound is at the beginning of the word or at the end of the word. Choral-read the word while you underline the **m** in red.

Moderate Support

Preparation: Use Light Support material.

Follow Light Support activity until, "Hold up a bright green marker...." Hold up a bright green marker. Ask for a volunteer to come up and circle an **m** in the poem. Point to the **m** and ask the class if the **m** sound is at the beginning of the word or at the end of the word. Choral-read the word and underline the **m** in red.

Substantial Support

Preparation: Use Light Support material.

Hold up the **m** card. Hold up an initial-letter **m** word card (e.g., man). Read the word. Trace an **m** shape in the air. Choral-read and trace with the students. Do the same for one more card. Hold up a card with a word with a final letter **m.** Use the same speak/trace steps as above. Point out that this word ends with **m.**

ELD.P1.K.I

Read Aloud and Shared Reading

(20 MIN.) RI.K.1, RI.K.10, RF.K.3a, SL.K.1a, SL.K.1b, L.K.1b

Read Aloud

To support the unit concept, use one of the Read-Aloud Handbook selections for Unit 1. As you read, model the metacognitive strategy for the unit, Ask Questions, guided by the samples provided. You may also wish to select a favorite read-aloud from your classroom or school library. To support the unit concept, use one of the suggested titles for Unit 1.

Shared Reading (iELD)

Reread the Informational Text

First reading. Read aloud the informational text fluently and expressively, pointing under each word.

Reread for Fluency: Accuracy/Self-Correct. Discuss what would happen if a reader added, skipped, or changed words while reading. As you read the text aloud, demonstrate adding, omitting, or changing some words and then self-correcting. Lead students to understand that accurate reading makes the meaning of the text more clear. Together, choral-read the text accurately at a steady pace. Provide corrective feedback and/or validate students' efforts.

Build Concepts: Following Rules

Pose questions to connect the informational text to the unit concept. For example:

* *Why do you think the author wrote the words "sit quietly" and "listen quietly"?*
* *Do you think listening to one another is important? Why or why not?*

Review Language: Verbs

Remind students that a verb is a word that names an action. Read aloud the first sentence and highlight the two verbs, **talks** and **pay.** Then read aloud the second sentence and ask volunteers to name the two verbs. (**sit, listen**) Call on other volunteers to use the verbs **sit** and **listen** in oral sentences.

Review: Final m

Highlight the word **from** in the last sentence. Have students read the word aloud with you. Ask volunteers to name the letter at the end of **from** and the sound the letter **m** stands for.

RI.K.1 With prompting and support, ask and answer questions about key details in a text., **RI.K.10** Actively engage in group reading activities with purpose and understanding., **RF.K.3a** Demonstrate basic knowledge of letter-sound correspondences by producing the primary or most frequent sound for each consonant., **SL.K.1a** Follow agreed-upon rules for discussions (e.g., listening to others and taking turns speaking about the topics and texts under discussion)., **SL.K.1b** Continue a conversation through multiple exchanges., **L.K.1b** Use frequently occurring nouns and verbs.

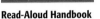

Read-Aloud Handbook   **Shared Reading Vol. 1, p. 5 "Rules for Talking and Listening"**

Student Objectives

I will be able to:
* Read along with the appropriate accuracy.
* Answer questions about rules for talking and listening.
* Use verbs in my writing.
* Identify final **m.**

(iELD) Integrated ELD

Light Support
Preparation: Poster-size copy of "Rules for Talking and Listening"; a large piece of paper with a question mark drawn inside a thought bubble. Add worksheets of the sentence-completion frames.
Read the title slowly.
Say: *I want to learn the rules for talking and listening. How can I learn the rules? Reading text accurately makes the meaning clear. Let's read this poem together accurately.*
Choral-read slowly. Act out the ideas. Put the poster of the poem and the sentence-completion poster side-by-side. Read the first frame.
Think aloud: *Hmm. I'm going to look and read carefully.*
Read the first two sentences in the poem aloud, pointing to each word. Say/point to the word **sit.** Pass out worksheets. Ask students to write **sit** on their worksheets in the appropriate location.
Have students complete the worksheet.

Moderate Support
Preparation: Use Light Support materials. Write the sentence-completion frames on a large sheet of paper. Follow Light Support activity until, "Pass out worksheets...." Write **sit** in the first sentence frame. Ask the group for help to complete the frames.

Substantial Support
Preparation: Use Light Support materials. Follow Light Support activity until, "Think aloud: Hmm."
Say: *Let's find out how accurately we read. Listen carefully and help me fill in the verb.*
When someone talks, we _____ quietly.
When someone talks, we _____ carefully.

ELD.PI.K.1, ELD.PI.K.5, ELD.PI.K.6, ELD.PI.K.9, ELD.PI.K.10, ELD.PI.K.11, ELD.PI.K.12

What Are Some Rules at School?

Identify and Use Text Features (10 MIN.)

RI.K.1, RI.K.5, SL.K.1a, SL.K.1b, SL.K.2, SL.K.6

Engage Thinking

Remind students that they have learned about a glossary and how readers use it. Tell them that today they will learn about using more parts of a book.

Ask: *What parts of a book do you know about?*

Model

Display page 6. Point to and read "Chapter 1" and the chapter title, "Rules Help You Learn." Model how readers use chapter titles.

Sample modeling: *This is the chapter title. Before I read this chapter, I read the chapter title and think about it. The chapter title is like the title of a book: it tells what the chapter will be about. When I read this chapter title, I know the chapter will tell about rules that help students learn.*

Repeat the procedure for Chapter 2.

Point to and read the caption on page 6. Model how readers use captions.

Sample modeling: *This is a caption. Photos often have a caption that tells what is happening in the photo. From this caption, I learn that this student is following one school rule by doing her homework.*

Point to and read the sidebar on page 7. Model how readers use sidebars.

Sample modeling: *Sometimes authors include extra text in a box on the page. This is called a sidebar. In this sidebar, there is a question for the reader. The author wants the reader to think about rules at his or her own school.*

Write each text feature and its purpose in a two-column chart.

Text Feature	Purpose
chapter title	tells what the chapter is about
caption	explains what the photo shows
sidebar	asks for or gives more information about the topic

Sample Text Features Chart

Guided Practice (iELD)

Ask students to locate the chapter titles on pages 10 and 12. Read aloud each title and ask students to explain what information each chapter title gives.

Display page 9. Ask students to locate the caption. Read aloud the caption. Ask students to explain what information the caption gives. Then ask students to locate the sidebar on page 9. Read it aloud. Ask students to explain how the sidebar asks for information from the reader.

Repeat the procedure for the caption and sidebar on page 11.

☑ Show Your Knowledge

Point to several chapter titles, captions, and sidebars in the text. Ask volunteers to name each feature and tell how it helps readers learn more about the topic of the book.

(iELD) Integrated ELD

Light Support

Preparation: Create a chart on a large sheet of paper (Column 1: Write "book title," "chapter title," "caption," and "sidebar" in separate rows. Column 2: Leave blank); large sticky notes, each with one vocabulary word.

Hold up the front cover of *What Are Some Rules at School?* Remind students that they have been learning about the parts of a book. Point to the title of the book. Ask/prompt for the words "book title."

Say: *Yes! This large text on the cover is the book title. It tells us what the book is about. [Read the title.] Now I know what this book is about!*

Put the "book title" sticky note next to the title and hold up the book.

Ask: *Do you see this word here? [Point to the chart and prompt for the correct word.]*

Underline "book title" on the chart in green.

Say: I don't want to forget how the book title helps me.

Show the class the remaining sticky notes. Read each word together. Show students an example of the book part. Say what the book part "tells" the reader.

Give each student a set of sticky notes. Have students place the notes in their copies of the book.

Have student volunteers show their work. Comment and reinforce as you complete the chart for each book part that volunteers identify. Choral-read the chart.

Moderate Support

Preparation: Use Light Support materials.

Follow Light Support activity until, "Show the class the...."

Show the class the remaining sticky notes. Read each word together. Show students an example of the book part. Say what the book part "tells" the reader.

Divide the class into small groups. Give each group one sticky note. Have the students work together to put their sticky notes on the book in an appropriate spot.

Have each group show the class where their sticky notes were placed.

Wrap up: Complete the prepared chart.

Substantial Support

Preparation: Use Light Support materials.

Follow Light Support Activity until, "Show the class the...."

Write the definition in C2, Row 1. Read and choral-read the definition. Complete the chart using the steps above.

ELD.PI.K.1, ELD.PI.K.3, ELD.PI.K.5, ELD.PI.K.6, ELD.PI.K.9, ELD.PI.K.11, ELD.PI.K.12

RI.K.1 With prompting and support, ask and answer questions about unknown words in a text., **RI.K.5** Identify the front cover, back cover, and title page of a book., **SL.K.1a** Follow agreed-upon rules for discussions (e.g., listening to others and taking turns speaking about the topics and texts under discussion)., **SL.K.1b** Continue a conversation through multiple exchanges., **SL.K.2** Confirm understanding of a text read aloud or information presented orally or through other media by asking and answering questions about key details and requesting clarification if something is not understood., **SL.K.6** Speak audibly and express thoughts, feelings, and ideas clearly.

What Are Some Rules at School?

Student Objectives

I will be able to:
- Write a list about ways to show respect.
- Use verbs in my writing.

(iELD) Integrated ELD

Light Support

Preparation: Large copy of page 10 and page 16 in *What Are Some Rules at School?* and large cards with verbs related to showing respect (**help, listen, wait, share**). Point to/read "Rules Teach Respect" on page 10.

Say: *We learned that following rules shows respect. But what is respect?* Show large copy of page 16. Remind students what a glossary is.

Say: *The glossary tells us what respect is! [Read/choral-read the definition.] What can we do to show care and concern?* Remind students that a verb is a word that names an action. Hold up and read a verb card (e.g., listen).

Say: *I can use this verb to show respect by listening to my friends. Who else can you listen to [e.g., teacher]?* Write simple sentences on the board for each verb. Divide the students into small groups. Give each group one verb card. Read the verb with the group. Check for comprehension. Have each group come up with two ways their verb can help people show respect. Write the idea on the list you started. Choral-read each idea before going on to the next.

Moderate Support

Preparation: Use Light Support prep. Follow Light Support activity until, "Divide students into small groups."

Divide the students into small work groups. Give each group one verb card. Read the verb with the group. Check for comprehension. Have each group come up with one way its verb can help people show respect. Choral-read each idea.

Substantial Support

Preparation: Use Light Support prep. Follow Light Support activity until, "Divide students into small groups."

ELD.PI.K.1, ELD.PI.K.3, ELD.PI.K.10, ELD.PII.K.2

Write a List about Respect (10 MIN.) W.K.2, W.K.8, L.K.1a, L.K.1b, SL.K.1a, SL.K.1b

Engage Thinking

Reread the Chapter 3 title and pages 10–11. Point out that schools have rules to teach respect.

Ask: *What is respect? How do you show respect to one another in school?*

Explain that today you will write a class list about respect.

💬 Collaborative Conversation: Share Ideas

Tell students that before writing, you would like them to turn and talk to a partner briefly. Ask them to talk about why and how we show respect to others in school. Model how to do this.

Sample modeling: *When I tell my partner about why and how we show respect, I say, "You show respect when you listen to others." When you speak to your partner, you can use that same sentence frame:* You show respect when you _____.

Write the sentence frame for students. Allow partners one minute for discussion. Then bring students together and ask volunteers to share their ideas.

Write as a Group

Collaborate with students to agree on ideas to write in the list. Rehearse each item orally and model how to write it. As you guide the writing, include at least one verb. Actively engage students in the writing process by thinking aloud and/or prompting them with questions. For example:

- *Who can show me where to start writing on the paper?*
- *How do we spell _____? We know that word.*
- *Are there any words we could add to make our writing better?*
- *Let's reread our list. Are there any ideas we want to change or add?*

Sample Shared Writing

You show respect when you:

take turns speaking.

raise your hand.

listen to your neighbor

walk in the halls

Build Language: Verbs

Circle a verb in your sample writing. Point out that this word is a verb. Remind students that a verb is a word that names an action. Ask volunteers to use each of the following verbs in an oral sentence: **speak, listen, wait, show.**

☑ Write Independently

Ask students to draw and label a picture to show how they show respect at school. Invite them to label and share their picture with the class.

Small-Group Differentiated Instruction (15 MIN. per Group)

Meet with Small Groups

Select small-group reading titles or activities based on students' needs. See the Small-Group Instructional Planner for titles that support a range of instructional levels within the unit topic. Remind students to apply skills and strategies they learned to their small-group reading experiences

Say: *As you listen to texts in your small groups today, look for chapter titles, captions, and sidebars. Remember to use these features to help you understand more about the text.*

Whole-Group Reflect and Share

Bring the class back together. Ask volunteers to tell about a text feature they noticed in their small-group text. Encourage them to tell what they learned from that text feature.

W.K.2 Use a combination of drawing, dictating, and writing to compose informative/explanatory texts in which they name what they are writing about and supply some information about the topic., **W.K.8** With guidance and support from adults, recall information from experiences or gather information from provided sources to answer a question., **L.K.1a** Print many upper- and lowercase letters., **L.K.1b** Use frequently occurring nouns and verbs., **SL.K.1a** Follow agreed-upon rules for discussions (e.g., listening to others and taking turns speaking about the topics and texts under discussion)., **SL.K.1b** Continue a conversation through multiple exchanges.

Pre-Decodable Reader: I

Student Objectives

I will be able to:
- Blend onset and rime.
- Read high-frequency word: **I.**
- Read pre-decodable text.

Additional Materials

- Pre-decodable reader: *I*

Weekly Presentation
- Picture cards: **man, map, mat, mitt, mop**
- High-frequency word card: *I*

Monitor Student Reading of Connected Text

As students chorally read the pre-decodable text and answer questions, ask these questions:

Are students able to . . .
- ❏ read the new high-frequency word with automaticity?
- ❏ demonstrate comprehension of the text by answering text-based questions?

Based on your observations, you may wish to support students' fluency, automaticity, and comprehension with additional decodable reading practice during intervention time.

Focus Skill: m/m/ (20 MIN.) RI.K.1, RI.K.10, RF.K.2c, RF.K.3c, RF.K.4

Phonological Awareness: Onset and Rime Blending

Model/Practice

Segment the word **mad** into its onset and rime: /**m**/ /**ad**/. Have students blend the sounds and say the word. Repeat with the words **mail** and **mask.** Then say the word **meat.**

Ask: *What is the onset or beginning sound? What is the rest of the word?*

Blend the sounds /**m**/ and /**eat**/ and say the word with the class.

Display the picture card **map.** Have students name the picture.

Ask: *What is the onset? What is the rest of the word? Let's blend the sounds /**m**/ and /**ap**/ and say the word:* **map.**

Repeat with picture cards: **man, mitt, mop, mat.**

High-Frequency Words

Review: *I*

Write the word **I.** Remind students that this is the word they have been practicing so that they can read it quickly. Have students read the word aloud several times.

Hold up the high-frequency word card **I** and call on individual students to quickly read the word. Then have the student use the word in an oral sentence. Have the other students clap when they hear the word **I.**

Pre-Decodable Reader: *I*

Introduce the Book

Point to the book's title, *I.* Have students read the word.

Ask: *What do you see on the cover? What are the children doing?*

Read the Book

Display the rebuses on pages 2-8 and discuss what each one stands for. Students should chorally read the story the first time through. Have them read the first sentence aloud so you can check their reading. Have students continue to read the high-frequency word quickly in the sentences.

Connect Phonics to Comprehension

When students have finished reading, ask:

- *What are some things that the children like to do?*
- *What **m** word is pictured on the inside back cover?*

Turn to a partner and retell the story.

RI.K.1 With prompting and support, ask and answer questions about unknown words in a text., **RI.K.10** Actively engage in group reading activities with purpose and understanding., **RF.K.2c** Blend and segment onsets and rimes of single-syllable spoken words., **RF.K.3c** Read common high-frequency words by sight (e.g., the, of, to, you, she, my, is, are, do, does)., **RF.K.4** Read emergent-reader texts with purpose and understanding.

Read Aloud and Shared Reading

(20 MIN.) RI.K.10, RF.K.3a, RF.K.3c, SL.K.1a, SL.K.1b, L.K.1b

Read Aloud

To support the unit concept, use one of the Read-Aloud Handbook selections for Unit 1. As you read, model the metacognitive strategy for the unit, Ask Questions, guided by the samples provided. You may also wish to select a favorite read-aloud from your classroom or school library. To support the unit concept, use one of the suggested titles for Unit 1.

Shared Reading (iELD)

Reread the Poem

First reading. Read aloud the informational text fluently and expressively, pointing under each word.

Reread for Fluency: Accuracy/Self-Correct. Model for students how to scan a text for unfamiliar words. Decode and discuss the meaning of any words students identified. Pronounce the words together several times. Then choral read the text, slowing the rate at unfamiliar words and allowing students to self-correct errors in pronunciations. Provide corrective feedback and/or validate students' efforts.

Build Concepts: Following Rules

Pose questions to connect the informational text to the unit concept. For example:

- *We walk in the classroom but where else it is important to walk in our school?*
- *How do you help clean up the classroom? Why is this important?*

Review Phonics: Initial and Final m

Highlight the word **my** in the first line. Have students read the word aloud with you. Ask volunteers to name the letter at the beginning of **my** and the sound the letter **m** stands for. Do the same for **me** in the last line. Use a similar procedure to have students identify the final **m** in **classroom.**

Review High-Frequency Words: *I*

Tell students that this text contains some words they have learned. Point to the previously-taught high-frequency word **I** in the third sentence. Ask students to turn to a partner and tell their partner the high-frequency word. Remind students to look for high-frequency words they know as they read a new text.

Read-Aloud Handbook   **Shared Reading Vol. 1, p. 4 "School Rules"**

Student Objectives

I will be able to:
- Read along with accuracy.
- Answer questions about listening to your partner.
- Identify initial and final **m.**
- Recognize the high-frequency word **I.**

(iELD) Integrated ELD

Light Support
Preparation: Enlarged copy of "School Rules"; large /**m**/ card; picture of a stop sign for each student. Add worksheets (poem in which all "**m**'s" are replaced with a short line to indicate the missing letter).
Remind students they have been learning about the letter **m.** Say the "mm" sound and have students repeat it. Read the poem once. Point to and emphasize each **m.** Divide students into four groups. Select one group to stand and choral-read the first line of the poem. After each group choral-reads a line, have students who are at their desks write in the missing **m**'s for the corresponding line on their worksheets.

Moderate Support
Preparation: Use Light Support prep.
Follow Light Support activity until, "Divide students into four groups." Divide students into four groups. Select one group to stand and choral-read the first line of the poem. After each choral-read, tell the other groups to listen carefully and hold up their stop signs when they hear the "mm" sound. Choral-read the line again. Ask a student in the group that is reading to underline the **m.**

Substantial Support
Preparation: Use Light Support prep.
Follow Light Support activity until, "Divide students into four groups." Point to/read the poem title. Hold up the /**m**/ card. Reread the first line of the poem. Point to the **m** in **classroom.** Read alone. Hold up a stop sign when you come to **classroom.** Repeat the word, emphasizing the final **m** sound. Underline the **m** and remind students the last letter is an **m.** Read the second line. Choral-read. Point to the **m** in **my.** Repeat the activity with **m** in **my.**

ELD.PI.K.1, ELD.PI.K.5, ELD.PI.K.6, ELD.PI.K.9, ELD.PI.K.10, ELD.PI.K.11, ELD.PI.K.12

Compare and Contrast Two Texts on the Same Topic (20 MIN.) RI.K.1, RI.K.9, SL.K.3, SL.K.4, SL.K.6

"Let's Play by the Rules!" and *What Are Some Rules at School?*

Student Objectives

I will be able to:
- Answer questions about following the rules.
- Recognize similarities and differences between two texts about understanding rules.

Additional Materials

Weekly Presentation
- Compare and Contrast Chart

Engage Thinking

Display "Let's Play by the Rules!" and *What Are Some Rules at School?* Remind students that they know both of these texts very well and now they are going to think about both texts together. They will think about how the two texts are alike and how they are different. Review with students that when they think about how two or more texts are similar to each other, they are comparing the texts. When they think about how two or more texts are different from each other, they are contrasting them. Display a pen and a pencil (or crayon).

Ask: *Can you tell me how these two things are the same? How are they different?*

Model

Use a three-column chart to create a compare and contrast chart for "Let's Play by the Rules!" and *What Are Some Rules at School?* Review that in the first and third columns you will list ways the two texts are different. In the middle column, you will list ways in which the two texts are similar. Use think-alouds such as the following samples to model how you compare and contrast texts.

Sample modeling: *To compare, I will think about how these two texts are alike. When I look at "Let's Play by the Rules!" I see that it has photos with captions.* What Are Some Rules at School? *also has photos with captions. That is a similarity, or comparison, between the two texts. They both have photos with captions. I will write that in the middle column of the chart.*

Sample modeling: *To contrast, I will think about how these two texts are different. I know that there are sidebars in* What Are Some Rules at School? *I look to see if* Let's Play by the Rules! *has sidebars. It does not. That is one way these two texts are different. I will write that down in the chart as a contrast.*

Guided Practice

Use directive and corrective prompts as needed to guide students to:

Compare and contrast genre and topics.

- *"Let's Play by the Rules!" is an informational text. Does that make it the same kind of text or a different kind of text than* What Are Some Rules at School?
- *What are "Let's Play by the Rules!" and* What Are Some Rules at School? *both about? What kind of rules is "Let's Play by the Rules!" about? What kind of rules is* What Are Some Rules at School? *about? Does that make the texts the same or different?*

Compare and contrast text features in the texts.

- What Are Some Rules at School? *has chapters. Does "Let's Play by the Rules!" have chapters?*
- What Are Some Rules at School? *has a table of contents, a glossary, and an index. Does "Let's Play by the Rules!" have these parts? How is it different?*

If necessary, continue to model how you think about the comparisons and contrasts. Collaborate with students to complete the chart. Reread the comparisons and contrasts together.

Let's Play by the Rules!	Both Texts	What Are Some Rules at School?
No sidebars	Photos with captions	Sidebars
About rules for team sports	Informational text	About rules at school
No chapters		Chapters
No table of contents, glossary, index		Table of contents, glossary, index

Compare and Contrast Chart

 Show Your Knowledge

Ask partners to take turns telling each other one way that the two selections are similar and different. Remind students to use complete sentences, such as *These texts are similar because _____. These texts are different because _____.*

iELD Integrated ELD

Light Support
Preparation: Select five text features most familiar to your students. Select two that are alike in the relevant texts, one that is different (e.g., photos, photo captions, glossary); write each word on a large sticky note; large 2-column poster (C1 header: Alike, C2 header: Different).

Hold up the cover of *What Are Some Rules at School?* Read the title and note that this is a familiar text. Hold up "Let's Play by the Rules!" Read the title and note that this is a familiar text. Ask if both texts are about the same main topic. Prompt and reinforce.
Read/choral-read another sticky note. Look through your text and ask students to look through theirs.
Say: *Yes! Both are about rules! The books are alike. Both books are about the same topic: rules! [Point to the C1 on the poster. Read "alike." Repeat definition and choral-read the word.] I'm going to write "same topic" under "Alike."*
Hold up and read the "photos" sticky note. Hold up one text at a time and look through it with students. For each, ask if there are photos in each text. Reinforce "Yes!" both times.
Say: *You told me there are photos in both texts. That's another way the texts are alike.*
Place the "photos" sticky note in C1 and explain why. Continue to show/ask/define with the remaining two sticky notes.
Ask students if the text feature is in both texts. Prompt and reinforce.
Ask for a volunteer to place the sticky note for the feature in the correct column.
Continue as above with the remaining notes.

Moderate Support
Preparation: Use Light Support prep, but select four text features.
Follow Light Support activity.

Substantial Support
Preparation: Use Light Support prep, but select three text features.
Follow Light Support activity.

ELD.PI.K.1, ELD.PI.K.3, ELD.PI.K.6, ELD.PI.K.9, ELD.PI.K.11, ELD.PI.K.12, ELD.PII.K.1, ELD.PII.K.2, ELD.PII.K.3, ELD. PII.K.4, ELD.PII.K.5

RI.K.1 With prompting and support, ask and answer questions about unknown words in a text., **RI.K.9** With prompting and support, identify basic similarities in and differences between two texts on the same topic (e.g., in illustrations, descriptions, or procedures)., **SL.K.3** Ask and answer questions in order to seek help, get information, or clarify something that is not understood., **SL.K.4** Describe familiar people, places, things, and events and, with prompting and support, provide additional detail., **SL.K.6** Speak audibly and express thoughts, feelings, and ideas clearly.

Mentor Read-Aloud Topic
Introduction pp. 2-3

Student Objectives

I will be able to:
- Plan a response to the essential question about rules.
- Write a first draft as a class activity about rules.

Additional Materials

Weekly Presentation
- Planning Guide

iELD Integrated ELD

Light Support
Preparation: Large sheet of paper titled, "Our Ideas about Rules." Below the title, write "Reasons." Leave space, then write "Rules"; large cards with concepts from *What Are Some Rules at School?* (e.g., **reasons:** show respect, be safe; **rules:** walk, listen).
Point to and read "Our Ideas about Rules."
Explain that authors need reasons for what they write. Ask students for their reasons to have rules. Prompt with "reason" cards as needed. Below "Reasons," on the large sheet, write, "Rules help us [complete with student/card ideas]."
After writing the first reason, divide students into work groups. Give each work group two "reason" and two "rule" cards. Have the group come up with a related reason and report to the class. Write their reasons on the sheet. Repeat with "rule" cards.

Moderate Support
Preparation: Use Light Support prep.
Follow Light Support activity until, "After writing the first reason...."
Divide students into work groups. Give each work group one "reason" card. Have the group come up with a related reason and report to the class. Write their reasons on the sheet. Repeat with "rule" card.

Substantial Support
Preparation: Use Light Support prep.
Follow Light Support activity until, "After writing the first reason...." Use this procedure for three rules.

ELD.PI.K.1, ELD.PI.K.3, ELD.PI.K.10, ELD.PII.K.2

Plan and Draft a Response to the Essential Question (10 MIN.) W.K.2, W.K.5, W.K.8, SL.K.1a,

SL.K.1b, SL.K.3, SL.K.6, L.K.1a, L.K.1b

Engage Thinking

Display and reread the unit essential question. Explain to students that today you will plan and draft a response to the question. Remind students that the essential question does not have a right or wrong answer. Today they will think of a response to the question that they can support with evidence from the selections they have read.

Why do we have rules?

Plan iELD

Explain what happens in the planning stage of writing. Tell students that during this stage, writers think about ideas and organize them. Use a think-aloud to model how writers generate a response.

Sample modeling: *In the selections we read, we learned a lot about different kinds of rules. To answer the essential question, I think about why we need all those rules. Those rules help us to learn and to behave well towards one another. That is information I will include in my main idea statement.*

Display a blank planning guide and write your main idea statement. Then think aloud to model how writers support their ideas with reasons.

Sample modeling: *Now I need to give reasons to support, or back up, my main idea. I think about one way rules help us. Rules for playing team sports help us be team players. Rules make playing sports fair for everyone. By following rules at school, we are able to learn. We learn to take care of pets by following rules. Following rules is also a way for us to respect others, both at school and on sports teams.*

Add reasons to the planning guide. Then point out that your text will need a conclusion. Tell students that a conclusion is a way to wrap up, or end, the text. The conclusion usually tells the writer's main idea in different words.

Main Idea Statement:
We need rules so we can learn and be fair to others.
Supporting Details
Rules help us be good players. Rules help us learn at school. Rules help us learn how to care for pets. Rules help us be fair and respectful to others.
Conclusion:
We need rules to be good citizens.

Sample Planning Guide

Draft

Tell students that when writers draft, they just try to get their ideas on paper. They don't worry about spelling or punctuation at this time. Think aloud to model how you use the information on your planning guide to help you draft your response.

Sample modeling: *The first thing I write is a main idea statement. Then I will write reasons to support my main idea. I will include the reasons why we need rules.*

Sample Draft

We need rules so we can learn and be fair to others. With rules, we can be team players. With rules, we can learn at school. We can learn how to care for our pets by following rules. Rules help us be fair to others. Rules help us respect others. We need rules to be good citizens.

Write Independently

Ask students to draw a picture to show an idea they would include in the draft. Encourage them to write a label for their picture.

Small-Group Differentiated Instruction (15 MIN. per Group)

Meet with Small Groups

Select small-group reading titles or activities based on students' needs. See the Small-Group Instructional Planner for titles that support a range of instructional levels within the unit topic. Remind students to apply skills and strategies they learned to their small-group reading experiences.

Say: *Think about how the book in your small group you are listening to today adds to what you know about why we have rules to follow.*

Whole-Group Reflect and Share

Bring the class back together. Invite volunteers to share new ideas about following rules based on the texts they listened to.

W.K.2 Use a combination of drawing, dictating, and writing to compose informative/explanatory texts in which they name what they are writing about and supply some information about the topic., **W.K.5** With guidance and support from adults, respond to questions and suggestions from peers and add details to strengthen writing as needed., **W.K.8** With guidance and support from adults, recall information from experiences or gather information from provided sources to answer a question., **SL.K.1a** Follow agreed-upon rules for discussions (e.g., listening to others and taking turns speaking about the topics and texts under discussion)., **SL.K.1b** Continue a conversation through multiple exchanges., **SL.K.3** Ask and answer questions in order to seek help, get information, or clarify something that is not understood., **SL.K.6** Speak audibly and express thoughts, feelings, and ideas clearly., **L.K.1a** Print many upper- and lowercase letters., **L.K.1b** Use frequently occurring nouns and verbs.

Pre-Decodable Reader: *I*

Student Objectives

I will be able to:
- Categorize **/m/** words.
- Practice letter-sound correspondences for **m/m/**.
- Read previously taught high-frequency word: **I.**
- Write legibly.
- Read decodable text.

Additional Materials

- Pre-decodable reader: *I*
- Letter card: **m**

Weekly Presentation
- Picture cards: **cat, dog, drum, man, monkey, moon, mop, tiger**
- High-frequency word card: *I*

Focus Skill: m/m/ (20 MIN.) RI.K.1, RI.K.10, RF.K.2d, RF.K.3a, RF.K.3c, RF.K.4, L.K.1a

Phonological Awareness: Phoneme Categorization

Model

Say: *I will say three words. Which two words end with the same sound?* ***Swim, cap, farm. Swim*** *and* ***farm*** *end with the same sound, /m/.* ***Cap*** *does not end with the /m/ sound. It does not belong.*

Practice

Say: *Listen as I say some more words. Which words have the same sound at the end?*

Use the following words: ***name, Sam, hit; lamb, race, Kim; him, word, ham; gym, jam, Jake.***

Letter-Sound Correspondences

Review

Display letter card **m.**

Say: *This is the letter* ***m.*** *The letter* ***m*** *stands for /mmm/. What is the letter? What sound does this letter stand for?*

Place **m** in a pocket chart. Hold up the picture card **moon.**

Say: *This is a picture of the moon. The word* ***moon*** *begins with the /m/ sound. The letter* ***m*** *stands for the /m/ sound. I will put the picture of the moon under the letter* ***m.***

Hold up the picture card **tiger.**

Say: *This is a picture of a tiger. Does* ***tiger*** *begin with /m/? No,* ***tiger*** *does not belong under the letter* ***m.***

Continue with the following picture cards: **cat, mop, man, dog.**

Picture Sort m/m/

Review

Place the picture cards of the **monkey** and the **drum** next to each other in the pocket chart.

Say: *What sound is at the beginning of **monkey?** What letter stands for the /**m**/ sound at the beginning of a word? What is the sound at the end of **drum?** What letter stands for the /**m**/ sound at the end of a word?*

Then give each student two index cards.

Say: *On one of the cards, draw a picture of something whose name begins with /**m**/. On the other card, draw a picture of something whose name ends with /**m**/.*

When finished, have students sort their pictures .

Say: *What is the name of your picture? Is /**m**/ at the beginning of its name? Is /**m**/ at the end of its name? Place your picture in the pocket chart to show where /**m**/ is.*

High-Frequency Words (iELD)

Review: *I*

Write the word **I**. Have students spell the word. Then erase the word, say the word, and have students spell it on their own.

Decodable Text

Write the letters **M** and **m** and the word **I**. Then have volunteers name each letter and read the word.

M	m
I	

Pre-Decodable Reader: *I*

Reread

Have partners reread *I* together. Circulate and listen in. Note students' speed, accuracy, and intonation. Based on the group as a whole, provide some general feedback and validate successes. If students need additional practice to read the text, provide support during small-group reading instruction.

(iELD) Integrated ELD

Light Support
Preparation: Enlarged copy of the poem "School Rules." Add a worksheet of the poem for each student (replace **I**'s with _).
Point to and read the title of the poem.
Choral-read the poem. Point to the **I** each time you read the word.
Give each student a worksheet. Choral-read each sentence. Underline the **I** in green on the large sheet. Ask students to fill in the missing **I** on their worksheets. Use the same procedure for each sentence with an **I**.

Moderate Support
Preparation: Use Light Support prep. Point to and read the title of the poem.
Choral-read the poem. Point to the **I** each time you read the word.
Say: *Now I am going to ask you questions. Every answer has to start with* **I***! Do you run in the classroom?* Prompt with, "No," then pause. Point to yourself/ mouth the word **I**. Point to "don't run in my classroom" and read/choral-read with students.
Use the same procedure for lines 2 and 3 (e.g., *What do you do when you want to talk? What do you do when you're done working?*).
Complete the poem in this way, and then choral-read the poem, underlining each **I** in green as you read.

Substantial Support
Preparation: Use Light Support prep.
Point to and read the title of the poem.
Say: *I [point to yourself] see children following the rules in this photo. I [point to yourself] can also read about how they follow the rules. Do you know where I look in the text to find out? [Prompt/reinforce]*
Read the poem. Point to the **I** each time you read the word. Tell students they are going to read the **I** now without you.
Choral-read. In the first line, point to/read the initial **I**. Point to, but do not say, the second **I** in the line (_ walk.). As you point to and drop out of saying each *I*, place your hand over your mouth as a prompt.
Complete the poem in this way, and then choral-read the poem, underlining each **I** in green as you read.

ELD.PI.K.5, ELD.PI.K.6, ELD.PI.K.8, ELD.PIII.K.3c

RI.K.1 With prompting and support, ask and answer questions about unknown words in a text., **RI.K.10** Actively engage in group reading activities with purpose and understanding., **RF.K.2d** Demonstrate understanding of spoken words, syllables, and sounds (phonemes). Isolate and pronounce the initial, medial vowel, and final sounds (phonemes) in three-phoneme (consonant-vowel-consonant, or CVC) words. (This does not include CVCs ending with /l/, /r/, or /x/.), **RF.K.3a** Demonstrate basic knowledge of letter-sound correspondences by producing the primary or most frequent sound for each consonant., **RF.K.3c** Read common high-frequency words by sight (e.g., the, of, to, you, she, my, is, are, do, does)., **RF.K.4** Read emergent-reader texts with purpose and understanding., **L.K.1a** Print many upper- and lowercase letters.

Week 3 Skills at a Glance

	Day 1	Day 2
Reading Mini-Lessons	**Mentor Read-Alouds:** Topic Introduction, pp. 2–3 **Build Knowledge and Review Week 1 Strategies (10 Min.), p. 80** RL.K.3, RL.K.7, SL.K.1a, SL.K.1b, SL.K.2 **Read-Aloud Handbook** **Shared Readings:** "No Dogs Allowed in School," p. 6 **Read Aloud and Shared Reading (20 Min.), p. 81** RL.K.10, RL.K.10a, RL.K.10b, RF.K.1b, RF.K.3a • Fluency: Prosody/Expression • Build Concepts: Following Rules • Review Print Concepts: Print Conveys Meaning • Review Phonics: Initial and Final m Rules Are Cool **"Rules Are Cool": Listen and Retell Key Events (10 Min.), p. 82** RL.K.1, RL.K.2, RL.K.5, RL.K.10, RL.K.10a, RL.K.10b, SL.K.1a, SL.K.1b, SL.K.3	**Read-Aloud Handbook** **Shared Readings:** "No Dogs Allowed in School," p. 6 **Read Aloud and Shared Reading (20 Min.), p. 88** RL.K.10, RF.K.3b, RF.K.3c, SL.K.1a, SL.K.1b • Fluency: Prosody/Expression • Build Concepts: Following Rules • Review Phonics: Short a Rules Are Cool **Make Connections Between Illustrations and Events in the Text (10 Min.), p. 89** RL.K.1, RL.K.7, SL.K.3 **Identify the Author and Illustrator and Define Their Roles (10 Min.), p. 90** RL.K.1, RL.K.6, SL.K.3
Writing Mini-Lessons	**Write Key Events (10 Min.), p. 84** W.K.2, W.K.8, SL.K.1a, SL.K.1b, L.K.1b • Build Language: Nouns	**Write an Opinion (10 Min.), p. 92** W.K.1, W.K.8, SL.K.1a, SL.K.1b, L.K.1a, L.K.1b • Build Language: Nouns
Phonics Mini-Lessons	**Focus Skill: a/a/ (20 Min.), p. 86** RF.K.2d, RF.K.3a, RF.K.2c, L.K.1a • Phonological Awareness: Phoneme Isolation • High-Frequency Words: *like, I*	**Focus Skill: m/m/ (20 Min.), p. 94** RF.K.2d, RF.K.3a, RF.K.2c, L.K.1a • Phonological Awareness: Phoneme Isolation • High-Frequency Words: *like*

Extended Read 2: "Rules Are Cool!"

Realistic Fiction

Quantitative	Lexile® 500L
Qualitative Analysis of Text Complexity	

Purpose and Levels of Meaning ❶
• Story purpose is simple: to show the importance of rules at school.

Structure ❷
• Narrative structure is sequential, with information conveyed logically and clearly.

Language Conventionality and Clarity ❶
• Sentences are simple, language is colloquial, and all vocabulary is familiar.

Knowledge Demands ❶
• No prior knowledge is needed for understanding.

Day 3	Day 4	Day 5
Read-Aloud Handbook **Shared Readings:** "Five Little Monkeys," p. 7 **Read Aloud and Shared Reading (20 Min.), p. 96** RL.K.10, RL.K.10a, RL.K.10b, RF.K.1b, RF.K.3a • Fluency: Prosody/Expression • Build Unit Concepts: Following Rules • Review Print Concepts: Print Conveys Meaning • Review Phonics: Initial m Rules Are Cool **Identify Characters in a Story (10 Min.), p. 97** RL.K.1, RL.K.3, RF.K.1a, SL.K.1a, SL.K.3	**Read-Aloud Handbook** **Shared Readings:** "Five Little Monkeys," p. 7 **Read Aloud and Shared Reading (20 Min.), p. 101** RL.K.1, RF.K.3a, SL.K.1a, SL.K.1b, L.K.1b • Fluency: Prosody/Expression • Build Concepts: Following Rules • Review Phonics: Initial m • Review Language: Nouns Rules Are Cool **Compare and Contrast a Story and an Informational Text (15 Min.), p. 102** RL.K.9, RF.K.1a, SL.K.1a	**Read-Aloud Handbook** **Shared Readings:** "No Dogs Allowed in School," p. 6 **Read Aloud and Shared Reading (20 Min.), p. 107** RL.K.10, RF.K.3b, RF.K.3c, SL.K.1a, SL.K.1b • Fluency: Prosody/Expression • Build Concepts: Following Rules • Review Phonics: Short a • Review High-Frequency Words: I, like Unit 1 Video **Reflect on Unit Concepts (20 MIN.), p. 112** SL.K.1, SL.K.2, SL.K.2a, SL.K.3, SL.K.4, SL.K.6
Write a Class Letter (10 Min.), p. 98 W.K.3, W.K.8, SL.K.1a, SL.K.1b, L.K.1a, L.K.1b • Build Language: Nouns	**Write a Comparison and Contrast Text (15 Min.), p. 104** RF.K.1a, W.K.2, W.K.8, SL.K.1a, SL.K.1b, SL.K.3, L.K.1a, L.K.1b, • Build Language: Verbs	**Revise and Edit a Response to the Essential Question (15 Min.), p. 108** W.K.2, W.K.5, W.K.6, L.K.1a, L.K.1b
Focus Skill: a/a/ (20 Min.), p. 100 RF.K.2d, RF.K.3a, RF.K.3c • Phonological Awareness: Phoneme Isolation • High-Frequency Words: *like, I*	**Pre-Decodable Reader:** *I Like* **Focus Skill: a/a (20 Min.), p. 106** RI.K.1, RI.K.10, RF.K.2a, RF.K.3a, RF.K.3c, RF.K.4 • Phonological Awareness: Listen and Produce Rhyme • High-Frequency Words: *I, like*	**Pre-Decodable Reader:** *I Like* **Focus Skill: a/a/ (20 Min.), p. 110** RI.K.1, RI.K.10, RF.K.2e, RF.K.3a, RF.K.3c, RF.K.4, L.K.1a • Phonological Awareness: Phoneme Blending • High-Frequency Words: *like, I*

**Mentor Read-Aloud Topic
Introduction Vol. 1, pp. 2-3**

Student Objectives

I will be able to:
- Discuss materials I have listened to or read.
- Take part in discussions by asking and answering questions about characters and illustrations.
- Review reading strategies I have learned.

 **Integrated ELD**

Light Support

Ask: *Who do you see in the picture?*
Help students respond with sentences such as "I see Ben in the picture" and "I see Ben's mom in the picture." Then ask questions such as "Who do you see with red hair?" and "Who do you see in a pink shirt?" Have students answer using the sentence frame below.
- *The person with _____ is Ben/Ben's mom.*

Moderate Support

Ask: *Who is in the picture?*
Help students respond with sentences such as "Ben is in the picture" and "Ben's mom is in the picture." Then ask questions such as "Who has red hair?" and "Who has a pink shirt?" Have students answer in full sentences, such as "Ben has red hair" or "Ben's mom has a pink shirt."

Substantial Support

Work with sentences beginning with *who*. Display "A New Pet." Point to the picture of Ben.
Ask: *Who is this?*
Model answering by saying, "This is Ben."
Have students repeat as you touch the illustration, saying both question and answer. Repeat with the picture of Ben's mom.
Say: *This is Ben's mom.*
Have individual students come forward. Have them touch the picture of Ben. Help them address the rest of the group and say "Who is this?" Help the rest of the group answer "This is Ben." Repeat with other students. Then repeat the activity with Ben's mom.

ELD.PI.K.1, ELD.PI.K.5, ELD.PII.K.6,

Build Knowledge and Review Week 1
Strategies (10 MIN.) RL.K.3, RL.K.7, SL.K.1a, SL.K.1b, SL.K.2

Discuss the Essential Question

Display the Topic 1 Introduction and read aloud the essential question. Then flip through the selections from Week 1. Ask students to turn and talk to a partner about three things they learned about why we have rules at home and at school. Provide a sentence frame for students to use:

I learned that _____.

Ask volunteers to share what their partners said.

Review Week 1 Strategies (iELD)

Identify Characters in a Story. Remind students that they learned about characters in a story.

Say: *We learned that characters are the people or animals that a story is about. And most stories have a main character whom the story is mainly about. Review how students can look for what characters say, think, feel, and do in the story. Display* A New Pet *and have a volunteer discuss the story characters.*

Make Connections between Illustrations and Text. Remind students that they also learned how to use illustrations to better understand the events in a story.

Say: *Remember how we looked at the illustrations in* A New Pet *to see how they went along with the text? We learned information from the illustrations that helped us understand the story.*

Display and read aloud a page from *A New Pet.* Ask students to explain how the illustration on the page connects with the text.

Tell students that being able to identify story characters and make connections between illustrations and text are two strategies that will help them understand the extended text you will read aloud this week.

RL.K.3 With prompting and support, identify characters, settings, and major events in a story., **RL.K.7** With prompting and support, describe the relationship between illustrations and the text in which they appear (e.g., what moment in a story an illustration depicts)., **SL.K.1a** Follow agreed-upon rules for discussions (e.g., listening to others and taking turns speaking about the topics and texts under discussion)., **SL.K.1b** Continue a conversation through multiple exchanges., **SL.K.2** Confirm understanding of a text read aloud or information presented orally or through other media by asking and answering questions about key details and requesting clarification if something is not understood.

Read Aloud and Shared Reading (20 MIN.) RL.K.10, RL.K.10a, RL.K.10b, RF.K.1b, RF.K.3a

Read Aloud

To support the unit concept, use one of the Read-Aloud Handbook selections for Unit 1. As you read, model the metacognitive strategy for the unit, Ask Questions, guided by the samples provided. You may also wish to select a favorite read-aloud from your classroom or school library. To support the unit concept, use one of the suggested titles for Unit 1.

Shared Reading (iELD)

Introduce the Story

Display "No Dogs Allowed in School." Read aloud the title of the story as you point under each word. Invite students to look at the illustration and then turn to a partner and tell what they predict the story will be about. Invite a few students to share their predictions with the whole class.

Read the Story

First reading. Read aloud the text fluently and expressively, pointing under each word.

Reread for Fluency: Prosody/Expression. Point to the exclamation point in the last sentence and tell students that this is a signal to read this sentence with excitement. Ask students to listen as you reread the story. Model reading each sentence with appropriate emphasis and expression. Demonstrate your change in expression when you read the last sentence. Invite students to echo-read the story. Provide corrective feedback and/or validate students' efforts.

Build Concepts: Following Rules

Pose questions to connect the story to the unit concept. For example:

- *Why did Max have to leave school?*
- *Is "No dogs allowed at school" a good rule? Why do you think so?*

Review Print Concepts: Print Conveys Meaning

Display page 6. Ask a volunteer to point to the illustration on the page and describe how the dog Max feels as he leaves school. Ask another volunteer to point to the words that describe how he feels. Remind students that the print, or words, carries the author's message.

Review Phonics: Initial and Final m

Highlight the word **My** in the first sentence. Have students read the word aloud with you. Ask volunteers to name the letter at the beginning of **My** and the sound the letter **m** stands for. Do the same for **Max**, **me**, **Mom**. Ask students to identify the final letter and its sound in **Mom**.

Read-Aloud Handbook

Shared Reading Vol. 1, p. 6 "No Dogs Allowed in School"

Student Objectives

I will be able to:
- Read along with expression.
- Answer questions about rules at school.
- Understand that print has meaning.
- Identify initial and final **m**.

(iELD) Integrated ELD

Light Support
Say: *I wonder why the dog left school. Why did the dog leave school?*
Point out that we say, "Why did the dog leave school?" We do not say, "Why the dog left school?" Remind students that when you ask a question with *why*, the answer usually includes the word *because*. Guide students to answer "The dog left school because no dogs are allowed at school." Have students ask each other *why* questions.

Moderate Support
Ask: *Why did the dog leave school?*
Have students repeat the question.
Say: *When you ask why, the answer uses the word because.*
Use the sentence frame below to model answering the *why* question.
- *The dog left school because _____.*
Then have students fill in a possible reason. Encourage them to ask each other simple *why* questions.

Substantial Support
Display "No Dogs Allowed in School." Point to the illustration of the dog leaving the school.
Say: *The dog had to leave the school. The dog had to go away. Why did the dog go away?*
Emphasize the word *why* as you speak.
Say: *The rule said NO DOGS ALLOWED IN SCHOOL. The dog went away because _____.*
Help students complete the sentence with "dogs could not be in school." Close the book.
Ask: *Why did the dog go away?*
Have students repeat your words. Help them ask the question with expression if possible.

ELD.PI.K.3, ELD.PI.K.12a, ELD.PII.K.1

RL.K.10 Actively engage in group reading activities with purpose and understanding., **RL.K.10a** Activate prior knowledge related to the information and events in texts. CA, **RL.K.10b** Use illustrations and context to make predictions about text. CA, **RF.K.1b** Recognize that spoken words are represented in written language by specific sequences of letters., **RF.K.3a** Demonstrate basic knowledge of letter-sound correspondences by producing the primary or most frequent sound for each consonant.

Rules Are Cool

Student Objectives

I will be able to:
- Recognize features of realistic fiction.
- Make predictions about a new classmate.
- Listen for a purpose.
- Link my ideas to the ideas of others.
- Retell key events about rules at school.

Additional Materials

Weekly Presentation
- Two Column Chart
- Story Events Chart

☑ Observation Checklist for Collaborative Conversation

As partners discuss the key details from each chapter, use the questions below to evaluate how effectively students communicate with each other. Based on your answers, you may wish to plan future core lessons to support the collaborative conversation process.

Do partners . . .

- ❑ stay on topic throughout the discussion?
- ❑ listen respectfully?
- ❑ build on the comments of others appropriately?
- ❑ pose or respond to questions to clarify information?
- ❑ support their partners to participate?

Rules Are Cool: Listen and Retell Key Events (10 MIN.) RL.K.1, RL.K.2, RL.K.5, RL.K.10, RL.K.10a, RL.K.10b, SL.K.1a, SL.K.1b, SL.K.3

Preview the Genre

Display the cover of *Rules Are Cool* and read aloud the title and name of the author and illustrator. Point out that this selection is a story. It is realistic fiction, which means the characters are like real people and the events could happen in real life. Ask partners to look at the illustrations and make predictions about the story. Invite partners to share their ideas with the group.

Have students turn and talk to a partner and name features they observe and predictions they have. Make sure they explain what text or graphic feature helped them formulate their predictions. Use this opportunity to discuss specific features students may not be able to name (such as speech balloons or thought bubbles).

Sample Realistic Fiction Features	Sample Predictions
• title • speech balloons • thought bubbles • illustrations	I predict that in this story… • a girl will have fun at school. • a girl will make friends. • a girl will learn rules.

Read Aloud the Text

Ask students to listen carefully to find out what events take place in the story. Explain that this is their purpose for listening. Read aloud the text with minimal interruption. Model how you read with expression and use different voices for dialogue and the text in the speech balloons and thought bubbles. Review the predictions students made before reading.

 Collaborative Conversation: Partners (iELD)

Ask students to recall key events from the text about rules at school. Model how students can build on partners' talk by listening carefully and linking their ideas to what they have said. For example, *[Name] mentioned _____. Another key event is _____. I agree with [Name] that _____ is a key event. Another key event is _____.*

Share

Invite students to share the key events they recalled. Record them on a class story events and reread the part of the text where the event was mentioned.

Beginning:	A new girl, Roma, joins the class.
Middle:	A classmate shows Roma the school rules. Roma learns the rules.
End:	Roma realizes the school rules keep her safe and happy.

Sample Story Events Chart

Reinforce or Reaffirm the Strategy

Provide modeling and/or engage students in self-reflection to build metacognitive awareness.

IF…	THEN…
students need support to retell key events…	**Model to reinforce the strategy.** • *My purpose for reading was to identify the key events in the story. The first important event happens right at the beginning of the story. Roma is a new girl who joins the class.* • *I keep reading to find the next key event. I learn from the text and the illustration that a classmate shows Roma the school rules. That is an important event in the story.* Continue to model how to find key events.
students independently retell key events…	**Invite partners to reflect on their strategy by discussing the following questions:** • *How did retelling the key events help you understand the story?* • *What happened in the beginning, middle, and end of the story?* Ask partners to name the key events they identified and explain how they found them.

☑ Show Your Knowledge

Tell children to draw a picture to show one key event about rules at school. Ask them to write a simple label or caption.

ⓘELD Integrated ELD

Light Support

Say: *The friend looks nice. Who agrees with me?* Guide students to say "I agree with you" or "I don't agree with you." Have them follow up by saying "I think the friend looks nice/does not look nice."

Turn to a new page. Have students make statements about the picture. They should ask the rest of the group, "Do you agree with me?"

Students respond individually in a complete sentence.

Moderate Support

Say: *The friend looks nice. Do you agree?* Have students respond "I agree" or "I don't agree." Help them complete the rest of the thought by using this sentence frame:

• *I think the friend _____ (looks nice/does not look nice).*

Turn to a new page. Ask students to say something they like in the picture. Help them phrase their observation as a sentence if possible. Have each student respond by saying "I agree" or "I don't agree."

Substantial Support

Say: *This book has many key events. Here is one key event: Roma makes a new friend.*

Point to the illustration on page 2 of *Rules Are Cool*, showing Roma and another girl.

Then say: *The friend looks nice. Do you agree?* Explain that *agreeing* is thinking the same thing as somebody else. Have children respond "yes" if they think that the friend looks nice.

Say: *_____ agrees with me. He/she thinks that the friend looks nice.*

Have them respond "no" if they do not.

Say: *_____ does not agree with me. He/she does not think that the friend looks nice.*

Repeat with other key events in the story, such as building on page 5.

Say: *That looks like fun. Do you agree?* Encourage children to formulate their own opinions and ask if others agree.

ELD.PI.K.1 ELD.PI.K.3, ELD.PII.K.6

RL.K.1 With prompting and support, ask and answer questions about key details in a text., **RL.K.2** With prompting and support, retell familiar stories, including key details, **RL.K.5** Recognize common types of texts (e.g., storybooks, poems, fantasy, realistic text). **CA**)., **RL.K.10** Actively engage in group reading activities with purpose and understanding., **RL.K.10a** Activate prior knowledge related to the information and events in texts. CA, **RL.K.10b** Use illustrations and context to make predictions about text. CA, **SL.K.1a** Follow agreed-upon rules for discussions (e.g., listening to others and taking turns speaking about the topics and texts under discussion)., **SL.K.1b** Continue a conversation through multiple exchanges., **SL.K.3** Ask and answer questions in order to seek help, get information, or clarify something that is not understood.

Rules Are Cool

Student Objectives

I will be able to:
- Identify and share key events about rules at school.
- Write a key event.
- Use nouns.

(iELD) Integrated ELD

Light Support
Remind students that a noun is a person, a place, or a thing.
Say: *Look at the pictures in the book* Rules Are Cool. *Look for a person, a place, or a thing.*
Help students name objects they see, such as *book*, *girl*, or *hat*. They should answer in a complete sentence. Have them create a sentence for each noun.

Moderate Support
Remind students that a noun is a person, a place, or a thing. Page slowly through the book *Rules Are Cool*.
Say: *Look at the pictures in the book. Who can find a hat? Who can find a book? Who sees a girl?*
Help students identify these and other objects. Write the words on the board. Explain that these words are all nouns. Help children create simple sentences using this sentence frame:
- *A(n) ____ is ____.*

Substantial Support
Tell students that some words are called nouns.
Say: *Nouns can be people. Nouns can be places. Nouns can be things.*
Explain that people can draw pictures of many nouns. Write the word *girl* on the board and read it aloud.
Say: *A girl is a person. ____ is a girl. ____ is a girl.*
Sketch a simple drawing of a girl.
Ask: *Who else can draw a picture of a girl? Sum up by saying: Girl is a noun. We can draw a picture of this noun.*
Repeat with the following nouns mentioned or shown in the book *Rules Are Cool*: *book, hat, chair, pencil.*

ELD.PI.K.2, ELD.PI.K.10, ELD.PII.K.4

Write Key Events (10 MIN.) W.K.2, W.K.8, SL.K.1a, SL.K.1b, L.K.1b

Engage Thinking

Display and reread the story events chart with students. Remind them that they have learned and retold important events from a story about school rules.

Ask: *How did finding the key events help you understand how rules keep you safe?*

💬 Collaborative Conversation: Peer Groups

Tell students that before writing, you would like them to turn and talk to a partner briefly. Ask them to share an event from the story they found especially interesting, an event they would like to write down. Model how you do this.

Sample modeling: *When I tell my partner about an interesting event, I say, "The most interesting event was when Roma joined the class." When you talk with your partner, you can start your sentence the same way:* The most interesting event was _____.

Write the sentence frame for students. Allow students one minute to discuss their ideas. Then bring them together and ask volunteers to share the key events they found interesting.

Write as a Group

Work with students to agree on one key event for the shared writing. Rehearse the message orally and model how you write the sentence. As you guide the writing, include at least one noun. Actively engage students in the writing process by thinking aloud and/or prompting them with questions. For example:

- *What is the first word in our sentence?*
- *What do I need to do when I start the first word in the sentence?*
- *Who knows how we spell the word _____?*
- *What is a better word we could use here?*
- *Now let's read our writing. Did we include all the words we needed in our sentence?*

Sample Shared Writing
Roma is a new girl in our school.
A classmate showed Roma the rules.
Our class helped Roma learn the rules.

Build Language: Nouns

Circle a noun in your sample writing. Explain that this word is a noun. Remind students that a noun is a word that names a person, place, or thing. Name a few nouns from *Rules Are Cool* and ask volunteers to use each one in an oral sentence. For example: **girl, class, job, fun.**

☑ Write Independently

Ask students to choose another key story event about the rules at school. Tell them to draw and label the event.

Small-Group Differentiated Instruction (15 Min. per Group)

Meet with Small Groups

Select small-group reading titles or activities based on students' needs. See the Small-Group Instructional Planner for titles that support a range of instructional reading levels within the unit topic. Remind students to apply what they learned to their small-group reading experiences.

Say: *Today we practiced finding the key events in a story. If you are listening to a literary text, pay attention to the key events. If you are listening to an informational text today, pay attention to the important details. Use strategies we have learned to help you understand the key events and details. You can look back at the text in order to remember ideas.*

Whole-Group Reflect and Share

Bring the class back together. Ask volunteers to share examples of key events they found in their small-group reading texts. Encourage them to explain how they knew which were the most important events.

W.K.2 Use a combination of drawing, dictating, and writing to compose informative/explanatory texts in which they name what they are writing about and supply some information about the topic., **W.K.8** With guidance and support from adults, recall information from experiences or gather information from provided sources to answer a question., **SL.K.1a** Follow agreed-upon rules for discussions (e.g., listening to others and taking turns speaking about the topics and texts under discussion)., **SL.K.1b** Continue a conversation through multiple exchanges., **L.K.1b** Use frequently occurring nouns and verbs.

Focus Skill: a/a/ (20 MIN.) RF.K.2d, RF.K.3a, RF.K.2c, L.K.1a

Phonological Awareness: Phoneme Isolation

Model/Practice

Display the frieze card for **Aa**.

Say: *Listen for the sound at the beginning of apple: /aaa/. Say the sound with me, /aaa/. What is the sound?*

Read the poem "Apple Pie," emphasizing the /a/ sound at the beginning of words. Reread the poem and have students say /aaa/ when they hear /a/ at the beginning of a word.

Review /m/

Display the picture card for **mop**.

Say: *This is a mop. The beginning sound in mop is /m/. What is the beginning sound in mop?*

Show the following picture cards and have students say the sound they hear at the beginning of the word: **ax, map, ant.**

Letter-Sound Correspondences

Introduce: Aa

Display frieze card **Aa**.

Say: *This is the apple card. The name of this letter is **a**. The letter **a** stands for the /aaa/ sound. The /aaa/ sound is spelled with the letter **a**. Say the sound with me, /aaa/. This is the sound at the beginning of **apple**. What is the name of this letter?* (**a**) *What sound does it stand for?* (**/aaa/**)

Model: Aa

Read the poem "Apple Pie." Reread the title and point out that **Apple** begins with **A.**

Practice: Aa

Have students point to words in the poem that begin with **Aa.** Say each word aloud and have students say the words with you.

Student Objectives

I will be able to:
- Isolate initial sound /a/.
- Identify letter-sound correspondence for **a/a/.**
- Practice the sound /m/.
- Blend sounds /a/, /m/.
- Learn new high-frequency word: **like**
- Read previously taught high-frequency word: **I**
- Write **Aa**.

Additional Materials

- Poetry poster: "Apple Pie"
- Letter cards: **a, m**
- Sound-spelling card **Aa**
- For additional practice, see Pre-Decodable Reader: *I Am*

Weekly Presentation
- Picture cards: **ant, apple, ax, map, mop**
- Frieze card: **Aa**
- High-frequency word cards: **I, like**

Blend Sounds

Review: Mm

Hold up frieze card **Mm** and ask students to say the sound the letter stands for.

Model: am

Place letter cards **a, m** in a pocket chart. Point to the letter **a.**

Say: *This is the letter **a**. The letter **a** stands for /**aaa**/. Say /**aaa**/. This is the letter **m**. The letter **m** stands for /**mmm**/. Say /**mmm**/. Listen as I blend the two sounds together, /**aaammm**/. Blend the sounds with me.*

Practice: am

Have students blend the sounds in the word **am**. Provide support as necessary.

High-Frequency Words (iELD)

Introduce/Practice: *like*

Display the high-frequency word card. Point to it and read the word.

Use the following routine: Point to each letter in the word and have students say the letter name with you. Say the word together.

Say: *When I say the word **like**, I will hold up the word card. Read the word with me. **I like apples. Sam and I like to run.***

Review: *I*

Display the high-frequency word card and have students read the word.

Handwriting

Write and identify the uppercase and lowercase **Aa**. Hold up your writing hand. Write the uppercase and lowercase **Aa**. Trace the letters as you say /**aaa**/.

Then have students write **A** and **a** in the air as they say /**aaa**/ several times. Finally have students write both forms of the letter several times, saying /**aaa**/ every time they write the letter.

(iELD) Integrated ELD

Light Support
Write this sentence frame on the board:
• *I like _____.*
Underline *like*. Read the sentence with the students.
Say: *Carrots and apples are good. I like to eat carrots and apples.*
Have students repeat after you. Help them form sentences of their own. Include two foods they like joined by the word *and*.
Have students work in pairs. Have them ask each other what they like to eat. The response should include the names of two foods.

Moderate Support
Write this sentence frame on the board:
• *I like _____.*
Underline the word *like*. Read the sentence with the students. Pantomime eating a carrot.
Say: *I like to eat carrots. What do you like to eat?*
Guide students to respond using this sentence frame:
• *I like to eat _____.*
The rest of the group should respond using this sentence frame:
• _____ *likes to eat _____.*
Have students work in pairs. Have one ask the other what they like to eat. The other should respond, *I like to eat _____.*

Substantial Support
Write the word *like* on the board. Read it with students. Pantomime eating a carrot.
Say: *I like carrots. What do you like?*
Have students respond with one-word answers of foods they like to eat. Have them draw the foods on the board if they are not sure of the English word. Help them say "I like _____." Point to the word like on the board when they say *like*. Then have the rest of the group say "_____ likes _____."
You may wish to make a book of these pictures titled *Things We Like*.

ELD.PI.K.1, ELD.PI.K.10, ELD.PII.K.3

RF.K.2d Isolate and pronounce the initial, medial vowel, and final sounds (phonemes) in three-phoneme (consonant-vowel-consonant, or CVC) words. (This does not include CVCs ending with /l/, /r/, or /x/.), **RF.K.3a** Demonstrate basic knowledge of letter-sound correspondences by producing the primary or most frequent sound for each consonant., **RF.K.2c** Blend and segment onsets and rimes of single-syllable spoken words., **L.K.1a** Print many upper- and lowercase letters.

Read-Aloud Handbook

Shared Reading Vol. 1, p. 6
"No Dogs Allowed in School"

Student Objectives

I will be able to:
- Answer questions about rules at school.
- Identify short **a**.
- Recognize the high-frequency word **like**.

Additional Materials

Weekly Presentation: Unit 1, Week 3

(iELD) Integrated ELD

Light Support

Tell children that the word *what* often comes at the beginning of questions. Model by asking the following question: *What things do you see in our classroom?* Answer by saying "I see a _____ in our classroom." Repeat the question and have children give an answer that makes sense to them, using the frame above.

Moderate Support

Ask: *What do you see in the picture?*
Help children answer, using this sentence starter: *I see _____*. Explain that the word **what** is often used at the beginning of questions. Tell children that people say "What is…" or "What does…" when they want to know something. Model asking a question with **what** at the beginning. Have children raise their hands when they hear the word. Hold up various classroom items. Have children ask "What is this?" They should call on a classmate to answer "This is a _____."

Substantial Support

Have children work with the word **what** as a question word. Display the book about Max, and model use of the word **what** by asking "What do you see?" and answering the question with something in the picture. Then reinforce use of the word **what**. Hold up a pencil. **Say:** *What is this? This is a pencil.* Repeat with other common objects such as a paintbrush, a marker, and a toy car. Then repeat the activity, only this time ask the question with children and have them raise their hands when they say the word *what*. Provide the following sentence frame: *This is a _____*. Have children complete the sentence by naming the object.

ELD.PI.K.5, ELD.PI.K.6, ELD.PII.K.4

Read Aloud and Shared Reading

(20 MIN.) **RL.K.10, RF.K.3b, RF.K.3c, SL.K.1a, SL.K.1b,**

Read Aloud

To support the unit concept, use one of the Read-Aloud Handbook selections for Unit 1. As you read, model the metacognitive strategy for the unit, Ask Questions, guided by the samples provided. You may also wish to select a favorite read-aloud from your classroom or school library. To support the unit concept, use one of the suggested titles for Unit 1.

Shared Reading (iELD)

Reread the Story

First rereading. Read aloud the story fluently and expressively, pointing under each word.

Reread for Fluency: Prosody/Expression. Ask students to listen as you read the story one sentence at a time. Then divide students into two groups. Ask the first group to choral-read the first two sentences and the second group to choral-read the second two sentences. Encourage students to match your tone and expression as they read. Provide corrective feedback and/or validate students' efforts.

Build Concepts: Following Rules

Pose questions to connect the story to the unit concept. For example:

- *What would happen if Max stayed at school? What would his day be like?*
- *Would there be special school rules for Max? What would they be?*

Review Phonics: Short a

Highlight the name **Max** in the first sentence. Ask students to read the name aloud with you. Point to the letter **a**. Call on a volunteer to name the letter. Ask another volunteer to tell the sound the letter **a** stands for in the name **Max**.

Review High-Frequency Words: like

Tell students that this text contains some words they have learned. Point to the previously taught high-frequency word **like**. Ask students to turn to a partner and tell their partner the high-frequency word. Remind students to look for high-frequency words they know when they read a new text.

RL.K.10 Actively engage in group reading activities with purpose and understanding., **RF.K.3b** Associate the long and short sounds with the common spellings (graphemes) for the five major vowels.(Identify which letters represent the five major vowels (Aa, Ee, Ii, Oo, and Uu) and know the long and short sound of each vowel. More complex long vowel graphemes and spellings are targeted in the grade 1 phonics standards.) CA, **RF.K.3c** Read common high-frequency words by sight (e.g., the, of, to, you, she, my, is, are, do, does)., **SL.K.1a** Follow agreed-upon rules for discussions (e.g., listening to others and taking turns speaking about the topics and texts under discussion)., **SL.K.1b** Continue a conversation through multiple exchanges.

Make Connections between Illustrations and Events in the Text

(10 MIN.) RL.K.1, RL.K.7, SL.K.3

Engage Thinking

Remind students that they have learned that the illustrations in a story go along with the words.

Ask: *How did looking at the illustrations and thought bubbles in* A New Pet *help you understand what Max wanted?*

Model

Display pages 2–3. Model for students how to make a connection between the illustration and the words.

Sample modeling: *In the text, I read that Roma joined the class and a classmate was going to help her. From the illustration, I see who Roma is and who her classmate is. I also see that the class has girls and boys who are doing their work at their tables.*

Then display page 7. Model how to interpret the thought bubble.

Sample modeling: *I see that on this page, the text is inside a thought bubble over Roma's head. That lets me know that the words are what Roma is thinking. She is thinking about one of the rules: Be Nice.*

Guided Practice (iELD)

Display pages 8–9. Read aloud the text and ask students to examine the illustrations. Use directive prompts to guide students to make the connection between the illustrations (including the thought bubble) and the words. For example:

- *The text says the children invite Roma to build with them. What does the illustration show the children are building?*
- *The text in the thought bubble says, "Take Turns." How does that connect to the illustration?*

☑ Show Your Knowledge

Display and read aloud pages 10–11. Ask students to tell how the illustrations go along with the text. Remind them to think about the thought bubble as they respond.

Challenge Activity On pages 14–15, ask students to explain how the text in each thought bubble matches the corresponding illustration.

RL.K.1 With prompting and support, ask and answer questions about key details in a text., **RL.K.7** With prompting and support, describe the relationship between illustrations and the text in which they appear (e.g., what moment in a story an illustration depicts)., **SL.K.3** Ask and answer questions in order to seek help, get information, or clarify something that is not understood.

EXTENDED READ 2 MINI-LESSON

Rules Are Cool

Student Objectives

I will be able to:
- Describe how illustrations and text are connected.

Additional Materials

Weekly Presentation: Unit 1, Week 3

iELD Integrated ELD

Light Support
Display page 3, and read the text with children, marking the words with your finger. Tell children that the words and the pictures often go together in stories.
Ask: *What can you read?*
Have children answer using a complete sentence. Help children identify the book in the picture. Continue through the book, helping children look for words and pictures that go together. Remind them to use whole sentences.

Moderate Support
Display page 3, and read the line of text with children, touching below each word as you say it. Touch the word **read**.
Say: *What can you read? Do you read a car? Do you read a dog? No, you read a…*
Pause to allow children to say **book**.
Say: *Sometimes the picture and the words go together. The words say read. Can you see a book in the picture? Say with children: You read a book.*
Touch the word and the picture as appropriate. Then repeat, using the words and pictures on page 10.

Substantial Support
Display page 3 of *Rules Are Cool*. Pantomime reading a book.
Say: *Who can see a book in the picture?*
Help children locate a book in the picture.
Say: *We found the book!*
Explain that the pictures often help readers understand the words in a story. Read the speech bubble "Come read with us and join the fun with children." Touch the words as you say them. Emphasize the word **read**.
Say: *When you read, you might read a book. The story says read. The picture shows books. The words and the pictures go together.*
Touch the word **read** and have children identify it.

ELD.PI.K.1, ELD.PI.K.5, ELD.PII.K.3b

Rules Are Cool

Additional Materials

Weekly Presentation
- Author Illustrator Chart

Identify the Author and Illustrator and Define Their Roles (10 MIN.) RL.K.1, RL.K.6, SL.K.3

Engage Thinking

Display *Rules Are Cool.* Explain that most stories contain words and pictures and have an author and illustrator. Explain that both the words and the pictures tell the story.

Ask: *Do you have a favorite storybook that you enjoy reading and learning from the illustrations?*

Model (iELD)

Point to the name **Brenda Parkes** on the cover of the book, and explain that the person who writes the words is called the **author**. Next, point to the name **Sarah Jennings** on the cover of the book, and explain that the person who creates the pictures is called the **illustrator**. Explain that both the words and the pictures tell the story.

Say: *Brenda Parkes is the **author** of this book. That means she wrote the words. Sarah Jennings is the **illustrator** of this book. That means she drew the pictures.*

Explain to students that *Rules Are Cool* contains words and pictures on every page. The words were written by the author, and the pictures were created by the illustrator. Tell students that both the words and the pictures tell the story.

Sample modeling: *Display page 2. This page has words and pictures. [Point to and read the words. These are the words.] They were written by the author, Brenda Parkes. Point to the illustrations. These are the pictures. They were drawn by the illustrator, Sarah Jennings. [Display page 3.] This page also has words and pictures. [Point to and read the words.] These are the words. They were written by the author, Brenda Parkes. [Point to the illustrations.] These are the pictures. They were drawn by the illustrator, Sarah Jennings. Display both pages 2 and 3. The author and illustrator have different jobs, but they both work to tell the story. For example, on page 2, the author uses words to tell me that Roma is a new student in the class. The illustrator didn't tell me that Roma is new, but showed me that Roma is smiling. I can read the words and look at the pictures to better understand the story.*

Guided Practice

Ask students to continue to identify the author's and illustrator's roles in creating the book *Rules Are Cool*. Use directive and corrective prompts to support their comprehension. For example:

- *On what page can you find out the name of the author and the illustrator?*
- *[Point to the author's name.] Whose name is this? What does an author do?*
- *[Point to the illustrator's name.] Whose name is this? What does an illustrator do?*
- *Who wrote the words on page 12? What about on page 13?*
- *Who drew the pictures on page 12? What about on page 13?*
- *How do both the author and the illustrator tell the story?*

	Author	Illustrator
Name	Brenda Parkes	Sarah Jennings
Their job	To tell the story with words	To tell the story with pictures
An example from the book	"My job is to help her as we work and play." (page 3)	A picture of Roma thinking and smiling (page 7)

Sample Author Illustrator Chart

Show Your Knowledge

Call on volunteers to do the following:

- Point to the author's name on the front cover. Tell what an author does.
- Point to the illustrator's name on the front cover. Tell what an illustrator does.

Challenge Activity Choose a classroom storybook. Ask students to find and name the book parts just discussed in the core lesson.

iELD Integrated ELD

Light Support

Challenge children to find the author's name on the cover of a book. Point out that it usually comes after the word **by**.

Say: _____ *is the author of this book. If you write the book, you are the author.*

Help children make a list of things an author might do. Have them use complete sentences to express their ideas. Possible answers might be "An author uses a computer" or "An author has good ideas."

Moderate Support

After showing children a book from the classroom library, find the author's name and read it aloud.

Say: _____ *is the author of this book. That means he/she wrote the book. He/she put the words in. What does an author do?*

Reinforce this information by asking the following questions and having children answer "yes" or "no" to each. Help them conclude each "no" sentence with "an author writes a book."

- *Does an author draw a picture? (no)*
- *Does an author fix a car? (no)*
- *Does an author write a book? (yes)*
- *Does an author work in a store? (no)*

Substantial Support

Model what an author is and what authors do by displaying a book from the classroom library.

Say: *Somebody wrote this book.*

Show children the author's name.

Say: _____ *is the author of the book. An author writes a book. What does an author do?*

Teach children to sing "An author writes a book, an author writes a book..." to the tune of "Farmer in the Dell." Have them pretend to write while they sing.

Repeat with other books from the classroom, locating each author's name and identifying each author as the person who wrote the book.

ELD.PI.K.5, ELD.PI.K.12b, ELD.PII.K.4

RL.K.1 With prompting and support, ask and answer questions about key details in a text., **RL.K.6** With prompting and support, name the author and illustrator of a story and define the role of each in telling the story., **SL.K.3** Ask and answer questions in order to seek help, get information, or clarify something that is not understood.

Rules Are Cool

Student Objectives

I will be able to:
- Write an opinion about *Rules Are Cool.*
- Use nouns in my writing.

iELD Integrated ELD

Light Support

Tell students that they can state what they think by saying *My opinion is that _____.* Write the words on the board and read them aloud. Model completing the sentence with *soccer is fun.* Write it on the board, and read the whole sentence with students. Have students take turns asking each other *What is your opinion about _____?* Students should answer *My opinion is that _____.* Write the sentences on the board. Read them with children. Ask students to help you identify the nouns.

Moderate Support

Tell students that they can give an opinion by saying *I think that _____.* Write the words on the board, and read them aloud with students. Model completing the sentence with *soccer is fun.* Write that sentence part on the board, and read the whole sentence with students.

Say: *That is my opinion. What is your opinion? I think that _____.*

Write their answers on the board in complete sentences. Read them all with students. Follow up by circling the nouns.

Substantial Support

Tell students that an opinion is something you believe or think. Write the phrase "I like" on the board and read it aloud. Then pantomime kicking a soccer ball.

Say: *I like soccer. That is my opinion. What do you like?*

I like _____. Make a list of the things children say. Read the list with the students, touching below each word as you move your finger along. Then circle any nouns.

Say: *These are people, places, or things. They are nouns.*

ELD.PI.K.2, ELD.PI.K.3, ELD.PII.K.4

Write an Opinion (10 MIN.) W.K.1, W.K.8, SL.K.1a, SL.K.1b, L.K.1a, L.K.1b

Engage Thinking

Briefly review with students the story *Rules Are Cool.*

Ask: *What did you like about this story? What didn't you like about it?*

Explain that students will give their opinion, or tell what they think, about *Rules Are Cool.* Remind them that when they give their opinion, they should give a reason that they think that way.

Collaborative Conversation: Peer Group

Separate students into peer groups. Tell students that before writing, you would like them to turn and talk to members of their group briefly. Ask them to talk about whether they liked or disliked *Rules Are Cool.* Remind them that when they tell their opinion, they should give a reason to back it up. Model how to do this.

Sample modeling: *When I tell my partner my opinion about the story, I say, "I liked* Rules Are Cool *because it reminded me of our school." Notice that I included a reason for my opinion. When you speak to your partner, you can use that same sentence frame:* I think *Rules Are Cool* is _____ because _____.

Write the sentence frame for students. Provide two minutes for peer discussion. Then bring students together and ask groups to share the opinions they discussed.

Write as a Group (iELD)

Collaborate with students to agree on an opinion for the shared writing. Rehearse the sentence orally and model how to write it. As you guide the writing, include at least one noun. Actively engage students in the writing process with question prompts. For example:

- How do I begin the first word in our sentence?
- Is there a better word we can use here? What is it?
- What punctuation mark should we write at the end of the sentence?
- Is there anything we want to change in our sentence?

Sample Shared Writing

We liked *Rules Are Cool* because:

The book reminds us of our class.

The class has the same rules as our class.

The students in our class think rules are cool, too!

Build Language: Nouns

Circle a noun in your sample writing. Point out that this word is a noun. Remind students that a noun is a word that names a person, place, or thing. Ask volunteers to use each of the following nouns in an oral sentence: **school, room, friend, rule.**

 Write Independently

Ask students to draw what they liked about the story. Encourage them to write a simple label for their picture.

Small-Group Differentiated Instruction (15 MIN. per Group)

Meet with Small Groups

Select small-group reading titles or activities based on students' needs. See the Small-Group Instructional Planner for titles that support a range of instructional reading levels within the unit topic. Remind students to apply what they learned to their small-group reading experiences.

Say: *Today we practiced making connections between illustrations and text. We learned how the illustrations and text go together and how to get more information from the illustrations. When you listen to literary or informational texts in your small groups today, think about how the illustrations and the text are connected.*

Whole-Group Reflect and Share

Bring the class back together. Invite volunteers to tell how the illustrations and the text were connected in some of their small-group texts. Encourage students to share any additional information the illustrations provided.

W.K.1 Use a combination of drawing, dictating, and writing to compose opinion pieces in which they tell a reader the topic or the name of the book they are writing about and state an opinion or preference about the topic or book (e.g., My favorite book is...)., **W.K.8** With guidance and support from adults, recall information from experiences or gather information from provided sources to answer a question., **SL.K.1a** Follow agreed-upon rules for discussions (e.g., listening to others and taking turns speaking about the topics and texts under discussion)., **SL.K.1b** Continue a conversation through multiple exchanges., **L.K.1a** Print many upper- and lowercase letters., **L.K.1b** Use frequently occurring nouns and verbs.

Focus Skill: a/a/ (20 MIN.) RF.K.2d, RF.K.3a, RF.K.2c, L.K.1a

Phonological Awareness: Phoneme Isolation

Student Objectives

I will be able to:
- Isolate initial and medial sound **/a/.**
- Practice letter-sound correspondences for **a/a/, m/m/**.
- Blend sounds **/a/, /m/**.
- Learn new high-frequency word: **like.**
- Read previously taught high-frequency word: **I.**
- Write **Aa**.

Additional Materials

- Poetry poster: "Apple Pie"
- Letter cards: **a, m**

Weekly Presentation
- Frieze card: **Aa**
- High-frequency word cards: **I, like**

Model

Say: *Listen for the beginning sound in the word* **apple**. *Apple has /aaa/ in the beginning. What is the sound?*

Now we are going to listen to the middle sound in the word **cat**. **Cat** has /aaa/ in the middle. What is the sound?

Practice

Show students the picture on the back of the poetry poster and have them name all the objects in the picture. Point to the ax in the picture and say the word **ax**.

Ask: *What sound do you hear at the beginning of the word* **ax**?

Have students point to other things in the picture whose name has **/aaa/** at the beginning.

Say: *Now listen as I say the word* **bat**. *I can hear the /aaa/ sound in the middle of the word* **bat**. *I'm going to say some words. If you hear /aaa/ at the beginning of the word, stamp your feet. If you hear /aaa/ in the middle of the word, clap your hands.*

Use the following words: **ant, can, apple, man.**

Blend Words

Model: *sit*

Display letter cards for one word at a time. Model blending the sounds. For example:

Say: *This is the letter* **s**. *It stands for /s/. Say it with me: /s/. This is the letter* **i**. *It stands for /i/. Listen as I blend the sounds: /sssiii/. This is the letter* **t**. *It stands for /t/. Listen as I blend all three sounds together: /sssiiittt/,* **sit**. *Say the word with me:* **sit**.

Practice: *pig, dim, sick*

Have students place the following letter cards on their desks: **c, d, g, i, k, m, p, s**. Then have them blend and read each word with you.

Letter-Sound Correspondences

Review: a/a/, m/m/

Hold up frieze cards **Aa** and **Mm** one at a time, and have students tell you the sounds the letters stand for. Encourage students to think of words that start with **/aaa/**. Record the words, underlining the letter **a**. Then have students think of words that have **/aaa/** in the middle. Record these words, underlining the letter **a**.

Next, have students think of words that start or end with the **/mmm/** sound. Write these words and circle the **m**. Reread the poem "Apple Pie," emphasizing words with the initial and medial **/aaa/** sound. Have volunteers locate all the words with the **/aaa/** sound.

Blend Sounds

Model: *am*

Place letter cards **a, m** in a pocket chart. Point to the letter **a**.

Say: *This is the letter **a**. The letter **a** stands for /aaa/. Say /aaa/. This is the letter **m**. The letter **m** stands for /mmm/. Say /mmm/. Listen as I blend the two sounds together, /aaammm/. Blend the sounds with me. Now blend the sounds to read the word, **am**.*

Practice: *am*

Repeat the steps for the word **am**. Move your hand from left to right under the word. Have students blend and read the word **am.**

High-Frequency Words

Introduce/Practice: *like*

Display the high-frequency word card **like** and read the word. Point to each letter in the word and have students say the letter name with you. Say the word together.

Say: *I am going to read some sentences. When I say the word **like**, I will hold up the word card. Read the word with me***. *I like to read. Jacob and Lily like to swim.*

Review: *I*

Display the high-frequency word card **I** and have students read the word. Then have the students use the word in an oral sentence.

Handwriting

Have students write the uppercase and lowercase **Aa**. Observe students' pencil grip and paper position. Have students say **/a/** every time they write the letters **Aa**.

iELD Integrated ELD

Light Support
Explain that the names for all the objects on the poetry poster include the sound **/a/**.
Say: *What are these objects? We're going to play a guessing game to find out. I'm thinking of something that you can use to cut wood. It has a handle. It is _____.*
Invite students to name the object (in this case, an ax) if they know the name; otherwise, have them point to the object in question, and say the name for them. Help students use each word in a simple sentence. Continue until all objects on the poster have been named.

Moderate Support
Display the poetry poster.
Say: *All these words have the same sound: /a/. What are these objects?*
Challenge students to name the objects. Have them touch an object and say *This is a(n) _____.* Then help children create a sentence about the object. Use prompting questions such as *What can you do with a(n) _____?* or *What is a(n) _____ made of?* Have the group as a whole repeat each word and, if possible, the sentence. If there are words that no one knows, follow the procedure described above to cover these words. Close with a review of all the words.

Substantial Support
Help students build vocabulary by naming each object on the poetry poster. Point to each object as you say its name. Then say a short sentence for each object. For **ax**, for example, say, *You can use an ax to cut wood.* Have students say **ax** and pantomime using an ax to chop wood. Repeat for the other objects on the poster. Emphasize that every word contains the sound **/a/**. Review the vocabulary by naming an object and asking students to repeat the word. Then point to the picture of it on the poster. If possible, ask students to complete a sentence about each object as well. For example, say, *You can chop wood with an _____,* and have students fill in the missing word *ax*.

ELD.PI.K.1, ELD.PI.K.5, ELD.PII.K.4

RF.K.2d Isolate and pronounce the initial, medial vowel, and final sounds (phonemes) in three-phoneme (consonant-vowel-consonant, or CVC) words.1 (This does not include CVCs ending with /l/, /r/, or /x/.), **RF.K.3a** Demonstrate basic knowledge of letter-sound correspondences by producing the primary or most frequent sound for each consonant., **RF.K.2c** Blend and segment onsets and rimes of single-syllable spoken words., **L.K.1a** Print many upper- and lowercase letters.

Read-Aloud Handbook

Shared Reading Vol. 1, p. 7 "Five Little Monkeys"

Student Objectives

I will be able to:
- Read along with the appropriate expression.
- Answer questions about rules
- Understand that print has meaning.
- Identify initial **m**.

(iELD) Integrated ELD

Light Support

Read the "Five Little Monkeys" poem with students. Reread it, leaving out the following key words the first time they appear: **monkeys, bed, head,** and **doctor.** Have children supply the missing words.

Moderate Support

Act out words in the poem. Repeat as necessary.

Five little monkeys	Have five children stand.
Jumping on the bed	Have them jump.
One fell off	Have one sit back down.
And bumped his head	Have that child rub his or her head.
Mama called the doctor	Have children pretend to make a phone call.
And the doctor said	Switch "phones" to the other ear.
No more monkeys	Wiggle forefingers.

Substantial Support

Act out words in the poem. Repeat as necessary.

Little	Hold your finger and thumb close together.
Jumping	Move hand rapidly up and down.
Bed	Spread hands to indicate a flat surface.
Fell	Have your hand drop to your side.
Called	Imitate making a phone call.
Doctor	Pretend to use a stethoscope.

ELD.PI.K.5, ELD.PI.K.12a, ELD.PII.K.6

Read Aloud and Shared Reading

(20 MIN.) RL.K.10, RL.K.10a, RL.K.10b, RF.K.1b, RF.K.3a

Read Aloud

To support the unit concept, use one of the Read-Aloud Handbook selections for Unit 1. As you read, model the metacognitive strategy for the unit, Ask Questions, guided by the samples provided. You may also wish to select a read-aloud from your classroom or school library. To support the unit concept, use one of the suggested titles for Unit 1.

Shared Reading (iELD)

Introduce the Poem

Display "Five Little Monkeys." Read aloud the title as you point under each word. Invite students to look at the illustration and then turn to a partner and tell what they predict the poem will be about. Invite a few students to share their predictions with the whole class.

Read the Poem

First reading. Read aloud the poem fluently and expressively, pointing under each word.

Reread for Fluency: Prosody/Expression.

Before rereading the poem, ask students to listen for the flow and rhythm of the lines. Read the poem expressively, emphasizing the rhyming words. Model using a different voice for the dialogue at the end, and reading the exclamation with excitement and urgency. Choral-read the poem with students several times, encouraging them to read as you do and clap to the rhythm. Provide corrective feedback and/or validate students' efforts.

Build Concepts: Following Rules

Pose questions to connect the poem to the unit concept. For example:

- *What gave the monkeys the idea to jump on the bed?*
- *What do you think the monkeys learned about following rules?*

Review Print Concepts: Print Conveys Meaning

Display page 7. Call on a volunteer to point to the illustration on the page. Describe the illustration: it shows five monkeys having fun jumping on a bed. Ask another volunteer to point to the words. Remind students that it is the print, not the illustration, that carries the author's message.

Review Phonics: Initial m

Highlight the word **monkeys** in the first line. Ask students to read the word aloud with you. Ask volunteers to name the letter at the beginning of **monkeys** and the sound the letter **m** stands for. Do the same for **Mama, more.**

Identify Characters in a Story (10 MIN.) RL.K.1,

RL.K.3, RF.K.1a, SL.K.1a, SL.K.3

Engage Thinking

Remind students that characters are the people or animals that a story is about. Recall the story "A New Pet."

Ask: *Who are the characters in "A New Pet"?*

Model

Display and read aloud page 2. Model for students how to identify a character in the story.

Sample modeling: *To find out who the characters are in this story, I pay attention to the words and I look at the illustrations. On this page, I read about a new girl named Roma. I see Roma wearing a name tag in the illustration. Roma is one of the people this story is about. She is a character in this story.*

Guided Practice (iELD)

Continue to review the story to have students identify other characters. Provide directive and corrective feedback as needed. For example:

- *Who is standing with Roma in the illustration on page 2? What do you know about this girl? Is she a character in the story? Why do you think so?*
- *On page 6, which two children speak to Roma? What do they say? Are they characters in the story? Why do you think so?*

☑ Show Your Knowledge

Ask students to explain what a character is. Then direct them to complete these sentence frames orally: "One character in *Rules Are Cool* is _____. Other characters are her _____."

Challenge Activity Choose a familiar classroom storybook. Ask students to name the characters in the story.

Rules Are Cool

Student Objectives

I will be able to:
- Identify the characters in a story.

(iELD) Integrated ELD

Light Support
Read *Rules Are Cool* with students.
Say: *This book has one main character. Remember, a character is a person or an animal in a book. Who is the character?*
Say: *Roma is a character in the book. She is a girl.*
Review pages 12 and 13 and have students identify the other characters in the book and then say one piece of information about how those characters help Roma.

Moderate Support
Remind students that the people and animals in a story are called **characters**. Read *Rules Are Cool* with children.
Ask: *Who is a person in the book?*
Elicit that Roma is the character in the book.
Say: *Yes, Roma is a person in the book. She is a character in the book.*
Reread pages 10 and 11 and ask, *Who are the other characters that speak to Roma?* Ask students who the other characters are on pages 10 and 11 and how they help Roma. Elicit *They are her classmates.*
Help students complete the sentence frame:
Roma's classmates help her _____.

Substantial Support
Read the book *Rules Are Cool* with students. Then do a picture walk of the book with children.
Say: *This is a person in the story. Her name is Roma. She is a character in the book.*
Reread pages 8 and 9 and ask, *Who are the other characters who speak to Roma?*
Help students complete the sentence frame: *One character in the book is _____.*

ELD.PI.K.1, ELD.PI.K.6, ELD.PII.K.1

Rules Are Cool

Student Objectives

I will be able to:
• Write a class letter.
• Use nouns.

iELD Integrated ELD

Light Support
Ask students to remember important classroom rules. Have them refer to readings such as *Rules Are Cool* for assistance if needed. Then have children state the rules in their own words. For each rule, have students complete this sentence:
This is a good rule because _____.
Write the rules and their sentences on the board or on chart paper, and read them with students.

Moderate Support
Ask students to remember important classroom rules. Use books such as *Rules Are Cool* to help jog students' memories. Then help them phrase the rules as sentences, using these sentence frames:
One rule is _____.
Another rule is _____.
Write the sentences, including the frames, on the board or on chart paper. Help students read the sentences with you. Close by having students tell a partner one of the rules they remember.

Substantial Support
Explain that words on the page are spoken words written down. Display books such as *Rules Are Cool*, and review some of the rules mentioned in the readings.
Say: *We can work together to write down these rules.* Say one of the rules aloud, such as "Use indoor voices." Have students repeat the rule. Then write the words and read the sentence back to students, touching the words as you say them.
Say: *Use indoor voices—that's a rule!*
Repeat with other rules. If students are willing, have them try saying "That's a rule!" on their own.

ELD.PI.K.2, ELD.PI.K.10, ELD.PII.K.1

Write a Class Letter (10 MIN.) W.K.3, W.K.8, SL.K.1a, SL.K.1b, L.K.1a, L.K.1b

Engage Thinking

Review with students the rules they learned about in *Rules Are Cool*: be nice, take turns, give a helping hand, use indoor voices.

Ask: *How do you follow these rules in our school?*

💬 Collaborative Conversation: Partners

Tell students that before writing, you would like them to turn and talk to a partner briefly. Ask them to talk about a rule from the book that the class follows, one they would like to write about in a letter to the principal. Model how to do this.

Sample modeling: *When I tell my partner about a rule we follow, I say, "We follow the rule to use indoor voices in the cafeteria." When you speak to your partner, you can start your sentence the same way:* We follow the rule to _____.

Write the sentence frame for students. Provide one minute for partner discussion. Then bring students together and ask volunteers to share the ideas they discussed.

Write as a Group (iELD)

Collaborate with students to agree on sentences to write. Rehearse the message orally and model how to write it. Briefly discuss the parts of the letter: greeting, message, closing. As you guide the writing, include at least one noun. Actively engage students in the writing process by prompting them with questions. For example:

• *What do I need to do when I start the first word in the sentence?*
• *Is there a better word we can use here? What is it?*
• *Here is the end of the sentence. What punctuation mark do we need at the end of this sentence?*
• *Let's read our letter. Is there anything we want to add or change?*

Sample Shared Writing

Dear Mrs. Sanchez,

Our class received a new computer. The computer helps us with our writing.

All the students wanted to use it at the same time.

We followed the rule to take turns and respect one another.

Sincerely,

Mrs. Green's class

Build Language: Nouns

Circle a noun in your sample writing. Point out that this word is a noun. Remind students that a noun is a word that names a person, place, or thing. Ask volunteers to use each of the following nouns in an oral sentence: **teacher, student, playground, desk.**

 **Write Independently**

Ask students to draw a picture showing a rule they follow at school. They can add a simple label or caption.

Small-Group Differentiated Instruction (15 MIN. per Group)

Meet with Small Groups

Select small-group reading titles or activities based on students' needs. See the Small-Group Instructional Planner for titles that support a range of instructional reading levels within the unit topic. Remind students to apply what they learned to their small-group reading experiences.

Say: *Today we practiced identifying the characters in a story following the class rules. Knowing who the story is about helps us understand the story better. If you listen to a book with characters today in your small group, pay attention to what the characters do and say. Remember that characters can be people or animals.*

Whole-Group Reflect and Share

Bring the class back together. Ask volunteers to name and describe characters in small-group texts they listened to.

Focus Skill: a/a/ (20 MIN.) RF.K.2d, RF.K.3a, RF.K.3c

Phonological Awareness: Phoneme Isolation

Model/Practice

Say the words **can** and **wag.** Have students repeat the words.

Ask students to clap twice if they hear the same middle sound in each word pair. Then ask them to identify the middle sound that is the same in both words: **/aaa/.**

Continue with the word pairs **man/kit** and **pat/ran.** Each time students clap twice, have them say the two words and identify the middle sound that is the same.

Repeat the process with the following word pairs: **fan/lap, Sam/Tim, sat/pan, tap/ran, tip/fan, bat/tag.**

Letter-Sound Correspondences (iELD)

Review with Picture Cards

Place picture cards **ax** and **monkey** in the pocket chart. Have students say the names of the pictures and the sound at the beginning of each name.

Show students picture card **apple** and ask them what sound they hear at the beginning of the word. Place picture card **apple** under picture card **ant.**

Repeat with picture cards **map, antelope, astronaut,** and **mop.**

Replace picture card **monkey** with picture card **cat.** Place letter cards **a** under **ax** and **cat.** Ask students where they hear the /**a**/ sound in the words **ax** and **cat.**

Show students picture cards **apple, bat, mat,** and **ant.** Have them sort the pictures in the pocket chart according to the beginning or medial /**a**/ sound.

Blend Sounds

Review: *am*

Have students blend the word **am** using the routine from Day One.

High-Frequency Words

Review: *like*

Write the word **like.** Read aloud the word. Then without students seeing, erase a letter in one of the words. Ask students which letter is missing. Replace the letter as students read the word.

Review: *I*

Display high-frequency word card **I.** Have students read the word as fast as they can.

Student Objectives

I will be able to:
• Isolate initial and medial sound /**a**/.
• Practice letter-sound correspondences for **a/a/, m/m/.**
• Sort picture names with initial **a/a/** and **m/m/.**
• Sort picture names with initial and medial **a/a/.**
• Blend sounds **a/a/, m/m/.**
• Read previously taught high-frequency words: **I, like.**

Additional Materials

• Letter cards: **a, m**

Weekly Presentation
• Picture cards: **ant, antelope, apple, astronaut, ax, bat, cat, map, mat, monkey, mop**
• High-frequency word cards: **like, I**

(iELD) Integrated ELD

Light Support
Write **map** on the board and read it aloud.
Say: *What sound do you hear first in* **map***?*
Encourage student answers. Continue with **a/a/** and the middle of the word.

Moderate Support
Write the word **map** on the board and display the picture card.
Say: *This word has a beginning letter and a middle letter. What letter is the beginning of the word?*
Encourage student answers. Have students say /**m**/. Say /**mmmmmap**/ and have students repeat. Repeat with **a** as the middle letter, saying /**maaaaap**/ and explaining that **a** comes after the beginning of the word.

Substantial Support
Write the word **map** on the board and display the picture card. Then point to the **m.**
Say: *This letter is* **m***. It goes with the sound* /**m**/*. The* **m** *is at the beginning of the word* **map***. It comes first. It is the beginning.*
Repeat with **a/a/** and the word *middle.*
Ask: *Is* /**m**/ *the beginning of map? (yes) Is* /**m**/ *the middle of map? (no)*
Repeat with the **a.**

ELD.PI.K.1, ELD.PI.K.5, ELD.PII.K.4

Read Aloud and Shared Reading

(20 MIN.) RL.K.1, RF.K.3a, SL.K.1a, SL.K.1b, L.K.1b

Read Aloud

To support the unit concept, use one of the Read-Aloud Handbook selections for Unit 1. As you read, model the metacognitive strategy for the unit, Ask Questions, guided by the samples provided. You may also wish to select a favorite read-aloud from your classroom or school library. To support the unit concept, use one of the suggested titles for Unit 1.

Shared Reading (iELD)

Reread the Poem

First rereading. Read aloud the poem fluently and expressively, pointing under each word.

Reread for Fluency: Prosody/Expression. Invite students to choral-read the poem fluently and in a lively tone. Model appropriate intonation and pitch, particularly for the exclamation. Choral-read the poem with students several times. Provide corrective feedback and/or validate students' efforts.

Build Concepts: Following Rules

Pose questions to connect the poem to the unit concept. For example:

- Why do you think the doctor said, "No more monkeys jumping on the bed"?
- Do you think the Monkeys and their Mama will have new rules about jumping on the bed? If so, what would they be?
- What are things you can do on your bed? And why?

Review Phonics: Initial m

Highlight the word **monkeys** in the first line. Ask students to read the word aloud with you. Ask volunteers to name the letter at the beginning of **monkeys** and the sound the letter **m** stands for. Do the same for **Mama, more.**

Review Language: Nouns

Point out that the word **monkeys** is a noun. Remind students that a noun is a word that names a person, place, or thing. Ask a volunteer to use the word **monkeys** in an oral sentence. Do the same for the nouns **bed, head,** and **doctor.**

Read-Aloud Handbook   **Shared Reading, Vol. 1, p. 7 "Five Little Monkeys"**

Student Objectives

I will be able to:
- Read along with expression.
- Answer questions about rules.
- Identify initial **m**.
- Use nouns.

(iELD) Integrated ELD

Light Support
Say: *If I ask you a question, you tell me the answer.* Remind students that many questions begin with **what, why,** or **who.** Model by asking children "What color is your shirt?" Then display "Five Little Monkeys."
Ask: *What do you see?*
Model responding: *I see a monkey dressed in red.* Have students work in pairs and ask each other the question "What do you see?"

Moderate Support
Remind students that people ask questions when they want to know an answer.
Say: *When I ask you a question, you tell me the answer.*
Add that many questions, but not all, begin with *what, why,* or *who.* Display "Five Little Monkeys."
Say: *I'm going to ask you a question. What do you see in the picture? Now you say the answer.*
Have students name objects in the picture. Help children formulate sentences to give complete answers to the question.

Substantial Support
Tell students that you ask a question when you want to know something. Explain that a question can often begin with **what** or **why.** Model that your voice usually goes up in pitch when you ask a question.
Say: *You can answer a question when someone asks it.*
Display "Five Little Monkeys." Touch the monkey on the top.
Say: *What is this? This is a monkey.* Say the question with me: *What is this?* Now say the answer with me: *This is a monkey.*
Repeat, this time leaving out the word *monkey* for students to fill in orally.

ELD.PI.K.1, ELD.PI.K.5, ELD.PII.K.2

RL.K.1 With prompting and support, ask and answer questions about key details in a text., **RF.K.3a** Demonstrate basic knowledge of letter-sound correspondences by producing the primary or most frequent sound for each consonant., **SL.K.1a** Follow agreed-upon rules for discussions (e.g., listening to others and taking turns speaking about the topics and texts under discussion)., **SL.K.1b** Continue a conversation through multiple exchanges., **L.K.1b** Use frequently occurring nouns and verbs.

Compare and Contrast a Story and an Informational Text (15 MIN.) RL.K.9, RF.K.1a, SL.K.1a

What Are Some Rules at School? and *Rules Are Cool*

Student Objectives

I will be able to:
- Answer questions about details in texts.
- Recognize similarities and differences between two texts.

Additional Materials

Weekly Presentation
- Compare and Contrast Chart

Engage Thinking (iELD)

Display *What Are Some Rules at School?* and *Rules Are Cool*. Remind students that they know both of these texts very well and now they are ready to compare and contrast the texts to learn even more about them. Discuss how readers often compare and contrast the author's purpose and text features in different texts to get a better understanding of the information in each one. What is one thing that is similar about both texts? What is one thing that is different?

Model

Use a three-column chart to create a compare and contrast chart for *What Are Some Rules at School?* and *Rules Are Cool*. Review that in the first and third columns you will list ways the two texts are different. In the middle column, you will list ways in which the two texts are similar. Use think-alouds, such as the following samples to model how you compare and contrast texts.

Sample modeling: *To compare, I will think about what is the same about both these texts.* What Are Some Rules at School? *tells about rules students should follow at school, including rules to stay safe and to treat others with respect.* Rules Are Cool *also tells about rules for students in school. It tells about rules for students to be nice to others and to be safe. Since I found these same ideas in both texts, I will write them as comparisons in the middle column of the chart.*

Sample modeling: *To contrast, I will think about what is different about these two texts. In* What Are Some Rules at School?*, the text tells about rules for taking care of a school.* Rules Are Cool *does not mention these kinds of rules. That is one way the two texts are different. I will write that down as a contrast between the two texts.*

Guided Practice

Use directive and corrective prompts as needed to guide students to:

Compare and contrast genre.

- *In* Rules Are Cool, *there are characters and story events. Does* What Are Some Rules at School? *have these things? How is it different?*
- *What Are Some Rules at School?* is an informational text, because it gives facts and information. Is *Rules Are Cool* an informational text, too? What kind of text is it? How do you know?*

Compare and contrast text features.

- *Do both* What Are Some Rules at School? *and* Rules Are Cool *have photos? How are they different?*
- *There are four chapters in* What Are Some Rules at School? *Is that the same or different from* Rules Are Cool?
- *What Are Some Rules at School?* has a table of contents, a glossary, and an index. Does *Rules Are Cool* have these parts, too? Does that make the two texts the same or different?*

If necessary, continue to model how you think about the comparisons and contrasts. Collaborate with students to complete the chart. Reread the comparisons and contrasts together.

What Are Some Rules at School?	**Both Texts**	**Rules Are Cool**
Tells about rules for taking care of a school	Tell about school rules for students	Does not tell about rules for taking care of a school
No characters, story events	Tell about school rules for staying safe and respecting others	Characters, story events
Informational text		Story
Photos		No photos
Four chapters		No chapters
Table of contents, index, glossary		No table of contents, index, glossary

Sample Compare and Contrast Chart

 Show Your Knowledge

Ask students to talk with a partner about one way the two texts are similar and different. Students can use sentence frames such as, *These texts are similar because _____. These texts are different because _____.*

iELD Integrated ELD

Light Support

Review the meanings of **alike** and **different.**

Say: *Things are alike if they are mostly the same. They are different if they are mostly not the same.*

Display two markers, one red and one blue. Have students explain how they are alike. Then display the pencil and the eraser, and ask children to explain how they are different. Encourage them to use connecting words such as **because** in their sentences.

Moderate Support

Display two markers, one red and one blue.

Say: *These markers are alike. They are both markers. You can draw with both of them. They are alike.*

Then display the pencil and the eraser.

Say: *These are not alike. You write with a pencil. You erase with an eraser.*

Model both actions as you say them.

Say: *The pencil is long. The eraser is short. They are different.*

Display two other objects. Ask students if the objects are alike or different. Help them respond in complete sentences, such as *The toy cars are alike* or *The block and the hat are different.*

Substantial Support

Display two markers, one red and one blue. Hold one marker up.

Say: *This is a marker.*

Then hold up the other marker.

Say: *This is a marker, too. They are both markers. So, they are alike.*

Display a pencil and an eraser. Hold the pencil up.

Say: *This is a pencil.*

Hold up the eraser.

Say: *This is an eraser. They are not alike. They are different.*

Place the markers on one side of you and the pencil and eraser on the other.

Say: *Point to the ones that are alike.*

Model by pointing to the markers. Repeat with **different**, pointing to the pencil and the eraser. Repeat several times, mixing up the order as needed. Then ask children to point to one set of objects and say either **alike** or **different** to describe them.

ELD.PI.K.3, ELD.PI.K.12b, ELD.PII.K.2

RL.K.9 With prompting and support, compare and contrast the adventures and experiences of characters in familiar stories., **RF.K.1a** Follow words from left to right, top to bottom, and page by page., **SL.K.1a** Follow agreed-upon rules for discussions (e.g., listening to others and taking turns speaking about the topics and texts under discussion).

What Are Some Rules at School? **and** ***Rules Are Cool***

Student Objectives

I will be able to:
- Write a comparison and contrast text.
- Use verbs in my writing.

iELD Integrated ELD

Light Support

Review the two books with students.

Say: *We will write how these books are alike.*
Model finding a similarity by pointing to one book and saying, *This book tells about rules and why we have them.* Point to the other book.

Say: *This book also tells about ___.*
Have students finish the sentence with *rules and why they have them.*

Say: *They both tell about rules and why we have them. You can use the word* **both** *when you tell how two things are alike.*
Then write the sentence beginning *They both . . .* on the board. Have children read it with you.

Moderate Support

Review the two books with students. Tell students that they are looking for things that are alike in the two books. Then model finding a similarity by displaying one book and saying *This book tells about rules,* and then doing the same for the other book.

Say: *They both _____.*
Ask: *How are these books alike?*
Have students answer by using the words in the sentence.

Substantial Support

Review the two books with students. Model how to find similarities by displaying the books in turn and saying, *Does this book tell about rules? Yes, it does. Does this book tell about rules? Yes, it does. They both tell about rules.*

Write the sentence *They both tell about rules,* and read it with students. Then read it again, having students say the words **both** and **rules** chorally.

Say: *These books are alike. They both tell about rules.*

ELD.PI.K.2, ELD.PI.K.6, ELD.PII.K.1

Write a Comparison and Contrast Text (15 MIN.) RF.K.1a, W.K.2, W.K.8, SL.K.1a, SL.K.1b, SL.K.3, LK.1a, LK.1b

Engage Thinking

Remind students that they talked about how *What Are Some School Rules?* and *Rules Are Cool* were the same and different. Reread both texts, asking students to carefully examine the images in each one. Then ask:

- *What topic did both books tell about?*
- *What did you notice about the images in the two texts?*
- *What did you learn from them?*

Collaborative Conversation: Partners iELD

Tell students that before writing, you would like them to turn and talk to a partner briefly. Ask them to talk about the information they learned from the photos and the illustrations in each book and how it was the same. Model how you do this.

Sample modeling: *When I tell my partner about the photos and illustrations, I say, "Both the photos and the illustrations show a rule about taking turns." When it is your turn to speak to your partner, you can use the same sentence frame:* Both the photos and the illustrations show a rule about _____.

Write the sentence frame for students. Give partners one minute for discussion. Then gather all students and ask volunteers to share their ideas.

Write as a Group

Collaborate with students to agree on a sentence to write as a class. Rehearse the sentence orally and model how to write it. As you guide the writing, include at least one verb. Actively engage students in the writing process by prompting them with questions. For example:

- *What is the first word in our sentence?*
- *I will leave a space before I write the next word. Why do I do that?*
- *Let's go back to the text to find the word _____. How do we spell it? We can use what we know about letters and sounds.*
- *Are there any words we could add to make our sentence better?*
- *Let's reread our sentence. Is there anything we should change?*

Sample Shared Writing

We read both books. The photos and the illustrations show a rule about how students should help others.

Build Language: Verbs

Circle a verb in your sample writing. Tell students that this word is a verb. Remind them that a verb is a word that names an action. Name a few verbs and ask students to act out each one, such as **tap, smile, bend, jump.**

Write Independently

Ask students to name another rule that both the photos and the illustrations show. Encourage them to find the photos and illustrations they mention in each book.

Small-Group Differentiated Instruction (15 MIN. per Group)

Meet with Small Groups

Select small-group reading titles or activities based on students' needs. See the Small-Group Instructional Planner for titles that support a range of instructional reading levels within the unit topic. Remind students to apply what they learned to their small-group reading experiences.

Say: *We have used many strategies in this unit as we've learned about following the rules at home and school. We have learned about connecting illustrations to events. We have learned about identifying the main topic in informational text and identifying characters in stories. Remember to use these and other strategies as you listen to texts.*

Whole-Group Reflect and Share

Bring the class back together. Invite volunteers to share the strategies they applied as they listened to small-group texts.

RF.K.1a Follow words from left to right, top to bottom, and page by page., **W.K.2** Use a combination of drawing, dictating, and writing to compose informative/explanatory texts in which they name what they are writing about and supply some information about the topic., **W.K.8** With guidance and support from adults, recall information from experiences or gather information from provided sources to answer a question., **SL.K.1a** Follow agreed-upon rules for discussions (e.g., listening to others and taking turns speaking about the topics and texts under discussion)., **SL.K.1b** Continue a conversation through multiple exchanges., **SL.K.3** Ask and answer questions in order to seek help, get information, or clarify something that is not understood., **L.K.1a** Print many upper- and lowercase letters., **L.K.1b** Use frequently occurring nouns and verbs.

Pre-Decodable Reader: *I Like*

Student Objectives

I will be able to:
- Listen for and produce rhyme.
- Read previously taught high-frequency words: **like, I**
- Read decodable text.

Additional Materials

- Pre-decodable reader: *I Like*

Weekly Presentation
- High-frequency word cards: **I, like**

Monitor Student Reading of Connected Text

As students chorally read the decodable text and answer questions, ask these questions:

Are students able to . . .

As students chorally read the pre-decodable text and answer questions, ask these questions:

Are students able to . . .
- ❑ blend and read short **a** words in the text?
- ❑ read new high-frequency words with automaticity?
- ❑ demonstrate comprehension of the text by answering text-based questions?

Based on your observations, you may wish to support students' fluency, automaticity, and comprehension with additional decodable reading practice during intervention time.

Focus Skill: a/a/ (20 MIN.) RI.K.1, RI.K.10, RF.K.2a, RF.K.3a, RF.K.3c, RF.K.4

Phonological Awareness: Listen and Produce Rhyme

Model/Practice

Say the words **bat** and **sat**. Tell students that these words rhyme because they end with the same sounds.

Say: *Listen to these words:* **bat, sat.** *I hear* /**aaat**/ *at the end of* **bat,** *and* /**aaat**/ *at the end of* **sat.** *Say the words with me and listen to the ending sounds.*

Reread the poem "Apple Pie," and have students listen for the word that rhymes with **can.** Have students say the word aloud: **pan.** Then say these word pairs and have students clap if they rhyme: **hat/pat; man/mop; ham/Sam.** Ask students for other words that rhyme with **hat** and **pat.**

High-Frequency Words (iELD)

Review: *I, like*

Write the words **I** and **like.** Remind students that these are words they have been practicing so that they can read them quickly. Have students read the words aloud several times.

Hold up the high-frequency word card **I,** and call on individual students to quickly read the word. Then have the student use the word in an oral sentence. Have the other students clap when they hear **I.** Repeat for the high-frequency word **like.**

Pre-Decodable Reader: *I Like*

Introduce the Book

Point to the book's title, *I Like,* and have students read the words as you run your finger under them.

Ask: *What do you see on the cover? What is the boy doing?*

Read the Book

Discuss what the rebuses on pages 2-8 stand for. Turn to page 2, and have students read the sentence aloud so you can check their reading. Have students continue to read, reading the high-frequency words quickly and blending the decodable word, **am.**

Connect Phonics to Comprehension

When students have finished reading, ask:

- *What was the boy making?*
- *What was he happy about at the end of the story?*

Turn to a partner and retell the story.

RI.K.1 With prompting and support, ask and answer questions about unknown words in a text., **RI.K.10** Actively engage in group reading activities with purpose and understanding., **RF.K.2a** Recognize and produce rhyming words., **RF.K.3a** Demonstrate basic knowledge of letter-sound correspondences by producing the primary or most frequent sound for each consonant., **RF.K.3c** Read common high-frequency words by sight (e.g., the, of, to, you, she, my, is, are, do, does)., **RF.K.4** Read emergent-reader text with purpose and understanding.

©2017 Benchmark Education Company, LLC

Read Aloud and Shared Reading

(15 MIN.) RL.K.10, RF.K.3b, RF.K.3c, SL.K.1a, SL.K.1b

Read Aloud

To support the unit concept, use one of the Read-Aloud Handbook selections for Unit 1. As you read, model the metacognitive strategy for the unit, Ask Questions, guided by the samples provided. You may also wish to select a favorite read-aloud from your classroom or school library. To support the unit concept, use one of the suggested titles for Unit 1.

Shared Reading (iELD)

Reread the Story

First rereading. Read aloud the story fluently and expressively, pointing under each word.

Reread for Fluency: Prosody/Expression. Call attention to the exclamation point in the last sentence that tells a reader to read with excitement. Invite students to join in as you read the story, using the same expression they hear from you. Provide corrective feedback and/or validate students' efforts.

Build Concepts: Following Rules

Pose questions to connect the story to the unit concept. For example:

- Do you think Max followed the rules when he followed the boy to school?
- Should there be rules for dogs? What would they be?

Review Phonics: Short a

Highlight the name **Max** in the first sentence. Ask students to read the name aloud with you. Then point to the letter **a** and call on a volunteer to name the letter. Ask another volunteer to tell the sound the letter **a** stands for in the name **Max**.

Review High-Frequency Words: *like*

Tell students that this text contains some words they have learned. Point to the previously taught high-frequency word **like.** Ask students to turn to a partner and tell their partner the high-frequency word. Remind students to look for high-frequency words they know when they read a new text.

RL.K.10 Actively engage in group reading activities with purpose and understanding., RF.K.3b Associate the long and short sounds with the common spellings (graphemes) for the five major vowels.(Identify which letters represent the five major vowels (Aa, Ee, Ii, Oo, and Uu) and know the long and short sound of each vowel. More complex long vowel graphemes and spellings are targeted in the grade 1 phonics standards.) CA, RF.K.3c Read common high-frequency words by sight (e.g., the, of, to, you, she, my, is, are, do, does)., SL.K.1a Follow agreed-upon rules for discussions (e.g., listening to others and taking turns speaking about the topics and texts under discussion)., SL.K.1b Continue a conversation through multiple exchanges.

Read-Aloud Handbook

Shared Reading Vol. 1, p. 6
"No Dogs Allowed in School"

Student Objectives

I will be able to:
- Read along with expression.
- Identify short **a**.
- Answer questions about rules.
- Recognize the high-frequency word **like.**

(iELD) Integrated ELD

Light Support
Read the story with students, focusing on the words **followed** and **called.** Explain that these two words tell about something that already happened.
Say: *You can change the words a little bit to show you are doing something now.*
Model calling a friend and then putting the pretend phone down.
Say: *I called my friend.*
Repeat, but this time say *I am calling my friend* as you pretend to push the buttons on the phone. Have children say these sentences as they act them out. Repeat with **followed** and **am following.**

Moderate Support
Read the story with students, pausing to explain the meanings of **followed, called, unhappy,** and **stay.** When you are finished, say one of the words at random. Have children take turns acting out the action. Then help them say the sentence you used, such as *I called my friend* or *I am unhappy.*

Substantial Support
Read the story with students, pausing to demonstrate the meanings of these words:

Followed	Have a child walk forward while you walk after that child. **Say:** *I followed _____.*
Called	Pantomime using a cell phone. **Say:** *I called my friend.*
Unhappy	Frown and look sad. **Say:** *I am unhappy.*
Stay	Walk up and down, and then stop. **Say:** *I will stay right here.*

Have children say and act out the words.

ELD.PI.K.5, ELD.PI.K.6, ELD.PII.K.6

Mentor Read-Aloud Topic Introduction Vol. 1, pp. 2-3

Student Objectives

I will be able to:
- Revise a first draft about why we have rules.
- Edit a first draft to create a final copy.
- Use a word processing program and printer to publish writing.

Additional Materials

- Sample Draft from Day 2
- Access to computer/word-processing program/printer

Weekly Presentation
- Editing Checklist

 **Integrated ELD**

Light Support

Write *I saw a cat* on the board, and read it aloud. Explain that you would like to make the sentence more interesting. Tell students that you can revise the sentence to tell what the cat was doing. Model by adding "climbing a tree" to the sentence. Read the new sentence aloud. Have students suggest additions to the sentence that follow the same format.

Moderate Support

Write the following sentence on the board and read it aloud: *I saw a cat.* Explain that this sentence makes sense, but that it is not interesting. Model using a describing word such as **big, little,** or **brown** to revise the sentence. Write the new sentence on the board.
Say: *Let's read this sentence together.*
Then have students offer words of their own to revise.

Substantial Support

Write the following sentence on the board and read it aloud: *The cat played the dog.* Shake your head.
Say: *This doesn't sound right. I know what a cat is.*
Have students use words or gestures to describe a cat.
Say: *I know what a dog is.*
Repeat, having students describe a dog.
Say: *But "the cat played the dog" isn't right.*
Show how to revise the sentence so it says *The cat played with the dog.* Read the sentence aloud, and have students say it with you.
Say: *I revised the sentence and now it sounds right!*

ELD.PI.K.2, ELD.PI.K.10, ELD.PII.K.2

Revise and Edit a Response to the Essential Question (15 MIN.) W.K.2, W.K.5, W.K.6, L.K.1a, L.K.1b

Engage Thinking

Display the text you drafted with students on Day 5, Week 2. Remind students that this is a first draft. Explain that in this lesson you will show them how a skillful writer revises and edits a draft to create a final version to publish or share with others.

Revise (iELD)

Review what happens in this key step in the writing process. Students should understand that during the revision stage, writers reread their work and focus on how to make it better by adding details to make ideas more clear and combining sentences to make the writing smoother.

Reread the sample draft from Week 2. Use a think-aloud to model how you evaluate the text critically and find ways to improve it. As you think aloud, make revisions to the draft to demonstrate what writers do. Use the sample think-alouds provided as a model of how to think aloud about the text you drafted.

Sentence	Sample Modeling
1	*I think my main idea sentence is clear. I do not need to make any changes to this sentence.*
2	*This sentence tells that rules help us to be good team players. I want readers to understand that I mean sports teams, so I will add the words **in sports** at the end of the sentence.*
3	*This sentence tells that rules help us learn at school. I will add a detail to make my idea more clear. After the word **learn,** I will add the words **and do our best** because that is an important part of the idea, too.*
5 and 6	*These two short sentences start out the same way. I will combine them into one longer sentence: "Rules help us be fair to others and respect others." This sentence sounds smoother.*

Edit

Remind students that they have been working on incorporating correct language in their writing. Explain that after revising, a writer edits his or her work. This means going back and correcting any errors in grammar, punctuation, or spelling. Display and read aloud the editing checklist, and use it with students to edit your revised text.

I capitalized the first word in every sentence.

I wrote complete sentences.

I used nouns and verbs.

I spelled all words correctly.

I used correct punctuation for each sentence.

Editing Checklist

Publish

You may wish to use a word-processing program to model how you turn your revised and edited text into a final copy for publication or sharing. Discuss with students many ways in which writers share their writing—in print, online, or audios or videos.

Sample revised and edited text

We need rules to help us learn and be safe. We learn how to care for our pets by following rules. Rules help us be fair and respect others. We need rules to be good citizens.

Write Independently

Ask students to draw and label a picture to show their response to the essential question.

Small Group Differentiated Instruction (15 MIN. per Group)

Meet with Small Groups

Select small-group reading titles or activities based on students' needs. See the Small-Group Instructional Planner for titles that support a range of instructional reading levels within the unit topic. Remind students to apply what they learned to their small-group reading experiences.

Say: *Remember all the strategies we have learned in this unit. Use them when you listen to texts in small groups. You can use these strategies when you listen to texts in our next unit, too.*

Whole-Group Reflect and Share

Bring the class back together. Invite volunteers to share the strategies they applied during small-group reading.

W.K.2 Use a combination of drawing, dictating, and writing to compose informative/explanatory texts in which they name what they are writing about and supply some information about the topic., **W.K.5** With guidance and support from adults, respond to questions and suggestions from peers and add details to strengthen writing as needed., **W.K.6** With guidance and support from adults, explore a variety of digital tools to produce and publish writing, including in collaboration with peers., **L.K.1a** Print many upper- and lowercase letters., **L.K.1b** Use frequently occurring nouns and verbs.

Pre-Decodable Reader: *I Like*

Student Objectives

I will be able to:
- Blend phonemes.
- Practice letter-sound correspondences for **a/a/, m/m/.**
- Blend sounds **/a/, /m/.**
- Write legibly.
- Read previously taught high-frequency words: **I, like.**
- Read decodable text.

Additional Materials

- Pre-decodable reader: *I Like*
- Letter cards**: a, m**

Weekly Presentation
- High-frequency word cards: **I, like**

Focus Skill: a/a/ (15 MIN.) RI.K.1, RI.K.10, RF.K.2e, RF.K.3a, RF.K.3c, RF.K.4, L.K.1a

Phonological Awareness: Phoneme Blending

Model

Say: *I am going to say the sounds in a word. Listen as I say each sound: /m/ /a/ /t/. I can blend these sounds together: /mmmaaat/, **mat.** Now you blend the sounds with me: /mmm//aaa/ /t/ /mmmaaat/* **mat.** *Say the word with me:* **mat.**

Practice

Say: *I will say the sounds in a word. Listen as I say each sound. Then blend the sounds together to say the word.*

/j/ /a/ /m/, /m/ /a/ /d/, /p/ /a/ /t/, /h/ /a/ /d/

Letter-Sound Correspondences

Review: a/a/

Display letter card **a.**

Say: *This is the letter* **a.** *The letter* **a** *stands for* **/aaa/.** *What sound does this letter stand for?*

Repeat for the letter **m.**

Blend Sounds

Review: am

Have students blend the word **am.** Place letter cards **a, m** in a pocket chart. Point to the letter **a.**

Say: *This is the letter* **a.** *The letter* **a** *stands for* **/aaa/.** *Say* **/aaa/.** *This is the letter* **m.** *The letter* **m** *stands for* **/mmm/.** *Say* **/mmm/.** *Listen as I blend the two sounds together* **/aaammm/.** *Now blend the sounds to read the word,* **am.**

Dictation

Review

Dictate these sounds for students to spell. Have them repeat the sound and then write the letter that stands for the sound: **/a/, /m/.**

Dictate the following word for students to spell: **am.**

Say: *When I say the word* **am,** *I hear two sounds,* **/a/ /m/.** *I know the letter* **a** *stands for* **/aaa/** *and the letter* **m** *stands for* **/mmm/.** *I will write the letters* **a** *and* **m** *to spell the word* **am.**

After students have written the word, have them correct their papers.

High-Frequency Words

Review: like, I

Write the words **like, I.** Focusing on one word at a time, have students spell the word as you point to each letter. Then erase the word, say the word, and have students spell it on their own.

Decodable Text

Say: *Let's read the words together:* **I am.** *What word could you add to make this sentence tell something about you? You could say* **I am happy.**

Have students take turns reading **I am** and adding a word. Repeat for **I like.** Then have students choose one of the sentences to write and fill in with a word that tells something about them.

| I am _____. |
| I like _____. |

Pre-Decodable Reader: *I Like*

Reread

Have partners reread aloud *I Like.* Circulate and listen in. Note students' speed, accuracy, and intonation. Based on the group as a whole, provide some general feedback and validate successes. If students need additional practice in reading the text, provide support during small-group reading instruction.

iELD Integrated ELD

Light Support

Use the following list of words: **am**, **is**, **ran**, **can**, **sit**, **had**, and **bit**. Say each word slowly and carefully, and have students tell you whether the word contains the sound /a/, using this form:

_____ *has/does not have the sound /a/.*

Then ask students to use each word in a short sentence. Help them make their sentences grammatically correct. Point out that all the words used are verbs, or action words, and that you use them to tell what someone is doing.

Moderate Support

Use words and brief sentences to help students distinguish which words have the sound /a/ and which do not. Say the following words carefully and slowly, and follow the word with the sentence given. Have students respond "_____ has the sound /a/" or "_____ does not have the sound /a/."

am	I am a grown-up.
is	She is a child.
ran	The girl ran fast.
can	A cat can meow.
sit	We will sit down.
had	I had a good time.
bit	I bit the apple.

Tell students that all of these words are verbs, or action words.

Substantial Support

The sound /a/ is common in English, but there are a number of languages in which it does not appear, including Spanish. Students from these language backgrounds may have a more difficult time hearing and distinguishing this sound. Tell students that you will say some words. Say that some of them have the sound /a/ and some do not. Say the words below slowly and carefully, having students say "yes" if the word has /a/ and "no" if it does not.

at, am, in, ax, it

map, mitt, cat, pin, man

Have students repeat each word after you. Have them pay special attention to how people hold their mouths when they say /a/.

ELD.PI.K.1, ELD.PI.K.5, ELD.PII.K.3

RI.K.1 With prompting and support, ask and answer questions about unknown words in a text., **RI.K.10** Actively engage in group reading activities with purpose and understanding., **RF.K.2e** Add or substitute individual sounds (phonemes) in simple, one-syllable words to make new words., **RF.K.3a** Demonstrate basic knowledge of letter-sound correspondences by producing the primary or most frequent sound for each consonant., **RF.K.3c** Read common high-frequency words by sight (e.g., the, of, to, you, she, my, is, are, do, does)., **RF.K.4** Read emergent-reader text with purpose and understanding., **L.K.1a** Print many upper- and lowercase letters.

Reflect on Unit Concepts (20 MIN.) SL.K.1, SL.K.2,

SL.K.2a, SL.K.3, SL.K.4, SL.K.6

Mentor Read-Aloud Topic
Introduction Vol. 1, pp. 2-3

Student Objectives

I will be able to:
- Share an answer to *Why do we have rules?*
- Take turns during a collaborative conversation about rules.
- Ask and answer questions about rules.

Additional Materials

Weekly Presentation
- Unit 1 Video
- Essential Question and Answer Chart

Engage Thinking

Say: *Over the past three weeks we have read and listened to informational texts, stories, and poems about why we have rules. What do you remember about those texts?*

Lead students to recall and retell information from the texts they have read and listened to in the unit. Invite all students to contribute to the discussion, reminding them to speak clearly. If students need support as they think about texts from the unit, display the texts for review.

Display the Unit 1 Opener and read aloud the essential question.

Essential Question: Why do we have rules?

Say: *Everyone may have different ideas about why we have rules, based on the texts from the unit and on what you already know about rules. Today we will talk more about this important question.*

View Multimedia

Remind students that they watched a short video at the beginning of the unit before they read any of the selections. Show the video to students again. Prompt students to discuss how the video fits with the unit and the essential question. Ask them to share how their viewing experience was different than their first viewing.

Collaborative Conversation: Peer Group

Divide students into peer groups of four to six students. Tell students that you would like them to collaborate to develop a group answer to the essential question.

Use a think-aloud to model one step you would like students to follow during this collaborative conversation:

Sample modeling: *In our conversation today, there is one direction we need to follow. We need to take turns, speaking one at a time. One person will begin the conversation while everyone else listens carefully. Then it will be the next person's turn to speak. Each person will have a turn to speak.*

Ensure that all students understand the step before groups begin their conversations. Have a volunteer from each group restate the step in his or her own words.

Give students approximately five minutes to share their ideas and develop their answer. As they converse, monitor their conversations to ensure that they follow directions, stay on task, and that all students in the group participate.

Share

Bring groups together. Call on a spokesperson for each group to present his or her group's answer to the essential question. If necessary, review your directions for what should happen as student groups share their ideas. For example:

1. *As students share ideas, others listen carefully to make sure they understand what is being said.*
2. *Students raise a hand and ask questions if they don't understand something.*

Ask a few students to restate these ideas in their own words.

As group spokespeople present ideas, capture their ideas in an Essential Question and Answers Chart. At the end of the unit, post the chart in your classroom.

Why do we have rules?

Rules help everyone.

The rules at school help us learn.

The rules at school help us treat others with respect.

If we don't follow the rules, we can get in trouble.

Rules are made to keep us safe.

It is important to learn the rules for sports.

Rules make us good speakers and listeners.

Sample Essential Question and Answers Chart

Use Digital Media

Ask each group of students to choose one important rule they learned about in the unit. Direct them to practice acting out how the rule is put into practice. After sufficient practice, assist students in making a video that shows them acting out the rule.

Observe and Assess

As students reflect on unit concepts and present ideas, use the following questions to informally assess students' understanding.

- *Do students recognize why we have rules?*
- *Do students understand that there are important rules for home, school, and other areas of life?*
- *Were students able to support their responses to the essential question?*

iELD Integrated ELD

Light Support

Help build vocabulary and sentence structure by helping students form sentences telling about the readings for the week. Review the essential question with students. Ask them to name or describe texts that they read. Display the texts as they are mentioned. Ask comprehension questions, such as *Who are the characters?* and *What happens in the story?* Have students answer in complete sentences. Review that all the texts are about rules.

Moderate Support

Help build vocabulary for use in group discussions. Review the essential question with students. Then display one of the texts you read during the week. Ask students to help you read the title of the text; then have students tell you something they remember about the text. Help by providing words as needed. Encourage them to form complete sentences, such as *Max went to school* or *Ben wanted a pet*. Accept shorter phrases as well. Repeat with other readings. Remind children that the readings all focused on rules.

Substantial Support

Support students by providing them with vocabulary to use in their discussions. Review the essential question with students. Remind them that the readings were about rules. Display several of the readings.

Say: *Do you remember the story about Max? Max was a _____.*

Pause and let students fill in the missing word **dog**, or guide children to say **dog** with you.

Say: *Max went to _____.*

Pause and let students fill in the missing word **school**, or guide them to say it with you.

Say: *Max had to leave school. No dogs allowed! That's the _____.*

Help students fill in **rule.** Repeat for other texts, guiding students to remember the key details of the readings and helping them say the important words.

ELD.PI.K.1, ELD.PI.K.9, ELD.PII.K.6

SL.K.1 Participate in collaborative conversations with diverse partners about kindergarten topics and texts with peers and adults in small and larger groups:, **SL.K.2** Confirm understanding of a text read aloud or information presented orally or through other media by asking and answering questions about key details and requesting clarification if something is not understood., **SL.K.2a** Understand and follow one- and two-step oral directions. CA, **SL.K.3** Ask and answer questions in order to seek help, get information, or clarify something that is not understood., **SL.K.4** Describe familiar people, places, things, and events and, with prompting and support, provide additional detail., **SL.K.6** Speak audibly and express thoughts, feelings, and ideas clearly.

UNIT 2 Formative Assessment Opportunities

	Minute-By-Minute Observation	*Daily* Performance Monitoring	*Weekly* Progress Monitoring
Reading/Writing Mini-lessons	• Collaborative Conversations • Guided Practice	• Show Your Knowledge • Write Independently • Student Conferences	• Weekly Assessments *See back of Unit 2 Tab for skills assessed*
Phonics Mini-lessons	• Practice	• Independent practice activities • Read Decodable Text	• Spelling Assessment and Dictation
Small-Group Reading	• Observe and monitor student reading	• Retelling • Graphic organizers • Text-Evidence Questions	• *Conduct oral reading records as appropriate*

Recommended observation forms:
• Speaking and listening observation form
• Small-Group Reading Observation Records
• Individual Reading Conference Form

UNIT 2 Vocabulary and Spelling

	Domain-Specific	General Academic		Instructional	High-Frequency Words	Spelling
Week 1		crawled cried dashed gnawed laughed mighty raced	roared skipped slowpoke speedy trousers walked windowsill	contrast infer similar theme	the we	the we
Week 2	porridge	angry argued called cried growled grumbled said	smelled slice surprise upstairs whispered	draft features	go see	go see
Week 3	flour mill ripened wheat	barked cut grunted meowed said wagging watched		demonstrate highlight	go I like see the we	go I like see the we

Week 1 Skills at a Glance

	Day 1	Day 2
Reading Mini-Lessons	**Mentor Read-Alouds:** Topic Introduction, pp. 12-13 **Unit 2 Video** **Introduce Unit 2: Every Story Has Characters (10 Min.), p. 116** SL.K.1a, SL.K.1b, SL.K.2 **Read-Aloud Handbook** **Shared Readings:** "Sad Ladybug, Glad Ladybug," p. 8 **Read Aloud and Shared Reading (20 Min.), p. 117** RL.K.1, RL.K.5, RL.K.10, RL.K.10a, RL.K.10b, RF.K.1a, RF.K.3b, RF.K.4, SL.K.1a, SL.K.1b • Fluency: Rate/Pausing • Build Concepts: Every Story Has Characters • Model Print Concepts: Directionality: Left to Right • Review Phonics: Initial and Medial Short *a* **Mentor Read Alouds:** "The Tortoise and the Hare," pp. 14-17 **"The Tortoise and the Hare": Listen and Retell Key Events (10 Min.), p. 118** RI.K.1, RI.K.2, RI.K.5, RI.K.10, RI.K.10a, RI.K.10b, SL.K.1a, SL.K.1b, SL.K.2	**Read-Aloud Handbook** **Shared Readings:** "Sad Ladybug, Glad Ladybug," p. 8 **Read Aloud and Shared Reading (20 Min.), p. 126** RL.K.1, RF.K.1a, RF.K.3c, RF.K.3c, RF.K.4, SL.K.1a, SL.K.1b • Fluency: Rate/Pausing • Build Concepts: Every Story Has a Character • Review Phonics: Initial *s* **Mentor Read-Alouds:** "The Tortoise and the Hare," pp. 14-17 **Identify Genre: Fantasy (10 Min.), p. 127** RL.K.1, RL.K.5, SL.K.2, SL.K.3 **Identify and Describe Story Characters (10 Min.), p. 128** RL.K.1, RL.K.3, SL.K.2, SL.K.3
Writing Mini-Lessons	**Write Key Events (10 Min.), p. 120** W.K.2, W.K.8, SL.K.1a, SL.K.1b, SL.K.4, L.K.1a, L.K.1c • Build Language: Form Regular Plural Nouns	**Write an Opinion (10 Min.), p. 130** W.K.1, W.K.8, SL.K.1a, SL.K.1b, SL.K.4, L.K.1a, L.K.1c • Build Language: Form Regular Plural Nouns
Phonics Mini-Lessons	**Focus Skill: /s/ (20 Min.), p. 124** RF.K.2d, RF.K.3a, RF.K.c, L.K.1a • Phonological Awareness: Phoneme Isolation • High-Frequency Words: *the*	**Focus Skill: /s/ (20 Min.), p. 132** RF.K.2c, RF.K.2d, RF.K.3a, L.K.1a • Phonological Awareness: Phoneme Isolation • High-Frequency Words: *we*

Mentor Read-Aloud 1: "The Tortoise and the Hare"

Fable

Quantitative	Lexile 480L

Qualitative Analysis of Text Complexity

Purpose and Levels of Meaning ②
• The story has a simple plot, but comprehending the moral—slow and steady wins the race—requires the reader to make an inference.

Structure ①
• The story has a chronological narrative structure.

Language Conventionality and Clarity ②
• Story includes a few complex and compound sentences.

Knowledge Demands ①
• The story is likely familiar, and requires no prior knowledge of actual animal behavior.

Day 3	**Day 4**	**Day 5**
Read-Aloud Handbook **Shared Readings:** "Diddle, Diddle, Dumpling," p. 9 **Read Aloud and Shared Reading (20 Min.), p. 134** RL.K.1, RL.K.3, RL.K.5, RL.K.10, RL.K.10a, RL.K.10b, SL.K.1a, SL.K.1b, SL.K.3, SL.K.6 • Fluency: Rate/Pausing • Build Unit Concepts: Every Story Has Characters • Model Poetic Features: Rhyming Words • Review High-Frequency Words: *the* **Mentor Read-Alouds:** "The Little Helper," pp. 18-21 **"The Little Helper": Listen and Retell Key Details (10 Min.), p. 135** RL.K.1, RL.K.3, RL.K.5, RL.K.10, RL.K.10a, RLK.10b, SL.K.1a, SL.K.1b, SL.K.3, SL.K.6 **Make Inferences About Characters (10 Min.), p. 136** RL.K.1, RL.K.3	**Read-Aloud Handbook** **Shared Readings:** "Diddle, Diddle, Dumpling," p. 9 **Read Aloud and Shared Reading (20 Min.), p. 141** RL.K.1, RF.K.1a, RF.K.2a, RF.K.3a, RF.K.4, SL.K.3 • Fluency: Rate/Pacing • Build Concepts: Every Story Has Characters • Review Phonics: Initial s • Review Poetic features: Rhythm **Mentor Read-Alouds:** "The Little Helper," pp. 18-21 **Build Vocabulary: Shades of Meaning (10 Min.), p. 142** RL.K.4, L.K.5d, L.K.6 **Identify Major Story Events (10 Min.), p. 143** RL.K.1, RL.K.3	**Read-Aloud Handbook** **Shared Readings:** "Sad Ladybug, Glad Ladybug," p. 8 **Read Aloud and Shared Reading (20 Min.), p. 147** RL.K.1, RF.K.1a, RF.K.3b, RF.K.3c, RF.K.4, SL.K.3 • Fluency: Rate/Pacing • Build Concepts: Every Story Has Characters • Review Phonics: Initial s • Review High-Frequency Words: *the* **Mentor Read-Alouds:** "The Tortoise and the Hare," pp. 14-17 "The Little Helper," pp. 18-21 **Compare and Contrast Adventures of Two Characters (20 Min.), p. 148** RL.K.3, RL.K.9, SL.K.1a
Write About a Character (10 Min.), p. 138 W.K.2, W.K.5, W.K.8, L.K.1a, L.K.1c • Build Language: Form Regular Plural Nouns	**Write a Monologue (10 Min.), p. 144** W.K.3, W.K.8, SL.K.1a, SL.K.1b, SL.K.2, L.K.1a, L.K.1c • Build Language: Form Regular Plural Nouns	**Write to Compare and Contrast Two Characters (10 Min.), p. 150** W.K.2, W.K.8, L.K.1a, L.K.1c • Build Language: Form Regular Plural Nouns
Focus Skill: s/s/ (20 Min.), p. 140 RF.K.2d, RF.K.3a, RF.K.3c • Phonological Awareness: Phoneme Isolation • High-Frequency Words: *the, we, I, like*	**Pre-Decodable Reader:** *I Am Sam* **Focus Skill: s/s (20 Min.), p. 146** RL.K.1, RL.K.10, RF.K.2a, RF.K.3a, RF.K.3c, RF.K.4 • Phonological Awareness: Recognize and Produce Rhyme • High-Frequency Words: *I, like, we, the*	**Pre-Decodable Reader:** *I Am Sam* **Focus Skill: s/s/ (20 Min.), p. 152** RL.K.1, RL.K.10, RF.K.2.c, RF.K.3a, RF.K.3c, RF.K.4, L.K.1a • Phonological Awareness: Blend Onset and Rime • High-Frequency Words: *I, like, the, we*

Mentor Read-Aloud 2: "The Little Helper"

The Little Helper

One day, a tiny mouse crawled up a little hill. But the hill was a big, mighty lion who had been fast asleep.

"Who dares to wake me, the King of Beasts?" roared the lion. He grabbed the little mouse in his great big paw.

The little mouse trembled and shook. "Forgive me, Your Majesty!" he cried. "Please let me live! I may be able to help you someday."

Realistic Fiction

Quantitative	Lexile® 610L
Qualitative Analysis of Text Complexity	

Purpose and Levels of Meaning ①
• The story has a simple moral: heart matters more than size.

Structure ①
• The story has a chronological narrative structure and tight, cause-and-effect plot.

Language Conventionality and Clarity ①
• Sentences are simple, language is common usage and vocabulary is familiar.

Knowledge Demands ①
• This story may feel familiar to readers because it is derived from Aesop, but requires no prior knowledge.

Introduce Unit 2: Every Story Has Characters (10 MIN.) SL.K.1a, SL.K.1b, SL.K.2

Mentor Read-Aloud Topic Introduction Vol. 1, pp. 12-13

Student Objectives

I will be able to:

- Ask **what**, **when**, **where**, **why**, and **how** questions about how people are different.
- Share what I know about how people are different.
- Take turns when speaking.

(iELD) Integrated ELD

Light Support

Have each student in a pair tell you the names of three objects he or she sees in the room (nouns or noun phrases). Write each object on a card. Place the six cards face down on a table or desk.

In a separate pile, face down, place word cards for **Who, What, When, Where, Why,** and **How.**

Have partners take turns turning over a card from each pile and asking and answering a question based on the card.

Moderate Support

Provide partners with word cards for **Who, What, When, Where, Why,** and **How.** Have partners turn the cards over and shuffle them. Taking turns, each student should turn over a card and pose a question that begins with the word on the card. If they need help, suggest that students use a verb or a noun from the Word Bank in each question.

The partner should answer the question. Then the card should be returned to the pile, again face down.

Word Bank

[verbs] do like think feel eat see hear
[nouns] family animal story outfit food color

Substantial Support

Create six word cards for **Who, What, When, Where, Why,** and **How.** Use them to help partners form questions they could ask each other. Guide partners to take turns asking and answering the questions.

ELD.PI.K.1, ELD.PII.K.3, ELD.PII.K.4

Pose the Essential Question

Display the Topic 2 Introduction and read aloud the essential question. Explain to students that they will be thinking about this question over the next few weeks.

How are people different?

State Unit Objectives

Say: *In this unit, we will learn about people. Some people, like you and me, are real. Some people are make-believe characters and not real characters. Let's look at the characters on these pages. Can you name them? All of these characters are not real. They are all different, too. For example, some of them are animals, one is a girl, one is an egg, and one character is made of wood!*

Link to Prior Knowledge

Ask students to tell a partner one way they know people can be different, such as their hair or eye color.

View Multimedia

Display or have students access the Unit 2 video on their devices.

Collaborative Conversation: Partners (iELD)

Tell student that you would like them to share questions they have about the unit theme. Model how you ask questions about how people are different.

Say: *When I ask a question, I start with a question word. Question words are **who, what, when, where, why,** and **how.** To ask a question about the unit theme, I could say, "What is one way people are different?" When I talk with a partner, I take turns speaking and listening. I also keep talking about the same thing. I do not change and talk about something else.*

Share

Ask volunteers to share a question with the class. Make a list of the questions. Post them in your classroom to refer to and add to during the unit. Reinforce the idea that asking and answering questions will help students learn new information.

SL.K.1a Follow agreed-upon rules for discussions (e.g., listening to others and taking turns speaking about the topics and texts under discussion)., **SL.K.1b** Continue a conversation through multiple exchanges., **SL.K.2** Confirm understanding of a text read aloud or information presented orally or through other media by asking and answering questions about key details and requesting clarification if something is not understood.

Read Aloud and Shared Reading (20 MIN.)

RL.K.1, RL.K.5, RL.K.10, RL.K.10a, RL.K.10b, RF.K.1a, RF.K.3b, RF.K.4, SL.K.1a, SL.K.1b

Read Aloud

To support the unit concept, use one of the Read-Aloud Handbook selections for Unit 2. As you read, model the metacognitive strategy for the unit, Visualize, guided by the samples provided. You may also wish to select a favorite read-aloud from your classroom or school library. To support the unit concept, use one of the suggested titles for Unit 2.

Shared Reading (iELD)

Display "Sad Ladybug, Glad Ladybug." Read aloud the title as you point under each word. Briefly discuss the illustration. Encourage students to share their prior knowledge about ladybugs. Invite students to turn to a partner and tell what they think the story will be about. Ask them to explain their predictions.

Read the Realistic Fiction

First rereading. Read aloud the text fluently and expressively, pointing under each word.

Reread for fluency: Rate/Pausing. Read with appropriate pauses. Leave a brief pause at the end of each sentence. Invite students to choral read the first sentence of the passage with you, emphasizing pausing at the period. Provide corrective feedback and/or validate students' efforts.

Build Concepts: Every Story Has Characters

Pose questions to connect the realistic fiction to the unit concept. For example:

- *Characters are the people in a story. Who are the characters in this story?*

- *How are the two characters different?*

- *Could these characters and story be real?*

Model Print Concepts: Directionality: Left to Right

Remind students that we read from left to right. Ask a volunteer to show you where to begin reading the selection. Then point to the first word, read it aloud, and ask students to show where to read next.

Review Phonics: Initial and Medial Short a

Point out the word **sad** in the title. Read the word aloud and ask students to identify the sound in the middle of the word. Ask them to say the letter that represents the sound /a/. Repeat with **glad** in the title and **Pam** in sentence 2.

Read-Aloud Handbook

**Shared Reading Vol. 1, p. 8
"Sad Ladybug, Glad Ladybug"**

Student Objectives

I will be able to:
- Answer questions about characters in a story.
- Read along with the appropriate pauses.
- Read along from left to right.
- Identify initial and medial short **a.**

(iELD) Integrated ELD

Light Support
Challenge students to answer the questions below about the characters and their actions in the story.
Ask: *Who are the two people in the story? Where are the people in the story? How do the people feel about the ladybug? What does Pam do to help the ladybug?* Have students share their opinions about the story by answering this question: *What do you think the story tells us about the characters?*

Moderate Support
Pose questions about the characters in the story using the sentence frames below. Encourage students to answer in complete sentences. Model how to use the question to form a complete sentence in response.
Say: *Who is Pam? Pam is the girl in the chair.*
Write responses on the board, and have students repeat them with you.
Ask: *Who is the other person in the picture? How are the people different? Why does Pam open the window?*

Substantial Support
Pose questions about the characters in the story. Elicit answers of single words or gestures. Allow students to point to the illustration in response.
Ask: *Who is Pam? How are the people different? Where is the ladybug? Why does Pam open the window? When is the ladybug happy?*

ELD.PI.K.1, ELD.PI.K.3, ELD.PII.K.1

RL.K.1 With prompting and support, ask and answer questions about key details in a text., **RL.K.5** Recognize common types of texts (e.g., storybooks, poems, fantasy, realistic text). CA., **RL.K.10** Actively engage in group reading activities with purpose and understanding., **RL.K.10a** Activate prior knowledge related to the information and events in texts. CA, **RL.K.10b** Use illustrations and context to make predictions about text. CA, **RF.K.1a** Follow words from left to right, top to bottom, and page by page., **RF.K.3b** Associate the long and short sounds with the common spellings (graphemes) for the five major vowels. (Identify which letters represent the five major vowels (Aa, Ee, Ii, Oo, and Uu) and know the long and short sound of each vowel. More complex long vowel graphemes and spellings are targeted in the grade 1 phonics standards.) CA, **RF.K.4** Read emergent-reader texts with purpose and understanding., **SL.K.1a** Follow agreed-upon rules for discussions (e.g., listening to others and taking turns speaking about the topics and texts under discussion)., **SL.K.1b** Continue a conversation through multiple exchanges., **SL.K.3** Ask and answer questions in order to seek help, get information, or clarify something that is not understood.

"The Tortoise and the Hare": Listen and Retell Key Events (10 MIN.) RI.K.1, RI.K.2, RI.K.5, RI.K.10, RI.K.10a, RI.K.10b, SL.K.1a, SL.K.1b, SL.K.2

Mentor Read-Aloud Vol. 1, pp. 14-17
"The Tortoise and the Hare"

Student Objectives

I will be able to:
- Identify characters in a fictional text.
- Make predictions about characters
- Listen for a purpose.
- Link my ideas to the ideas of others.
- Retell key details.

Additional Materials

Weekly Presentation
- Story Events Chart

Observation Checklist for Collaborative Conversation

As partners discuss the key events in the selection, use the questions below to evaluate how effectively students communicate with each other. Based on your answers, you may wish to plan future core lessons to support the collaborative conversation process.

Do partners . . .

- ❏ stay on topic throughout the discussion?
- ❏ listen respectfully?
- ❏ build on the comments of others appropriately?
- ❏ pose or respond to questions to clarify information?
- ❏ support their partners to participate?

Preview the Genre (iELD)

Display "The Tortoise and the Hare," and read aloud the title as you point under each word. Direct students' attention to the illustrations in the selection. Point out features, such as illustrations, that indicate the selection is fiction, or a made-up, story. Then have students turn and talk to a partner and name features they observe and predictions they have. Students should state their prediction in a sentence, such as, *I predict _____ because _____*. Call on volunteers to report their partners' predictions. Record students' ideas.

Sample Fiction Features	Sample Predictions
• illustrations • animals as main characters • animal characters doing things they cannot do in real life	I predict that in this story • Tortoise and Hare will race. • Tortoise will win. • Hare will be upset that Tortoise wins.

Read Aloud the Text

Ask student to listen carefully to learn key details about how the characters in the story are different. Tell them that is their purpose for listening. Read aloud the text with minimal interruption. Model using a different tone of voice for dialogue and reading exclamations with excitement.

Collaborative Conversations: Partners

Lead partners to retell key events from the story. Remind students to build on partners' talk. Provide a model.

Sample modeling: *[Name] said Hare challenges all animals to race him. I remember what happens next. Tortoise tells Hare she will race.*

Share

As students recall key events, record them. Include simple illustrations to help students read the chart. As students name key events, reread the part of the story where the event was mentioned.

Beginning:	Hare challenges all the animals to a race. Tortoise accepts.
Middle:	Hare thinks he will win. The race starts. Hare is winning, so he takes a rest. While Hare naps, Tortoise passes him.
End:	Hare wakes up, but he is too late. Tortoise wins the race.

Sample Story Events Chart

Reinforce or Reaffirm the Strategy

Provide modeling and/or engage students in self-reflection to build metacognitive awareness.

IF...	THEN...
students need support to retell key events from the text...	**Model to reinforce the strategy**. • *To find key events, I ask myself questions about the story. My questions begin with* **who, what, when, where, why,** *and* **how**. *For example, "What happens first?" This is the beginning of the story. I reread page 14 to remember what happens at the beginning.* • *I know at the end of the story, Tortoise wins the race. What happens in between the beginning and the end is the middle of the story. I look at page 15. I retell events from this page. This page is part of the middle of the story.* • Turn to page 16. *This page tells more events from the middle of the story. I can look at the illustration and reread the text. Hare rests because he is far ahead.* Continue to model how you identify important events as needed.
students independently retell key events...	**Invite partners to reflect on their strategy by discussing one of the following questions:** • *How did you retell key events?* • *Did retelling the key events help you understand the story? How?* Have partners present their key events and explain how they found them.

Show Your Knowledge

Invite partners to be Hare and Tortoise. Ask them to act out an event from the story.

Integrated ELD

Light Support

Ask students to study the title of the story and the illustration on page 14. Challenge them to complete the following sentence frames based on the illustration. Encourage them to use words and phrases from the Word Bank in their sentences.

In a race, I think _____ _____.

I think this will happen because _____ can _____ and _____ can only _____.

Word Bank

fast slow run walk Tortoise Hare will win

Moderate Support

Direct students' attention to the title of the story and the illustration on page 14.

Ask: *Which animal is fast, and which animal is slow? Which animal do you think will win a race?*

Give students the following sentence frames. Have them use words and phrases from the Word Bank to complete the sentences.

Hare is _____.

Tortoise is _____.

Hare can _____.

Tortoise can only _____.

I think _____ _____ a race.

Word Bank

fast slow run walk Tortoise Hare will win

Substantial Support

Before reading the story, use the illustration on page 14 to help students practice simple sentence structures and verb tenses. Have students name the two animals (rabbit, turtle), and explain that in this story the rabbit is called Hare and the turtle is called Tortoise.

Ask: *Which animal is fast? Which animal is slow?* Have students point to the picture and say the animal's name. Turn students' answers into complete sentences and have students repeat them with you: *Hare is fast. Tortoise is slow.*

ELD.PI.K.3, ELD.PI.K.12b, ELD.PII.K.3

RI.K.1 With prompting and support, ask and answer questions about unknown words in a text., **RI.K.2** With prompting and support, identify the main topic and retell key details of a text., **RI.K.5** Identify the front cover, back cover, and title page of a book., **RI.K.10** Actively engage in group reading activities with purpose and understanding., **RI.K.10a** Activate prior knowledge related to the information and events in texts. CA, **RI.K.10b** Use illustrations and context to make predictions about text. CA, **SL.K.1a** Follow agreed-upon rules for discussions (e.g., listening to others and taking turns speaking about the topics and texts under discussion)., **SL.K.1b** Continue a conversation through multiple exchanges., **SL.K.2** Confirm understanding of a text read aloud or information presented orally or through other media by asking and answering questions about key details and requesting clarification if something is not understood.

Mentor Read-Aloud Vol. 1, pp. 14-17
"The Tortoise and the Hare"

Student Objectives

I will be able to:
- Identify and share key events about fictional characters.
- Help write key events about fictional characters.
- Form plural nouns orally.

(iELD) Integrated ELD

Light Support

Challenge students to describe each illustration in the story using the plural form of each word in the list below. Tell them to work from the beginning of the story to the end and to explain what happens in each illustration.

Word List

animal

ear

hill

eye

Moderate Support

Read aloud the following sentence stems for each illustration in the story, and have students offer one or more responses to complete each stem.

p. 14: In this picture, I see two _____.

p. 15: This picture shows one _____. It also shows one _____. That means that the picture shows two _____.

p. 16: The hare sleeps under one _____.

Across the road there are many _____.

p. 17: I see many _____.

At the finish line there are two _____.

Substantial Support

On the board, write the words *Hare, Tortoise,* and *race.* Use the following sentence stems to help students orally practice making regular plural nouns:

One animal is called _____.

One animal is called _____.

Tortoise and Hare are two _____.

One event is the start of the _____.

One event is the end of the _____.

The start and end of the race are two _____.

ELD.PI.K.6, ELD.PII.K.1, ELD.PII.K.4

Write Key Events (10 MIN.) W.K.2, W.K.8, SL.K.1a, SL.K.1b, SL.K.4, L.K.1a, L.K.1c

Engage Thinking

Display and reread the Story Events Chart with students.

Say: *Remember, we retold key details from the beginning, middle, and end of "The Tortoise and the Hare." Today we will write a key event from the story. What was your favorite event that happened in the story? Why?*

Collaborative Conversation: Peer Groups

Divide students into peer groups. Tell students that before they begin writing, you want them to talk with their group about the story they enjoyed most. Model how you do this.

Sample modeling: *To tell my group the event I enjoyed the most, I would say, "My event was when Tortoise was waiting at the finish line for Hare. Hare was so mad, he stamped his foot!" When you talk to your group members, you can use the same sentence frame: "My event was _____."*

Write as a Group

Collaborate with students to agree on their favorite part of the story to write about as a class. Work with students to generate a sentence orally that they could write. Rehearse the message orally so that students internalize it, and then model how you write the sentences. As you guide the writing, include at least one plural noun. Actively engage students in the writing process by thinking aloud and/or prompting them with questions. For example:

- *What kind of letter should we use to begin the sentence?*
- *We write words from left to right. Did we write this sentence correctly?*
- ***Animals** is a noun in the sentence. Does this word stand for one or more than one? How do you know?*
- *How do we show we have finished the sentence? What mark goes at the end?*

Sample Shared Writing

Hare did not think any of the animals could beat him.

Tortoise slowly walked along as tortoises do.

Build Language: Form Regular Plural Nouns

Tell students that a noun is a word that names a person, place, or thing. Provide an example, such as **rabbit, race,** and **park.** Explain that these nouns name one thing: one rabbit, one race, and one park. Then tell students that when you want to talk about more than one rabbit, you add **–s** to the end of the word. The word **rabbits** means more than one rabbit. Say a singular noun. Use the word in a sentence. Then ask students to orally form the plural by adding /s/ (**–s, –es**) to the end of the word. Use the plural noun in a sentence. Possible nouns and sentences are in the chart below.

Singular Noun	Plural Noun
tortoise (The tortoise walks slowly.)	tortoises (The tortoises walk slowly.)
tree (The tree has green leaves.)	trees (The trees have green leaves.)
race (The animals had a race.)	races (The animals had many races.)
wish (The tortoise made a wish.)	wishes (The tortoise made three wishes.)

☑ Write Independently

Guide students to draw a picture to show another key event from the story. Invite students to label their drawing.

Small-Group Differentiated Instruction (15 MIN. per Group)

Meet with Small Groups

Select small-group reading titles or activities based on students' needs. See the Small-Group Instructional Planner for titles that support a range of instructional levels within the unit topic. Remind students to apply skills and strategies they learned to their small-group reading experiences.

Say: *Today we practiced finding key events in "The Tortoise and the Hare." To find key details, you can ask* **who, what, when, where,** *and* **how** *questions. You can look back at the beginning, middle, and end of the story. If you are reading or listening to story today, pay attention to the key events.*

Whole-Group Reflect and Share

Bring the class back together. Invite them to share some of the key events they read about. Ask volunteers to describe how they identified the key events.

W.K.2 Use a combination of drawing, dictating, and writing to compose informative/explanatory texts in which they name what they are writing about and supply some information about the topic., **W.K.8** With guidance and support from adults, recall information from experiences or gather information from provided sources to answer a question., **SL.K.1a** Follow agreed-upon rules for discussions (e.g., listening to others and taking turns speaking about the topics and texts under discussion)., **SL.K.1b** Continue a conversation through multiple exchanges., **SL.K.4** Describe familiar people, places, things, and events and, with prompting and support, provide additional detail., **L.K.1a** Print many upper- and lowercase letters., **L.K.1c** Form regular plural nouns orally by adding /s/ or /es/ (e.g., dog, dogs; wish, wishes).

Focus Skill: s/s/ (20 MIN.) RF.K.2d, RF.K.3a, RF.K.3c, L.K.1.a

Phonological Awareness: Phoneme Isolation

Model/Practice

Display the frieze card for **Ss**.

Say: *Listen for the sound at the beginning of this word,* **sun**. *Say the sound with me,* **/sss/**. **Sun** *has* **/sss/** *at the beginning.*

Say the words **sit, Sam, silly** and have students repeat. Emphasize the **/s/** sound.

Say: *I am going to read the poem "Seven Silly Sailors." Listen to the* **/s/** *sound in this sentence:* Seven Silly Sailors sat beside the sea.

Reread the poem.

Say: *Tap your feet each time you hear* **/s/** *at the beginning of a word. Clap each time you hear* **/s/** *at the end of a word.*

Letter-Sound Correspondences

Introduce: Ss

Display frieze card **Ss**.

Say: *This is the sun card. The sound is* **/s/**. *The* **/s/** *sound is spelled with the letter* **s**. *Say the sound with me,* **/sss/**. *This is the sound at the beginning of the word* **sun**. *What is the name of this letter?* (**s**) *What sound does this letter stand for?* (/**s**/)

Model: Ss

Reread the poem "Seven Silly Sailors" and invite students to read along with you. Point to words in the poem that begin with the letter **s**. Say each word aloud.

Practice: Ss

Place letter cards **m** and **s** in the pocket chart.

Place picture cards **magnet** and **sun** under the corresponding letters while you say the name of the letter and picture.

Hold up the picture card **sub**. Have students say **sub** with you. Ask if **sub** begins like **magnet** or **sun**.

Place picture card **sub** under the letter card **s**.

Say: Sssssub *begins like* **sssun**, *so I am putting picture card* **sub** *under the letter* **s**.

Repeat with picture cards **sandwich, sock, mop, map,** and **mitten.**

Blend Sounds

Review: *Aa, Mm*

Hold up frieze cards **Aa** and **Mm** and ask students to say the sound each letter stands for.

Model: *Sam*

Place letter cards **S, a, m** in a pocket chart. Point to the letter **S**.

Say: *This is the letter* **S**. *The letter* **S** *stands for* **/sss/**. *Say* **/sss/**. *This is the letter* **a**. *The letter* **a** *stands for* **/aaa/**. *Say* **/aaa/**. *Listen as I blend the two sounds together,* **/sssaaa/**. *Blend the sounds with me. This is the letter* **m**. *The letter* **m** *stands for* **/mmm/**. *Say* **/mmm/**. *Listen as I blend all three sounds together,* **/sssaaammm/**. *Now blend the sounds to read the word,* **Sam**.

Practice: *am*

Repeat the routine for the word **am**. Move your hand from left to right under the word. Have students blend and read the word.

High-Frequency Words

Introduce/Practice: *the*

Display the high-frequency word card. Point to it and read the word.

Use the following routine: Point to each letter in the word and have students say the letter name with you. Say the word together. Guide children to name the letter that **the** begins with.

Say: *When I say the word* **the**, *I will hold up the word card. Read the word with me. I see* **the** *playground. The children see* **the** *swings.*

Review: *like, I*

Display each card and have students read the word.

Handwriting

Write and identify the uppercase and lowercase **Ss**. Hold up your writing hand. Write the uppercase and lowercase **Ss**. Trace the letters as you say **/s/**.

Then have students write **S** and **s** in the air as they say **/s/** several times. Finally have students write both forms of the letter several times, saying **/s/** every time they write the letter.

Integrated ELD

Light Support

Tell students to listen closely as you say each pair of words below. Have them tell you whether the **/s/** is at the beginning or end of the word:

slowpoke   tortoise
speedy   spoke
stamping   animals

Challenge pairs of students to take turns generating sentences about *The Tortoise and the Hare* that include the words **speedy, slow,** and **race**.

Moderate Support

Read aloud page 16 of "The Tortoise and the Hare." Have students clap when they hear an initial **/s/** (**soon, slowpoke, stop, stretched, side, slowly**). Read the page again, and have students clap when they hear a final **/s/** (**tortoise, tortoises**).

Write on the board several words from page 16 that begin with **Ss**. Say each one aloud and have students repeat it with you. Write the word **tortoise** on the board and circle the **s**. Say the word and have students repeat it with you.

Substantial Support

Say the following word pairs. Have students clap when they hear the initial **/s/**. Then have them repeat each **/s/** word with you.

fed   said
sore   for
fly   sly

Say these word pairs, and have students clap when they hear the final **/s/**. Then have them repeat each **/s/** word with you.

raze   race
grass   graph
pass   patch

ELD.PI.K.1, ELD.PI.K.5, ELD.PII.K.6

RF.K.2d Isolate and pronounce the initial, medial vowel, and final sounds (phonemes) in three-phoneme (consonant-vowel-consonant, or CVC) words. (This does not include CVCs ending with /l/, /r/, or /x/.), **RF.K.3a** Demonstrate basic knowledge of letter-sound correspondences by producing the primary or most frequent sound for each consonant. , **RF.K.3c** Read common high-frequency words by sight (e.g., the, of, to, you, she, my, is, are, do, does)., **L.K.1.a** Print many upper- and lowercase letters.

Read-Aloud Handbook

**Shared Reading Vol. 1, p. 8
"Sad Ladybug, Glad Ladybug"**

Student Objectives

I will be able to:
- Read along with appropriate pausing.
- Identify the letter **s** and the sound /**s**/.
- Recognize words I know in different texts.

(iELD) Integrated ELD

Light Support

Hold up "Sad Ladybug, Glad Ladybug" and point out the title and the story. Point to the comma in the title and the periods in the story, and explain that these marks tell the reader to pause.

Read aloud the story, beginning with the title.

Ask: *Did I stop reading for a moment after the title? Why do you think I did that?*

Ask: *Did I stop reading for a moment after each period?*

Moderate Support

Hold up "Sad Ladybug, Glad Ladybug" and point out the title. Then read the title aloud, pausing after the comma. Point to the comma, and tell students that this mark means a reader should pause. Read aloud the title.

Ask: *Did I stop reading for a moment after the comma? Why do you think I did that?*

Point to the periods after the first three sentences of the story. Explain that a period means a sentence has ended and a new one will begin. Have students echo-read the story with you, clearly pausing after each period.

Substantial Support

Hold up "Sad Ladybug, Glad Ladybug," and point out the title and the story. Then read it aloud, beginning with the title.

Ask: *Did I stop reading for a moment after the title? Why do you think I did that?*

Point to the periods after the first three sentences. Explain that a period means a sentence has ended and a new one will begin. Have students echo-read the story with you, clearly pausing after each period.

ELD.PI.K.1, ELD.PII.K.1, ELD.PII.K.2

Read Aloud and Shared Reading

(20 MIN.) RL.K.1, RF.K.1a, RF.K.3a, RF.K.3c, RF.K.4, SL.K.1a, SL.K.1b

Read Aloud

To support the unit concept, use one of the Read-Aloud Handbook selections for Unit 2. As you read, model the metacognitive strategy for the unit: Fix-Up/Monitoring Strategies guided by the samples provided. You may also wish to select a favorite read aloud from your classroom or school library. To support the unit concept, use one of the suggested titles for Unit 2.

Shared Reading (iELD)

Reread the Realistic Fiction

First rereading. Read aloud the text fluently and expressively, pointing under each word.

Reread for Fluency: Rate/Pausing Point out that end punctuation in a text cues readers when to stop. Explain that pausing briefly at end marks maintains the steady rate of the text. Choral-read the text, emphasizing rate and stopping briefly at the end of each sentence. Provide corrective feedback and/or validate students' efforts.

Build Concepts: Every Story Has Characters

Pose questions to connect the realistic fiction to the unit concept. For example:

- *What do you think the relationship is between the two characters?*
- *Why do you think the girl wanted the ladybug to fly outside?*

Review Phonics: Initial s

Highlight the word **Sad** in the title. Ask students to identify the first letter and its sound. Lead students in reading the word aloud. Then repeat with the words **saw** and **so**.

Review High-Frequency Words: the

Tell students that this text contains some words they have learned. Point to the previously-taught high-frequency word **the** in the third sentence. Ask students to turn to a partner and tell their partner the high-frequency word. Remind students to look for high-frequency words they know as they read a new text

RL.K.1 With prompting and support, ask and answer questions about key details in a text., **RF.K.1a** Follow words from left to right, top to bottom, and page by page., **RF.K.3a** Demonstrate basic knowledge of letter-sound correspondences by producing the primary or most frequent sound for each consonant., **RF.K.3c** Read common high-frequency words by sight (e.g., the, of, to, you, she, my, is, are, do, does)., **RF.K.4** Read emergent-reader texts with purpose and understanding. **SL.K.1a** Follow agreed-upon rules for discussions (e.g., listening to others and taking turns speaking about the topics and texts under discussion). **SL.K.1b** Continue a conversation through multiple exchanges.

Identify Genre: Fantasy (10 MIN.) RL.K.1, RL.K.5, SL.K.2, SL.K.3

Mentor Read-Aloud Vol. 1, pp. 14-17
"The Tortoise and the Hare"

Engage Thinking

Display pages 14 and 15 from "The Tortoise and the Hare." Remind students that they have heard this story.

Ask: *Could this story happen in real life? Why or why not?*

Model

Tell students that there are different kinds of stories. Some stories could really happen. We call them realistic fiction. Explain that "Sad Ladybug, Glad Ladybug" is an example of realistic fiction, or a story that could really happen. Another kind of story is called a fantasy. It has characters, settings, and events that could never happen in the real world. Model identifying "The Tortoise and the Hare" as a fantasy and could not happen in real life.

Sample modeling: *When I read "The Tortoise and the Hare," I notice right away that the hare talks. This cannot happen in real life. The tortoise answers the hare. This could not happen in real life. I think the story is a fantasy.*

Guided Practice (iELD)

Ask students to name additional examples from the story that identify it as a fantasy. Use directive and corrective prompts to support their comprehension. For example:

- *Could a hare and a tortoise plan to race each other?*
- *Look at the illustrations. How do they help you know this story is a fantasy?*
- *Let's reread page 16. What events happen on this page that could not happen in the real world?*
- *Hare takes a rest on page 16. Could a hare sleep in real life? What does your answer tell you about the events in a fantasy?*

☑ Show Your Knowledge

Ask students to name one example from the story that helps them understand the story is a fantasy.

Student Objectives

I will be able to:
- Recognize characteristics of a fantasy.
- Identify a story as a fantasy.

(iELD) Integrated ELD

Light Support

Ask partners to explain in complete sentences why the story of the tortoise and the hare is called a fantasy. Challenge them to find three examples in the story, in the words or in the illustrations, that support their answer. Provide the following sentence starter as a prompt, and offer the verbs in the Word Bank as possible vocabulary to include in their sentences.
This story is a fantasy because _____.

Word Bank

brag, race, joke, plod, nap, run, win, grin, shriek, dash, stamp

Moderate Support

Have students work in pairs with pages 16 and 17 of "The Tortoise and the Hare." Have them ask and answer questions about the illustrations, answering in complete sentences.
Do real worms have eyes?
Do real hares suck their thumbs?
Do real tortoises walk on their back legs?
Do real hares and tortoises have races?
Then have partners form a sentence to answer the following question:
Why is this story called a fantasy?

Substantial Support

Focus on the illustrations on pages 16 and 17 of "The Tortoise and the Hare." Point to the appropriate part of each illustration as you ask the questions below. After students answer each question, have them complete the corresponding sentence frame.
Do real worms have eyes?
Real worms do not have _____.
Do real hares suck their thumbs?
Real hares do not _____.
Do real birds hop up and down?
Real birds _____.

ELD.PI.K.1, ELD.PI.K.5, ELD.PII.K.3

RL.K.1 With prompting and support, ask and answer questions about key details in a text., **RL.K.5** Recognize common types of texts (e.g., storybooks, poems).)., **SL.K.2** Confirm understanding of a text read aloud or information presented orally or through other media by asking and answering questions about key details and requesting clarification if something is not understood., **SL.K.3** Ask and answer questions in order to seek help, get information, or clarify something that is not understood.

Identify and Describe Story Characters (10 MIN.) RL.K.1, RL.K.3, SL.K.2, SL.K.3

Mentor Read-Aloud Vol. 1, pp. 14-17
"The Tortoise and the Hare"

Student Objectives

I will be able to:
• Describe story characters.

Additional Materials

Weekly Presentation
• Two-Column Chart

Engage Thinking

Display pages 14 and 15 of "The Tortoise and the Hare."

Ask: *Who are the characters in the story? Which character did you like better?*

Tell students that today they will learn how to describe, or tell about, characters in a story.

Model

Display a blank two-column chart. Tell students that you are going to reread parts of the story in order to learn more about the characters Hare and Tortoise. Read aloud paragraph 1 on page 14. Use your voice to emphasize Hare's superior attitude.

Sample modeling: *In the first sentence, I read that Hare always talks about how fast he runs. He brags to the other animals about how speedy he is. Then he challenges them. He does not think anyone can beat him in a race. He thinks he is faster than anyone. Hare is a bragger and a show off. He thinks a lot of himself. I'll write this in the chart to tell about Hare.*

Write descriptive words for Hare in the chart.

Guided Practice (iELD)

Ask students to listen as you continue to reread excerpts from the story that help you describe each character. For example, reread paragraph 2 on page 14 to help students identify Tortoise as calm and confident. As students talk about each character, use directive and corrective prompts to support their comprehension.

For example:

- *Why do you think Tortoise agrees to race Hare?*
- *Does Tortoise seem afraid of Hare's ability?*
- *How does Hare respond to Tortoise's response?*
- *Why does Hare take a nap? What does that tell you about his character?*

Add students' ideas to the chart. Point out the differences between the two characters.

Hare	Tortoise
bragger	calm
show off	confident
thinks he is better than everyone else	does not give up
rude	
sore loser	

Sample Two Column Chart

 Show Your Knowledge

Ask partners to take turns pretending to be Hare and Tortoise. Partners should interact in a way that shows their character traits.

Integrated ELD

Light Support

Choral read page 16 and study the illustration. Then ask the following questions:

What does Hare think about Tortoise before he goes to sleep?

What does Tortoise think when she sees Hare?

Provide the sentence frames below to get students started. Encourage students to use as many detail words as they can.

Hare acts _____ about Tortoise.

Tortoise acts _____ toward Hare.

Moderate Support

Have partners turn to page 16 of "The Tortoise and the Hare" to focus on how the tortoise and the hare behave. Read aloud the paragraphs and point to the illustration. Ask the questions below after the relevant paragraphs. Encourage students to use words from the Word Bank.

Where is Hare?

What does Hare think is going to happen?

What does Hare do?

What does Tortoise do?

Why does Tortoise do this?

Word Bank: under a tree down the road ahead of Tortoise after a nap

Substantial Support

Ask students the questions below to elicit descriptions of the characters in "The Tortoise and the Hare." Lead students from specific text-based responses to generalizations about the characters. Provide the words and phrases in the Word Bank to help students express generalizations.

What does Hare say to the other animals?

What does Hare always talk about?

What does Tortoise say to Hare in the beginning?

What does Tortoise say to Hare at the end?

How does Tortoise talk?

Word Bank: boastfully proudly about himself politely thoughtfully about herself

ELD.PI.K.9, ELD.PI.K.12, ELD.PII.K.5

RL.K.1 With prompting and support, ask and answer questions about key details in a text., **RL.K.3** With prompting and support, identify characters, settings, and major events in a story., **SL.K.2** Confirm understanding of a text read aloud or information presented orally or through other media by asking and answering questions about key details and requesting clarification if something is not understood., **SL.K.3** Ask and answer questions in order to seek help, get information, or clarify something that is not understood.

Write an Opinion (10 MIN.) W.K.1, W.K.8, SL.K.1a, SL.K.1b, SL.K.4, L.K.1a, L.K.1c

Mentor Read-Aloud Vol. 1, pp. 14-17
"The Tortoise and the Hare"

Student Objectives

I will be able to:
- State an opinion about a text.
- Form plural nouns orally.

(iELD) Integrated ELD

Light Support

Challenge students to form and write words, with assistance, that give nuanced opinions in sentences that begin with *I think the story was, I think Tortoise was,* or *I think Hare was.* Tell students to include the reason or reasons for their opinions.

Moderate Support

Remind students that they know the words **I** and **like.**
Say: *when you say you like something, you are expressing a feeling or an opinion. People also express an opinion by saying "I think" and giving the reasons they think that way.*
Have students work in pairs to generate words that give an opinion about one of the characters in "The Tortoise and the Hare," such as *bossy, proud, boastful,* and *calm.*

Substantial Support

Remind students that they know the words **I** and **like.** Explain that when they say they like something, they are expressing a feeling or an opinion. Point out that people usually can give reasons that explain why they feel a certain way about a topic.
Say: *Now I want you to give your opinion of the Hare in "The Tortoise and the Hare."*
Give students the following sentence frames:
I like Hare because _____.
I do not like Hare because_____.
Help students complete their statements with reasons for their opinions.

ELD.PI.K.3, ELD.PI.K.11, ELD.PII.K.6

Engage Thinking

Quickly page through "The Tortoise and the Hare."

Ask: *What was your favorite part of the story?*

Tell students that today they will write an opinion about the story. Remind them that an opinion is what you think about something. There is no right or wrong answer.

💬 Collaborative Conversation: Partners (iELD)

Tell students that before writing, you would like them to turn and talk to a partner briefly. Ask them to share their opinion of the story. Students should answer the questions, "Did you like this story? Why or why not?" Model how you do this.

Sample modeling: *When I talk to my partner, I say, "I liked the story because Tortoise beat Hare." First, I say whether or not I liked the story. Then I say why I liked or didn't like it. When you talk to your partner, you can use that same sentence frame: I (liked/did not like) the story because _____.*

Write the sentence frame for students and lead them in reading it aloud. Give students one minute to share their ideas. Then bring them together and ask volunteers to share their partner's opinion and reason.

Write as a Group

Collaborate with students to agree on an opinion and a reason to write as a class. Work with students to generate a sentence orally. Rehearse the message orally so that students internalize it, and then model how you write the sentence. Actively engage students in the writing process by thinking aloud and/or prompting them with questions. For example:

- *We can use the sentence frame to help us write the beginning of the sentence.*
- *Tortoise is a long name. How can we make sure we spell it correctly?*
- *How do we end the sentence?*
- *Let's reread the sentence. Do we give our opinion? Do we give a reason for why we liked the story?*

Sample Shared Writing

I liked the story because Tortoise wins the race and the animals cheer.

Build Language: Form Regular Plural Nouns

Remind students that a noun is a word that names a person, place, or thing. Provide example, such as **girl, school,** and **tree**. Point out that these nouns name one thing: one girl, one school, and one tree. Then tell students that when you want to talk about more than one girl, you add **–s** to the end of the word. The word **girls** means more than one girl. Say a singular noun. Use the word in a sentence. Then ask students to orally form the plural by adding /s/ *(–s, –es)* to the end of the word. Use the plural noun in a sentence. Possible nouns and sentences are in the chart below.

Singular Noun	Plural Noun
nap (Hare took a nap.)	naps (Hare took two naps today.)
prize (Tortoise won a prize.)	prizes (Tortoise won three prizes.)
animal (The animal watched the race.)	animals (The animals watched the race.)
kiss (Mom gave Tortoise a kiss.)	kisses (Mom gave Tortoise a lot of kisses.)

 **Write Independently**

Ask students to draw a happy face if they liked the story and a sad face if they did not. Invite them to dictate a reason to support their opinion.

Small-Group Differentiated Instruction (15 MIN. per Group)

Meet with Small Groups

Select small-group reading titles or activities based on students' needs. See the Small-Group Instructional Planner for titles that support a range of instructional levels within the unit topic. Remind students to apply skills and strategies they learned to their small-group reading experiences.

Say: *Today we learned that the characters and events in a fantasy could not happen in real life. We know that people are different, so we practiced telling about different characters. As you read and listen to stories today, ask yourself, "Is this a fantasy?" Listen for details that help you tell about a character.*

Whole-Group Reflect and Share

Bring the class back together. Ask volunteers to tell about characters in their small-group texts.

W.K.1 Use a combination of drawing, dictating, and writing to compose opinion pieces in which they tell a reader the topic or the name of the book they are writing about and state an opinion or preference about the topic or book (e.g., My favorite book is...)., **W.K.8** With guidance and support from adults, recall information from experiences or gather information from provided sources to answer a question., **SL.K.1a** Follow agreed-upon rules for discussions (e.g., listening to others and taking turns speaking about the topics and texts under discussion)., **SL.K.1b** Continue a conversation through multiple exchanges., **SL.K.4** Describe familiar people, places, things, and events and, with prompting and support, provide additional detail., **L.K.1a** Print many upper- and lowercase letters., **L.K.1c** Form regular plural nouns orally by adding /s/ or /es/ (e.g., dog, dogs; wish, wishes).

Focus Skill: s/s/ (15 MIN.) RF.K.2c, RF.K.2d, RF.K.3a, L.K.1a

Phonological Awareness: Phoneme Isolation

Model/Practice

Show students the picture on the back of the poetry poster, and have them name all the objects in the picture. Point to the sun in the picture and say the word **sun**.

Ask: *What sound do you hear at the beginning of the word?*

Have volunteers point to things in the picture whose name starts with /s/.

Say: *Now listen as I say the word **bus**. I can hear the /s/ sound at the end of the word **bus**. I am going to say some words. If you hear /s/ at the beginning of the word, raise your hand. If you hear /s/ at the end of the word, clap your hands.*

Use the following words: **side, yes, sale, soap, gas, suit.**

Letter-Sound Correspondences

Review: m/m/, a/a/, s/s/

Hold up frieze cards **Mm** and **Aa** one at a time, and have students tell you the sounds the letters stand for. Encourage students to think of words that start with /m/. Record the words, underlining the letter **m**. Then have students think of words that end with /m/. Record these words, underlining the letter **m**.

Next, have students think of words that have the /a/ sound at the beginning and in the middle. Write these words and circle the **a**.

Hold up the frieze card **Ss**, and have students say the letter name and the letter sound.

Reread the poem "Seven Silly Sailors," emphasizing the initial /s/ sounds. Have volunteers find words that begin and end with /s/.

Blend Sounds

Model: *Sam*

Place letter cards **S, a, m** in a pocket chart. Point to the letter **S**.

Say: *This is the letter **S**. The letter **S** stands for /**sss**/. Say /**sss**/. This is the letter **a**. The letter **a** stands for /**aaa**/. Say /**aaa**/. Listen as I blend the two sounds together, /**sssaaa**/. Blend the sounds with me. This is the letter **m**. The letter **m** stands for /**mmm**/. Say /**mmm**/. Listen as I blend all three sounds together, /**sssaaammm**/. Now blend the sounds to read the word, **Sam.***

Practice: *am*

Repeat the routine for the word **am**. Move your hand from left to right under the word. Have students blend and read the word **am**.

Student Objectives

I will be able to:
- Isolate initial and final /**s**/.
- Review letter-sound correspondences for **s**/**s**/, **a**/**a**/, **m**/**m**/.
- Blend sounds /**s**/, /**a**/, /**m**/.
- Learn new high-frequency word: **we**.
- Read previously taught high-frequency words: **the, like, I**.
- Write **Ss**.

Additional Materials

- Poetry poster: "Seven Silly Sailors"
- Letter cards: **a, m, S, s**

Weekly Presentation
- Frieze cards: **Aa, Mm, Ss**
- High-frequency word cards: **I, like, the, we**

High-Frequency Words ⓘELD

Introduce/Practice: *we*

Display high-frequency word card **we** and read the word. Point to each letter in the word and have students say the letter name with you. Say the word together.

Say: *I am going to read some sentences. When I say the word* **we***, I will hold up the word card. Read the word with me.* **We** *go to the playground. Can* **we** *go on the swings?*

Review: *I, like, the*

Display each card and have students read the word. Then have the students use each word in an oral sentence.

Handwriting

Have students write the uppercase and lowercase **Ss**. Observe students' pencil grip and paper position. Have students say /s/ every time they write the letters **Ss**.

ⓘELD Integrated ELD

Light Support
Show students the word cards for **I, like, the,** and **we.** Have students copy the words onto a piece of paper. Then challenge them to form sentences that include one, two, three, and then all four of the words. Students may write their sentences, with spelling assistance, as well as present their sentences orally.

Moderate Support
Give pairs of students the word cards for **I, like, the,** and **we.** Have them place the cards face down on a table or a desk. Taking turns, partners turn over a card and form a sentence using the card. Encourage students to incorporate nouns and noun phrases from the Word Bank in their sentences.

Word Bank
silly sentence our classmates night
summer vacation my friends carrots
train trip big families farm
soccer game holiday parties cow

Substantial Support
Show students the word cards for **I, like, the,** and **we.** Have students complete the sentence frames below. Write down each student's sentence, and have the student copy what you have written.
I like the _____ I saw today.
We learned about the _____ in school today.

ELD.PI.K.1, ELD.PI.K.2, ELD.PII.K.4

RF.K.2c Blend and segment onsets and rimes of single-syllable spoken words., **RF.K.2d** Isolate and pronounce the initial, medial vowel, and final sounds (phonemes) in three-phoneme (consonant-vowel-consonant, or CVC) words.1 (This does not include CVCs ending with /l/, /r/, or /x/.), **RF.K.3a** Demonstrate basic knowledge of letter-sound correspondences by producing the primary or most frequent sound for each consonant., **L.K.1a** Print many upper- and lowercase letters.

Read-Aloud Handbook

**Shared Reading Vol. 1, p. 9
"Diddle, Diddle, Dumpling"**

Student Objectives

I will be able to:
- Read along with the appropriate pausing.
- Answer questions about a character in a poem.
- Identify rhyming words in a poem.
- Recognize the high-frequency word *the*

(iELD) Integrated ELD

Light Support

Tell students to imagine that someone is talking in the poem "Diddle, Diddle, Dumpling." Explain that we call that person the poem's speaker. Ask students to listen carefully as you read the poem once. Ask students to imagine that they are the person talking. Pose the questions: *How does the person talking feel about John? Who is the person talking in the poem?*

Moderate Support

Tell students to imagine that someone is talking in the poem "Diddle, Diddle, Dumpling." Explain that we call that person the poem's speaker. Ask students to listen carefully as you read the poem. Then pose the following questions: *Where is John? Who is in the pictures over John's bed?* Ask pairs of students to pose questions to each other about John and his relationship to the speaker of the poem. Finally, have students complete the following sentence: *The speaker is John's _____ because the speaker calls John "my son."*

Substantial Support

Tell students to imagine that someone is talking in the poem "Diddle, Diddle, Dumpling." Ask students to listen carefully as you read the poem. Then pose the following questions: *Where is John? What is John wearing? What is John doing? Why does the speaker call the boy "My son John"? Who is the speaker, if the boy is the son?*

Then ask students to complete the following sentence: *The person saying the poem is John's _____.*

ELD.PI.K.1, ELD.PI.K.7, ELD.PII.K.2

Read Aloud and Shared Reading

(20 MIN.) RL.K.1, RL.K.3, RL.K.5, RL.K.10, RL.K.10a, RL.K.10b, SL.K.1a, SL.K.1b, SL.K.3, SL.K.6

Read Aloud

To support the unit concept, use one of the Read-Aloud Handbook selections for Unit 2. As you read, model the metacognitive strategy for the unit, Visualize, guided by the samples provided. You may also wish to select a favorite read-aloud from your classroom or school library. To support the unit concept, use one of the suggested titles for Unit 2.

Shared Reading (iELD)

Introduce the Poem

Display "Diddle, Diddle, Dumpling." Read aloud the title of the poem as you point under the words. Ask students if they have ever heard the poem before. Point out the illustration. Invite students to turn to a partner and tell what they predict the poem will be about. Invite a few students to share their predictions with the whole class.

Read the Poem

First reading. Read aloud the text fluently and expressively, pointing under each word.

Second reading: Rate/Pausing. Model reading the poem at a lively rate. Pause appropriately after each comma, semicolon, and period. Prompt students to echo read the text in the same way. Model appropriate intonation and rate as you read. Provide corrective feedback and/or validate students' efforts.

Build Concepts: Every Story Has Characters

Pose questions to connect the poem to the unit concept. For example:

- *Who are the characters in the poem?*
- *Why do you think John went to bed with one shoe off and the other one on?*
- *Why do you think the parent uses the term **diddle, diddle, dumpling**?*

Model Poetic Features: Rhyming Words

Remind students that rhyming words are words that have the same ending sounds. Explain that the poem has words that rhyme at the end of the lines. Read the first two lines aloud, emphasizing the rhyming words **John** and **on**. Ask students to repeat the rhyming words.

Review High-Frequency Words: *the*

Tell students that this text contains some words they have learned. Point to the previously taught high-frequency word **the** in the third line. Ask students to turn to a partner and tell their partner the high-frequency word. Remind students to look for high-frequency words they know as they read a new text.

RL.K.1 With prompting and support, ask and answer questions about key details in a text., **RL.K.3** With prompting and support, identify characters, settings, and major events in a story., **RL.K.5** Recognize common types of texts (e.g., storybooks, poems, fantasy, realistic text). CA, **RL.K.10** Actively engage in group reading activities with purpose and understanding., **RL.K.10a** Activate prior knowledge related to the information and events in texts. CA, **RLK.10b** Actively engage in group reading activities with purpose and understanding., **SL.K.1a** Follow agreed-upon rules for discussions (e.g., listening to others and taking turns speaking about the topics and texts under discussion)., **SL.K.1b** Continue a conversation through multiple exchanges., **SL.K.3** Ask and answer questions in order to seek help, get information, or clarify something that is not understood., **SL.K.6** Speak audibly and express thoughts, feelings, and ideas clearly.

"The Little Helper": Listen and Retell
Key Details (10 MIN.) RL.K.1, RL.K.3, RL.K.5, RL.K.10, RL.K.10a, RL.K.10b, SL.K.1a, SL.K.1b, SL.K.3, SL.K.6

Introduce the Fantasy

Display "The Little Helper" and read aloud the title. Talk about what it means to be a helper. Page through the selection, briefly talking about the illustrations. Lead students make predictions about the characters and story events based on the title and illustration.

Read Aloud the Fantasy

Ask students to listen carefully to identify the characters and important events in the story. Remind them that this is their purpose for listening. Read aloud the text with minimal interruption. Read the lion's quotations with a deep voice and the mouse's words with a squeaky voice.

Collaborative Conversation: Retell Key Events (iELD)

Give partners about two minute to tell each other three events from the story. Call on students to share story events with the whole class. Encourage them to think about the most important events at the beginning, middle, and end of the story. Make a list of the events students retell.

Reinforce or Reaffirm the Strategy

Provide modeling and/or engage students in self-reflection to build metacognitive awareness.

IF…	THEN…
students need support to retell key events from the text…	**Model to reinforce the strategy.** • *At the beginning of the story, mouse climbs up what he thinks is a hill, but it is a lion! When mouse climbs on the sleeping lion, it wakes the lion. This is a very important event.* • *The mouse begs the lion to let him go. He says he can help the lion one day. This is another important event in the story.* • *The lion does not believe the mouse could ever help him, but he lets him go because mouse made him laugh.* Continue to model how to find key events at the end of the story.
students independently retell key events…	**Invite partners to reflect on their strategy by discussing one of the following questions:** • *What helped you remember the important events in the story?* • *How did the illustrations help you tell the key events?* • *How did you know this event was important to the story?* Have partners present their key events and explain how they found them.

RL.K.1 With prompting and support, ask and answer questions about key details in a text., **RL.K.3** With prompting and support, identify characters, settings, and major events in a story., **RL.K.5** Recognize common types of texts (e.g., storybooks, poems, fantasy, realistic text). CA)., **RL.K.10** Actively engage in group reading activities with purpose and understanding. **RL.K.10a** Activate prior knowledge related to the information and events in texts. CA, **RL.K.10b** Actively engage in group reading activities with purpose and understanding., **SL.K.1a** Follow agreed-upon rules for discussions (e.g., listening to others and taking turns speaking about the topics and texts under discussion)., **SL.K.1b** Continue a conversation through multiple exchanges., **SL.K.3** Ask and answer questions in order to seek help, get information, or clarify something that is not understood., **SL.K.6** Speak audibly and express thoughts, feelings, and ideas clearly.

MENTOR READ 2 MINI-LESSON

The Little Helper

Mentor Read-Aloud Vol. 1, pp. 18–21
"The Little Helper"

Student Objectives

I will be able to:
• Identify features of a fantasy.
• Make predictions about characters in a story.
• Listen for a purpose.
• Link my ideas to the ideas of others.
• Retell key events about characters in a story.

(iELD) Integrated ELD

Light Support
Explain to students that events are the main things that happen in a story. Reread "The Little Helper" to students. Pause after each page to ask, *What happens on this page?* Ask students to agree on an answer.

Moderate Support
List the numbers 1 through 4 on the board, vertically. Draw four blank lines next to each number. Each line represents one page in the story.
Reread "The Little Helper" to students page by page, pointing to the pictures. For each page, ask: *What happens to the lion on this page? What happens to the mouse?* Ask students to agree on an answer, and then write the answer on the list.
Explain that the numbered lines represent events, or things that happen, in the story. Ask students to use the list to retell the sequence of events using the words *First, Next, Then*, and *At last*.

Substantial Support
Make a simple chart on the board with four numbered rows and four blank lines in each row, such as:
1. _____ _____ _____ _____
Each row represents one page of the story.
Reread "The Little Helper" to partners page by page, pointing to the pictures. For each page, ask: *What is the lion doing? How does the lion feel? What is the mouse doing? How does the mouse feel?* Use the Word Bank to help students choose words. Explain that the rows represent events, or things that happen, in the story. Discuss the sequence of events with students using the words *First, Next, Then*, and *At last*.

Word Bank
roaring, eating, crying, chewing, smiling, talking, angry, scared, happy, grateful, worried

ELD.PI.K.6, ELD.PI.K.12, ELD.PII.K.2

The Little Helper

Mentor Read-Aloud Vol 1, pp. 18-21
"The Little Helper"

Student Objectives

I will be able to:
- Make inferences about characters' feelings.
- Answer questions about characters in a story.

Additional Materials

Weekly Presentation
- Two Column Chart

Make Inferences about Character

(10 MIN.) RL.K.1, RL.K.3

Engage Thinking

Remind students that they learned how to describe, or tell about, Tortoise and Hare.

Ask: *What words did you use to describe Hare? Why did you choose those words?*

Tell students that today, they will continue to practice telling about characters. Today, they will think about the story and describe the mouse and the lion.

Model

Display a blank two-column chart. Tell students that they you are going to reread parts of "The Little Helper" to learn more about the characters. Read aloud the first two paragraphs on page 18. Think aloud to model making an inference about the lion's feelings.

Sample modeling: *I know that an author does not always tell me everything I need to know about a character. Sometimes I have to make an inference, or a guess, about a character's feelings. To make an inference, I think about what I know and what the author tells me in the story. After I read the first two paragraphs, I understand that the mouse woke the lion. The author uses the word **roared** to tell how the lion spoke to the mouse. The lion asks in a very loud voice, "Who dares to wake me..." These are clues that the lion was angry. I can infer that the lion was angry about the mouse waking him up.*

Record the inference in the chart.

Guided Practice

Ask students to listen as you continue to reread excerpts from the story that help you describe each character's feelings at different times in the story. For example, reread paragraph 3 on page 18 to help students infer that the mouse feels afraid. As students talk about each character and make inferences, use directive and corrective prompts to support their comprehension. For example:

- *The author says the "mouse trembled and shook." What does this help you understand about how the mouse feels?*
- *Why does the lion laugh after the mouse says he can help the lion one day?*
- *The author does not say how the lion feels when he is trapped in a hunter's net. Look at the illustration on page 20. Think about how an animal might feel if it were trapped in a net. What inference can you make about the way the lion feels?*

Add students' ideas to the chart. Point out the differences between the two characters.

Lion	Mouse
feels angry when the mouse wakes him	feels very afraid when the lion has him
feels disbelief that the mouse could ever help him	feels grateful the lion let him go
feels happy because the mouse made him laugh	feels confident he can help the lion
feels sad and scared that he is trapped	
feels grateful the mouse freed him	

Sample Two-Column Chart

Show Your Knowledge

Reread an excerpt from the story that allows students to make an inference about a character's feelings. Have students make a face to convey the emotion the character feels.

---

iELD Integrated ELD

Light Support
Read aloud "The Little Helper." Point to the word **grateful** on pages 19 and 21. Explain that the mouse and the lion both feel grateful in the story. Challenge students to complete the following sentences stems orally:
The mouse is grateful on p. 19 because _____.
The lion is grateful on p. 21 because _____.

Moderate Support
Remind students that they have listened to "The Little Helper" and have thought about the events and characters in the story. Read each page aloud. After finishing each page, ask students the questions below about how the characters feel.
Define words for students as necessary. Encourage them to answer you in complete sentences.
p. 18: *Why does the lion roar at the mouse? Why does the mouse tremble?*
p. 19: *Why does the lion let the mouse go? Why is the mouse grateful?*
p. 20: *Why is the mouse skipping? Why is the lion crying?*
p. 21: *Why is the lion grateful? Why is the mouse smiling?*

Substantial Support
Remind students that they have listened to "The Little Helper" and have thought about the events and characters in the story. Show students the words in the word bank. Turn the pages of the story and have students point to these words. For each word, ask: *What does this word tell you about feelings?*
Turn the pages of the story again, read each one aloud, and ask **Why** questions about the words in the word bank. For example, on page 19, ask, *Why does the lion laugh?* and *Why is the mouse grateful?* Define words for students as necessary.

Word Bank
dares trembled grabbed shook laughed grateful
Please Forgive skipping Thank you

ELD.PI.K.1, ELD.PI.K.5, ELD.PII.K.3

RL.K.1 With prompting and support, ask and answer questions about key details in a text., RL.K.3 With prompting and support, identify characters, settings, and major events in a story.

Write about a Character (10 MIN.) W.K.2, W.K.5, W.K.8, L.K.1a, L.K.1c

The Little Helper

One day, a tiny mouse crawled up a little hill. But the hill was a big, mighty lion who had been fast asleep.

"Who dares to wake me, the King of Beasts?" roared the lion. He grabbed the little mouse in his great big paw.

The little mouse trembled and shook. "Forgive me, Your Majesty!" he cried. "Please let me live! I may be able to help you someday."

The lion laughed and laughed.

"How could a tiny creature like you ever help the King of Beasts?" he said. "But you have put me in a good mood, so I will let you go."

The grateful mouse thanked the lion and raced off as fast as he could.

Mentor Read-Aloud Vol. 1, pp. 18–21
"The Little Helper"

Student Objectives

I will be able to:
- Write about characters in a story.
- Form plural nouns orally.

(iELD) Integrated ELD

Light Support
Make and hand out individual word cards for **mighty, lion, tiny,** and **mouse.** Challenge students to create sentences about the characters that include the words on the cards. Tell them to think of sentences that describe who the characters are, and then to think of sentences that explain how the characters feel.

Moderate Support
Have students work in pairs. Make individual word cards for **big, mighty, lion, trapped, tiny, little, mouse,** and **helped.** Give one student the **lion** card and the other student the **mouse** card.
Ask: Which words describe the lion?
After students respond, explain that they need to choose just two words to use in a sentence about the lion. Have them decide whether to use the word **big** or the word **mighty** in the sentence. Encourage them to explain their decision. Give the selected word cards to the student with the **lion** card.
Repeat the process for the mouse using the words **tiny** and **little.**

Substantial Support
Create a two-column chart on the board. Label one column "Lion" and the other column "Mouse." Ask students to listen for words that tell about the characters' size and power as you read aloud "The Little Helper." Pause after each paragraph, and have students tell you which words they heard.

Lion	Mouse
big	tiny
mighty	little
king	trembled
roared	shook

ELD.PI.K.8, ELD.PI.K.12, ELD.PII.K.6

Engage Thinking

Display page 20 in "The Little Helper."

Ask: *Look at the illustration and describe how the lion is feeling.*

Explain that today, you will write to explain why the mouse helps the lion.

Collaborative Conversation: Peer Groups (iELD)

Separate students into peer groups. Tell students that before writing, you would like them to turn and talk to members of their group about why they think the mouse chooses to help the lion. Provide a model.

Sample modeling: *Before I talk to my partner, I think about what happens at the beginning of the story. I remember how scared the mouse was. He told the lion that if the lion let him go, he may be able to help the lion one day. Then later, the mouse sees the lion is trapped. I think the mouse chooses to help the lion because the mouse remembers what he told the lion. He keeps his word and helps the lion. When you speak to your partner, you can use the same sentence frame: I think the mouse chooses to help the lion because _____.*

Give students two minutes to share their ideas. Then bring them together and ask volunteers to share their ideas.

Write as a Group

Collaborate with students to agree on one reason to write about as a class. Work with students to generate a sentence orally. Then model how you write it. Actively engage students in the writing process by thinking aloud and/or prompting them with questions. For example:

- *We know how to spell the word **the**. Did we spell the word correctly in the sentence?*
- *We have reached the end of the sentence. What do we need?*
- *Does our sentence make sense? Should we change the sentence to help a reader understand what we mean?*
- *What nouns did we use? Are the nouns plural?*

Sample Shared Writing
The mighty mouse chewed the ropes to set the lion free. Even tiny creatures can be brave.

Build Language: Form Regular Plural Nouns

Remind students that a singular noun names one person, place, or thing. Provide examples, such as *one lion* and *one net*.

Say: *When you want to describe more than one of something, you add /s/ to the end of the word. This makes a plural noun. For example,* **lion** *means one lion. If I want to tell about more than one lion, I add /s/ to the end of* **lion** *to make the word* **lions.** *The word* **lions** *tells about more than one lion.*

Say a singular noun. Use the word in a sentence. Then ask students to orally form the plural by adding /s/ (**–s, –es**) to the end of the word. Use the plural noun in a sentence. Possible nouns and sentences are in the chart below.

Singular Noun	Plural Noun
net (The mouse chewed through a net.)	nets (The mouse chewed through three nets.)
friend (The lion did not have a friend.)	friend (The lion has many friends.)
box (The mouse sleeps in a box.)	boxes (The mouse has three boxes.)

 **Write Independently**

Ask students to draw a picture of the mouse helping the lion. They can write or dictate a sentence to explain why the mouse helps the lion.

Small-Group Differentiated Instruction (15 MIN. per Group)

Meet with Small Groups

Select small-group reading titles or activities based on students' needs. See the Small-Group Instructional Planner for titles that support a range of instructional levels within the unit topic.

Say: *Today we read a new story and practiced retelling key events. We also learned more about making inferences about characters. Remember when you make an inference about the way a character feels, you think about what you know. You can imagine how you would feel if you were the character. You also think about the words the author tells you in the story. Practice making inferences about characters' feelings when you read and listen to stories today.*

Whole-Group Reflect and Share

Bring the class back together. Ask volunteers to tell about the characters and their feelings from the readings today.

W.K.2 Use a combination of drawing, dictating, and writing to compose informative/explanatory texts in which they name what they are writing about and supply some information about the topic., **W.K.5** With guidance and support from adults, respond to questions and suggestions from peers and add details to strengthen writing as needed., **W.K.8** With guidance and support from adults, recall information from experiences or gather information from provided sources to answer a question., **L.K.1a** Print many upper- and lowercase letters., **L.K.1c** Form regular plural nouns orally by adding /s/ or /es/ (e.g., dog, dogs; wish, wishes).

Focus Skill: s/s/ (20 MIN.) RF.K.2d, RF.K.3a, RF.K.3c

Phonological Awareness: Phoneme Isolation

Model/Practice

Say the words **man, mitt,** and **sit**. Have students repeat the words.

Ask students what two words have the same beginning sound. Then ask them to identify the sound.

Say the words **silly, sun,** and **sink**. Have students repeat the words. Ask students if they hear the same sound at the beginning of each word. Then ask what sound is the same in all three words. Repeat the process with the words **sit, save, Sarah; mind, find, map; see, sick, sat**.

Letter-Sound Correspondences

Review with Picture Cards

Place picture cards **apple, sun,** and **magnet** in the pocket chart. Have students say their names and the sounds at the beginning of each name. Show students picture card **ax** and ask them what sound they hear at the beginning of the word. Place picture card **ax** under picture card **apple**. Repeat with picture cards **ant, antelope, mop, map, mitten, sock, sub,** and **sandwich**.

Replace picture cards **sun** and **magnet** with picture card **pan**. Place a letter card **a** under **apple** and **pan**. Ask students where they hear the **/a/** sound in the words **apple** and **pan**. Show students picture cards **map, bat, pan, ax, ant,** and **antelope**. Have them sort the pictures by the beginning or medial **/a/** sound.

Blend Sounds

Review: *am, Sam*

Have students blend the words **am** and **Sam,** using the routine from Day One.

High-Frequency Words (iELD)

Review: *the, we*

Write the words **the** and **we**. Read aloud each word. Then without students seeing, erase a letter in one of the words. Ask students which letter is missing. Replace the letter as students read the word. Repeat with the second word.

Review: *I, like*

Display each high-frequency word card.

Point quickly to each card, at random, and have students read the word as fast as they can.

Student Objectives

I will be able to:
- Isolate initial sound **/s/**.
- Review letter-sound correspondences for **s/s/, a/a/, m/m/**.
- Sort picture names with **s/s/, a/a/** and **m/m/**.
- Blend sounds **s/s/, a/a/, m/m/**.
- Read previously taught high-frequency words: **the, we like, I**.

Additional Materials

- Letter cards: **a, m, S**

Weekly Presentation
- Picture cards: **ant, antelope, apple, ax, bat, magnet, map, mitten, mop, pan, sandwich, sock, sub, sun**
- High-frequency word cards: **I, like, the, we**

(iELD) Integrated ELD

Light Support

Write the high-frequency word *the* on the board. Read aloud *"The Little Helper,"* and ask students to clap each time they hear the word. Let pairs of students read the story on their own. When they see a sentence that begins with the word **the,** challenge them to read the sentence aloud together. Offer help as needed.

Moderate Support

Read aloud paragraph 2 on page 20 of "The Little Helper." Ask students to listen closely as you read it again and to clap when they hear the high-frequency words *the* and *I*. Write the following sentence on the board:

"I can help you, Your Majesty!" the little mouse cried.
Erase the words **help you** and draw a line in their place. Invite students to suggest substitute action words to go on the line.

Substantial Support

Read aloud "The Little Helper," and have students clap when they hear the high-frequency word **I**. For each appearance, repeat the sentence and have students echo-read it with you. Write the first of the sentences (page 18) on the board.
Write: *I may be able to help you someday.*
Erase the words **help you** and draw a line in their place. Invite students to suggest substitute words.

ELD.PI.K.1, ELD.PI.K.10, ELD.PII.K.3

RF.K.2d Isolate and pronounce the initial, medial vowel, and final sounds (phonemes) in three-phoneme (consonant-vowel-consonant, or CVC) words. (This does not include CVCs ending with /l/, /r/, or /x/.), RF.K.3a Demonstrate basic knowledge of letter-sound correspondences by producing the primary or most frequent sound for each consonant., RF.K.3c Read common high-frequency words by sight (e.g., the, of, to, you, she, my, is, are, do, does).

Read Aloud and Shared Reading

(20 MIN.) RL.K.1, RF.K.1a, RF.K.2a, RF.K.3a, RF.K.4, SL.K.3

Read-Aloud Handbook

Shared Reading Vol. 1, p. 9 "Diddle, Diddle, Dumpling"

Read Aloud

To support the unit concept, use one of the Read-Aloud Handbook selections for Unit 2. As you read, model the metacognitive strategy for the unit, Visualize, guided by the samples provided. You may also wish to select a favorite read-aloud from your classroom or school library. To support the unit concept, use one of the suggested titles for Unit 2.

Shared Reading (iELD)

Reread the Poem

First rereading. Read aloud the text fluently and expressively, pointing under each word.

Reread for fluency: Rate/Pacing. Model reading the poem at a comfortable pace. Point out that you continue the steady pace unless there's a punctuation mark. Echo-read the selection several times, allowing students time to read at a pace that reflects the rhythm of the poem. Provide corrective feedback and/or validate students' efforts.

Build Concepts: Every Story Has Characters

Pose questions to connect the poem to the unit concept. For example:

- *Do you go to bed with your trousers on? Why or why not?*
- *Why do you think John's dad wrote this poem?*

Review Phonics: Initial *s*

Highlight the word **son** in the first line.

Ask: *What is the first letter in this word? What is its sound?*

Guide students to read the word aloud.

Review Poetic Features: Rhythm

Tell students that poems have a rhythm. The rhythm, or pattern, makes the poems fun to read. Read the poem again using a correct rhythm and pace. Clap the rhythm as you read. Encourage students to clap the rhythm along with you.

Student Objectives

I will be able to:
- Read a poem with appropriate pacing.
- Identify words with initial **s**.
- Recognize rhythm in a poem.

(iELD) Integrated ELD

Light Support
Read aloud the poem with proper pacing. Ask students to tell you what they learn in each line and what they notice about the first and last lines. Challenge them to ask you a question about the meaning of the first and last lines. Echo-read the poem line by line with students. Then choral-read the poem.

Moderate Support
Point out the structure of the poem, showing students that the first and last lines match. Tell students that the phrase **Diddle, diddle, dumpling** is a nonsense phrase that will help them understand the pace at which they should read the poem. Read aloud the poem with proper pacing. Clap your hands for each word, and clap without speaking at the end of lines 1, 2, and 3 to demonstrate a pause. Ask students what happens in lines 2 and 3, prompting them to answer with the following sentence stem:
In line 2, I learn that _____.
Echo-read the poem and invite students to clap along.

Substantial Support
Point out the structure of the poem, showing students that the first and last lines match. Draw their attention to the comma at the end of the first line and the period at the end of the last line. Explain that these are punctuation marks and that each mark means a reader should pause while reading the poem aloud.
Ask: *Where are the pauses in this poem?*
Have students point to all the punctuation marks and answer with the following sentence frame:
I see a _____ here.
Read aloud the poem, carefully pausing at each punctuation mark. Then have students echo the words **diddle, dumpling,** and **trousers.**

ELD.PI.K.5, ELD.PI.K.9, ELD.PII.K.2

RL.K.1 With prompting and support, ask and answer questions about key details in a text., RF.K.1a Follow words from left to right, top to bottom, and page by page., RF.K.2a Recognize and produce rhyming words., RF.K.3a Demonstrate basic knowledge of letter-sound correspondences by producing the primary or most frequent sound for each consonant., RF.K.4 Read emergent-reader texts with purpose and understanding., SL.K.3 Ask and answer questions in order to seek help, get information, or clarify something that is not understood.

Mentor Read-Aloud Vol. 1, pp. 18-21
"The Little Helper"

Student Objectives

I will be able to:
• Act out the meaning of verbs with similar meanings.

iELD Integrated ELD

Light Support

Have students work in pairs. Remind them that the lion and the mouse have two different encounters in "The Little Helper." Ask them to describe what happens the first time the animals meet and what happens the second time the animals meet. Challenge them to use one word from each pair of words below.

crawled   tiptoed
grabbed   crushed
skipped   danced
chomped   gnawed

Then have partners select and act out one of the scenes.

Moderate Support

Draw students' attention to page 20 of "The Little Helper." Read aloud the page, and ask students to explain to you what happens. Then write the following sets of verbs and verb phrases on the board:

skip   hop
come upon   discover
cry   yell
gnaw   chew

Ask a volunteer to act out each set, showing how the two actions are different. Provide vocabulary support as needed. Then invite students to act out the events on the page as you read the paragraphs aloud.

Substantial Support

Remind students that in "The Little Helper," when the lion grabbed the mouse, "the little mouse trembled and shook."

Ask: *What is it like to tremble?*
Mime trembling by shaking as if you are shivering.
Ask: *What is it like to shake?*
Mime shaking by shaking more dramatically. Prompt students to act out the difference between trembling and shaking.

ELD PI.K.6, ELD.PI.K.12, ELD.PII.K.3

Build Vocabulary: Shades of Meaning (10 MIN.) RL.K.4, L.K.5d, L.K.6

Engage Thinking

Display pages 18 and 19 of "The Little Helper." Tell students that the writer used different verbs, or action words, to describe how characters spoke. Explain that today, students will act out the meaning of action words that have similar meanings.

Say: *The words **shouted** and **whispered** are both ways to speak. How are they different?*

Model

Reread sentence 1 in paragraph 1 and circle the word **crawled.** Invite a student to stand and act out how the mouse moved on the sleeping lion. Then read the last sentence on page 19. Circle the word **raced**. Invite a different student to demonstrate what it looks like to "race off." Then think aloud to model how you pay attention to the shades of meaning among these verbs.

Sample modeling: *When I read the first paragraph, I can form a picture in my head of exactly how the mouse moved up the lion. The author says the mouse crawled. Then, when the lion lets the mouse go, the author says the mouse "raced off." This helps me visualize the action. I know the mouse ran as hard as he could. He did not crawl, and he did not walk. Both **crawled** and **raced** describe movement. The author chose each word to tell exactly how the mouse moved.*

Guided Practice iELD

Reread paragraphs 2–4 and ask students to listen for three verbs that describe how a character speaks (**roared, cried, laughed**). Help students identify the words. Prompt students to think critically about the word meanings. Ask students to demonstrate each manner of speaking. Provide prompts as necessary. For example:

• *What does it sound like when a lion roars? What would it mean if someone "roared" when they spoke to you?*
*Does **cried** in this sentence mean the mouse had tears running down his face? How can you cry when you speak?*

• *Have you ever laughed while you spoke?*

☑ Show Your Word Knowledge

Ask students to listen carefully as you say an action word. Ask students to act out the meaning of the word. Repeat with related verbs. Use **walked, raced, skipped.**

RL.K.4 Ask and answer questions about unknown words in a text. (See grade K Language standards 4-6 for additional expectations.) CA **L.K.5d** Distinguish shades of meaning among verbs describing the same general action (e.g., walk, march, strut, prance) by acting out the meanings. **L.K.6** Use words and phrases acquired through conversations, reading and being read to, and responding to texts.

©2017 Benchmark Education Company, LLC

Identify Major Story Events (10 MIN.) RL.K.1,

RL.K.3

Engage Thinking

Display "The Little Helper."

Ask: *How does the mouse feel in the beginning of the story?*

Model

Think aloud to model identifying major events from the beginning of the story.

Sample modeling: *I know a story has a beginning, a middle, and an end. The beginning is what happens first. I know page 18 is the beginning of the story. It is the first page. I reread and look at the illustration. I can identify the major events from the beginning of the story. The mouse accidentally climbs on the sleeping lion. The lion wakes up angry. He grabs the mouse. The mouse begs to be let go and tells the lion he can help the lion one day. Next I read the middle of the story. Then I read the end, or what happens last. I read to find major events in the middle and end of the story.*

Guided Practice (iELD)

Review the text on pages 19–21. Use directive and corrective feedback to help students identify major events from the middle and end of the story. For example:

- *We identified the major events from the beginning of the story. What happens next is the middle of the story. What are the important events?*
- *How can the illustration help you understand a major event?*
- *At the end of the story, a character usually solves a problem. The lion has a problem. He is trapped. How is the problem solved? This is an important event from the end of the story.*

☑ Show Your Knowledge

Name an event from the beginning, middle, or end of the story. Have students identify the part of the story in which the event occurs.

Mentor Read-Aloud Vol. 1, pp. 18–21
"The Little Helper"

MENTOR READ 2 MINI-LESSON

Student Objectives

I will be able to:
- Identify major events from the beginning, middle, and end of a story.

(iELD) Integrated ELD

Light Support
Draw three boxes on the board and label them **Beginning, Middle,** and **End.** Have students copy the organizer on their own paper.
Ask: *What happens first in "The Little Helper"?*
Prompt students to draw or write the first event in the **Beginning** box, showing or using at least one action word. Have students complete their organizers with drawings or words that show actions. Then have them retell the story, using their organizers as a resource.

Moderate Support
Draw three boxes on the board and label them **Beginning, Middle,** and **End.** Have students copy the organizer on their own paper.
Ask: *What happens first in "The Little Helper"?*
Prompt students to draw or write the first event in the **Beginning** box.
Ask: *What happens last in the story?*
Have students draw or write the final event in the **End** box. Then have students to fill in the **Middle** box. Coach students to tell the story using their organizers.

Substantial Support
Ask students to tell you what happens in "The Little Helper." As they talk, draw a set of three boxes on the board and label them **Beginning, Middle,** and **End.**
Ask: *What happens first in the story?*
Prompt students to describe how the mouse wakes the lion. In the **Beginning** box, write *mouse wakes lion.*
Ask: *What is the action word?*
Circle **wakes** as students respond.
Ask: *What happens last in the story?*
Prompt students to describe how the mouse saves the lion. Write *mouse saves lion* in the **End** box.
Ask: *What is the action word?*
Circle **saves** as students respond.
Ask: *What happens in the middle of the story?*
Write one or more answers in the **Middle** box, and have students identify the action word or words.

ELD.PI.K.6, ELD.PI.K.12, ELD.PII.K.3

RL.K.1 With prompting and support, ask and answer questions about key details in a text., **RL.K.3** With prompting and support, identify characters, settings, and major events in a story.

Mentor Read-Aloud Vol. 1, pp. 18-21
"The Little Helper"

Student Objectives

I will be able to:
- Write about a character's feelings.
- Form plural nouns orally.

(iELD) Integrated ELD

Light Support

Have students work in pairs. Challenge them to choose one event from "The Little Helper" and then to complete the sentence frame below, using a variety of words to name feelings and explain their causes.
When _____, the lion feels _____ because _____, and the mouse feels _____ because _____.

Moderate Support

Ask students to think about the different ways the lion feels during the story "The Little Helper." Prompt them to tell you how the lion feels when the mouse wakes him up, when the mouse says he may be able to help the lion someday, while he is trapped in the hunter's net, and while the mouse is gnawing at the hunter's net. Have students complete the sentence frame below using one word from the Word Bank and an explanation of their own choosing.
The lion feels _____ because _____.

Word Bank

angry irritated amused teased afraid hopeful

Substantial Support

Ask students to think about the different ways the mouse feels during the story "The Little Helper." Provide students with the chart of choices below. Read and explain the choices. Then have students complete the sentence frame below using one word from the left column and one phrase from the right column.
The mouse feels _____ because _____.

Feeling	Reason
scared	the lion grabs him
happy	the lion lets him go
worried	he is skipping through the grass
serious	the lion is trapped in a net

ELD.PI.K.10, ELD.PI.K.12, ELD.PII.K.6

Write a Monologue (10 MIN.) W.K.3, W.K.8, SL.K.1a, SL.K.1b, SL.K.2, L.K.1a, L.K.1c

Engage Thinking

Display page 18 of "The Little Helper." Direct students' attention to the illustration. Tell students that today they are going to imagine they are the little mouse. They will work together to write what they felt when the lion grabbed them!

Ask: *How do you think the mouse felt when the lion grabbed him?*

Collaborative Conversation: Partners

Tell students that before writing, you would like them to turn and talk to a partner briefly. Ask them to share their ideas about how the mouse felt when the lion grabbed him. Before beginning, reread paragraphs 1 and 2 on page 18. Then model how students should talk with their partner.

Sample modeling: *I imagine I am the mouse. I think I'm walking on a small hill. Then the hill roars at me! It's a huge lion. The King of Beasts is yelling at me! Then he grabs me in his huge paw. I want to tell my partner what the mouse would say about his feelings. I might say, "I think the mouse would say, 'I was terrified!'" When you speak to your partner, you can use the same sentence frame: I think the mouse would say, "___."*

Give students two minutes to share their ideas. Then bring them together and ask volunteers to share their partner's ideas.

Write as a Group (iELD)

Collaborate with students to agree on sentences that tell what the mouse would say about when the lion grabbed him. Rehearse the sentences orally and model how to write them. Invite volunteers to dictate the sentences. Engage students in the writing process by prompting them with questions. For example:

- *We are pretending we are the mouse, so we use the words **I** and **me**. Did we use these words?*
- ***Paw** is a noun. How can we make a plural noun to name more than one paw?*
- *This sentence has strong feeling. Let's add an exclamation mark. This tells the reader to read this sentence with a lot of feeling.*
- *I'm not sure how to spell this word. How can we make sure we spell it correctly?*

Sample Shared Writing

The lion grabbed me tightly in one of his paws. I was terrified! I thought he was going to eat me!
In the end, he did not eat me and we became friends.

Build Language: Form Regular Plural Nouns

Remind students that you have been practicing adding **/s/** to the end of a noun to make plural nouns. Review that a plural noun names more than one. Continue naming a singular noun and have students add **/s/** to form the plural. Encourage students to use the plural nouns in a sentence.

Singular Noun	Plural Noun
animal	animals (The animals helped each other.)
hill	hills (The mouse climbed over three hills.)
friend	friends (The lion and the mouse became friends.)

 Write Independently

Ask students to draw the mouse with a face that shows the mouse's feelings when the lion caught him. Students can write or dictate a sentence to tell about the mouse's feelings.

Small-Group Differentiated Instruction (15 MIN. per Group)

Meet with Small Groups

Select small-group reading titles or activities based on students' needs. See the Small-Group Instructional Planner for titles that support a range of instructional levels within the unit topic. Remind students to apply skills and strategies they learned to their small-group reading experiences.

Say: *One important strategy we practiced today was identifying major events from the beginning, middle, and end of a story. As you read and listen to stories today, ask yourself, "What happens at the beginning of the story? What happens next? What happens at the end of the story?" You can also read and listen for verbs, or action words, that tell you exactly how a character moves or speaks. These words can help you picture the action in your mind.*

Whole-Group Reflect and Share

Bring the class back together. Ask volunteers to identify major story events they read about. Ask them to tell events from the beginning, middle, and end of the story.

W.K.3 Use a combination of drawing, dictating, and writing to narrate a single event or several loosely linked events, tell about the events in the order in which they occurred, and provide a reaction to what happened., **W.K.8** With guidance and support from adults, recall information from experiences or gather information from provided sources to answer a question., **SL.K.1a** Follow agreed-upon rules for discussions (e.g., listening to others and taking turns speaking about the topics and texts under discussion)., **SL.K.1b** Continue a conversation through multiple exchanges. ,**SL.K.2** Confirm understanding of a text read aloud or information presented orally or through other media by asking and answering questions about key details and requesting clarification if something is not understood., **L.K.1a** Print many upper- and lowercase letters., **L.K.1c** Form regular plural nouns orally by adding /s/ or /es/ (e.g., dog, dogs; wish, wishes).

Pre-Decodable Reader: *I Am Sam*

Student Objectives

I will be able to:
- Recognize and produce rhyme.
- Read previously taught high-frequency words: **I, like, we, the.**
- Read decodable text.

Additional Materials

- Pre-decodable reader: *I Am Sam*

Weekly Presentation
- High-frequency word cards: **I, like, the, we**

Monitor Student Reading of Connected Text

As students chorally read the pre-decodable text and answer questions, ask these questions:

Are students able to . . .
- ❏ blend and read **s** words in the text?
- ❏ read new high-frequency words with automaticity?
- ❏ demonstrate comprehension of the text by answering text-based questions?

Based on your observations, you may wish to support students' fluency, automaticity, and comprehension with additional decodable reading practice during intervention time.

Focus Skill: s/s/ (20 MIN.) RL.K.1, RL.K.10, RF.K.2a, RF.K.3a, RF.K.3c, RF.K.4

Phonological Awareness: Recognize and Produce Rhyme

Model/Practice

Say the words **cat** and **mat**. Tell students that these words rhyme because they have the same sounds at the end.

Say: *Listen to these words:* **cat, mat***. I hear* **/at/** *at the end of* **cat***, and* **/at/** *at the end of* **mat***. Say the words with me and listen to the ending sounds.*

Say pairs of words and have students clap if the pairs rhyme: **fan, pan; hit, had; moon, spoon; cake, can.** Have students say other words that rhyme with **fan** and **pan**.

High-Frequency Words

Review: *I, like, we, the*

Write the words **I, like, we, the.** Remind students that these are words they have been practicing so that they can read them quickly. Have students read the words aloud several times.

Hold up the high-frequency word card **the** and call on individual students to quickly read the word. Then have the student use the word in an oral sentence. Have the other students clap when they hear **the**. Repeat for the other high-frequency words.

Pre-Decodable Reader: *I Am Sam*

Introduce the Book

Point to the book's title, *I Am Sam*. Have students sound out each word as you run your finger under it.

Ask: *What do you see on the cover? Where is Sam?*

Read the Book

Display the rebuses on pages 2–7 and discuss what each stands for. Turn to page 2, and have students blend the decodable words and read the first sentence aloud so you can check their reading. Have students continue to read, blending the decodable words and reading the high-frequency words quickly.

Connect Phonics to Comprehension

When students have finished reading, ask:

- *What are some things that Sam likes?*
- *Who likes Sam?*

Turn to a partner and retell the story.

RL.K.1 With prompting and support, ask and answer questions about key details in a text., **RL.K.10** Actively engage in group reading activities with purpose and understanding., **RF.K.2a** Recognize and produce rhyming words. **RF.K.3a** Demonstrate basic knowledge of letter-sound correspondences by producing the primary or most frequent sound for each consonant., **RF.K.3c** Read common high-frequency words by sight (e.g., the, of, to, you, she, my, is, are, do, does)., **RF.K.4** Read emergent-reader texts with purpose and understanding.

Read Aloud and Shared Reading

(20 MIN.) RL.K.1, RF.K.1a, RF.K.3b, RF.K.3c, RF.K.4, SL.K.3

Read-Aloud Handbook   **Shared Reading Vol. 1, p. 8 "Sad Ladybug, Glad Ladybug"**

Read Aloud

To support the unit concept, use one of the Read-Aloud Handbook selections for Unit 2. As you read, model the metacognitive strategy for the unit, Visualize, guided by the samples provided. You may also wish to select a favorite read-aloud from you classroom or school library. To support the unit concept, use one of the suggested titles for Unit 2.

Shared Reading (iELD)

Reread the Realistic Fiction

First rereading. Read aloud the text fluently and expressively, pointing under each word.

Reread for fluency: Rate/Pacing. Read with appropriate pacing. Point out that you do not read the text too quickly or too slowly. Lead them to pause at the end of a sentence. Invite students to choral read the text at a good pace. Provide corrective feedback and/or validate students' efforts.

Build Concepts: Every Story Has Characters

Pose questions to connect the realistic fiction "Sad Ladybug, Glad Ladybug" to the unit concept about how people are different. For example:

- *How is Pam the same and different from you?*
- *If Pam was a student in your class, what are some ways she could help you and what are some way you could help her?*
- *How can we be respectful of Pam's needs?*

Review Phonics: Initial s

Highlight the word **Sad** in the title. Ask students to identify the first letter and its sound. Lead students in reading the word aloud. Then repeat with the words *saw* and *so*.

Review High-Frequency Words: *the*

Tell students that this text contains some words they have learned. Point to the previously taught high-frequency word **the** in the third sentence. Ask students to turn to a partner and tell their partner the high-frequency word. Remind students to look for high-frequency words they know as they read a new text.

Student Objectives

I will be able to:
- Read a along with appropriate pacing.
- Answer questions about how people are different.
- Identify the letter **s** and the sound **/s/.**
- Recognize words I know in different texts.

(iELD) Integrated ELD

Light Support
Remind students that they have learned to find the word **the** when they read. Show students "Sad Ladybug, Glad Ladybug," and have them point to the word **the.**
Have students work in pairs. Challenge them to tell each other sentences about the story that begin with **The.** Ask partners to write one of their sentences on a sheet of paper.

Moderate Support
Remind students that they have learned to find the word **the** when they read. Show students "Sad Ladybug, Glad Ladybug," and have them point to the word **the.** Have students work in pairs. Ask them to choose one of the sentence frames below and complete the sentence.
The ladybug _____.
The windowsill _____.

Substantial Support
Remind students that they have learned to find the word **the** when they read. Read aloud "Sad Ladybug, Glad Ladybug," and have students clap each time they hear the word **the.** Have students work in pairs. Read aloud the four noun phrases below and have students repeat them after you. Then have partners choose one of the phrases to use as the beginning of a sentence. Have partners collaborate on their sentence and then dictate the sentence to you. Write the sentence.
the ladybug
the windowsill
the big window
the happy ladybug

ELD.PI.K.1, ELD.PI.K.10, ELD.PII.K.1

RL.K.1 With prompting and support, ask and answer questions about key details in a text., RF.K.1a Follow words from left to right, top to bottom, and page by page., RF.K.3b Associate the long and short sounds with the common spellings (graphemes) for the five major vowels. (Identify which letters represent the five major vowels (Aa, Ee, Ii, Oo, and Uu) and know the long and short sound of each vowel. More complex long vowel graphemes and spellings are targeted in the grade 1 phonics standards.) CA, RF.K.3c Read common high-frequency words by sight (e.g., the, of, to, you, she, my, is, are, do, does)., RF.K.4 Read emergent-reader texts with purpose and understanding., SL.K.3 Ask and answer questions in order to seek help, get information, or clarify something that is not understood.

Compare and Contrast Adventures of Two Characters (20 MIN.) RL.K.3, RL.K.9, SL.K.1a

Engage Thinking

Display "The Tortoise and the Hare" and "The Little Helper." Ask students to think about the characters and their adventures.

Ask: *Who are the characters in "The Tortoise and the Hare" and "The Little Helper"?*

Say: *Today you are going to compare characters from each story and their adventures.*

Model

Display a three-column chart and read the column heads. Explain that in the far left and right columns you will list ways the characters are different. In the middle column, you will list ways in which the two characters are similar. Model how to compare and contrast the different things about characters, such as the way they look, their actions, and their adventures.

Sample modeling: *To compare, I will think about how the mouse and the tortoise adventures are alike. They both live in the wild. I will write this similarity in the chart. They also talk and do other things animals in the real world cannot do.*

Sample modeling: *To contrast, I will think about how the mouse and the tortoise adventures are different. The mouse gnawed on the ropes with his sharp teeth to set the lion free and the tortoise walked slowly to win the race.*

Mentor Read-Aloud Vol. 1, pp. 14–21
"The Tortoise and the Hare" and "The Little Helper"

Student Objectives

I will be able to:
- Answer questions about two different characters in a text.
- Recognize and describe similarities and differences between two characters.

Additional Materials

Weekly Presentation
- Compare-and-Contrast Chart

Guided Practice (iELD)

Use directive and corrective prompts as needed to guide students to compare and contrast the mouse and Tortoise.

- *What do both characters prove during their adventure?*
- *The mouse is small. Is the tortoise big? What does the tortoise have that the mouse does not?*
- *What is Tortoise's problem?*
- *What happens when Mouse finds the lion trapped in a net? What inference can we make about his character?*
- *Tortoise never stops putting one foot in front of the other. What inference can we make about her character?*

As students participate in the discussion, remind them to follow rules for discussion, such as listening to others, waiting for a turn to speak, and adding to the ideas of others.

Mouse	Both	Tortoise
• Gnawed on the ropes with his teeth to set the lion free • Has fur and a long tail • Is small • Helps a mighty lion • Is scared at the beginning • Does what he says he will do	• Live in the wild • Talk and do other things animals in the real world cannot do • Prove they can do things that no one thinks they can do • Are honest • Are characters in a fantasy	• Walked slowly to win the race. • Has a shell and a short tail • Is large • Is slow • Beats fast Hare in a race • Is calm • Doesn't give up

Sample Compare-and-Contrast Chart

 Show Your Knowledge

Read various entries from the chart. Have students cup their hand, palm down to make a shell if the description tells only about Tortoise. Have them wiggle their nose like a mouse if the description tells only about the mouse. Have them say **both** if the description relates to both characters. For example:

- *This character is slow.*
- *This character does something a real animal cannot do.*
- *This character helps a mighty lion.*

(iELD) Integrated ELD

Light Support

Ask partners to recall "The Tortoise and the Hare" and "The Little Helper." Challenge them to decide how the tortoise and the mouse are alike and different. Provide them with the following categories to discuss:

how the animals look

how the animals behave

how the animals feel

As partners talk, encourage them to use examples from the stories to support their decisions.

Moderate Support

Have students page through "The Tortoise and the Hare."

Ask: *What does the Tortoise say she always tries to do?*

Have students answer with a complete sentence.

Have students page through "The Little Helper."

Ask: *What does the mouse do that surprises the lion?*

Have students complete the following sentence stem:

The mouse surprises the lion by _____.

Finally, ask whether the mouse, like Tortoise, always tries to do his best. Have student respond using the following sentence frame:

_____, *because* _____.

Substantial Support

Hold up "The Tortoise and the Hare" and "The Little Helper." Tell students you will help them decide how the tortoise and the mouse are alike and different. Page through "The Tortoise and the Hare."

Ask: *How many legs does Tortoise have?*

Page through "The Little Helper."

Ask: *How many legs does the mouse have?*

Ask students to tell you whether they see any other ways that the two characters are alike.

Provide the sentence frame below and help students complete it.

Tortoise and the mouse are _____ because _____.

ELD.PI.K.7, ELD.PI.K.8, ELD.PII.K.6

RL.K.3 With prompting and support, identify characters, settings, and major events in a story., **RL.K.9** With prompting and support, compare and contrast the adventures and experiences of characters in familiar stories., **SL.K.1a** Follow agreed-upon rules for discussions (e.g., listening to others and taking turns speaking about the topics and texts under discussion).

Mentor Read-Aloud Vol. 1, pp. 14-21
"The Tortoise and the Hare" and "The Little Helper"

Student Objectives

I will be able to:
- Discuss how two characters are alike and different.
- Write comparison and contrast sentences about two story characters.
- Form plural nouns orally.

Integrated ELD

Light Support

Challenge students to write a sentence that tells how the mouse in "The Little Helper" and "Tortoise in The Tortoise and the Hare" are alike and different. Have students sketch a Venn diagram with the labels Mouse, Tortoise, and Both. Give students time to add descriptive nouns and noun phrases to the diagram. Then have them use the details to produce a sentence that compares and contrasts the characters.

Moderate Support

Sketch a Venn diagram with the labels Mouse, Tortoise, and Both. Ask students to recall the two stories and suggest words to write in each part of the diagram. Encourage them to use descriptive noun phrases such as **small animal, polite animal, skipping animal,** and **plodding animal.** Use the following sentence frame: *Both Tortoise and the mouse are _____, but Tortoise is _____ and the mouse is _____.*

Substantial Support

Remind students that they know a lot about the mouse in "The Little Helper" and Tortoise in "The Tortoise and the Hare." Sketch a Venn diagram with the labels Mouse, Tortoise, and Both.
Ask: *Are both the mouse and Tortoise animals?*
As students respond, write animals in the diagram under Both.
Ask: *Is the mouse a girl or a boy?*
Help students find the answer. Write *boy* in the Mouse circle.
Ask: *Is Tortoise a girl or a boy?*
Have students answer, and then write *girl* in the Tortoise circle. Use this sentence frame:
Both Tortoise and the mouse are _____, but Tortoise is a _____ and the mouse is a _____.

ELD.PI.K.6, ELD.PI.K.10, ELD.PII.K.4

Write to Compare and Contrast Two Characters (10 MIN.) W.K.2, W.K.8, L.K.1a, L.K.1c

Engage Thinking

Display "The Tortoise and the Hare" and "The Little Helper." Also display the Compare and Contrast chart. Remind students that you just worked together to compare two characters–the mouse and Tortoise. Explain that today they will write one way the characters are alike and one way they are different.

Ask: *Why do you think it is important to compare characters in two different stories?*

Point out how comparing and contrasting characters will help students understand and remember the characters.

Collaborative Conversation: Peer Groups

Separate students into peer groups. Lead them to take turns talking to members of their group to identify ways the mouse and Tortoise are alike and different. Tell partners that they will report their ideas to the class. Before partners begin, model what you might say to group members.

Sample modeling: *When I compare and contrast the mouse and Tortoise with my partner, I say, "Both the mouse and Tortoise do things no one thinks they can do. The characters are different, too. The mouse is small, but Tortoise is slow." When you talk with your partner, you can use the sentence frame: Both the mouse and Tortoise _____. The mouse _____, but Tortoise _____.*

Give groups two minutes to compare and contrast with their partner. Then bring them together and ask volunteers to share their ideas about the characters' similarities and differences.

Write as a Group (iELD)

Collaborate with students to agree on one similarity and one difference between the characters. Rehearse the message orally and model how you write the sentences. Engage students in the writing process by prompting them with questions. For example:

- *Let's start by giving a comparison. What word can we use to show we are telling how the mouse and Tortoise are alike?*
- *We wrote what Mouse's problem is. What word can we use to show that now we are going to contrast Mouse's problem and Tortoise's?*
- *Let's read our sentences. Are there any changes we want to make? Did we tell one way the characters are alike and one way they are different?*

Sample Shared Writing

The mouse and Tortoise are creatures who live in the wild.
The mouse is small and brave. The Tortoise is large and does her best.

Build Language: Form Regular Plural Nouns

Tell students that you will say a singular noun. Remind them that a singular noun names one person, place, or thing. Ask students what they add to the end of a noun to make the noun mean more than one. Then say a singular noun and have students add /s/ to the end to form the plural noun. Encourage students to use the plural nouns in a sentence.

Singular Noun	Plural Noun
tortoise	tortoises (The are five tortoises in the pen.)
paw	paws (The lion has four paws.)
road	roads (Tortoise and Hare raced on two roads.)

Write Independently

Ask students to draw and label a picture to show one way the characters are different. Students can label their drawing.

Small-Group Differentiated Instruction (15 MIN. per Group)

Meet with Small Groups

Select small-group reading titles or activities based on students' needs. See the Small-Group Instructional Planner for titles that support a range of instructional levels within the unit topic. Remind students to apply skills and strategies they learned to their small-group reading experiences.

Say: *Today we practiced comparing and contrasting two characters. When you read or listen to a story, compare a character to another character you have read about. Remember, every story has characters. Like real people, characters have some things in common, but they are different in many ways.*

Whole-Group Reflect and Share

Bring the class back together. Ask volunteers to share comparisons and contrasts they made to a character in a new story to a character in a story they are more familiar with.

W.K.2 Use a combination of drawing, dictating, and writing to compose informative/explanatory texts in which they name what they are writing about and supply some information about the topic., W.K.8 With guidance and support from adults, recall information from experiences or gather information from provided sources to answer a question., L.K.1a Print many upper- and lowercase letters., L.K.1c Form regular plural nouns orally by adding /s/ or /es/ (e.g., dog, dogs; wish, wishes).

Pre-Decodable Reader: *I Am Sam*

Student Objectives

I will be able to:
- Blend onset and rime.
- Review letter-sound correspondences for **s/s/, a/a/, m/m/.**
- Blend sounds **/s/, /a/, /m/.**
- Spell words **am** and **Sam.**
- Write legibly.
- Read previously taught high-frequency words: **I, like, we, the.**
- Read decodable text.

Additional Materials

- Pre-decodable reader: *I Am Sam*
- Letter cards: **S, s, a, m**

Weekly Presentation
- Picture cards: **ant, map, mop, sail, soap**
- High-frequency word cards **I, like, the, we**

Focus Skill: s/s/ (20 MIN.) RL.K.1, RL.K.10, RF.K.2c, RF.K.3a, RF.K.3c, RF.K.4, L.K.1a

Phonological Awareness: Blend Onset and Rime

Model/Practice

Segment the word **Sam** into its onset and rime: **/s/ /am/.** Have students blend the sounds and say the word.

Repeat with the words **sit, sink, sock,** and **six.** Then say the word **sun.**

Ask: *What is the onset or beginning sound? What is the rest of the word?*

Blend the sounds **/s/** and **/un/** and say the word with the class.

Display the picture card **sail.** Have the students name the picture.

Ask: *What is the onset or beginning sound? What is the rest of the word? Let's blend the sounds* **/s/** *and* **/ail/** *and say the word:* **sail.**

Repeat with the picture cards **soap, map, mop, ant.**

Letter-Sound Correspondences

Review
Display Letter Card **m.**

Say: *This is the letter* **m.** *The letter* **m** *stands for /***mmm***/. What is the letter? What sound does this letter stand for?*

Repeat for **a** and **s.**

Give each student three blank index cards. Have students draw a picture of something that begins like **mitten, apple,** and **sun.** Then have students sort their pictures under the correct letter card.

Say: *What sound does the name of your picture begin with? Place your picture under the letter that stands for that sound.*

Blend Sounds

Review

Have students blend the word **Sam.** Place letter cards **S, a, m** in a pocket chart. Point to the letter **S.**

Say: *This is the letter* **S.** *The letter* **S** *stands for* **/sss/.** *Say /***sss***/. This is the letter* **a.** *The letter* **a** *stands for* **/aaa/.** *Say* **/aaa/.** *Listen as I blend the two sounds together* **/sssaaa/.** *Blend the sounds with me. This is the letter* **m.** *The letter* **m** *stands for /* **mmm/.** *Say* **/mmm/.** *Listen as I blend all three sounds together,* **/sssaaammm/.** *Now blend the sounds to read the word,* **Sam.**

Repeat the steps for the word **am.** Move your hand from left to right under the word. Have students blend and read the word **am.**

Dictation (iELD)

Review

Dictate these sounds for students to spell: **/s/ /a/ /m/**. Have them repeat the sound and then write the letter that stands for the sounds.

Dictate the following words for students to spell: **am, Sam**. Model how to segment each word.

Say: *When I say the word* **am***, I hear two sounds,* **/a/ /m/***. I know the letter* **a** *stands for* **/a/** *and the letter* **m** *stands for* **/m/***. I will write the letters* **a** *and* **m** *to spell the word* **am***.*

Repeat for the word **Sam**. When children finish, write the words and have them correct their papers.

High-Frequency Words

Review: *I, like, the, we*

Write **I, like, the, we.** Focusing on one word at a time, have students spell the word as you point to each letter. Then erase one letter, say the word, and have students identify the missing letter. Replace the letter and have students read the word.

Decodable Text

Write the words and sentences. Guide students with blending the first two words. Then have volunteers read the sentences.

Sam	am
I am Sam.	
We like Sam.	

Pre-Decodable Reader: *I Am Sam*

Reread

Have partners reread *I Am Sam* together. Circulate and listen in. Note student's speed, accuracy, and intonation. Based on the group as a whole, provide some general feedback and validate successes. If students need additional practice to read the text, provide support during small-group reading instruction.

(iELD) Integrated ELD

Light Support
On the board, write the letters **T, t,** and **m** and the word **the**. Remind students about the two stories they listened to this week, "The Tortoise and the Hare" and "The Little Helper."
Ask: *Who is the little helper?*
As they respond, write *the mouse* on the board. Challenge students to write one sentence to describe an event or a character from one of the stories. Check their work and help them improve their handwriting as necessary.

Moderate Support
Show students the letter cards **T, t,** and **m** as well as the word card **the**.
Say: *You heard two stories this week, "The Tortoise and the Hare" and "The Little Helper."*
Ask: *What word do you hear in both titles?*
Say: *Let's write that word.*
Write *the* on the board and have students copy it. Show students the sentence frame with partial words below. Have students copy and complete it on their own. Check their work. If they have difficulty writing any of the words, help them form the letters or allow them to trace your printing.

___he ___ouse and ___ortoise are in different stories.

Substantial Support
Show students the letter cards **T, t,** and **m** and the word card **the**. Remind them about the two stories they listened to this week, "The Tortoise and the Hare" and "The Little Helper."
Ask: *What word do you hear in both titles?*
Say: *Let's write that word.*
Ask students the name of the turtle in the first story.
Say: *Let's write that name.*
Write *Tortoise* on the board and have students copy it. Point to the capital **T** and have students name the letter.
Ask students what the tiny animal in the other story is called.
Say: *Let's write that name.*
Hold up the **m** card and write *mouse* on the board.

ELD.PI.K.2, ELD.PI.K.10, ELD.PII.K.2

RL.K.1 With prompting and support, ask and answer questions about key details in a text., **RL.K.10** Actively engage in group reading activities with purpose and understanding., **RF.K.2c** Demonstrate understanding of spoken words, syllables, and sounds (phonemes). Blend and segment onsets and rimes of single-syllable spoken words., **RF.K.3a** Demonstrate basic knowledge of letter-sound correspondences by producing the primary or most frequent sound for each consonant., **RF.K.3c** Read common high-frequency words by sight (e.g., the, of, to, you, she, my, is, are, do, does)., **RF.K.4** Read emergent-reader texts with purpose and understanding., **L.K.1a** Print many upper- and lowercase letters.

Week 2 Skills at a Glance

	Day 1	Day 2
Reading Mini-Lessons	**Mentor Read-Alouds:** Topic Introduction, pp. 12-13 **Build Knowledge and Review Week 1 Strategies (10 Min.), p. 156** RL.K.3, RL.K.5, SL.K.1a, SL.K.1b **Read-Aloud Handbook** **Shared Readings:** "A Birthday Cat," p. 10 **Read Aloud and Shared Reading (20 Min.), p. 157** RL.K.1, RL.K.10, RL.K.10a, RL.K.10b, RF.K.1.a, RF.K.3a, RF.K.4, SL.K.2, SL.K.3 • Fluency: Accuracy/Use Context • Build Concepts: Every Story Has Characters • Model Print Concepts: Directionality: Top to Bottom • Review Phonics: Initital s Goldilocks and the Three Bears **Goldilocks and the Three Bears: Listen and Retell Key Events (10 Min.), p. 158** RL.K.1, RL.K.2, RL.K.3, RL.K.5, RL.K.6, RL.K.10, RL.K.10a, RL.K.10b, SL.K.1a, SL.K.1b, SL.K.2, SL.K.3, SL.K.6	**Read-Aloud Handbook** **Shared Readings:** "A Birthday Cat," p. 10 **Read Aloud and Shared Reading (20 Min.), p. 164** RL.K.1, RL.K.3, RF.K.1a, RF.K.3a, RF.K.3c, RF.K.4, SL.K.3 • Fluency: Accuracy/Use Context • Build Concepts: Every Story Has Characters • Review Phonics: Initial and Final t • Review High-Frequency Words: see Goldilocks and the Three Bears **Identify Story Characters (10 Min.), p. 165** RL.K.1, RL.K.3, SL.K.1a **Find Text Evidence: Make Inferences About Character (10 Min.), p. 166** RL.K.1, RL.K.3
Writing Mini-Lessons	**Write Key Events (10 Min.), p. 160** W.K.2, W.K.8, SL.K.1a, SL.K.1b, L.K.1a, L.K.1d • Build Language: Understand and Use Question Words	**Write an Opinion (10 Min.), p. 168** W.K.1, W.K.8, L.K.1a, L.K.1d • Build Language: Understand and Use Question Words
Phonics Mini-Lessons	**Focus Skill: t/t/ (20 Min.), p. 162** RF.K.2d, RF.K.3a, RF.K.3c, L.K.1a • Phonological Awareness: Phoneme Isolation • High-Frequency Words: see	**Focus Skill: t/t/ (20 Min.), p. 170** RF.K.2d, RF.K.3a, RF.K.3c, L.K.1a • Phonological Awareness: Phoneme Isolation • High-Frequency Words: go

Extended Read 1: "Goldilocks and the Three Bears"

Fable

Quantitative	Lexile® 500L
Qualitative Analysis of Text Complexity	

Purpose and Levels of Meaning ❶
• The story has a simple, very familiar plot.

Structure ❶
• Story has a strictly sequential narrative structure.

Language Conventionality and Clarity ❷
• Vocabulary is familiar from traditional fables, but there are a few compound sentences.

Knowledge Demands ❶
• This familiar story, retold in a straightforward way, requires no prior knowledge for comprehension.

Day 3	Day 4	Day 5
Read-Aloud Handbook **Shared Readings:** "Bear and Fox," p. 11 **Read Aloud and Shared Reading (20 Min.), p. 172** RL.K.1, RL.K.5, RL.K.10, RL.K.10a, RL.K.10b, RF.K.1a, RF.K.3c, RF.K.4, SL.K.3, L.K.1d • Fluency: Accuracy/Use Context • Build Unit Concepts: Every Story Has Characters • Model Print Concepts: Directionality: Top to Bottom • Review Language: Understand and Use Question Words Goldilocks and the Three Bears **Build Vocabulary: Shades of Meaning (10 Min.), p. 173** RL.K.1, L.K.5d, L.K.6 **Find Text Evidence: Story Events (10 Min.), p. 174** RL.K.1, RL.K.3, SL.K.3	**Read-Aloud Handbook** **Shared Readings:** "Bear and Fox," p. 11 **Read Aloud and Shared Reading (20 Min.), p. 179** RL.K.1, RL.K.3, RL.K.5, RF.K.1a, RF.K.3b, RF.K.4, SL.K.3 • Fluency: Accuracy/Context • Build Concepts: Every Story Has Characters • Review Phonics: Short *a* • Review High-Frequency Words: *the* Goldilocks and the Three Bears **Find Text Evidence: Text Type: Fantasy (15 Min.), p. 180** RL.K.1, RL.K.5, SL.K.3	**Read-Aloud Handbook** **Shared Readings:** "Bear and Fox," p. 11 **Read Aloud and Shared Reading (20 Min.), p. 185** RL.K.1, RL.K.5, RF.K.1a, RF.K.3a, RF.K.3c, RF.K.4, SL.K.3 • Fluency: Accuracy/Use Context • Build Concepts: Every Story Has Characters • Review Phonics: Final t • Review High-Frequency Words: *the* **Mentor Read-Alouds:** "The Little Helper," pp. 18-21 Goldilocks and the Three Bears **Compare and Contrast Fantasy Characters (15 Min.), p. 186** RL.K.1, RL.K.9, SL.K.3, SL.K.4, SL.K.6
Write a New Ending (10 Min.), p. 176 W.K.3, W.K.8, L.K.1a, L.K.1d • Build Language: Understand and Use Question Words	**Write an Opinion (15 Min.), p. 182** W.K.1, W.K.8, L.K.1a, L.K.1d • Build Language: Understand and Use Question Words	**Plan and Draft a Response to the Essential Question (15 Min.), p. 188** W.K.2, W.K.5
Focus Skill: t/t/ (20 Min.), p. 178 RF.K.2d, RF.K.3a, RF.K.3c • Phonological Awareness: Phoneme Isolation • High-Frequency Words: *see, go, the, we*	**Pre-Decodable Reader:** *I See* **Focus Skill: t/t (20 Min.), p. 184** RL.K.1, RL.K.10, RF.K.2a, RF.K.3a, RF.K.3c, RF.K.4 • Phonological Awareness: Recognize and Produce Rhyme • High-Frequency Words: *I, like, the, we, see, go*	**Pre-Decodable Reader:** I See **Focus Skill: t/t/ (20 Min.), p. 190** RL.K.1, RL.K.10, RF.K.2c, RF.K.2d, RF.K.3a, RF.K.3c, RF.K.4, L.K.1a • Phonological Awareness: Blend Onset and Rime • High-Frequency Words: *I, like, the, we, see, go*

Mentor Read-Aloud Topic Introduction Vol. 1, pp. 12-13

Student Objectives

I will be able to:
- Reflect on strategies I have learned to help me understand how characters are different.
- Identify fantasy stories
- Discuss story events.

iELD Integrated ELD

Light Support
Challenge students to briefly recount the story events in the order they happened. Encourage them to use verbs and verb phrases from the text, such as **was talking, challenge, will race, plodded, woke up, was waiting,** and **stamping**. Record their responses on the board, and have students practice reading them aloud.

Moderate Support
Focus students on the key verbs from "The Tortoise and the Hare." Ask questions that probe the reading and help students review recounting story events in order.
Ask: *Before the race, what does Hare talk about? During the race, what does Hare do? What does Tortoise do?*
After the race, how does Hare act? How does Tortoise act?

Substantial Support
Have students review "The Tortoise and the Hare" to practice using verbs and recounting story events. Highlight important text verbs such as **race, stop, woke,** and **waiting**. Have students act out each word. Together, use some of the verbs to fill out a chart like the one below, showing what happened during the beginning, middle, and end of the story. Students can use picture cues and gestures as needed.

Beginning	race	Tortoise races Hare
Middle	stop	Hare stops to take a nap.
End	woke waiting	Hare wakes up. Tortoise is waiting for him at the finish line.

ELD.PI.K.12, ELD.PII.K.1, ELD.PII.K.3b

Build Knowledge and Review Week 1 Strategies (10 MIN.) RL.K.3, RL.K.5, SL.K.1a, SL.K.1b

Discuss the Essential Question

Show students the Topic 2 Introduction and read aloud the essential question. Then flip through the selections from Week 1. Ask students to turn and talk to a partner about what they have learned about ways people are different. Tell them to use the sentence frame:

I learned that _____.

Ask volunteers to share what their partners said. Then tell students that in Week 2, they will read more stories to learn about characters and people.

Review Week 1 Strategies iELD

Identify Genre: Fantasy. Remind students that during Week 1, they learned to identify fantasy.

Say: *Remember we read* "The Tortoise and the Hare." *We learned that the story is a fantasy because it has characters that do things that cannot happen in real life.*

Display pages 14 and 15 of "The Tortoise and the Hare." Read aloud page 14 and call attention to the illustrations. Guide students to identify at least two things that identify the story as a fantasy, such as a hare and tortoise speaking.

Identify Story Events. Remind students that they also learned how to find major events at the beginning, middle, and end of a story.

Say: *Remember we found the major events in "The Tortoise and the Hare." Sometimes the illustrations can help us identify major events. What happens at the beginning of the story?*

Continue to page through the story guiding students to identify events in the middle and end of the story.

Tell students that as they listen to and read stories this week, they should practice identifying important story events from the beginning, middle, and end of the story. Tell them they will also decide if each story is a fantasy.

RL.K.3 With prompting and support, identify characters, settings, and major events in a story., **RL.K.5** Recognize common types of texts (e.g., storybooks, poems, fantasy, realistic text). CA)., **SL.K.1a** Follow agreed-upon rules for discussions (e.g., listening to others and taking turns speaking about the topics and texts under discussion)., **SL.K.1b** Continue a conversation through multiple exchanges.

Read Aloud and Shared Reading

(20 MIN.) RL.K.1, RL.K.10, RL.K.10a, RL.K.10b, RF.K.1a, RF.K.3a, RF.K.4, SL.K.2, SL.K.3

Read Aloud

To support the unit concept, use one of the Read-Aloud Handbook selections for Unit 2. As you read, model the metacognitive strategy for the unit, Visualize, guided by the samples provided. You may also wish to select a favorite read aloud from you classroom or school library. To support the unit concept, use one of the suggested titles for Unit 2.

Shared Reading (iELD)

Introduce the Realistic Fiction
Display "A Birthday Cat." Read aloud the title of the realistic fiction as you point under each word. Ask a few volunteers to tell what they know about birthdays. Invite students to turn to a partner and tell what they predict the text will be about. Invite a few students to share their predictions with the whole class.

Read the Realistic Fiction
First reading. Read aloud the text fluently and expressively, pointing under each word.

Reread for Fluency: Accuracy/Use Context. As you read, model using context to read words accurately. Choose an "unfamiliar" word, such as **presents,** and demonstrate how to use surrounding words to read the word correctly. Encourage students to chime in with you, using the same rate and expression as you do. Provide corrective feedback and/or validate students' efforts.

Build Concepts: Every Story Has Characters
Pose questions to connect the realistic fiction to the unit concept. For example:

- *Who are the characters in the story?*
- *What can you tell about Tim from reading the story?*
- *What can you tell about Gram from reading the story?*

Model Print Concepts: Directionality: Top to Bottom
Point to the title. Tell students we begin reading at the top of the page. Read the title aloud, pointing under each word. Stop at the last word in the title. Ask students to tell where you should start reading next. Remind students that when we read, we read from top to bottom.

Review Phonemic Awareness and Phonics: Initial s
Highlight the word **sad** in sentence 3. Ask students to identify the first letter and sound. Lead students in reading the word aloud. Repeat for **surprise** and **see.**

Read-Aloud Handbook | Shared Reading Vol. 1, p. 10 "A Birthday Cat"

Student Objectives

I will be able to:
- Answer questions about characters in a text.
- Read along with accuracy.
- Follow words from left to right and top to bottom.
- Identify words with initial **s**.

(iELD) Integrated ELD

Light Support
Look at "A Birthday Cat" with students. Challenge students to make inferences about the characters based on the text and picture.
Ask: *Who are the most important characters in the story?*
How would you describe Tim? How do Tim's feelings change in the story? How would you describe Gram? What details about the characters do you learn from the picture?

Moderate Support
Look at "A Birthday Cat" with students. Have partners use nouns and adjectives from the word bank to answer the questions about the characters.
Ask: *Who is the main character in the story? Who is another character in the story? How does Tim feel after he opens his presents? How does Tim feel after Gram shows him the surprise?*
Word Bank: Gram, Tim, sad, surprised, happy, excited

Substantial Support
Look at "A Birthday Cat" with students. Have students use the sentence frames and nouns and adjectives from the word bank to answer the questions and describe the characters.
Ask: *Who is the story mostly about?*
The story is mostly about a _____ named _____.
Ask: *Who is the other main character in the story?*
The other main character is _____.
Ask: *How does Tim feel after he opens his presents?*
Tim feels _____.
Ask: *How do you think Tim feels after the surprise?*
I think Tim feels _____.
Word Bank: Gram, boy, Tim, sad, happy

ELD.PI.K.5, ELD.PI.K.6, ELD.PII.K.4

RL.K.1 With prompting and support, ask and answer questions about key details in a text., RL.K.10 Actively engage in group reading activities with purpose and understanding., RL.K.10a Activate prior knowledge related to the information and events in texts. CA, RL.K.10b Use illustrations and context to make predictions about text. CA, RF.K.1a Follow words from left to right, top to bottom, and page by page., RF.K.3a Demonstrate basic knowledge of letter-sound correspondences by producing the primary or most frequent sound for each consonant., RF.K.4 Read emergent-reader texts with purpose and understanding., SL.K.2 Confirm understanding of a text read aloud or information presented orally or through other media by asking and answering questions about key details and requesting clarification if something is not understood., SL.K.3 Ask and answer questions in order to seek help, get information, or clarify something that is not understood.

Goldilocks and the Three Bears

Student Objectives

I will be able to:
- Identify and name characters in a fantasy.
- Make predictions about Goldilocks and the three bears.
- Listen for a purpose.
- Link my ideas to the ideas of others about characters in a story.
- Retell key events from *Goldilocks and the Three Bears*.

Additional Materials

Weekly Presentation
- Key Events Chart

Observation Checklist for Collaborative Conversation

As groups discuss the story events, use the questions below to evaluate how effectively students communicate with each other. Based on your answers, you may wish to plan future core lessons to support the collaborative conversation process.

Do partners . . .
- ❏ stay on topic throughout the discussion?
- ❏ listen respectfully?
- ❏ build on the comments of others appropriately?
- ❏ pose or respond to questions to clarify information?
- ❏ support their group member to participate?

Goldilocks and the Three Bears: Listen and Retell Key Events (10 MIN.) RL.K.1, RL.K.2, RL.K.3, RL.K.5, RL.K.6, RL.K.10, RL.K.10a, RL.K.10b, SL.K.1a, SL.K.1b, SL.K.2, SL.K.3, SL.K.6

Preview the Genre

Display the cover of *Goldilocks and the Three Bears*. Read aloud the title. Ask students if they know the story. Read the name of the author. Remind students that the author is the person who wrote the words in the story. Explain that the words **retold by** let us know that the story is a familiar story that has been told before. The author, Brenda Parkes, retells the familiar story in her own way. Read aloud the name of the illustrator. Remind students that the illustrator is the person who drew the illustrations.

Preview the pages. Guide students as they consider the genre. Ask students to turn and tell a partner the name of the author and illustrator and their roles. Also ask them to predict what kind of story they will read and what it will be about.

Sample Fantasy Feature	Sample Predictions
• title • illustrations • some characters are animals with human characteristics	I predict the story... • will be a fantasy. • will be about a girl who comes to a bear family's house while they are not at home.

Read Aloud the Text

Ask students to listen carefully for the characters and major events in the story. Explain that this is their purpose for listening. Read aloud with minimal interruption. Model using an appropriate voice for each character. Also model reading the words in bold type in a voice that matches the words. Remind students of their predictions. Have them tell if their predictions were correct.

Collaborative Conversation: Peer Groups

Divide students into three groups. Ask students to recall key events from the text. Remind students to build on group members' talk by listening carefully and linking their ideas to what they have said. Record students' ideas on the key events chart.

Share

Invite groups to share the key events they recalled. Record them on a class key events chart and reread the part of the text where the idea was mentioned. Draw simple illustrations.

Beginning:	The bear family lives in the woods. One day Mama Bear made porridge. It was too hot to eat, so they went for a walk.
Middle:	Goldilocks smelled the porridge while she was walking in the woods. She was hungry, so she went inside. She ate all the porridge in Baby Bear's bowl. She broke Baby Bear's chair. She fell asleep in Baby Bear's bed.
End:	The bears come back and find Goldilocks asleep in the bed. She wakes up and runs out the door.

Sample Key Events Chart

Reinforce or Reaffirm the Strategy

Provide modeling and/or engage students in self-reflection to build metacognitive awareness.

IF…	THEN…
students need support to retell key events from the text…	**Model to reinforce the strategy.** • *To identify the major events at the beginning of the story, I ask myself, "What happens?" I look back at the beginning of the story. The author tells us about the bear family. I'll note this in the chart.* • *The first event occurs on pages 6 and 7. I know this is an important event because it is very important to the story that the bears leave the house while their porridge cools. I'll record this event in the beginning row.* • *I know I have identified the major events from the beginning of the story. I know what happens after the bears leave is the middle of the story. I look for events in the middle, but I make sure I do not identify key events from the end of the story.* Continue to model how you identify and differentiate between important and unimportant events as needed.
students independently retell key details…	**Invite groups to reflect on their strategy by discussing one of the following questions:** • *How do you know what happened at the beginning, middle, and end of the story?* • *How did the illustrations help you identify major events?* • *How did you decide if an event or detail was important or not?* Have partners present their key events and explain how they found them.

 ## Show Your Knowledge

Name a story event and ask students to act it out. Then have them tell if the event is from the beginning, middle, or end of the story.

(iELD) Integrated ELD

Light Support
Have students in small groups orally retell the events from pages 6–9 in order using signal words **first, next, then, after that,** and **finally**. Students take turns, with each student telling the next event in the sequence.

Moderate Support
Have partners use the signal words to show the events of pages 6–9 in order. Point out that some signal words and phrases, such as **next, then,** and **after that** can be used anywhere in the middle, just not first or last.

_____, *Mama Bear makes porridge for breakfast.*
_____, *the porridge is too hot.*
_____, *the bears go for a walk to let the porridge cool.*
_____, *Goldilocks is walking in the woods.*
_____, *Goldilocks smells the porridge and goes into the house.*

Substantial Support
Help students practice using signal (linking) words to organize events in time order, or the order they happened. Focus on a short passage, pages 6–9, to model the concept. Read the events aloud, and have students determine their order, drawing or recording the events in correct order. Then have students repeat the sentences using the signal words.

Events
The porridge is too hot.
Goldilocks is walking in the woods.
The bears go for a walk.
Goldilocks goes into the bears' house.
Mama Bear makes breakfast.
1. First, _____.
2. Next, _____.
3. Then, _____.
4. After that, _____.
5. Finally, _____.

ELD.PI.K.12, ELD.PII.K.1, ELD.PII.K.2

RL.K.1 With prompting and support, ask and answer questions about key details in a text., **RL.K.2** With prompting and support, retell familiar stories, including key details., **RL.K.3** With prompting and support, identify characters, settings, and major events in a story., **RL.K.5** Recognize common types of texts (e.g., storybooks, poems, fantasy, realistic text). CA)., **RL.K.6** With prompting and support, name the author and illustrator of a story and define the role of each in telling the story., **RL.K.10** Actively engage in group reading activities with purpose and understanding., **RL.K.10a** Activate prior knowledge related to the information and events in texts. CA, **RL.K.10b** Use illustrations and context to make predictions about text. CA, **SL.K.1a** Follow agreed-upon rules for discussions (e.g., listening to others and taking turns speaking about the topics and texts under discussion). ,**SL.K.1b** Continue a conversation through multiple exchanges., **SL.K.2** Confirm understanding of a text read aloud or information presented orally or through other media by asking and answering questions about key details and requesting clarification if something is not understood., **SL.K.3** Ask and answer questions in order to seek help, get information, or clarify something that is not understood., **SL.K.6** Speak audibly and express thoughts, feelings, and ideas clearly.

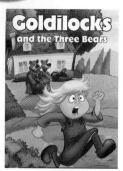

Goldilocks and the Three Bears

Student Objectives

I will be able to:
- Identify and share key events about characters in a fantasy.
- Write a key event from a fantasy.
- Use question words in my writing.

iELD Integrated ELD

Light Support
Have partners ask and answer questions about the text. One partner asks a question using a question word and verb. The other partner answers the question using the same verb. Record questions and answers on the board and together read them aloud.
Question Words: who, what, where, when, why
Verbs: go, see, like, run

Moderate Support
Have students ask and answer the following **wh-**questions. Have them answer the questions using the sentence frames. Model the first exercise as an example.
Ask: *When does Goldilocks go into the bears' house?*
She goes there when she is hungry.
Ask: *What does Goldilocks see in the bears' house?*
She _____ _____.
Ask: *Where does Goldilocks like to sit?*
She _____ to sit _____.
Ask: *Who does Baby Bear see in his bed?*
He _____ _____ in his bed.

Substantial Support
Give students practice with key verbs by using question words and word cards. Write these nouns on cards: **Goldilocks, porridge, chair, bed, Baby Bear, bears**. Write these verbs on cards: **goes, sees, likes**. Have students choose one noun card and one verb card to help answer each question.
Ask: *When does Goldilocks go into the bears' house?*
What does Goldilocks see in the bears' house?
Where does Goldilocks like to sit?
Who does Baby Bear see in his bed?

ELD.PI.K.1, ELD.PI.K.10, ELD.PII.K.3

Write Key Events (10 MIN.) W.K.2, W.K.8, SL.K.1a, SL.K.1b, L.K.1a, L.K.1d

Engage Thinking

Display and reread the key events chart with students. Tell them that today, you will work together to write key events from the story.

Ask: *What was your favorite event from the story?*

Collaborative Conversation: Partners

Tell students that before you begin writing, you would like them to turn and talk to a partner briefly. Ask them to share their favorite event from the story. Model how you do this.

Sample modeling: *When I talk to my partner about my favorite event from the story, I might say, "My favorite event from the story is when Goldilocks runs out the door." When you talk to your partner, you can start your sentence the same way: "My favorite event from the story is when _____."*

Write the sentence frame for students. Give them one minute to share their ideas. Then bring them together and ask volunteers to share their favorite key events.

Write as a Group

Work with students to agree on key events to write about. Then work with students to generate an oral sentence. Model writing sentences. As you write, involve students in the writing process by thinking aloud and/or prompting them with questions. For example:

- *Our task is to write key events from the story. Is our event important to the story?*
- *When we write, we need to tell our readers who and what we are telling about. Do we answer the question, "Who did what?"*
- *When we write the name of a person or a character, we begin with a capital letter. Let's make sure we write the character names Baby Bear and Goldilocks with a capital letter.*
- *Goldilocks is a long name! How can we make sure we spell it correctly?*
- *What nouns are in our sentence? Verbs?*

Sample Shared Writing

When Goldilocks went for a walk, she smelled Mama Bear's Porridge.
She walked right in to the bears house.
Baby Bear finds Goldilocks sleeping in his bed.
Goldilocks ran all the way home.

Build Language: Understand and Use Question Words (IELD)

Tell students that some words are question words. We use these words to begin a question. Write the words on the board and read them aloud: **who, what, when, where, why, how.** Explain that good writers keep these questions in mind when they write a story. Good writers tell **who** the characters are and **where** and **when** the story takes place. They tell **what** happens. Good writers also tell **why** and **how** characters do certain things.

Tell students to ask a question about *Goldilocks and the Three Bears.* Remind them to begin each question with a question word. Quickly locate the answer in the story.

Sample Question	Sample Answer
Who lives in the house?	The bears live in the house.
What does Mama Bear do at the beginning of the story?	Mama Bear makes porridge at the beginning of the story.
When does the story take place?	The story takes place in the daytime.
Where does the story take place?	Most of the story takes place in the bears house in the woods.
Why does Goldilocks go in the house?	Goldilocks goes in the house because she is hungry and smells the porridge.
How does Baby Bear find Goldilocks?	Baby Bear finds Goldilocks asleep in his bed.

Write Independently

Ask students to choose key event and write it on their own. Tell them they can label or dictate a sentence or draw a picture and label it.

Small-Group Differentiated Instruction (15 MIN. per Group)

Meet with Small Groups

Select appropriate small-group reading titles or reinforcement activities based on students' needs. See the Small-Group Instructional Planner for titles that support a range of instructional reading levels within the unit topic. Remind students to apply what they learned to their small-group reading experiences.

Say: *Today we recalled the key details in an informational text. Whether if you are reading informational or literary text it is important to find the key details to help you understand the text. You can look back at the text to help you remember ideas.*

Whole-Group Reflect and Share

Bring the class back together. Ask volunteers to share key events from stories they read or heard today. Ask them which key event they enjoyed the most.

W.K.2 Use a combination of drawing, dictating, and writing to compose informative/explanatory texts in which they name what they are writing about and supply some information about the topic., **W.K.8** With guidance and support from adults, recall information from experiences or gather information from provided sources to answer a question., **SL.K.1a** Follow agreed-upon rules for discussions (e.g., listening to others and taking turns speaking about the topics and texts under discussion)., **SL.K.1b** Continue a conversation through multiple exchanges., **L.K.1a** Print many upper- and lowercase letters., **L.K.1d** Understand and use question words (interrogatives) (e.g., who, what, where, when, why, how).

Focus Skill: t /t/ (20 MIN.) RF.K.2d, RF.K.3a, RF.K.3c, L.K.1a

Phonological Awareness: Phoneme Isolation

Model/Practice

Display frieze card **Tt.**

Say: *Listen for the sound at the beginning of this word,* ***tiger****. Say the sound with me,* */t/.* ***Tiger*** *has* */t/* *at the beginning.*

Say the words **ten, tiny, turtle** and have students repeat. Emphasize the /t/ sound.

Say: *I am going to read the poem "Turtles." Listen to the* */t/* *sound in this sentence:* Ten tiny turtles sit on a tabletop.

Reread the poem.

Say: *Touch your head when you hear* */t/* *at the beginning of a word. Tap your feet when hear* */t/* *at the end of a word.*

Letter-Sound Correspondences (iELD)

Introduce: *Tt*

Display frieze card **Tt.**

Say: *This is the tiger card. The sound is* */t/. The* */t/* *sound is spelled with the letter* **t.** *Say the sound with me,* */t/. This is the sound at the beginning of the word* **tiger**. *What is the name of this letter?* (**t**) *What sound does this letter stand for?* (*/t/*)

Model: *Tt*

Reread the poem "Turtles" and invite students to read along with you. Point to words in the poem that begin with the letter **t.** Say each word aloud.

Practice: *Tt*

Place letter cards **t, m,** and **s** in the pocket chart.

Place picture cards **tiger, sandwich,** and **map** under the corresponding letters while you say the name of the letter and picture.

Hold up the picture card **top**. Have students say **top** with you. Ask if **top** begins like **sandwich, tiger,** or **map**.

Place picture card *top* under the letter card **t.**

Say: ***Top*** *begins like* ***tiger****, so I am putting picture card* ***top*** *under the letter* **t.**

Repeat with picture cards **tent, tub, magnet, mitten, sub,** and **sock.**

Student Objectives

I will be able to:
- Isolate initial and final sound **/t/.**
- Identify letter-sound correspondences for **t/t/.**
- Practice the sounds **/m/, /a/,** and **/s/.**
- Sort picture names with initial **t/t/, m/m/,** and **s/s/.**
- Blend sounds **/t/, /a/, /m/, /s/.**
- Learn new high-frequency word: **see**.
- Read previously taught high-frequency words: **I, like, the, we.**
- Write **Tt.**

Additional Materials

- Poetry poster: "Turtles"
- Letter cards: **a, m, s, t**
- Sound-spelling cards: **Aa, Mm, Tt**
- For additional practice, see Pre-Decodable Readers: *Tam and Sam, Go, Go, Go!*

Weekly Presentation
- Picture cards: **magnet, map, mitten, sandwich, sock, sub, tent, tiger, top, tub**
- Frieze cards: **Aa, Mm, Ss,Tt**
- Student letter cards: **a, m, s, t**
- High-frequency word cards: **I, like, see, the, we**

Blend Sounds

Review: *Aa, Mm*
Hold up frieze cards **Aa, Mm, Ss,**and **Tt** and ask students to say the sound each letter stands for.

Model: *tam*
Place letter cards **t, a, m** in a pocket chart. Point to the letter **t**.

Say: *This is the letter **t**. The letter **t** stands for **/t/**. Say **/t/**. This is the letter **a**. The letter a stands for **/aaa/**. Say **/aaa/**. Listen as I blend the two sounds, **/taaa/**. Blend the sounds with me. This is the letter **m**. The letter **m** stands for **/mmm/**. Say /mmm/. Listen as I blend all three sounds, **/taaammm/**. Now blend the sounds to read the word, **tam**. Tell students that a **tam** is a type of hat.*

Practice: *at, mat,* and *sat*
Repeat the routine for the words **at, mat**, and **sat**. Move your hand from left to right under the word. Have students blend and read the words **at, mat,** and, **sat.**

High-Frequency Words

Introduce/Practice: *see*
Display the high-frequency word card. Point to and read the word.

Use the following routine: Point to each letter in the word and have students say the letter name. Say the word together. Guide students to name the letter that **see** begins with.

Say: *When I say the word **see**, I will hold up the word card. Read the word with me. I **see** the cat. I **see** the dog. Do you **see** fish?*

Review: *I, like, the, we*
Display each card and have students read the word.

Handwriting

Write and identify the uppercase and lowercase **Tt**. Hold up your writing hand. Write the uppercase and lowercase **Tt**. Trace the letters as you say **/t/**.

Then have students write **T** and **t** in the air as they say **/t/** several times. Finally have students write both forms of the letter several times, saying **/t/** every time they write the letter.

(iELD) Integrated ELD

Light Support
Have students identify the words in the pictures on the **Tt** frieze card as well as other initial **t** words around the room.

Model the initial stop sound /**t**/. Point to random pictures or objects that begin with **t** and have volunteers say the words.

Challenge students to name other words they know that begin with the **t** sound. Write words on the board, or have volunteers write them if they can. Have students then use as many of the **t** words as possible in sentences.

Moderate Support
Have partners identify the words in the pictures of the **Tt** frieze card or around the classroom.

Model the initial /**t**/ stop sound, pronouncing it /**t**/, not /**tuh**/. Say each **t** word slowly and have students repeat after you. Practice with different words until students can pronounce the /**t**/ sound correctly.

Then write **t** words on the board. Partners take turns pointing to the picture (or object) for the word, saying the word, and underlining the initial **t** in the word written on the board. Encourage one partner to use a **t** word in an oral sentence. The other partner can add other **t** words to embellish the original sentence. (Example: *tiger; The tiger is Tom; The tall tiger is Tom*.)

Substantial Support
Work with students to identify the words on the picture side of the **Tt** frieze card. Point to the picture and have a volunteer say the word. Repeat to model and reinforce correct pronunciation. Introduce the words yourself if necessary.

Model the /**t**/ sound while pointing to objects in the room that begin with **Tt**. Make sure to model the stop sound /**t**/ correctly (as /**t**/, not /**tuh**/). Have students say the word chorally. Write each word on the board, and have volunteers underline the initial **t** in each word. Use the word in a sentence, and encourage volunteers to do the same, using gestures or pictures if needed.

ELD.PI.K.1.,ELD.PI.K.9

RF.K.2d Isolate and pronounce the initial, medial vowel, and final sounds (phonemes) in three-phoneme (consonant-vowel-consonant, or CVC) words.* (This does not include CVCs ending with /l/, /r/, or /x/.), **RF.K.3a** Demonstrate basic knowledge of letter-sound correspondences by producing the primary or most frequent sound for each consonant., **RF.K.3c** Read common high-frequency words by sight (e.g., the, of, to, you, she, my, is, are, do, does)., **L.K.1a** Print many upper- and lowercase letters.

Read-Aloud Handbook

**Shared Reading Vol. 1, p. 10
"A Birthday Cat"**

Student Objectives

I will be able to:
- Read along with accuracy.
- Identify characters in a story.
- Identify words with initial and final **t**.
- Recognize words I know in different texts.

iELD Integrated ELD

Light Support

Model reading the story once or twice for students, focusing on accuracy. Then, have students choral-read and practice reading sentences on their own. Finally, have students briefly summarize story events using linking words, such as **first, next**, and **at the end** to ensure comprehension. Challenge students to read the two or more sentences accurately on their own.

Moderate Support

Partners preview the text and identify unfamiliar words and punctuation. Then model reading the text once at a moderate rate.

Next, choral-read the text twice with students. Have partners practice reading the story aloud, alternating sentences. They should focus on accuracy, tracking the print as they read. Offer corrective feedback.

Substantial Support

Explain that reading accurately means reading all words correctly, without skipping, adding, or changing any words. Point out punctuation, and remind students to pause briefly for commas and longer for periods. Preview the story with students. Model previewing the story and identifying any difficult words, such as **birthday, presents,** or **surprise.** Pronounce these words before reading the text. Next, model reading the text line by line. Have students echo-read each sentence, tracking the print as they read.

ELD.PI.K.5, ELD.PI.K.9, ELD.PII.K.2

Read Aloud and Shared Reading

(20 MIN.) RL.K.1, RL.K.3, RF.K.1a, RF.K.3a, RF.K.3c, RF.K.4, SL.K.3

Read Aloud

To support the unit concept, use one of the Read-Aloud Handbook selections for Unit 2. As you read, model the metacognitive strategy for the unit: Visualize, guided by the samples provided. You may also wish to select a favorite read aloud from your classroom or school library. To support the unit concept, use one of the suggested titles for Unit 2.

Shared Reading iELD

Reread the Realistic Fiction

First rereading. Read aloud the text fluently and expressively, pointing under each word.

Reread for Fluency: Accuracy/Use Context. Tell students that as they read, they should think about the context, or what the selection is about. This will help them read with accuracy. Tell students you will read the selection on phrase at a time. Ask them to echo read after you. Provide corrective feedback and/or validate students' efforts.

Build Concepts: Every Story Has Characters

Pose questions to connect the realistic fiction to the unit concept. For example:

- *Why do you think Tim felt sad when he was opening up presents on his birthday?*
- *Did Tim get the present he wanted? How did this happen?*

Review Phonics: Initial and Final *t*

Point to the word **Tim** in the first sentence. Have students identify the first letter and sound. Guide students in reading the word with you. Repeat for final **t** with the words **cat, got, but,** and **what.**

Review High-Frequency Words: *see*

Tell students that this text contains some words they have learned. Point to the previously-taught high-frequency word *see* in the third sentence. Ask students to turn to a partner and tell their partner the high-frequency word. Remind students to look for high-frequency words they know as they read a new text.

RL.K.1 With prompting and support, ask and answer questions about key details in a text., **RL.K.3** With prompting and support, identify characters, settings, and major events in a story., **RF.K.1a** Follow words from left to right, top to bottom, and page by page., **RF.K.3a** Demonstrate basic knowledge of letter-sound correspondences by producing the primary or most frequent sound for each consonant., **RF.K.3c** Read common high-frequency words by sight (e.g., the, of, to, you, she, my, is, are, do, does)., **RF.K.4** Read emergent-reader texts with purpose and understanding. ,**SL.K.3** Ask and answer questions in order to seek help, get information, or clarify something that is not understood.

Identify Story Characters (10 MIN.) RL.K.1, RL.K.3,

SL.K.1a

Engage Thinking

Tell students that today you are going to learn more about the characters in a story.

Ask: *Why was the mouse an important character in "The Little Helper"?*

Model

Display *Goldilocks and the Three Bears*. Read aloud pages 2 and 3. Model identifying the characters as you read.

Sample modeling: *As I read, I name the characters that are important to the story. On page 2, I read that there were three bears. One bear, Papa Bear is "great big." I find the great big bear in the illustration. This is Papa Bear. I read Mama Bear is "middle-sized," and Baby Bear is little. I find Mama Bear and Baby Bear in the illustration. This helps me remember each character.*

Guided Practice (iELD)

Continue reading aloud and guiding students to identify characters in the story. Use directive and corrective prompts to support students' comprehension. For example:

- *What characters are named on these pages? Are these new characters in the story?*
- *What do we learn about Papa Bear, Mama Bear, and Baby Bear on these pages?*
- *We meet a new character on this page. What is her name? How do you know she is an important character?*

☑ Show Your Word Knowledge

Ask students to use their fingers to show you how many characters are in the story. Encourage them to name each character with a partner.

Goldilocks and the Three Bears

Student Objectives

I will be able to:
- Identify characters in a story.

(iELD) Integrated ELD

Light Support

Have students review the story and complete a character and details chart. Encourage them to focus not only on what the characters look like, but also on the characters' feelings. For example, focus on page 16. Help students answer the questions using noun phrases when possible.

Ask: *How does Papa Bear feel after he sees that someone has been eating his porridge? How do you know?*
How does he feel after he sees that someone was sleeping in his bed?
What pattern do you see?

Moderate Support

Have partners review the text and pictures to identify and describe key characters. Have them fill out a character and details chart like the one below, recording characters' names and key details using pictures, labels, and noun phrases.

Character	Details
Papa Bear	"great big"

Have partners share their charts and check that their details are based on the text and pictures.

Substantial Support

Help students review the text and pictures in *Goldilocks and the Three Bears* to identify and describe story characters. Remind them that characters are the people or animals that the story is about.
Start by focusing on pages 2–3. Point to each bear on the pages.
Ask: *Who is this?*
Then point to the boldface type on page 2 that describes each bear.
Ask: *How big is Papa Bear? Mama Bear? Baby Bear?*
Then have students focus on the pictures.
Ask what other details students learn about each bear by looking at the pictures.

ELD.PI.K.6, ELD.PI.K.1, ELD.PII.K.4

RL.K.1 With prompting and support, ask and answer questions about key details in a text. **RL.K.3** With prompting and support, identify characters, settings, and major events in a story. **SL.K.1a** Follow agreed-upon rules for discussions (e.g., listening to others and taking turns speaking about the topics and texts under discussion).

Goldilocks and the Three Bears

Student Objectives

I will be able to:
• Make inferences about characters' feelings.

Observation Checklist for Productive Engagement

Is the Productive Engagement Productive?

As partners discuss make inferences about characters, look for evidence that they are truly engaged in the task.

Partners are engaged productively if…

❑ they ask questions and use feedback to address the task.

❑ they demonstrate engagement and motivation.

❑ they apply strategies with some success.

❑ *If the discussion is productive, continue the task.*

Partners are not engaged productively if…

❑ they apply no strategies to the task.

❑ they show frustration or anger.

❑ they give up.

❑ *If the discussion is unproductive, end the task, and provide support.*

Find Text Evidence: Make Inferences About Character (10 MIN.) RL.K.1, RL.K.3

Engage Thinking

Explain that students will now learn more about the characters in the story. Ask a volunteer to come to the front of the room. Quietly direct the volunteer to cross his or her arms and make an angry face.

Ask: *How does _____ feel right now? How do you know?*

Point out that no one told students how the volunteer felt. Students were able to tell his or her feelings based on what they know about what an angry person looks like.

Model (iELD)

Display and read aloud the text evidence questions. Help students identify words in the question that help them know what to look for in the text. Explain that they will have to make inferences about the characters in order to answer the questions. Remind them that when they make an inference, they think about words the author uses and what they already know.

> **Text Evidence Question:** How does Papa Bear feel on page 16?
> **Text Evidence Question:** How does Mama Bear feel on page 16?
> **Text Evidence Question:** How does Baby Bear feel on page 16?

Ask students to listen carefully as you read page 16. Then model how you make inferences about characters to answer the questions.

Sample modeling: *I'm going make an inference about the way Papa Bear feels on page 16. I think about what the author tells me. I read the Papa Bear sees that someone has been eating his porridge. The author writes that Papa Bear **growled** when he spoke. If Papa Bear growled, he is probably angry. I also think about what I know. If I had gone on a walk waiting for my porridge to cool, I would be very angry if someone ate some of it while I was gone. So I know Papa Bear feels angry on page 16.*

Continue modeling in the same way to identify Mama Bear and Baby Bear's feelings.

Guided Practice

Display and read aloud the text-evidence question. Review the words in the questions that help students know what evidence to look for in the text.

> **Text Evidence Question:** How does Goldilocks feel at the end of the story?

Tell students you will reread pages 22 and 23. Remind them to think about what the author tells them and what they already know to make an inference about how Goldilocks feels. Provide directive feedback as necessary. For example:

- *What does Goldilocks do when she first wakes up and sees the bears? Why do you think she does this?*
- *What does Goldilocks do on page 23?*
- *Think about what you know. How would you feel if you were Goldilocks? Why would you feel that way?*

Highlight the evidence in the text and reread it with students.

Productive Engagement: Partner Activity

Display and read aloud a third question. Remind students to listen for words in the question that will help them know what information to look for in the text.

> **Text Evidence Question:** What are the three bears thinking at the end of the story?

Reread page 23 and have partners discuss what Mama Bear, Papa Bear and Baby Bear are thinking about what just happened. Have partners share their answers with the group.

☑ Show Your Knowledge

Read aloud page 20. Ask students to tell how Papa Bear feels and why.

ⓘELD Integrated ELD

Light Support

Have partners review page 17 and answer questions to make inferences about the characters' feelings.

- *How does Papa Bear talk?*
- *What does this detail tell you about him?*
- *How does Papa Bear act?*
- *When do people talk and act this way?*
- *How do you think Papa Bear feels?*

Repeat the questions for the other characters.

Moderate Support

Have partners focus on page 17 of the story and complete the sentence frames to describe the characters based on the text and pictures. Make sure students focus on the verbs (actions) to help infer what these actions tell about the characters' feelings.

Ask: *How does Papa Bear talk?*

He _____.

This word shows he is _____.

In the picture, Papa Bear _____.

I talk and act like Papa Bear when I feel _____, so I think Papa Bear must feel _____.

Repeat the questions for the other characters.

Substantial Support

Focus on page 17 of *Goldilocks and the Three Bears.* With students, highlight verbs in the text that tell how each bear felt (**growled, grumbled, cried**). Model how to use the text and pictures to make an inference about how the characters feel.

Ask: *Which word describes what Papa Bear/Mama Bear/Baby Bear said?*

*What does **growled/grumbled/cried** mean?* [Have students act out or describe the meaning and when they might feel that way.]

*How is the word **growled/grumbled/cried** different from the word **said**?*

What does the picture show you about how Papa Bear/Mama Bear/Baby Bear feels?

ELD.PI.K.6, ELD.PI.K.8, ELD.PII.K.3a

RL.K.1 With prompting and support, ask and answer questions about key details in a text., **RL.K.3** With prompting and support, identify characters, settings, and major events in a story.

Goldilocks and the Three Bears

Student Objectives

I will be able to:
- Write an opinion about Goldilocks.
- Use question words to begin an oral question.

(iELD) Integrated ELD

Light Support

Allow partners to share questions based on their observations and predictions about Goldilocks to cue verbs. Model and provide sentence frames as needed. *How did Goldilocks show she was brave? When did Goldilocks show she was afraid? What will Goldilocks do if she sees the bears again?* Have partners ask questions, including one prediction question. Then have students answer their questions orally.

Moderate Support

Post question words, as well as cards with verb phrases for partners.
How / When / Where / Why / What…
…did / didn't
…Goldilocks…
do first? / go inside? / act brave? / seem scared? / fall asleep? / run away? / make the bears mad?
Model simple questions, such as *Why didn't Goldilocks seem scared?*
Have partners write down as many questions as they can. Then choose a question for them to answer using drawings and captions.

Substantial Support

Give students practice generating questions about Goldilocks using **wh-** words and simple verbs. Post question words, and picture cards with captions for Goldilocks and each verb phrase.
How / When / Where / Why / What…did…
Goldilocks…
do first? / go inside? / act brave? / fall asleep?
Model simple questions, such as *How does Goldilocks act brave?*
Work through several examples with students orally. Then choose one question for students to answer using drawings or dictation.

ELD.PI.K.6, ELD.PI.K.10, ELD.PII.K.3b

Write an Opinion (10 MIN.) W.K.1, W.K.8, L.K.1a, L.K.1d

Engage Thinking

Display pages 8 and 9. Explain that today the class will write an opinion. Remind students that an opinion is what we think or feel about something. There is no right or wrong answer.

Ask: *Do you think Goldilocks was brave?*

Point out the words **Do you think** and say that these words are asking for the reader's opinion.

Collaborative Conversation: Partners (iELD)

Have students turn and talk to a partner to answer the question, Do you think Goldilocks was brave? Encourage them to use complete sentences as they answer the question and provide examples to support their opinion. Provide a model.

Sample modeling: *When I talk to my partner, I will answer the question, "Do you think Goldilocks was brave?" I'll also give at least one example from the story to explain why I think the way I do. I might say, "I think Goldilocks was brave because she went into the house. She was hungry and she smelled something delicious, so she went in." When you talk to your partner, you can use the same sentence frame: I think Goldilocks (was/was not) brave because _____.*

Give students two minutes to share their ideas. Then bring them together and ask volunteers to share their opinions and examples.

Write as a Group

After students have shared their opinions, work together to decide on the opinion of the majority. This will be the opinion for the shared writing. Continue working with students to agree on a supporting reason for the opinion. Then lead students in a shared writing. Actively engage students in the writing process by thinking aloud and/or prompting them with questions. For example:

- *We are writing an opinion. Let's use the words **I think** to let readers know we are writing an opinion.*
- *When we tell an opinion, we need to give a reason to support it. Let's write the word **because** and then tell why we think the way we do. We'll write one example from the story that shows Goldilocks being brave.*
- *What do we write at the end of a sentence to let readers know the sentence is over?*

Sample Shared Writing
Why do I think Goldilocks was brave? I think Goldilocks was brave because she tried out all the beds and fell asleep in the one she liked best.

Build Language: Understand and Use Question Words

Write question words **who, what, when, where, why,** and **how** on the board. Read them aloud with students. Remind students that they can use these words to begin a question. Say a question word and have students take turns asking a partner a question about the story. Students should use the word you call to begin their questions. For each question word, invite partners to share their questions.

✓ Write Independently

Ask students to draw a picture to show why they think Goldilocks was brave. Students can label or dictate a sentence to go with their picture.

Small-Group Differentiated Instruction (15 MIN. per Group)

Meet With Small Groups

Select appropriate small-group reading titles or reinforcement activities based on students' needs. See the Small-Group Instructional Planner for titles that support a range of instructional reading levels within the unit topic. Remind students to apply what they learned to their small-group reading experiences.

Say: *Today we practiced naming characters in a story. We also practiced making inferences about the way the characters feel. We wrote an opinion, too. If you read a story today, think about the characters and how they feel. You can tell your opinion about the story, too. Did you like it? Why? This is your opinion.*

Whole-Group Reflect and Share

Bring the class back together. Ask volunteers to share inferences they made about characters' feelings. Ask them to share their opinion of the texts they read and heard.

W.K.1 Use a combination of drawing, dictating, and writing to compose opinion pieces in which they tell a reader the topic or the name of the book they are writing about and state an opinion or preference about the topic or book (e.g., My favorite book is...)., **W.K.8** With guidance and support from adults, recall information from experiences or gather information from provided sources to answer a question., **L.K.1a** Print many upper- and lowercase letters., **L.K.1d** Understand and use question words (interrogatives) (e.g., who, what, where, when, why, how).

Focus Skill: t/t/ (20 MIN.) RF.K.2d, RF.K.3a, RF.K.3c, L.K.1a

Phonological Awareness: Phoneme Isolation

Model/Practice

Show students the picture on the back of the poetry poster, and have them name all the objects in the picture. Point to the tiger in the picture and say the word **tiger**.

Ask: *What sound do you hear at the beginning of the word?*

Have volunteers point to things in the picture whose name starts with /t/.

Say: *Now listen as I say the word **cat**. I can hear the /t/ sound at the end of the word **cat**. I am going to say some words. If you hear /t/ at the beginning of the word touch the top of your head. If you hear /t/ at the end of the word, touch your knees.*

Use the following words: **tap, sit, tail, time, pet.**

Letter-Sound Correspondences

Review: m/m/, a/a/, s/s/, t/t/

Hold up frieze cards **Mm, Aa, Ss** one at a time. Have students say the sounds the letters stand for. Have students say words that start with /**m**/. Record the words, underlining **m**. Then have students think of words that end with /**m**/. Record them, underlining **m**.

Next, have students say words that have /**a**/ at the beginning and in the middle. Write these words and circle **a**.

Then have students say words with /**s**/ at the beginning and the end. Write them and circle **s**.

Hold up frieze card **Tt**. Have students say the letter name and letter sound.

Reread the poem "Turtles," emphasizing the initial and ending /t/ sounds. Have volunteers find words that begin or end with /t/.

Blend Sounds (iELD)

Model: *tam*

Place letter cards **t, a, m** in a pocket chart. Point to the letter **t**.

Say: *This is the letter **t**. The letter **t** stands for /**t**/. Say /**t**/. This is the letter **a**. The letter **a** stands for /**aaa**/. Say /**aaa**/. Listen as I blend the two sounds together, /**taaa**/. Blend the sounds with me. This is the letter **m**. The letter **m** stands for /**mmm**/. Say /**mmm**/. Listen as I blend all three sounds together, /**taaammm**/. Now blend the sounds to read the word **tam**.*

Practice: *sat*

Have students place the following letter cards on their desks: **a, s, t**. Then have them blend and read the word with you. Provide support as necessary.

Student Objectives

I will be able to:
- Isolate initial and final /t/.
- Practice letter-sound correspondences for **t/t/, s/s/, a/a/, m/m/**.
- Blend sounds /t/, /a/, /m/ and /s/, /a/, /t/.
- Learn new high-frequency word: *go.*
- Read previously taught high-frequency words: *I, like, the, we, see.*
- Write **Tt**.

Additional Materials

- Poetry poster: "Turtles"
- Letter cards: **a, m, s, t**

Weekly Presentation
- Frieze cards: **Aa, Mm, Ss, Tt**
- Student letter cards: **a, s, t**
- High-frequency word cards: **go, I, like, see, the, we**

High-Frequency Words

Introduce/Practice: *go*

Display high-frequency word card **go** and read the word. Point to each letter and have students say the letter name with you. Say the word together.

Say: *I am going to read some sentences. When I say the word* **go***, I will hold up the word card. Read the word with me. We* **go** *to school. We* **go** *on the bus.*

Review: *I, like, the, we, see*

Display each card and have students read the word. Then have the students use each word in an oral sentence.

Handwriting

Have students write uppercase and lowercase **Tt**. Observe student's pencil grip and paper position. Have students say **/t/** every time they write the letters **Tt**.

(iELD) Integrated ELD

Light Support
1. Read the following sentences aloud slowly, pausing after each word. Have students raise their hands when they hear each word with the final **/t/** sound. Have them touch their knees if they hear the beginning **/t/** sound. Repeat the words aloud to reinforce the **/t/** sounds.
- *Go get a tan mat.*
- *I met a cat who sat on a tall pot.*
- *She will pat Tom's pet rat.*

2. Then have students create new sentences using the final **/t/** verbs (**get, met, pat**).

Moderate Support
1. Read the following sentences aloud slowly, pausing after each word. Have students raise their hands when they hear each word with the **/t/** sound at the end. Repeat each final **/t/** word to reinforce the sound.
- *I hit a ball with a tall bat.*
- *Put a tan dot on my mat.*
- *Tom got a cat named Spot.*

2. Read the sentences again, but this time have students raise their hands for words with only the beginning **/t/** sound.

3. Then have partners write or say new phrases or sentences using the final **/t/** verbs (**hit, put, got**) and as many other final **/t/** words as they can.

Substantial Support
1. Give students practice identifying the final **/t/** sound. Read a sentence aloud. (If possible, display a simple picture card or drawing to show what the sentence describes.)
- *The cat sat on a bed.*
- *Put that pot on a chair.*
- *The bat got in Dan's tent.*

2. Then reread the sentence a second time, pausing after each word. Have students raise their hand if the word has the **/t/** sound at the end, as in **cat.** Repeat each final **/t/** word to reinforce the sound.

3. Then work with students to create a new phrase or sentence with one of the verbs (**sat, put, got**) using another final **/t/** word.

ELD.PI.K.1, ELD.PI.K.10, ELD.PII.K.3a

RF.K.2d Isolate and pronounce the initial, medial vowel, and final sounds (phonemes) in three-phoneme (consonant-vowel-consonant, or CVC) words. * (This does not include CVCs ending with /l/, /r/, or /x/.), **RF.K.3a** Demonstrate basic knowledge of letter-sound correspondences by producing the primary or most frequent sound for each consonant., **RF.K.3c** Read common high-frequency words by sight (e.g., the, of, to, you, she, my, is, are, do, does)., **L.K.1a** Print many upper- and lowercase letters.

Read-Aloud Handbook

Bear and Fox

Bear baked a delicious apple pie.
Fox came by and asked him for a slice.
"I'll get you a plate," said Bear.
But sneaky Fox ran off with the pie!

Shared Reading Vol. 1, p. 11 "Bear and Fox"

Student Objectives

I will be able to:
- Answer questions about animal characters.
- Use question words.
- Read along from left to right and top to bottom.

(iELD) Integrated ELD

Light Support

Partners work together to answer the questions about the first sentence of "Bear and Fox."

What words tell you about the pie? Do these details make you want to eat the pie? Why?

Is Bear a good cook? How do you know?

Then have students practice adding details with prepositional phrases using the sentence frame below.

Where / When / How does Bear make the pie? Bear makes the pie _____.

Moderate Support

Ask questions to give students practice adding details with prepositional phrases. Have students complete each sentence using the phrases. Finally, read the complete sentences aloud together.

Ask: *Where does Bear make the pie? Bear makes the pie _____.*

Ask: *When does Bear make the pie? Bear makes the pie _____.*

Ask: *How does Bear make the pie? Bear makes the pie _____.*

Phrases: at home, before Fox comes, with apples

Substantial Support

Display "Bear and Fox." Read the story aloud. Ask questions to help students focus on the words the author uses to present the character, Bear, and his pie.

Ask: *What did Bear do? What words describe Bear's pie? How do these words help you see the pie? Smell the pie? Taste the pie? What does the first sentence tell you about Bear?*

Have students use gestures and words to answer the questions. Record answers on the board.

ELD.PI.K.1, ELD.PI.K.7, ELD.PII.K.5

Read Aloud and Shared Reading

(20 MIN.) RL.K.1, RL.K.5, RL.K.10, RL.K.10a, RL.K.10b, RF.K.1a, RF.K.3c, RF.K.4, SL.K.3, L.K.1d

Read Aloud

To support the unit concept, use one of the Read-Aloud Handbook selections for Unit 2. As you read, model the metacognitive strategy for the unit, Visualize, guided by the samples provided. You may also wish to select a favorite read aloud from you classroom or school library. To support the unit concept, use one of the suggested titles for Unit 2.

Shared Reading (iELD)

Introduce the Animal Fantasy

Display "Bear and Fox." Read aloud and point under the title of the story. Invite students tell a partner what they predict the poem will be about. Invite a few students to share their predictions with the whole class.

Read the Animal Fantasy

First reading. Read aloud the story fluently and expressively, pointing under each word.

Reread for Fluency: Accuracy/Use Context. As you read, model using context to read words accurately. Choose an "unfamiliar" word, such as **delicious** or **sneaky** and demonstrate how to use surrounding words to read the word correctly. Point to each word as you read aloud the text again. Encourage students to choral read with you, using the same rate and expression as you. Provide corrective feedback and/or validate students' efforts.

Build Concepts: Every Story Has Characters

Pose questions to connect the animal fantasy to the unit concept. For example:

- *Who are the characters in the story?*
- *What words would you use to tell about Bear?*
- *How is Fox different from Bear?*

Model Print Concepts: Directionality: Top to Bottom

Ask students to tell where you should start reading on a page. Ask a volunteer to point to each word as you read it aloud. Emphasize the top to bottom directionality as the student moves from line to line.

Review Language: Understand and Use Question Words

Say a question word. Ask students to use the word to begin a question about the story. Encourage other students to answer the question based on the story.

RL.K.1 With prompting and support, ask and answer questions about key details in a text., **RL.K.5** Recognize common types of texts (e.g., storybooks, poems, fantasy, realistic text). CA)., **RL.K.10** Actively engage in group reading activities with purpose and understanding. **RL.K.10a** Activate prior knowledge related to the information and events in texts. CA **RL.K.10b** Use illustrations and context to make predictions about text. CA, **RF.K.1a** Follow words from left to right, top to bottom, and page by page., **RF.K.3c** Read common high-frequency words by sight (e.g., the, of, to, you, she, my, is, are, do, does)., **RF.K.4** Read emergent-reader texts with purpose and understanding., **SL.K.3** Ask and answer questions in order to seek help, get information, or clarify something that is not understood., **L.K.1d** Understand and use question words (interrogatives) (e.g., who, what, where, when, why, how).

Build Vocabulary: Shades of Meaning (10 MIN.) RL.K.1, L.K.5d, L.K.6

Goldilocks and the Three Bears

Engage Thinking

Remind students that they have learned that authors use certain verbs, or action words, to let readers know exactly what a character is doing.

Ask: *Running* and *walking* are both ways to get from place to place. If you were Goldilocks, would you walk or run away? Why?

Tell students today they will learn more about different verbs that tell about the same action.

Model

Display page 16. Point out the three quotations. Explain that these are the exact words a character says. Read aloud Papa Bear's quotation. Then think aloud to model how you pay attention to the shades of meaning among verbs.

Sample modeling: *The author uses the word **growled** to tell how Papa Bear spoke. The author could have used the word **said,** but **said** does not tell me exactly how Papa Bear sounded. A bear growls loudly. I can imagine Papa Bear saying the words in a loud, angry voice. Using the word **growled** helps me understand that Papa Bear is angry.*

Read Papa Bear's quotation in a loud, angry voice.

Guided Practice (iELD)

Reread Mama Bear and Baby Bear's quotations on page 16. Ask students to listen for the verbs that describe how each character spoke **(grumbled, cried).** Help students identify the words. Prompt students to think critically about the word meanings. Ask students to demonstrate each manner of speaking. Provide prompts as necessary. For example:

- *Have you ever grumbled? When might someone grumble?*
- *How does grumbling sound different from growling?*
- *Baby Bear **cried** when he spoke. The picture does not show he is crying tears. How can you cry when you speak?*
- *Why do you think the author used the word **cried**? What does it help us understand about Baby Bear's feelings?*

Show Your Word Knowledge

Ask students to listen carefully as you say an action word related to speaking. Ask students to act out the meaning of the word. Repeat with related verbs. Use **whispered, called, argued.**

Student Objectives

I will be able to:
- Identify verbs that describe how characters feel.
- Act out the meaning of verbs with similar meanings.

(iELD) Integrated ELD

Light Support

Display pages 20–21 of *Goldilocks and the Three Bears.* Ask questions to help students recognize how the words **growled, grumbled,** and **cried** show shades of meaning. *How is growling different from talking? What people or animals usually growl? Why? How is grumbling different from growling?*

Moderate Support

Display pages 20–21 of *Goldilocks and the Three Bears.* Point out the words **growled, grumbled,** and **cried.** Have partners take turns acting out the words and describing them. Use the sentence frames below. *People and animals _____ when they feel very angry. People _____ when they feel mad or annoyed.*

Then work with the group to fill out the chart.

Verb	Picture Details	Similar Verbs
growled	sharp teeth, mad face	barked, roared
grumbled	frown, hand on hip, mad face	complained, whined
cried	surprised face, mouth open	sobbed, screamed

Substantial Support

Display pages 20–21 of *Goldilocks and the Three Bears.* Point out the words **growled, grumbled,** and **cried.** To help students understand the word meanings, model saying each quotation the way that the character says it. Fill out the chart.

Ask: *What are the feelings?*

Word	Feelings	Picture Details
growled	mad, scary	sharp teeth, mad face
grumbled	complaining, annoyed	frown, hand on hip, mad face
cried	sad, upset	surprised face, mouth open

ELD.PI.K.7, ELD.PI.K.8, ELD.PII.K.3

RL.K.1 With prompting and support, ask and answer questions about key details in a text., **L.K.5d** Distinguish shades of meaning among verbs describing the same general action (e.g., walk, march, strut, prance) by acting out the meanings., **L.K.6** Use words and phrases acquired through conversations, reading and being read to, and responding to texts.

Goldilocks and the Three Bears

Find Text Evidence: Story Events (10 MIN.)

RL.K.1, RL.K.3, SL.K.3

Engage Thinking

Remind students that they have practiced identifying major events in *Goldilocks and the Three Bears*. Explain that today, they will use the strategy to answer a question.

Ask: *What is a major story event? How do you know an event is important to the story?*

Model

Display and read aloud a text evidence question. Remind students to listen carefully for any words in the question that would help them know what evidence to look for in the text. Students should recognize the question word **What**. Guide them to identify the key words **major events** and **beginning.**

> **Find Text Evidence:** What major events happen to Goldilocks and the three bears at the beginning of the story?

Ask students to listen carefully for this information as you reread pages 2–7. Then model how you use the text to answer the question.

Sample modeling: *I reread the beginning of the story because the question asks me to identify major events from the beginning of the story. As I read pages 2 and 3, I look for major events. I learn about the family and where they live, but no major events happen. So I keep reading. On pages 4 and 5, I learn about their chairs and beds. On pages 6 and 7, two very important events happen. Mama Bear makes porridge, but it is too hot. The family takes a walk in the woods while the porridge cools. I know these are important events because if the family did not leave, the rest of the story could not happen.*

Guided Practice (iELD)

Display and read aloud a text evidence question. Ask students to again listen for words in the question that will help them know what information to look for in the text. Students should recognize that the key words **major, events,** and **middle**.

> **Find Text Evidence:** What major events happen to Goldilocks and the three bears in the middle of the story?

Ask students to listen carefully for the information they need as you reread pages 8–21. Provide directive feedback as needed. For example:

- *Is this an important event? How do you know?*
- *How can this illustration help you understand the major event in this part of the story?*
- *How do you know this is an event from the middle of the story and not the end?*

Highlight the evidence in the text and reread it with students. Then use the text evidence to answer the close reading question.

Productive Engagement: Partner Activity

Display and read aloud a third question. Remind students to listen for words in the question that will help them know what information to look for in the text.

> **Find Text Evidence:** What major events happen in *Goldilocks and the Three Bears* at the end of the story?

Reread the text on pages 22-23. After reading, ask students to turn and talk to a partner. Partners should talk about the major events at the end of the story. Have partners share their answers with the class.

☑ Show Your Knowledge

Ask students to draw a picture of a major event. Students can label or dictate the word **beginning, middle,** or **end** to identify the part of the story in which the event occurs. Students can also write or dictate a sentence identifying the event.

(iELD) Integrated ELD

Light Support
Have partners organize the major events in the story, from beginning to end. Have them go back to the text to organize their ideas. Have them retell two or three major events from the beginning, the middle, and the end. Encourage them to use the following sentence starters as a guide:
In the beginning of the story, _____. Then, _____.
In the middle of the story, _____. Then, _____.
At the end of the story, _____. Finally, _____.
After they finish, have students share their events orally.

Moderate Support
Have partners focus on the beginning and middle events of the story, organizing the following events in order using the sentence starters.
Events:
the bears go for a walk
Goldilocks walks into the bears' house
the porridge is too hot
Goldilocks falls asleep in Baby Bear's bed
Mama Bear makes porridge
1. First, _____.
2. Second, _____.
3. Next, _____.
4. Then, _____.
5. After that, _____.

Substantial Support
Write the following question on the board: *What major events happen in the beginning of* Goldilocks and the Three Bears?
Circle the key words **major, events,** and **beginning,** and check students' understanding of these key words. Then provide students with sentence starters and possible events. Have them say the events in order using the sentence starters.
Events:
the bears go for a walk
the porridge is too hot
Mama Bear makes porridge
1. The first event happens when ___.
2. The second event happens when ___.
3. The third event happens when ____.

ELD.PI.K.3, ELD.PI.K.12a, ELD.PII.K.1

RL.K.1 With prompting and support, ask and answer questions about key details in a text., **RL.K.3** With prompting and support, identify characters, settings, and major events in a story., **SL.K.3** Ask and answer questions in order to seek help, get information, or clarify something that is not understood.

Goldilocks and the Three Bears

Student Objectives

I will be able to:
- Write a new ending for *Goldilocks and the Three Bears.*
- Use question words.

(iELD) Integrated ELD

Light Support
Have partners answer questions about the ending of the story. Then challenge them to combine answers using the word **because**.
Ask: *Who is the most important character in the story? Why is this character so important? Where does Goldilocks go after she wakes up? Why does she go here? What if Goldilocks did not run away? How would this change the story?*

Moderate Support
Have partners use the sentence starters to answer **wh-** questions about the ending of *Goldilocks and the Three Bears.*
Ask: *Who is the most important character in the story?*
The most important character is _____.
Ask: *Why is this character so important?*
_____ is important because _____.
Ask: *Where does Goldilocks go after she wakes up?*
Goldilocks goes _____.
Ask: *Why does she go here?*
She goes here because _____.
Record partners' responses on the board. Then model how to combine ideas.

Substantial Support
Have students use the sentence starters to answer **wh-** questions about the ending of *Goldilocks and the Three Bears.*
Ask: *How does Goldilocks feel when she wakes up?*
Goldilocks feels _____.
Goldilocks also feels _____.
Ask: *What does Goldilocks do after she wakes up?*
Goldilocks _____ .
Goldilocks also _____.
Have students respond using gestures and words. Record their responses on the board.

ELD.PI.K.1, ELD.PI.K.5, ELD.PII.K.6

Write a New Ending (10 MIN.)  W.K.3, W.K.8, L.K.1a, L.K.1d

Engage Thinking

Display pages 22 and 23 of *Goldilocks and the Three Bears.* Briefly retell the beginning and middle of the story.

Ask: *What happens at the end of the story?*

Tell students that today they will write a new ending to the story.

🗪 Collaborative Conversation: Share Ideas

Ask: *What if Goldilocks did not run out of the house?*

Tell students that before writing, you want them to turn and talk to a partner about ideas for answering the question. Provide a model.

Sample modeling: *I want to talk to my partner about a new ending for* Goldilocks and the Three Bears. *I can say, "If Goldilocks had not run out of the house, she might have stayed and made friends with the three bears. They might even have eaten porridge together." When you talk to your partner, you can start by saying, "If Goldilocks had not run out of the house ____." You could also say, "The story could end with ____."*

Give students two minutes to share their ideas for a new ending. Then bring them together and ask volunteers to share their ideas.

Write as a Group

After hearing students' ideas, work with them to decide on a new ending for the story. Guide students' writing and involve them in the writing process by thinking aloud and/or prompting them with questions. For example:

- *What kind of letter do we use to begin a sentence?*
- *We know how to spell the word* **the.** *It is a high-frequency word. How do we spell the word* **the**?
- *We are writing about more than one bear.* **Bear** *is a noun. What do we add to the end of* **bear** *to mean more than one bear?*
- *What sound do you hear at the beginning of the word* **sorry**? *Let's write an* **s** *for /**s**/.*
- *Let's reread our sentence. Do we tell what might happen if Goldilocks did not run out of the house at the end of the story? Is there anything we want to change?*

Sample Shared Writing
If Goldilocks had not run out of the house, she may have stayed and had a conversation with the three bears. She might explain that while she was walking in the wood she got tired and hungry. And that is why she walked into the their home, ate, and fell asleep. She thanked the bears for their food and the baby bear invited her to come back and visit.

Build Language: Understand and Use Question Words (IELD)

Remind students that we use question words to begin a question. Ask students to name question words. Record them in a column on the board. Make sure students name question words **who, what, when, where, why,** and **how.** Then ask students to ask questions about the new ending. Encourage them to begin each question with a question word. Record the questions next to the corresponding question word.

Question Word	Possible Question
who	Who spoke to the bears?
what	What did Goldilocks say?
when	When did the bears return?
where	Where did the bears find Goldilocks?
why	Why did the bears forgive Goldilocks?
how	How did Goldilocks apologize?

 **Write Independently**

Tell students draw a picture of a new ending. Ask students to label or dictate a sentence to tell about the alternate ending.

Small-Group Differentiated Instruction (15 MIN. per Group)

Meet with Small Groups

Select small-group reading titles or activities based on students' needs. See the Small-Group Instructional Planner for titles that support a range of instructional levels within the unit topic. Remind students to apply what they learned in the mini-lessons to their small-group reading experiences.

Say: *As you read and listen in small groups today, identify story events at the beginning, middle, and end of the story. Ask yourself questions to make sure you understand what you read. Remember to ask questions that begin with* **who, what, when, where, why,** *and* **how.**

Whole-Group Reflect and Share

Bring the class back together. Invite volunteers to identify story events they recall. Ask them to describe how they asked and answered questions about their reading.

W.K.3 Use a combination of drawing, dictating, and writing to narrate a single event or several loosely linked events, tell about the events in the order in which they occurred, and provide a reaction to what happened., **W.K.8** With guidance and support from adults, recall information from experiences or gather information from provided sources to answer a question., **L.K.1a** Print many upper- and lowercase letters., **L.K.1d** Understand and use question words (interrogatives) (e.g., who, what, where, when, why, how).

Student Objectives

I will be able to:
- Isolate initial sound /t/.
- Practice letter-sound correspondences for **t/t/,** **s/s/,** a/a/, m/m/.
- Sort picture names with **t/t/,** **s/s/,** a/a/, and **m/m/.**
- Blend sounds **a/a/,** **t/t/,** m,/m/, s/s/.
- Read previously taught high-frequency words: **see, go, the, we.**

Additional Materials

- Letter cards: *a, m, s, t*

Weekly Presentation
- Picture cards: *ant, apple, ax, cat, hat, magnet, map, mitten, nut, sandwich, sock, sub, sun, tent, tiger, top, tub*
- High-frequency word cards: *go, see, the, we*

(iELD) Integrated ELD

Light Support
Have students use blank Elkonin boxes and letter tiles or cards for **t, s, a,** and **p** to create words.

	a	

Moderate Support
Use Elkonin boxes with students to help them generate words with the /t/, /s/, /a/, and /m/ sounds. Have multiple letter tiles or cards available for **t, s, a,** and **m.** Focus on changing the final position.

s	a	

- What word can we make for a man's name?
1. What letter can I add? (**m**)
2. What sound does this letter make? (/**m**/)
3. Let's say the word. (/**sssaaammm**/)

Substantial Support
Use Elkonin boxes with students to help them generate words with the /t/, /s/, /a/, and /m/ sounds. Have multiple letter tiles or cards available for **t, s, a,** and **m.** Focus on changing the initial position.

	a	t

- What word can we make for "something soft that is put on the floor"?
1. What letter can I add? (**m**)
2. What sound does this letter make? (/**m**/)
3. Let's say the word. (/**mmmaaat**/)

ELD.PI.K.1, ELD.PII.K.3a, ELD.PII.K.4

Focus Skill: t/t/ (20 MIN.) RF.K.2d, RF.K.3a, RF.K.3c

Phonological Awareness: Phoneme Isolation

Model/Practice
Say the words **tiger, table,** and **sun.** Have students repeat the words.

Ask students if they hear the same sound at the beginning of each word. Then ask them to identify the word that starts with a different sound. Say the words **teach, tiny,** and **tap.** Have students repeat the words.

Ask students if they hear the same sound at the beginning of each word. Then ask what sound is the same in all three words.

Repeat with **tooth, toe, touch; turtle, monkey, turkey; toy, ten, top.**

Letter-Sound Correspondences

Review with Picture Cards
Place picture cards **sun, apple, magnet,** and **tub** in the pocket chart. Have students say their names and the sound at the beginning of each name.

Show students picture card **sock** and ask them what sound they hear at the beginning of the word. Place picture card **sock** under picture card **sun.** Repeat with picture cards **ant, ax, map, mitten, sub, sandwich, tiger, tent, top.**

Replace picture cards **sun, apple,** and **magnet** with picture card **hat.** Place a letter card **t** under **tub** and **hat.** Ask students where they hear the /t/ sound in the words **tub** and **hat.** Show students picture cards **top, cat, nut,** and **tiger.** Have them sort the pictures by the beginning or ending /t/ sound.

Blend Sounds

Review: *at, mat, sat*
Have students blend the words **at, mat,** and **sat,** using the routine from Day One.

High-Frequency Words

Review: *see, go*
Write the words **see** and **go.** Read aloud each word. Then without students seeing, erase a letter in one of the words. Ask students which letter is missing. Replace the letter as students read the word. Repeat with the second word.

Review: *the, we*
Display each High-Frequency Word Card.

Point quickly to each card, at random, and have students read the word as fast as they can.

RF.K.2d Isolate and pronounce the initial, medial vowel, and final sounds (phonemes) in three-phoneme (consonant-vowel-consonant, or CVC) words.* (This does not include CVCs ending with /l/, /r/, or /x/.), RF.K.3a Demonstrate basic knowledge of letter-sound correspondences by producing the primary or most frequent sound for each consonant., RF.K.3c Read common high-frequency words by sight (e.g., the, of, to, you, she, my, is, are, do, does).

Read Aloud and Shared Reading

(20 MIN.) RL.K.1, RL.K.3, RL.K.5, RF.K.1a, RF.K.3b, RF.K.4, SL.K.3

Read Aloud

To support the unit concept, use one of the Read-Aloud Handbook selections for Unit 2. As you read, model the metacognitive strategy for the unit, Visualize, guided by the samples provided. You may also wish to select a favorite read aloud from your classroom or school library. To support the unit concept, use one of the suggested titles for Unit 2.

Shared Reading (iELD)

Reread the Animal Fantasy

First rereading. Read aloud the story fluently and expressively, pointing under each word.

Reread for first reading. Read aloud the text fluently and expressively, pointing under each word.

Reread the text: Accuracy/Context. Point to the title and read it aloud. Encourage students to echo-read the text one sentence at a time, using the same rate and expression. Lead students to look for words they don't know before beginning the selection. Explain that scanning for unfamiliar words and using surrounding words with help them understand the word. This will help them read fluently and accurately without stopping to figure out words. Provide corrective feedback and/or validate students' efforts.

Build Concepts: Every Story Has Characters

Pose questions to connect the animal fantasy to the unit concept. For example:

- *What tells you that the Bear and the Fox are friends? Explain your thinking.*
- *What do you think the bear did after the fox ran off with the pie?*
- *When the bear sees the fox again what do you think he will say to his friend?*

Review Phonics: Short *a*

Highlight the word **ran** in the last sentence. Have students listen for the medial sound as you read the word.

Ask: *What letter stands for the sound /a/ in **ran**?*

Review High-Frequency Words: *the*

Tell students that this text contains some words they have learned. Point to the previously taught high-frequency word *the* in the third sentence. Ask students to turn to a partner and tell their partner the high-frequency word. Remind students to look for high-frequency words they know as they read a new text.

RL.K.1 With prompting and support, ask and answer questions about key details in a text., RL.K.3 With prompting and support, identify characters, settings, and major events in a story., RL.K.5 Recognize common types of texts (e.g., storybooks, poems, fantasy, realistic text). CA)., RF.K.1a Follow words from left to right, top to bottom, and page by page., RF.K.3b Associate the long and short sounds with the common spellings (graphemes) for the five major vowels.(Identify which letters represent the five major vowels (Aa, Ee, Ii, Oo, and Uu) and know the long and short sound of each vowel. More complex long vowel graphemes and spellings are targeted in the grade 1 phonics standards.) CA, RF.K.4 Read emergent-reader texts with purpose and understanding., SL.K.3 Ask and answer questions in order to seek help, get information, or clarify something that is not understood.

Read-Aloud Handbook

Shared Reading Vol. 1, p. 11 "Bear and Fox"

Student Objectives

I will be able to:
- Read along with accuracy.
- Answer questions about the bear and foxes relationship.
- Identify words with medial short **a**.
- Recognize the high-frequency word *the*.

(iELD) Integrated ELD

Light Support
Display "Bear and Fox." Have students answer the following questions to describe and compare/contrast the characters. *What does Fox do when he sees Bear? What does Bear do for Fox? What does this tell you about Bear? What does Fox do when Bear turns his back?*

Moderate Support
Display "Bear and Fox." Have partners fill out the chart below with verb phrases to better understand each character.

Bear's Action	Fox's Actions

Ask: *How are Bear and Fox different? Is Bear a good friend? How do you know? Is Fox a good friend? How do you know?*
Phrase Bank: takes the pie, bakes a pie, asks for a slice, gets a plat, shares the pie

Substantial Support
Display "Bear and Fox." Help students describe each character and determine how the characters are similar and different. Have students answer the questions using the story illustration and verbs from the word bank to complete the sentence frames.
Ask: *What does Bear do first?*
- *Bear _____ a pie.*
Ask: *What does Fox do?*
- *Fox _____ for a slice.*
Ask: *What does Bear do for Fox?*
- *Bear _____ a plate for Fox.*
Ask: *What does this tell you about Bear?*
Word Bank: takes   shares   gets   bakes   asks   is

ELD.PI.K.5, ELD.PI.K.7, ELD.PII.K.3

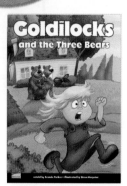

Goldilocks and the Three Bears

Student Objectives

I will be able to:
- Identify fantasy characteristics in *Goldilocks and the Three Bears*.

Find Text Evidence: Text Type: Fantasy (15 MIN.) RL.K.1, RL.K.5, SL.K.3

Engage Thinking

Display *Goldilocks and the Three Bears.* Remind students that they have learned about a special kind of story called a fantasy.

Ask: *Is* Goldilocks and the Three Bears *a story that can really happen?*

Explain that in this lesson, you will show students how to closely reread the text to answer a question about fantasy.

Model

Display and read aloud a text evidence question. Ask students what words in the question can help them know what to look for in the text. Point out the question word **How.** Lead students to recognize that the question is asking for an example of what makes the story a fantasy.

> **Text Evidence Question:** What tells you that *Goldilocks and the Three Bears* is a fantasy?

Ask students to listen carefully as you read pages 2 and 3. Use a think aloud to model how identify the story as fantasy.

Say: *The story begins with the words "Once upon a time." I know that these words usually begin stories that are fantasies, but I keep reading. I read about the three bears. They live together in a house in the woods. Real bears do not live in houses. I look at the illustration. The bears do not look like real bears. Mama Bear is cooking and wearing a necklace. Papa Bear is reading. Baby Bear is playing with dolls. None of these things can happen in real life.*

Guided Practice (iELD)

Display and read aloud a second question. Ask students to listen carefully for the words in the question that will help them find evidence in the text.

> **Text Evidence Question:** How do you know *Goldilocks and the Three Bears* is a fantasy?

Discuss with students that the question is the same. Guide them to recognize that they need to find another example of what makes the story a fantasy. Ask students to listen as you read aloud pages 16 and 17. Then ask students to turn and talk to a partner to answer the text evidence question. If necessary, provide directive feedback. For example:

- *What do you learn about the bears on these pages?*
- *Could real bears do this in real life?*
- *How do the illustrations help you answer the questions?*

Call on partners to share their answers to the question.

Productive Engagement: Partner Activity

Display and read aloud another question.

> **Text Evidence Question:** What do you learn about the three bears on pages 20 and 21 that tells you this story is a fantasy?

Reread pages 18–21. After reading, ask students to turn and talk to a partner. Partners should discuss reasons that support their answer to the question. Invite students to share their ideas with the class.

☑ Show Your Knowledge

Ask students to draw a picture to show one way they know the story is a fantasy. Students can write or dictate a description for the picture.

(iELD) Integrated ELD

Light Support
Partners use the prepositional phrases from the phrase bank to write or dictate responses to the questions.
Ask: *Where do the three bears live?*
Where do real bears live?
Where are the bears sitting?
Where do real bears sit?
What do the bears wear on their bodies?
What are the bears doing on these pages?
How are these bears different from real bears?
How are they similar to people?
Phrase Bank
on a chair
in the woods
at a book
in a house

Moderate Support
Partners ask and answer questions about the text and pictures on pages 4–5 using sentence stems and prepositional phrases.
Where do the three bears live?
The bears live _____.
Where do real bears live?
Real bears live _____.
Where is Mama Bear sitting?
The bears are sitting _____.
What is Baby Bear looking at?
Baby Bear is looking _____.
Phrase Bank
on a chair
in the woods
at a book
in a house
Have partners take turns drawing or dictating their responses.

Substantial Support
Display pages 4–5 of *Goldilocks and the Three Bears*. Ask the questions in the chart. Together, have students use the words from the word bank or draw pictures to answer the questions.

1. Where do the three bears live?	The bears live in a _____.
2. Where do the three bears sit?	The bears sit on _____.
3. What is Baby Bear wearing?	Baby Bear wears a _____ on his _____.

Word Bank
hat house head chairs
Ask: *Do these bears look and act more like people or real bears?*

ELD.PI.K.1, ELD.PI.K.10, ELD.PII.K.5

RL.K.1 With prompting and support, ask and answer questions about key details in a text., **RL.K.5** Recognize common types of texts (e.g., storybooks, poems, fantasy, realistic text). CA)., **SL.K.3** Ask and answer questions in order to seek help, get information, or clarify something that is not understood.

Goldilocks and the Three Bears

Student Objectives

I will be able to:
- Help write an opinion about the three bears.
- Use question words.

(iELD) Integrated ELD

Light Support

Ask: *Should Goldilocks have fixed the chair she broke?*

Have partners combine opinions and reasons to form a complete compound sentence. Have students follow the model.

Question: *Was it okay for the bears to leave their door open?*

Opinion*: yes*

Reason: *They were not going far.*

Combined: *I think it was okay for the bears to leave their door open because they were not going far.*

Moderate Support

Have partners work together to respond to the following questions. Have them use sentence frames to state an opinion, and use words or short phrases as reasons. Have partners then alternate reading aloud their complete sentences.

Ask: *Was it okay for the bears to leave their door open?*

I think it was/wasn't a good idea to leave the door open because _____.

Ask: *Should Goldilocks have fixed the chair she broke?*

I think Goldilocks should/should not have fixed the chair because _____.

Substantial Support

Display *Goldilocks and the Three Bears.* As a group, help students orally form opinions about the text using the questions below and sentence frames. Write responses on the board.

Ask: *Was it okay for the bears to leave their door open?*

I think it was/wasn't a good idea to leave the door open.

Ask: *Why or why not?*

Then model how to join opinions and reasons using conjunctions, and have students repeat after you.

ELD.PI.K.2, ELD.PI.K.3, ELD.PII.K.6

Write an Opinion (15 MIN.) W.K.1, W.K.8, L.K.1a, L.K.1d

Engage Thinking

Review the text and illustrations on pages 22 through 24.

Ask: *How do the bears' feelings change? Why do you think they feel this way?*

Tell students that today they will write an opinion. They will tell if they think the bears were happy or sad at the end of the story. Remind them that an opinion is not right or wrong. An opinion is what you think or feel. When you give an opinion, you give at least one reason why you think the way you do.

Collaborative Conversation: Share Opinions and Reasons (iELD)

Tell students that to begin, you want them to discuss their opinions with a partner. Provide a model.

Sample modeling: *I want to tell my partner if I think the three bears were happy or sad to see Goldilocks leave. I look at the pictures. I think about my opinion. I think about my reason. Now I know what I want to say. I'll tell my partner, "I think the bears were sad to see Goldilocks leave because they wanted to find out why she was in their house." When you talk to your partner, use the same sentence starter: I think the bears were (happy/sad) to see Goldilocks leave because ___.*

Write as a Group

Take a class vote to agree on an opinion. Decide on one reason to write. Rehearse the message orally. Explain that when writers write an opinion text, they begin by stating their opinion clearly. Then they provide reasons for the opinion. Engage students in the writing process by prompting them to use strategies they have been learning and practicing. For example:

- *What words can we use at the beginning of the sentence to let readers know we are writing an opinion?*
- *What word can we use to let readers know we are giving a reason for why we feel the way we do?*
- *What punctuation do we use for the end of the sentence?*
- *Let's reread our sentence. Does it tell an opinion, or what we think? Does it give a reason for our opinion?*

Sample Shared Writing

When Goldilocks left the bears' house, I think the bears were sad to see her go. I think the bears wanted to know why Goldilocks was in their house and if she needed any help.

Build Language: Understand and Use Question Words

Have students hold up their hand. Explain that just as we have five fingers on one hand, there are five question words we can use to begin a question. Assign a question word **who, what, when, where,** and **why,** to each finger. Have students practice pointing to each finger and saying a question word. Then have them use each question word to begin a question related to *Goldilocks and the Three Bears.*

 ## Write Independently

Ask students to draw a picture of a bear with a happy or sad face to tell if they believe the bears were happy or sad when Goldilocks left. Encourage them to dictate or write a label.

Small-Group Differentiated Instruction (15 MIN. per Group)

Meet with Small Groups

Select small-group reading titles or activities based on students' needs. See the Small-Group Instructional Planner for titles that support a range of instructional levels within the unit topic. Remind students to apply skills and strategies they learned to their small-group reading experiences.

Say: *We spent more time today learning about fantasies. We found examples in* Goldilocks and the Three Bears *that help us identify the story as a fantasy. We also wrote an opinion. We told what we think about character feelings. In small group today, decide if what you are reading and listening to is a fantasy. Think about your opinion. Do you like the story? Why or why not?*

Whole-Group Reflect and Share

Bring the class back together. Ask volunteers to tell about any fantasies they read and heard. Encourage students to give their opinions about the selections and support their opinions with examples from the text.

W.K.1 Use a combination of drawing, dictating, and writing to compose opinion pieces in which they tell a reader the topic or the name of the book they are writing about and state an opinion or preference about the topic or book (e.g., My favorite book is...)., **W.K.8** With guidance and support from adults, recall information from experiences or gather information from provided sources to answer a question., **L.K.1a** Print many upper- and lowercase letters., **L.K.1d** Understand and use question words (interrogatives) (e.g., who, what, where, when, why, how).

Pre-Decodable Reader: *I See*

Student Objectives

I will be able to:
- Recognize and produce rhyme.
- Read previously taught high-frequency words: **I, like, the, we, see, go.**
- Read decodable text.

Additional Materials

- Pre-decodable reader: *I See*

Weekly Presentation
- High-frequency word cards: **go, I, like, see, the, we**

Monitor Student Reading of Connected Text

As students chorally read the pre-decodable text and answer questions, ask these questions:

Are students able to . . .
❏ blend and read **t** words in the text?
❏ read new high-frequency words with automaticity?
❏ demonstrate comprehension of the text by answering text-based questions?

Based on your observations, you may wish to support students' fluency, automaticity, and comprehension with additional decodable reading practice during intervention time.

Focus Skill: t/t/ (20 MIN.) RL.K.1, RL.K.10, RF.K.2a, RF.K.3a, RF.K.3c, RF.K.4

Phonological Awareness: Recognize and Produce Rhyme (iELD)

Model/Practice

Say the words **big** and **fig**. Tell students that these words rhyme because they have the same sounds at the end.

Say: *Listen to these words: **big**, **fig**. I hear **/ig/** at the end of **big**, and **/ig/** at the end of **fig**. Say the words with me and listen to the ending sounds.*

Say pairs of words and have students clap if the pair rhymes: **bat, hat; sick, ball; feet, neat; cot, lot.** Have students say other words that rhyme with **bat** and **hat**.

High-Frequency Words

Review: *I, like, the, we, see, go*

Write **I, like, the, we, see, go.** Remind students that they have been practicing these words so that they can read them quickly. Have students read the words aloud several times.

Hold up the high-frequency word card **see** and call on individual students to quickly read the word.

Then have a student use the word in an oral sentence. Have the other students clap when they hear **see**. Repeat for the other words.

Pre-Decodable Reader: *I See*

Introduce the Book

Point to the book's title, *I See,* and have students read it.

Ask: *What do you see on the cover? What does the boy see?*

Read the Book

Discuss what the rebuses on pages 5, 6, 7, and 8 stand for. Turn to page 2, and have students blend the decodable words and read the sentence aloud so you can check their reading. Have students continue to read, blending the decodable words and reading the high-frequency words quickly.

Connect Phonics to Comprehension

When students have finished, ask:

- *What did Tam see? What did Sam see?*
- *What did they take home?*

Turn to a partner and retell the story.

RL.K.1 With prompting and support, ask and answer questions about key details in a text., **RL.K.10** Actively engage in group reading activities with purpose and understanding., **RF.K.2a** Recognize and produce rhyming words., **RF.K.3a** Demonstrate basic knowledge of letter-sound correspondences by producing the primary or most frequent sound for each consonant., **RF.K.3c** Read common high-frequency words by sight (e.g., the, of, to, you, she, my, is, are, do, does)., **RF.K.4** Read emergent-reader texts with purpose and understanding.

Read Aloud and Shared Reading

(20 MIN.) **RL.K.1, RL.K.5, RF.K.1a, RF.K.3a, RF.K.3c, RF.K.4, SL.K.3**

Read Aloud

To support the unit concept, use one of the Read-Aloud Handbook selections for Unit 2. As you read, model the metacognitive strategy for the unit, Visualize, guided by the samples provided. You may also wish to select a favorite read aloud from your classroom or school library. To support the unit concept, use one of the suggested titles for Unit 2.

Shared Reading (iELD)

Reread the Animal Fantasy

First reading. Read aloud the story fluently and expressively, pointing under each word.

Reread for Fluency: Accuracy/Use Context. Point to and read aloud the title. Lead students in an echo-reading of the text. Read one sentence at a time and have students echo you. Remind students that when they come to a word they don't know, they can use surrounding words to help them read it. Model reading aloud each sentence with fluency and accuracy. Provide corrective feedback and/or validate students' efforts.

Build Concepts: Every Story Has Characters

Pose questions to connect the animal fantasy to the unit concept. For example:

- *If you were Bear what would you say to Fox the next time you see him?*
- *What words would you use to tell about Fox?*
- *Do you think Bear and Fox can be friends in the future? Why or why not?*

Review Phonics: Final *t*

Highlight the word **get** in sentence 3. Ask students to identify the last letter and its sound. Then guide students in sounding out the word aloud.

Review High-Frequency Words: *the*

Tell students that this text contains some words they have learned. Point to the previously taught high-frequency word **the** in the third sentence. Ask students to turn to a partner and tell their partner the high-frequency word. Remind students to look for high-frequency words they know as they read a new text.

Read-Aloud Handbook   **Shared Reading Vol. 1, p. 11 "Bear and Fox"**

Student Objectives

I will be able to:
- Echo read a story fluently and accurately.
- Answer questions about characters in a story.
- Identify words with final *t*.
- Recognize the high-frequency word *the*.

(iELD) Integrated ELD

Light Support
Have partners respond to questions based on details from the text and pictures.

Ask: *How does Bear/Fox look? What does Bear/Fox do? What does Bear/Fox say? How do you think Bear's feelings about Fox change in the story? Why do you think Fox ran away?*

Moderate Support
Display "Bear and Fox." Have partners fill out the chart below for each character to answer the following questions:
How does Bear/Fox look? What does Bear/Fox do? What does Bear/Fox say?

Character	Bear	Fox
Looks	big and soft	smiling sneaky
Acts	bakes pie shares pie	steals pie runs away
Says	"I'll get you a plate"	asks for a slice of pie

Have partners create oral sentences based on, *Bear/Fox…looks/acts/says.*

Substantial Support
Display "Bear and Fox." First, provide students with cards including the following captions and, if possible, pictures: **big and soft, smiling, sneaky, bakes pie, shares pie, asks for pie, steals pie, runs away.**
Have students sort the cards into two piles: **Bear** and **Fox.**
Next, have students organize cards within each group based on whether the details describe how the character *looks* or how the character *acts*.
Have students create sentences to respond to the following questions: *How does Bear/Fox look? What does Bear/Fox do?*

ELD.PI.K.5, ELD.PI.K.6, ELD.PII.K.4

RL.K.1 With prompting and support, ask and answer questions about key details in a text., **RL.K.5** Recognize common types of texts (e.g., storybooks, poems, fantasy, realistic text). **CA).**, **RF.K.1a** Follow words from left to right, top to bottom, and page by page., **RF.K.3a** Demonstrate basic knowledge of letter-sound correspondences by producing the primary or most frequent sound for each consonant., **RF.K.3c** Read common high-frequency words by sight (e.g., the, of, to, you, she, my, is, are, do, does)., **RF.K.4** Read emergent-reader texts with purpose and understanding., **SL.K.3** Ask and answer questions in order to seek help, get information, or clarify something that is not understood.

Compare and Contrast Fantasy Characters (15 MIN.) RL.K.1, RL.K.9, SL.K.3, SL.K.4, SL.K.6

Mentor Read-Aloud Vol. 1, pp. 18-21
"The Little Helper" and
Goldilocks and the Three Bears

Student Objectives

I will be able to:
- Compare and contrast the adventures and experiences of two characters.
- Participate in a group discussion about how characters are alike and different.

Additional Materials

Weekly Presentation
- Compare and Contrast Chart

Engage Thinking

Display "The Little Helper" and *Goldilocks and the Three Bears.* Remind students that they know both of these texts very well and now they are going to think about how characters in the stories are alike and how they are different.

Say: *When we compare two characters we are looking for how they are alike. When we contrast two characters we are looking on how they are different.*

Ask: *Name one way the Mouse and Goldilocks are the same and one way they are different.*

Model

Use a three-column chart to create a compare and contrast chart for the mouse in "The Little Helper" and *Goldilocks.* Review that in the left column and the right column, you will write how the characters are different. In the middle, you will list ways the two characters are alike. Display each text as you think aloud to model how you compare and contrast mouse and Goldilocks' adventures and experiences.

Sample modeling: *I want to compare the mouse and Goldilocks. I think about experiences they both had that are similar. Both the mouse and Goldilocks were caught doing something. I'll note that in the chart. I'll write it in the middle column because that's where we write ways the characters are the same.*

Sample modeling: *A lion caught the mouse when the mouse accidentally climbed on the lion. The three bears caught Goldilocks sleeping in Baby Bear's bed. This is a difference I can write in the chart. I'll write what happened to the mouse under the column that says "the mouse." This column tells mouse's experiences and adventures that are different from Goldilocks's. I'll write what happened to Goldilocks under the column that says "Goldilocks."*

Guided Practice

Use directive and corrective prompts as needed to guide students to compare and contrast the mouse and Goldilocks and their adventures and experiences.

- *The mouse is an animal character. How is Goldilocks different?*
- *Goldilocks is a character in a fantasy. Is mouse?*
- *How does the mouse feel about lion when lion catches him? How does Goldilocks feel about the bears when they catch her?*
- *Goldilocks eats the bears' food. She uses their furniture. Is this something the mouse does? Explain.*
- *What does the mouse do for the lion at the end of the story? How does this compare to what Goldilocks does at the end of the story?*

If necessary, continue to model how you make comparisons and contrasts between the mouse and Goldilocks. Collaborate with students to complete the chart. Reread the comparisons and contrasts together.

The Mouse	Both	Goldilocks
Lion caught the mouse when he accidentally climbed on the sleeping lion.	Caught doing something	The bears caught Goldilocks while she slept in Baby Bear's bed.
An animal character (mouse)	Characters in a fantasy	A human character (girl)
Does not take or use things that belong to the lion.	Scared of the character that caught him/her	Takes and uses things that belong to the bears, not her.
Helps the lion later in the story.	Ran away	Does not return to the bears' home in the story.

Sample **Compare and Contrast Chart**

✓ Show Your Knowledge

Point to either the mouse or Goldilocks. Ask students to tell an experience or adventure unique to the character. Then point to both characters at the same time and have students tell one way they are alike.

 Integrated ELD

Light Support

Have partners fill out the chart to answer the question, *How are the mouse and Goldilocks similar and different?*

	similar	different
feelings		
events		
actions		

Then have partners work together to create one compound sentence to compare the mouse and Goldilocks using **and** and one compound sentence to contrast the mouse and Goldilocks using **but**.

Compare: *The mouse _____, and Goldilocks _____.*

Contrast: *The mouse _____, but Goldilocks _____.*

Moderate Support

Have partners work together, using the chart above to help them answer the question, *How are the mouse and Goldilocks similar and different?* They can focus on the characters' feelings, story events, and the characters' actions.

Substantial Support

Talk with students about how the mouse from "The Little Helper" and Goldilocks from *Goldilocks and the Three Bears* are alike. Focus on comparing experiences and reinforcing similarities. Use guiding questions and sentence frames that include conjunctions to help students compare the characters.

Ask: *What similar feeling do both the mouse and Goldilocks feel in the stories?*

The mouse feels _____, and Goldilocks also feels _____. (fear)

Ask: *What makes both the mouse and Goldilocks feel this way?*

The mouse is _____ by the lion, and Goldilocks is _____ by the bears. (caught)

Ask: *What do both characters do after that?*

The mouse _____ _____, and Goldilocks _____ _____ too. (runs away).

ELD.PI.K.2, ELD.PI.K.5, ELD.PII.K.6

RL.K.1 With prompting and support, ask and answer questions about key details in a text., RL.K.9 With prompting and support, compare and contrast the adventures and experiences of characters in familiar stories., SL.K.3 Ask and answer questions in order to seek help, get information, or clarify something that is not understood., SL.K.4 Describe familiar people, places, things, and events and, with prompting and support, provide additional detail., SL.K.6 Speak audibly and express thoughts, feelings, and ideas clearly.

Plan and Draft a Response to the Essential Question (15 MIN.) W.K.2, W.K.5

Engage Thinking

Display and reread the unit essential question. Explain to students that today you will plan and draft a response to the question. You will guide students to think of a response to the question that they can support with evidence from the selections they have read so far.

How are people different?

Plan (iELD)

Remind students that there are different stages of writing. Today they will work on the first stage, which is to generate ideas and organize them. Use a think aloud to model how writers generate a response to a question.

Sample modeling: *There are many ways that people are different. I cannot write about all of them. I will write about the ones that I think are the most important. I will write about how people look and act different.*

Display a blank planning guide and write your main idea statement. Then think aloud to model how writers support their ideas with reasons.

Sample modeling: *I need to give one or more reasons or examples to support my main idea. I have read a lot of stories with characters. Although the characters in this unit's stories have mostly been animals, they act like people. Like people, the characters look different. For example, the mouse is small, but the lion is big. Tortoise tries his best, but Rabbit does not.*

Add reasons to the planning guide. Then explain that your text will need a conclusion. Remind students that a conclusion often restates the writer's main idea in a different way.

Main Idea Statement:
People look and act different from each other.
Supporting Details:
Some people are tall. Some are short.
People have different color hair, eyes, and skin.
Some people always try their best. Some people do not.
Some people are helpful. Some people are not.
Conclusion:
People do not look or act the same.

Sample Planning Guide

Every Story Has
Characters

Essential Question
How are people different?

Mentor Read-Aloud Topic Introduction Vol. 1, pp. 12-13

Student Objectives

I will be able to:
• Help plan and write a response to how people are different.

Additional Materials

Weekly Presentation
• Planning Guide

Integrated ELD

Light Support
Have students complete the main idea and details chart from Moderate Support. Students should generate words to complete the frames on their own.

Moderate Support
Write the Essential Question, *How are people different?*, on the board and read it aloud. Then have partners work together to draw a main idea and detail chart, using the word bank to complete the frames for main idea and details. Guide students to think about how particular characters looked or acted differently.

Main Idea:	People ___ and ___ different from each other.
Detail 1	**Look**: Some people are ____, but some people are ____.
Detail 2	**Act**: Some people are ____, but some people are ____.

Word Bank: act kind big look small not

Substantial Support
Write the Essential Question, *How are people different?*, on the board and read it aloud.
Ask: *Which words are most important in the Essential Question?* (**people, different**)
Circle them. Have students think about the stories they have read this week.
Ask: *What were some important ways that the characters were different?*
Elicit examples, such as Bear baking the pie and Fox taking it, or the tiny mouse compared to the large lion. Elicit that the characters both looked differently and acted differently.

ED.PI.K.1, ELD.PI.K.10, ELD.PII.K.6

Draft

Remind students that when writers draft, they do not worry about correct spelling and end punctuation. They simply want to get their ideas on paper. Think aloud to model how you use the information on your planning guide to help you draft a response.

Sample modeling: *The main idea statement should be my first sentence. Then I will give reasons to support my main idea. I will give examples of how people look and act differently. I'll end my writing with a concluding sentence.*

Rehearse each sentence before you write it, and engage students in the writing process using question prompts. Reread the draft. Save it to return to in Week 3 to model the revision and editing stages of the writing process.

> **Sample Draft**
> People look and act differently. Some people are tall. Others are short. People have different hair. Some people try hard. Some people are helpful. People are different in many ways.

 Write Independently

Ask students to write or dictate their own main idea statement in response to the question. Students can write or draw a reason to the support the statement.

Small-Group Differentiated Instruction (15 MIN. per Group)

Meet with Small Groups

Select appropriate small-group reading titles or reinforcement activities based on students' needs. See the Small-Group Instructional Planner for titles that support a range of instructional reading levels within the unit topic. Ask students to think about the unit topic and essential question as they read their small-group text.

Say: *Today we practiced comparing and contrasting two characters. We also thought about the question **How are people different?** As you read and listen to new stories today, think about how the characters are like characters you have read about in this unit. How are they different? Also consider how the stories help you understand ways people are different.*

Whole-Group Reflect and Share

Bring the class back together. Invite volunteers to share comparisons and contrasts they made. Also encourage students to expand on the Essential Question based on their reading in small group.

W.K.2 Use a combination of drawing, and writing to compose informative/explanatory texts in which they name what they are writing about and supply some information about the topic., **W.K.5** With guidance and support from adults, respond to questions and suggestions from peers and add details to strengthen writing as needed.

Pre-Decodable Reader: *I See*

Student Objectives

I will be able to:
- Blend onset and rime.
- Practice letter-sound correspondences for **t/t/, s/s/, a/a/, m/m/.**
- Blend sounds **/m/, /a/, /t/.**
- Spell words **tam** and **sat.**
- Write legibly.
- Read previously taught high-frequency words: **I, like, the, we, see, go.**
- Read decodable text.

Additional Materials

- Pre-decodable reader: *I See*
- Letter cards: **a, m, s, t**

Weekly Presentation
- Picture cards: **bat, tag, tape, top, tub**
- High-frequency word cards: **go, I, like, see, the, we**

Focus Skill: t/t/ (20 MIN.) RL.K.1, RL.K.10, RF.K.2c, RF.K.2d, RF.K.3a, RF.K.3c, RF.K.4, L.K.1a

Phonological Awareness: Blend Onset and Rime

Model/Practice

Segment the word **tam** into its onset and rime: **/t/ /am/.** Have students blend the sounds and say the word.

Repeat with the words **mat, sat, tap, ten,** and **tug.** Then say the word **tip.**

Ask: *What is the onset or beginning sound? What is the rest of the word?*

Blend the sounds **/t/** and **/ip/** and say the word with the class.

Display the picture card **top.** Have the students name the picture.

Ask: *What is the onset or beginning sound? What is the rest of the word? Let's blend the sounds **/t/** and **/op/** and say the word:* **top.**

Repeat with the picture cards **tape, tag, tub,** and **bat.**

Letter-Sound Correspondences

Review

Display letter card **s.**

Say: *This is the letter **s**. The letter **s** stands for **/sss/**. What is the letter? What sound does this letter stand for?*

Repeat for **m, a,** and **t.**

Give each student an index card. Have each student write **s, m, a,** or **t** on the card. Say the sound one of the letters stands for. Have students with that letter hold up their cards.

Say: *What sound does your letter stand for? When I say that sound, hold up your card.*

Blend Sounds

Review

Have students blend the word **mat.** Place letter cards **m, a, t** in a pocket chart. Point to the letter **m.**

Say: *This is the letter **m**. The letter **m** stands for **/mmm/**. Say **/mmm/**. This is the letter **a**. The letter **a** stands for **/aaa/**. Say **/aaa/**. Listen as I blend the two sounds together **/mmmaaa/**. Blend the sounds with me. This is the letter **t**. The letter **t** stands for **/t/**. Listen as I blend all three sounds together, **/mmmaaat/**. Now blend the sounds to read the word, **mat**.*

Repeat the steps for the word **sat.** Move your hand from left to right under the word. Have students blend and read the word **sat.**

Dictation

Review

Dictate these sounds for students to spell. Have them repeat the sound and then write the letter that stands for the sound: **/t/, /s/, /a/, /m/.**

Dictate these words for students to spell: **tam, sat.** Model how to segment each word.

Say: *When I say **tam**, I hear three sounds, /t/ /a/ /m/. I know the letter **t** stands for /t/, the letter **a** stands for /a/, and the letter **m** stands for /m/. I will write the letters **t, a,** and **m** to spell **tam.***

Repeat for **sat**. When children finish writing the words, have them correct their papers.

High-Frequency Words

Review: *I, like, the, we, see, go*

Write **I, like, the, we, see, go**. Focusing on one word at a time, have students spell the word as you point to each letter. Then erase one letter, say the word, and have students identify the missing letter. Replace the letter and have students read the word.

Decodable Text

Write the words and sentences. Guide students with blending the first two words. Then have volunteers read the sentences.

Tam	sat
I see Tam.	
Tam sat.	

Pre-Decodable Reader: *I See*

Reread

Have partners reread aloud *I See* together. Circulate and listen in. Note student's speed, accuracy, and intonation. Based on the group as a whole, provide some general feedback and validate successes. If students need additional practice to read the text, provide support during small-group reading instruction.

(iELD) Integrated ELD

Light Support

Give partners a set of onset cards and rime cards. Include onset cards, each labeled as follows: **t, m, s, short e,** and **u.** Include rime cards, each labeled **am, at, ap, ip, op, om, et, en, ug, um.** First, hold up each onset or rime card and pronounce it together as a group. Then have students create their own words by blending onset and rime. Call on volunteers to share their words. Then challenge students to use the words in an original sentence.

Moderate Support

Provide students with cards to practice blending onset and rime. Each card should be labeled as follows: **t, m, s.** Include rime cards, each labeled **am, at, ap, ip, op.**

Hold up a picture card and say the word, such as **/tam/.** Repeat the word, but break the sounds into onset and rime, **/t/ /aaaaam/.** Repeat the onset again, and guide students to find the correct onset card (**t**). Then repeat the rime, and guide students to find the correct rime card (**am**). Say the word again with students, blending the onset and rime: **/tam/.**

Have partners join the onset cards and rime cards to create their own words, such as **tam, tap, tip, top, Tom, mat.** Have students blend the onset and rime orally. Correct pronunciation as needed.

Substantial Support

Provide students with cards to practice blending onset and rime. Each card should be labeled as follows: **t, m, s.** Include rime cards, each labeled **am, at, ap, ip, op.**

Hold up a picture card and say the word, such as **/map/.** Repeat the word, but break the sounds into onset and rime, **/mmm/ /aaaaap/.** Repeat the onset again, and guide students to find the correct onset card (**m**). Then repeat the rime, and guide students to find the correct rime card (**ap**). Say the word again with students, blending the onset and rime: **/map/.**

Follow the routine for other words, such as **tam, tap, tip, top, Tom, mat, mop, mom, Sam, sat, sap,** and **sip.**

ELD.PI.K.1, ELD.PII.K.3a, ELD.PII.K.4

RL.K.1 With prompting and support, ask and answer questions about key details in a text., **RL.K.10** Actively engage in group reading activities with purpose and understanding., **RF.K.2c** Blend and segment onsets and rimes of single-syllable spoken words., **RF.K.2d** Isolate and pronounce the initial, medial vowel, and final sounds (phonemes) in three-phoneme (consonant-vowel-consonant, or CVC) words.* (This does not include CVCs ending with /l/, /r/, or /x/.), **RF.K.3a** Demonstrate basic knowledge of letter-sound correspondences by producing the primary or most frequent sound for each consonant., **RF.K.3c** Read common high-frequency words by sight (e.g., the, of, to, you, she, my, is, are, do, does)., **RF.K.4** Read emergent-reader texts with purpose and understanding., **L.K.1a** Print many upper- and lowercase letters.

Week 3 Skills at a Glance

	Day 1	Day 2
Reading Mini-Lessons	**Mentor Read-Alouds:** Topic Introduction, pp. 12-13 **Build Knowledge and Review Week 1 Strategies (10 Min.), p. 194** RL.K.3, SL.K.1a, SL.K.1b **Read-Aloud Handbook** **Shared Readings:** "New Friends," p. 12 **Read Aloud and Shared Reading (20 Min.), p. 195** RL.K.1, RL.K.3, RL.K.10, RL.K.10a, RL.K.10b, RF.K.1a, RF.K.3a, RF.K.4, SL.K.3 • Fluency: Prosody/Pitch • Build Concepts: Every Story Has Characters • Model Print Concepts: Directionality: Left to Right • Review Phonics: Initital and Final *t* The Little Red Hen **The Little Red Hen: Listen and Retell Key Details (10 Min.), p. 196** RL.K.1, RL.K.2, RL.K.5, RL.K.6, RL.K.10, RL.K.10a, RL.K.10b, SL.K.1a, SL.K.1b, SL.K.2, SL.K.3, SL.K.6	**Read-Aloud Handbook** **Shared Readings:** "New Friends," p. 12 **Read Aloud and Shared Reading (20 Min.), p. 202** RL.K.1, RL.K.3, RF.K.3a, RF.K.3c, RF.K.4, SL.K.3 • Fluency: Prosody/Pitch • Build Concepts: Every Story Has Characters • Review Phonics: Initial and Final n • Review High-Frequency Words: *the, like* The Little Red Hen **Build Vocabulary: Shades of Meaning (10 Min.), p. 203** RL.K.1, L.K.5d **Find Text Evidence Story Events (15 Min.), p. 204** RL.K.1, RL.K.2, RL.K.3, SL.K.3
Writing Mini-Lessons	**Write Key Events (10 Min.), p. 198** W.K.2, W.K.6, W.K.8, SL.K.1a, SL.K.1b, SL.K.4, L.K.1a, L.K.1c • Build Language: Form Regular and Plural Nouns	**Write Story Events (10 Min.), p. 206** RL.K.1, RL.K.2, RL.K.3, W.K.3, W.K.8, L.K.1c • Build Language: Form Regular Plural Nouns
Phonics Mini-Lessons	**Focus Skill: n/n/ (20 Min.), p. 200** RF.K.2d, RF.K.3a, RF.K.3c, L.K.1.a • Phonological Awareness: Phoneme Isolation • High-Frequency Words: *I, like, the, we, see, go*	**Focus Skill: n/n/ (20 Min.), p. 208** RF.K.2d, RF.K.3a, RF.K.3c, L.K.1a • Phonological Awareness: Phoneme Isolation • High-Frequency Words: *I, like, the, we, see, go*

Extended Read 2: *The Little Red Hen*

Animal Fantasy

Quantitative	Lexile® 340L

Qualitative Analysis of Text Complexity

Purpose and Levels of Meaning ①
• Story theme is simple: those who do the work should reap the benefits.

Structure ①
• The narrative is chronological, with a repetitive sequence of events.

Language Conventionality and Clarity ①
• Test uses common language, with few complex sentences.

Knowledge Demands ①
• Some prior knowledge of how bread is derived from wheat would help in comprehension.

Day 3	Day 4	Day 5
Read-Aloud Handbook **Shared Readings:** "Little Bo-Peep," p. 13 **Read Aloud and Shared Reading (20 Min.), p. 210** RL.K.5, RL.K.10, RL.K.10a, RL.K.10b, RF.K.1a, RF.K.3a, RF.K.4, SL.K.3 • Fluency: Prosody/Pitch • Build Unit Concepts: Every Story Has Characters •Review Print Concepts: Directionality: Top to Bottom • Review Phonics: Initial and Final t The Little Red Hen **Find Evidence: Make Inferences About Character (10 Min.), p. 211** RL.K.1, RL.K.3, SL.K.3	**Read-Aloud Handbook** **Shared Readings:** "Little Bo-Peep," p. 13 **Read Aloud and Shared Reading (20 Min.), p. 215** RL.K.1, RL.K.3, RF.K.3b, RF.K.4, SL.K.3, L.K.1c • Fluency: Prosody/Pitch • Build Concepts: Every Story Has Characters • Review Phonics: Initial and Medial Short a • Review Language: Form Regular Plural Nouns Goldilocks and the Three Bears The Little Red Hen **Compare and Contrast Fantasy Characters (15 Min.), p. 216** RL.K.9, SL.K.2, SL.K.3	**Read-Aloud Handbook** **Shared Readings:** "New Friends," p. 12 **Read Aloud and Shared Reading (20 Min.), p. 221** RL.K.1, RL.K.3, RF.K.3a, RF.K.3c, RF.K.4 • Fluency: Prosody/Pitch • Build Concepts: Every Story Has Characters • Review Phonics: Initial and Final n • Review High-Frequency Words: *the, like* **Unit 2 Video** **Reflect on Unit Concepts (20 Min.), p. 226** SL.K.2, SL.K.2a, SL.K.3, SL.K.4, SL.K.6
Write an Opinion (10 Min.), p. 212 W.K.1, W.K.8, SL.K.1a, SL.K.1b, L.K.1c • Build Language: Form Regular Plural Nouns	**Write a Comparison and Contrast Text (15 Min.), p. 218** RL.K.9, W.K.2, W.K.8, L.K.1c • Build Language: Form Regular Plural Nouns	**Revise and Edit a Response to the Essential Question (15 Min.), p. 222** W.K.2, W.K.5, W.K.6, W.K.8, L.K.1a, L.K.1b
Focus Skill: n/n/ (20 Min.), p. 214 RF.K.2d, RF.K.3a, RF.K.3c • Phonological Awareness: Phoneme Isolation • High-Frequency Words: *I, like, the, we, see, go*	**Focus Skill: n/n/ (20 Min.), p. 220** RL.K.1, RL.K.10, RF.K.2a, RF.K.3a, RF.K.3c, RF.K.4 • Phonological Awareness: Recognize and Produce Rhyme • High-Frequency Words: *I, like, the, we, see, go*	**Focus Skill: n/n/ (20 Min), p. 224** RL.K.1, RL.K.10, RF.K.2c, RF.K.3a, RF.K.3c, RF.K.4, L.K.1a • Phonological Awareness: Blend Onset and Rime • High-Frequency Words: *I, like, the, we, see, go*

Build Knowledge and Review Week 1
Strategies (10 MIN. RL.K.3, SL.K.1a, SL.K.1b

**Mentor Read-Aloud Topic
Introduction Vol. 1, pp. 12-13**

Student Objectives

I will be able to:
- Discuss materials I have listened to or read.
- Take part in discussions by asking and answering questions.
- Review reading strategies I have learned.

(iELD) Integrated ELD

Light Support

Have students answer questions to retell the events of "The Little Helper" in order.

Ask: *What major events happened in the beginning of the story? What happened in the middle? What happened at the end?*

Moderate Support

Have partners review story events for "The Little Helper" by listing major events in order in the chart below using the signal words. When they finish, have them alternate telling the events in order.

First,	the mouse	
Then,	the lion	
Next,	the mouse	
The next day,	the lion	
Finally,	the mouse	

Substantial Support

Review major story events for "The Little Helper" with students by collaborating to fill in the sentence frames below.

Ask: *What were the major events?*
Remind students to put events in the correct order.
Have students choral-read the completed sentences.

1. First, the mouse _____ the lion.
2. Then, the lion _____ the mouse.
3. Next, the mouse _____ the lion to let him go.
4. The next day, the lion gets _____ in a net.
5. Finally, the mouse _____ the lion.

Word Bank: begs, helps, grabs, trapped, wakes

ELD.PI.K.1, ELD.PI.K.12a, ELD.PII.K.1

Discuss the Essential Question

Display the Topic 2 Introduction and read aloud the essential question. Then flip through the Week 1 selections. Ask students to turn and talk to a partner what they have learned about how characters and people are different. Tell them to use the sentence frame:

I learned _____.

Ask volunteers to share what their partners said. Then explain that in Week 3, students will read stories with different characters.

Review Week 1 Strategies (iELD)

Identify Major Story Events. Remind students that during Week 1, they learned how to identify major story events. Display "The Little Helper."

Say: *Remember we named important events that happened at the beginning, middle, and end of the story. At the beginning of the story, the mouse went up what he thought was a hill, but it was the sleeping lion's back! The lion grabbed the mouse.*

Page through the rest of the story with students as you guide them to identify major events from the middle and end of the story.

Make Inferences about Character. Also remind students that they practiced making inferences about characters.

Say: *When we read a story, we have to make inferences about characters. An inference is a conclusion. Like a detective, you look for clues. You think about what the author tells you about the character. You also think about what you know. Then you make an inference about what the character feels or why the character acts a certain way.*

Reread the second paragraph on page 18 and help students recall the inference they made about the lion's feelings, based on the author's use of the word **roared**.

Tell students this week they will continue to practice identifying story events and making inferences about character. Doing so will help them understand the text they will hear this week.

RL.K.3 With prompting and support, identify characters, settings, and major events in a story., **SL.K.1a** Follow agreed-upon rules for discussions (e.g., listening to others and taking turns speaking about the topics and texts under discussion)., **SL.K.1b** Continue a conversation through multiple exchanges.

Read Aloud and Shared Reading

(20 MIN.) RL.K.1, RL.K.3, RL.K.10, RL.K.10a, RL.K.10b, RF.K.1a, RF.K.3a, RF.K.4, SL.K.3

Read Aloud

To support the unit concept, use one of the Read-Aloud Handbook selections for Unit 2. As you read, model the metacognitive strategy for the unit, Visualize, guided by the samples provided. You may also wish to select a favorite read-aloud from your classroom or school library. To support the unit concept, use one of the suggested titles for Unit 2.

Shared Reading (iELD)

Introduce the Realistic Fiction

Display "New Friends." Read aloud the title as you point under each word. As a few volunteers to tell what they know about making new friends. Then invite students to turn to a partner and tell what they predict the story will be about. Invite a few students to share their predictions with the whole class.

Read the Realistic Fiction

First reading. Read aloud the realistic fiction fluently and expressively, pointing under each word.

Reread for Fluency: Prosody/Pitch. Read aloud the text and emphasize the rising pitch in your voice as you read the question at the end of the text. Explain that your voice goes up at the question mark at the end of a sentence. Choral read the last sentence. Provide corrective feedback and/or validate students' efforts.

Build Concepts: Every Story Has Characters

Pose questions to connect the text to the unit concept. For example:

- *How are the characters alike?*
- *How are the characters different?*
- *Could these characters exist in real life? How do you know?*

Model Print Concepts: Directionality: Left to Right

Remind students that we read from left to right. Ask a volunteer to show you where to begin reading the selection. Then point to the first word, read it aloud, and ask students to show where to read next. Encourage volunteers to point under each word to emphasize reading from left to right.

Review Phonics: Initial and Final *t*

Highlight the word *to* in the first sentence. Read the word aloud. Then have students read the word aloud with you. Ask a volunteer to name the letter at the beginning of *to*. Then ask another volunteer to say the sound the letter *t* stands for. Repeat with *town, tag,* and *Tess.* Then repeat for final *t* using the words *sat* and *at.*

Read-Aloud Handbook   **Shared Reading Vol. 1, p. 12 "New Friends"**

Student Objectives

I will be able to:
- Answer questions about characters in a story.
- Read along with the correct pitch.
- Follow words from left to right and top to bottom.
- Identify words with initial and final *t.*

(iELD) Integrated ELD

Light Support
Display the story and read it aloud. Model raising your pitch as you read the question. Have partners alternate reading the sentences aloud for the group. Then have partners extend practice by making up questions and statements about the story and saying them orally with correct pitch (inflection).

Moderate Support
Display "New Friends." Read it aloud. Point out the question mark and how you raised your pitch to read the question. Choral-read with the whole group 2–3 times. Then have partners practice alternating reading each sentence. Correct pronunciation and inflection as needed.

Substantial Support
Display "New Friends." Read it aloud. After you finish, call attention to the question mark and how you raised your pitch to read the question. Then choral-read "New Friends" with students. Model using expression in your voice. Have volunteers reread the last two sentences in succession to emphasize the difference in pitch (inflection) between a statement and a question.

ELD.PI.K.9, ELD.PI.K.12a, ELD.PII.K.2

RL.K.1 With prompting and support, ask and answer questions about key details in a text., **RL.K.3** With prompting and support, identify characters, settings, and major events in a story., **RL.K.10** Actively engage in group reading activities with purpose and understanding., **RL.K.10a** Activate prior knowledge related to the information and events in texts. CA, **RL.K.10b** Use illustrations and context to make predictions about text. CA, **RF.K.1a** Follow words from left to right, top to bottom, and page by page., **RF.K.3a** Demonstrate basic knowledge of letter-sound correspondences by producing the primary or most frequent sound for each consonant., **RF.K.4** Read emergent-reader texts with purpose and understanding., **SL.K.3** Ask and answer questions in order to seek help, get information, or clarify something that is not understood.

The Little Red Hen

Student Objectives

I will be able to:

- Identify and name features of fantasy.
- Make predictions about *The Little Red Hen*.
- Listen for a purpose.
- Link my ideas to the ideas of others.
- Retell key events about the hen's actions.

Additional Materials

Weekly Presentation

- Story Events Chart

Observation Checklist for Collaborative Conversation

As partners discuss the key events from the story, use the questions below to evaluate how effectively students communicate with each other. Based on your answers, you may wish to plan future core lessons to support the collaborative conversation process.

Do partners . . .

❏ stay on topic throughout the discussion?

❏ listen respectfully?

❏ build on the comments of others appropriately?

❏ pose or respond to questions to clarify information?

❏ support their partners to participate?

The Little Red Hen: Listen and Retell
Key Details (10 MIN.) RL.K.1, RL.K.2, RL.K.5, RL.K.6, RL.K.10, RL.K.10a, RL.K.10b, SL.K.1a, SL.K.1b, SL.K.2, SL.K.3, SL.K.6

Preview the Genre

Display the cover of *The Little Red Hen*. Read aloud the title. Ask students if they know the story. Read the name of the author. Remind students that the author is the person who wrote the words in the story. Explain that the words **retold by** let us know that the story is a familiar story that has been told before. The author, Brenda Parkes, retells the familiar story in her own way. Read aloud the name of the illustrator. Remind students that the illustrator is the person who drew the illustrations. Read each name aloud again and have students repeat.

Preview the pages. Guide students as they consider the genre. Ask students to turn and tell a partner the name of the author and illustrator and their roles. Also ask them to predict what kind of story they will read and what it will be about.

Sample Fantasy Feature	Sample Predictions
• title • illustrations • some characters are animals with human characteristics	I predict the story... • will be a fantasy • will be about a hen that plants wheat and makes her own bread.

Read Aloud the Text (iELD)

Tell students that you will read the selection aloud. Ask them to listen carefully to identify characters and major events in the story. Explain that this is their purpose for listening. Read aloud with minimal interruption. Model using an appropriate voice for each character. Also model reading the words in bold type in a voice that matches the words. Remind students of their predictions. Invite them to tell if their predictions were correct.

💬 Collaborative Conversation: Peer Group

Ask students to recall key events from the text. Model how students can build on the group's talk by listening carefully and linking their ideas to what they have said. For example, *I agree with _____ that _____ happened at the beginning of the story. _____ is another important event that happened at the beginning of the story.*

Share

Invite students to share the key events they recalled. Record them on a class key events chart and reread the part of the text where the idea was mentioned. Draw simple illustrations.

Beginning:	Little Red Hen found a grain of wheat. She asked the duck, the dog, the cat, and the pig to help her plant it. None of them would help. She plants it herself.
Middle:	Little Red Hen asks her friends, "Who will help me cut the wheat?" They all say, "Not I," so she cuts it herself. Little Red Hen asks her friends, "Who will help take the wheat to the mill?" They all say, "Not I," so she takes it herself. Little Red Hen asks her friends who will help her make and bake the bread. They all say, "Not I," so she makes and bakes it herself.
End:	Little Red Hen asks her friends, "Who will help me eat the bread?" They all say, "I will," but she eats it herself.

Sample Story Events Chart

Reinforce or Reaffirm the Strategy

Provide modeling and/or engage students in self-reflection to build metacognitive awareness.

IF…	THEN…
students need support to retell key events from the text…	**Model to reinforce the strategy.** • *I need to retell important events from the beginning, middle, and end of the story. First, I think about what happened at the beginning. Little Red Hen found a grain of wheat. That's what started all of the other events, so I know it is important. I'll write that in the chart.* • *I look back at the story and the illustrations. The hen asks each of her friends to help plant the wheat. They all tell her no, so she plants it herself.* • *This story is a pattern. The hen asks her friends for help, and they tell her know. Recognizing this pattern helps me remember the events in the middle of the story.* Continue to model how to find key events in the rest of the story.
students independently retell key events…	**Invite partners to reflect on their strategy by discussing the following questions:** • *How did you decide what important events happened at the beginning of the story?* • *How did you separate the middle events from the events that occurred at the end of the story?* • *Explain how you decided _____ was a key event.* Lead partners to present their key events and explain how they found them.

☑ Show Your Knowledge

Name a story event and ask students to act it out. Then have them tell if the event is from the beginning, middle, or end of the story.

 Integrated ELD

Light Support

Have partners work together to make predictions based on the illustrations and text.

Do you think the animals will help Red Hen plant the seed? Why or why not?

Do you think anyone will ever help Red Hen? Why or why not?

What change do you see in the illustrations at the end? How does this you make predictions?

Encourage partners to connect their reasons and predictions using **so** and **because**.

Moderate Support

Display "The Little Red Hen." Have partners preview the text and make predictions based on the illustrations and boldface words. Have them use sentence frames to organize their opinions.

1. *I think that Red Hen will plant the seed with others/ by herself because _____.*
2. *I think that Red Hen will cut the wheat with others/ by herself because _____.*
3. *I think the other animals will help Red Hen when _____.*

Have students ask yes/no questions to identify their reasons.

What do the animals' faces show?
What are the animals doing?
What is Red Hen doing?
Who is helping her?
When do the animals change?

Substantial Support

Display "The Little Red Hen." Have students preview the text and make predictions based on the illustrations. Have them use sentence frames to organize their opinions.

I think that Red Hen will plant the seed with others/by herself because _____ and _____.

Then ask yes/no questions to help students identify their reasons.

Ask: *Does the duck seem like it wants to help?*
Does the dog seem like it wants to help?
Does the cat seem like it wants to help?
Does the pig seem like it wants to help?
Is the little Red Hen alone or with others when she digs a hole?

ELD.PI.K.3, ELD.PI.K.11, ELD.PII.K.6

RL.K.1 With prompting and support, ask and answer questions about key details in a text., RL.K.2 With prompting and support, retell familiar stories, including key details., RL.K.5 Recognize common types of texts (e.g., storybooks, poems, fantasy, realistic text). CA)., RL.K.6 With prompting and support, name the author and illustrator of a story and define the role of each in telling the story., RL.K.10 Actively engage in group reading activities with purpose and understanding., RL.K.10a Activate prior knowledge related to the information and events in texts. CA, RL.K.10b Use illustrations and context to make predictions about text. CA, SL.K.1a Follow agreed-upon rules for discussions (e.g., listening to others and taking turns speaking about the topics and texts under discussion)., SL.K.1b Continue a conversation through multiple exchanges., SL.K.2 Confirm understanding of a text read aloud or information presented orally or through other media by asking and answering questions about key details and requesting clarification if something is not understood., SL.K.3 Ask and answer questions in order to seek help, get information, or clarify something that is not understood., SL.K.6 Speak audibly and express thoughts, feelings, and ideas clearly.

The Little Red Hen

Student Objectives

I will be able to:
- Identify and share key events from "The Little Red Hen".
- Write key events about what happened to the little red hen.
- Form plural nouns orally.

Integrated ELD

Light Support

Read aloud each statement.

The hen asked many <u>animal</u> to help her plant the wheat. (animals)

None of her <u>friend</u> wanted to help. (friends)

Then have students correct each sentence by using plural nouns as needed. Have volunteers say the correct sentences orally.

Moderate Support

Have students form pairs. Using the sentences shown above, read each sentence aloud and repeat the underlined noun. Have one partner say the plural for the noun. Then have the other partner say the sentence again, this time replacing the singular noun with the plural form. Provide corrective feedback as needed.

Substantial Support

Read the following key event statements from "The Little Red Hen" aloud.

The hen asked many <u>animal</u> to help her plant the wheat. (animals)

None of her <u>friend</u> wanted to help. (friends)

Tell students which noun to make plural. Have students say the plural form of the noun aloud. Then choral-read the sentence using the plural form of the noun.

ELD.PI.K.12a, ELD.PII.K.3a, ELD.PII.K.4

Write Key Events (10 MIN.) W.K.2, W.K.6, W.K.8, SL.K.1a, SL.K.1b, SL.K.4, L.K.1a, L.K.1c

Engage Thinking

Display and reread the key events chart with students. Remind them that they retold events from the beginning, middle, and end of the story. Tell them that today, you will work together to write key events from the story.

Ask: *What event did you most enjoy? Why?*

Collaborative Conversation: Partner

Ask students to turn and talk to a partner. They should tell their partner one event from the story that they enjoyed hearing. Model sentence frames students may use in their conversation.

Sample modeling: *My partner and I take turns talking. I listen when my partner talks. When it is my turn to talk, I tell an event from the story. I might say, "I liked it when the little Red Hen asked her friends, 'Who will help me eat the bread?' Her friends all said, 'I will,' but she ate it herself!" You can start your sentence with, "I liked it when..."*

Give students two minutes to share their ideas. Then bring them together and ask volunteers to share the key events they discussed with their partners.

Write as a Group

Work with students to agree on an event to write as a class. Rehearse the sentences to help students internalize them. Then model how you write each sentence. As you write, engage students in the writing process by modeling and/or prompting them with questions. For example:

- *Do we tell an important event?*
- *Did name the important character?*
- *Let's make sure we started our sentence with a capital letter.*
- *How do we end our sentence?*

When the writing is complete, read the sentences aloud fluently as you point under each word.

Sample Shared Writing

The hen found a grain of wheat.
None of her friends helped her plant it, take it to the mill, or make the bread.
She ate the bread herself.

Build Language: Form Regular Plural Nouns

Remind students that a noun is a word that names a person, place, or thing. Explain that *hen* is a noun. It names one animal. If you want to tell about more than one hen, you add *–s* to the end of the word. *Hens* means more than one hen. Say a singular noun. Use the word in a sentence. Then ask students to orally form the plural by adding /s/ or /z/ *(–s, –es)* to the end of the word. Use the plural noun in a sentence. Possible nouns and sentences are in the chart below

Singular Noun	Plural Noun
friend (I have one friend.)	friends (Today I made two friends.)
grain (The hen found one grain of wheat.)	grains (The farmer has many grains of wheat.)
house (The hen went to one house.)	hen (The hen went to four houses.)
box (The hen had a box of sugar.)	boxes (The hen had two boxes of sugar.)

☑ Write Independently

Tell students that during independent time, you would like for them to draw one key event. Tell them they label or dictate a sentence for their picture.

Small-Group Differentiated Instruction (15 MIN. per Group)

Meet with Small Groups

Select small-group reading titles or activities based on students' needs. See the Small-Group Instructional Planner for titles that support a range of instructional levels within the unit topic. Remind students to apply skills and strategies they learned to their small-group reading experiences.

Say: *Remember that finding key events helps you understand and remember a story. Finding key events in an informational text helps you understand the information. As you listen and read texts today, ask yourself, "What are the key details or events?" Look at the illustrations or photos to help you learn the key events and details.*

Whole-Group Reflect and Share

Bring the class back together. Ask volunteers to share key details or key events they read or heard today. Ask them how they identified each key detail or event.

W.K.2 Use a combination of drawing, dictating, and writing to compose informative/explanatory texts in which they name what they are writing about and supply some information about the topic., **W.K.6** With guidance and support from adults, explore a variety of digital tools to produce and publish writing, including in collaboration with peers., **W.K.8** With guidance and support from adults, recall information from experiences or gather information from provided sources to answer a question., **SL.K.1a** Follow agreed-upon rules for discussions (e.g., listening to others and taking turns speaking about the topics and texts under discussion)., **SL.K.1b** Continue a conversation through multiple exchanges., **SL.K.4** Describe familiar people, places, things, and events and, with prompting and support, provide additional detail., **L.K.1a** Print many upper- and lowercase letters., **L.K.1c** Form regular plural nouns orally by adding /s/ or /es/ (e.g., dog, dogs; wish, wishes).

Student Objectives

I will be able to:
- Isolate initial sound **/n/**.
- Identify letter-sound correspondences for **n/n/**.
- Review the sounds **/t/, /s/, /m/,** and **/a/**.
- Sort picture names with initial **n /n/, t /t/, s /s/,** and **m/m/**.
- Blend sounds **/m/, /a/, /n/** and **/t/, /a/, /n/**.
- Read previously taught high-frequency words: **I, like, the, we, see, go.**
- Write **Nn**.

Additional Materials

- Poetry poster: "Nip the Newt"
- Letter cards: **a,m, n, t**
- Sound-spelling cards: **Aa, Mm, Nn, Ss, Tt**
- For additional practice, see Pre-Decodable Readers: *We Like Baseball, We Plant*

Weekly Presentation
- Picture cards: **napkin, nest, notebook, nut, sandwich, sock, sun, tiger, top, tub**
- Frieze cards: **Aa, Mm, Nn, Ss, Tt**
- High-frequency word cards: **I, like, the, we, see, go**

Focus Skill: n/n/ (20 MIN.) RF.K.2d, RF.K.3a, RF.K.3c, L.K.1a

Phonological Awareness: Phoneme Isolation

Model/Practice
Display frieze card **Nn**.

Say: *Listen for the sound at the beginning of this word,* **nest.** *Say the sound with me,* **/nnn/. Nest** *has* **/nnn/** *at the beginning.*

Say the words **newt, nice, nap** and have students repeat. Emphasize the **/n/** sound.

Say: *I am going to read the poem Nip the Newt. Listen to the* **/n/** *sound in this sentence:* **Nip the Newt is nice and neat.**

Reread the poem.

Say: *Touch your nose each time you hear* **/n/** *at the beginning of a word. Touch your chin when you hear* **/n/** *at the end of a word.*

Letter-Sound Correspondences

Introduce: *Nn*
Display frieze card **Nn**.

Say: *This is the* **nest** *card. The sound is* **/n/**. *The* **/n/** *sound is spelled with the letter* **n**. *Say the sound with me,* **/nnn/**. *This is the sound at the beginning of the word* **nest**. *What is the name of this letter?* (**n**) *What sound does this letter stand for?* (**/n/**)

Model: *Nn*
Reread the poem "Nip the Newt" and invite students to read along with you. Point to words in the poem that begin with the letter **n**. Say each word aloud.

Practice: *Nn*
Place letter cards **n, t,** and **s** in the pocket chart.

Place picture cards **nest, tiger,** and **sun** under the corresponding letters while you say the name of the letter and picture.

Hold up the picture card **napkin**. Have students say **napkin** with you. Ask if **napkin** begins like **nest, tiger,** or **sun**.

Place picture card **napkin** under the letter card **n**.

Say: Nnnapkin *begins like* **nnnest,** *so I am putting picture card* **napkin** *under the letter* **n**.

Repeat with picture cards **notebook, nut, top, tub, sandwich,** and **sock**.

Blend Sounds

Review: *Mm, Aa, Ss, Tt, Nn*

Hold up frieze cards *Mm, Aa, Ss, Tt,* and *Nn*. Ask students to say the sound each letter stands for.

Model: *man*

Place letter cards *m, a, n* in a pocket chart. Point to the letter *m*.

Say: *This is the letter* **m**. *The letter* **m** *stands for* /**mmm**/. *Say* /**mmm**/. *This is the letter* **a**. *The letter* **a** *stands for* /**aaa**/. *Say* /**aaa**/. *Listen as I blend the two sounds together,* /**mmmaaa**/. *Blend the sounds with me. This is the letter* **n**. *The letter* **n** *stands for* /**nnn**/. *Say* /**nnn**/. *Listen as I blend all three sounds together,* /**mmmaaannn**/. *Now blend the sounds to read the word* **man**.

Practice: *tan*

Repeat the routine for the word *tan*. Move your hand from left to right under the word. Have students blend and read *tan*.

High-Frequency Words

Review: *I, like, the, we, see, go*

Display the high-frequency word card *go*. Point to it and read the word.

Use the following routine: Point to each letter in the word and have students say the letter name with you. Guide children to read *go*.

Repeat with the words *I, like, the, we, see.*

Handwriting

Write and identify uppercase and lowercase *Nn.* Hold up your writing hand. Write uppercase and lowercase *Nn*. Trace the letters as you say /**nnn**/.

Then have students write *N* and *n* in the air as they say /**nnn**/ several times. Finally have students write both forms of the letter several times, saying /**nnn**/ every time they write the letter.

(iELD) Integrated ELD

Light Support

Students identify the words on the picture side of the **Nn** frieze card as well as other initial **n** words around the room.

Model the initial continuous sound /**n**/. Point to pictures or objects that begin with **n** and have volunteers say the words.

Challenge students to name other words they know that begin with the **n** sound. Write words on the board, or have volunteers write them if they can. Have students then use as many of the **n** words as possible in original sentences.

Moderate Support

Have partners identify the words on the picture side of the **Nn** frieze card or other words with the initial /**n**/ around the classroom.

Model the initial /**n**/ sound (/**nnnn**/). Say each **n** word slowly and have students repeat after you. Practice with different words until students can pronounce the initial /**n**/ sound correctly.

Then write **Nn** words on the board. Partners take turns pointing to the picture (or object) for the word, saying the word, and underlining the initial **n** in the word written on the board. Encourage one partner to use an **n** word in an oral sentence. The other partner can add other **n** words to embellish the original sentence. (Example: notebook; That is a nice notebook; That is a nice new notebook.)

Substantial Support

Work with students to identify the words on the picture side of the **Nn** frieze card. Point to the picture and have a volunteer say the word. Repeat to model and reinforce correct pronunciation. Introduce the words yourself if necessary.

Model the /**n**/ sound while pointing to objects in the room that begin with **Nn**. Model the continuous /**n**/ sound (/**nnnn**/) to emphasize the sound. Have students say the words chorally. Write each word on the board, and have volunteers underline the initial **n** in each word. Use each word in a sentence, and encourage volunteers to do the same, using gestures or pictures if needed

ELD.PIII.K.2d, ELD.PIII.K.3a

RF.K.2d Isolate and pronounce the initial, medial vowel, and final sounds (phonemes) in three-phoneme (consonant-vowel-consonant, or CVC) words.*(This does not include CVCs ending with /l/, /r/, or /x/.), **RF.K.3a** Demonstrate basic knowledge of letter-sound correspondences by producing the primary or most frequent sound for each consonant., **RF.K.3c** Read common high-frequency words by sight (e.g., the, of, to, you, she, my, is, are, do, does)., **L.K.1a** Print many upper- and lowercase letters.

Read-Aloud Handbook

New Friends

Nick had just moved to town.
He sat and watched the kids play tag.
Tess saw Nick and waved at him.
"Would you like to play?" she called.

**Shared Reading Vol. 1, p. 12
"New Friends"**

Student Objectives

I will be able to:
• Read along with the correct pitch.
• Answer questions about friends.
• Identify initial and final *n*.
• Recognize words I know in different texts.

(iELD) Integrated ELD

Light Support
Challenge students to make inferences about the characters based on the text and picture.
Ask: *Who are the most important characters in the story? How would you describe Nick? How would you describe Tess? Do you think Nick had fun playing with the children?*

Moderate Support
Have partners use nouns and adjectives from the word bank to answer the questions about the characters.
Ask: *Who is the main character in the story? Who is another character in the story? How does Nick feel after Tess waves at him?*
Word Bank: Boy, Nick, Tess, sad, happy.

Substantial Support
Look at "New Friends" with students. Have students use sentence frames and the word bank to answer the questions and describe the characters.
Ask: *Who is the story mostly about?*
The story is mostly about a _____ named _____.
Ask: *Who is the other main character in the story?*
The other main character is _____.
Ask: *How does Nick feel when watching the other children play?*
Nick feels _____.
Ask: *How do you think Nick feels after Tess waves at him?*
I think Nick feels _____
Word Bank: Boy, Nick, Tess, sad, happy.

ELD.PI.K.5, ELD.PI.K.6, ELD.PII.K.4

Read Aloud and Shared Reading

(20 MIN.) RL.K.1, RL.K.3, RF.K.3a, RF.K.3c, RF.K.4, SL.K.3

Read Aloud

To support the unit concept, use one of the Read-Aloud Handbook selections for Unit 2. As you read, model the metacognitive strategy for the unit, Visualize, guided by the samples provided. You may also wish to select a favorite read-aloud from your classroom or school library. To support the unit concept, use one of the suggested titles for Unit 2.

Shared Reading (iELD)

Reread the Realistic Fiction
First rereading. Read aloud the realistic fiction fluently and expressively, pointing under each word.

Reread for Fluency: Prosody/Pitch. Read aloud the text emphasizing using a lower pitch for the first and second sentences to stress the loneliness. Read the third sentence with a higher pitch, and read the question with rising inflection. Explain when reading a text you can stress emotions with the tone of your voice. Have the class choral read the second and third sentences with you. Provide corrective feedback and/or validate students' efforts.

Build Concepts: Every Story Has Characters
Pose questions to connect the text to the unit concept. For example:

• *How would you describe Tess's actions towards Nick?*
• *Have you ever felt like Nick?*
• *Do you think Nick joined the others for a game of tag? Why or why not?*

Review Phonics: Initial and Final *n*
Highlight the word *New* in title. Read the word aloud. Then ask students to read the word aloud with you. Ask volunteers to name the letter at the beginning of *New*. Point out that it is a capital *N*. Ask students to say the sound the letter *n* stands for. Repeat with *Nick*. Then repeat for final *n* using the word *town*.

Review High-Frequency Words: *the, like*
Tell students that this text contains some words they have learned. Point to the previously taught high-frequency word *the*. Ask students to turn to a partner and tell their partner the high-frequency word. Repeat with the word *like*. Remind students to look for high-frequency words they know when they read a new text.

RL.K.1 With prompting and support, ask and answer questions about key details in a text., **RL.K.3** With prompting and support, identify characters, settings, and major events in a story., **RF.K.3a** Demonstrate basic knowledge of letter-sound correspondences by producing the primary or most frequent sound for each consonant., **RF.K.3c** Read common high-frequency words by sight (e.g., the, of, to, you, she, my, is, are, do, does)., **RF.K.4** Read emergent-reader texts with purpose and understanding., **SL.K.3** Ask and answer questions in order to seek help, get information, or clarify something that is not understood.

©2017 Benchmark Education Company, LLC

Build Vocabulary: Shades of Meaning (10 MIN.) RL.K.1, L.K.5d

Engage Thinking

Remind students that they practiced using verbs, or action words, that tell about the same action.

Ask: *What are some different ways you can move from one place to another?*

Review that verbs such as walk, run, craw, and jog all tell about different ways we move.

Model

Display *The Little Red Hen*. Begin by reading aloud page 2. Model how to identify verbs that identify how the characters speak.

Sample modeling: *The author says the hen "asked the duck." The word* **asked** *tells me the hen asked a question. I keep reading. The author writes, "Not I," quacked the duck.* **Quacked** *tells me how the duck answered. In this story,* **asked** *and* **quacked** *are both verbs that tell how the characters spoke.*

Guided Practice (iELD)

Continue reading pages 3–6. Guide students to identify all of the verbs the author uses to name how the characters speak (barked, meowed, grunted, said). Identify the character associated with each verb. Provide prompts as necessary. For example:

- *What does a dog sound like in real life? Is the dog in the story talking?*
- *The author uses an animal sound to tell how each character speaks, except for the hen. Why might the author use the word* **said** *to tell us how the hen speaks?*

Verb	Character	Reason for use
barked	dog	It is what we would expect from a dog. The dog speaks, but in a short, barky way.
meowed	cat	It is what we would expect from a cat. The cat speaks, but in a long, whiny way.
grunted	pig	It is what we would expect from a pig. The pig speaks, but in a messy, lazy way.
said	hen	The hen does not cluck or make a sound like a hen. The author uses *said* to let readers know the hen is serious.

☑ Show Your Word Knowledge (iELD)

Ask partners to imitate a character from the story and speak in a way that matches the verb the author used for that character.

Challenge Activity Have partners name another action word that tells how a character might speak.

RL.K.1 With prompting and support, ask and answer questions about key details in a text., L.K.5d Distinguish shades of meaning among verbs describing the same general action (e.g., walk, march, strut, prance) by acting out the meanings.

The Little Red Hen

Student Objectives

I will be able to:
- Understand the meaning of verbs with similar meanings.

(iELD) Integrated ELD

Light Support

Have students work in pairs. Have them repeat the following sentence after you:
The duck was quacking.
Point out that the action word "quacked" from the story is now "was quacking." Use the clause in a sentence.
Ask: *When was the duck making this noise?*
Prompt students to respond with a past-tense verb, for example "When the hen asked for help." Challenge students to turn the other three action words (**barked, meowed, grunted**) into the corresponding past participle.

Moderate Support

Have students work in pairs. Review with them the past-tense verbs **quacked, barked, meowed**, and **grunted**. Have them repeat the following sentences after you:
The duck quacked. The dog barked.
The cat meowed.   The pig grunted.
Have partners take turns making the sound of each animal and naming the sound in a complete sentence. Model an appropriate dialogue.
Question: *What animal made this sound?*
Answer: *The [duck] made that sound. The [duck quacked].*

Substantial Support

Have students work in pairs. Review with them the present-tense verbs **quack, bark, meow**, and **grunt**. Have them repeat the following sentences after you:
Quack! says the duck. Bark! says the dog.
Meow! says the cat.   Grunt! says the pig.
Ask partners to take turns making one of the animal sounds and naming the sound using one of the verbs they have rehearsed.

ELD.PI.K.1, ELD.PI.K.5, ELD.PII.K.3b

The Little Red Hen

Student Objectives

I will be able to:
- Identify characters, setting, and the sequence of major events.
- Use evidence from the text to support my answers.

Additional Materials

Weekly Presentation: Unit 2 Week 3

Observation Checklist for Productive Engagement

Is the Productive Engagement Productive?

As partners discuss story events, look for evidence that they are truly engaged in the task.

Partners are engaged productively if...

- ❏ they ask questions and use feedback to address the task.
- ❏ they demonstrate engagement and motivation.
- ❏ they apply strategies with some success.
- ❏ *If the discussion is productive, continue the task.*

Partners are not engaged productively if...

- ❏ they apply no strategies to the task.
- ❏ they show frustration or anger.
- ❏ they give up.
- ❏ *If the discussion is unproductive, end the task, and*

Find Text Evidence: Story Events (15 MIN.)

RL.K.1, RL.K.2, RL.K.3, SL.K.3

Engage Thinking

Remind students that they have learned to identify the characters and setting in a story. They have also learned to identify major story events from the beginning, middle, and end of a story.

Ask: *How are events arranged in a story? Why does their order matter?*

Explain that students will practice using text evidence to answer questions about a story's events, characters, and setting.

Model

Display and read aloud a text evidence question. Tell students that they first need to understand what the question is asking. Highlight the term *important characters.* Explain that these words help students know they are to identify the important characters. Explain that to answer the second question, students have to tell where the story takes place.

> **Text Evidence Question:** Who are the important characters in the story? What is the setting?

Ask students to listen carefully as you read pages 2–5. Then model how you use the text to help you answer the question.

Sample modeling: *We met many characters. The main character is the Little Red Hen. Other characters are duck, dog, cat, and pig. The author tells us on page 2 that the story takes place in spring. She does not tell us where the story takes place, but I look at the illustrations and think about where a hen, duck, dog, cat, and pig might live. I think the story takes place on a farm.*

Guided Practice

Display and read aloud a second text evidence question. Guide them to focus on the words that will help them answer the question *(major events, beginning)*.

> **Text Evidence Question:** What major events happened to the hen at beginning of the story?

Ask students for events at the beginning of the story as you read aloud pages 2–6. Remind students that a problem is often identified at the beginning of a story. If necessary, reread the text and provide directive feedback. For example:

- *When we tell what events happen at the beginning of the story, we tell what happened first. What happened first in the story?*
- *How do you know this event is from the beginning of the story?*
- *How can the illustrations help you retell important events?*
- *Is this an important event or just an interesting event?*

Highlight the evidence in the text and reread it with students. Then use the text evidence to answer the question.

 Productive Engagement: Partner Activity (iELD)

Display and read aloud a third question. Remind student to listen for words in the question that will help them know what information to look for in the text. Remind them that what happens in the middle of a story is what happens between the beginning events and the end events.

> **Text Evidence Question:** What important events happened to the hen in the middle of the story?

Reread pages 7–14. After reading, ask students to turn and talk to a partner. Partners should discuss the text that supports their answer to the question. Have partners share their findings with the group.

☑ Show Your Knowledge

Ask students to tell the events that happen at the end of the story.

Challenge Activity Ask students to tell how they know which events occur in the middle of the story.

(iELD) Integrated ELD

Light Support

Ask: *What are the steps for making bread from a grain of wheat?*

Encourage students to use ideas from "The Little Red Hen." Have students repeat this statement: *The hen worked to get the bread.* Ask students to give details from the story to support the statement.

Moderate Support

Remind students that at the beginning of "The Little Red Hen," the hen finds a grain of wheat, and at the end, the hen eats some bread.

Ask: *How did the hen get the bread to eat?*

Invite responses. Then, beginning with page 6, turn the pages of the story.

Ask: *What is the hen doing?*

Have students describe each of the hen's actions. When they are done, review the hen's actions in sequence: **planting grain, cutting wheat, taking wheat to the mill, making the bread,** and **baking the bread.**

Have students repeat this statement: The hen worked to get the bread. Then have them give details from the story to support the statement.

Substantial Support

Remind students of what happens at the beginning and the end of "The Little Red Hen."

Say: *At the beginning, the hen finds a grain of wheat. At the end, the hen eats some bread.*

Ask: *How did the hen get the bread to eat?*

Invite responses. Then, beginning with page 6, turn the pages of the story, and encourage students to describe each of the hen's actions. If they have the vocabulary, invite them to also describe the setting of each activity. When they are done, read aloud the following sequence of events and have students repeat after you:

She plants the grain.

She cuts the wheat.

She takes the wheat to the mill.

She makes the bread.

She bakes the bread.

Ask: *What do these steps help the hen do at the end?*

ELD.PI.K.1, ELD.PI.K.6, ELD.PII.K.2

RL.K.1 With prompting and support, ask and answer questions about key details in a text., **RL.K.2** With prompting and support, retell familiar stories, including key details., **RL.K.3** With prompting and support, identify characters, settings, and major events in a story., **SL.K.3** Ask and answer questions in order to seek help, get information, or clarify something that is not understood.

The Little Red Hen

Student Objectives

I will be able to:
• Identify and key events in order.
• Write key events in order from *The Little Red Hen*.
• Form plural nouns orally.

(iELD) Integrated ELD

Light Support
Have students work in pairs. Write the words below on the board, point out that each one is an animal, and have students copy the words. Challenge partners to complete the following sentence frame for each animal, adding descriptive details as they are able:
One _____ [animal] met another _____ [same animal], and then there were two _____ [plural animals].
ladybug, lion, hare, dog

Moderate Support
Write the noun phrases below on the board. After you write each phrase, say it aloud and have students repeat after you. Then ask: How can we say "more than one [sad ladybug]?" As students respond, affirm correct answers and write an **s** at the end of the corresponding word.
sad ladybug, proud hare, selfish duck, happy horse
Ask students to work in pairs. Have each pair take turns pronouncing the singular and plural forms of each noun phrase from the list. Invite students to experiment with forming plurals of other animals from the stories they have heard.

Substantial Support
Write the words below on the board one at a time. After you write each word, say: *This is the word for one [lion]. If there are two, the word is [lions]. What sound do you hear at the end of that word?* (/z/ or /s/)
Complete the list of words. Then say each plural aloud and have students repeat after you.
Ask: *What is the word for "more than one [lion]?"*
As students respond, affirm correct answers.
lion, hare, bear, duck, horse

ELD.PI.K.2, ELD.PI.K.5, ELD.PII.K.4

Write Story Events (10 MIN.) RL.K.1, RL.K.2, RL.K.3, W.K.3, W.K.8, L.K.1c

Engage Thinking

Display pages 2–3 of *The Little Red Hen*. Remind students that they practiced identifying story events from the beginning, middle, and end of the story.

Ask: *How does retelling story events in order help you understand the story?*

Tell students that today they will write story events in order.

💬 Collaborative Conversation: Peer Group

Draw a three-column chart on the board with headings "Beginning," "Middle," and "End." Read the headings with students. Tell them that before you begin to write together, you want them to talk in peer groups for two minutes to discuss the what happened first, next, and last in the story.

Sample modeling: *You may wish to model using sentence frames to support students as they discuss the sequence of events. First _____. Next _____. Last _____.*

Write as a Group

Collaborate with students to agree on events to write. Rehearse the message orally and model how you write in the chart. Engage students in the writing process with question prompts. For example:

• *We start with events that happened at the beginning. Did this event happen first?*
• *The Little Red Hen asked more than one friend to help her. What do we add to the end of **friend** to show more than one?*
• *What do we need at the end of this sentence?*
• *What sound do you hear at the end of the word **hen**? What letter stands for /n/? Let's write it.*
• *Did we tell what happens in the middle of the story?*

Beginning (First)	Middle (Next)	End (Last)
The Little Red Hen found a grain of wheat. She asked her friends to help her plant it. None of them would help her. She planted it herself.	The Little Red Hen asked her friends to help her cut the wheat, take it to the mill, make the bread, and bake the bread. None of them would help her. She did it all herself.	The Little Red Hen asked her friends to help her eat the bread. All of her friends wanted to eat the bread. She ate it by herself!

Build Language: Form Regular Plural Nouns

Remind students that a noun names a person, place, or thing. A plural noun names more than one person, place, or thing. To make a noun plural, we add /s/ or /z/ to the end of the word. Say a sentence and guide students to find the singular noun(s). Ask them to add /s/ or /z/ to the end of the word to form the plural.

Sentence	Plural
The **hen** lives on a **farm**.	hens, farms
The **duck** has a **wish**.	duck, wishes
The **hen** ate one **piece**.	hens, pieces

☑ Write Independently

Tell students that during independent time, you would like them to draw a key event. Tell them they can label or dictate a sentence for their drawing. Students should also identify if the event is from the beginning, middle, or end of the story.

Small-Group Differentiated Instruction (15 MIN. per Group)

Meet With Small Groups

Select small-group reading titles or activities based on students' needs. See the Small-Group Instructional Planner for titles that support a range of instructional levels within the unit topic. Remind students to apply what they learned to their small-group reading experiences.

Say: *Today we continued to practice telling what happened at the beginning, middle, and end of a story. We learned more about identifying characters and setting in a story. We also practiced identifying words that name the same action. As you read and hear stories in small groups, identify the characters, setting, and events. Pay attention to words the author uses to name an action.*

Whole-Group Reflect and Share

Bring the class back together. Ask volunteers to share the characters and setting in stories they read or heard. Encourage them to retell what happened first, next, and last.

RL.K.1 With prompting and support, ask and answer questions about key details in a text., **RL.K.2** With prompting and support, retell familiar stories, including key details., **RL.K.3** With prompting and support, identify characters, settings, and major events in a story., **W.K.3** Use a combination of drawing, dictating, and writing to narrate a single event or several loosely linked events, tell about the events in the order in which they occurred, and provide a reaction to what happened., **W.K.8** With guidance and support from adults, recall information from experiences or gather information from provided sources to answer a question., **RL.K.1c** Form regular plural nouns orally by adding /s/ or /es/ (e.g., dog, dogs; wish, wishes).

Focus Skill: n/n/ (20 MIN.) RF.K.2d, RF.K.3a, RF.K.3c, L.K.1a

Phonological Awareness: Phoneme Isolation

Model/Practice

Show students the picture on the back of the poetry poster and have them name all the objects in the picture. Point to the net in the picture and say the word *net*.

Ask: *What sound do you hear at the beginning of the word?*

Have volunteers point to things in the picture whose name starts with **/n/**.

Say: *Now listen as I say the word* **man**. *I can hear the* /n/ *sound at the end of the word* **man**. *I am going to say some words. If you hear* /n/ *at the beginning of the word, touch your nose. If you hear* /n/ *at the end of the word, touch your chin.*

Use the following words: ***nut, pen, fan, name, night, win.***

Letter-Sound Correspondences (iELD)

Review: a/a/, s/s/, t/t/, n/n/

Hold up frieze cards *Tt, Ss,* and *Aa* one at a time, and have students tell you the sounds the letters stand for. Have students think of words that start with **/t/**. Record the words, underlining the letter *t*. Repeat with words that end with **/t/**. Repeat for **s/s/.**

Next, have students think of words that have the **/a/** sound at the beginning and in the middle. Write these words, circling the **a**.

Hold up frieze card *Nn*, and have students say the letter name and the letter sound.

Reread the poem "Nip the Newt," emphasizing the initial **/n/** sounds. Have volunteers find words that begin with **/n/**. Then find the word that ends with **/n/.**

Blend Sounds

Model: *man*

Place letter cards *m, a, n* in a pocket chart. Point to the letter *m.*

Say: *This is the letter* **m**. *The letter* **m** *stands for* /mmm/. *Say* /mmm/. *This is the letter* **a**. *The letter* **a** *stands for* /aaa/. *Say* /aaa/. *Listen as I blend the two sounds together,* /mmmaaa/. *Blend the sounds with me. This is the letter* **n**. *The letter* **n** *stands for* /nnn/. *Say* /nnn/. *Listen as I blend all three sounds together,* /mmmaaannn/. *Now blend the sounds to read the word, man.*

Practice: *tan*

Repeat the steps for the word *tan*. Move your hand from left to right under the word. Have students blend and read the word *tan.*

Student Objectives

I will be able to:
• Isolate initial and final sound **/n/**.
• Review letter-sound correspondences for *n* **/n/**, *t* **/t/**, *s* **/s/**, *a* **/a/**.
• Blend sounds **/m/, /a/, /n/** and **/t/, /a/, /n/**.
• Read previously taught high-frequency words: ***I, like, the, we, see, go***.
• Write ***Nn***.

Additional Materials

• Poetry poster: "Nip the Newt"
• Letter cards: ***a, m, n, t***

Weekly Presentation
• Frieze cards ***Aa, Nn, Tt, Ss***
• High-frequency word cards: ***I, like, the, we, see, go***

High-Frequency Words

Review: *I, like, the, we, see, go*

Display high-frequency word card *see.* Say the word together.

Say: *I am going to read a sentence. When I say the word* **see***, raise your hand. Then I will hold up the word card. Read the word with me.* **I see my backpack.**

Repeat the routine with each word card and sentence. **I get my coat.** We **get on the bus. I ride** the **bus. We** go **to school. I like school.**

Handwriting

Have students write uppercase and lowercase *Nn*. Observe students' pencil grip and paper position. Have students say **/nnn/** every time they write the letters *Nn*.

iELD Integrated ELD

Light Support

Challenge students to find the sounds **/s/, /t/, /n/,** and **/a/** in the story "New Friends." Ask students to raise their hands when they find one of the sounds. Call on students and have them speak the words, emphasizing the sounds. Write each word on the board.

Have each student come to the board and point to a letter corresponding to one of the sounds. Ask the student to complete the following sentence:
I know that this letter makes the sound _____ because the word is pronounced _____.

Moderate Support

Write **n, t, s,** and **a** on the board. Point to each letter and say the corresponding sound.

Have students listen for the sounds as you read line 3 of "New Friends": *Tess saw Nick and waved at him.* Read each word by itself, and have students tell you when they hear a sound that corresponds to one of the letters on the board.

Finally, read **saw** and **waved.**

Ask: *Does the **a** in these words sound like the **a** in* **and** *and* **at***?*

Have students support their responses with evidence.

Substantial Support

Ask students to listen for **/s/** in the following words and tell you which one has the sound: **Tess, kids.** Repeat as necessary to help students distinguish the **/s/** in **Tess** from the **/z/** in **kids.**

Remind students that they know a story called "New Friends." Speak each word below and ask the questions shown. Affirm each correct answer, write the word, and circle the letter.

New *What is the sound at the beginning of* **New***? What letter shows that sound?*

Town *What is the sound at the beginning of* **Town***? What letter shows that sound?*

Sat *What is the sound at the beginning of* **Sat***? What letter shows that sound?*

Had *What is the sound in the middle of* **Had***? What letter shows that sound?*

ELD.PI.K.5, ELD.PI.K.6, ELD.PI.K.11

RF.K.2d Isolate and pronounce the initial, medial vowel, and final sounds (phonemes) in three-phoneme (consonant-vowel-consonant, or CVC) words *. (This does not include CVCs ending with /l/, /r/, or /x/.), **RF.K.3a** Demonstrate basic knowledge of letter-sound correspondences by producing the primary or most frequent sound for each consonant., **RF.K.3c** Read common high-frequency words by sight (e.g., the, of, to, you, she, my, is, are, do, does)., **L.K.1a** Print many upper- and lowercase letters.

Read-Aloud Handbook

**Shared Reading Vol. 1, p. 13
"Little Bo-Peep"**

Student Objectives

I will be able to:
- Answer questions about a character in a poem.
- Identify words with initial and final *t*.

(iELD) Integrated ELD

Light Support

Have students review the poem and complete the character and details chart.

Character	Details
Bo-Peep	
sheep	

Then ask the following questions:
- *How do you think Bo-Peep feels about losing her sheep? How do you know?*
- *Do you think Bo-Peep should be worried? Why or why not?*
- *Do you think the sheep will come home? Tell why or why not.*

Then have students predict what they think will happen to Bo-Peep and her sheep.

Moderate Support

Have partners review the text and pictures to identify and describe key characters. Have them fill out a chart like the one above, recording characters' names and key details using pictures, labels, and noun phrases.

Substantial Support

Display "Little Bo-Peep." Read the poem aloud. Remind students that characters are the people or animals that the poem is about.
- Point to the girl on the page and ask, "Who is this?"
- Then ask, "Which other characters are in the poem?" Have students name the sheep or point to the sheep in the illustration.
- "Why can't Little Bo-Peep find her sheep?" Have students use details from the picture to answer.

As you work with students, record characters (Bo-Peep and the sheep) and details in the chart above, using pictures, labels, and/or short noun phrases.

ELD.PI.K.6, ELD.PI.K.11, ELD.PII.K.4

Read Aloud and Shared Reading

(20 MIN.) RL.K.5, RL.K.10, RL.K.10a, RL.K.10b, RF.K.1a, RF.K.3a, RF.K.4, SL.K.3

Read Aloud

To support the unit concept, use one of the Read-Aloud Handbook selections for Unit 2. As you read, model the metacognitive strategy for the unit, Visualize, guided by the samples provided. You may also wish to select a favorite read-aloud from your classroom or school library. To support the unit concept, use one of the suggested titles for Unit 2.

Shared Reading (iELD)

Introduce the Poem

Display "Little Bo-Peep." Read aloud the title of the poem as you point under each word. Ask students if they know the poem. Direct them to the illustration. Then ask them to turn to a partner and predict what they think the poem will be about. Invite partners to share their predictions with the class.

Read the Poem

First reading. Read aloud the poem fluently and expressively, emphasizing the rhythm.

Reread for Fluency: Prosody/Pitch. Model using a low pitch at the beginning of the poem to emphasize the poem's mood and feeling. Read the second two lines with a higher pitch to emphasize the hope and assurance. Reread the poem and invite students to chime in. Provide corrective feedback and/or validate students' efforts.

Build Concepts: Every Story Has Characters

Pose questions to connect the poem to the unit concept. For example:

- *Who is the character in this poem?*
- *What problem does she have?*
- *Does she remind you of another character you have read about? How is she similar? How is she different?*

Review Print Concepts: Directionality: Top to Bottom

Remind students that you read from the top to the bottom. Ask a volunteer to point to the title. Emphasize that the title is what you read first. It is at the top of the page. Read the title, pointing to each word. Then ask another volunteer to tell you where to read next. Continue in this manner until you have read to the end of the poem.

Review Phonics: Initial and Final *t*

Highlight the word **tell** in the second sentence. Read the word aloud. Then have students read the word aloud with you. Ask a volunteer to name the letter at the beginning of **tell**. Then ask another volunteer to say the sound the letter **t** stands for.

RL.K.5 Recognize common types of texts (e.g., storybooks, poems, fantasy, realistic text). CA., **RL.K.10** Actively engage in group reading activities with purpose and understanding., **RL.K.10a** Activate prior knowledge related to the information and events in texts. CA, **RL.K.10b** Use illustrations and context to make predictions about text. CA, **RF.K.1a** Follow words from left to right, top to bottom, and page by page., **RF.K.3a** Demonstrate basic knowledge of letter-sound correspondences by producing the primary or most frequent sound for each consonant., **RF.K.4** Read emergent-reader texts with purpose and understanding., **SL.K.3** Ask and answer questions in order to seek help, get information, or clarify something that is not understood.

Find Evidence: Make Inferences About Character (10 MIN.) RL.K.1, RL.K.3, SL.K.3

Engage Thinking

Invite a volunteer to the front of the room. Ask him or her privately to pretend to cry.

Ask: *How does _____ feel right now? How do you know?*

Model

Display and read aloud the text evidence questions. Help students identify words in the question that help them know what to look for in the text. Explain that they will have to make inferences about the characters in order to answer the questions.

> **Text Evidence Question:** Why does the Little Red Hen repeat, "Then I will do it myself"?

Ask students to listen carefully as you read pages 7-14. Then model how you make an inference about the Little Red Hen to answer the question.

Sample modeling: *I'm going make an inference about why the Little Red Hen repeats, "Then I will do it myself." On page 7, she asks friends for help in cutting the wheat. No one helps her. She says she will do it herself, and she does. I think the Little Red Hen is determined. She wants to make bread. Even though no one will help her with the hard work, she does not give up. She keeps doing the work herself.*

Guided Practice (iELD)

Display and read aloud the text evidence question. Review the words in the questions that help students know what evidence to look for in the text.

> **Text Evidence Question:** Is the Little Red Hen proud of her bread on page 13?

Tell students you will reread pages 10–13. Remind them to think about what the author tells them and what they already know to make an inference about how the Little Red Hen feels about her bread.

- *What has the Little Red Hen done so far to make the bread?*
- *Look at the hen's face in the illustration on page 12. How can you tell she is concentrating and working hard?*
- *How would you feel about bread you had made all by yourself? Look at the hen's face in the illustration on page 13. Is that the way you think Hen feels? Why?*

Show Your Knowledge

Read aloud page 15. Ask students to tell why the Little Red Hen's friends changed their answer to her persistent questions.

RL.K.1 With prompting and support, ask and answer questions about key details in a text., RL.K.3 With prompting and support, identify characters, settings, and major events in a story., SL.K.3 Ask and answer questions in order to seek help, get information, or clarify something that is not understood.

The Little Red Hen

Student Objectives

I will be able to:
- Make inferences about characters.

(iELD) Integrated ELD

Light Support
Have partners review pages 2–8 and make inferences about the characters' actions and feelings. Guide students by asking questions such as the following.
- *What does the hen ask each animal?*
- *How do all the animals respond?*
- *How are their responses different?*

Moderate Support
Have partners focus on pages 2–8 of the story and complete the sentence frames to describe the characters based on the text and pictures. Make sure students focus on the verbs (actions) in the text and what the pictures show to help infer what these words tell about the characters.
- *The hen asks each animal to _____ her plant the grain of wheat. Each animal tells her, "_____ _____."*
- *The animals say they have _____ things to do.*
Ask: *How does each animal say the same thing in different ways?*
Direct students' attention to verbs, such as **quacked** and **barked**.

Substantial Support
Focus on pages 2–8 of *The Little Red Hen*. Display the text. Point out some of the verbs in the text that tell how each animal responds to the hen (**quacked, barked, meowed, grunted**). Have students act out or describe the meaning of each verb.
Ask: *Why would the author use these words instead of the word "said"?*
Direct students' attention to the animals' expressions.
Ask: *What feelings do they show?*
Have students act out the feelings or use words to respond.

ELD.PI.K.6, ELD.PI.K.8, ELD.PII.K.3a

The Little Red Hen

Student Objectives

I will be able to:
- Help write an opinion about *The Little Red Hen*.
- Form regular plural nouns orally.

Integrated ELD

Light Support

Have partners answer the questions orally to create an opinion statement.
What does the hen do to help make the bread?
What do the other animals do?
What does this tell you about the hen? About the other animals?
Does the hen have enough bread for all the animals?
I think it _____ right for the animals to ask for the bread because _____.

Moderate Support

Display *The Little Red Hen.* Have partners complete the chart to draw conclusions about the hen and the other animals.

Action	Hen	Others
plants the grain		
cuts the wheat		
takes wheat to the mill		
bakes bread		
wants to eat bread		

Help students draw the conclusion that the hen does all the work, but the other animals want to share the bread. Have partners complete an opinion statement.

Substantial Support

Display *The Little Red Hen.* Work with students to develop an opinion based on details in the text. Provide picture cards for each animal in the story, including the hen. For each question, have students use the cards to answer the question.
Ask: *Who plants the grain of wheat?*
Who takes the wheat to the mill?
Was it right for the animals to ask for some bread?

ELD.PI.K.3, ELD.PI.K.11, ELD.PII.K.6

Write an Opinion (10 MIN.) W.K.1, W.K.8, SL.K.1a, SL.K.1b, L.K.1c

Engage Thinking (iELD)

Display page 16. Remind students that they made an inference about why the Little Red Hen ate the bread by herself. Explain that today, they will write an opinion about her decision.

Ask: *Do you think the Little Red Hen was right to eat the bread all by herself?*

💬 Collaborative Conversation: Peer Group

Before writing, divide students into peer groups for two minutes to discuss their opinion. Remind students that an opinion is what you believe. There is no right or wrong answer. Provide a model for how to give an opinion about the hen's decision.

Sample modeling: *When I speak in my group, I wait my turn. When I tell my opinion, I can say, "In my opinion, it was right for the Little Red Hen to eat the bread by herself because she did all the work to make it." When you give your opinion, you can start your sentence the same way. "In my opinion, it was (right/wrong) for the Little Red Hen to eat the bread by herself because _____."*

Write as a Group

Collaborate with students to agree on opinion sentences to write. Rehearse the sentences orally and model how to write them. Engage students in the writing process by prompting them with questions. For example:

- *What kind of letter do we use to begin a sentence?*
- *How do we show readers this is the end of a sentence?*
- *When we give our opinion, we have to explain why we think the way we do. What reason can we give to support our opinion?*
- *Is there anything we want to add to our writing?*

Sample Shared Writing
We think the Little Red Hen was right to eat the bread all by herself because she did all the work. She asked her friends to help with the jobs in making the bread but one would help her do the work. So she did not share the bread.

Build Language: Form Regular Plural Nouns

Remind students of the definition of a noun. Ask them to explain how to make a noun mean more than one. Reread the Shared Writing and guide students to identify any plural nouns. Say additional nouns and ask students to add /s/ or /z/ to make each noun plural.

Noun	Plural
slice	slices
grain	grains
pig	pigs

 **Write Independently**

Ask students to draw a picture of the Little Red Hen eating the bread. Then have them label or dictate a sentence to explain their opinion about her eating it by herself.

Small-Group Differentiated Instruction (15 MIN. per Group)

Meet with Small Groups

Select small-group reading titles or activities based on students' needs. See the Small-Group Instructional Planner for titles that support a range of instructional levels within the unit topic. Remind students to apply what they learned to their small-group reading experiences.

Say: *As you read stories in your small groups today, practice making inferences about why characters do they things they do. Remember to think about what the characters say and what you know from your own experiences to make an inference.*

Whole-Group Reflect and Share

Bring the class back together. Ask volunteers to identify characters from the stories they read or heard today. Invite them to tell any inferences they made about the characters' actions or feelings.

W.K.1 Use a combination of drawing, dictating, and writing to compose opinion pieces in which they tell a reader the topic or the name of the book they are writing about and state an opinion or preference about the topic or book (e.g., My favorite book is...)., **W.K.8** With guidance and support from adults, recall information from experiences or gather information from provided sources to answer a question., **SL.K.1a** Follow agreed-upon rules for discussions (e.g., listening to others and taking turns speaking about the topics and texts under discussion)., **SL.K.1b** Continue a conversation through multiple exchanges., **L.K.1c** Form regular plural nouns orally by adding /s/ or /es/ (e.g., dog, dogs; wish, wishes).

Focus Skill: n/n/ (20 MIN.) RF.K.2d, RF.K.3a, RF.K.3c

Phonological Awareness: Phoneme Isolation

Model/Practice

Say the words *nose, nap*, and *time*. Have students repeat the words.

Ask students if they hear the same sound at the beginning of each word. Then ask them to identify the word that starts with a different sound.

Say the words *nice, name,* and *nut*. Have students repeat the words.

Ask students if they hear the same sound at the beginning of each word. Then ask what sound is the same in all three words. Repeat the process with the words *soup, note, nip; noise, night, news; nest, tape, need*.

Letter-Sound Correspondences

Review with Picture Cards

Place picture cards *nest, tub, sun*, and *apple* in the pocket chart. Have students say their names and the sound at the beginning of each name.

Show students picture card *top* and ask them what sound they hear at the beginning of the word. Place picture card *top* under picture card *tub*.

Repeat with picture cards *ant, antelope, tiger, tent, sock, sub, nut, notebook, and napkin*.

Using picture cards *nest* and *sun*, place a letter card *n* under each. Ask students where they hear the /n/ sound in the words *nest* and *sun*. Show students picture cards *pan, nut, notebook*, and *mitten*. Have them sort the pictures by the beginning or ending /n/ sound.

Blend Sounds

Review: *man, tan*

Have students blend the words *man* and *tan*, using the routine from Day One.

High-Frequency Words

Review: *I, like, the, we, see, go*

Write *I, like, the, we, see,* and *go*. Read aloud each word. Then without students seeing, erase a letter in one of the words. Ask students which letter is missing. Replace the letter as students read the word.

Review *I, like, the, we, see, go*

Display each high-frequency word card. Point quickly to each card, at random, and have students read the word as fast as they can.

Student Objectives

I will be able to:
- Isolate initial sound **/n/**.
- Review letter-sound correspondences for **n/n/, t/t/, s/s/, a/a/**.
- Sort picture names with **n/n/, t/t/, s/s/, a/a/**.
- Blend sounds **m/m/, a/a/, n /n/,** and **t/t/, a/a/, n/n/**.
- Read previously taught high-frequency words: **I, like, the, we, see, go**.

Additional Materials

- Letter cards: **a, m, n, t**

Weekly Presentation
- Picture cards: **ant, antelope, apple, mitten, napkin, nest, notebook, nut, pan, sock, sub, sun, tent, tiger, top, tub**
- High-frequency word cards: **I, like, the, we, see, go**

(iELD) Integrated ELD

Light Support

Have students use blank Elkonin boxes and letter cards for **t, s, a, m, n,** and **p** to create as many of their own words as they can. Have students record all the words they create.

Moderate Support

Have multiple letter cards available for **t, s, a, m, n,** and **p**, and make Elkonin boxes to generate new words. Focus on changing the final position.

	a	n

Say: *What word can we make for "a light brown color"?*
1. *What letter can I add? (t)*
2. *What sound does this letter make? (/t/)*
3. *Let's say the word. (/taaannn/)*

Substantial Support

Use Elkonin boxes with students to help them generate words with the /t/, /s/, /a/, /m/, /p/, and /n/ sounds. Have multiple letter cards available for **t, s, a, m, p,** and **n**, and have students follow the routine to make new words.

	a	p

Say: *What word can we make for "a short rest"?*
1. *What letter can I add? (n)*
2. *What sound does this letter make? (/n/)*
3. *Let's say the word. (/nnnaaap/)*

ELD.PI.K.1, ELD.PII.K.3a, ELD.PII.K.4

RF.K.2d Isolate and pronounce the initial, medial vowel, and final sounds (phonemes) in three-phoneme (consonant-vowel-consonant, or CVC) words.* (This does not include CVCs ending with /l/, /r/, or /x/.), **RF.K.3a** Demonstrate basic knowledge of letter-sound correspondences by producing the primary or most frequent sound for each consonant., **RF.K.3c** Read common high-frequency words by sight (e.g., the, of, to, you, she, my, is, are, do, does).

Read Aloud and Shared Reading

(20 MIN.) RL.K.1, RL.K.3, RF.K.3b, RF.K.4, SL.K.3, L.K.1c

Read Aloud

To support the unit concept, use one of the Read-Aloud Handbook selections for Unit 2. As you read, model the metacognitive strategy for the unit, Visualize, guided by the samples provided. You may also wish to select a favorite read-aloud from your classroom or school library. To support the unit concept, use one of the suggested titles for Unit 2.

Read-Aloud Handbook

Shared Reading Vol. 1, p. 13 "Little Bo-Beep"

Shared Reading (iELD)

Reread the Poem

First rereading. Read aloud the poem fluently and expressively, emphasizing the rhythm.

Reread for Fluency: Prosody/Pitch. Model using a low pitch at the beginning of the poem to emphasize the poem's mood and feeling. Read the second two lines with a higher pitch to emphasize the hope and assurance. Reread the poem and invite students to chime in. Provide corrective feedback and/or validate students' efforts.

Build Concepts: Every Story Has Characters

Pose questions to connect the poem to the unit concept. For example:

- *Why do you think the sheep will come home?*
- *What does the author mean by "Wagging their tails behind them"?*
- *Could Little Bo-Peep exist in real life? How do you know?*

Review Phonics: Initial and Medial Short *a*

Highlight the word **has** in the first line of the poem. Read the word and ask students to read it with you. Ask volunteers to name the letter in the middle of **has** and the sound the letter **a** stands for. Repeat for short **a** in **can't** and **wag**.

Review Language: Form Regular Plural Nouns

Point out the word **sheep**. Explain that **sheep** can name one animal. It is also the plural for more than one sheep. Then call attention to the plural noun **tails**. Explain that **tails** means more than one **tail**.

Student Objectives

I will be able to:
- Read along with the appropriate pitch.
- Answer questions about characters in a poem.
- Identify initial and medial short *a*.
- Recognize plural nouns.

(iELD) Integrated ELD

Light Support
Read aloud "Little Bo-Peep." Ask questions to help students discuss how Bo-Peep is supposed to feel at the beginning and at the end of the poem.

Challenge pairs of students to recite the poem with appropriate pitch to express the emotions behind the words. Ask one partner to recite the first two lines and the other to recite the last two lines.

Moderate Support
Read aloud the first two lines of "Little Bo-Peep."
Ask: *What has happened to Bo-Peep? What has happened to her sheep?*
Write **lost** on the board. Ask students to tell you how this experience feels to Bo-Peep. Read the lines again with appropriate distress. Then ask students to recite the lines and match your pitch.

Read aloud lines three and four of "Little Bo-Peep."
Ask: *What do these lines tell Bo-Peep to do? How is Bo-Peep supposed to feel when she hears this advice?*
Read the lines again with a comforting tone. Invite students to speak the lines with you, matching their pitch to yours.

Substantial Support
Read aloud the first two lines of "Little Bo-Peep."
Ask: *What has happened to Bo-Peep? What has happened to her sheep?*
After students respond, write **lost** on the board. Ask students how this experience makes Bo-Peep feel. Reread the first line and emphasize the word **lost**. Have students repeat it after you. Read the second line with exaggerated emotion, and have students repeat. Place students in pairs, and have them practice speaking the lines to each other with the proper pitch.

ELD.PI.K.1, ELD.PI.K.12a, ELD.PII.K.1

RL.K.1 With prompting and support, ask and answer questions about key details in a text., RL.K.3 With prompting and support, identify characters, settings, and major events in a story., RF.K.3b Associate the long and short sounds with the common spellings (graphemes) for the five major vowels.(Identify which letters represent the five major vowels (Aa, Ee, Ii, Oo, and Uu) and know the long and short sound of each vowel. More complex long vowel graphemes and spellings are targeted in the grade 1 phonics standards.) CA, RF.K.4 Read emergent-reader texts with purpose and understanding. SL.K.3 Ask and answer questions in order to seek help, get information, or clarify something that is not understood., L.K.1c Form regular plural nouns orally by adding /s/ or /es/ (e.g., dog, dogs; wish, wishes).

Compare and Contrast Fantasy Characters (15 MIN.) RL.K.9, SL.K.2, SL.K.3

The Little Red Hen

Goldilocks and the Three Bears

Student Objectives

I will be able to:
- Answer compare and contrast questions about two main characters.
- Recognize similarities and differences between Goldilocks and The Little Red Hen.

Additional Materials

Weekly Presentation
- Compare and Contrast Chart

Engage Thinking

Display *Goldilocks and the Three Bears* and *The Little Red Hen.* Remind students that they know both of these texts very well and now they are going to think about both texts together.

Ask: *Who is the main character in each story?*

Tell students in this lesson they will think about how these two characters are alike and how they are different.

Model

Use a three-column chart to create a compare and contrast chart for Goldilocks and the little Red Hen. Review that in the left column and the right column, you will write how the characters are different. In the middle, you will list ways the two characters are alike. Display each text as you think aloud to model how you compare and contrast the two characters.

Sample modeling: *First I'll think about ways the two characters are the same. They are both characters in a fantasy. I'll record that in the chart.*

Sample modeling: *Now I'll think about how the characters are different. The first thing I notice is that the hen is an animal, but Goldilocks is a girl. That's one difference I can write about in the chart.*

Guided Practice (iELD)

Use directive and corrective prompts as needed to guide students to compare and contrast the little Red Hen and Goldilocks.

- *What does the little Red Hen do in the story? What does Goldilocks do? Why?*
- *The little Red Hen asks for help, but she has to do everything for herself. Does anyone help Goldilocks? Is that a similarity or a contrast?*
- *What lesson does the little Red Hen teach her friends? Does Goldilocks teach a lesson? What does she learn?*
- *Are the Little Red Hen and Goldilocks main characters?*

If necessary, continue to model how you make comparisons and contrasts between the little Red Hen and Goldilocks. Collaborate with students to complete the chart. Reread the comparisons and contrasts together.

The Little Red Hen	Both	Goldilocks
An animal character (hen)	Characters in a fantasy	A human character (girl)
Plants wheat and makes bread	Do things on their own	Goes into the bears' home to eat and rest
Teaches her friends a lesson about helping and sharing	Main Character	Learns a lesson about not using what does not belong to you

Sample Compare and Contrast Chart

☑ Show Your Knowledge

Invite partners to take turns telling each other one way the two characters are similar and different. Provide sentence frames, such as *Both the little Red Hen and Goldilocks _____. The little Red Hen _____, but Goldilocks _____.*

(iELD) Integrated ELD

Light Support
Ask: *Does Goldilocks like to eat? Does the Little Red Hen like to eat?*
Challenge students to discuss the different ways the two characters go about getting food. Ask them to use words from the Word Bank in their discussion.

Word Bank

into	out of	with
in	after	from
to	outside	inside
off		

Moderate Support
Ask: *Does Goldilocks like to eat food? Does the Little Red Hen like to eat food?*
Have students orally complete the following sentence frame to respond: *Both Goldilocks and the Little Red Hen _____.*
Ask students to use the stories to describe how the Little Red Hen and Goldilocks get food to eat. Begin with page 14 of *The Little Red Hen*.
Ask: *What did the hen do when the bread was cooked?*
Continue with page 9 of Goldilocks.
Ask: *How did Goldilocks decide which porridge to eat?*
Urge students to use the prepositions **out of, on, with,** and **into** to describe how the two characters got their food.

Substantial Support
Ask: *Does Goldilocks like to eat food? Does the Little Red Hen like to eat food?*
When students respond, have them orally complete this sentence frame: *Both Goldilocks and the Little Red Hen _____.*
Point out that the two main characters do different things and visit different places to get their food. Have students work in pairs. Ask them to use the pictures to retell how Goldilocks and the Little Red Hen get their food. Encourage them to use the prepositions **to**, **into**, and **in** in their narration. Offer sentence stems such as these:
The Little Red Hen went to _____.
She baked the bread in _____.
Goldilocks went into _____.
The bears found Goldilocks in _____.

ELD.PI.K.1, ELD.PI.K.12b, ELD.PII.K.5

RL.K.9 With prompting and support, compare and contrast the adventures and experiences of characters in familiar stories., **SL.K.2** Confirm understanding of a text read aloud or information presented orally or through other media by asking and answering questions about key details and requesting clarification if something is not understood., **SL.K.3** Ask and answer questions in order to seek help, get information, or clarify something that is not understood.

The Little Red Hen

Goldilocks and the Three Bears

Student Objectives

I will be able to:
- Write a comparison and contrast text about two characters in fantasies.
- Use question words.

Additional Materials

Weekly Presentation
- Two Column Chart

Integrated ELD

Light Support

Have students copy the words **Who, What, When, Where, Why,** and **How** on a sheet of paper. Ask students to take turns using the words, along with action words they know, to form questions about the animals and events in *The Little Red Hen*.

Moderate Support

Have students practice asking questions about the animals in *The Little Red Hen*. Write this list on the board:

Who _____? What _____?
When _____? Where _____?
Why _____? How _____?

Help students orally compose questions using each of the question words. Then have the group choose one question for you to write on the board. Write it, have students copy it on their own paper, and have students practice asking it independently.

Substantial Support

Have students practice asking and answering questions about *The Little Red Hen*. Begin by having students repeat each question below with you. After each question, let students answer.

Who helps the Little Red Hen?
When do the animals visit the Little Red Hen?
Why won't the Little Red Hen share the bread?

Point out the question words **Who, When,** and **Why.**

What _____?
Where _____?
How _____?

ELD.PI.K.1, ELD.PI.K.2, ELD.PII.K.3a

Write a Comparison and Contrast Text (15 MIN.) RL.K.9, W.K.2, W.K.8, L.K.1c

Engage Thinking

Display the compare and contrast chart you developed with students, and reread the comparison and contrast information about the little Red Hen and Goldilocks. Tell students that today they will turn information in the chart into an informative/explanatory text that compares and contrast.

Ask: *How can the chart help you plan what you want to write?*

 ## Collaborative Conversation: Partner

Have students turn and talk to a partner briefly to tell one way the little Red Hen and Goldilocks are alike and one way they are different. Encourage students to use complete sentences. Provide a model.

Sample modeling: *I will tell my partner one way the two characters are alike. I can say, "Both the little Red Hen and Goldilocks are the main characters in a fantasy." I also will tell one way the characters are different. I can say, "The little Red Hen made bread by herself but Goldilocks found food and a place to sleep in someone else's house." You can use the same sentence frames when you talk to your partner. Both the little Red Hen and Goldilocks _____. The little Red Hen _____, but Goldilocks _____.*

Have students turn and talk to a partner. Bring students together after two minutes and invite volunteers to share their ideas.

Write as a Group (iELD)

Work with students to agree on a comparison and contrast to write. Rehearse the sentences orally and model how to write it. Encourage students in the writing process by prompting them with questions. For example:

- *We know how to spell the high-frequency word **the**. Let's spell it together.*
- ***Things** is a plural noun. How do we make sure we form a plural noun?*
- *What can we add to this sentence to tell a contrast?*
- *What do we add to the end of the sentence to let readers know the sentence is complete?*
- *Let's reread our sentences. Do we tell one way the characters are alike? Do we tell one way they are different?*

Sample Shared Writing

Both the little Red Hen and Goldilocks do things on their own.
The little Red hen teaches her friends a lesson, but Goldilocks learns a lesson.

Build Language: Understand and Use Question Words

Remind students that they learned to use question words **who, what, when, where, why, how**. Remind them they can use the words to begin a question. Write the words on the board and read them aloud. Explain that good writers keep these questions in mind when they write. Guide students to ask questions related to their writing and the two characters. Remind them to begin each question with a question word.

Sample Question	Sample Answer
Who are we comparing and contrasting?	The little Red Hen and Goldilocks.
What is one way they are alike?	They are both characters in a fantasy.
When does Goldilocks learn a lesson about using things that are not hers?	Goldilocks learns a lesson at the end of the story when the bears wake her up.
Where is Goldilocks in the story?	Goldilocks is in the bears' home in the woods.
Why doesn't the little Red Hen share her bread?	The little Red Hen's friends would not help her make the bread, so she would not share it with them.
How are the little Red Hen and Goldilocks different?	The little Red Hen is an animal, and Goldilocks is a girl.

Sample Two Column Chart

 Write Independently

Tell students that during independent time, they will be able to draw a comparison and contrast about the little Red Hen and Goldilocks. Students can label or dictate their comparisons and contrasts.

Small-Group Differentiated Instruction (15 MIN. per Group)

Meet with Small Groups

Select small-group reading titles or activities based on students' needs. See the Small-Group Instructional Planner for titles that support a range of instructional levels within the unit topic. Remind students to apply what they learned to their small-group reading experiences.

Say: *We have been learning a lot of strategies to help us understand stories. We've practiced identifying characters and story events. We've made inferences about characters. These strategies help us understand the story events. Remember to use these strategies as you listen to texts.*

Whole-Group Reflect and Share

Bring the class back together. Invite volunteers to share the strategies they used during in small-group reading. Guide them to explain inferences they made about characters.

RL.K.9 With prompting and support, compare and contrast the adventures and experiences of characters in familiar stories., **W.K.2** Use a combination of drawing, dictating, and writing to compose informative/explanatory texts in which they name what they are writing about and supply some information about the topic., **W.K.8** With guidance and support from adults, recall information from experiences or gather information from provided sources to answer a question., **L.K.1c** Form regular plural nouns orally by adding /s/ or /es/ (e.g., dog, dogs; wish, wishes).

Pre-Decodable Reader: *I See Nat*

Student Objectives

I will be able to:
- Recognize and produce rhyme.
- Read previously taught high-frequency words: *I, like, the, we, see go.*
- Read decodable text.

Additional Materials

- Pre-decodable reader: *I See Nat*

Weekly Presentation
- High-frequency word cards: *go, I, like, see, the, we*

Monitor Student Reading of Connected Text

As students chorally read the pre-decodable text and answer questions, ask these questions:

Are students able to . . .
- ❏ blend and read *n* words in the text?
- ❏ read new high-frequency words with automaticity?
- ❏ demonstrate comprehension of the text by answering text-based questions?

Based on your observations, you may wish to support students' fluency, automaticity, and comprehension with additional decodable reading practice during intervention time.

Focus Skill: n/n/ (20 MIN.) RL.K.1, RL.K.10, RF.K.2a, RF.K.3a, RF.K.3c, RF.K.4

Phonological Awareness: Recognize and Produce Rhyme (iELD)

Model/Practice
Say the words *fan* and *man*. Tell students that these words rhyme because they have the same sounds at the end.

Say: *Listen to these words:* **fan, man**. *I hear* **/an/** *at the end of* **fan**, *and* **/an/** *at the end of* **man**. *Say the words with me and listen to the ending sounds.*

Say pairs of words and have students repeat the words if the pairs rhyme: *hip, nip; nut, book; bone, phone; net, nice.* Have students say other words that rhyme with **fan** and **man**.

High-Frequency Words

Review: *I, like, the, we, see, go*
Write the words *I, like, the, we, see, go.* Remind students that these are words they have been practicing so that they can read them quickly. Have students read the words aloud several times.

Hold up the high-frequency word card *go* and call on individual students to quickly read the word. Then have the student use the word in an oral sentence. Have the other students clap when they hear *go*. Repeat for the other high-frequency words.

Pre-Decodable Reader: *I See Nat*

Introduce the Book
Point to the title, *I See Nat.* Have students sound out **Nat** as you run your finger under it and then read the title.

Ask: *What do you see on the cover? What does the girl see?*

Read the Book
Display the title page and discuss where Nat is and what he is doing. Students should chorally read the story. Start by having them read the first sentence aloud, blending the decodable word so you can check their reading. Then have students continue to read, blending the decodable words and reading the high-frequency words quickly.

Connect Phonics to Comprehension
When finished reading, ask:

- *What does each person have? What are they watching?*
Turn to a partner and retell the story.

RL.K.1 With prompting and support, ask and answer questions about key details in a text., RL.K.10 Actively engage in group reading activities with purpose and understanding., RF.K.2a Recognize and produce rhyming words., RF.K.3a Demonstrate basic knowledge of letter-sound correspondences by producing the primary or most frequent sound for each consonant., RF.K.3c Read common high-frequency words by sight (e.g., the, of, to, you, she, my, is, are, do, does)., RF.K.4 Read emergent-reader texts with purpose and understanding.

Read Aloud and Shared Reading

(15 MIN.) RL.K.1, RL.K.3, RF.K.3a, RF.K.3c, RF.K.4

Read Aloud

To support the unit concept, use one of the Read-Aloud Handbook selections for Unit 2. As you read, model the metacognitive strategy for the unit, Visualize, guided by the samples provided. You may also wish to select a favorite read aloud from your classroom or school library. To support the unit concept, use one of the suggested titles for Unit 2.

Shared Reading (iELD)

Read the Realistic Fiction

First reading. Read aloud the text fluently and expressively, pointing under each word.

Reread for Fluency: Prosody/Pitch. Remind students that you can use the pitch of your voice to emphasize the feelings in the story. Read the text using a lower pitch for the first two sentences and a higher pitch for the last two sentences. Read the text again and encourage students to join in, matching your pitch. Provide corrective feedback and/or validate students' efforts.

Build Concepts: Every Story Has Characters

Pose questions to connect the poem to the unit concept. For example:

- *Why do you think Tess was concerned about Nick sitting by himself?*
- *Can you describe what it is like to be the new child in town and not know anyone?*

Review Phonics: Initial and Final *n*

Highlight the word **New** in title. Read the word aloud. Then ask students to read the word aloud with you. Ask volunteers to name the letter at the beginning of **New**. Point out that it is a capital **N**. Ask students to say the sound the letter **n** stands for. Repeat with **Nick**. Then repeat for final **n** using the word **town**.

Review High-Frequency Words: *the, like*

Tell students that this text contains some words they have learned. Point to the previously taught high-frequency word **the**. Ask students to turn to a partner and tell their partner the high-frequency word. Repeat with the word **like.** Remind students to look for high-frequency words they know when they read a new text.

RL.K.1 With prompting and support, ask and answer questions about key details in a text., RL.K.3 With prompting and support, identify characters, settings, and major events in a story., RF.K.3a Demonstrate basic knowledge of letter-sound correspondences by producing the primary or most frequent sound for each consonant., RF.K.3c Read common high-frequency words by sight (e.g., the, of, to, you, she, my, is, are, do, does)., RF.K.4 Read emergent-reader texts with purpose and understanding.

READ ALOUD & SHARED READING

Read-Aloud Handbook   **Shared Reading Vol. 1, p. 12 "New Friends"**

Student Objectives

I will be able to:
- Read along with the appropriate pitch.
- Answer questions about friendship.
- Identify initial and final **n**.
- Recognize words I know in different texts.

(iELD) Integrated ELD

Light Support
Have partners answer the following questions about the story using the text and illustrations. Then challenge them to combine answers using conjunctions such as **and**, **because**, and **so**.
Who is the main character in the story?
Who is another important character?
What makes Nick different?
How does this make him feel?

Moderate Support
Have partners use the sentence starters to answer **wh**-questions about the story.
Ask: *Who are the main characters in the story?*
The main characters are _____ and _____.
Ask: *How is Nick different from the others in the story?*
Nick is different because _____.
Ask: *What does Tess do? Why?*
Tess _____ because _____.
Record partners' responses on the board. Then point out how to use conjunctions to combine ideas. For example, *Nick is different because he is sitting alone.*

Substantial Support
Have students use the sentence starters to answer **wh**-questions about "New Friends."
Ask: *What can you tell about Nick from the text?*
Nick had just _____.
He _____ the other kids play.
Ask: *What can you tell Nick from the pictures?*
Nick is _____.
Ask: *What can you tell about Tess from the text and pictures?*
Tess _____ at Nick. She asks Nick to _____.
Have students respond using words from the Word Bank.
Word Bank: watched, play, alone, waves, moved

ELD.PI.K.1, ELD.PI.K.5, ELD.PII.K.6

Mentor Read-Aloud Topic Introduction Vol. 1, pp. 12-13

Student Objectives

I will be able to
- Revise a first draft.
- Edit a first draft to create a final copy.
- Use a word processing program and printer to publish writing.

Additional Materials

- Sample Draft from Week 2
- Access to computer/word-processing program/ printer

Weekly Presentation
- Editing Checklist

(iELD) Integrated ELD

Light Support
Have partners add descriptive adjectives to revise the following sentences. Have students read aloud their sentences. *Carlos has short hair. Kim has long hair. Yoshi is small. Kate is large.*

Moderate Support
Provide partners with sentence frames and the Word Bank. Have them add precise details and descriptions to their sentences.
People have different hair. Some have _____, _____ hair. Others have _____, _____ hair. People are different sizes. Some people are _____ and _____. Others are _____ and _____. People have different eyes. Some have _____, _____ eyes. Others have _____, _____ eyes.

Word Bank:

long, straight	short, curly
wavy, thick	thin, brown
black, red, silver	blond, gray, white

Substantial Support
Provide students with the sentence frames below and a set of adjective cards to add detail to descriptions. Include the following adjective cards, with pictures if possible: **long, short, straight, curly, wavy, thin, thick, brown, black, blond, red, gray**. Have students complete the sentences using the cards. Then read the sentences together as a group.
People have different hair. Some people have __ hair. Others have _____ hair. Some people have _____, _____ hair. Others have _____, _____ hair.

ELD.PI.K.8, ELD.PI.K.12c, ELD.PII.K.4

Revise and Edit a Response to the Essential Question (15 MIN.) W.K.2, W.K.5, W.K.6, W.K.8, L.K.1a, L.K.1b

Engage Thinking

Display the text you drafted with students on Week 2, Day 5. Remind students that this is a first draft. Explain that in this lesson you will show them how a skillful writer revises and edits a draft to create a final version to publish or share with others.

Ask: *What is one thing you look for when you revise and edit?*

Revise (iELD)

Remind students of the purpose of the revision stage of writing. Students should understand that during the revision stage, writers reread their work and focus on how to make it better by making sure their ideas are clear, adding details to give more information, and using complete sentences with nouns and verbs.

Reread the sample draft from Week 2. Model how you evaluate the text critically and find ways to improve it. As you model, make revisions to the draft to demonstrate what writers do. Use the sample modeling provided.

Sentence	Sample Modeling
1	I think my main idea statement is clear and it says what I want it to say. I will not change it.
After sentence 1	The first part of my writing tells about how people look different. I'll add a sentence to help readers understand my ideas. I'll add, "People are different heights."
After sentence 3	I will add examples of different hair. I might say, "Some people have red, straight hair. Some have black, curly hair."
After sentence 4	The next examples are about how people act differently. I can add a sentence to help readers understand my ideas. I'll add, "People have different characteristics."

Edit

Remind students that they have been working on incorporating correct language in their writing. Explain that after revising, a good writer edits his or her work. This means going back and correcting any errors in grammar, punctuation, or spelling. Display and read aloud the editing checklist, and use it with students to edit your revised text.

Editing Checklist

- I capitalized the first word in every sentence.
- I used nouns correctly.
- I wrote complete sentences.
- I spelled all words correctly.
- I used correct end punctuation for each sentence.

Publish

You may wish to use a word-processing program to model how you turn your revised and edited text into a final copy for publication or sharing. Discuss with students many ways in which writers share their writing—in print, online, or as audios or videos.

> **Sample revised and edited text:**
> People look and act differently. For example, people are different heights. Some people are tall. Others are short. People have different color skin and types of hair. Some people have red, straight hair. Some have black, curly hair. People have different characteristics. Some people try hard. Some people are helpful. People do not look or act the same.

 Write Independently

Ask students to draw and label a picture to show their response to the essential question. Students can dictate their ideas.

Small-Group Differentiated Instruction (15 MIN. per Group)

Meet with Small Groups

Select small-group reading titles or activities based on students' needs. See the Small-Group Instructional Planner for titles that support a range of instructional levels within the unit topic. Remind students to apply what they learned to their small-group reading experiences.

Say: *Remember all the strategies we have learned in this unit. Use them when you read in small groups and independently. Take them into our next unit and use them there as well.*

Whole-Group Reflect and share

Bring the class back together. Invite volunteers to share the strategies they applied during small-group reading.

W.K.2 Use a combination of drawing, dictating, and writing to compose informative/explanatory texts in which they name what they are writing about and supply some information about the topic., **W.K.5** With guidance and support from adults, respond to questions and suggestions from peers and add details to strengthen writing as needed., **W.K.6** With guidance and support from adults, explore a variety of digital tools to produce and publish writing, including in collaboration with peers., **W.K.8** With guidance and support from adults, recall information from experiences or gather information from provided sources to answer a question., **L.K.1a** Print many upper- and lowercase letters., **L.K.1b** Use frequently occurring nouns and verbs.

Focus Skill: n/n/ (20 MIN.) RL.K.1, RL.K.10, RF.K.2c, RF.K.3a, RF.K.3c, RF.K.4, L.K.1a

Phonological Awareness: Blend Onset and Rime

Model/Practice

Segment the word ***man*** into its onset and rime: **/m/ /an/**. Have students blend the sounds and say the word.

Repeat with the words ***net, nine, pin,*** and ***note***. Then say the word ***nap***.

Ask: *What is the onset or beginning sound? What is the rest of the word?*

Blend the sounds **/n/** and **/ap/** and say the word with the class.

Display the picture card ***nut***. Have the students name the picture.

Ask: *What is the onset or beginning sound? What is the rest of the word? Let's blend the sounds* **/n/** *and* **/ut/** *and say the word:* **nut.**

Repeat with the picture cards **mop, sun, tub, nest**.

Letter-Sound Correspondences

Review

Display Letter Card ***n***.

Say: *This is the letter* **n**. *The letter* **n** *stands for* **/nnn/**. *What is the letter? What sound does this letter stand for?*

Repeat for **a, s,** and **t**.

Give each student three blank index cards. Have them draw a picture of something that begins like **apple, sun, tiger,** and **nest**. Then have students sort their pictures under the correct letter card.

Say: *What sound does the name of your picture begin with? Place your picture under the letter that stands for that sound.*

Blend Sounds

Review

Have students blend the word ***man***. Place letter cards ***m, a, n*** in a pocket chart. Point to the letter ***m***.

Say: *This is the letter* **m**. *The letter* **m** *stands for* **/mmm/**. *Say* **/mmm/**. *This is the letter* **a**. *The letter* **a** *stands for* **/aaa/**. *Say* **/aaa/**. *Listen as I blend the two sounds together* **/mmmaaa/**. *Blend the sounds with me. This is the letter* **a**. *The letter* **a** *stands for* **/aaa/**. *This is the letter* **n**. *The letter* **n** *stands for* **/nnn/**. *Say* **/nnn/**. *Listen as I blend all three sounds together,* **/mmmaaannn/**. *Now blend the sounds to read the word,* **man**.

Repeat the steps for the word ***tan***. Move your hand from left to right under the word. Have students blend and read the word ***tan***.

Pre-Decodable Reader: *I See Nat*

Student Objectives

I will be able to:
- Blend onset and rime.
- Review letter-sound correspondences for ***m/m/, a/a/, n/n/, t/t/***.
- Build words.
- Blend sounds **/m/, /a/, /n/** and **/t/, /a/, /n/**.
- Spell words ***man*** and ***tan***.
- Write legibly.
- Read previously taught high-frequency words: ***I, like, we, the, see, go***.

Additional Materials

- Pre-decodable reader: *I See Nat*
- Letter cards: **a, n, s, t**

Weekly Presentation
- Picture cards: ***mop, nest, nut, sun, tub***
- High-frequency word cards: ***go, I, like, see, the, we***

Dictation

Review

Dictate these sounds for students to spell: **/m/ /a/ /n/**. Have them repeat the sound and then write the letter that stands for the sound.

Dictate the following words for students to spell: **man, tan**. Model how to segment each word.

Say: *When I say the word* **man**, *I hear three sounds*, **/m/ /a/ /n/**. *I know the letter* **m** *stands for* **/m/**, *the letter* **a** *stands for* **/a/**, *and the letter* **n** *stands for* **/n/**. *I will write the letters* **m, a,** *and* **n** *to spell the word* **man**.

Repeat for the word **tan**. When students finish writing the words, have them correct their papers.

High-Frequency Words (iELD)

Review: *I, like, the, we, see, go*

Write the words *I, like, the, we, see, go*. Focusing on one word at a time, have students spell the word as you point to each letter. Then erase the word, say the word, and have students spell it on their own.

Decodable Text

Write the words and sentences. Guide students with blending the first two words. Then have volunteers read the sentences.

man	tan
We see the man.	
I like the tan mat.	

Pre-Decodable Reader: I See Nat

Reread

Have partners reread *I See Nat* together. Circulate and listen in. Note students' speed, accuracy, and intonation. Based on the group as a whole, provide some general feedback and validate successes. If students need additional practice to read the text, provide support during small-group reading instruction.

(iELD) Integrated ELD

Light Support
Remind students that they have read a story called "New Friends." Write **I, like, see, we, the,** and **go** on the board. Point to each word and have students read it aloud. Ask students to compose sentences about "New Friends" that begin with **We** and **I**. Tell them to use the other words in the sentences as often as they can. Encourage them to use different action words in their sentences as well.

Moderate Support
Write the following sentences on the board:
We know the story about Pam.
Pam opens the window so the ladybug can go out.
I like to see happy bugs.
Have students take turns coming to the board to identify the words **I, like, see, we, the,** and **go.** Underline the words.
Provide students with the sentence frames below. Encourage them to use the underlined words and new action words from the word bank to complete the sentences.
We see _____.
I go _____.
Cats like _____.
Word Bank:
drink splash pour swim play smell hear
Ask: *Does the* **a** *in these words sound like the* **a** *in* **and** *and* **at**?

Substantial Support
Write the following sentences on the board:
We see the trees.
I like to go swimming.
Have students take turns coming to the board to identify the words **I, like, see, we, the,** and **go.** Underline the words.
Provide students with the sentence frames below. Encourage them to use the underlined words as well as action words from the Word Bank to complete the sentences.
We _____ ducks swimming.
I _____ to _____ water.
_____ ducks _____ in _____ water.
When ducks _____ water, they want to _____.
Word Bank:
drink splash pour swim play smell hear

ELD.PI.K.6, ELD.PI.K.12a, ELD.PII.K.3a

RL.K.1 With prompting and support, ask and answer questions about key details in a text., **RL.K.10** Actively engage in group reading activities with purpose and understanding., **RF.K.2c** Blend and segment onsets and rimes of single-syllable spoken words., **RF.K.3a** Demonstrate basic knowledge of letter-sound correspondences by producing the primary or most frequent sound for each consonant., **RF.K.3c** Read common high-frequency words by sight (e.g., the, of, to, you, she, my, is, are, do, does).,**RF.K.4** Read emergent-reader texts with purpose and understanding., **L.K.1a** Print many upper- and lowercase letters.

Mentor Read-Aloud Topic
Introduction Vol. 1, pp. 12-13

Student Objectives

I will be able to
• Share an answer to how people are different.
• Take turns during a collaborative conversation.
• Present ideas in a clear, audible voice.

Additional Materials

Weekly Presentation
• Unit 2 Video
• Essential Question and Answer Chart

Reflect on Unit Concepts (20 MIN.) SL.K.2, SL.K.2a, SL.K.3, SL.K.4, SL.K.6

Engage Thinking

Say: *Over the past three weeks we have read and listened to stories and a poem with characters. What do you remember about those texts?*

Encourage a brief whole-group discussion in which students recall and retell characters and major events from what they have read and listened to in the unit. You can display some of the titles to support students' thinking.

Display the Unit 2 Opener and read aloud the essential question.

Essential Question: How are people different?

Say: *Each of you may have different ideas based on the texts and on what you already know about characters and people. Today we will continue to share ideas about this important question.*

View Multimedia

Remind students that they watched a short video at the beginning of the unit before they read any of the selections. Show the video to students again. Prompt students to discuss how the video fits with the unit and the essential question. Ask them to share how their viewing experience was different from their first viewing.

Collaborative Conversation: Peer Group

Divide students into peer groups of 4 to 6 students. Tell students that you would like them to collaborate to develop a group answer to the essential question.

Model the steps you would like students to follow during this collaborative conversation:

Sample modeling: *Remember to follow the two directions. Step 1 is to use our own words when it is your turn to speak. Step 2 is to speak in an audible voice when expressing your ideas in a clear manner. We do not want to say exactly what someone else in the group said.*

Ensure that all students understand the two step directions have a volunteer from each group restate the directions.

Give students approximately five minutes to share their ideas and develop their answer. As they converse, monitor their conversations to ensure that they follow directions, stay on task, and that all students in the group participate.

Share (iELD)

Bring groups together. Call on a spokesperson for each group to present his or her group's answer to the essential question. If necessary, review your directions for what should happen as student groups share their ideas. For example:

1. *The spokesperson tells the class how they answered the question.*
2. *Other students listen attentively and ask questions if something is not clear.*
Ask a few students to restate these ideas in their own words.

As group spokespeople present ideas, capture their ideas in an Essential Question and Answers Chart. At the end of the unit, post the chart in your classroom.

> **How are people different?**
> People look different.
> Some people are boys, others are girls.
> People are good at different things.
> People enjoy doing different things.
> People live in different places.

Sample Essential Question and Answers Chart

Use Digital Media

Guide students to find and print images from the Internet showing how people are different. Students can use the images to make a collage to display in the classroom.

Observe and Assess

As students reflect on unit concepts and present ideas, use the following questions to informally assess students' understanding.

- *Do students understand how are look different?*
- *Do students understand ways characters are different?*
- *Were students able to support their responses to the essential question?*

(iELD) Integrated ELD

Light Support
Make sure students understand that in their groups, they must give their own opinions, or ideas, about how people are different. Write **I think** on the board and tell students to begin their ideas with these words. Provide this sentence frame to students and challenge them to complete the sentence with their own ideas:
I think some people _____ and other people _____.

Moderate Support
Explain to students that in their groups, they will give their opinions, or their own ideas, about how people are different. Write *I think* on the board and have students read the words with you. Tell them to begin their ideas with these words.
Provide this sentence stem to students and have them complete the sentence with their own ideas:
I think people are different because they _____.

Substantial Support
Remind students that they have been asked to give their opinions, or their own ideas, about characters in the stories they have heard. Explain that in their groups, they will give their own ideas about how people are different. Write *I think* on the board and have students read the words with you. Tell them to begin their ideas with these words.
Provide the sentence frames below to students and let them choose one. Have them complete the sentence they choose with their own ideas.
I think people are different because some are _____ and some are _____.
I think people are different because some have _____ and some have _____.

ELD.PI.K.3, ELD.PI.K.12b, ELD.PII.K.6

SL.K.2 Confirm understanding of a text read aloud or information presented orally or through other media by asking and answering questions about key details and requesting clarification if something is not understood., **SL.K.2a** Understand and follow one- and two-step oral directions. CA, **SL.K.3** Ask and answer questions in order to seek help, get information, or clarify something that is not understood., **SL.K.4** Describe familiar people, places, things, and events and, with prompting and support, provide additional detail., **SL.K.6** Speak audibly and express thoughts, feelings, and ideas clearly.

Introduction

The *Connect Across Disciplines Inquiry Projects* are designed to deepen students' understanding of the Unit Concepts and Essential Questions through inquiry-based learning. The projects promote the integration of the strands of English Language Arts (reading, writing, speaking and listening, and language). They also promote the integration of the language arts with content areas.

All projects are aligned to the *California Common Core State Standards for English Language Arts* as well as the *Next Generation Science Standards (NGSS)* and/or *History-Social Science Standards for California (HSS).*

Inquiry-Based Learning

Each project presents an opportunity for students to investigate a real-world problem or challenge. While accomplishing each task, students develop 21st century skills, such as the use of technology, collaboration, communication, problem solving, critical thinking, innovation, and creativity.

The projects all share four main tasks:

Investigate

Students generate questions, make observations, explore, and research. They locate information through a variety of ways, including digital and paper sources and interviews. They engage in meaningful interactions with sources and with each other.

Create

Students create a product, which can include videos, audio recordings, journals, experiments, charts, graphs, maps, galleries, artworks, posters, flyers, and brochures, achieved both on paper and digitally.

Present

Students share their products with peers in many ways. They may present videos, role-plays, share a web page, or guide a tour though an exhibition. The audiences are prompted to ask questions and the presenting groups provide answers and explanations.

Reflect and Respond

After projects are completed and presented, students reflect on what they have learned from their own experiences as well as what they have learned from presentations by other groups.

Assigning Projects and Roles

Students are more motivated when they engage in experiences that are relevant to their interests, everyday life, or important current events. You may wish to have students select which project they will work on based on their own personal interests. You may also wish to assign groups based on your social studies and science curriculum.

After students are organized into small groups, facilitate the efficacy of the project by assigning roles. Depending on the nature of the project, students may take on authentic roles such as Lead Researcher, Project Manager, Head Engineer, Main Presenter, Chief Designer, and so on.

HSS Draw a Comic Strip about Rules

ELA W.K.3, W.K.8, SL.K.1a, SL.K.5, SL.K.6, L.K.1d, L.K.1f, L.K.6 HSS K.1.1

Student Objectives

I will be able to:
- Understand how to follow rules.
- Know the consequences of breaking rules.
- Create a comic strip about rules in school.

Materials

Paper • Drawing materials (crayons and colored pencils) • Tape
• Dolls or puppets

Investigate

- Remind students that they learned about the importance of following rules at school. Ask groups of three students to think about a particular rule they follow at school and why they follow it.

- Guide students to discuss the consequences of not following these rules. Provide the following sentence starter: *What would happen if _____?* Encourage students to take turns while they talk.

Create

- Give each student a piece of blank paper. Explain that they will be drawing a comic strip together as a group, and that each student in the group will draw one panel. Draw an outline of a three-panel comic strip on the board as an example.

- Tell one student to draw the first panel, showing an example of a school rule he or she thinks is important. Tell another student to draw the second panel, showing someone not following this rule. Tell the third student in the group to draw the third panel, showing the consequences of not following the rule.

Present

- Ask students to display their comic strips. Allow each group member to discuss one panel. Suggest that group members use one of the following sentence frames to discuss their rule: *Never _____ in school* or *Always _____ in school.*

- Allow time for groups to act out their comic strip with dolls or puppets. Remind them to speak and express their ideas clearly.

Reflect and Respond

Ask students to reflect on how their school day would be different if people broke the school rules.

HSS Be a "Rules" Reporter

ELA W.K.7, W.K.8, SL.K.1a, SL.K.6, L.K.1d, L.K.1f, L.K.6 HSS K.1.1

Student Objectives

I will be able to:
- Interview people about rules at home during mealtimes.
- Learn why people need to follow rules at home.

Materials

Picture books illustrating rules • Audio recorder and microphone
• Video recorder (optional)

Investigate

- Share picture books about rules with students. Invite volunteers to describe the rules they see in the pictures.

- Prompt a discussion about these rules and how they relate to the rules students follow in their own homes. Encourage students to listen to what everyone shares.

Create

- Invite small groups to formulate a question they can use to interview people about rules they follow during mealtimes at home. Model an example question, such as: *What rules do you follow when you eat dinner at home?*

- Students can take turns using the microphone as they become the "rules" reporter and ask people the question. Other group members can use audio or video equipment to record the interviews.

Present

- Invite groups to share the question they used in their interviews.
- Replay the recordings students made.

Reflect and Respond

Ask students to reflect on the similarities and differences among the interview questions and answers. Encourage students to discuss the values of rules and why people need to follow rules at home. Remind students to try and use complete sentences in their responses.

 **Make a Science Safety Rule Poster**

ELA W.K.5, W.K.7, SL.K.5, L.K.6 HSS K.1.1, NGSS K-2-ETS1-1

Student Objectives

I will be able to:
• Talk about the ways scientists study the world.
• Discuss safety rules scientists follow during experiments.
• Make a poster to show an important safety rule for scientists.

Materials

Books or websites illustrating science experiments • Poster board
• Drawing materials (such as crayons and colored markers)

Investigate

• Share books or websites that show several different types of science experiments students can conduct. Invite students to discuss the various ways scientists study the world, and the tools they use to do it.

• Then ask students to notice the safety equipment and safety rules for each experiment. Guide them to discuss the reasons why scientists have safety equipment and need to follow certain rules.

Create

• Ask students to choose one safety rule used in a scientific experiment.
• Invite students to create a poster showing why it is important to follow the rule they chose.

Present

• Invite students to present their posters and describe their safety rule.

• Allow time for students to ask questions about the consequences of not following the rules on the posters.

Reflect and Respond

Ask students to reflect on one another's posters and suggest changes to make the rules depicted clearer and more accurate. Remind students to use words and phrases they learned from listening to the different scientific experiments.

Useful Resources

Know and Follow Rules by Cheri J. Meiners
Kevin Knows the Rules by Molly Dowd
Kindergators: Hands Off, Harry! by Rosemary Wells
Kitchen Science Lab for Kids by Liz Lee Heinecke

CCSS for English Language Arts

ELA W.K.3 Use a combination of drawing, dictating, and writing to narrate a single event or several loosely linked events, tell about the events in the order in which they occurred, and provide a reaction to what happened. **W.K.5** With guidance and support from adults, respond to questions and suggestions from peers and add details to strengthen writing as needed. **W.K.7** Participate in shared research and writing projects (e.g., explore a number of books by a favorite author and express opinions about them). **W.K.8** With guidance and support from adults, recall information from experiences or gather information from provided sources to answer a question. **SL.K.1a** Follow agreed-upon rules for discussions (e.g., listening to others and taking turns speaking about the topics and texts under discussion). **SL.K.5** Add drawings or other visual displays to descriptions as desired to provide additional detail. **SL.K.6** Speak audibly and express thoughts, feelings, and ideas clearly. **L.K.1d** Understand and use question words (interrogatives) (e.g., who, what, where, when, why, how). **L.K.1f** Produce and expand complete sentences in shared language activities. **L.K.6** Use words and phrases acquired through conversations, reading and being read to, and responding to texts.

History–Social Science Content Standards

HSS K.1.1 Follow rules, such as sharing and taking turns, and know the consequences of breaking them.

Next Generation Science Standards

NGSS K-2-ETS1-1 Ask questions, make observations, and gather information about a situation people want to change to define a simple problem that can be solved through the development of a new or improved object or tool.

HSS Make a "Worker" Puppet

ELA W.K.7, SL.K.1a, SL.K.4, SL.K.5, SL.K.6, L.K.5c HSS K.3

Student Objectives

I will be able to:
• Make a "worker" puppet.
• Describe the work people do at their jobs.

Materials

Picture books or websites about jobs people do, such as Kids.gov pages about jobs • Paper bags • Drawing materials (crayons and markers) • Tape and/or glue • Craft supplies (yarn, plastic eyes, buttons) • Scissors

Investigate

• Point out that the title of your job is "Teacher." Elicit from students the names of other jobs workers have at their school and in their community.

• Display websites or picture books showing different jobs, and read the descriptions of jobs people do. Invite students to take turns talking about how the workers in the books or websites are like workers in their school and community.

Create

• Ask each student to choose the worker they find most interesting. Tell them that they will make a puppet representing this worker.

• Help students use craft supplies to create a paper bag puppet. Students may also refer to the illustrations or photographs of workers to get ideas. Remind students to look carefully at any uniform their worker wears and to "dress" their puppet similarly.

Present

• Ask students to use their worker puppets to tell a short description of their job. Guide students to use the following sentence frames if needed: *Hello, I am a _____. When I do my job, I have to _____.*

• Encourage students to give as many details about their worker's job as possible. Remind them to include facts about where the job takes place, the responsibilities of the worker, and any special equipment or uniforms the worker needs to perform his or her job.

Reflect and Respond

Invite students to ask each worker puppet questions about their job.

HSS Act Out an American Legend

ELA W.K.7, SL.K.1a, SL.K.6 HSS K.6.2

Student Objectives

I will be able to:
• Learn about important people in American legends.
• Play a character in an American legend.
• Answer questions about why people in American legends acted in certain ways.

Materials

Picture books or websites about American legends • Supplies for making masks and costumes (paper plates, hole punch, string, fabric, felt, yarn, glue, crayons or markers)

Investigate

• Read students brief tales about a variety of American legends.

• Ask questions to prompt a discussion about the main character in each legend and what makes the character important in American history. For example: *What special thing did _____ do? How did this affect other people?* Encourage students to take turns sharing in the discussion.

Create

• Divide the class into two groups and assign one legend to each group. Help students choose roles in order to act out the legend. Discuss the main characters and events in each legend that groups will act out.

• Ask students to choose or make costumes or masks to represent the different characters.

• Allow time for groups to quietly rehearse the main events in their legend.

Present

• Invite groups to perform their legends for each other.

Reflect and Respond

After each group's performance, tell the other group to ask questions of the characters. Suggest the following sentence frames: *How did you feel when _____ happened? What made you do _____?*

NGSS Map People Around the World   Challenge

ELA W.K.7, L.K.1a, L.K.6 HSS K.4.4, NGSS K-ESS3-1

Student Objectives

I will be able to:
• Understand what people need to live.
• Find out how people get what they need from their environment.
• Make a map to show where and how people get what they need.

Materials

Books or websites explaining how people live around the world • Paper • Drawing materials (such as crayons and colored markers) • World map or globe • Tape

Investigate

• Share books or websites that describe how people live in various regions around the world.

• Guide students to discuss the illustrations and important details about each environment. Help students see the connection between where people live and the types of food, shelter, and clothing they use to live.

Create

• Ask students to choose one way people in a particular region use their environment to satisfy a basic need, such as food, clothing, shelter, water, or medical care.

• Invite students to draw a picture of this relationship.

Present

• Help students locate the region they drew about on a world map or globe.

• Work with students to use the classroom wall or board to create a world map. Help them place their drawings on the map in the appropriate locations.

Reflect and Respond

Ask students to compare and contrast the way people around the world use their environment to meet their basic needs. Guide them to use complete sentences, such as: *In _____, people get their food by _____. They build their homes by _____. They get their clothes by _____.*

Useful Resources

Jobs People Do by Felicity Brooks
What Do People Do All Day? by Richard Scarry
American Legends and Tall Tales by Steven James Petruccio
Families Around the World by Margriet Ruurs

CCSS for English Language Arts

ELA W.K.7 Participate in shared research and writing projects (e.g., explore a number of books by a favorite author and express opinions about them). **SL.K.1a** Follow agreed-upon rules for discussions (e.g., listening to others and taking turns speaking about the topics and texts under discussion). **SL.K.4** Describe familiar people, places, things, and events and, with prompting and support, provide additional detail. **SL.K.5** Add drawings or other visual displays to descriptions as desired to provide additional detail. **SL.K.6** Speak audibly and express thoughts, feelings, and ideas clearly. **L.K.1a** Print many upper- and lowercase letters. **L.K.5c** Identify real-life connections between words and their use (e.g., note places at school that are colorful). **L.K.6** Use words and phrases acquired through conversations, reading and being read to, and responding to texts.

History–Social Science Content Standards

HSS K.3 Students match simple descriptions of work that people do and the names of related jobs at the school, in the local community, and from historical accounts. **K.4.4** Construct maps and models of neighborhoods, incorporating such structures as police and fire stations, airports, banks, hospitals, supermarkets, harbors, schools, homes, places of worship, and transportation lines. **K.6.2** Know the triumphs in American legends and historical accounts through the stories of such people as Pocahontas, George Washington, Booker T. Washington, Daniel Boone, and Benjamin Franklin.

Next Generation Science Standards

NGSS K-ESS3-1 Use a model to represent the relationship between the needs of different plants or animals (including humans) and the places they live.

Table of Contents

Retelling Routine AR7

Phonological Awareness Routine. AR8

Letter-Sound Correspondence Routine. AR9

Blending Routine AR10

Word Building Routine AR11

High-Frequency Words Routine AR12

Fluency Routine AR13

Vocabulary Routine: Define/Example/Ask AR14

Vocabulary Routine: Academic Vocabulary AR15

Retelling Routine

Retelling requires students to remember as much as they can about what they read or heard. The ability to retell is a critical early reading skill and connected to the development of higher order thinking skills. It is a precursor to summarizing. Model retelling, then provide weekly practice with read-alouds or student texts.

STEP 1: Read Aloud

Display a book or read-aloud. Activate prior knowledge using the cover, title, and a few illustrations/photos in the book. Read aloud the book. Ask students to listen carefully and "remember as much as possible."

STEP 2: Prompt Retelling and Record

Ask questions to prompt student retellings. Ask questions such as: *What happened (did you find out) first? What happened (did you learn) next? Can you tell me more?* Record students' retellings on the board or chart paper.

STEP 3: Reread and Revise

Prompt students to add to their retellings. Model look-backs and/or reread the text. Ask students to listen for anything they left out of their retellings. Use their responses to add to the retelling you recorded on the board or chart paper.

STEP 4: Connect to Lives

Encourage students to make personal and across-text connections to the text. Model an example, such as how the information in a nonfiction text connects to facts you read in another text on the topic or how a fiction story connects to something that happened in your life.

Teacher Tips

- Retelling is a great partner activity and increases students' use of new language. Prompt students to retell the selection to a partner before you record class retellings.

- Provide engaging ways to retell. For example, draw a story path on a large sheet of paper. Mark the sheet beginning, middle, and end. Have students draw pictures to remind them of key events in each part of the story. Then have students "walk the story" by walking the story path and using the pictures to aid in retelling.

Phonological Awareness Routine
Pose Essential Question

Phonological awareness involves the understanding that words are made up of discrete sounds and the ability to identify, blend, segment, and manipulate these sounds in spoken words. Key phonological awareness tasks include rhyme, phoneme isolation, phoneme categorization, oral blending, oral segmentation, and phonemic manipulation (addition, deletion, substitution).

STEP 1: Introduce

Explain to students the target phonological awareness task.

Example: (Rhyme) *We will be listening for words that rhyme. Rhyming words have the same ending sounds.*

Example: (Blending) *We will be listening to a series of sounds, then blend, or string together, the sounds to make words.*

STEP 2: Model

Model the target phonological awareness task with 2–3 examples. Clearly state the sounds. Stretch, elongate, or emphasize them, as needed.

Example: (Rhyme) *I'm going to say two words. Listen and tell me if they rhyme: sat, mat. Do sat and mat rhyme? [Wait for students to respond.] That's right, sat and mat rhyme because they both end in /at/. Listen: /s/ /at/, sat; /m/ /at/, mat. We hear /at/ at the end of sat and mat. So, sat and mat rhyme.*

Example: (Blending) *I'm going to say three sounds. Listen carefully. Blend, or put together, the sounds to make a word. The sounds are: /sss/ . . . /aaa/ . . . /t/. What word do you get when you put together these sounds? [Wait for students to respond.] That's right, when I put /sss/ . . . /aaa/ . . . /t/ together I get /sssaaat/, sat. The word is sat.*

STEP 3: Practice

Have students practice the target phonological awareness task using multiple examples. Do one or two with students, then have them do the remaining examples as a class.

Example: (Rhyme) *Now it's your turn. I will say two words. Tell me if they rhyme: man/fan, mop/top, boat/coat, sad/pin, read/seed, lick/pack.*

Example: (Blending) *Now it's your turn. I will say a series of sounds. Put the sounds together to make a word: /s/ /a/ /d/, /m/ /o/ /p/, /l/ /i/ /p/, /r/ /u/ /n/.*

Letter-Sound Correspondence Routine

STEP 1: Introduce

Display the frieze card for the target sound-spelling (e.g., Dd). Say the sound and letter. Have students repeat. Ask: What is the sound? What letter stands for the sound?

Example: *Display the Dd frieze card. This is the dog card. The sound is /d/. Say the sound with me: /d/. This is the sound at the beginning of the word dog. The /d/ sound is spelled with the letter d. What is the name of the letter? (d) What sound does the letter stand for? (/d/)*

STEP 2: Model

Point to the picture on the frieze card. Say the picture name, write it on the board, and underline the letter that stands for the target sound. Review the letter-sound correspondence. If you are reading a poem, have students find all the words in the poem that contain the target letter-sound. Write the words on the board, underline the target letter, and reinforce the letter-sound correspondence.

Example: *Look at the word I wrote: d-o-g. I see the letter d. It stands for the /d/ sound. Listen as I read the word: dog. What sound do you hear at the beginning of the word? What letter stands for that sound?*

STEP 3: Practice

Display picture cards whose names contain the target letter-sound, and a few that do not. Have students sort the picture cards (e.g., by beginning sound if that is where the target letter-sound occurs in the picture card names).

Teacher Tips

- Review previously taught letter-sounds frequently throughout the week to build mastery.

- Create additional activities with the frieze, letter, and picture cards to reinforce letter-sound correspondences (e.g., matching games, concentration, timed activities, etc).

Teacher Tips

- When time is limited for Practice, write the words on the board for students to blend instead of using letter cards.

- Select words to blend from upcoming Decodable Texts and other high-utility words containing the target letter-sounds.

Blending Routine

Blending is the main strategy readers use to decode, or sound out, words. When blending, students string together the sounds in a word to read it. It is a strategy that must be frequently modeled (with each new phonics skill) and applied both in isolation and in connected text.

STEP 1: Model

Select a word with the target phonics skill. Display letter cards for the word you want to model blending. Point to each letter card as you say the sound. Then blend the sounds together to make the word.

Example: Display the letter cards s-a-t. *This is the letter s. The letter s stands for the /s/ sound. This is the letter a. The letter a stands for the /a/ sound. Let's blend these two sounds together: /sssaaa/. This is the letter t. The letter t stands for the /t/ sound. Let's blend all the sounds together: /sssaaat/. The word is sat.*

STEP 2: Practice

Distribute letter cards to students and have them place the letter card set for the day's blending on their desks. Make a word using the letter cards, but do not say the word. Have students repeat. Then ask students to blend the sounds to read the word. Continue with other words.

Example: Have students place the following letter cards on their desks: a, m, s, t, p, o. Place the letter cards m-a-t in order in a pocket chart. Have students repeat on their desks. Then ask them to blend the sounds to read the word mat.

STEP 3: Apply

Guide students through a reading of the Decodable Text focusing on the lesson's target phonics skill. Have students chorally read the story the first time through. Stop and model sounding out words students misread. Ask comprehension questions to check students' understanding. Have students reread the story a second time with partners or in small groups.

Word Building Routine

Word building helps increase students' word awareness, improves the ability to fully analyze words, provides practice flexibly using learned sound-spellings, and aids in general reading and spelling growth.

STEP 1: Model

Display letter cards for a word containing the target phonics skill (e.g., mop for /o/). Model how to add, replace, or delete one or more letters to make a new word. Make a series of 3–5 words.

Example: Display the letter cards for mop. Then say the following:

• *Let's blend all the sounds together to read the word: /mmmooop/, mop.*

• *Replace m with t. [Replace the letter m with t.] Let's blend all the sounds to read the new word: /tooop/, top.*

• *Replace t with h. [Replace the letter t with h.] Let's blend all the sounds together: / hooop/, hop.*

• *Replace the p with t. [Replace the letter p with t.] Let's blend all the sounds together: / hooot/, hot.*

STEP 2: Practice

Provide a series of words to guide student practice. Say one word at a time and the letter or letters to be added, removed, or changed. Ask students to blend and say the new word formed before moving on to the next word (e.g., sat, mat, map, mop).

Teacher Tips

• Begin with simple replacement of letters in one position of the word (e.g., beginning). Progress to replacing beginning and ending sounds, then add on medial sounds as students are able.

• Create a series of 4–8 words for student practice.

• Add in words with review sound-spellings when appropriate to build mastery.

Teacher Tips

- Review last week's words using the Read/Spell/Write routine to extend practice over a two-week period. This will increase mastery.

- Add the words to a Word Wall.

- Have students record the words in their notebooks or on a separate sheet of paper to take home for review. Encourage them to write a sentence for each word. Reviewing the words in context is especially beneficial for English learners.

High-Frequency Words Routine

High-frequency words are the most common words in English. Some contain irregular spelling patterns. Others are used in stories before students learn the phonics skills needed to decode them. Therefore, these words must be taught as sight words.

STEP 1: Read

Display the high-frequency word card. Point to the word and read it aloud. Ask students to repeat after you.

Example: *This is the word was. What is the word?*

STEP 2: Spell

Spell each letter in the word as you point to it. Then ask students to chorally read and spell aloud the word.

Example: *The word was is spelled w-a-s. Spell the word as I point to each letter: w-a-s.*

STEP 3: Write

Write the word as you spell it aloud. Then have students write the word several times as they say each letter.

Example: *Watch as I write the word was. I will write w-a-s. Now you write the word was three times.* **Say** *each letter as you write the word.*

STEP 4: Apply

Have students use the word in an oral sentence.

Example: *Turn to a partner and use the word was in a sentence. You might begin your sentence with I was _____.*

Fluency Routine

In order to achieve mastery, students will need fluency instruction and practice at the sound, letter, word, and sentence level. Use one or more of the following fluency-building activities each week based on the week's skill focus.

Letter-Sound Fluency

As a warm-up or transition activity, display a set of letter cards. Use the letters taught up to that point in the year. Display the cards one at a time as students say the letter name. Repeat at varying speeds. Then mix the cards and ask students to say the letter's sound.

Word Fluency

As a warm-up or transition activity, display a set of word cards with words containing the letter-sounds taught up to that point in the year. Write 2–3 words for each letter-sound taught. Display the cards one at a time as students chorally read the words. Repeat at varying speeds. Periodically mix the cards so students don't become overly familiar with the sequence.

Sentence Fluency

Have students do repeated readings of the Decodable Texts to build fluency. Repeated readings can include partner reading, independent reading (where you circulate and listen in on students), and rereadings at home. Include decodable stories from previous weeks to extend practice of previously taught phonics skills and build mastery.

Model Fluent Reading

Fluency includes a student's ability to read accurately (correct decoding), at an appropriate rate/speed, and with the proper expression/intonation. Each week, select an aspect of fluency to model, such as intonation. Model with sentences from student texts. Have students repeat. For example, model how you read sentences with different punctuation marks (e.g., raise your voice slightly at the end of a question). Read a sentence with the proper intonation and have students echo your reading.

Teacher Tips

• Review new and previously taught words daily using the Define/Example/Ask routine and other vocabulary follow-up activities (e.g., act out, teach cognates, focus on synonyms and antonyms, semantic maps).

• In addition to introducing new words each week, teach word-learning strategies such as wide reading, using context clues, learning from read-alouds.

Vocabulary Routine: Define/Example/Ask

This routine, developed by Isabel Beck, is ideal for introducing new words to students. It provides a student-friendly definition, connects the word to students' experiences, and asks students to use the word in speaking to check understanding.

STEP 1: Define

Provide a student-friendly definition of the vocabulary word.

Example: *The word huge means "very big."*

STEP 2: Example

Provide an example sentence using the word. Use an example related to students' experiences.

Example: *An elephant is a huge animal.*

STEP 3: Ask

Ask students a question that requires them to use the new word in their answer. Provide sentence frames for students needing additional support.

Example: *Name something you have seen that is huge.*

I saw a huge _____ .

Vocabulary Routine: Academic Vocabulary

This routine, developed by Kate Kinsella, is an alternate routine for working with new words. It is especially strong for English learners and can be used to extend vocabulary work after the initial Define/Example/Ask introduction.

STEP 1: Introduce the Word

Write the new word on the board (or display a vocabulary card) and pronounce the word. Have students repeat. Then introduce the following features of the word, as appropriate for students' level.

- Provide a student-friendly definition. (Compare *means "to show how things are the same or almost the same."*)
- Provide a synonym for the word. (*alike, similar*)
- Provide the various forms of the word. (*compare, comparison, comparing, comparative*)
- Provide word partners and/or sentences. (*compare/contrast*)

STEP 2: Verbal Practice

Talk about the word. Read a sentence frame using the word. Have students discuss several ways to complete the frame. Then have them say their favorite idea to complete the frame.

Example: *We will compare a _____ to a _____ to see how they are alike.*

When we compare two things, we _____ .

STEP 3: Written Practice

Have students use the word in writing. Do one or more of the following:

- **Collaborate** Have students work with a partner to complete simple sentence frames using the word.
- **Your Turn** Have students work independently to complete sentence frames.
- **Be an Academic Author** Have students work independently to write two sentences using the word. Each sentence should use a different form of the word (e.g., singular and plural, noun and verb).

Teacher Tips

- When introducing a word, focus on correct pronunciation and point out any common spelling patterns or known letter-sounds in the word.
- Prompt students to create their own explanation of the word to share with the class.
- Have students create nonlinguistic representations of the word (e.g., pictures).

Small-Group Texts for Reteaching Strategies and Skills

Title	Unit	Letter Level	Number Level	Lexile Level	Theme	Text Type/Genre
I Follow Rules at School	1	A	1	BR	Rules at Home and School	Informational Text: Social Studies
Good Citizens Can Help	1	A	1	BR	Rules at Home and School	Informational Text: Social Studies
My Backpack	1	A	1	BR	Rules at Home and School	Literary Text: Realistic Fiction
My Book	1	A	1	BR	Rules at Home and School	Informational Text: Social Studies
Playing Sports	1	B	2	BR	Rules at Home and School	Informational Text: Social Studies
Day Camp	1	B	2	BR	Rules at Home and School	Informational Text: Social Studies
Eating Well	1	B	2	70L	Rules at Home and School	Informational Text: Science
Families Have Rules	1	C	3	30L	Rules at Home and School	Informational Text: Social Studies
King Midas's Gold	2	A	1	BR	Every Story Has Characters	Literary Text: Myth
The Elves and the Shoemaker	2	A	1	BR	Every Story Has Characters	Literary Text: Fairy Tale
The Enormous Turnip	2	A	1	60L	Every Story Has Characters	Literary Text: Folktale
Peter and the Wolf	2	A	1	BR	Every Story Has Characters	Literary Text: Folktale
We Fish	2	B	2	BR	Every Story Has Characters	Literary Text: Realistic Fiction
Goldilocks and the Three Bears	2	B	2	50L	Every Story Has Characters	Literary Text: Fairy Tale
Tim's Trip	2	B	2	150L	Every Story Has Characters	Literary Text: Realistic Fiction
Jin and Pedro Get to Work!	2	C	4	330L	Every Story Has Characters	Literary Text: Realistic Fiction
Animal Colors	3	A	1	BR	Plants and Animals Have Needs	Informational Text: Science
The Best Things in Nature Are Blue	3	A	1	BR	Plants and Animals Have Needs	Opinion Text
My Bird-Watching Journal	3	A	1	10L	Plants and Animals Have Needs	Narrative Nonfiction: Science
Animal Homes	3	B	2	BR	Plants and Animals Have Needs	Informational Text: Science
At the Pond	3	B	2	BR	Plants and Animals Have Needs	Informational Text: Science

First Reading Focus	Close Reading 1	Close Reading 2	Close Reading 4
Identify Main Topic and Retell Key Details (RI.K.2)	Determine Main Topic and Key Supporting Details (RI.K.2)	Integrate Information from Text and Illustrations to Understand Key Details (RI.K.7)	Identify Real-Life Connections Between Words and Their Uses (RI.K.4, L.K.5c)
Identify Main Topic and Retell Key Details (RI.K.2)	Use Text Evidence to Draw Inferences from the Text (RI.K.1)	Integrate Information from Text and Illustrations to Understand Key Details (RI.K.7)	Identify New Meanings for Familiar Words and Apply Them Correctly (RI.K.4, L.K.4a)
Retell Key Details in a Story (RL.K.2)	Use Text Evidence to Ask and Answer Questions (RL.K.1)	Identify Characters in a Story (RL.K.3)	Identify Real-Life Connections Between Words and Their Uses (RL.K.4, L.K.5c)
Identify Main Topic and Retell Key Details (RI.K.2)	Describe Connections Between Events in a Text (RI.K.3)	Define the Role of the Author of a Text (RI.K.6)	Use Words and Phrases Acquired Through Conversations, Reading and Being Read To, and Responding to Texts (RI.K.4, L.K.6)
Identify Main Topic and Retell Key Details (RI.K.2)	Describe Connections in a Text (RI.K.3)	Define the Role of the Author and Illustrator of a Text (RI.K.6)	Identify Real-Life Connections Between Words and Their Uses (RI.K.4, L.K.5c)
Identify Main Topic and Retell Key Details (RI.K.2)	Identify and Describe a Sequence of Events (RI.K.3)	Define the Roles of the Author and the Illustrator of a Text (RI.K.6)	Identify Real-Life Connections Between Words and Their Uses (RI.K.4, L.K.5c)
Retell Key Details (RI.K.2)	Integrate Information from Text and Illustrations to Understand Key Details (RI.K.7)	Identify and Describe Connections (RI.K.3)	Sort Common Objects into Categories (L.K.5a)
Determine Main Topic and Key Supporting Details (RI.K.2)	Retell Key Details of a Text (RI.K.2)	Integrate Information from Text and Illustrations to Understand Key Details (RI.K.7)	Use Frequently Occurring Affixes as a Clue to the Meaning of an Unknown Word (RI.K.4, L.K.4b)
Retell Key Story Details (RL.K.2)	Identify Characters in a Story (RL.K.3)	Make Connections Between Illustrations and Events in a Text (RL.K.7)	Identify New Meanings for Familiar Words and Apply Them Correctly (RL.K.4, L.K.4a)
Retell Key Story Details (RL.K.2)	Identify Characters in a Story (RL.K.3)	Use Text Evidence to Ask and Answer Questions (RL.K.1)	Use Frequently Occurring Inflections and Affixes as a Clue to the Meaning of an Unknown Word (RI.K.4, L.K.4b)
Retell Key Story Details (RL.K.2)	Identify Key Events in a Story (RL.K.1, RL.K.3)	Make Connections Between Illustrations and Events in a Text (RL.K.7)	Identify Real-Life Connections Between Words and Their Uses (RL.K.4, L.K.6)
Retell Key Story Details (RL.K.2)	Identify Characters in a Story (RL.K.3)	Use Text Evidence to Draw Inferences from a Text (RL.K.1)	Sort Common Objects Into Categories to Gain a Sense of the Concepts and Categories Represented (RL.K.4, L.K.5a)
Retell Key Story Details (RL.K.2)	Use Text Evidence to Ask and Answer Questions (RL.K.1)	Identify Settings in a Story (RL.K.3)	Identify New Meanings for Familiar Words and Apply Them Correctly (RL.K.4, L.K.4a)
Retell Key Story Details (RL.K.2)	Identify Characters in a Story (RL.K.3)	Make Connections Between Illustrations and Events in a Text (RL.K.7)	Sort Common Objects into Categories to Gain a Sense of the Concepts and Categories Represented (RL.K.4, L.K.5a)
Retell Key Details (RL.K.2)	Describe the Role of the Author and Illustrator (RL.K.6)	Ask Questions to Identify and Describe Story Elements (RL.K.3)	Use Frequently Occurring Inflections and Affixes as a Clue to Word Meaning (L.K.4b)
Retell Key Details (RL.K.2)	Make Connections Between Illustrations and Events (RL.K.7)	Identify Characters and Key Story Events (RL.K.3)	Identify New Meanings for Familiar Words (L.K.4a)
Identify Main Topic and Retell Key Details (RI.K.2)	Describe Relationship Between Photographs and Text (RI.K.2)	Ask and Answer Questions About Key Details (RI.K.1)	Sort Common Objects into Categories (RI.K.4, L.K.5a)
Identify Main Topic and Retell Key Details (RI.K.2)	Identify an Author's Reasons to Support a Point (RI.K.8)	Describe Relationship Between Photographs and Text (RI.K.7)	Use Acquired Words and Phrases (RI.K.4, L.K.6)
Identify Main Topic and Retell Key Details (RI.K.2)	Describe the Relationship Between the Illustrations and the Text (RI.K.7)	Define Role of Author and Illustrator (RI.K.6)	Sort Objects into Categories to Understand Concepts (RI.K.4, L.K.5a)
Identify Main Topic and Retell Key Details (RI.K.3)	Identify and Describe Comparisons and Contrasts (RI.K.3)	Define the Role of the Author of a Text (RI.K.6)	Sort Common Objects into Categories to Gain a Sense of the Concepts and Categories Represented (RI.K.4, L.K.5a)
Identify Main Topic and Retell Key Details (RI.K.3)	Identify Connections in a Text (RI.K.3)	Integrate Information from Text and Illustrations to Understand Key Details (RI.K.7)	Sort Common Objects into Categories to Gain a Sense of the Concepts and Categories Represented (RI.K.4, L.K.5a)

Small-Group Texts for Reteaching Strategies and Skills

Title	Unit	Letter Level	Number Level	Lexile Level	Theme	Text Type/Genre
Look at the Animals	3	C	4	BR	Plants and Animals Have Needs	Informational Text: Science
Animal Treats	3	C	4	BR	Plants and Animals Have Needs	Informational Text: Science
A Plant Has Parts	3	C	4	30L	Plants and Animals Have Needs	Informational Text: Science
Going Bananas for Apples	4	A	1	BR	Writers Tell Many Stories	Literary Text: Animal Fantasy
The Three Tates	4	A	1	BR	Writers Tell Many Stories	Literary Text: Realistic Fiction
Hat Day at the Zoo	4	B	2	BR	Writers Tell Many Stories	Literary Text: Animal Fantasy
I Like	4	B	2	BR	Writers Tell Many Stories	Literary Text: Realistic Fiction
Two Owls in Paris	4	B	2	BR	Writers Tell Many Stories	Literary Text: Animal Fantasy
Wishing With Pennies	4	B	2	30L	Writers Tell Many Stories	Literary Text: Animal Fantasy
Frank in a Tank	4	C	3	110L	Writers Tell Many Stories	Literary Text: Animal Fantasy
Sam Sleeps	4	C	4	200L	Writers Tell Many Stories	Narrative Fiction: Fantasy
People Use Tools	5	A	1	BR	Technology at Home and School	Informational Text: Social Studies
Let's Go	5	B	2	BR	Technology at Home and School	Informational Text: Social Studies
Old and New	5	B	2	BR	Technology at Home and School	Informational Text: Social Studies
Schools Then and Now	5	B	2	BR	Technology at Home and School	Informational Text: Social Studies
On the Playground	5	B	2	BR	Technology at Home and School	Informational Text: Social Studies
Clock Watch	5	C	3	BR	Technology at Home and School	Informational Text: Social Studies
Making a House	5	C	4	40L	Technology at Home and School	Informational Text: Social Studies
Technology Brings Us Together	5	D	6	120L	Technology at Home and School	Opinion Text
Mouse and Lion	6	A	1	BR	Stories Have a Message	Literary Text: Fable

First Reading Focus	Close Reading 1	Close Reading 2	Close Reading 4
Identify Main Topic and Retell Key Details (RI.K.2)	Describe Connections in a Text (RI.K.3)	Identify the Parts of a Book (RI.K.5)	Sort Common Objects into Categories to Gain a Sense of the Concepts and Categories Represented (RI.K.4, L.K.5a)
Identify Main Topic and Retell Key Details (RI.K.2)	Use Text Evidence to Draw Inferences from the Text (RI.K.1)	Integrate Information from Text and Illustrations to Understand Key Details (RI.K.7)	Sort Common Objects into Categories to Gain a Sense of the Concepts and Categories Represented (RI.K.4, L.K.5a)
Retell Key Details (RI.K.2)	Retell Key Details of a Text (RI.K.2)	Integrate Information from Text and Illustrations to Understand Key Details (RI.K.7)	Identify Real-Life Connections Between Words and Their Uses (RI.K.4, L.K.5c)
Retell Key Story Details (RL.K.2)	Identify Characters and Key Events in a Story (RL.K.3)	Describe Relationship Between Illustrations and Events in a Text (RL.K.7)	Identify New Meanings for Familiar Words and Apply Them Correctly (RL.K.4, L.K.4a)
Retell Key Story Details (RL.K.2)	Identify Characters and Major Events (RL.K.3)	Ask and Answer Questions About Key Details (RL.K.1)	Identify New Meanings for Familiar Words (RL.K.4, L.K.4a)
Retell Key Story Details (RL.K.2)	Recognize Common Types of Texts (RL.K.5)	Identify Characters, Setting, and Events in a Story (RL.K.3)	Identify Real-Life Connections Between Words and Their Uses (RL.K.4, L.K.5c)
Retell Key Story Details (RL.K.2)	Use Text Evidence to Ask and Answer Questions (RL.K.1)	Identify Major Events in a Story (RL.K.3)	Sort Common Objects into Categories to Gain a Sense of the Concepts and Categories Represented (RL.K.4, L.K.5a)
Retell Key Story Details (RL.K.2)	Identify the Setting of a Story (RL.K.3)	Describe the Role of the Author and Illustrator of a Text (RL.K.6)	Use Words and Phrases Acquired Through Conversations, Reading and Being Read To, and Responding to Texts (RL.K.4, L.K.6)
Retell Key Details in a Story (RL.K.2)	Integrate Information from Text and Illustrations to Understand Story Elements (RL.K.7)	Use Text Evidence to Ask and Answer Questions (RL.K.1)	Demonstrate Understanding of Frequently Occurring Verbs by Relating Them to Their Opposites (RL.K.4, L.K.5b)
Retell Key Details in a Story (RL.K.2)	Identify Key Events in a Story (RL.K.2)	Describe the Role of the Author and Illustrator of a Text (RL.K.6)	Identify New Meanings for Familiar Words and Apply Them Correctly (RL.K.4, L.K.4a)
Retell Key Story Details (RL.K.2)	Describe Relationship Between Illustrations and Events in the Text (RL.K.7)	Identify Characters in a Story Using Key Details (RL.K.3)	Demonstrate Understanding by Relating Verbs to Their Opposites (RL.K.4, L.K.5b)
Identify Main Topic and Retell Key Details (RI.K.2)	Use Text Evidence to Draw Inferences (RI.K.1)	Describe the Relationship Between Illustrations and the Text (RI.K.7)	Identify Real-Life Connections Between Words and Their Uses (RI.K.4, L.K.5c)
Identify Main Topic and Retell Key Details (RI.K.1)	Use Text Evidence to Draw Inferences (RI.K.1)	Describe the Relationship Between Illustrations and the Text (RI.K.7)	Sort Common Objects Into Categories (RI.K.4, L.K.5a)
Identify Main Topic and Retell Key Details (RI.K.2)	Ask and Answer Questions About Key Details in a Text (RI.K.1)	Describe Connections in a Text (RI.K.3)	Use Words Acquired Through Reading and Responding to Texts (RL.K.4, L.K.6)
Identify Main Topic and Retell Key Details (RI.K.3)	Identify and Describe Comparisons and Contrasts (RI.K.3)	Integrate Information from Text and Illustrations to Understand Key Details (RI.K.7)	Identify Real-Life Connections Between Words and Their Uses (RI.K.4, L.K.5c)
Identify Main Topic and Retell Key Details (RI.K.2)	Ask and Answer Questions in a Text (RI.K.1)	Describe Connections in a Text (RI.K.3)	Identify New Meanings for Familiar Words (RI.K.4, L.K.4a)
Identify Main Topic and Retell Key Details (RI.K.2)	Describe Connections in a Text (RI.K.3)	Describe the Relationship Between Illustrations and Text (RI.K.7)	Demonstrate Understanding of Frequently Occurring Adjectives by Relating Them to Their Opposites (RL.K.4, L.K.5b)
Identify Main Topic and Retell Key Details (RI.K.2)	Describe Connections in a Text (RI.K.3)	Identify the Parts of a Book (RI.K.5)	Identify Real-Life Connections Between Words and Their Use (RI.K.4, L.K.5c)
Retell Key Details (RI.K.2)	Identify an Author's Reasons to Support a Point (RI.K.8)	Identify and Describe Comparisons and Contrasts (RI.K.8)	Sort Common Objects into Categories (L.K.5a)
Retell Key Story Details (RL.K.2)	Identify Characters in a Story (RL.K.3)	Make Connections Between Illustrations and Events in a Text (RL.K.7)	Use Words and Phrases Acquired Through Conversations, Reading and Being Read To, and Responding to Texts (RL.K.4, L.K.6)

Small-Group Texts for Reteaching Strategies and Skills

Title	Unit	Letter Level	Number Level	Lexile Level	Theme	Text Type/Genre
The Ant and the Grasshopper	6	B	2	BR	Stories Have a Message	Literary Text: Fable
The Blind Men and the Elephant	6	B	2	BR	Stories Have a Message	Literary Text: Folktale
The Fox and the Crow	6	B	2	60L	Stories Have a Message	Literary Text: Fable
Stone Soup	6	C	3	20L	Stories Have a Message	Literary Text: Folktale
Why the Sea Is Salty	6	C	3	70L	Stories Have a Message	Literary Text: Folktale
The Crow and the Pitcher	6	C	4	230L	Stories Have a Message	Literary Text: Fable
Rikki-Tikki-Tavi	6	D	6	70L	Stories Have a Message	Literary Text: Animal Fantasy
The Flag	7	B	2	BR	Holidays and Celebrations	Informational Text: Social Studies
My Day at the Capital	7	B	2	BR	Holidays and Celebrations	Narrative Nonfiction: Social Studies
Jin and Pedro Celebrate!	7	B	2	150L	Holidays and Celebrations	Literary Text: Realistic Fiction
At the Birthday Party	7	C	3	BR	Holidays and Celebrations	Informational Text: Social Studies
Thanksgiving Then and Now	7	C	3	BR	Holidays and Celebrations	Informational Text: Social Studies
Costume Party	7	C	3	BR	Holidays/Celebrations	Literary Text: Realistic Fiction
A Party for Rabbit	7	C	3	40L	Holidays and Celebrations	Literary Text: Animal Fantasy
The Best Thanksgiving Ever	7	D	5	70L	Holidays and Celebrations	Literary Text: Realistic Fiction
A Week of Weather	8	B	2	BR	Weather and Seasons	Informational Text: Science
Let's Look Outside	8	B	2	BR	Weather and Seasons	Informational Text: Science
Life With Our Sun	8	C	3	BR	Weather and Seasons	Informational Text: Science
All Weather Is Fun!	8	C	3	BR	Weather and Seasons	Opinion Text
My Weather Log	8	C	3	BR	Weather and Seasons	Narrative Nonfiction: Science
Sam Can't Sleep	8	C	3	BR	Weather and Seasons	Literary Text: Realistic Fiction
The Seasons	8	D	5	BR	Weather and Seasons	Informational Text: Science

First Reading Focus	Close Reading 1	Close Reading 2	Close Reading 4
Retell Key Story Details (RL.K.2)	Identify the Settings of a Story (RL.K.3)	Use Text Evidence to Draw Inferences from a Text (RL.K.1)	Use Words and Phrases Acquired Through Conversations, Reading and Being Read To, and Responding to Texts (RL.K.4, L.K.6)
Retell Key Story Details (RL.K.2)	Identify Characters in a Story (RL.K.3)	Use Text Evidence to Draw Inferences from a Text (RL.K.1)	Sort Common Objects Into Categories to Gain a Sense of the Concepts and Categories Represented (RL.K.4, L.K.5a)
Retell Key Story Details (RL.K.2)	Identify the Setting in a Story (RL.K.3)	Use Text Evidence to Draw Inferences from a Text (RL.K.1)	Identify New Meanings for Familiar Words and Apply them Correctly (RL.K.4, L.K.4a)
Retell Key Story Details (RL.K.2)	Identify Characters in a Story (RL.K.3)	Use Text Evidence to Draw Inferences from a Text (RL.K.1)	Use Frequently Occurring Inflections and Affixes as a Clue to the Meaning of an Unknown Word (RL.K.4, L.K.4b)
Retell Key Story Details (RL.K.2)	Identify Characters in a Story (RL.K.3)	Use Text Evidence to Draw Inferences from a Text (RL.K.1)	Identify New Meanings for Familiar Words and Apply Them Correctly (RL.K.4, L.K.4a)
Retell Key Story Details (RL.K.2)	Identify the Setting of a Story (RL.K.1)	Make Connections Between Illustrations and Events in a Text (RL.K.7)	Identify Real-Life Connections Between Words and Their Uses (RL.K.4, L.K.5c)
Retell Key Story Details (RL.K.2)	Identify Characters, Settings, and Key Events in a Story (RL.K.3)	Make Connections Between Illustrations and Events in a Text (RL.K.1)	Identify New Meanings for Familiar Words and Apply Them Correctly (RL.K.4, L.K.4a)
Identify Main Topic and Retell Key Details (RI.K.2)	Identify Text Features (Front Cover, Back Cover, Title Page) (RI.K.5)	Determine Main Topic(s) and Key Supporting Details (RI.K.2)	Sort Common Objects into Categories to Gain a Sense of the Concepts and Categories Represented (RI.K.4, L.K.5a)
Retell Key Details (RI.K.2)	Determine Main Idea and Key Supporting Details (RI.K.2)	Name the Author and Define His Role in the Text (RI.K.6)	Identify Real-Life Connections Between Words and Their Uses (RI.K.4, L.K.5c)
Retell Key Story Details (RL.K.2)	Identify Settings and Key Events in a Story (RL.K.3)	Identify Characters in a Story (RL.K.3)	Distinguish Shades of Meaning Among Verbs (RL.K.4, L.K.5d)
Identify Main Topic and Retell Key Details (RI.K.2)	Describe Connections Between Concepts in a Text (RI.K.2)	Define the Roles of Author and Illustrator in Presenting the Information in a Text (RI.K.6)	Identify Real-Life Connections Between Words and Their Use (RI.K.4, L.K.5c)
Identify Main Topic and Retell Key Details (RI.K.2)	Ask and Answer Questions About Key Details in a Text (RI.K.2)	Describe Connections in a Text (RI.K.3)	Use Frequently Occurring Inflections and Affixes as a Clue to the Meaning of an Unknown Word (RI.K.4, L.K.4b)
Retell Key Story Details (RL.K.2)	Recognize Common Types of Texts (RL.K.5)	Make Connections Between Illustrations and Events in a Text (RL.K.7)	Identify Real-Life Connections Between Words and Their Uses (RL.K.4, L.K.5c)
Retell Key Story Details (RL.K.2)	Use Text Evidence to Draw Inferences from a Text (RL.K.1)	Recognize Common Types of Text (RL.K.5)	Sort Common Objects Into Categories to Gain a Sense of the Concepts and Categories Represented (RL.K.4, L.K.5a)
Retell Key Details (RL.K.2)	Identify Characters and Key Story Events (RL.K.3)	Recognize Common Types of Text (RL.K.5)	Sort Common Objects into Categories (L.K.5a)
Identify Main Topic and Retell Key Details (RI.K.2)	Use Text Evidence to Draw Inferences from the Text (RI.K.1)	Integrate Information from Text and Illustrations to Understand Key Details (RI.K.7)	Sort Words into Categories to Gain a Sense of the Concepts and categories Represented (RI.K.4, L.K.5a)
Identify Main Topic and Retell Key Details (RI.K.2)	Ask and Answer Questions About Key Details (RI.K.1)	Identify the Parts of a Book (RI.K.5)	Distinguish Shades of Meaning Among Verbs Describing the Same General Action (RI.K.4, L.K.5d)
Retell Key Details (RI.K.2)	Ask and Answer Questions About Key Details (RI.K.1)	Integrate Information from Text and Illustrations (RI.K.7)	Use Words Acquired Through Reading (L.K.6)
Retell Key Details (RI.K.2)	Identify an Author's Reasons to Support a Point (RI.K.8)	Integrate Information from Text and Illustrations (RI.K.7)	Demonstrate Understanding of Frequently Occurring Adjectives (L.K.5b)
Retell Key Details (RI.K.2)	Integrate Information from Text and Illustrations (RI.K.7)	Identify a Sequence of Events (RI.K.3)	Use Words Acquired Through Reading (L.K.6)
Retell Key Details (RL.K.2)	Identify Characters and Setting (RL.K.3)	Make Connections Between Illustrations and Events (RL.K.7)	Identify Real-Life Connections Between Words and Their Use (L.K.5c)
Identify Main Topic and Retell Key Details (RI.K.2)	Describe Connections in a Text (RI.K.2)	Describe the Relationship Between Illustrations and the Text (RI.K.7)	Identify New Meanings for Familiar Words and Apply Them Correctly (RI.K.4, L.K.4a)

Title	Unit	Letter Level	Number Level	Lexile Level	Theme	Text Type/Genre
Rainy Day, Sunny Day	8	D	6	120L	Weather and Seasons	Literary Text: Animal Fantasy
Saturday with Dad	9	B	2	50L	Meeting Our Needs and Wants	Narrative Nonfiction: Social Studies
Clothes	9	C	3	20L	Meeting Our Needs and Wants	Informational Text: Social Studies
Needs and Wants	9	C	4	BR	Meeting Our Needs and Wants	Informational Text: Social Studies
Jobs at School	9	C	4	BR	Meeting Our Needs and Wants	Informational Text: Social Studies
Can We Have a Pet?	9	C	4	120L	Meeting Our Needs and Wants	Literary Text: Realistic Fiction
Jobs in a Community	9	D	6	50L	Meeting Our Needs and Wants	Informational Text: Social Studies
The Yard Sale	9	D	6	190L	Meeting Our Needs and Wants	Literary Text: Realistic Fiction
Do We Need It? Do We Want It?	9	E	7	BR	Meeting Our Needs and Wants	Informational Text: Social Studies
How Animals Move	10	C	3	90L	Forces and Motion	Informational Text: Science
Up and Down the Hill	10	C	3	160L	Forces and Motion	Literary Text: Animal Fantasy
Magnets	10	C	3	200L	Forces and Motion	Informational Text: Science
What Is Slow? What Is Fast?	10	D	5	BR	Forces and Motion	Informational Text: Science
Little Cat Goes Fast	10	D	5	110L	Forces and Motion	Literary Text: Animal Fantasy
Hickory Dickory Dock	10	D	6	60L	Forces and Motion	Literary Text: Animal Fantasy
Jack Be Nimble	10	D	6	150L	Forces and Motion	Literary Text: Fantasy
Using Magnets	10	E	8	260L	Forces and Motion	Informational Text: Science

First Reading Focus	Close Reading 1	Close Reading 2	Close Reading 4
Retell Key Story Details (RL.K.2)	Identify Settings in a Story (RL.K.3)	Describe the Role of the Author and Illustrator of a Text (RL.K.6)	Use Affixes as a Clue to the Meaning of a Word (RL.K.4, L.K.4b)
Retell Key Details (RI.K.2)	Identify and Describe a Sequence of Events (RI.K.3)	Integrate Information from Text and Illustrations (RI.K.7)	Identify Real-Life Connections Between Words and Their Use (L.K.5c)
Identify Main Topic and Retell Key Details (RI.K.2)	Identify and Describe Comparisons and Contrasts (RI.K.3)	Define the Role of the Author of a Text (RI.K.6)	Sort Objects into Categories to Gain a Sense of the Concepts and Categories Represented (RI.K.4, L.K.5a)
Identify Main Topic and Retell Key Details (RI.K.2)	Identify Reasons an Author Gives to Support Points in a Text (RI.K.8)	Describe the Relationship Between Illustrations and the Text (RI.K.6)	Identify Real-Life Connections Between Words and Their Uses (RI.K.4, L.K.5c)
Retell Key Details (RI.K.2)	Determine Main Topic and Key Supporting Details (RI.K.2)	Define the Role of the Author of a Text (RI.K.6)	Use Frequently Occurring Inflections as Clues to the Meaning of an Unknown Word (RI.K.4, L.K.4b)
Retell Key Story Details (RL.K.2)	Use Text Evidence to Draw Inferences from a Text (RL.K.1)	Recognize Common Types of Texts (RL.K.5)	Sort Common Objects into Categories to Gain a Sense of the Concepts and Categories Represented (RL.K.4, L.K.5a)
Identify Main Idea and Retell Key Details (RI.K.2)	Determine the Main Topic and Key Supporting Details (RI.K.2)	Integrate Information from Text and Illustrations to Understand Key Details (RL.K.7)	Identify New Meanings for Familiar Words and Apply Them Correctly (RI.K.4, L.K.4a)
Retell Key Story Details (RL.K.2)	Describe Characters and How They Respond to Events in a Story (RL.K.3)	Integrate Information from the Text and Illustrations to Understand Story Elements (RL.K.7)	Use Words Acquired Through Conversation, Reading, and Being Read To (RL.K.4, L.K.6)
Identify Main Topic and Retell Key Details (RI.K.2)	Ask and Answer Questions About Key Details in a Text (RI.K.1)	Describe Connections Between Pieces of Information in a Text (RI.K.3)	Identify New Meanings for Familiar Words (RI.K.4, L.K.5a)
Identify Main Topic and Retell Key Details (RI.K.2)	Identify and Describe Causes and Their Effects (RI.K.3)	Integrate Information from Text and Photographs to Understand Key Details (RI.K.7)	Identify Real-Life Connections Between Words and Their Uses (RI.K.4, L.K.6)
Retell Key Story Details (RL.K.2)	Use Text Evidence to Ask and Answer Questions (RL.K.1)	Identify Characters in a Story (RL.K.3)	Sort Common Objects into Categories to Gain a Sense of the Concepts and Categories Represented (RL.K.4, L.K.5a)
Identify Main Topic and Retell Key Details (RI.K.2)	Use Text Evidence to Draw Inferences from the Text (RI.K.1)	Describe Connections in a Text (RI.K.3)	Identify New Meanings for Familiar Words and Apply Them Correctly (RI.K.4, L.K.4a)
Identify Main Topic and Retell Key Details (RI.K.2)	Use Text Evidence to Ask and Answer Questions (RI.K.1)	Make Connections in the Text (RI.K.3)	Sort Common Objects into Categories to Gain a Sense of the Concepts and Categories Represented (RI.K.4, L.K.5a)
Retell Key Story Details (RL.K.2)	Ask and Answer Questions in a Text (RL.K.1)	Identify Characters in a Story (RL.K.3)	Demonstrate Understanding of Frequently Occurring Adjectives by Relating Them to Their Opposites (RL.K.4, L.K.5b)
Retell Key Details (RL.K.2)	Use Text Evidence to Ask and Answer Questions (RL.K.1)	Make Connections Between Illustrations and Events in a Text (RL.K.7)	Distinguish Shades of Meaning Among Verbs Describing the Same General Action (RL.K.4, L.K.5d)
Retell Key Details (RL.K.2, RL.K.3)	Identify Characters and Setting (RL.K.3)	Describe the Role of the Author and Illustrator (RL.K.6)	Identify New Meanings for Familiar Words (RL.K.4, L.K.4a)
Identify Main Topic and Retell Key Details (RI.K.2)	Use Text Evidence to Make Inferences (RI.K.1)	Describe the Relationship Between Illustrations and the Text (RI.K.7)	Distinguish Shades of Meaning Among Verbs Describing the Same General Action (RI.K.4, L.K.5d)

Maximizing the Quality of Classroom Collaborative Conversations

by Jeff Zwiers, Ed.D.

> "The richest conversations have ideas that become clearer and stronger as students talk—such that all participating students walk away from the conversation with more insight and clarity than they had before they conversed."
>
> *Jeff Zwiers*

Productive classroom conversations include many features and require many skills. Fortunately, most of these features and skills can be modeled and scaffolded. The mini-lessons in your *Benchmark Advance* Teacher Resource System offer a wide range of conversational opportunities and helpful scaffolds to support rich conversations. For these conversations to be successful learning experiences, however, teachers must adapt lessons to meet the unique needs of their students. This article outlines several teacher habits, skills, and ideas for maximizing the quality of students' collaborative conversations in every unit of the program.

There are two common types of conversations that take place in the classroom. In the first, participants build up an idea together. In the second, participants discuss multiple ideas in order to choose one idea over another. An idea can take many forms: an answer to an essential question, an opinion, an inference, a hypothesis, a description of a complex process, a solution to a problem, a theme in a story, a comparison, etc.

Teachers and students can better understand how to improve conversations with the tools that accompany the *Benchmark Advance* program. The first tool, the **Conversation Blueprint**, is a visual guide to help teachers scaffold students' conversations. This tool shows the structure of the two main types of conversations that should happen during lessons.

The tools especially designed for students are the **Think-Speak-Listen Bookmarks** for grades K–1 and the *Think-Speak-Listen Flip Book* for Grades 2–6. These tools offer sentence stems for various skills within a conversation. Each bookmark focuses on a specific conversation skill. The flip book provides stems for expressing and eliciting general ideas as well as stems for clarifying, supporting, and discussing the choice of one idea over others.

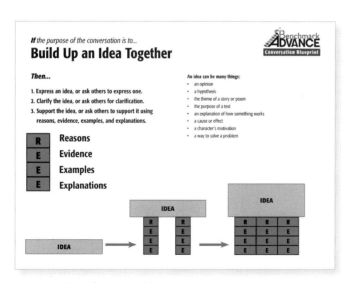

Conversation Blueprint, side 1

Think-Speak-Listen Bookmarks and Flip Books for Students

Building up an idea together

To support the first type of conversation, three key skills are needed: expressing an idea, clarifying the idea, and supporting the idea with reasons, evidence, examples, and explanations. First, students express an idea relevant to the conversation prompt. Then students clarify the idea by defining and explaining what they mean as they use appropriate academic terms. They can also refer to the stems in the Think-Speak-Listen tools for language structures to help them pose and clarify ideas. A vital part of building up an idea is supporting the idea with **reasons**, **evidence**, and **examples**. Usually, students need to **explain** how the reasons, evidence, and examples support the idea.

For example, at the end of Grade 1, Unit 3 (*Plants and Animals Grow and Change*), the teacher prompts students to talk about the essential question, "Why do living things change?" Students talk in small groups to build up their ideas together in preparation for writing about the topic. Before and during the conversations, the teacher reminds students to stay on topic, listen respectfully, and build on one another's comments. Here is an example.

Carlos:	Based on what I read, an idea that I have is living things change because they want to live. (*Expresses an idea*)
Nina:	What do you mean? (*Asks for clarification*)
Carlos:	They change so they won't die. Like to eat and move. (*Clarifies*)
Ana:	Like the frog? Remember? It was in an egg in water so it wouldn't dry and die, then it grew a tail to swim. (*Supports Carlos's idea with an example*)
David:	Yeah, with no tail it dies cuz it can't eat. But then it loses its tail. (*Adds clarity to the example*)
Nina:	Why? (*Connects back to prompt; clarifies*)
David:	Maybe so it can jump better. To get away from snakes.
Ana:	I hate snakes.
Carlos:	So do frogs. Are we done?
Ana:	No. That's just one animal. What about another animal change? (*Asks for another example; gets back on topic*)
Nina:	Butterfly. (*Provides another example*)
David:	Why does it change to stay alive? It could just stay a caterpillar. (*Asks for clarification focused on prompt*)
Nina:	I don't think it will live long like that. Butterflies can fly to warm places and get away from birds.

Notice how the students use the skills of expressing, clarifying, and supporting to build up an idea during the conversation. These skills help them stay on topic and solidify their knowledge of how living things change.

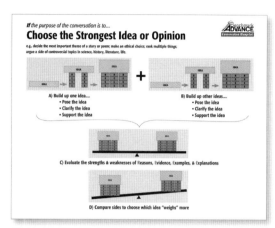

Conversation Blueprint, side 2

Choosing one idea over others

The second type of conversation builds on the first type. Students first build up one idea as just described, and after it is built up, they build up a second idea, and even others, if needed. After building up two or more ideas, the students converse to decide which idea is "stronger." A good example of this type of conversation is an argument. In an argument, a person often takes a side (i.e., makes a case for one idea) and supports it to show how it outweighs the other side(s). Learning to choose one idea over others—and respectfully and effectively argue about it—is a vital skill for life, one that students should work on every year in school.

The Conversation Blueprint illustrates how to structure a rich conversation that helps participants choose one idea over another. Students must first build up one idea with clarifications, reasons, evidence, examples, and explanations. Students then build up a second idea, and so on. Only after students have clarified and built up each idea are they ready to evaluate the strengths and weaknesses of the reasons, evidence, examples, and explanations that support each idea. Evaluation means deciding how valuable, or "heavy," the support is for an idea. For example, when conversing about the prompt, "What is the most important reason to read stories?" a group of students built up two ideas: (1) we read stories to show us how to be better people; and (2) we read stories to learn about others. They came up with examples for both ideas, and in some cases the same stories were used on both sides. They found more examples for the second idea, but one student, Brenda, argued that being better people was very heavy, even if there were more examples on the other side.

Then they compared the two ideas to choose which was "heavier"—that is, which idea had more convincing evidence. Manuel said he also thought that being better people weighed more than just learning about others. "I think we need to have better people, not just people who know more stuff about others." They chose the first idea but conceded that the second idea was important, too. Indeed, this is what the teacher wanted. She didn't care what idea they ultimately chose, but she did want them to think carefully about each idea and argue each side. Also, notice that this prompt forced students to choose an idea. If it had been, "Why do we read stories?" students could have just come up with a list of reasons and not done the cognitive work of evaluating and comparing the two ideas.

Let's look at a sample conversation between two 4th grade students who were discussing the prompt, "Do earthquakes have a more positive or negative impact on our lives?" To set up the conversation, students were given time to research the positive and negative impacts of earthquakes. Again, notice how the prompt, which asked for an argument-based choice as a result of the conversation, spurred students to clarify, support, and evaluate ideas more than if they had been prompted just to describe how earthquakes impact people.

Daniela: What negative impacts do earthquakes have on us?

Nico: Buildings fall down. (*Expresses one idea*)

Daniela: Can you elaborate? (*Asks for clarification*)

Nico: The ground shakes and buildings fall down. People die and lose their homes and their things get all smashed up. (*Clarifies*)

Daniela: What's the evidence of that? (*Asks for support*)

Nico: For example, Emma Burke's account of the San Francisco earthquake told about the damage for that family. And it said like 80 percent of the city was destroyed. That's a lot. (*Provides evidence from a text*)

Daniela: And the fire it started. And in the news lots of people still die in earthquakes. And earthquakes cause tsunamis that flood people. They are hard to predict. (*Adds to evidence*)

Nico: What about positive impact? Is there any?

Daniela: I read that the earthquake plates move and bring up oil and minerals that we use. That's a good impact. We need oil. (*Provides reason for positive impact and an explanation about the importance of oil*)

Nico: So is the impact more good or bad?

Daniela: I don't know. Maybe we... I don't know. Let's see how heavy each idea is.

Nico: OK, the bad impact is destruction of buildings and lots of people dying from it. And fires and floods. People dying is very heavy. (*Evaluates the "weight" of first idea*)

Daniela: And for good impacts, the plates help us get minerals and oil. We need these things for energy and cars, so it's heavy. (*Evaluates the "weight" of second idea*)

Nico: So it's like people dying on one side and minerals and oil on the other? What's heavier? (*Begins to compare weights of two ideas*)

Daniela: I think people dying. We need oil and minerals, but they aren't as important as people's lives. (*Compares ideas using the criterion of human life*)

Nico: I agree because think if it was you or your family in a falling building. You don't care about oil or minerals, just staying alive. (*Final explanation of choice*)

Students will never have this exact conversation, and no two conversations among students will ever be the same. This is what makes collaborative conversation so exciting and unpredictable. Just remember to keep the structures, features, and skills in mind. Use the tools as needed, but remember to reduce student reliance on them during the year. Build a culture in the classroom that values conversation and the ideas of others. In *Benchmark Advance*, you will find a wealth of opportunities to build such a culture, and in doing so, you will equip students with not only highly valuable knowledge and literacy skills, but also the priceless abilities to communicate with other humans and work together to build up ideas that are unique and generative.

If the purpose of the conversation is to...

Build Up an Idea Together

Then...

1. Express an idea, or ask others to express one.

2. Clarify the idea, or ask others for clarification.

3. Support the idea, or ask others to support it using reasons, evidence, examples, and explanations.

R	**Reasons**
E	**Evidence**
E	**Examples**
E	**Explanations**

An idea can be many things:

- an opinion
- a hypothesis
- the theme of a story or poem
- the purpose of a text
- an explanation of how something works
- a cause or effect
- a character's motivation
- a way to solve a problem

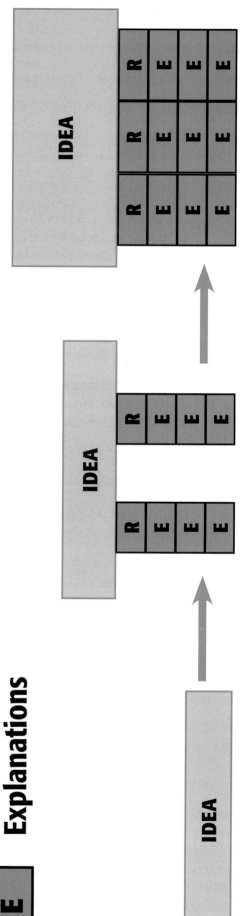

Benchmark ADVANCE
Conversation Blueprint

If the purpose of the conversation is to...

Choose the Strongest Idea or Opinion

e.g., decide the most important theme of a story or poem; make an ethical choice; rank multiple things; argue a side of controversial topics in science, history, literature, life.

Then...

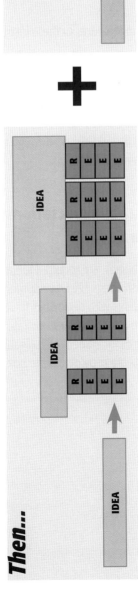

A) Build up one idea.
- **Pose the idea.**
- **Clarify the idea.**
- **Support the idea.**

+

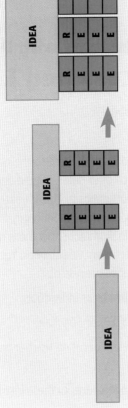

B) Build up other ideas.
- **Pose the idea.**
- **Clarify the idea.**
- **Support the idea.**

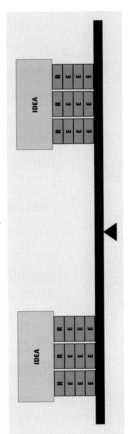

C) Evaluate the strengths and weaknesses of Reasons, Evidence, Examples, and Explanations.

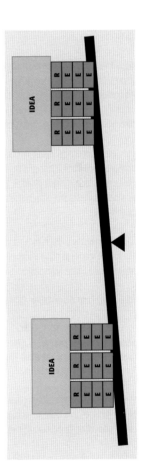

D) Compare sides to choose which idea "weighs" more.

Meeting the Needs of Students with Disabilities:
The Power of Access and Equity

By Erin Marie Mason and Marjorie McCabe, Ph.D.

Benchmark Advance is designed to support you in meeting the needs of all learners through systematic, evidence-based methods which offer differentiated and scaffolded instruction for students. Each lesson offers multiple opportunities to individualize and/or customize learning through ongoing assessment and progress monitoring, flexible grouping, and scaffolding. The purpose of this article is to illuminate how these materials can assist you in providing access and equity for your students with disabilities. You will find step-by-step guidelines to support you in the collaborative process of:

- getting to know your students with disabilities as individuals;

- using the Individual Education Program (IEP) or 504 Plan;

- building collaboration between the general education teacher and special education teacher;

- utilizing the differentiation and scaffolding features of these instructional materials;

- implementing appropriate and effective accommodations and modifications to enhance learning; and

- providing culturally and linguistically responsive instruction and accommodations.

Benchmark Advance will help you maximize access to the Common Core and elevate engagement for students with disabilities by guiding you through the instructional planning process and by directing you to recommended resources.

What are the national and state expectations for students with disabilities and the Common Core?

All students, including students with disabilities, are required to have access to the Common Core for English Language Arts and English Language Development. There are national and state recommendations for ensuring students with disabilities have appropriate access to the Common Core. In fact, the Common Core State Standards include a section on how to best provide appropriate access to the standards for student with disabilities, entitled Application to Students with Disabilities. Key elements are provided in the box on left.

How/where can I learn more about the types of disabilities of my students?

In alignment with the federal Individuals with Disabilities Education Improvement Act (IDEA), reauthorized in 2004, California schools provide special education and other related services as a part of a guaranteed free appropriate public education to students who qualify under one of the following categories (presented alphabetically): autism, deafness, deaf-blindness, emotional disturbance, hearing impairment, intellectual disability, multiple disabilities, orthopedic impairment, other health impairment, specific learning disability, speech or language impairment, traumatic brain injury, or visual impairment, including blindness.

However, approximately two-thirds of the students in special education qualify under speech and language impairment or specific learning disabilities (California Department of Education, Data Quest, 2011). Furthermore, the area of literacy is the area most affected by learning disabilities. The goals and objectives addressed in many IEPs are very often in reading and written expression.

Create safe, respectful, and stimulating learning environments for all students, including students with disabilities.

According to the California Framework, "…some groups of students experience a low level of safety and acceptance in schools for reasons including cultural, ethnic, and linguistic background; disability; sexual orientation; economic; and other factors. Students must be provided . . . settings that are physically and psychologically safe, respectful, and intellectually stimulating."

The first step in helping students with disabilities to achieve their highest potential is to address the learning environment to make sure it is physically and psychologically safe, respectful and intellectually stimulating. Without this foundation in place, students will not be able to focus on academic instruction. All students need to feel safe, respected, and welcomed in school. Students with disabilities will not be successful if they are anxious or intimidated. The California Framework emphasizes this point.

The teacher must build a culture of valuing individual differences (in learning, culture, ethnicity, language, etc). Model inclusive language and behavior. Discuss and role play situations that make students with disabilities feel included, as well as situations that may be offensive to students with disabilities. Educate all students about the types of disabilities of classmates. Have zero tolerance for any type of teasing or bullying. Reinforce the value of individual differences.

Recommended Resource:

For more information on these disabilities, refer to the National Dissemination Center for Children with Disabilities http://nichcy.org/disability/categories.

Application to Students with Disabilities, http://www.corestandards.org/assets/application-to-students-with-disabilities.pdf.

Recommended Resource:

Individualized Education Program (IEP) http://www.ncld.org/learning-disability-resources/videos/video-what-is-an-iep

504 plan http://specialchildren.about.com/od/504s/qt/sample504.htm

How do I plan, deliver, and assess instruction for the students with disabilities in my class?

1. Get to know your students with disabilities as individuals.

Students with disabilities represent the full range of diversity regarding culture, language, socioeconomic background, sexual orientation, age, gender, and more, and they are simultaneously members of these multiple demographic groups. The challenges they face may be compounded if their individual differences are not appreciated. In fact, an asset-oriented approach is essential to successful learning for students with disabilities. Like all students, they want to fit in and feel included as part of the class. No modifications, accommodations, or expert lesson plans can mitigate the feeling of not being accepted. Getting-to-know-you activities for all students are very important.

2. Utilize the Individual Education Program (IEP) or 504 Plan.

All students eligible for special education services are required to have an IEP, according to federal law. It is important to view the IEP as a working document. The IEP is developed by a multidisciplinary team in which "parents are considered equal partners with school personnel," according to the Individual with Disabilities Education Information Act, (IDEIA, 2004). In addition to demographic information, including the category of program eligibility and signature page, it is critical for teachers to be very familiar with the following IEP components and utilize them in instructional planning:

• student's current level of educational performance and social-emotional functioning;

• measurable goals and objectives to address individual needs;

• related services and program modification/supports;

• the extent to which the student will not participate in general education;

• the level of participation in district/state assessments and testing modification and accommodations, if any;

• transition services at age 16 (14 in California).

Of particular use in instructional planning are the IEP sections on current levels, goals and objectives, and modifications and supports.

3. Build collaboration between the general education and special education teachers.

It is required that students with disabilities be educated in the least restrictive environment. While that environment varies depending on the individual needs of the student, most students with mild and moderate disabilities are included in general education classrooms for much of the day with support from the special education teacher. Effective collaboration between the general education teacher and the special education teacher is essential. The general education teacher is often viewed as the grade-level curriculum expert while the special education teacher often provides resources and suggests modifications and accommodations. This collaboration should include co-designing instruction, joint progress monitoring, shared assessments, and co-teaching. For collaboration to be effective, it is very important that time be specifically given for this process.

4. See *Accommodating Students with Special Needs Throughout the Literacy Block* to learn more about how to differentiate instruction using the specially designed features in *Benchmark Advance*.

This literacy program includes flexible grouping and differentiation for all students as well as repeated opportunities to individualize for a heterogeneous student population, including students with disabilities in English and Spanish. Numerous evidence-based instructional strategies that are effective for all learners are repeated throughout the Teacher Resource Systems. This section highlights features of the instruction that provide opportunities to differentiate content, process, and assessment. With this type of instructional materials, accommodations and modifications are a natural match. Teachers will find these carefully constructed differentiation strategies very helpful when planning and implementing literacy or biliteracy instruction.

There is no such thing as a one-size-fits-all accommodation or modification. You will want to strategically select the accommodation or modification that fits your individual student, maximizes on his/her strengths, and minimizes the impact of the disability.

As noted in the California Framework, "*accommodations* are changes that help a student to overcome or work around the disability. Accommodations do not reduce the learning or performance expectations but allow the student to complete an assignment or assessment with a change in presentation, response, setting, timing, or scheduling so that learners are provided equitable access during instruction and assessment.

"Unlike accommodations, *modifications* are adjustments to an assignment or assessment that changes what is expected or measured. Modifications should be used with caution as they alter, change, lower, or reduce learning expectations and can increase the gap between the achievement of students with disabilities and expectations for proficiency. Examples of modifications include the following:

- Reducing the expectations of an assignment or assessment (completing fewer problems, amount of materials, or level of problems to complete);

- Making assignments or assessment items easier;

- Providing clues to correct responses;

- Strategic use of primary language.

Accommodations and modifications should be designed on an individual student basis, not on the basis of category of disability.

When a student is taught by multiple teachers, it is recommended that accommodations and modifications be the same across instruction classroom tests. However, some accommodations and modifications may be appropriate only for instructional use and may not be appropriate for standardized assessments. It is very important that teachers are well informed about state policies regarding accommodations for state assessments.

What do I need to do differently for English learners with special needs?

Individual Education Programs for English learners with disabilities should include linguistically appropriate goals and objectives in addition to all the supports and services the student may require due to his or her disability. Typically, sheltering strategies are very powerful accommodations for students with special needs who are also English learners. Choose the strategies that meet both the learning need due to the disability and the current stage of English language development. Remember to think about the many aspects of the individual (culture, age, home language, socioeconomic level, and more). For example, wait time is both a common accommodation for students with disabilities who need additional time to process information and for English learners who require additional time to process the second language. Some of the strategies include visuals (photos, diagrams with labels, illustrations), manipulatives, realia (real objects), hands-on activities, total physical response (TPR), gestures, graphic organizers, sentence frames, and other accommodations that minimize language barriers and maximize comprehension of the concepts. It is important to note that under the Individuals with Disabilities Education Improvement Act (IDEA), a student who is performing below grade level may not be determined to have a specific learning disability if the student's performance is primarily a result of limited English proficiency or is due to a lack of appropriate instruction.

What types of support are needed for students with Autism Spectrum Disorders?

As noted in Chapter 9 of the California ELA/ELD Framework, students with Autism Spectrum Disorders (ASD) represent the fastest growing population of students with disabilities. Students with ASD experience many challenges, especially in the area of social awareness—understanding how their behavior and actions affect others and interpreting the nonverbal cues (body language) of others (Constable, Grossi, Moniz, and Ryan 2013). Having difficulty recognizing and understanding the thoughts, feelings, beliefs, and intentions of others can be problematic in terms of achieving the Common Core English Language Arts standards that require communication and collaboration as well as those that require interpreting the feelings, thoughts, and intentions of characters or real persons. Teachers of students with ASD need to understand how these difficulties manifest themselves in the classroom in relation to the standards as well as how to provide instruction for these students to comprehend and write narratives related to the task at hand. Although some students with ASD are able to answer questions such as who, what, and where, they often struggle answering questions asking how and why. These issues become progressively more challenging as the demands to integrate information for various purposes increase at the secondary level. Teachers can find supports to enhance comprehension and ameliorate potentially anxious and stressful experiences by incorporating cognitive behavioral strategies identified by the National Professional Development Center on Autism Spectrum Disorders. Among important considerations are the following:

• Physically positioning oneself for face-to-face interactions and establishing attention;

• Providing verbal models for specific tasks;

• Responding to students' verbal and nonverbal initiations;

• Providing meaningful verbal feedback;

• Expanding students' utterances;

• Ensuring students have the prerequisite skills for a task;

• Breaking down tasks into manageable components;

• Knowing and using what students find motivating;

• Ensuring the use of appropriately challenging and interesting tasks.

Meeting the Needs of Students Who Are Advanced Learners

By Marjorie McCabe, Ph.D. and Erin Marie Mason

How can I recognize a range of advanced learners in my class?

In this section, we are focusing on students who perform or demonstrate the capacity to perform significantly above age-level peers in English Language Arts and English Language Development. Although it is up to each district to establish their own criteria for formal identification of advanced or gifted and talented learners, it is important for teachers to learn to recognize a range of advanced learners in their class and differentiate instruction to meet their needs whether formal identification exists or not. These students comprise a highly heterogeneous population, in terms of culture, language, ethnicity, socioeconomic level, gender, sexual orientation, age, and neurodiversity. It is especially common for advanced learners to go unrecognized when students exhibit their advanced learning in unfamiliar or inconsistent ways. In addition to the more familiar image of the "A" student who regularly masters grade-level concepts significantly faster than age-level peers, there is a much broader variety of advanced learners whose gifts and talents may go unnoticed on traditional measures of performance.

> **Advanced Learners**
> Students who perform or have the potential to perform significantly above their age group. They may be formally identified as gifted and talented or not but demonstrate the capacity.

Tips for recognizing a range of advanced learners:

- Advanced learners do not necessarily demonstrate advanced performance uniformly across all areas. Advanced learning may present itself in spikes of achievement in the areas of talent or interest.

- Consider the stage of English language development for English learners, as well as their rate of progress. For example, imagine an English learner who begins the year with emerging English proficiency and is translating for peers by the end of the school year. This student may not demonstrate advanced abilities on typical English Language Arts tests yet. However, he or she may be best served by strategies for advanced learners since the student is exhibiting accelerated learning and talent in second language acquisition (or English language development).

- English learners will need sheltered instruction techniques to access the content and demonstrate their learning. Non-sheltered instructional strategies and assessments may not provide true opportunity to learn and may not reveal their advancement or talents.

- Students with disabilities can be twice exceptional. A student may have a disability that affects one area and may be gifted and talented in another.

- Students with behavioral challenges may exhibit significantly accelerated learning but may do so intermittently depending on the impact of the challenging behavior.

These identifications are not mutually exclusive, and in California's culturally and linguistically diverse population, many students will share identification in a variety of categories. In many ways, teachers can look for students who not only exhibit achievement or the capacity to achieve significantly above age-level peers, but in relation to their demographic peers. For example, is an English learner performing significantly beyond other English learners of their age who entered school at the same stage of English language development?

As the California ELA/ELD Framework outlines:

"A synthesis of research (Rogers 2007) on the education of students identified as gifted and talented suggests that they should be provided the following:

• Daily challenge in their specific areas of talent

• Regular opportunities to be unique and to work independently in their areas of passion and talent

• Various forms of subject-based and grade-based acceleration as their educational needs require

• Opportunities to socialize and learn with peers with similar abilities

• Instruction that is differentiated in pace, amount of review and practice, and organization of content presentation

Instruction for advanced learners should focus on depth and complexity. Opportunities to engage with appropriately challenging text and content, conduct research, use technology creatively, and write regularly on topics that interest them can be especially valuable for advanced learners; these experiences allow students to engage more deeply with content and may contribute to motivation. Instruction that focuses on depth and complexity ensures cohesion in learning rather than piecemeal "enrichment."

California Framework, Chapter 9: Access and Equity

How can I differentiate instruction to meet the needs of advanced learners?

All students can benefit from the types of strategies that support advanced learners. However, too often, advanced learners stagnate in their learning trajectory because the content, pace, and instructional processes do not meet their needs. This can lead to behavior issues, loss of interest in school, and a sense of not belonging with peers.

Assessment is key to determining content, pace and instructional processes. Pre-assessments and ongoing evaluation may be conducted formally or informally. Teacher observation is a powerful tool in detecting evidence of advanced learning, since it may not always be reflected on traditional assessments. Progress monitoring is essential to keeping instruction in the student's zone of proximal development. Students who demonstrate advanced learning or the potential for advanced learning may require:

• compacted content (advancing to more complex skills/concepts within the grade level or standards from future grade levels);

• accelerated pace of instruction (introduction of grade-level concepts, but with less time spent on each concept, practice, or review);

• variety of instructional processes (novelty of process or product, enhanced creativity, opportunities to apply standards to student's individual interests);

• opportunities to demonstrate biliteracy abilities in creative ways (for example, contrastive analysis of thematically related poetry/literature/lyrics in two languages, role play situational biliteracy contexts in academic content areas such as explaining the parts of cells and their functions in two languages).

Because *Benchmark Advance* is built around differentiated opportunities for student learning, it is an ideal instructional resource to support your students who are advanced learners. For example:

• A variety of formal and informal assessments allow teachers to pinpoint a student's zone of proximal development in two languages.

• Flexible grouping and small-group instruction for most reading and writing activities allows teachers to group student with similar levels of advancement or similar talents/interests.

• Flexible pacing and If/Then "Reinforce or Reaffirm the Strategy" instruction within the mini-lessons allow teachers to compact the content and accelerate the instruction in each lesson, within each standard, as needed.

• Leveled readers and trade book recommendations on each unit topic or concept allow teachers to customize reading instruction.

• E-books allow extensive variety of texts on topics that add depth and complexity, as well as novelty and variety.

• Research and writing opportunities engage students in creatively pursuing their unique interests and passions.

• Collaborative conversations allow students to customize learning to their interests and level of advancement.

- A gradual release model (modeled, shared, guided, and independent activities) for speaking, listening, reading, and writing allows teachers to support a student's current stage of development while preparing them to master the next stage. Teachers can move students along a continuum of depth and complexity as needed.

- Project-based learning "Connect Across Disciplines" learning opportunities to promote innovation and social responsibility.

Accommodating Students with Special Needs Throughout the Benchmark Advance Literacy Block

As you get to know your individual students with disabilities and their current levels of performance, pay attention to the areas in which they struggle. If their disability manifests itself in one area, provide an alternate pathway for them to access the standards, while supporting growth as much as possible in the area of challenge. The chart on the following pages points out many of the opportunities for differentiated instruction already integrated into the Benchmark Advance literacy block, and it suggests some additional accommodations that can implemented within your whole- and small-group instruction. These accommodations will help you meet the needs of students with a range of disabilities as well as the needs of advanced learners.

Struggling readers will benefit by direct, explicit code instruction in phonemic awareness and word identification strategies as part of a balanced literacy instruction program. Also, the use of implicit instruction, which focuses on context clues and picture cues, will be valuable. The use of systematic phonemic awareness and phonics instruction and numerous opportunities for practice and review will be key to successful learning by students with disabilities.

It is essential to get to know your students as individuals. If they are students with disabilities, it is crucial to review the IEP or 504 Plan and build collaboration between the general education and special education teachers serving the student. The same strategy could soothe one student yet aggravate another, empower one child yet incapacitate another, depending on how the disability manifests itself. For example, a student with sensory processing issues may shut down with a sandpaper phonics activity, while a student without such sensitivities may require that stimulus and thrive with it. Your broader knowledge of the student, your detailed progress monitoring, and your collaboration will allow you to distinguish which strategies are the best fit for the student.

Benchmark Advance also includes intervention materials for efficient and effective use in tutorial or small-group instructional settings. These materials focus on students who need re-teaching and practice in one or more of the four identified key foundational skills in English and/or in Spanish that are part of the Reading Standards: Foundational Skills in the CA CCSS for ELA: (1) print concepts; (2) phonological awareness; (3) phonics and word recognition; and (4) fluency.

Many of the strategies included in the following chart were adapted from those recommended in *Strategies for Teaching Students with Learning and Behavior Problems* [Vaughn, S. & Bos, C. (2012). Boston, MA: Pearson].

Accommodating Students with Special Needs Throughout the Literacy Block–Grades K–2

Grades K–2 Literacy Block Component	Lesson activities to support through accommodations	Disabilities that affect oral language (speaking and listening)	Disabilities that affect decoding	
Interactive Read-Aloud	Listening to complex read-alouds	- Ask frequent questions to check for comprehension. - Provide visual cues such as photos, illustrations, gestures, and facial expressions. - Pause throughout the text to allow students to make connections and note their ideas in a journal.	n/a	
	Summarizing and responding to read-alouds	- Have students express ideas by developing drawings or selecting from pre-made photos and visuals. - Students may benefit from preparing and formulating a response with a partner. - Provide sentence frames. - Use technology, such as typing a response and sending it to the teacher or posting on an electronic chart realtime such as a wiki or discussion forum.	n/a	
Shared Reading	Developing concepts about print	- Use a pointer to model one-to-one correspondence between the actual features of the real book and the discussion.	n/a	
	Reading aloud to build fluency	- Scaffolding is built into the mini-lessons through picture walk, choral reading, and gradual release of teacher modeling (I do, we do). Students join choral reading as they are ready. - Repeated readings build confidence, familiarity, and fluency. - Add gestures, facial expressions, and total physical response to enhance comprehension.	- Scaffolding is built into the mini-lessons through picture walk, choral reading, and gradual release of teacher modeling. - Use a pointer to model one-to-one correspondence between oral and written words.	
	Developing language knowledge	- Use graphic organizers and charts that illustrate word patterns and features. - Highlight key words and word features written in the text using a frame in the big book or by using the highlighting or window shade features in the e-presenter version of the text.	- Provide opportunities to hear and discuss word patterns and features in cooperative groups or pairs.	
Reading/ Shared Writing Mini-Lessons	Participating in Collaborative Conversations	- Use the Observation Checklist for Collaborative Conversation (found in each week of instruction) to help you identify communication skills to model for your students. - Provide sentence frames to support the kind of conversation you expect. (You may wish to download copies of the Think-Speak-Listen Flip Book, which contains frames to support academic conversations.) - Allow students to write or draw to express their ideas during discussions. - Make laptops or tablets available for students to keyboard their responses to conversation prompts	n/a	
	Participating in Productive Engagement Activities	- Use the Observation Checklist for Productive Engagement (found in Weeks 2 and 3) to help you monitor students during learning tasks and make minute-by-minute instructional decisions based on their needs. - Based on your observations, adjust the content and pace of instruction. - Provide additional gradual release instruction using the model/guided practice or If/Then strategies.	- Use the Observation Checklist for Productive Engagement (found in Weeks 2 and 3) to help you monitor students during learning tasks and make minute-by-minute instructional decisions based on their needs. - Based on your observations, adjust the content and pace of instruction. - Provide additional gradual release instruction using the model/guided practice or If/Then strategies.	

Disabilities that affect reading comprehension	Disabilities that affect written expression	Accommodations for advanced learners
n/a	n/a	- Pause to allow students to make connections and note their ideas in a journal. - Adjust the pace to allow students to spend more time on a particular section that inspires them or to listen to longer segments and then analyze the whole.
- Provide pictures or visuals to aide with sequencing, main ideas and details, and retelling.	- Have students express ideas by developing drawings or selecting from pre-made photos and visuals. - Students may benefit from processing and formulating a response with a partner. - Provide sentence frames to support student responses. You may wish to download copies of the Think-Speak-Listen Flip Book	- Group students with like interests or similar accelerated learning needs in a think-pair-share or team discussion. - Ask students to compare the text with other complex texts, with other authors, or with texts on the same topic from other content areas, in order to identify patterns. - Invite students to consider multiple perspectives, such as the point of view of different characters or professionals from different disciplines related to the text.
n/a	n/a	- Formally or informally pre-assess to identify who has mastered these concepts at the start of instruction. (Screeners may be found in the K–2 Reading Foundational Skills Assessment Handbook.) - Teach a mini-lesson on more advanced concepts of print to those who need it. - Group students who have mastered these concepts and have them create their own book that includes key concepts of print that they have already mastered.
- Scaffolding is built into the mini-lessons through picture walk, choral reading, and gradual release of teacher modeling. - Add gestures, facial expressions, and total physical response (TPR) to enhance comprehension.	n/a	- Allow the students who decode fluently after the picture walk or first read to create gestures or actions to accompany the read-aloud. - Ask students who are decoding at an advanced level to focus on expressive reading, prosody (e.g., intonation, voice, and phrasing to convey their understanding of characters and mood).
- Use visual aids (photos, sketches, icons) to support comprehension of the key words being studied. - Use gestures and total physical response to support comprehension of the key words. - Use graphic organizers and charts that illustrate word patterns and features. - Highlight key words and word features written in the text.	- Students can express their ideas through verbal discussions or visual representations (diagrams or charts). - Use sentence frames to scaffold written expression. - Use graphic organizers to list key phrases, rather than full sentences or paragraphs in some cases. - Utilize assistive technology (writing on a computer, dictating to computer).	- Adjust the type of language students study in the lesson to meet their zone of proximal development. Provide more advanced content (language) or accelerate the pace and move to independent practice or application more quickly. - Strategically pair students for discussion with other students who share their passions or accelerated learning needs. - Ask students to think like a linguist or an author and identify new words that fit the pattern. They may use a graphic organizer or chart to expand on the lesson's ideas. - For advanced learners who are also English learners, ask them to apply the lesson to their primary language and chart examples from that language. Compare and contrast how the pattern in English is similar or different from the pattern in the primary language.
n/a	- Allow students to express their ideas in pictures or through role playing. - Provide a sentence frame for students to use. - Consider timekeeper, reporter, or discussion director as strategic roles.	- Provide opportunities for students to make connections across texts, authors, and genre. - Challenge students to pose new questions and to identify connections between the text and their other content area studies. - Provide more challenging group roles and responsibilities. - Use the Challenge Activities provided in many of the Weeks 2 and 3 Close Reading mini-lessons.
- Use the Observation Checklist for Productive Engagement (found in Weeks 2 and 3) to help you monitor students during learning tasks and make minute-by-minute instructional decisions based on their needs. - Based on your observations, adjust the content and pace of instruction. - Provide additional gradual release instruction using the model/guided practice or If/Then strategies.	- Use the Observation Checklist for Productive Engagement (found in Weeks 2 and 3) to help you monitor students during learning tasks and make minute-by-minute instructional decisions based on their needs. - Based on your observations, adjust the content and pace of instruction. - Provide additional gradual release instruction using the model/guided practice or If/Then strategies.	- Use the Observation Checklist for Productive Engagement (found in Weeks 2 and 3) to help you monitor students during learning tasks and make minute-by-minute instructional decisions based on their needs. - Accelerate the content based on progress monitoring. Move to above-grade-level content where/when indicated by formal and informal assessment. - Students may need all concepts taught but for a shorter time, with less repetition and at an accelerated pace. - Use progress monitoring to form a temporary, flexible group of students who are ready for advancement in a particular standard.

Accommodating Students with Special Needs Throughout the Literacy Block—Grades K–2

Grades K–2 Literacy Block Component	Lesson activities to support through accommodations	Disabilities that affect oral language (speaking and listening)	Disabilities that affect decoding	
Reading/Shared Writing Mini-Lessons	Text Annotation (Grade 2)	n/a	- Model text annotation skills as needed. Refer to the annotation symbols on the inside front cover of each unit's Texts for Close Reading. - Consider using a leveled reader that addresses the same content and concepts, but at the student's current reading level. Allow the student to annotate this leveled reader using sticky notes or the notetaking feature in the e-reader version on BenchmarkUniverse.com. - Allow partner or buddy reading and discussion while creating annotated notes.	
	Writing	n/a	- During the revising and editing process when decoding is most required, allow students to work in pairs. - Allow the use of electronic spelling and grammar checks to help students identify text that needs correction. - Use assistive technology so the device reads the written text back to the student for review.	
Phonics	Phonemic Awareness	- Use the Pre-Teach/Re-Teach Phonemic Awareness Routine to provide additional practice with phonemic awareness skills. - Use counters with the Elkonin boxes on the student work mats to visually and kinesthetically help students build awareness of the number and order of sounds they hear. - Try clapping or gesturing to count or mark sounds.	n/a	
	Letter/Sound Correspondence	- Use the Pre-Teach/Re-Teach Letter/Sound Correspondences Routine to provide additional instruction and practice. - Reinforce letter/sound correspondences using the Frieze Cards and other visuals. - Use letter tiles that can be manipulated and moved as students say each sound. - Provide longer and more frequent opportunities for modeled, guided, and independent practice. - Conduct more frequent progress monitoring to check for understanding and mastery.	- Use the Pre-Teach/Re-Teach Letter/Sound Correspondences Routine to provide additional instruction and practice. - Reinforce letter/sound correspondences using the Frieze Cards and other visuals. - Use letter tiles that can be manipulated and moved as students say each sound. - Provide longer and more frequent opportunities for modeled, guided, and independent practice. - Conduct more frequent progress monitoring to check for understanding and mastery.	
	Blending	- Use the Pre-Teach/Re-Teach Blending Routine to provide additional instruction and practice. - As you model blends, elongate the sounds as you pronounce them. - Use letter tiles that can be manipulated and moved as students say the sounds. - Provide longer and more frequent opportunities for modeled, guided, and independent practice. - Conduct more frequent progress monitoring to check for understanding and mastery.	- Use the Pre-Teach/Re-Teach Blending Routine to provide additional instruction and practice. - As you model blends, elongate the sounds as you pronounce them. - Use letter tiles that can be manipulated and moved as students say the sounds. - Provide longer and more frequent opportunities for modeled, guided, and independent practice. - Conduct more frequent progress monitoring to check for understanding and mastery.	

Disabilities that affect reading comprehension	Disabilities that affect written expression	Accommodations for advanced learners
- Model text annotation skills as needed. Refer to the annotation symbols on the inside front cover of each unit's Texts for Close Reading. - Teach students to note words that are not familiar. - Students may use the e-reader version of the text to highlight words or phrases they wish to clarify or practice, paraphrase them, or write notes.	- Students may highlight, underline, or circle key parts of text using the consumable or the e-reader version. - Annotated notes may be taken electronically in the e-reader version of the text. - Notes may take the form of diagrams, visuals, charts, or key phrases.	- Add complexity by allowing students to use text annotation to compare text elements or information with other texts or authors or across content areas. - Add complexity by asking students to analyze the text/information from the perspective of different characters or professions (disciplines), such as a historian, an economist, an ecologist, a lawyer, etc. - Add depth by asking students to note additional information based on their interests, cite other sources they have read, and compare/contrast information or opinions. - Add depth by asking students to cite key evidence in support of a particular overarching theme such as ethics, change, systems, etc. - (See Sandra Kaplan's *Icons of Depth and Complexity.*)
- n/a	- Allow the full writing process to take place using a computer or tablet. Avoid having students write or rewrite drafts by hand. - Pre-writes may be illustrated or use graphic organizers with key phrases. - Provide sentence frames specific to the genre or text structure. Practice them orally prior to using them in writing. - Provide models of the desired type of writing, anchor papers, and rubrics with examples. (See the exemplars provided in the mini-lessons and Informal Assessment Handbook.) - Use illustrated graphic organizers to explain the key elements of the text/genre, such as a checklist with a visual or icon to represent each item. - Allow students to work in pairs or teams. - Allow the use of spelling and grammar checks to help student's identify text that needs correction. - Use assistive technology so the device reads the written text back to the student for review.	- Allow the full writing process to take place using a computer or tablet. Avoid having students write or rewrite drafts by hand if it reduces their pace of thinking/production. - Support more sophisticated, advanced language through sentence frames. - Provide models of more advanced writing, anchor papers, and rubrics with examples from the current grade or the next grade level (See the Informal Assessment Handbook). - Allow students to work in pairs or teams by interest/passion or zone of proximal development. - Allow the use of spelling and grammar checks to help students identify text that needs correction and maintain the pace of their creative process and thought process. - Use assistive technology so the device reads the written text back to the student for review. - For students who are advanced learners and English learners, allow them to write any part of the pre-write or rough draft in the primary language to support the pace and sophistication of thinking/writing.
n/a	n/a	- Use progress monitoring to continually provide activities in students' zone of proximal development. Accelerate the pace of instruction as needed. Once automaticity is acquired, move on. - Provide more complex words and sound combinations.
n/a	- Try multimodality approaches such as writing the letter in sand or in shaving cream, tracing the letter with a finger on sandpaper or textured surface, placing moveable letters on the work mat or a magnetic board. - Use technology to allow students to select printed letters, manipulate them, and draw them on a screen. - Use assistive technology to dictate letters to the computer or tablet.	- Use progress monitoring to continually provide activities in students' zone of proximal development. Accelerate the pace of instruction as needed. Once automaticity is acquired, move on. - If students are decoding and comprehending text independently, proceed to small group and independent reading activities. - Provide more complex words and sound combinations.
n/a	- Try multimodality approaches such as writing the letter in sand or in shaving cream, tracing the letter with a finger on sandpaper or textured surface, placing moveable letters on a magnetic board. - Use technology to allow students to select printed letters, manipulate them, or draw them on a screen. - Use assistive technology to dictate letters to the computer or tablet.	- Use progress monitoring to continually provide activities in students' zone of proximal development. Accelerate the pace of instruction as needed. Once automaticity is acquired, move on. - Provide more complex words and sound combinations. - If students are decoding and comprehending text independently, proceed to small group and independent reading activities.

Accommodating Students with Special Needs Throughout the Literacy Block—Grades K–2

Grades K–2 Literacy Block Component	Lesson activities to support through accommodations	Disabilities that affect oral language (speaking and listening)	Disabilities that affect decoding	
Phonics	High-Frequency Word Instruction	- Use the Pre-Teach/Re-Teach High-Frequency Words Routine to provide additional instruction and practice. - Teach the most frequently occurring words. - Use words in meaningful contexts and make sure students understand word meaning. - Limit the number of words introduced in a single lesson. - Utilize multimodality systems, such as tracing, copying and writing from memory. - Provide multiple opportunities to practice words by building, reading, and writing words until automaticity occurs.	n/a	
	Spelling			
	Handwriting	If students have difficulty recognizing sounds they hear, it will affect their ability to write them.	n/a	

Disabilities that affect reading comprehension	Disabilities that affect written expression	Accommodations for advanced learners
- Use the Pre-Teach/Re-Teach High-Frequency Words Routine to provide additional instruction and practice. - Teach the most frequently occurring words. - Use words in meaningful contexts and make sure students understand word meaning. - Limit the number of words introduced in a single lesson. - Utilize multimodality systems, such as tracing, copying, and writing from memory. - Provide multiple opportunities to practice words by building, reading, and writing words until automaticity occurs.	- Try multimodality approaches such as writing the high-frequency word in sand or in shaving cream, tracing the letters with a finger on sandpaper or textured surface, or placing moveable letters on a magnetic board. - Use technology to allow students to select printed letters, manipulate them, or draw them on a screen. - Use assistive technology to dictate letters to the computer or tablet.	- Use progress monitoring to continually provide activities in students' zone of proximal development. - If students are decoding and comprehending text independently, proceed to small-group and independent reading activities. - Provide more complex words and sound combinations.
	- Analyze current level of functioning in students' written work and dictation by determining the type and pattern of errors. - Develop spelling instructional program based on individual needs as evidenced in assessment. - Look for error patterns. - Make sure students can read and understand the meaning of each spelling word. - Reduce the number of words introduced—no more than three words at a time - Spelling is taught concurrently with phonics in the program so that students see a connection between reading and spelling. Reinforce this as much as possible to scaffold them. - Teach words with same spelling patterns and include non-examples. - Give many opportunities to practice spelling complete words correctly using a model and self-checking for mastery. - Use the Re-teach/Pre-teach Spelling Routine to provide additional modeling and guided practice. - Provide frequent opportunities for seeing and using mastered words in context. - Review mastered words while introducing new words. - Avoid having students simply write the words over and over from memory without checking a model and getting feedback. - Use high-frequency words so students can see same words in reading texts. - Use a combination of approaches, such as multi-sensory, technology supports. - Have students say the words while writing it or spelling it aloud with a partner. - Have students write a spelling word while teacher or partner simultaneously displays the correct model. Then delay the amount of time before the correct model is shown until students write the word from memory. - Students compare their incorrectly spelled words with correct model.	- Use progress monitoring to continually provide activities in their zone of proximal development. - Provide more complex spelling words and sound combinations.
n/a	Have students write with a keyboard or a touch screen if they have sensory issues with the physical handwriting process.	- n/a

Accommodating Students with Special Needs Throughout the Literacy Block—Grades K–2

Grades K–2 Literacy Block Component	Lesson activities to support through accommodations	Disabilities that affect oral language (speaking and listening)	Disabilities that affect decoding	
Small Group Reading/ Independent & Collaborative Activities	Reading leveled texts	- Small-group reading may be conducted with fewer students. - Use buddy reading to alternate reading and listening activities, shorten the length of listening/decoding segments, and allow students to focus on comprehension.	- Precede a difficult book with an easier book on the same topic that uses similar language. - Reading books in a series is a tremendous support (same topic or characters). - Small reading groups may be conducted with fewer students. - Use partner reading to alternate reading and listening activities, shorten the length of listening/decoding segments, and allow students to focus on comprehension. - Allow more frequent and repeated readings of text. - Have students record themselves reading on a laptop or tablet, measure words per minute, and hear their intonation and prosody.	
	Reading reader's theater scripts	- Have students record themselves reading on a laptop or tablet, measure words per minute, and hear their intonation and prosody.	- Remind students to use the color-coding in their scripts to help them find and track their parts. - Have students record themselves reading on a laptop or tablet, measure words per minute, and hear their intonation and prosody. - Invite students to read along with the audio-highlighted e-reader version of the script.	
	Performing reader's theater scripts	- Explicitly teach presentation or public speaking skills including volume, intonation, eye contact, body positioning, facial expressions, and more. - Allow students to read aloud only when fully confident or give them small groups in which they perform. - Allow students to create an audio or video recording to capture the performance in which they are the most successful.	- Assign parts or roles to students based on their reading level. Match the role to the student's reading level using the Characters/Levels chart for each script (in the Reader's Theater Teacher Handbook). - Pair students to allow buddy reading as a pre-reading support before reading publicly to a larger group.	

Disabilities that affect reading comprehension	Disabilities that affect written expression	Accommodations for advanced learners
- Precede a difficult book with an easier book on the same topic that uses similar language. - Reading books in a series is a tremendous support (same characters or topic). - Use text-specific graphic organizers, story maps, or illustrations to chart key points for comprehension. - Provide visuals, such as diagrams, drawings, and photos from the text to support the student in discussing the text (sequence/retell/summarize). - Use buddy reading to alternate reading and listening activities, shorten the length of listening/decoding segments, and allow students to focus on comprehension.	n/a	- If students are decoding and comprehending text independently, provide texts at advanced levels, including above grade level. The small-group texts for each unit include titles at a range of guided reading levels. See also the list of trade book recommendations provided for each grade level. - Allow the students who decode fluently after the first read to create gestures or actions to accompany the read-aloud. - Ask students who are decoding at an advanced level to focus on expressive reading, prosody (e.g. intonation, voice, and phrasing to convey their understanding of characters and mood). - Students with similar interests and reading levels may form literature circles and research teams.
- Use the gradual release modeling and practice in the Reader's Theater Teacher Handbook lessons to support comprehension through read-aloud, shared reading, and discussion of the characters, plot, and key ideas or themes. - Use the explicit vocabulary instruction to support comprehension. - Extend think aloud to model metacognition to students. For example, provide repeated modeling on how to make connections between events and ideas in the text. - Explicitly teach students self-monitoring strategies for identifying words or language that is confusing or unknown. Then provide extended guided practice in applying the strategies. - Use graphic organizers to visually and explicitly teach connections between ideas in the text (cause and effect, inferences, author's intent, main idea, etc.).	n/a	- Have advanced learners read and rehearse the more challenging script provided for each unit. - Consult Characters/Levels chart for each script and assign advanced readers higher level roles or roles that require a more nuanced, expressive interpretation. - Allow more passionate, interested advanced readers to be understudies for other parts/roles. - Individuals or a group can create a text extension, an alternate plot twist, or interaction between texts.
- Acting out and role-playing scenes can provide total physical response and kinesthetic approach to enhance comprehension. - Chunk scenes into smaller segments to explain passages, phrases, or inferences that are challenging.	n/a	- Allow students to use technology to present reader's theater via podcast/audio presentation, video, puppet show. - Create an improvisational theater experience, based on the original script that asks students to create their own language/text in the style of the original with new events, ideas, and actions.

The Value of Contrastive Analysis

By Silvia Dorta-Duque de Reyes and Jill Kerper-Mora, Ph.D.

**Benchmark Advance
Contrastive Analysis Charts**

The Sound-Spelling Contrastive Analysis Charts compare the phonemes (sounds) and graphemes (letters) of English to nine world languages and enable teachers to compare various features at a glance, including:

- Categories of English spellings (grapheme types, such as short vowels)

- English sounds (phonemes)

- English letter(s) (the most common grapheme(s) used to represent the sound)

- Examples of English sounds in various positions in words (initial, medial, and final position)

- Whether that sound exists in each of the nine languages

- Whether the letter(s) that represent that sound exist in each language

Contrastive analysis is the systematic study of two languages to identify their similarities and differences. Contrastive analysis charts help educators recognize distinctions between a student's primary language and English. The Benchmark Advance Contrastive Analysis Charts address the similarities and differences between English and nine of the most common world languages spoken by English learners in California.

For both students and teachers, using a language construction process that recognizes the similarities and differences between a primary and secondary language, rather than an error correction procedure, builds students' awareness of how English works. In every contrastive analysis lesson, students benefit when their primary language is respected and tapped as a resource for learning English through an additive approach that honors their primary language.

All oral languages are comprised of phonemes, and each of those sounds is articulated in a particular position in the mouth. As teachers are helping students to recognize and pronounce the sounds of English (phonology), they need to know whether the students' primary language utilizes particular sounds. If the target sound is found in the student's primary language, it will be fairly easy for the student to articulate and use that sound in English. If, however, the sound is not found in the student's primary language, teachers will need to provide additional instruction and support to ensure that students "hear" (discriminate) and articulate the sound in English.

Students will need instruction in recognizing and distinguishing the sounds of English as compared to or contrasted with sounds in their primary language (e.g., vowels, consonants, consonant blends, syllable structures). An example is the short vowel sounds of English that are not equivalent to vowel sounds in Spanish. In an alphabetic language system, phonology and phonemic awareness are the foundation for reading and writing.

There are many writing systems in the world. Latin-based languages, such as English and Spanish, use a writing system that is based on the letters of the alphabet; words are formed by combining different letters. Other languages, such as Chinese, use a completely different system of writing. It is called the logographic system. Each character represents a meaningful (morphological) unit. Because these two systems are entirely different, there is not a basis for comparison of the writing systems. For students who have been taught to use the logographic system, an introduction to the alphabet is necessary, and the instruction needs to include the sound–symbol relationship.

The Structure of the Sound-Spelling Contrastive Analysis Charts

In order to support students who are acquiring new sounds and letters in a new language, it is important to map out which sounds and letters are familiar to students, the extent to which the sounds and letters are familiar, and which sounds and letters are new and unfamiliar. The charts indicate whether the English phonemes and graphemes exist in both languages (positive), are about the same (approximate), or have no equivalency.

Transfer Indicators in the Charts	What They Mean
Yes	There is an equivalent, or positive, transfer relationship between English and student's primary language.
Approximate	This term is used when referring to phoneme variants that are considered close enough to the corresponding English language sound not to cause confusion for English learners.
No	There is no equivalent or transfer relationship between English and the student's primary language.

Although some world languages use an alphabetic system for writing (e.g., Spanish, Vietnamese), they each vary in both sounds and symbols used to encode those sounds. Some sounds and spellings are fully transferable (e.g., sound /b/ can be encoded with letter *b* in both Spanish and English, as in [botón/button]). Some sounds that are transferable can be encoded in English using spelling patterns *not* found in primary language (e.g., /k/ spelled *ck* in English, as in *duck*).

The Structure of the Grammar-Syntax Charts

The Grammar-Syntax charts are aligned to the CCSS Language standards and compare the grammatical differences between English and each of the nine world languages. The charts are divided into the conventions of standard English grammar: verbs; nouns; word order; adverbs and adjectives; pronouns; and prepositions, conjunctions, and articles.

These charts provide teachers with information relating to potential error patterns that may result as students generalize what they know and use in their home language to English. Once teachers know which grammatical structures transfer to academic English conventions, and which do not, they can adjust instruction to provide maximum reinforcement for skills lessons on these structures. For example, English is an inflectional language. In an inflectional language, verbs change forms. For example, the verb "see" can appear as "see," "sees," "saw," "seen," or "seeing." Other languages, such as Chinese, are non-inflectional. Words/verbs do not change shapes. The word "see" 看 is always written as 看 and there is no change. In addition, the word "to" in front of an English "verb" such as "to go" is nonexistent.

When teachers learn to identify and capitalize on students' existing language skills, they are able to use positive transfer to support student in gaining English language proficiency and biliteracy. Instructional approaches that promote students' awareness of and understandings about language variety are particularly useful for supporting students' metalinguistic knowledge and positive language identity.

We extend our appreciation to the language consultants, educators, and linguists who reviewed these charts for accuracy and completeness, and we extend special recognition to Sandra Ceja, who compiled these charts.

Using Contrastive Analysis to Inform Instruction

The Contrastive Analysis Charts give teachers information about students' native language usages, structures, and grammar to enable them to accomplish the following:

1. Support students' overall understanding of how English works in ways that are similar to or different from usages in their native language.

2. Identify specific teaching points where metalinguistic knowledge of linguistic similarities and differences will enable students to self-monitor and correct errors and error patterns in English in both oral and written production. This includes teachers' use of phonological differences between students' primary language and English that impact their pronunciation and spelling.

3. Scaffold and support students' developing strategies in gaining word level meaning of English forms, such as nominalization (converting a verb to a noun) and noting the way English words are formed (morphology), such as prefixes, root word, and suffixes that support students in deciphering new vocabulary based on their knowledge of their native language. This is especially helpful in learning cognates.

4. Scaffold and support students in developing language learning strategies for increasing their ability in sentence and clause-level meaning-making strategies of sentence deconstruction ("unpacking sentences") and for understanding phrase level meaning conveyed through English grammar and syntax in informational and literary text.

Sound-Spelling: Consonants

	Sound (phoneme)	Most Common Spelling Patterns (graphemes)	Notes	Word Examples: initial	medial	final	Spanish Sound (phoneme) transfer?	Spanish Spelling pattern (grapheme) transfer?	Vietnamese Sound (phoneme) transfer?	Vietnamese Spelling pattern (grapheme) transfer?	Hmong Sound (phoneme) transfer?	Hmong Spelling pattern (grapheme) transfer?
Consonants				initial	medial	final						
The sound /b/ is used or approximated in all of these languages, but the spelling used to communicate /b/ varies.	/b/	b	Subject to medial consonant doubling. Consonant blends include bl and br. Spelling b(e) in long vowel syllables	button	cabin (bubble)	lab (cube)	yes	yes	yes	yes	approx.	no
The sound /k/ is used in all of these languages, but the spelling used to communicate /k/ varies.	/k/	c	Primarily followed by another consonant, or short/long a, o, u vowel sound. Consonant blends include cl and cr.	castle	act	music	yes	yes	yes	yes	yes	no
		k	Primarily followed by short/long e, i vowel sound	karate	monkey	mask		yes		yes		yes
		_ck	Following short vowel sound at the end of a syllable or word	(n/a)	blacksmith	duck		no		no		no
		-lk	Low frequency when preceded by o or a	(n/a)	chalky, yolks	talk, folk		no		no		no
		ch	Greek words	chorus,	echo	stomach, ache		no		no		no
		qu, que	French	quay	conquer	antique		yes (qu but not que)		no		no
The sound /d/ is used or approximated in most of these languages, but the spelling used to communicate /d/ varies.	/d/	d	Subject to medial consonant doubling. Consonant blends include dr and dw	dice	maiden (paddle)	mad (add)	approx.	yes	yes	yes	yes	yes
The sound /f/ is used or approximated in many of these languages, but the spelling used to communicate /f/ varies.	/f/	f	Subject to medial consonant doubling. Consonant blends include fr and fl.	family	after (baffle)	self, knife, muff	yes	yes	yes	no	yes	yes
		gh	-ough and -augh patterns	(n/a)	laughter	enough		no		no		no
		ph		photo	aphid	graph		no		yes		no
The sound /g/ is used or approximated in many of these languages, but the spelling used to communicate /g/ varies.	/g/	g	"Hard g" sound, mainly when followed by a, o, u. There are exceptions (girl, get and others). Subject to medial consonant doubling. Consonant blends include gr and gl. /gw/ sound spelled with gu (language, penguin)	goal	drags (baggage)	tag, (egg)	yes	yes	yes	yes	approx.	no
		gu ("silent u")	"Hard g" sound spelled gu when followed by e, I, or y to prevent "soft g" sound	guide	intrigued	(gue) league, plague		yes		no		
		gh		ghost	aghast			no		yes		no

Sound (phoneme)	Most Common Spelling Patterns (graphemes)	Tagalog Sound (phoneme) transfer?	Tagalog Spelling pattern (grapheme) transfer?	Korean Sound (phoneme) transfer?	Korean Spelling pattern (grapheme) transfer?	Cantonese Sound (phoneme) transfer?	Cantonese Spelling pattern (grapheme) transfer?	Mandarin Sound (phoneme) transfer?	Mandarin Spelling pattern (grapheme) transfer?	Farsi Sound (phoneme) transfer?	Farsi Spelling pattern (grapheme) transfer?	Arabic Sound (phoneme) transfer?	Arabic Spelling pattern (grapheme) transfer?
/b/	b	yes	yes	approx.	no	approx.	no	no	no	yes		yes	
/k/	c	yes	no	yes	no	yes	no	yes	no	yes	no	yes	no
	k		yes		no		no		no		no		no
	_ck		no		no		no		no		no		no
	-lk		no		no		no		no		no		no
	ch		no		no		no		no		no		no
	qu, que		no		no		no		no		no		no
/d/	d	yes	no	approx.	no	approx.	no	no	no	yes	no	yes	no
/f/	f	no	no	no	no	yes	no	yes	no	yes	no	yes	no
	gh		no		no		no		no		no		no
	ph		no		no		no		no		no		no
/0/	g	yes	yes	approx.	no	approx.	no	no	no	yes	no	no	no
	gu ('silent u')		no				no	no	no		no		no
	gh		no		no		no	no	no		no		no

Sound-Spelling: Consonants

	English						Spanish		Vietnamese		Hmong	
	Sound (phoneme)	Most Common Spelling Patterns (graphemes)	Notes	Word Examples			Sound (phoneme) transfer?	Spelling pattern (grapheme) transfer?	Sound (phoneme) transfer?	Spelling pattern (grapheme) transfer?	Sound (phoneme) transfer?	Spelling pattern (grapheme) transfer?
The sound /h/ is used or approximated in many of these languages, but the spelling used to communicate /h/ varies.	/h/	h_	/h/ sound in English occurs only at the beginning of a syllable and never as the final sound in a word. When not in the first syllable, it is paired with a consonant ch, gh, rh, ph, sh, th, or wh.	hip	enhance		approx.	no	yes	yes	yes	yes
The sound /j/ is used or approximated in some of these languages, but the spelling used to communicate /j/ varies.	/j/	j	j used at the beginning of a syllable. ge or dge used for /j/ at the end of a word or syllable. Few exceptions (algae, margarine)	jam	inject		no	no	approx.	no	no	no
		ge	"Soft g" when followed by e. Final /j/ sound when part of a long vowel/final e pattern.	gems	angel	page		no		no		no
		gi_	"Soft g" when followed by i	gist	margin			no		no		no
		gy	"Soft g" when followed by y	gym	biology			no		no		no
		_dge	Used as /j/ spelling at the end of a syllable when following a short vowel sound		badger	wedge		no		no		no
		du	More complex Latin words		gradual, educate			no		no		no
		di	Lower frequency, more complex words		soldier			no		no		no
The sound /l/ is used or approximated in all of these languages, and the common spelling used to communicate /l/ is l among the alphabetic languages.	/l/	l	Used as spelling for initial sound of a syllable and the last sound of a consonant blend (bl, cl, chl, fl, gl, pl, sl, spl). Doubled when adding suffix -ly (equal --> equally).	lion	melt, (follow)	girl	yes	yes	yes	yes	yes	yes
		ll	More frequently used than l at the end of a syllable after short vowel	yellow	bell			no		no		no
		-el	English suffix			tunnel		no		no		no
		_le	English suffix, used more often than -el. When added to a closed syllable, can influence consonant doubling (i.e., ap-ple, bab-ble).			maple		no		no		no
The sound /m/ is used or approximated in all of these languages, and the common spelling used to communicate /m/ is m among the alphabetic languages.	/m/	m	Most common spelling, can be subject to medial consonant doubling (hammock).	medal	hamper	ham, become	yes	yes	yes	yes	yes	yes
		mn	Low frequency. When adding affixes, can "cause" both letters to be pronounced (i.e., autumn --> autumnal)		condemned	hymn		no		no		no

Sound (phoneme)	Most Common Spelling Patterns (graphemes)	Tagalog Sound (phoneme) transfer?	Tagalog Spelling pattern (grapheme) transfer?	Korean Sound (phoneme) transfer?	Korean Spelling pattern (grapheme) transfer?	Cantonese Sound (phoneme) transfer?	Cantonese Spelling pattern (grapheme) transfer?	Mandarin Sound (phoneme) transfer?	Mandarin Spelling pattern (grapheme) transfer?	Farsi Sound (phoneme) transfer?	Farsi Spelling pattern (grapheme) transfer?	Arabic Sound (phoneme) transfer?	Arabic Spelling pattern (grapheme) transfer?
/h/	h_	yes	no	yes	no	yes	no	no	no	yes	no	yes	no
/j̆/	j	no	no	approx.	no	approx.	no	no	no	yes	no	yes	no
	ge		no		no		no		no		no		no
	gi_		no		no		no		no		no		no
	gy		no		no		no		no		no		no
	_dge		no		no		no		no		no		no
	du		no		no		no		no		no		no
	di		no		no		no		no		no		no
/l/	l	yes	yes	yes	no	yes	no	yes	no	yes	no	yes	no
	ll		no		no		no		no		no		no
	-el		no		no		no		no		no		no
	_le		no		no		no		no		no		no
/m/	m	yes	yes	yes	no	yes	no	yes	no	yes	no	yes	no
	mn		no		no		no		no		no		no

Sound-Spelling: Consonants

	Sound (phoneme)	Most Common Spelling Patterns (graphemes)	Notes	Word Examples			Spanish Sound (phoneme) transfer?	Spanish Spelling pattern (grapheme) transfer?	Vietnamese Sound (phoneme) transfer?	Vietnamese Spelling pattern (grapheme) transfer?	Hmong Sound (phoneme) transfer?	Hmong Spelling pattern (grapheme) transfer?
The sound /m/ is used or approximated in all of these languages, and the common spelling used to communicate /m/ is m among the alphabetic languages. *continued*	/m/	lm	Low frequency. Some regions do pronounce the l separately.	alms	calm			no		no		no
		mb	Low frequency. When adding affixes, can "cause" both letters to be pronounced (i.e., crumb --> crumble)	climber	lamb			no		no		no
The sound /n/ is used or approximated in most of these languages, and the common spelling used to communicate /n/ is n among the alphabetic languages.	/n/	n	Subject to consonant doubling (inn, connect)	nest	pants	fan	yes	yes	yes	yes	yes	yes
		kn_		knee				no		no		no
		gn	Initial Anglo-Saxon consonant blend that lost "g" sound over time, German, Scandinavian, Latin, Greek	gnome	designing	reign, assign, foreign		no		no		no
		pn	Consonant blend in Greek words that "lost" /p/ sound across languages	pneu-monia				no		no		no
The sound /p/ is used or approximated in most of these languages, and the common spelling used to communicate /p/ is p among the alphabetic languages.	/p/	p	subject to medial consonant doubling	paper	steps (happy)	help	yes	yes	yes	yes	approx.	yes
The sound /n/ is used or approximated in few of these languages.	/kw/	qu_		queen	liquid		yes	no	yes	yes	no	no
The sound /r/ is used or approximated in few of these languages. Many of these languages use a trilled version of /r/ that is not used in English (e.g., Spanish carro).	/r/	r	subject to medial consonant doubling	radio	carpet (arrow)	star	approx.	yes	approx.	no	no	no
		wr_		write	unwrap			no		no		no
		re	French, British low frequency			acre, theatre		no		no		no
		er, ur, ir (r-controlled vowels)	Syllables where /r/ is the sound requiring a vowel. Frequently misspelled without the vowel.	ermine, herbal, urgent, irk	interest	wonder, fir, fur				no		no
		rh	Greek words	rhyme	hemor-rhage			yes		no		no
		ear (r-controlled)		earth	learn			no		no		no
The sound /s/ is used or approximated in all of these languages, and the common spelling used to communicate /s/ is s among most of the alphabetic languages.	/s/	s		sun	past	gas	yes	yes	yes	yes	yes	no
		ss	Consonant team at the end of a root or last syllable after a short vowel (not a suffix)		lesson	bless, toss, pass		no		no		no
		se	At the end of word or syllable	horse	else, goose			no		no		no
		ce	"Soft c" /s/ when followed by e	cereal	paced	face		yes		yes		no
		ci_	"Soft c" /s/ when followed by i (very rarely at the end of a word, e.g. foci)	circle	incite, incident			yes		yes		no
		cy		cycle, cyst	bicycle	racy		no		no		no

Contrastive Analysis of English and Nine World Languages

Sound (phoneme)	Most Common Spelling Patterns (graphemes)	Tagalog Sound (phoneme) transfer?	Tagalog Spelling pattern (grapheme) transfer?	Korean Sound (phoneme) transfer?	Korean Spelling pattern (grapheme) transfer?	Cantonese Sound (phoneme) transfer?	Cantonese Spelling pattern (grapheme) transfer?	Mandarin Sound (phoneme) transfer?	Mandarin Spelling pattern (grapheme) transfer?	Farsi Sound (phoneme) transfer?	Farsi Spelling pattern (grapheme) transfer?	Arabic Sound (phoneme) transfer?	Arabic 'fer?
/m/	lm		no		no		no		no		no		no
	mb		no		no		no		no		no		no
/n/	n	no	yes	yes	no	yes	no	yes	no	yes	no	yes	no
	kn_		no		no		no		no		no		no
	gn		no				no		no		no		no
	pn		no		no		no		no		no		no
/p/	p	yes	yes	yes	no	yes	no	yes	no	yes	no	no	no
/kw/	qu_	no	no	yes	no	approx.	no	no	no	no	no	no	no
/r/	r	yes	yes	no	no	no	no	no	no	no	no	no	no
	wr_		no		no		no		no		no		no
	re		no		no		no		no		no		no
	er, ur, ir (r-controlled vowels)		no		no		no		no		no		no
	rh		no		no		no		no		no		no
	ear (r-controlled)		no		no		no		no		no		no
/s/	s	yes	yes	yes	no	yes	no	yes	no	yes	no	yes	no
	ss		no		no		no		no		no		no
	se		no		no		no		no		no		no
	ce		no		no		no		no		no		no
	ci_		no		no		no		no		no		no
	cy		no		no		no		no		no		no

Contrastive Analysis of English and Nine World Languages

Sound-Spelling: Consonants

	Sound (phoneme)	English — Most Common Spelling Patterns (graphemes)	Notes	Word Examples			Spanish — Sound (phoneme) transfer?	Spanish — Spelling pattern (grapheme) transfer?	Vietnamese — Sound (phoneme) transfer?	Vietnamese — Spelling pattern (grapheme) transfer?	Hmong — Sound (phoneme) transfer?	Hmong — Spelling pattern (grapheme) transfer?
The sound /s/ continued	/s/	sc		scene, science	descend, disciple			no		no		no
		ss	used at the end of a root or last syllable after a short vowel (not a suffix)		assess	grass, princess		no		no		no
The sound /t/ is used or approximated in all of these languages, and the common spelling used to communicate /t/ is t among most of the alphabetic languages.	/t/	t	initial, medial, and final sounds	telephone	after	just, wheat, late	approx.	yes	yes	yes	approx.	no
		tt			bitten, battle	mitt		no		no		no
		_ed	suffix			raced		no		no		no
		pt	few words of Greek origin	pterodactyl				no		no		no
		te, tte	French origin			suite, gazette		no		no		no
The sound /v/ is used or approximated in few of these languages.	/v/	v		van	flavor		no	no	yes	yes	yes	yes
		ve	Word or syllable endings; never end in solo v.		driven	give, brave		no		no		no
The sound /w/ is used or approximated in some of these languages.	/w/	w	Note that many vowel sounds are changed when following w.	Washington	away	cow	yes	approx.	no	no	no	no
The unvoiced sound /hw/ is not used or approximated in any of these languages.	/hw/	wh	Old English beginning of word or syllable. Many question words or whistling/whining sounds. Modern day /w/	why, whale	nowhere		no	no	no	no	no	no
The sound /ks/ is not used or approximated in a few of these languages.	/ks/	_x	Preceded by vowel. Latin prefix ex-. Distinguish between plurals and words (tax vs. tacks)		extra	fix	yes	yes	no	no	no	no
		-cks	plural			ducks		no		no		no
The sound /y/ is used or approximated in most of these languages, but the spelling used to communicate /y/ varies.	/y/	y_	Y is a consonant letter at the beginning of a word or syllable. Any other placement is a vowel.	yucca	lawyer		yes	yes	no	no	yes	yes
The sound /z/ is used, or approximated in some of these language but the spelling is not the same in the alphabetic languages.	/z/	z	subject to medial consonant doubling	zip	lazy (puzzle)		no	no	yes	no	yes	no
		ze	at the end of a word or syllable			ooze, haze		no		no		no
		_s	sm at the end of syllable or word, between 2 vowels, few HFWs (his, is, was, as, has). Suffix after vowel.		laser, prism	has, lens, bees, days		no		no		no
		_se	long vowel pattern with s (rise). Suffix after s, z, ch, sh			cheese, wise, passes, gazes, coaches, wishes		no		no		no
		s contractions				it's, she's he's		no		no		no
		x	at the beginning of a word	xylophone				no		no		no

Contrastive Analysis of English and Nine World Languages

Sound (phoneme)	Most Common Spelling Patterns (graphemes)	Tagalog Sound (phoneme) transfer?	Tagalog Spelling pattern (grapheme) transfer?	Korean Sound (phoneme) transfer?	Korean Spelling pattern (grapheme) transfer?	Cantonese Sound (phoneme) transfer?	Cantonese Spelling pattern (grapheme) transfer?	Mandarin Sound (phoneme) transfer?	Mandarin Spelling pattern (grapheme) transfer?	Farsi Sound (phoneme) transfer?	Farsi Spelling pattern (grapheme) transfer?	Arabic Sound (phoneme) transfer?	Arabic Spelling pattern (grapheme) transfer?
/s/	sc		no		no		no		no		no		no
	ss		no		no		no		no		no		no
/t/	t	yes	yes	yes	no	yes	no	yes	no	yes	no	yes	no
	tt		no		no		no		no		no		no
	_ed		no		no		no		no		no		no
	pt		no		no		no		no		no		no
	te, tte		no		no		no		no		no		
/v/	v	no	no	no	no	no	no	no	no	yes	no	no	no
	ve		no		no		no		no		no		no
/w/	w	yes	yes	yes	no	yes	no	no	no	no	no	yes	no
/hw/	wh	no	no	no	no	no	no	no	no	no	no	no	no
/ks/	_x	no	no	yes	no	no	no	no	no	no	no	no	no
	-cks		no		no		no		no		no		no
/y/	y_	yes	yes	yes	no	yes	no	no	no	yes	no	yes	no
/z/	z	no	no	no	no	no	no	no	no	yes	no	yes	no
	ze		no		no		no		no		no		no
	_s		no		no		no		no		no		no
	_se		no		no		no		no		no		no
	s contractions		no		no		no		no		no		no
	x		no		no		no		no		no		no

Sound-Spelling: Consonant Digraphs

English						Spanish		Vietnamese		Hmong	
Sound (phoneme)	Most Common Spelling Patterns (graphemes)	Notes	Word Examples			Sound (phoneme) transfer?	Spelling pattern (grapheme) transfer?	Sound (phoneme) transfer?	Spelling pattern (grapheme) transfer?	Sound (phoneme) transfer?	Spelling pattern (grapheme) transfer?
			initial	medial	final						
/ch/	ch		chile	satchel	inch	yes	yes	yes	no	no	no
	_tch	Used after short vowel in root.		hatchet	crutch		no		no		no
	tu	Latin origin. Unstressed long u impacts the /t/ sound.		culture, situate, fortunate, mutual			no		no		no
	ci, ce	Small number of foreign words commonly used in English	cello	concerto, ancient, financial			no		no		no
/sh/	sh		sheep	ashes	wish	no	no	yes	no	no	no
	ch	French words	chef, chic	machine	mustache		no		no		no
	ci	Latin (-cial, -scious, -cious)		social, efficient			no		no		no
	ti			nation, patience, initial			no		no		no
	ssi	Latin, unstressed i before a vowel. Adding /shun/ after ss.		passion, (express) expression			no		no		no
	-su-	Usually sh sound, sometimes /zh/	sure	insure, pressure			no		no		no
	si	Latin. Unstressed i before a vowel.		mansion, tension			no		no		no
/hw/	wh_		when	nowhere		no	no	no	no	no	
/th/ (voiced)	th	Native English words, most in beginning reader level words. Often "pointing" words (this, there, thy, thee, theirs)	these	feather	bathe, smooth	approx.	no	no	no	no	

Contrastive Analysis of English and Nine World Languages

Sound (phoneme)	Most Common Spelling Patterns (graphemes)	Tagalog Sound (phoneme) transfer?	Tagalog Spelling pattern (grapheme) transfer?	Korean Sound (phoneme) transfer?	Korean Spelling pattern (grapheme) transfer?	Cantonese Sound (phoneme) transfer?	Cantonese Spelling pattern (grapheme) transfer?	Mandarin Sound (phoneme) transfer?	Mandarin Spelling pattern (grapheme) transfer?	Farsi Sound (phoneme) transfer?	Farsi Spelling pattern (grapheme) transfer?	Arabic Sound (phoneme) transfer?	Arabic Spelling pattern (grapheme) transfer?
/ch/	ch	yes	no	no	no	no	no	approx.	no	yes	no	no	no
	_tch		no		no		no		no		no		no
	tu		no		no		no		no		no		no
	ci, ce		no		no		no		no		no		no
/sh/	sh	yes	yes	no	no	no	no	approx.	no	no	no	yes	no
	ch		no		no		no		no		no		no
	ci		no		no		no		no		no		no
	ti		no		no		no		no		no		no
	ssi		no		no		no		no		no		no
	-su-		no		no		no		no		no		no
	si		no		no		no		no		no		no
/hw/	wh_	no	no		no	no	no	no	no	no	no	no	no
/th/ (voiced)	th	no	no	no	no	no	no	no	no	no	no	yes	no

Sound-Spelling: Consonant Digraphs

	English					Spanish		Vietnamese		Hmong	
Sound (phoneme)	Most Common Spelling Patterns (graphemes)	Notes		Word Examples		Sound (phoneme) transfer?	Spelling pattern (grapheme) transfer?	Sound (phoneme) transfer?	Spelling pattern (grapheme) transfer?	Sound (phoneme) transfer?	Spelling pattern (grapheme) transfer?
/th/ (unvoiced)	th	At the beginning of nouns, verbs, adjectives. In Greek words between vowels. Beyond children's book words, most are unvoiced.	think	panther	math	approx.	no	no	no		no
/ng/	ng (a few exceptions such as tongue)			mango	hang	yes	yes	yes	yes		no
	n (followed by /k/)			uncle, conquer, sphinx	thank		no		no		no
/zh/	-si-	/s/ changed to /zh/ when followed by unsressed i before a vowel			vision, division, version	no	no	partial	no		no
	ge, gi	French "soft g" before e, I, y	gendarme	regime	garage		no		no		no
	-su-	Usually sh sound		usual, visual, closure			no		no		no
	z	Unstressed I or long u before vowel		azure, brazier			no		no		no
/gz/	ex	When syllable ending in x is unstressed and the next syllable begins with a vowel or silent h	exhaust, exact	unexampled		no	no	no	no		no

Sound (phoneme)	Most Common Spelling Patterns (graphemes)	Tagalog		Korean		Cantonese		Mandarin		Farsi		Arabic	
		Sound (phoneme) transfer?	Spelling pattern (grapheme) transfer?	Sound (phoneme) transfer?	Spelling pattern (grapheme) transfer?	Sound (phoneme) transfer?	Spelling pattern (grapheme) transfer?	Sound (phoneme) transfer?	Spelling pattern (grapheme) transfer?	Sound (phoneme) transfer?	Spelling pattern (grapheme) transfer?	Sound (phoneme) transfer?	Spelling pattern (grapheme) transfer?
/th/ (un-voiced)	th	no	no	no	no	no	no	no	no	no	no	yes	no
/ng/	ng (a few exceptions such as tongue)	yes	yes	no	no	yes	no	yes	no	no	no	no	no
	n (followed by /k/)		no		no		no		no		no		no
/zh/	-si-	no	no	no	no	no	no	no	no	no	no	no	no
	ge, gi		no		no		no		no		no		no
	-su-		no		no		no		no		no		no
	z		no		no		no		no		no		no
/gz/	ex	no	no		no	no	no	no	no		no		no

Sound-Spelling: Short and Long Vowels

Short Vowels

Sound (phoneme)	Most Common Spelling Patterns (graphemes)	Notes	Word Examples initial	medial	final	Spanish Sound (phoneme) transfer?	Spanish Spelling pattern (grapheme) transfer?	Vietnamese Sound (phoneme) transfer?	Vietnamese Spelling pattern (grapheme) transfer?	Hmong Sound (phoneme) transfer?	Hmong Spelling pattern (grapheme) transfer?
/ā/	a	closed syllables	apple	cab		no	no	approx.	yes	yes	yes
/ĕ/	e	closed syllables	egg	pet		yes	yes	approx.	yes	no	no
/ĭ/	i	closed syllables	igloo	bit		no	no	no	no	no	no
/ŏ/	o	closed syllables	octopus	rock		no	no	approx.	yes	approx.	yes
	ough		ought	bought		approx.			no		no
	augh		aught	daughter, caught					no		no
/ŭ/	u	closed syllables	under	munch		no	no	yes	no	no	no

Long Vowels

Sound (phoneme)	Spelling Pattern	Notes	initial	medial	final	Spanish Sound	Spanish Spelling	Vietnamese Sound	Vietnamese Spelling	Hmong Sound	Hmong Spelling
/ā/	a	open syllable	able	caper		yes	no	approx.	no	approx.	no
	ai_		aim	stair			no		no		no
	_ay				stay		no		no		no
	a_e		ale	baseball	paste		no		no		no
	eigh		eight	neighbor	weigh		no		no		no
/ē/	e	open syllable	ether	defend	me	yes	no	yes	no	yes	no
	ee			seed	knee		no		no		no
	ea		east	wheat			no		no		no
	e_e		*eke		these		no		no		no
	_y				happy		no		no		no
	_ie_						no		no		no
	igh			light	sigh		no		no		no
/ī/	i	open syllable	item	bicycle	*hi	yes	no	yes	no	yes	no
	i_e		ice	tired	bik1		no		no		no
	_y			myself	fly		no		no		no
	igh			bright	high		no		no		no
	_ie				tie		no		no		no
/ō/	o	open syllable	open	motor		yes	yes	approx.	no	no	no
	oa		oath	boat			no		no		no
	_oe				toe		no		no		no
	ow				bow		no		no		no
	o_e		ode		globe		no		no		no
	ough	low frequency			though		no		no		no
/ū/	u	open syllable	unicorn	cucumber		yes	no	no	no	no	no
	_ue				rescue		no		no		no
	u_e				cube		no		no		no
	_ew				few		no		no		no

Table 1

Sound (phoneme)	Most Common Spelling Patterns (graphemes)	Tagalog Sound (phoneme) transfer?	Tagalog Spelling pattern (grapheme) transfer?	Korean Sound (phoneme) transfer?	Korean Spelling pattern (grapheme) transfer?	Cantonese Sound (phoneme) transfer?	Cantonese Spelling pattern (grapheme) transfer?	Mandarin Sound (phoneme) transfer?	Mandarin Spelling pattern (grapheme) transfer?	Farsi Sound (phoneme) transfer?	Farsi Spelling pattern (grapheme) transfer?	Arabic Sound (phoneme) transfer?	Arabic Spelling pattern (grapheme) transfer?
/ā/	a	no	no	yes	no	no	no	no	no	approx.	no	approx.	no
/ĕ/	e	yes	no	yes	no	approx.	no	approx.	no	approx.	no	approx.	no
/ĭ/	i	no	no	yes	no	approx.	no	approx.	no		no	approx.	no
/ŏ/	o	no	no	approx.	no	approx.	no	approx.	no	approx.	no	approx.	no
/ŏ/	ough		no		no		no		no		no		no
/ŏ/	augh		no		no		no		no		no		no
/ū/	u	yes	no	no	no	approx.	no	approx.	no	no	no	yes	no

Table 2

Sound (phoneme)	Graphemes	Tagalog Sound	Tagalog Spelling	Korean Sound	Korean Spelling	Cantonese Sound	Cantonese Spelling	Mandarin Sound	Mandarin Spelling	Farsi Sound	Farsi Spelling	Arabic Sound	Arabic Spelling
/ā/	a	no	no	yes	no	approx.	no	approx.	no	yes	no	yes	no
/ā/	ai_		no		no		no		no		no		no
/ā/	_ay		no		no		no		no		no		no
/ā/	a_e		no		no		no		no		no		no
/ā/	eigh		no		no		no		no		no		no
/ē/	e	yes	no	yes	no	yes	no	approx.	no	yes	no	yes	no
/ē/	ee		no		no		no		no		no		no
/ē/	ea		no		no	approx.	no		no		no		no
/ē/	e_e		no		no		no		no		no		no
/ē/	_y		no		no		no		no		no		no
/ē/	_ie_		no		no		no		no		no		no
/ē/	igh		no		no		no		no		no		no
/ī/	i	no	no	yes	no	approx.	no	approx.	no	no	no	approx.	no
/ī/	i_e		no		no		no		no		no		no
/ī/	_y		no		no		no		no		no		no
/ī/	igh		no		no		no		no		no		no
/ī/	_ie		no		no		no		no		no		no
/ō/	o	yes	no	yes	no	approx.	no	approx.	no	approx.	no	no	no
/ō/	oa		no		no		no		no		no		no
/ō/	_oe		no		no		no		no		no		no
/ō/	ow		no		no		no		no		no		no
/ō/	o_e		no		no		no		no		no		no
/ō/	ough		no		no		no		no		no		no
/ū/	u	no	no	yes	no	approx.	no	approx.	no	no	no	no	no
/ū/	_ue		no		no		no		no		no		no
/ū/	u_e		no		no		no		no		no		no
/ū/	_ew		no		no		no		no		no		no

Sound-Spelling: R-Controlled Vowels, Other Vowel Patterns

			English			Spanish		Vietnamese		Hmong	
R-Controlled Vowels			initial	medial	final						
	/är/	ar	arm	barn	far	approx.**	yes	no	no	no	no
	/ûr/	er	ernest	fern	teacher	no	no	no	no	no	no
		ir	irk	girl	fir		no		no		no
		ur	urn	curl	fur		no		no		no
		ear	early,	pearl			no		no		no
			initial	medial	final						
Other Vowel Patterns	/oi/	oi	oil	broil		yes	yes	approx.	yes	no	no
		_oy	*oyster		boy		yes		no		no
	/ou/	ow	owl	brown	how	yes	no	yes	no	approx.	no
		ou_	out	cloud			no		no		no
	/ô/	aw	awful	crawl	draw	approx.	no	yes	no	approx.	no
		au_	augment				no		no		no
	/ôl/	al	also			approx.	yes	yes	no	no	no
		all	all		hall		no		no		no
		ol		follow			no		no		no
		awl	crawl				no		no		no
	/ōō/	oo	ooze	moon	boo	yes	no	yes	no	yes	no
		u_e	ruler				no		yes		yes
		_ew	flew				no		no		no
		_ue	blue				no		no		yes
		ui	suit				no		no		yes
		ough			through		no		no		no
	/oo/	oo		book		no	no	approx.	no	no	no

		Tagalog		Korean		Cantonese		Mandarin		Farsi		Arabic	
R-Controlled Vowels	/är/	no	no	no	no	no	no	no	no	no	no	no	no
	/ûr/				no		no		no		no		no
		no		no	no	approx.	no	approx.	no	no	no		no
			no		no		no		no		no		no
					no		*no*		*no*		*no*		*no*
Other Vowel Patterns	/oi/	yes	no	yes	no	approx.	no	no	no	no	no	no	no
			no		no		no		no		no		no
	/ou/	no		yes	no	approx.	no	approx.	no	yes	no	no	no
			no		no		no		no		no		no
	/ô/	yes	no	approx.	no	yes	no	no	no	no	no	no	no
					no		no		no		no		no
	/ôl/		no		no		no		no		no		no
		yes	no	approx.	no	approx.	no	no	no	no	no	no	no
			no		no		no		no		no		no
			no		no		no		no		no		no
	/ōō/		no		no		no		no		no		no
		yes	no	yes	no	approx.	no	yes	no	yes	no	yes	no
			no		no		no		no		no		no
			no		no		no		no		no		no
			no		no		no		no		no		*no*
			no		no		no		no		no		*no*
	/oo/	no	no	approx.	no	approx.	no	approx.	no	no	no	no	no

Syntax and Grammar: Verbs
Differences and Potential Errors for English Learners

English Grammar	Spanish	Vietnamese	Hmong	Tagalog
VERBS				
Use of **infinitives*** (*He wants them to learn quickly.*)	Clause "that" is used rather than an infinitive (*He wants that they learn quickly.*)		Clause "that" is used rather than an infinitive (*He wants that they learn quickly.*)	
Use of **infinitives to express** purpose (*We go out to have dinner.*)				
Verbs are separated with punctuation or other words (*I throw, catch, and kick the ball*).		Verbs can be used together without punctuation or other words (*I throw catch kick the ball.*)	Verbs can be used together without punctuation or other words (I throw catch kick the ball.)	
Use of **gerund**** (-ing) /infinitive distinction). (*She enjoys cooking.*)	No use of gerund (-ing)/ infinitive distinction. (*She enjoys to cook.*)	No use of gerund (-ing)/ infinitive distinction. (*She enjoys to cook.*)	No use of gerund (-ing)/ infinitive distinction. (She enjoys to cook.)	
Use of the **verb "to be"** (*He is walking. They are coming to school.*).		Be can be omitted. (*He walking. They coming to school.*)	Be can be omitted. (*He walking. They coming to school.*)	Be can be omitted. (*He walking. They coming to school.*)
Use of the verb "to be" for adjectives or places (*The lock is strong. The book is on the desk.*)		The verb "to be" is not used for adjectives or places (*The lock strong. The book on the desk.*)	The verb "to be" is not used for adjectives or places (*The lock strong. The book on the desk.*)	The verb "to be" is not used for adjectives or places (*The lock strong. The book on the desk.*)
Use of the **verb "to be" to express states of being** such as hunger or age).	The verb "to have" can be used to express states of being (age, hunger, etc.). She *has* ten years. They *have* hunger.			
Use of **"there is/are,was/ were"** (*In school, there are many students."*)	Can use "have" (*In school they have many students.*) or "there are" (*In school, there are many students.*)	Use of "have" instead of "there is/ are,was/were" (*In school, have many students."*)	Use of "have" instead of "there is/ are,was/were" (*In school, have many students."*)	
Change in verb "to be" in past perfect form. (*They are climbing --> They climbed*).				
Use of **verb "to have"** (*I have one book.*)				
Verb inflection for person and number. (*Everyone cooks food. She has a large cat.*)		Verbs are not inflected for person and number. (*Everyone cook food. She have a large cat.*)	Verbs are not inflected for person and number. (*Everyone cook food. She have a large cat.*)	
Verb tenses change within the same sentence. (*When we eat, we will be full.*)			Verb tenses do not change within the same sentence. (*When we eat, we full.*)	
Use of **tense boundaries** (*I will study here for a year. When she was young, she played with dolls.*)		Tense can be indicated by context or an expression of time rather than through the verb tense. (*I study here for a year. When she is young, she play with dolls.*)	Tense indicated by use of infinitive of verb with an expression of time rather than through the verb tense.	
Use of **future tense** (*I will go tomorrow*) and **present perfect** tense (*I have been there many times.*)	Present tense can replace future tense (*I go there tomorrow*) and can replace present perfect (*I go there many times*).		Present tense can replace future tense (*I go there tomorrow*) and can replace present perfect (*I go there many times*).	
Use of **passive tense** (*Their window was broken.*)		Different limits for use of passive tense (*They were broken their window.*)		

*An infinitive can be considered the "base verb" that can be conjugated into different forms to represent past, present, future (e.g., to run, to sing, to eat, to be).

**A gerund is a verb that functions as a noun in a sentence. Gerunds end in -ing (e.g., Running is great exercise. In this sentence, the verb (in infinitive form) to run is functioning as a noun and the verb is (conjugated from the infinitive to be) functions as the verb.

Contrastive Analysis of English and Nine World Languages

Common Core Language Standard 1:
Demonstrate command of the conventions of standard English grammar and usage when writing or speaking.

L.K.1b. Use frequently occurring nouns and verbs.
L.1.1 e. Use verbs to convey a sense of past, present, and future.
L.2.1 d. Form and use the past tense of frequently occurring irregular verbs.
L.3.1 d. Form and use regular and irregular verbs.
L.3.1 e. Form and use the simple verb tenses.

L.4.1 b. Form and use the progressive verb tenses.
L.4.1 c. Use modal auxiliaries to convey various conditions.
L.5.1 b. Form and use the perfect verb tenses.
L.5.1 c. Use verb tense to convey various times, sequences, states, and conditions.
L.5.1 d. Recognize and correct inappropriate shifts in verb tense.*

English Grammar	Korean	Cantonese	Mandarin	Farsi	Arabic
VERBS					
Use of **infinitives*** (He wants them to learn quickly.)					
Use of **infinitives to express** purpose (We go out to have dinner.)	Infinitives not used to express purpose (We go out for having dinner.)				
Verbs are separated with punctuation or other words (I throw, catch, and kick the ball).					
Use of **gerund**** (-ing) /infinitive distinction). (She enjoys cooking.)	No use of gerund (-ing)/ infinitive distinction. (She enjoys to cook.)	No use of gerund (-ing)/ infinitive distinction. (She enjoys to cook.)	No use of gerund (-ing)/ infinitive distinction. (She enjoys to cook.) Tense is expressed by adding adverbs of time instead of changing the verb form.	No use of gerund (-ing)/ infinitive distinction. (She enjoys to cook.)	No use of gerund (-ing)/ infinitive distinction. (She enjoys to cook.)
Use of the **verb "to be"** (He is walking. They are coming to school.)	Be can be omitted. (He walking. They coming to school.)	Be can be omitted. (He walking. They coming to school.) Tense is expressed by adding adverbs of time instead of changing the verb form.	Be can be omitted. (He walking. They coming to school.) Adjectives an be directly used as verbs.		Be can be omitted. (He walking. They coming to school.)
Use of the verb "to be" for adjectives or places (The lock is strong. The book is on the desk.)					
Use of the **verb "to be" to express states of being** such as hunger or age).				The verb "to have" can be used to express states of being (age, hunger, etc.). She has ten years. They have hunger.	
Use of **"there is/are,was/ were"** (In school, there are many students.")					
Change in verb "to be" in past perfect form. (They are climbing --> They climbed).				Past perfect form for "to be" changes differently. (They are climbing --> They were climbed.)	Past perfect form for "to be" changes differently. (They are climbing --> They were climbed.)
Use of **verb "to have"** (I have one book.)	The verb "to have" can be substituted with "to be" (I am book.)				
Verb inflection for person and number. (Everyone cooks food. She has a large cat.)	Verbs are not inflected for person and number. (Everyone cook food. She have a large cat.) In Korean verbs are inflected for age or status.	Verbs are not inflected for person and number. (Everyone cook food. She have a large cat.)	Verbs are not inflected for person and number. (Everyone cook food. She have a large cat.)		
Verb tenses change within the same sentence. (When we eat, we will be full.)					
Use of **tense boundaries** (I will study here for a year. When she was young, she played with dolls.)		Tense can be indicated by context or an expression of time rather than through the verb tense. (I study here for a year. When she is young, she play with dolls.)	Tense can be indicated by context or an expression of time rather than through the verb tense. (I study here for a year. When she is young, she play with dolls.)		Tense can be indicated by context or an expression of time rather than through the verb tense. (I study here for a year. When she is young, she play with dolls.)
Use of **future tense** (I will go tomorrow) and **present perfect** tense (I have been there many times).				Present tense can replace future tense (I go there tomorrow) and can replace present perfect (I go there many times).	
Use of **passive tense** (Their window was broken.)	Different limits for use of passive tense (They were broken their window.)				Different limits for use of passive tense (They were broken their window.)

Syntax and Grammar: Nouns
Differences and Potential Errors for English Learners

English Grammar	Spanish	Vietnamese	Hmong	Tagalog
NOUNS				
Nouns and adjectives use different forms (*They felt safe in their home.*)	Suffixes can be added to nouns (e.g. -ito, -oso) to combine description with a noun.		Nouns and adjectives can use the same form (*They felt safety in their home.*)	
Nouns and verbs are distinct.			Nouns and verbs may not be distinct.	Nouns and verbs may not be distinct.
Use of **proper names** in first, middle, last order (*George Lucas Smith*).		Proper names can be ordered in last, first, middle order or last, middle, first. First and last names can be confusing to teachers and students.	Proper names can be ordered in last, first, middle order, or last, middle, first. First and last names can be confusing to teachers and students.	Depends on familiarity.
Use of 's for **possessive nouns** (*This is Holly's box.*)	Possessive nouns are formed with an "of phase" (*This is the box of Holly.*)	Possessive nouns are formed with an "of phase" (*This is the box of Holly.*)	Possessive nouns are formed with an "of phase" (*This is the box of Holly.*)	Possessive nouns are formed with an "of phase" (*This is the box of Holly.*)
Use of **plural nouns** (*She makes many friends. He has few questions.*)		No use of plural nouns (*She make many friend. He has few question.*) Plurals can be expressed through an adjective quantifier.	No use of plural nouns (*He has few question.*) Plurals are used for nouns related to people such as "friends." Plurals can be expressed through an adjective quantifier.	No use of plural nouns (*She make many friend. He has few question.*) Plurals can be expressed through an adjective quantifier.
Use of **plural forms** after a number (*We go home in two weeks. They are bringing five shirts.*)		Use of plural forms after a number (*We go home in two week. They are bringing five shirt.*)	Use of plural forms after a number (*We go home in two week. They are bringing five shirt.*)	Use of plural forms after a number (*We go home in two week. They are bringing five shirt.*)
Use of -es to make **plural nouns** only used after nouns ending in consonants s, x, ch, sh, and z. (*passes, foxes, catches, wishes, buzzes*) Nouns ending in y change the y to i before adding -es. (*candies*)	Use of -es to make plural nouns for all nouns that end in consonants or y (walls --> walles, pay --> payes)			
Use of **noncount nouns** that do not have plurals such as *weather, homework, money, rain,* etc. (*We have different types of weather. We have a lot of homework.*)		Confusion with noncount nouns that do not have plurals (*We have different types of weathers. We have a lot of homeworks.*)	Confusion with noncount nouns that do not have plurals (*We have different types of weathers. We have a lot of homeworks.*)	Confusion with noncount nouns that do not have plurals (*We have different types of weathers. We have a lot of homeworks.*)

Common Core Language Standard 1:
Demonstrate command of the conventions of standard English grammar and usage when writing or speaking.
L.K.1b. Use frequently occurring nouns and verbs.
L.K.1c. Form regular plural nouns orally by adding /s/ or /es/ (e.g., dog, dogs; wish, wishes).
L.1.1 b. Use common, proper, and possessive nouns.
L.1.1 c. Use singular and plural nouns with matching verbs in basic sentences (e.g., He hops; We hop).
L.2.1 a. Use collective nouns (e.g., group).
L.2.1 b. Form and use frequently occurring irregular plural nouns (e.g., feet, children, teeth, mice, fish).
L.3.1 b. Form and use regular and irregular plural nouns.
L.3.1 c. Use abstract nouns (e.g., childhood).

English Grammar	Korean	Cantonese	Mandarin	Farsi	Arabic
NOUNS					
Nouns and adjectives use different forms (They felt <u>safe</u> in their home.)		Nouns and adjectives can use the same form (They felt <u>safety</u> in their home.)	Nouns and adjectives can use the same form (They felt <u>safety</u> in their home.)		
Nouns and verbs are distinct.		Nouns and verbs overlap, may not be distinct.	Nouns and verbs overlap, may not be distinct.	Nouns and verbs may not be distinct.	
Use of **proper names** in first, middle, last order (George Lucas Smith).	Proper names can be ordered in last, first, middle order, or last, middle, first. First and last names can be confusing to teachers and students.	Proper names can be ordered in last, first, middle order, or last, middle, first. First and last names can be confusing to teachers and students. (Chinese: Always last name first)	Proper names can be ordered in last, first, middle order, or last, middle, first. First and last names can be confusing to teachers and students. (Chinese: Always last name first)		
Use of 's for **possessive nouns** (This is <u>Holly's</u> box.)		Possessive nouns are consistently formed (<u>Holly's</u> box.)			
Use of **plural nouns** (She makes <u>many friends</u>. He has <u>few questions</u>.)	No use of plural nouns (She make <u>many friend</u>. He <u>has few question</u>.) Plurals can be expressed through an adjective quantifier. In Korean, nouns related to people (e.g., *children*) have plural forms, but not other nouns.	No use of plural nouns (She make <u>many friend</u>. He has <u>few question</u>.) Plurals can be expressed through an adjective quantifier.	No use of plural nouns (She make <u>many friend</u>. He has <u>few question</u>.) Plurals can be expressed through an adjective quantifier or number word.		
Use of **plural forms** after a number (We go home in <u>two weeks</u>. They are bringing <u>five shirts</u>.)	Use of plural forms after a number (We go home in <u>two week</u>. They are bringing <u>five shirt</u>.) Students may add a word rather than adding -s to a noun.	Use of plural forms after a number (We go home in <u>two week</u>. They are bringing <u>five shirt</u>.)	Use of plural forms after a number (We go home in <u>two week</u>. They are bringing <u>five shirt</u>.)	Use of plural forms after a number (We go home in <u>two week</u>. They are bringing <u>five shirt</u>.)	
Use of -es to make **plural nouns** only used after nouns ending in consonants s, x, ch, sh, and z. (*passes, foxes, catches, wishes, buzzes*) Nouns ending in y change the y to i before adding -es. (*candies*)					
Use of **noncount nouns** that do not have plurals such as *weather, homework, money, rain*, etc. (We have different <u>types of weather</u>. We have a lot <u>of homework</u>.)	Confusion with noncount nouns that do not have plurals (We have different types of <u>weathers</u>. We have a lot of <u>homeworks</u>.)	Confusion with noncount nouns that do not have plurals (We have different types of <u>weathers</u>. We have a lot of <u>homeworks</u>.)	Confusion with noncount nouns that do not have plurals (We have different types of weathers. We have a lot of homeworks.)	Confusion with noncount nouns that do not have plurals (We have different types of <u>weathers</u>. We have a lot of <u>homeworks</u>.)	

Syntax and Grammar:
Word Order and Sentence Structure
Differences and Potential Errors for English Learners

English Grammar	Spanish	Vietnamese	Hmong	Tagalog
WORD ORDER				
Subject-Verb-Object and, Object-Verb-Subject order can be used. (*Every student in the class received good grades. Good grades were received by every student in the class.*)	Word order can change and can change the emphasis.	The usual word order is subject-verb-object.	The usual word order is subject-verb-object.	The word order is subject-verb-object, or object-verb-subject.
Use of subject pronouns (*They are coming. He is running.*)	Optional use of subject pronouns when the subject is understood (*They coming. He running*).	Optional use of subject pronouns when the subject is understood (*They coming. He running*).	Optional use of subject pronouns when the subject is understood (*They coming. He running*).	Optional use of subject pronouns when the subject is understood (*They coming. He running*).
Pronouns used as Indirect objects precede the direct object (*He gave her an umbrella.*)			Direct objects precede pronouns used as Indirect objects (*He gave an umbrella her*).	
Verbs precede adverbs and adverbial phrases (*She runs quickly. They travel to work by train.*)				Adverbs and adverbial phrases precede verbs (She quickly runs. They by train travel to work).
Sentences always include a subject. (*Is this your chair? Yes, it is. Is it raining?*)	Sentences do not always include a subject (*Is this your chair? Yes, is. Is raining?*)			
Subjects and verbs can be inverted (*He is cooking and so am I.*)	Verbs can precede subject (Good grades were received by every student in the class).		Subjects and verbs are rarely inverted, so one might be deleted or flipped in English (*He is cooking and so am. He is cooking and so I am*).	
Relative clause or restrictive phrase follows a noun it modifies (*The student enrolled in community college.*)				

Language Standard 1:

Demonstrate command of the conventions of standard English grammar and usage when writing or speaking.

L.K.1d. Understand and use question words (interrogatives) (e.g., who, what, where, when, why, how).

L.K.1f. Produce and expand complete sentences in shared language activities.

L.1.1 c. Use singular and plural nouns with matching verbs in basic sentences (e.g., He hops; We hop).

L.1.1 j. Produce and expand complete simple and compound declarative, interrogative, imperative, and exclamatory sentences in response to prompts.

L.2.1 f. Produce, expand, and rearrange complete simple and compound sentences (e.g., The boy watched the movie; The little boy watched the movie; The action movie was watched by the little boy).

L.3.1 a. Explain the function of nouns, pronouns, verbs, adjectives, and adverbs in general and their functions in particular sentences.

L.3.1 f. Ensure subject-verb and pronoun-antecedent agreement.*

L.3.1 i. Produce simple, compound, and complex sentences.

L.4.1 d. Order adjectives within sentences according to conventional patterns (e.g., a small red bag rather than a red small bag).

L.4.1 g. Correctly use frequently confused words (e.g., to, too, two; there, their).*

L.4.1 f. Produce complete sentences, recognizing and correcting inappropriate fragments and run-ons.*

L.5.1 a. Explain the function of conjunctions, prepositions, and interjections in general and their function in particular sentences.

English Grammar	Korean	Cantonese	Mandarin	Farsi	Arabic
WORD ORDER					
Subject-Verb-Object and, Object-Verb-Subject order can be used. *(Every student in the class received good grades. Good grades were received by every student in the class.)*	Verbs are placed last in a sentence. The usual word order is subject-object-verb *(Every student in the class good grades received).*	The most common word order is subject-verb-object but object-subject-verb is used to emphasize the object.	The most common word order is subject-verb-object but object-subject-verb is used to emphasize the object.	Verbs are placed last in a sentence. The usual word order is subject-object-verb *(Every student in the class good grades received.)*	Verbs can precede subject and subject can precede verbs in Arabic. When the subject precedes verb, the sentence is nominative. When the verb precedes subject, the sentence is verbal. *(Good grades received every student in the class.)*
Use of subject pronouns *(They are coming. He is running.)*	Optional use of subject pronouns when the subject is understood *(They coming. He running).* Korean: Can omit the subject pronoun "you."	Optional use of subject pronouns when the subject is understood *(They coming. He running).*	Optional use of subject pronouns when the subject is understood *(They coming. He running.)*	Optional use of subject pronouns when the subject is understood *(They coming. He running.)*	
Pronouns used as Indirect objects precede the direct object *(He gave her an umbrella.)*		Direct objects precede pronouns used as Indirect objects *(He gave an umbrella her).*	Direct objects precede pronouns used as Indirect objects *(He gave an umbrella her).*	Direct objects precede pronouns used as Indirect objects *(He gave an umbrella her.)*	
Verbs precede adverbs and adverbial phrases *(She runs quickly. They travel to work by train.)*	Adverbs and adverbial phrases precede verbs *(She quickly runs. They by train travel to work).*	Adverbs and adverbial phrases precede verbs *(She quickly runs. They by train travel to work).*	Adverbs and adverbial phrases precede verbs *(She quickly runs. They by train travel to work).*	Adverbs and adverbial phrases precede verbs *(She quickly runs. They by train travel to work.)*	Some adverbs can precede or follow verbs. *(Sometimes he studies. He studies sometimes. They travel by train. By train they travel.)*
Sentences always include a subject. *(Is this your chair? Yes, it is. Is it raining?)*					Sentences do not always include a subject *(Is this your chair? Yes, is. Is raining?)*
Subjects and verbs can be inverted *(He is cooking and so am I.)*	Subjects and verbs are rarely inverted, so one might be deleted or flipped in English *(He is cooking and so am. He is cooking and so I am).*	Subjects and verbs are rarely inverted, so one might be deleted or flipped in English *(He is cooking and so am. He is cooking and so I am).*	Subjects and verbs are rarely inverted, so one might be deleted or flipped in English *(He is cooking and so am. He is cooking and so I am).*	Subjects and verbs are rarely inverted, so one might be deleted or flipped in English *(He is cooking and so am. He is cooking and so I am).*	
Relative clause or restrictive phrase follows a noun it modifies *(The student enrolled in community college.)*	Relative clause or restrictive phrase precedes a noun it modifies *(The enrolled in community college student).*	Relative clause or restrictive phrase precedes a noun it modifies *(The enrolled in community college student.)*	Relative clause or restrictive phrase precedes a noun it modifies *(The enrolled in community college student.)*		

Syntax and Grammar: Word Order and Sentence Structure
Differences and Potential Errors for English Learners

English Grammar	Spanish	Vietnamese	Hmong	Tagalog
QUESTIONS				
Yes/No questions usually begin with a question word. *(Do you eat broccoli? Is this your sweater?)*	Yes/No questions can be formed by adding an element to the end of a declarative statement. *(You eat broccoli, yes? This is your sweater, no?)*	Yes/No questions can be formed by adding an element to the end of a declarative statement. *(You eat broccoli, yes? This is your sweater, no?)* Vietnamese can also use a statement followed by the phrase: "or not."	Yes/No questions can be formed by adding an element to the end of a declarative statement *(You eat broccoli, yes? This is your sweater, no?)* Yes/No questions can be formed by adding the question word between the pronoun and the verb. (You [question word] take the bus?)	Yes/No questions can be formed by adding an element to the end of a declarative statement *(You eat broccoli, yes? This is your sweater, no?)*
Yes/No questions can be formed by adding a verb followed by its negative at the end of a statement. *(Do you like to go to the beach or not?)*		Yes/No questions can be formed by adding a verb followed by its negative within a statement. *(Do you not like to go to the beach?)*	Yes/No questions can be formed by adding a verb followed by its negative within a statement. *(Do you not like to go to the beach?)*	
Questions words are usually placed at the beginning of the sentence. *(Where is the book? What did my sister tell you?)*		Question words are placed according to the position of the answer. For example, if the answer functions as an object, the question words are placed in the regular object position *(The book is where? My sister told you what?)*	Question words are placed according to the position of the answer. For example, if the answer functions as an object, the question words are placed in the regular object position. *(The book is where? My sister told you what?)*	
Yes and no answers are used in a consistent manner. *(Do you play soccer? Yes. Do you play hockey? No.)*			The answers yes and no vary depending upon the verb used in the question. Students may substitute a verb for a yes-no answer *(Do you play soccer? Soccer. Do you play hockey? No hockey.)*	The answers yes and no vary depending upon the verb used in the question. Students may substitute a verb for a yes-no answer *(Do you play soccer? Soccer. Do you play hockey? No hockey.)*
COMMANDS				
Commands are formed consistently. *(Stop it now!)*		Commands can be formed by adding an adverb after the verbs to be emphasized. *(Stop right now!)* Commands can be formed by adding the verb "go" for emphasis at the end of the sentence. (Get my slippers, go!)	Commands can be formed by adding an adverb after the verbs to be emphasized. *(Stop now!)*	
Commands do not require a time indicator after the verbs to be emphasized *(Take out the trash).*			Commands can be formed by adding a time indicator after the verbs to be emphasized. *(Take out the trash at 9:00.)*	
Commands use consistent verb form *(Show it to me).*				Commands can be formed by changing the verb ending *(Show[ing] it to me).*
NEGATIVES AND NEGATIVE SENTENCES				
Double negatives are not used *(She doesn't eat anything).*	Double negatives are routinely used to reinforce the thought *(She doesn't eat nothing).*			
The negative marker goes after the verb phrase *(They have not been there before).*	The negative marker goes before the verb phrase *(They not have been there before.).*		The negative marker goes before the verb phrase *(They not have been there before.)*	The negative marker goes before the verb phrase *(They not have been there before).*

English Grammar	Korean	Cantonese	Mandarin	Farsi	Arabic
QUESTIONS					
Yes/No questions usually begin with a question word. (*Do you eat broccoli? Is this your sweater?*)	Yes/No questions can be formed by adding an element to the end of a declarative statement (*You eat broccoli, yes? This is your sweater, no?*)	Yes/No questions can be formed by adding an element to the end of a declarative statement. (*You eat broccoli, yes? This is your sweater, no?*)	Yes/No questions can be formed by adding an element to the end of a declarative statement. (*You eat broccoli, yes? This is your sweater, no?*)	Yes/No questions can be formed by adding an element to the end of a declarative statement. (*You eat broccoli, yes? This is your sweater, no?*)	Yes/No questions can be formed by adding "or not" to the end of a declarative statement. (*You eat broccoli, or not? This is your sweater, or not?*)
Yes/No questions can be formed by adding a verb followed by its negative at the end of a statement. (*Do you like to go to the beach or not?*)		Yes/No questions can be formed by adding a verb followed by its negative within a statement. (Do you not like to go to the beach?)	Yes/No questions can be formed by adding a verb followed by its negative within a statement. (Do you not like to go to the beach?)		
Questions words are usually placed at the beginning of the sentence. (*Where is the book? What did my sister tell you?*)	Question words are placed according to the position of the answer. For example, if the answer functions as an object, the question words are placed in the regular object position (*The book is where? My sister told you what?*)	Question words are placed according to the position of the answer. For example, if the answer functions as an object, the question words are placed in the regular object position (*The book is where? My sister told you what?*)	Question words are placed according to the position of the answer. For example, if the answer functions as an object, the question words are placed in the regular object position. (*The book is where? My sister told you what?*)	Question words are placed according to the position of the answer. For example, if the answer functions as an object, the question words are placed in the regular object position. (*The book is where? My sister told you what?*)	
Yes and no answers are used in a consistent manner. (*Do you play soccer? Yes. Do you play hockey? No.*)				The answers yes and no vary depending upon the verb used in the question. Students may substitute a verb for a yes-no answer (*Do you play soccer? Soccer. Do you play hockey? No hockey.*)	
COMMANDS					
Commands are formed consistently. (*Stop it now!*)			Commands can be formed by adding an adverb after the verbs to be emphasized. (*Stop now!*)		
Commands do not require a time indicator after the verbs to be emphasized (*Take out the trash*).			Commands can be formed by adding a time indicator after the verbs to be emphasized (*Take out the trash at 9:00*).	Commands can be formed by adding a time indicator after the verbs to be emphasized (*Take out the trash at 9:00*).	
Commands use consistent verb form (*Show it to me*).			Commands can be formed by changing the verb ending (*Show[ing] it to me*).	Commands can be formed by changing the verb ending (*Show[ing] it to me*).	
NEGATIVES AND NEGATIVE SENTENCES					
Double negatives are not used (*She doesn't eat anything*).		Double negation is usually used in reverted sentence order with "nothing" and a word of emphasis before the verb (*They nothing have not been there before*).	Double negation is usually used in reverted sentence order with "nothing" and a word of emphasis before the verb (*They nothing have not been there before*).	Double negatives are routinely used (*She doesn't eat nothing*).	Double negatives are sometimes used. (*He doesn't drink coffee never*).
The negative marker goes after the verb phrase (*They have not been there before*).	The negative marker goes before the verb phrase (*They not have been there before*) Korean: used regularly in informal situations.			The negative marker goes before the verb phrase (*They not have been there before*).	

Syntax and Grammar: Adverbs and Adjectives
Differences and Potential Errors for English Learners

English Grammar	Spanish	Vietnamese	Hmong	Tagalog
ADVERBS				
Use of adverbs to describe an adjective or a verb *(I ate __really__ fast. I ran __quickly__ to the store).*			Adverbs are not used. Two adjectives or two verbs can be used to describe an adjective or verb *(I ate __fast fast__. I __ran ran__ to the store).*	
ADJECTIVES				
Adjectives precede nouns they modify *(We live in a __coastal__ city. She has a __yellow__ shirt.)*	Adjectives follow nouns they modify *(We live in a city __coastal__. She has a shirt __yellow__).* The adjective position can also reflect meaning.	Adjectives follow nouns they modify *(We live in a city __coastal__. She has a shirt __yellow__).*	Adjectives follow nouns they modify *(We live in a city coastal. She has a shirt __yellow__).*	
Use of **possessive adjectives** used to indicate ownership *(This is __her__ sweater. She wears __her__ sweater).*		Omission of possessive adjectives when ownership is clear *(She wears sweater).*	Use of another word, article or character used to indicate ownership *(This is __she__ sweater).*	
Comparative adjectives change form *(He is __taller than__ me. They are __slower than__ him).*	Comparative adjectives change form *(He is __more tall__ than me. They are __more slow__ than him).*		Comparative adjectives change form *(He is __more tall__ than me. They are __more slow__ than him).*	Comparative adjectives change form *(He is __more tall__ than me. They are __more slow__ than him).*
Nouns and adjectives have different forms *(They want to be __independent__).*				
Adjectives do not reflect gender or number of nouns they modify *(They have __sharp__ teeth).*	Adjectives reflect gender and number of nouns they modify *(They have __sharps__ teeth).*			Adjectives reflect gender and number of nouns they modify *(They have __sharps__ teeth).*
Use of **possessive adjectives** used for parts of the body *(The boy skinned __his__ knee).*	Use of definite article instead of possessive adjectives used for parts of the body *(The boy skinned __the__ knee).*			
Distinction between personal pronouns and possessive adjectives *(This is __my__ friend).*		Distinction between personal pronouns and possessive adjectives *(This is friend I).*		

English Grammar	Korean	Cantonese	Mandarin	Farsi	Arabic
ADVERBS					
Use of adverbs to describe an adjective or a verb *(I ate _really_ fast. I ran _quickly_ to the store)*.					
ADJECTIVES					
Adjectives precede nouns they modify *(We live in a _coastal_ city. She has a _yellow_ shirt)*.				Adjectives follow nouns they modify *(We live in a city coastal. She has a shirt yellow)*. The adjective position can also reflect meaning.	Adjectives follow the nouns they modify.
Use of **possessive adjectives** used to indicate ownership *(This is _her_ sweater. She wears _her_ sweater)*.	Omission of possessive adjectives when ownership is clear *(She wears sweater)*.	Use of another word, article or character used to indicate ownership *(This is _she_ sweater)*.	Use of another word, article or character used to indicate ownership *(This is _she_ sweater)*.		
Comparative adjectives change form *(He is _taller than_ me. They are _slower than_ him)*.	Comparative adjectives change form *(He is _more tall_ than me. They are _more slow_ than him)*.				
Nouns and adjectives have different forms *(They want to be _independent_)*.		Some nouns and adjectives use the same forms *(They want to be _independence_)*.	Some nouns and adjectives use the same forms *(They want to be _independence_.)*		
Adjectives do not reflect gender or number of nouns they modify *(They have _sharp_ teeth)*.					Adjectives agree with the gender and number of nouns they modify.
Use of **possessive adjectives** used for parts of the body *(The boy skinned _his_ knee)*.					
Distinction between personal pronouns and possessive adjectives *(This is _my_ friend)*.					

Syntax and Grammar: Pronouns
Differences and Potential Errors for English Learners

English Grammar	Spanish	Vietnamese	Hmong	Tagalog
PRONOUNS				
Distinction between **subject and object pronouns** (He gave it to *me*. We spent the time with *her*).	No distinction between subject and object pronouns (He gave it to *I*. We spent the time with *she*.)	No distinction between subject and object pronouns (He gave it to *I*. We spent the time with *she*).	No distinction between subject and object pronouns (He gave it to *I*. We spent the time with *she*).	
Distinction between **subject and object** forms of pronouns (I gave the book to *him*).	No distinction between subject and object forms of pronouns (I gave the book to *he*).		No distinction between subject and object forms of pronouns (I gave the book to *he*.)	
Use of **pronoun "it" as a subject** (*It is* four o'clock now. What time *is it*?)		Optional use of pronoun "it" as a subject (Four o'clock now. What time?)	Optional use of pronoun "it" as a subject. (Four o'clock now. What time?)	Optional use of pronoun "it" as a subject. (Four o'clock now. What time?)
Distinction between **object, subject, simple, compound, and reflexive pronouns** (He is *my* cousin. The pencil is *mine*. I can do it by *myself*).		Reflexive pronoun is formed by adding "oneself" to the verb phrase.	No distinction between object, subject, simple, compound, and reflexive pronouns (He is *I* cousin. The pencil is *I*. I can do it *I*.)	
Use of **gender specific third person singular pronouns** (Go talk to the man and ask *him* for directions).	No use of gender specific third person singular pronouns (Go talk to the man and ask *it* for directions).	No use of gender specific third person singular pronouns (Go talk to the man and ask *it* for directions). Vietnamese uses familiar form of third person singular.	No use of gender specific third person singular pronouns (Go talk to the man and *ask* it for directions).	No use of gender specific third person singular pronouns (Go talk to the man and ask *it* for directions).
Use of **relative pronouns** (Go get the book *that is* on the desk. If you want to drive, there are three ways to get there).		No use of relative pronouns (Go get the book is on the desk).		
Use of **human/nonhuman distinction for relative pronouns** (who/which) (She is the one *who wants* to go. The neighbors *who* just moved in are at the door).	*Quien* is a relative pronoun used specifically for humans.		No human/nonhuman distinction for relative pronouns (who/which) (*She* is the one *which* wants to go. The neighbors *which* just moved in are at the door).	
Use of **possessive pronouns** to indicate ownership (The shorts are *his*. These snacks are *theirs*).		A separate word or character is used before a pronoun to indicate ownership (The shorts are *(of) him*. These snacks are *[of] them*). Omission of possessive pronoun when association is clear (He raised his hand).	Use of a possessive character between pronoun and noun to indicate ownership (He *[possessive character]* shorts. Snacks *[possessive character]* them). Possessive pronoun can come after the noun. Omission of possessive pronoun when association is clear (He raised his hand).	
Personal pronouns are not restated (*Your sister wants to go too*).				
No use of **pronoun object at the end of a relative clause** (*The mouse that ran by was small*).				

Common Core Language Standard 1:

Demonstrate command of the conventions of standard English grammar and usage when writing or speaking.

L.1.1 d. Use personal (subject, object), possessive, and indefinite pronouns (e.g., I, me, my; they, them, their; anyone, everything). CA

L.2.1 c. Use reflexive pronouns (e.g., myself, ourselves)

L.3.1 k. Use reciprocal pronouns correctly. CA

L.4.1 a Use interrogative, relative pronouns (who, whose, whom, which, that) and relative adverbs (where, when, why). CA

English Grammar	Korean	Cantonese	Mandarin	Farsi	Arabic
PRONOUNS					
Distinction between **subject and object pronouns** (*He gave it to me. We spent the time with her*).		No distinction between subject and object pronouns (*He gave it to I. We spent the time with she*).	No distinction between subject and object pronouns (*He gave it to I. We spent the time with she*).	No distinction between subject and object pronouns (*He gave it to I. We spent the time with she*).	
Distinction between **subject and object** forms of pronouns (*I gave the book to him*).	No distinction between subject and object forms of pronouns (*I gave the book to he*).		No distinction between subject and object forms of pronouns (*I gave the book to he*).	No distinction between subject and object forms of pronouns (*I gave the book to he*).	
Use of **pronoun "it"** as a **subject** (*It is four o'clock now. What time is it?*)	Optional use of pronoun "it" as a subject. (*Four o'clock now. What time?*)	Optional use of pronoun "it" as a subject. (*Four o'clock now. What time?*)	Optional use of pronoun "it" as a subject. (*Four o'clock now. What time?*)		
Distinction between **object, subject, simple, compound, and reflexive pronouns** (*He is my cousin. The pencil is mine. I can do it by myself*).		Uses possession words to distinguish.	Uses possession words to distinguish.		
Use of **gender specific third person singular pronouns** (*Go talk to the man and ask him for directions*).		No use of gender specific third person singular pronouns (*Go talk to the man and ask it for directions*).	No use of gender specific third person singular pronouns (*Go talk to the man and ask it for directions*).	No use of gender specific third person singular pronouns (*Go talk to the man and ask it for directions*).	
Use of **relative pronouns** (*Go get the book that is on the desk. If you want to drive, there are three ways to get there*).	No use of relative pronouns (*Go get the book is on the desk. If you want to drive, three ways to get there*). In Korean, a modifying clause can function as a relative clause.				
Use of **human/nonhuman distinction for relative pronouns** (who/which) (*She is the one who wants to go. The neighbors who just moved in are at the door*).				No human/nonhuman distinction for relative pronouns (who/which) (*She is the one which wants to go. The neighbors which just moved in are at the door*).	No human/nonhuman distinction for relative pronouns (who/which) (*She is the one which wants to go. The neighbors which just moved in are at the door*).
Use of **possessive pronouns** to indicate ownership (*The shorts are his. These snacks are theirs*).	Omission of possessive pronoun when association is clear (*He raised his hand*).	Use of a possessive character between pronoun and noun to indicate ownership (*He (possessive character) shorts. Snacks (possessive character) them.*) Character sometimes omitted.	Use of a possessive character between pronoun and noun to indicate ownership (*He [possessive character] shorts. Snacks [possessive character] them*). Omission of possessive character when association is clear or to limit redundancy (*He raised [possessive character] hand*).	No distinction between personal and possessive pronouns (*The shorts are him. These snacks are they*).	
Personal pronouns are not restated (*Your sister wants to go too*).					Personal pronouns are restated (*Your sister she wants to go too*).
No use of **pronoun object at the end of a relative clause** (*The mouse that ran by was small*).					Pronoun object added at the end of a relative clause (*The mouse that ran by it was small*).

Syntax and Grammar:
Prepositions, Conjunctions, Articles
Differences and Potential Errors for English Learners

English Grammar	Spanish	Vietnamese	Hmong	Tagalog
PREPOSITIONS				
Use of prepositions (*The movie is on the DVD*).	Use of prepositions may be different than in English (*The movie is in the DVD*).			
CONJUNCTIONS				
Only one conjunction is needed (*Although, I know her, I don't know what she likes. OR I know her but I don't know what she likes*).				
ARTICLES				
Use of articles.			Classifiers take the place of articles in Hmong.	
Use of **indefinite articles** (*I bought an orange. Do they go to a market for groceries?*)		No use of indefinite articles (*I bought one orange. Do they go to market for groceries?*)	Plural form of classifiers take the place of articles. (*I bought one orange. Do they go to market for groceries?*)	
Use of **indefinite articles** before a profession (*She is a brilliant scientist. He is an electrician*).	Use of indefinite articles before a profession is optional (*She is brilliant scientist. He is electrician*).	No use of indefinite articles before a profession (*She is brilliant scientist. He is electrician*).	In Hmong, professions have unique classifiers, although some are shared. (*She is brilliant scientist. He is electrician.*)	
Consistent use of **definite articles** (*I have the piece of paper. She has a pencil*).	Definite articles can be omitted or used (*I have [a] piece of paper. She has [a] pencil*).		Definite articles can be omitted. (*I have piece of paper. She has pencil.*)	Definite articles can be omitted (*I have piece of paper. She has pencil*).
No use of **definite article** for generalization (*Eating vegetables is healthful for people*).	Use of definite article for generalization (*Eating the vegetables is healthful for the people*).		Use of definite article for generalization (*Eating the vegetables is healthful for the people*).	Use of definite article for generalization (*Eating the vegetables is healthful for the people*).
No use of **definite articles** with a profession (*Doctor Sanchez is at the hospital*).	Optional use of definite articles with a profession (*The Doctor Sanchez is at the hospital*).		Optional use of definite articles with a profession (*The Doctor Sanchez is at the hospital*).	Optional use of definite articles with a profession (*The Doctor Sanchez is at the hospital*).
No use of **definite articles** with months, sometimes not used with places (*We will go in May. She is in bed*).	Use of definite article with months, sometimes not used with places. (*We will go in the May. She is in the bed.*)		Use of definite article with months, sometimes not used with places. (*We will go in the May. She is in the bed.*)	

Common Core Language Standard 1:

Demonstrate command of the conventions of standard English grammar and usage when writing or speaking.

L.K.1e. Use the most frequently occurring prepositions (e.g., to, from, in, out, on, off, for, of, by, with).
L.1.1 g. Use frequently occurring conjunctions (e.g., and, but, or, so, because).
L.1.1 h. Use determiners (e.g., articles, demonstratives).
L.1.1 i. Use frequently occurring prepositions (e.g., during, beyond, toward).
L.3.1 h. Use coordinating and subordinating conjunctions.
L.4.1 e. Form and use prepositional phrases.
L.5.1 e. Use correlative conjunctions (e.g., either/ or, neither/nor).

English Grammar	Korean	Cantonese	Mandarin	Farsi	Arabic
PREPOSITIONS					
Use of prepositions (*The movie is on the DVD*).					
CONJUNCTIONS					
Only one conjunction is needed (*Although, I know her, I don't know what she likes. OR I know her but I don't know what she likes*).		Conjunctions occur in pairs (*Although, I know her but I don't know what she likes*).	Conjunctions occur in pairs (*Although, I know her but I don't know what she likes*).		Coordination favored over subordination (frequent use of and and so).
ARTICLES					
Use of articles.		Use of articles to be very clear and definite.	Use of articles to be very clear and definite.	No use of articles.	
Use of **indefinite articles** (*I bought an orange. Do they go to a market for groceries?*)	No use of indefinite articles (*I bought one orange. Do they go to one market for groceries?*) Depends on the context.	No use of indefinite articles (*I bought one orange at the store. Do they go to one market for groceries?*)	No use of indefinite articles (*I bought one orange at the store. Do they go to one market for groceries?*)		No use of indefinite articles (*I bought one orange. Do they go to market for groceries?*)
Use of **indefinite articles** before a profession (*She is a brilliant scientist. He is an electrician*).	No use of indefinite articles before a profession (*She is brilliant scientist. He is electrician*).	No use of indefinite articles before a profession (*She is brilliant scientist. He is electrician*).	No use of indefinite articles before a profession (*She is brilliant scientist. He is electrician*).	No use of indefinite articles before a profession (*She is brilliant scientist. He is electrician*).	No use of indefinite articles before a profession (*She is brilliant scientist. He is electrician*).
Consistent use of **definite articles** (*I have the piece of paper. She has a pencil*).		Definite articles can be omitted (*I have piece of paper. She has pencil*).	Definite articles can be omitted (*I have piece of paper. She has pencil*).		
No use of **definite article** for generalization (*Eating vegetables is healthful for people*).					
No use of **definite articles** with a profession (*Doctor Sanchez is at the hospital*).				Optional use of definite articles with a profession (*The Doctor Sanchez is at the hospital*).	The definite article is used with names of professions before a proper noun (*The Doctor Sanchez is at the hospital*).
No use of **definite articles** with months, sometimes not used with places (*We will go in May. She is in bed*).					Use of definite article with days, months, places, idioms (*We will go in the May. She is in the bed*).

African American English

African American English (AAE) is also termed African-American Vernacular English (AAVE), African American language, Black English Vernacular, Black Language, Black Dialect, or U.S. Ebonics (Chisholm and Godley 2011; Perry and Delpit 1998). Like all other natural linguistic systems, AAE is governed by consistent linguistic rules and has evolved in particular ways based on historical and cultural factors (Trumbull, E., & Pacheco, M. [2005]). As a dialect of American English it is important to understand that:

- Some (not all) African Americans speak AAE;

- Some non-African Americans speak AAE;

- AAE may be spoken by both Standard English Learners and standard English speakers who are able to code-switch based on a given situation and discourse community and can be considered bi-dialectical;

- As a natural linguistic system, AAE maintains a consistent set of linguistic rules and has evolved in particular ways based on historical and cultural factors;

- AAE has evolved and continues to evolve based on historical and cultural factors;

- African American English is fully capable of serving all of the intellectual and social needs of its speakers.

African American English speakers who are able to code-switch can flexibly shift the variety of English they use, adjusting it to the expectations of particular discourse communities (such as work, school, family, peers). It is essential for educators to understand that while ethnic-specific dialects differ from Standard English in spelling, grammar, pronunciation and/or vocabulary, they represent a common and accepted form of communication in the homes and communities of those who speak them (Trumbull, E., & Pacheco, M. 2005).

Language and culture are inextricably linked, and students' dispositions toward school learning are affected by the degree to which schools convey that students' cultural and linguistic heritage are valued. Therefore, teachers should allow—and indeed encourage—their students to use their primary language(s) and dialects when appropriate in the classroom and infuse cultural and linguistic heritage into the curriculum (Gay 2000).

Culturally and Linguistically Responsive Instruction

Research has shown that pedagogical approaches that support students to become bi-dialectal, or proficient users of both Standard English and African American English (and other dialects of English), are those practices that explicitly acknowledge the value and linguistic features of AAE, build on students' knowledge of AAE to improve their learning opportunities, and ensure that students have the linguistic resources necessary to meet the expectations of school contexts (Chisholm and Godley 2011; Delpit 2006; Hill 2009; Thompson 2010).

Culturally and Linguistically Responsive instruction impacts all facets of instruction, and contrastive analysis strategies support the acquisition of Standard American and Academic English by making explicit the structural and grammatical differences between African American Language and the language of school, Standard American and/or Academic English (LeMoine, N. 2014). In acknowledging and affirming students' linguistic heritage, LeMoine provides the following classroom practices among others:

[1] California English Language Arts/English Language Development (ELA/ELD) Framework, California Department of Education, Sacramento, CA. 2014

1. Provide texts that affirm and validate students' culture, language, and experiences.

- Using literature, poetry, songs, plays, student-elicited sentences, or prepared story scripts that incorporate examples of specific AAE forms, students perform contrastive analysis translations to determine the underlying rules that distinguish the two language forms.

- Reading passages out loud, students compare the way people talk with the ways they write and suggest ways of making a text more authentic. Discuss and compare spelling systems.

2. Explore situational appropriateness in language.

- Students contrast and analyze the mainstream and non-mainstream versions of targeted language forms with an emphasis on situational appropriateness, i.e., communication, environment, audience, purpose, and function.

- Students should be given an opportunity to decide, prior to a given activity, the type of communication behaviors that would be most appropriate.

- Let students use their home variety in various classroom activities: classroom discussions, role-playing, writing in journals, or acting out plays with dialogue in the variety.

- Help students feel comfortable. Accept and appreciate the idea of style-shifting and have them think of situations in their own lives in which it would be more appropriate to choose one variety over another.

3. Promote opportunities to explore cultural and linguistic heritage.

- Teacher elicits spontaneous verbalizations/responses from students about material read or presented and creates teachable moments for conducting contrastive analysis.

- Students collect language data from the speech community, transcribe it, and have students use it to answer questions about grammatical patterns.

- Students explore the grammatical rules of their home variety. Some activities for students: translating passages (poems, instructions, etc.) into the variety; creating lessons for teaching someone the variety; making up a test in the variety (e.g., with acceptable and unacceptable sentences).

- Over the course of an academic year, students are taught overtly about their language and its worth and beauty.

4. Support the development of Academic English.

- Classroom activities provide ample opportunities for students to engage in intellectually rich activities that motivate them to use academic language registers and use discipline-specific terms with confidence and understanding.

- Teachers actively support, model, and scaffold use of academic language, and structure academic conversations in heterogeneous collaborative groups.

Ensuring the academic achievement of African American students and improved pedagogical practices of those who serve them requires a collective approach, which leverages broad-based support and coordination from school leaders, teachers, parents, and community organizations.

Oral Language Production, Foundational Skills (Phonemic Awareness, Phonics), and Spelling of African American and Standard English

Dialectical differences between African American English (AAE) and Standard English (SE) may be present in the oral language of students, which can impact transfer from AAE to SE phonemic awareness, phonics, and spelling. For example, if a student pronounces a word in a way consistent with AAE, such as *aks*, for the word pronounced in SE as *ask*, the student may face challenges in orally blending and segmenting sounds /a/s/k/ as well as in decoding and spelling the word with the SE sequence of sounds and spellings. Some of the more common contrasts between AAE and SE are represented in the chart below. Educators should note that these may not all apply to every AAE speaker and that through analysis of the actual speech and writing production of the student, teachers can identify the specific contrasts to focus on.

	African American English (AAE) Pronunciation	Standard English (SE) Pronunciation	Sound or Spelling Pattern	Position/Occurrence	Notes
/l/	awe, coo', nickuh, I'uh or I'	all, cool, nickel, I'll	/l/ not pronounced or pronounced as /uh/	At the end of a word, after a vowel	Like an r-controlled vowel, an /uh/ sound can be added.
	hep, bet, mik, fawt	help, belt, milk, fault	/l/ not pronounced	Before a consonant and after a vowel	Mainly occurs before sounds /p/, /t/, or /k/.
	peopuh, coupuh, littuh	people, couple, little	/l/ pronounced as /uh/	In lieu of final -le	An /uh/ sound is pronounced instead of the SE final /l/
/r/	sto', fo', do'	store, for, door	/r/ not pronounced	At the end of a word, after a vowel	Words and syllables ending in r or re spellings are frequently pronounced without SE /r/ sound
	fawd, sawt, cawd	ford, sort, cord	/r/ controlled vowel pronounced as /aw/	/r/ after a vowel	
	fou'o'clock	four o'clock	/r/ not pronounced	Between two vowels and across adjacent words	
	Flo'ida, sto'y	Florida, story	/r/ not pronounced	Between two vowels and within a words	Not commonly used
	p'ofessor, th'ow, th'ough,	professor, throw, through	/r/ not pronounced	Before o or ou, after a consonant	Only applies to some AAE speakers and in some words

	African American English (AAE) Pronunciation	Standard English (SE) Pronunciation	Sound or Spelling Pattern	Position/Occurrence	Notes
/th/	ting	thing	/th/ unvoiced pronounced as /t/	At the beginning of words or syllables	More common with Caribbean or West African speakers.
	mont, bafroom, toof	month, bathroom, tooth	/th/ unvoiced not pronounced or pronounced as /f/	At the end of words or syllables	Voiceless /th/ can be replaced with unvoiced sounds /t/ or /f/
	bruvver, anuvver	brother, another	/th/ voiced pronounced as /v/	Initial or medial placements	Voiced /th/ can be replaced by voiced sounds /d/ or /v/.
	brudder, anudder	brother, another	/th/ voiced pronounced as /d/	Initial or medial placements	
	de, dis	the, this	/th/ voiced pronounced as /d/	At the beginning of words or syllables	Common pronunciation of function words such as this, them, their, the
/s/	bidness, idn't, hadn't	business, isn't, hasn't	/z/ spelled with s	preceding /n/	
/i/ /e/	him/him, pin/pin	him/hem, pin/pen	Short /e/ sound pronounced as short /i/ sound		Common among SE and SEL speakers of Southern dialects as well as SELs in other locations.
Consonant Blends	pas', pass'	past, passed	/st/	At the end of words or syllables	It is common in AAE to not pronounce the final consonant in a consonant cluster at the end of a word or syllable.
	was'	wasp	/sp/		
	des'	desk	/sk/		
	gif', stuff'	gift, stuffed	/ft/		
	rap'	wrapped, rapped	/pt/		
	han', ban'	hand, band	/nd/		
	dim'	dimmed	/md/		
	lap	lamp	/mp/		
	pat	pant	/nt/		
	sak	sank	/nk/		
/ing/	thang, sang, rang	thing, sing, ring	/ing/ pronounced /ang/	-ing used in a root	Primarily in Southern dialects
	playin', talkin'	playing, talking	/ing/ pronounced /in/	-ing used as a suffix	Occurs in informal language of SE speakers and SELs
Ask	aks, akst	ask, asked	Consonant blend sk flipped in the word ask	Occurs in any placement of the word	This is a standard pronunciation of the word.

Conventions of African American and Standard English

Dialectical differences between African American English (AAE) and Standard English (SE) may be present in the oral language of students, which can impact transfer from AAE to SE grammar, usage, and mechanics in oral and written language. Some of the more common contrasts between AAE and SE are represented in the chart below. Educators should note that these may not all apply to every AAE speaker and that through analysis of the actual speech and writing production of the student, teachers can identify the specific contrasts to focus on.

	African American English Pronunciation	Standard English Pronunciation	Sound, Spelling or Grammar/Usage/Syntax	Position/ Occurrence	Notes
Inflectional Endings	walk, tighten, skip, wash	walked, tightened, skipped, washed	Ending –ed represented by /t/ is not pronounced	End of past tense verbs	Sometimes past tense verbs are pronounced the same as present tense verbs in AAE.
	walkted, skipted, washted	walked, skipped, washed	Ending –ed represented by/t/ is pronounced as /ted/	End of past tense verbs.	
Use of the verb "to be"	Uhm	I'm	Unique pronunciation.	In any position in a word.	Use of the SE forms of *am, is, are,* in speech and writing may need to be explicitly taught and practiced.
	She goin' over there.	She is going over there.	Contracted form of the verb.		
	He reading.	He was reading.	Contracted form of the verb.		
	He always be playing around.	He is always playing around.	Different forms of the verb.		
Verb + to (Infinitive)	gonna hafta	going to have to	Merge of the verb + to	In any position in a sentence	This pattern occurs more often in oral language than in writing.
	They is going to the store. They going to the store.	They are going to the store.	Different forms of the verb.	In the middle of a sentence.	The SE usage of the verb "to be" can be very confusing across many groups of students.
Verbs Subject/verb	He nice. They be nice.	He is nice. They are nice.	Nonuse or different form of the verb.		
	You is smart.	You are smart.	Different forms of the verb.		
	They was walking.	They are walking.	Different forms of the verb.		
Past Tense Verbs	pickted pick	picked	Deletion of suffix -ed or addition of –ted to indicate past tense.	In any position in a sentence.	When AAE speakers delete the –ed ending, they generally understand the past tense but do not use it in speech or writing.
	I had given him a pencil.	I gave him a pencil.	Use of past perfect *had* in place of the past tense verb.	In any position in a sentence.	This is a very common pattern of using the past perfect tense for both past perfect and past tense.

Common Core State Standards

Language Standard 1: Demonstrate command of the conventions of standard English grammar and usage when writing or speaking.

VERBS

L.K.1b Use frequently occurring nouns and verbs.

L.1.1e Use verbs to convey a sense of past, present, and future
(e.g., Yesterday I walked home; Today I walk home; Tomorrow I will walk home).

L.2.1d Form and use the past tense of frequently occurring irregular verbs (e.g., sat, hid, told).

L.3.1d Form and use regular and irregular verbs.

L.3.1e Form and use the simple (e.g., I walked; I walk; I will walk) verb tenses.

L.4.1b Form and use the progressive (e.g., I was walking; I am walking; I will be walking) verb tenses.

L.4.1c Use modal auxiliaries (e.g., can, may, must) to convey various conditions.

L.5.1b Form and use the perfect
(e.g., I had walked; I have walked; I will have walked) verb tenses.

L.5.1c Use verb tense to convey various times, sequences, states, and conditions.

L.5.1d Recognize and correct inappropriate shifts in verb tense.*

	African American English Pronunciation	Standard English Pronunciation	Sound, Spelling or Grammar/Usage/ Syntax	Position/Occurrence	Notes
Plural Nouns	I have two test today, She love all her cat.	I have two tests today. She loves all her cats.	-s added to the end of a noun when plural	End of nouns	AAE speakers will likely understand that they are referring to more than one noun. Young students across language groups frequently have challenges with regular and irregular plurals.
	It cost ten dollars. He owe me fifteen dollas.	It costs ten dollars. He owes me fifteen dollars.			Most frequent in Southern dialects.
	childrens, mens, feets	children, men, feet	Irregular plurals	In any position in a sentence	Irregular plurals can be challenging across populations of students.
Possessive Nouns	That Cassie book. Cassie book is on the table.	That's Cassie's book. Cassie's book is on the table	's not pronounced	Usually the possessive 's is not pronounced when followed by a noun.	The 's is frequently not pronounced when the possessive is followed by a noun.
	That is mines.	That is mine.	's added to the word mine	Generally when the word mine comes at the end of a sentence.	
	Who book is that?	Whose book is that?	who is used instead of whose	whose is not usually used in AAE	

Common Core State Standards
Language Standard 1: Demonstrate command of the conventions of standard English grammar and usage when writing or speaking.
NOUNS

L.K.1b Use frequently occurring nouns and verbs.
L.K.1c Form regular plural nouns orally by adding /s/ or /es/
    (e.g., dog, dogs; wish, wishes).
L.1.1b Use common, proper, and possessive nouns.
L.1.1c Use singular and plural nouns with matching verbs in basic sentences
    (e.g., He hops; We hop).
L.2.1a Use collective nouns (e.g., group).

L.2.1b Form and use frequently occurring irregular plural nouns
    (e.g., feet, children, teeth, mice, fish).
L.3.1b Form and use regular and irregular plural nouns.
L.3.1c Use abstract nouns (e.g., childhood).
L.5.1c Use verb tense to convey various times, sequences, states, and conditions.
L.5.1d Recognize and correct inappropriate shifts in verb tense.*

Conventions of African American and Standard English (continued)

	African American English Pronunciation	Standard English Pronunciation	Sound, Spelling or Grammar/Usage/ Syntax	Position/Occurrence	Notes
Pronouns	Them can't sing.	They can't sing.	The SE personal pronoun *they* is replaced with *them*.	In any placement in a sentence.	
	He saw it for hisself.	He saw it for himself.	The reflexive SE pronoun *himself* is replaced with *hisself*.		
	They house is nice.	Their house is nice.	The SE possessive pronoun *their* is replaced by *they*.		
Prepositions, Conjunctions, Determiners	a apple, a elephant, a iguana, a octopus, a umbrella	an apple, an elephant, an octopus, an umbrella	Article an replaced by a	In any placement.	Nouns beginning with a vowel are preceded by an in Standard English. This is an SE pattern that most young readers/writers of English learn through formal instruction.

Common Core State Standards
Language Standard 1: Demonstrate command of the conventions of standard English grammar and usage when writing or speaking.

PRONOUNS

L.1.1d Use personal (subject, object), possessive, and indefinite pronouns (e.g., I, me, my; they, them, their; anyone, everything). CA
L.2.1c Use reflexive pronouns (e.g., myself, ourselves)
L.3.1k Use reciprocal pronouns correctly. CA

PREPOSITIONS, CONJUNCTIONS, DETERMINERS

L.K1e Use the most frequently occurring prepositions (e.g., to, from, in, out, on, off, for, of, by, with).
L.1.1g Use frequently occurring conjunctions (e.g., and, but, or, so, because).
L.1.1h Use determiners (e.g., articles, demonstratives).
L.1.1i Use frequently occurring prepositions (e.g., during, beyond, toward).
L.3.1h Use coordinating and subordinating conjunctions.
L.4.1e Form and use prepositional phrases.
L.5.1e Use correlative conjunctions (e.g., either/ or, neither/nor).

	African American English Pronunciation	Standard English Pronunciation	Sound, Spelling or Grammar/Usage/ Syntax	Position/ Occurrence	Notes
Double Negatives	Nobody never gets me nothing.	Nobody ever gets me anything.		In all positions in a sentence.	Understanding that two negatives cancel each other out in SE is a concept that many students need to learn in school. This is a consistent pattern in AAE.
	Can't nobody know this.	Nobody can know this.			
	They didn't get none. He didn't get nothing.	They didn't get any. He didn't get anything.			

Common Core State Standards

Language Standard 1: Demonstrate command of the conventions of standard English grammar and usage when writing or speaking.

ADJECTIVE

L.1.1f Use frequently occurring adjectives.

L.2.1e Use adjectives and adverbs, and choose between them depending on what is to be modified.

L.3.1g Form and use comparative and superlative adjectives and adverbs, and choose between them depending on what is to be modified.

L.4.1a Use interrogative, relative pronouns (who, whose, whom, which, that) and relative adverbs (where, when, why). CA

Specific contrasts between AAE and SE are not noted.

WORD ORDER AND SENTENCE STRUCTURE

L.K.1d Understand and use question words (interrogatives) (e.g., who, what, where, when, why, how).

L.K.1f Produce and expand complete sentences in shared language activities.

L.1.1c Use singular and plural nouns with matching verbs in basic sentences (e.g., He hops; We hop).

L.1.1j Produce and expand complete simple and compound declarative, interrogative, imperative, and exclamatory sentences in response to prompts.

L.2.1f Produce, expand, and rearrange complete simple and compound sentences (e.g., The boy watched the movie; The little boy watched the movie; The action movie was watched by the little boy).

L.3.1a Explain the function of nouns, pronouns, verbs, adjectives, and adverbs in general and their functions in particular sentences.

L.3.1f Ensure subject-verb and pronoun-antecedent agreement.*

L.3.1i Produce simple, compound, and complex sentences.

L.4.1d Order adjectives within sentences according to conventional patterns (e.g., a small red bag rather than a red small bag).

L.4.1g Correctly use frequently confused words (e.g., to, too, two; there, their).*

L.4.1f. Produce complete sentences, recognizing and correcting inappropriate fragments and run-ons.*

L.5.1a Explain the function of conjunctions, prepositions, and interjections in general and their function in particular sentences.

Unit 1

Week	Type	Vocabulary Word	Spanish Cognate* / Translation
1	A	playmate	compañero(a) de juegos
1	A	enormous	**enorme**
1	A	courteous	**cortés**
1	A	kick	patada (la)
1	A	winning	triunfo (el)
1	D	equipment	**equipo (el)**
2	A	clean	limpio(a)
2	A	attention	**atención (la)**
2	A	rules	reglas (las)
2	A	safe	seguro(a)
2	A	school	**escuela (la)**
2	D	citizens	ciudadanos(as)
2	D	community	**comunidad (la)**
2	D	respect	**respeto (el)**
3	A	everyone	todos(as)
3	A	joined	ingresó a (ingresar)
3	A	turns	turnos (los)
3	A	unhappy	triste
3	A	bumped	chocó (chocarr)

Unit 2

Week	Type	Vocabulary Word	Spanish Cognate* / Translation
1	A	windowsill	alféizar (el)
1	A	dashed	corrió (correr)
1	A	speedy	rápido(a)
1	A	trousers	pantalones (los)
1	A	gnawed	royó (roer)
1	A	mighty	poderoso(a)
1	A	crawled	gateó (gatear)
1	A	cried	lloró (llorar)
1	A	laughed	rio (reír)
1	A	raced	compitió (competir)
1	A	roared	rugió (rugir)
1	A	slowpoke	lento(a)
1	A	skipped	saltó (saltar)
1	A	walked	caminó (caminar)
2	A	angry	enojado(a)
2	A	smelled	olió (oler)
2	A	upstairs	escaleras arriba
2	A	surprise	**sorpresa (la)**
2	A	slice	trozo (el)
2	A	argued	discutió (discutió)
2	A	called	llamó (llamar)
2	A	cried	lloró (llorar)
2	A	growled	rugió (rugir)
2	A	grumbled	**gruñó (gruñir)**
2	A	said	dicho (decir)
2	A	whispered	susurró (susurrar)
2	D	porridge	sopa de avena (la)
3	A	cut	**corte (el)**
3	A	watched	vio (ver)
3	A	wagging	meneando (menear) la cola
3	A	barked	ladró (ladrar)
3	A	grunted	**gruñó (gruñir)**
3	A	meowed	**maulló (maullar)**
3	A	said	dicho (decir)
3	D	flour	harina (la)
3	D	mill	**molino (el)**
3	D	ripened	maduró (madurar)
3	D	wheat	trigo (el)

*Words in bold are cognates

Managing an Independent Reading Program

Independent reading is a critical component of the *Benchmark Advance* literacy block. It is the time during which students experience the joy of reading self-selected books based on their interests and reading abilities.

As students read widely, both literary and content-rich informational texts, "they increase their background knowledge and understanding of the world; they increase their vocabulary and familiarity with varied grammatical and text organizational structures; they build habits for reading and stamina; they practice their reading skills; and perhaps, most importantly, they discover interests they can carry forward into a lifetime of reading and enjoying books and texts of all types."[1]

Within *Benchmark Advance,* students may participate in daily independent reading during the Independent and Collaborative Activity block, while the teacher meets with small groups of students to conduct differentiated small-group reading instruction, model fluency skills through Reader's Theater, or reteach skills and strategies.

Explicit support for managing independent reading is provided in the online component *Managing Your Independent Reading Program*. This resource is available to read and/or download at benchmarkuniverse.com. It provides:

- guidance for setting up and managing a classroom reading program;

- strategies to help students self-select books and texts;

- ideas to support book-sharing, partner-reading, and discussion circles;

- activities to promote reflection and writing in response to reading;

- prompts, questions, and strategies to support engaging one-on-one conferencing between teacher and student;

- home-school letters.

Students may draw from many sources for independent reading including classroom-library and school-library books. In addition, a list of recommended, award-winning trade books is provided for every unit in *Benchmark Advance* (at the end of this section), with titles that expand on the unit concepts and essential questions.

---

[1] California English Language Arts/English Language Development (ELA/ELD) Framework, California Department of Education, Sacramento, Ca. 2014

Unit 1: Rules at Home and School

Title	Author	Genre	Summary Notes	Awards
No, David!	David Shannon	Realistic Fiction	In this boisterous exploration of naughtiness, Shannon and David, two troublemakers, do what they know best: color on the walls, track mud on the carpet, jump on the bed, and throw "one visual zinger after another."	Starred Reviews Caldecott Medal Honorees
No T. Rex in the Library	Toni Buzzeo	Fiction	T. Rex has escaped from his book in the library! Shelves are falling, pages are ripping, and books are being chewed. Tess knows that he needs to go back into his book, but does she have to say good-bye forever? Fortunately, she has a plan.	
Billy Twitters and His Whale Problem	Mac Barnett	Humorous Fiction/Animal Fantasy	Billy has a huge problem one day when his mother orders him a giant pet blue whale as punishment for not cleaning his room.	Starred Reviews Children's Core Collection, 20th ed. and Supplements
Ten Rules You Absolutely Must Not Break if You Want to Survive the School Bus	John Grandits	Fiction	It's Kyle's first trip on the school bus and he is nervous. Luckily, big brother, James, is there to give Kyle the advice he needs to avoid being pushed around. As Kyle rides the school bus, he keeps each rule his brother told him in mind, but discovers that the school bus isn't that bad! Kyle may even be able to teach his brother a few things about the bus.	Kirkus Books of Special Note Library Media Connection Starred Reviews School Library Journal Starred Reviews
A New Year's Reunion	Yu Li-Qiong	Realistic Fiction	A Chinese family celebrates the Chinese New Year when Father returns home.	ALSC Notable Children's Books School Library Journal Starred Reviews
Each Kindness	Jacqueline Woodson	Realistic Fiction	A new student arrives into a diverse rural classroom. Will she be accepted? Will those cruel to her ever get a chance to make it right?	Coretta Scott King Award Honorees Starred reviews
One World, One Day	Barbara Kearley	Informational Nonfiction	Compares the daily lives of children around the world via photographs and simple text. Thorough explanation at the end of the book.	Publishers Weekly Starred Reviews Teachers' Choices
Rules for School	Alec Greven	Informational Nonfiction	This book presents fifteen rules to help youngsters "get ready, take charge, and rule the school."	
Monsters Mind Your Manners	Elizabeth Spur	Fiction	Monsters will do what they want to do without thinking of others! Using illustrations and rhyming text, this book reveals the ways monsters will behave in one's home, on sidewalks, on a bus, or at school: like bad, bad monsters!	
Table Manners	Chris Raschka	Fiction	Why shouldn't you speak with your mouth full? Who is allowed to wave their napkin like a flag? What would happen if you don't chew your food? Find out the hilarious answers to these and other burning questions in this must-read book about table manners.	Starred Reviews

Unit 2: Every Story Has Characters

Title	Author	Genre	Summary Notes	Awards
A Sick Day for Amos McGhee	Philip C. Stead	Realistic Fiction/Animal Fantasy	The kind zoo-keeper stays home sick and the animals come to visit him.	Starred Reviews, Caldecott
Mr. Tiger Goes Wild	Peter Brown	Realistic Fiction/Animal Fantasy	Mr. Tiger decides that walking upright, wearing a top hat, and a coat and tie are just not for him. He wants to loosen up and be wild. The town animal-folk do not approve of his wild behaviour and banish him to the wilderness—which, for Mr. Tiger, is not such a bad place to be.	Starred Reviews
Big Mean Mike	Michelle Knudson	Realistic Fiction	Mike the bulldog has a rough and tough yet soft side that he tries to hide from the "guys." Only the cute bunnies that keep turning up in his Big Rig glove box will turn him around.	Children's Choices for 2013 SLJ's Best of 2012
Cecil the Pet Glacier	Matthea Harvey	Realistic Fiction/Fantasy	Desperate for normalcy but destined for weird, Ruby's longing for a simple pet dog is replaced by a pet glacier who sacrifices its own melting state to be the best (and strangest) pet the girl could ever hope for.	Cooperative Children's Book Center Choices, 2000–Present
The Hello, Goodbye Window	Norton Juster	Realistic Fiction	Recounted in a little girl's voice, the kitchen window at Nanna and Poppy's house is a magic gateway. Everything important happens near it, through it, or beyond it.	Starred Reviews Caldecott
Chicken Big	Keith Graves	Humorous Animal Fiction	What happens when a giant chicken pops out of a giant egg? Will the smaller chickens accept him?	Starred Reviews
A Good Day	Kevin Henkes	Animal Fiction	Nothing will ruin bird's, fox's, dog's, and squirrel's very good day! Read how this team of animal friends finds a way to overcome their setbacks.	
Interrupting Chicken	David Ezra Stein	Humorous Fiction/Animal Fantasy	Little chicken can't stop interrupting and finishing all of her dad's bedtime fairy tales.	Randolph Caldecott Medal Honorees Starred Reviews
Who Pushed Humpty Dumpty?: And Other Notorious Nursery Rhyme Mysteries	David Levinthal	Fairy Tales/Mysteries	Humorous questions about who was behind five of the biggest nursery tale mysteries.	Horn Book Guide Titles, Rated 1–4 Library Media Connection Starred Reviews
I Stink!	Kate McMullen	Fiction	What do garbage trucks do while you're asleep? This rowdy New York City garbage truck will tell you, "Eat you're TRASH, that's what." Join this hungry truck as he narrates this unlikely and thoroughly engaging story.	Children's Choices Cooperative Children's Book Center Choices, 2000–Present Starred Reviews